Defending Democracies

THE OXFORD SERIES IN ETHICS, NATIONAL SECURITY, AND THE RULE OF LAW

Series Editors
Claire Finkelstein and Jens David Ohlin
Oxford University Press

ABOUT THE SERIES

The *Oxford Series in Ethics, National Security, and the Rule of Law* is an interdisciplinary book series designed to address abiding questions at the intersection of national security, moral and political philosophy, and practical ethics. It seeks to illuminate both ethical and legal dilemmas that arise in democratic nations as they grapple with national security imperatives. The synergy the series creates between academic researchers and policy practitioners seeks to protect and augment the rule of law in the context of contemporary armed conflict and national security.

The book series grew out of the work of the Center for Ethics and the Rule of Law (CERL) at the University of Pennsylvania. CERL is a nonpartisan interdisciplinary institute dedicated to the preservation and promotion of the rule of law in twenty-first century warfare and national security. The only Center of its kind housed within a law school, CERL draws from the study of law, philosophy, and ethics to answer the difficult questions that arise in times of war and contemporary transnational conflicts.

Defending Democracies

Combating Foreign Election Interference in a Digital Age

Edited by

DUNCAN B. HOLLIS
JENS DAVID OHLIN

OXFORD
UNIVERSITY PRESS

OXFORD
UNIVERSITY PRESS

Oxford University Press is a department of the University of Oxford. It furthers the University's objective of excellence in research, scholarship, and education by publishing worldwide. Oxford is a registered trade mark of Oxford University Press in the UK and certain other countries.

Published in the United States of America by Oxford University Press
198 Madison Avenue, New York, NY 10016, United States of America.

Library of Congress Cataloging-in-Publication Data
Names: Hollis, Duncan B., 1970– editor. | Ohlin, Jens David, editor.
Title: Defending democracies : combating foreign election interference in a digital age / edited by Duncan B. Hollis, Jens David Ohlin.
Description: First edition. | New York, NY : Oxford University Press, [2021] |
Series: Ethics, national security, and the rule of law | Includes index.
Identifiers: LCCN 2020039406 (print) | LCCN 2020039407 (ebook) |
ISBN 9780197556979 (hardback) | ISBN 9780197556993 (epub) |
ISBN 9780197556986 (updf) | ISBN 9780197557006 (digital-online)
Subjects: LCSH: Election law. | Elections—Corrupt practices. | Self-determination, National. | Sovereignty. | Election law—United States. | Presidents—United States—Elections.
Classification: LCC K3304 .D44 2017 (print) | LCC K3304 (ebook) | DDC 342/.07—dc23
LC record available at https://lccn.loc.gov/2020039406
LC ebook record available at https://lccn.loc.gov/2020039407

DOI: 10.1093/oso/9780197556979.001.0001

Note to Readers

This publication is designed to provide accurate and authoritative information in regard to the subject matter covered. It is based upon sources believed to be accurate and reliable and is intended to be current as of the time it was written. It is sold with the understanding that the publisher is not engaged in rendering legal, accounting, or other professional services. If legal advice or other expert assistance is required, the services of a competent professional person should be sought. Also, to confirm that the information has not been affected or changed by recent developments, traditional legal research techniques should be used, including checking primary sources where appropriate.

(Based on the Declaration of Principles jointly adopted by a Committee of the American Bar Association and a Committee of Publishers and Associations.)

Contents

III. COMBATING FOREIGN ELECTION INTERFERENCE UNDER INTERNATIONAL LAW

IV. COMBATING FOREIGN ELECTION INTERFERENCE THROUGH OTHER MEANS

List of Contributors

Steven J. Barela is Senior Research Fellow at the University of Geneva in the Global Studies Institute and a member of the Law Faculty. He specializes in interdisciplinary scholarship on national security issues, has produced a monograph on counterterrorism and an edited volume on armed drones, and was the lead editor of a volume on interrogation and torture with Oxford University Press in 2020.

Sebastian Bay, MSc, is a researcher and project manager at the Swedish Defence Research Agency focusing on election security, hybrid threats, and disinformation.

Akhil Deo is a Junior Fellow with the Technology and Media Initiative at the Observer Research Foundation, New Delhi.

Kevin C. Desouza is a Professor of Business, Technology, and Strategy in the School of Management at the Queensland University of Technology. He is a Nonresident Senior Fellow in the Governance Studies Program at the Brookings Institution.

Evelyn Douek is a lecturer on law and a doctoral candidate at Harvard Law School and an Affiliate at the Berkman Klein Center for Internet & Society.

Jérôme Duberry is a Research Associate at the Albert Hirschman Centre for Democracy, Graduate Institute, and Postdoctoral Researcher at the Dusan Sidjanski Centre of Excellence in European Studies, GSI, University of Geneva. His research focuses on the use of emergent and digital technologies by civil society.

David P. Fidler is an adjunct senior fellow for cybersecurity and global health at the Council on Foreign Relations.

Alicia Fjällhed is a PhD student at the Department of Strategic Communication, Lund University.

Duncan B. Hollis is Laura H. Carnell Professor of Law at Temple University's James E. Beasley School of Law and a nonresident Fellow at the Carnegie Endowment for International Peace. He is an elected member of the American Law Institute and the OAS Inter-American Juridical Committee; in the latter role he serves as Rapporteur for a project on improving the transparency of how states apply international law in cyberspace. Professor Hollis also regularly consults with the Microsoft Corporation on its digital peace agenda.

Chimène I. Keitner is Alfred & Hanna Fromm Professor of International Law at UC Hastings Law in San Francisco. She previously served as Counselor on International Law in the U.S. Department of State and is an adviser on the American Law Institute's *Restatement (Fourth) of the Foreign Relations Law of the United States*.

Ido Kilovaty is the Frederic Dorwart and Zedalis Family Fund Assistant Professor of Law, University of Tulsa, College of Law and a Visiting Faculty Fellow, Center for Global Legal Challenges, Yale Law School.

Dov H. Levin is an Assistant Professor of International Relations at the University of Hong Kong. His main research topic is on the effects of foreign interference with a special focus on the causes, effects, and effectiveness of partisan electoral interventions.

Herbert Lin is senior research scholar for cyber policy and security at the Center for International Security and Cooperation and Hank J. Holland Fellow in Cyber Policy and Security at the Hoover Institution, both at Stanford University. His research interests relate broadly to policy-related dimensions of cybersecurity and cyberspace, and he is particularly interested in the security dimensions of information warfare and influence operations on national security. He is a member of the Science and Security Board of the Bulletin of Atomic Scientists. In 2016, he served on President Obama's Commission on Enhancing National Cybersecurity. He received his doctorate in physics from MIT.

Duncan MacIntosh is Chair of the Philosophy Department at Dalhousie University and a member of the Executive Board of the Center for Ethics and the Rule of Law, which is based at the University of Pennsylvania Law School.

Valeria Marcia is a lawyer and a PhD candidate of Comparative Private Law at the University of Milan-Bicocca.

Jan Neutze is Senior Director for Digital Diplomacy at Microsoft and heads the company's Defending Democracy Program. He joined Microsoft in 2011 from the United Nations, where he worked in the Executive Office of the Secretary-General and the Department for Political Affairs. Jan co-chaired the Global Future Council on Cybersecurity of the World Economic Forum from 2018 to 2019, and he is a Certified Information Security Systems Professional . Jan holds a German law degree from the University of Münster and an MA in Security Studies from the Walsh School of Foreign Service at Georgetown University.

Lawrence Norden is the director of the Election Reform Program at the Brennan Center for Justice at NYU School of Law. He leads the Center's work in a variety of areas, including its effort to bring balance to campaign funding and protect elections from foreign interference.

Jens David Ohlin is Vice Dean and Professor of Law at Cornell Law School. He is the author of a new casebook on international law called *International Law: Evolving Doctrine and Practice*, and his latest monograph is *Election Interference: International Law and the Future of Democracy* (2020). He is the co-editor, with Claire Finkelstein, of the Oxford Series on Ethics, National Security, and the Rule of Law.

James Pamment, PhD, is co-director of the Partnership for Countering Influence Operations at the Carnegie Endowment for International Peace. He is also associate professor of Strategic Communication at Lund University and a special adviser to the European Centre of Excellence for Countering Hybrid Threats.

Arun Mohan Sukumar is a PhD Candidate at the Fletcher School, Tufts University, and a Junior Fellow at the School's Centre for International Law and Governance.

Ian Vandewalker is senior counsel for the Democracy Program at the Brennan Center for Justice at NYU School of Law, where he works to address the influence of money in politics and foreign interference in U.S. elections.

James Van de Velde is a Booz Allen Hamilton consultant to U.S. Cyber Command, Associate Professor at the National Intelligence University, and Adjunct Faculty at Johns Hopkins and Georgetown Universities.

Jacqueline Van De Velde is an Associate at King & Spalding, LLP. She previously served as an Attorney Adviser for a U.S. District Court and clerked on a U.S. Court of Appeals and a U.S. District Court.

Introduction

Duncan B. Hollis and Jens David Ohlin

I. Why Care about Election Interference?

Election interference is one of the most widely discussed international phenomena of the last five years. Russian covert interference in the 2016 U.S. presidential election elevated the topic into a national priority.[1] But that experience was far from an isolated one. Evidence of election interference by foreign states or their proxies has become a regular feature of national elections (e.g., the 2017 French presidential elections[2]), regional elections (the 2019 EU Parliamentary elections[3]), not to mention national referenda (e.g., the Brexit Question,[4] Crimean annexation[5]). Paired with historical evidence of substantial and repeated foreign electoral interference throughout the Cold War (and beyond),[6] the issue is a constant and critical challenge to the very functions of democracy. It is, moreover, a problem likely to get worse in the near future; information and communication technologies afford those who would interfere with new tools that can operate (at scale) in ways previously unimaginable. Twitter bots, Facebook advertisements, closed social media platforms (e.g., 8chan), algorithms that prioritize extreme views, disinformation, misinformation, and malware that opens up access to previously secret campaign and candidate communications are all increasingly prominent features of electoral processes.

For all the attention and importance attached to foreign election interference, there is currently a massive gap in the legal literature on the topic (nor, frankly, are

[1] *See generally* Office of Dir. Nat'l Intelligence, *Assessing Russian Activities and Intentions in Recent U.S. Elections* (Jan. 6, 2017); Robert S. Mueller, III, *Report on the Investigation into Russian Interference in the 2016 Presidential Election* (Mar. 2019).

[2] *See, e.g.*, *French Prosecutors Investigate Hacking of Macron Campaign*, Reuters (May 9, 2017); Andy Greenberg, *The NSA Confirms It: Russia Hacked French Election "Infrastructure,"* Wired (May 9, 2017).

[3] *See, e.g.*, European Commission and High Representative of the Union for Foreign Affairs and Security Policy, *Report on the implementation of the Action Plan Against Disinformation*, JOIN(2019) 12 final (June 14, 2019) 3; Michael Birnbaum & Craig Timberg, *E.U.: Russians Interfered in Our Elections, Too*, Washington Post (June 14, 2019).

[4] Jeremy Kahn, *U.K. Probes Russian Social Media Influence in Brexit Vote*, Bloomberg (Nov. 2, 2017); Clare Llewellyn et al., *Russian Troll Hunting in a Brexit Twitter Archive*, in JCDL 2018—Proceedings of the 18th ACM/IEEE Joint Conference on Digital Libraries 361–362 (IEEE, 2018), *at* https://dl.acm.org/doi/pdf/10.1145/3197026.3203876.

[5] Kenneth Geers, *Strategic Analysis: As Russia-Ukraine Conflict Continues, Malware Activity Rises*, FireEye Blog (May 28, 2014); Jeffrey Carr, *Rival Hackers Fighting Proxy War over Crimea*, CNN (Mar. 25, 2014).

[6] Both the United States and Russia have a long history of election meddling. *See* Peter Beinart, *The U.S. Needs to Face Up to Its Long History of Election Meddling*, The Atlantic (July 22, 2018); *see also* Casey Michel, *Russia's Long and Mostly Unsuccessful History of Election Interference*, Politico (Oct. 26, 2019).

Duncan B. Hollis and Jens David Ohlin, *Introduction* In: *Defending Democracies*. Edited by Duncan B. Hollis and Jens David Ohlin, Oxford University Press (2021). © Duncan B. Hollis & Jens David Ohlin. DOI: 10.1093/oso/9780197556979.003.0001

other disciplines much further ahead).[7] The idea of a "gap in the literature" is a trope of many law review abstracts, but in this case, the statement is painfully true. While international lawyers continue to spill gallons of ink on the use of force and other traditional topics in international law, election interference has received insufficient scrutiny, despite almost universal recognition of its significance.

The present volume is designed as a corrective. *Defending Democracies: Combating Foreign Election Interference in a Digital Age* tackles the problem through an interdisciplinary lens. It focuses on three things: (1) defining the problem of foreign election interference; (2) exploring the solutions that international law might bring to bear; and (3) considering alternative regulatory frameworks for understanding and addressing the problem. The result is a deeply urgent examination of an old problem on social media steroids, one that implicates the most central institution of liberal democracy—elections.

Before continuing, we should note that the volume's methodology is interdisciplinary though largely weighted toward law. It seeks to bring domestic and international perspectives on elections and election law into conversation with other disciplinary frameworks. We hope that in doing so, this volume may offer a broader perspective, escaping the typical biases of lawyers encountered in both the domestic and international spheres. For many domestic lawyers, every problem calls out for a domestic legal solution, and international lawyers often have a corresponding bias preferring international legal solutions for issues of international relations. Yet, law has no monopoly on regulating threats, especially those as deeply political as democratic institutions and the electoral processes on which they rest. Hence, we invited a broader group of scholars to join us in this project to avoid reinforcing the familiar but untested responses (i.e., international lawyers calling for more treaties or domestic lawyers calling for reforms in administrative regulations) and to create space for alternative frameworks that might contribute to redressing or at least diluting the threat that foreign election interference poses.

Taken together, the chapters that follow represent, we believe, a far more faithful representation of the broad array of solutions that might be deployed, including international and domestic, legal and extralegal, ambitious and cautious. More fundamentally, the volume's chapters use different disciplinary and normative frameworks to help identify the specific harm foreign election interference threatens—a necessary prolegomenon before any solutions can be proposed or debated.

[7] There are exceptions, of course, including Michael N. Schmitt, *Virtual Disenfranchisement: Cyber Election Meddling in the Grey Zones of International Law*, 19 Chi. J. Int'l L. 30 (2018); Logan Hamilton, *Beyond Ballot-Stuffing: Current Gaps in International Law Regarding Foreign State Hacking to Influence a Foreign Election*, 35 Wis. Int'l L.J. 179 (2017). We each have written on this subject previously as well. *See, e.g.*, Jens D. Ohlin, Election Interference (2020); Duncan B. Hollis, *The Influence of War; the War for Influence*, 32 Temple Int'l & Comp. L.J. 31 (2018); Jens D. Ohlin, *Did Russian Cyber Interference in the 2016 Election Violate International Law*, 95 Tex. L. Rev. 1579 (2017). For work in other disciplines, *see* Robert K. Knacke, *Banning Covert Foreign Election Interference* (CFR, May 29, 2020), *at* https://www.cfr.org/report/banning-covert-foreign-election-interference; Securing American Elections: Prescriptions for Enhancing the Integrity and Independence of the 2020 U.S. Presidential Election and Beyond (Michael McFaul ed., Stanford University, June 2019); Ryan L. Boyd et al. *Characterizing the Internet Research Agency's Social Media Operations During the 2016 U.S. Presidential Election using Linguistic Analysis*, PsyArXiv (2018); Ian Vandewalker & Laurence Norden, Securing Elections from Foreign Interference (Brennan Center for Justice, 2017).

II. This Volume's Contribution to the Debate

In Part I, "Election Interference by Foreign Powers: Understanding Its History and Its Harm(s)," the volume begins with four chapters introducing the concept of foreign election interference with particular attention to its online manifestations. It critically evaluates key, basic questions: What is foreign election interference and why do states or their agents pursue it? Is it a new phenomenon or simply an old form of statecraft with new (cyber) methodology? How is election interference conducted in this new world of social media platforms and email hacking? What in particular about computer technology and information systems makes election interference particularly dangerous? How can the "foreign" aspect of election interference be isolated from the "domestic politics" that is a regular feature of democratic processes? And, finally, is foreign election interference even all that harmful in comparison to the alternatives? Why not simply allow foreign voices with an interest in electoral outcomes to weigh in on, and campaign for, a particular result alongside domestic actors?

In chapter 1, "Should We Worry about Partisan Electoral Interventions? The Nature, History, and Known Effects of Foreign Interference in Elections," Dov H. Levin focuses on the historical practice to help guide the central normative question, that is, whether and why election interference is problematic. In this sense, Levin seeks to broaden the focus from the specific example of Russia's interference in the 2016 election and instead situate that example within a much larger category of interventions against political processes in other states, including campaign funding and campaign assistance, to name just a few. What Levin uncovers is that election interference is a "longstanding common phenomenon" even as he (rightly) concedes that its ubiquity does not eliminate its problematic nature. Rather, Levin notes that it has disturbing impacts: increasing political polarization and altering election results through the deliberative process, though Levin admits that "most scholars of American politics are still highly skeptical about these arguments."[8] Levin concludes that whatever the motivation, a state's involvement in another state's political process will almost invariably have negative effects on the target state's democracy because the interventions "significantly increased the chances of a democratic breakdown in the targeted state in the following five years by a factor of 2.5 to 8 times."[9] The mechanism for this harm includes the loss of integrity of, and faith in, democratic institutions, as well as the promotion of corruption that can linger after an intervention. Finally, Levin finds a strong correlation between election interference and domestic instability (and even domestic violence) in its aftermath. The result is a chapter that situates foreign election interference as a historical tradition even as it emphasizes its highly problematic effects in the digital age.

In chapter 2, "Understanding Disinformation Operations in the Twenty-First Century," Steven J. Barela and Jérôme Duberry focus on Soviet-era disinformation campaigns as a way of understanding how today's election interference differs from its historical antecedents. The authors use a former Romanian intelligence chief as a case study for understanding the promise and perils of disinformation campaigns.

[8] *See* chapter 1, this volume, at 32.

[9] *Id.* at 33.

They combine these case studies with more contemporary examples of election interference to frame the concept of disinformation and the operations states undertake to spread it. Barela and Duberry conclude that "because disinformation aims to twist the truth in subtle ways when key facts remain secret and unavailable, exposing an operation becomes a tedious and difficult task."[10] The authors end their chapter by concluding that the opacity of the social media space—where it can be hard to trace the source of information—has made this task even more difficult in contemporary cases of election interference. In essence, their pessimistic story finds a difference in degree, but not in kind, between Soviet-era disinformation and modern disinformation over Twitter and Facebook. The digital tools of social media platforms allow for added "depth and precision" to disinformation operations when compared to historical antecedents even as many of the original concepts and strategies remain the same.

In chapter 3, "Weaponizing Information Systems for Political Disruption," Valeria Marcia and Kevin C. Desouza look, in the broadest possible way, at how information systems can be used to accomplish political disruption. Although they recognize the threat posed by cyberattacks, Marcia and Desouza focus on a wider array of examples where (even with adequate cybersecurity) information systems are threatened, including but not limited to election interference. The authors develop a novel explanatory framework—which they call ALERT—to categorize and systematize all forms of political disruption via information systems. The acronym stands for (1) Actor; (2) Lever; (3) Effect; and (4) Response, which can generate (5) Theories for understanding and predicting political disruptions. The goal of the ALERT framework is to provide a systematized taxonomy for understanding the core elements of political disruption via information systems. While the taxonomy itself does not entail normative conclusions, it provides a common "language" for scholars, experts, and policymakers alike. To provide one specific example, the authors suggest that the ALERT taxonomy could serve "as a reference point for developing uniform standards at the international level" that could set "minimum security requirements to be adopted by companies in order to reduce the risk of the weaponization of information systems."[11]

In chapter 4, "Protecting Democracy by Commingling Polities: The Case for Accepting Foreign Influence and Interference in Democratic Processes," philosopher Duncan MacIntosh proposes a counterintuitive solution to the problem of foreign election interference: allow it. MacIntosh wonders whether foreign participation in elections is all that bad and canvasses the various objections to allowing broader participation in elections. Operating from an implicitly cosmopolitan outlook, MacIntosh sees broader foreign participation in national elections as one avenue to broaden America's parochial perspective. Instead of trying to prevent outsiders from "infiltrating" American elections, he argues that the U.S. government should be working to alleviate the very conditions that lead outsiders to attempt to influence American politics in the first place. If the country were to take these foreign views more seriously, instead of being enthralled to a nationalist outlook, MacIntosh wonders if outsiders would still need to engage in election interference at all. Skeptics may read MacIntosh's perspective as overly utopian, but MacIntosh retains faith in the

[10] *See* chapter 2, this volume, at 42.
[11] *See* chapter 3, this volume, at 88.

power of reasoned dialogue to structure international relations and reduce or even eliminate the need for states to engage in election interference in the first instance. In a sense, MacIntosh believes we need to cure the disease rather than the symptom—the symptom is election interference, while the disease is the externalities of national policies and interests.

Part II, "Understanding Election Interference via a Comparative Lens," continues to explore the concept of foreign election interference but pivots from historical and taxonomic efforts to comparative analysis. As central and pivotal as the American experience with election interference may be, it would be a mistake to assume that it encapsulates the problem set completely or sufficiently. Looking at other countries' experiences alongside the U.S. experience expands our understanding of what states participate in election interference, the methods interfering states and their proxies pursue, as well as the different targets for their attention. These comparative conversations are important because the varying political dynamics, power structures, and legal cultures they reveal demonstrate that we need an understanding of election interferences (and potential responses to them) that accommodates the divergent contexts in which they occur.

For example, in chapter 5, "The Specter of Chinese Interference: Examining Beijing's Inroads into India's Digital Spaces and Political Activity," Arun Mohan Sukumar and Akhil Deo look at the potential for Chinese interference in Indian elections—a phenomenon that has largely been ignored in the American and European press (both of which have focused, perhaps understandably, on Russian interference). Sukumar and Deo ably demonstrate why such a myopic view is misplaced because there is much to learn from the example of Chinese interference efforts and the Indian context in which they may occur. The authors argue that in the Indian experience, increased scrutiny of social media information operations means that foreign election interference is almost always detected, making fully covert operations next to impossible. Yet, Sukumar and Deo note, China may take advantage of India's particular vulnerability to disinformation campaigns due to "near-continuous federal and local election cycles," "the country's young and internet-savvy demographic that has shown a voracious appetite for social media," and a "growing network of marketing agencies, political consultancies, influencer networks and analytics platforms."[12] China, moreover, has situated itself to uniquely perpetuate interference by the ubiquity of Chinese digital platforms in India, including their modification and adoption by India's youth in local languages. The prevalence of Chinese digital platforms might explain why Chinese disinformation campaigns are more likely to target India as opposed to other democracies, like the United States, that China may also wish to influence, but where it lacks such market penetration. Sukumar and Deo concede that "[p]olitical entrepreneurship that harvests tensions among communities, especially along religious lines, has always been a feature of Indian democracy." Nonetheless, "[t]he cost of exploiting social cleavages has lowered, with digital spaces offering anonymity and deniability to political outfits."[13] As a result, China has an established capacity to foment division across the Indian social and political space.

[12] *See* chapter 5, this volume, at 124.
[13] *Id.* at 130.

In chapter 6, "A Swedish Perspective on Foreign Election Interference," Alicia Fjällhed, James Pamment, and Sebastian Bay describe and evaluate Sweden's experience with election interference, including Swedish efforts to develop counterstrategies. The authors aim to identify what has worked (and what did not), so that other actors and other states may benefit when designing their own counterstrategies. The authors conceptualize the harm of election interference as "information influence," which the Swedish government defines as "deliberate interference in a country's internal affairs to create a climate of distrust between a state and its citizens" and to "further the interests of a foreign power through the exploitation of perceived vulnerabilities in society."[14] As an example, they highlight how outside actors have fostered political and social polarization in Sweden centered around the European migration crisis. They explain how a distinctive feature of the Swedish government—management through independent administrative agencies—meant that an independent agency operating at arm's-length from political oversight has taken responsibility for responding to election interference. Moreover, they highlight a particular strategy for doing so—that is, fostering the public's "resiliency" to potential information influence operations through agency communications designed to warn the public about the danger of misinformation on social media platforms. The authors conclude by emphasizing that the Swedish government assessed that the 2018 election—the first to be conducted with new counterstrategies in place—proceeded appropriately (though they concede that it is difficult to prove that the government strategies were the cause of such a success).

In chapter 7, "When Does Election Interference via Cyberspace Violate Sovereignty?," James Van de Velde analyzes the American experience with election interference. Van de Velde argues that interference should be assessed on whether there was "unauthorized use" of networks or systems rather than on its effects. His analysis leverages several distinctive features of the American political landscape, including the relative weakness of international legal constraints and the central role that the American presidency plays in making decisions about how to respond to national security threats. Van de Velde notes that a cyber operation that targets an election probably does not rise to the level of an armed attack and would not qualify as an act of war. However, Van de Velde also notes that in the U.S. system, it is the U.S. president who decides when to take the nation to war, so that whether a cyberattack constitutes an act of war is mostly decided by the executive branch. So far, presidents have not considered cyber operations targeting an election as acts of war, though he suggests that could change if subsequent presidents take a different view on the matter. Van de Velde concludes by suggesting that not only did Russia's 2016 interference not constitute an act of war but that it also was a failure, triggering more responsive actions and attitudes from the U.S. government than might have otherwise occurred.

The comparative analysis in these three chapters foregrounds the fact that the threat of election interference depends on the nature and tenor of the relevant political and social fault lines, which are different in each country. At the same time, these chapters reveal some commonalities: foreign actors seeking to leverage those fault lines and

[14] *See* chapter 6, this volume, at 141.

amplifying them, often to produce social division and distrust in the targeted government or in its electoral processes. Furthermore, these chapters show that national *responses* to election interference are also structured in part by local differences in political and legal cultures. So, for example, a country that grants strong independence to administrative agencies will tend to allow those agencies to protect democratic deliberations without too much political oversight, while countries with a tradition of strong political oversight of administrative agencies will often mean that those countries embroil the protection of elections in political controversies.

Part III of the volume, "Combating Foreign Election Interference under International Law," focuses most explicitly on how international legal frameworks evaluate foreign election interference. It includes a survey of all the relevant international legal rules and standards in both restricting how states may approach foreign electoral processes and how states that face interference may respond to it. We recognize that, in theory, a cyberattack could under certain circumstances constitute an illegal use of force in violation of either the *jus ad bellum* (e.g., Articles 2 and 51 of the UN Charter), or *jus in bello* (international humanitarian law). Yet, we and the chapters that follow are more focused on nonforceful interference and the extent to which it is restricted by (1) the principle of nonintervention, (2) sovereignty (whether as a concrete rule or a background principle), (3) human rights law (including, but not limited to, the right to privacy and freedom of expression), or (4) self-determination (i.e., the right of a people to select their own destiny through the democratic institution of a free election). The existing literature has largely focused on nonintervention as the dominant trope, although the chapters that follow suggest that this approach is too limiting, if not misplaced.

At the same time, Part III examines how international law may authorize responses to election interference—chiefly, countermeasures (otherwise illegal acts that international law permits when done in response to a prior internationally wrongful act). Countermeasures are, in theory, a legitimate means of self-help enforcement in the face of significant lawbreaking, but international lawyers have long worried about their power to justify what would otherwise be illegal conduct. For that reason, international law has developed robust procedural and substantive constraints on countermeasures that would regulate their use in fighting foreign election interference. Taken together, Part III's chapters thus map out the full range of frameworks that the international legal system might use to evaluate, regulate, and protect elections from foreign interference. In doing so, this part helps highlight areas where international law is contested (e.g., sovereignty operating as a stand-alone rule) or in need of further clarification (e.g., what interference in elections can qualify as coercion), as well as the potential need for new international law rules.

In chapter 8, "Foreign Election Interference and International Law," Chimène I. Keitner provides a general overview of the international legal regulation of election interference. Keitner starts out by noting that although international law is built on a Westphalian notion of state sovereignty, the exact contours of the nonintervention principle have escaped easy definition—though not without effort. Keitner discusses how states specifically ceded some control over their internal affairs by creating the United Nations and other international organizations. However, Keitner sees the 1960s and 1970s as the crucial time period when states sought to more precisely give content to the principle of nonintervention. Applying these efforts to the case of election interference is difficult, Keitner perceptively suggests, because "the terms 'interference,' 'influence,' and 'meddling' seem to have gained the most currency" but none "of these terms sound in a distinctly legal register."[15] After canvassing the various international legal paradigms for understanding election interference—nonintervention, sovereignty, and self-determination—Keitner ends with a tantalizing possibility: leaving the regulation of election interference exclusively to domestic law. Although this might sound like a concession or a defeat for international law, Keitner ends on a more hopeful note, highlighting that in international relations, "publicizing and stigmatizing disinformation campaigns and other efforts to manipulate public opinion might have as much effect as attempts to prohibit them."[16]

In chapter 9, "Cybersecurity Abroad: Election Interference and the Extraterritoriality of Human Rights Treaty Obligations," Ido Kilovaty focuses on the capacity of human rights law to regulate foreign election interference. In doing so, he engages with a particular conceptual and doctrinal obstacle—and one of the greatest controversies in international human rights law—the scope of extraterritorial obligations when a state acts outside of its borders. Extraterritoriality, for example, is the key question that determines whether human rights law might have a role to play in how states conduct an armed conflict (i.e., does a state owe human rights duties only to those within its territory, or do the duties extend to foreign nationals subject to its overseas operations or control). Kilovaty's contribution asks whether human rights law can regulate election interference given the alleged constraints of human rights law, requiring "control" or "jurisdiction" before human rights obligations apply extraterritorially. Kilovaty offers an innovative solution to this problem by advancing a notion of "virtual control," that is, a distinctive form of control that can apply during certain cyber operations. When combined with an "effects-based" approach to extraterritoriality, Kilovaty's modern gloss on the notion of control suggests that the right to self-determination (and other human rights obligations) may apply when a state engages in election interference on the territory of another state. So, for example, Russia might be responsible for violating human rights, even when acting outside of its borders, because it enjoys "virtual control" over the individuals that it targets. With this innovative proposal, Kilovaty brings debates over extraterritoriality into the twenty-first century.

In chapter 10, "The Dangers of Countermeasures as a Response to Cyber Election Interference," Jacqueline Van De Velde focuses on the responses available to a state that has been subject to foreign election interference. Specifically, Van De Velde looks at the requirements under international law for using "countermeasures." For example, after Russia interfered in the 2016 election, what countermeasures was the United States permitted to utilize in order to pressure Russia to stop meddling in future elections? Van De Velde notes that international law generally prohibits a state from using a countermeasure as a justification for the use of military force, which is generally only permitted under strict conditions (e.g., self-defense). Van De Velde concludes that the law of countermeasures must remain strictly construed as a nonforceful

[15] *See* chapter 8, this volume, at 188.
[16] *Id.* at 194.

response mechanism to prevent military situations from spiraling out of control. It would be a hollow victory if the price of stopping election interference was a new wave of military confrontations triggering armed conflicts and all the accompanying death and destruction. Consequently, Van De Velde rejects calls to change international law to make it easier for states to use the doctrine of countermeasures to justify military behavior in response to election interference deemed a use of force (but not an armed attack). In the absence of forcible, military countermeasures, she suggests that states need to resort to more traditional mechanisms to defend their democratic institutions. Like Chimène Keitner in her chapter, Van De Velde concludes with a call for the filing of more domestic criminal or civil cases regarding documented cases of election interference.

In chapter 11, "Election Interference: A Unique Harm Requiring Unique Solutions," Jens David Ohlin seeks to identify the distinctive harm of election interference. As in past work, Ohlin argues that international law's standard frameworks for evaluating election interference fail to adequately capture what is wrong with these information operations. Specifically, Ohlin suggests that cyberwar is a poor analogy for understanding the harm of election interference, because physical targets are not destroyed. Similarly, the legal principles of sovereignty and nonintervention are inapt because the harm of election interference is more political than territorial. Consequently, Ohlin argues that election interference should be regarded as a violation of the collective right of self-determination, that is, the right of a people to select their own destiny. In order to protect that right, and reduce the distortionary potential of information operations, Ohlin argues that the United States can and should enforce transparency regimes on the internet to identify foreign speech. Doing so would prevent foreign actors—such as Russian troll farms—from engaging in political speech while masquerading as Americans. For Ohlin, then, the unique harm of election interference pursued through social media is the infiltration and distortion of the deliberative process.

In addition to international *legal* responses, alternative frameworks exist for tackling the problem of foreign election interference—responses that rely less on the tools of international lawyers and more on tools commonly deployed by cybersecurity experts, social media companies, and information specialists. The international law literature on cyber-election interference is predisposed to focus on international law solutions; when you are a hammer, everything looks like a nail. However, in Part IV, "Combating Foreign Election Interference through Other Means," we explore mechanisms other than international law to redress the foreign election interference problem set. These chapters do not purport to offer an exhaustive list of alternative responses, but rather embrace a diversity of approaches, including:

1. social media standards for taking down offensive content (with attendant risks to freedom of speech and other values);
2. the use of international relations theory to understand and anticipate how foreign actors may seek to undermine democracies in the future;
3. the use of cybernorms that are not codified in hard-law instruments but nonetheless promise to help constrain the use of cyberattacks in some circumstances; as well as

4. the use of campaign finance regulations as a tool for protecting elections from foreign interference.

To be clear, these alternatives are not mutually exclusive with international law's responses, nor can they occur in a legal vacuum. Indeed, the last alternative emphasizes the power of an existing *domestic* regulatory regime in lieu of an international legal approach. Rather, Part IV offers candidates for combating foreign election interference that warrant analysis as possible supplements or substitutes for the extant international law. Taken together, these studies offer policymakers the potential to mix and match solutions to a problem set whose complexity and scale counsels against any single silver bullet solution.

In chapter 12, "The Free Speech Blind Spot: Foreign Election Interference on Social Media," Evelyn Douek explores responses to election interference on social media and evaluates them against the backdrop of free speech norms. This inquiry is especially relevant because free speech norms—not just constitutional requirements but also more nebulous background values—were instrumental in the creation of internet culture, a place where anyone can say virtually anything without restriction. Douek argues that the removal of election interference material on social media implicates free speech norms in ways that the election law and cyberlaw literature has failed to grasp. Although Douek leaves open the possibility that, in some circumstances, removal and censorship of election interference speech on the internet might be proportional to the harm that it might otherwise cause, she concludes that basing such a decision on the basis of the "foreignness" of speech alone is misplaced and should be rare. In any event, her chapter demonstrates that proponents of censorship on social media have not come close to satisfying her standard for removing offending content. In addition, Douek complains that the need to police election interference speech has fallen to private firms—the operators of social media platforms—with the result that the public has not engaged in an adequate public dialogue regarding the nature and danger of censorship on the internet. Her chapter explains what private firms are doing, and not doing, regarding election interference—protocols that are largely opaque and not well publicized. The result is a cautionary narrative about solutions that may be worse than the underlying disease.

In chapter 13, "Foreign Election Interference and Open-Source Anarchy," David P. Fidler studies foreign election interference through the lens of international relations (IR) theory. By surveying the four standard theories of realism, institutionalism, liberalism, and constructivism, Fidler concludes that none of them adequately explain the phenomenon of election interference and argues that new theories are required. Fidler is particularly interested in the concept of anarchy that plays a major role in neo-Hobbesian IR theories, particularly realism. Fidler argues that the nature of anarchy has changed with the advent of the digital age and is now best understood as a form of "open-source anarchy." One function of this new form of anarchy is that "weaker" states are able to leverage information technologies to produce strategic outcomes, even though these states have less capacity when defined against traditional metrics, such as military power or economic resources. The result is more anarchy, and less structure, to international relations than in prior eras. Fidler concludes that his theory of open-source anarchy offers a theory that helps explain why, since 2016, the United States has had difficulty "preventing, protecting against, and responding to foreign election interference," and why therefore, it has struggled to achieve "effective defenses and credible deterrence, with the U.S. government resorting . . . to offensive cyber operations to disrupt capabilities and preempt anticipated threats."[17]

In chapter 14, "Defending Democracies via Cybernorms," Duncan B. Hollis and Jan Neutze argue that the most prominent mechanisms for combating foreign election interference today—international law, domestic law, and technical measures—are inadequate to the threat posed. They proffer an additional regulatory tool—cybernorms (i.e., shared expectations of proper behavior for actors with a shared identity)—to add to the current menu of responses. Cybernorms could tell states what not to do vis-à-vis foreign elections or how to cooperate to help victims of such interference when it occurs. Hollis and Neutze concede that cybernorms are not a "salve for all wounds." Just as the international legal order allows for existential and interpretative disputes that are not easily overcome given the law's inherently consensual structure, cybernorms may do little to reign in rogue states that reject a shared identity while cybernorms' social quality limits the availability of concrete "coercive" tools for their implementation. Nevertheless, Hollis and Neutze conclude that "[l]ike-minded states and other stakeholders have already begun to embrace the cybernorms project for foreign election interference" and that the adoption and internalization of cybernorms may be part of "a broad, multilayered and multidisciplinary response to the threat of foreign election interference."[18]

In chapter 15, "Using Campaign Finance Reform to Protect U.S. Elections from 'Dark Money' and Foreign Influence," Ian Vandewalker and Lawrence Norden argue that domestic campaign finance law might be used to help combat foreign election interference. Vandwalker and Norden note that campaign finance law has long banned foreign contributions, but they note the frustrating fact that many loopholes have allowed "dark money" from foreign sources to flow into American political campaigns. The authors argue that closing these loopholes will make a substantial contribution to ending foreign election interference, since foreign funding is one of the avenues through which that illicit interference occurs. For example, Russia spent substantial funds to operate social media troll farms under the aegis of the Internet Research Agency; enforcing a ban on foreign expenditures would help stop organized troll farm efforts that necessarily involve organized expenditures by foreign sources. Vandewalker and Norden propose specific reforms to update U.S. campaign finance regulations, including the expansion of rules regarding issue advertisements to include candidate "mentions" online, broader disclaimer requirements, the creation of a public database for internet political ads, and a requirement that advertisement sellers do more to block foreign purchases. The authors conclude with a major policy reform—a proposal for eliminating dark money in political campaigns. Taken together, their suggestions offer a policy and regulatory road map for updating campaign finance regulations for an era of organized social media disinformation.

Finally, in chapter 16, "Conclusion: An Outsider Looks In," Herbert Lin reviews all the volume's contributions and offers some concluding thoughts. He makes the

[17] *See* chapter 13, this volume, at 311.

[18] *See* chapter 14, this volume, at 316.

important point that understanding foreign election interference requires engagement with social cognition research. He uses it to challenge the idea among American political scholars that Russia's 2016 election interference had no meaningful impact, noting that regardless of whether those operations tipped the election, they clearly undermined trust in U.S. electoral processes and its democratic project. For Lin, foreign election interference online is a new threat at a scale demanding new responses. He critically engages with many of the existing response proposals, including those favoring transparency, free speech, and autonomous bureaucratic efforts. Lin's critiques, however, lead him to generate his own set of research questions. He lays out an agenda for further study, including: (1) the impact of social cognition on potential remedies to foreign election interference; (2) the disjunction and commonalities between foreign election interference and domestic politics; (3) possible further evolutions of international law to regulate foreign election interference; (4) the relationship between norms and customary international law; (5) the development of domestic norms against foreign election interference; and (6) business models to combat foreign election interference. Taken together, Lin's conclusion shows the complexity and diversity of the foreign election interference problem as it exists in today's digital age. His questions, moreover, reaffirm our original agenda. They help provide a foundation for research and regulatory responses to this critically important and rising threat matrix. Our ultimate goal remains—to offer those within the international legal discipline (as well as those, like Lin, from outside it) a launching pad for much needed further analysis, policy proposals, and legal reforms.

III. Future Directions

Thus, for all its conclusions, this volume remains, at its core, an opening salvo in the engagement of international law with the problem of foreign election interference. It does not aspire to fully and finally define that problem set nor the ways international law (or other regulatory approaches) may best respond to it. Our ambitions are more modest—to offer an initial, yet still in-depth, treatment of the subject from a variety of perspectives (e.g., historical, conceptual, comparative, legal, political, social); to explore international law's potential (and problems) in regulating this area; and the availability of alternative or supplementary solutions. In doing so, we hope, like Herbert Lin, that our volume will not just offer some preliminary conclusions and ideas but also spawn further areas for research and dialogue. Looking across the contributions to this volume, for example, five future areas appear ripe for more attention: that is, the (1) cognitive; (2) informational; (3) domestic; (4) facilitative; and (5) responsive aspects of combating foreign election interference.

For starters, when we focus on foreign election interference, we assume that the behavior in question—the spread of misinformation, disinformation, and other aspects of an influence operation—has at least some potential to be effective. The concern with foreign election interference rests, at bottom, on the idea that when interference occurs, it risks changes to electoral outcomes or, more broadly, undermines trust (and thus the legitimacy and power) of democratic institutions. And certainly, history catalogs a number of examples, where one state has clearly interfered with—and disrupted—the political will expressed by the people of another state.[19] The question is how such risks translate into the digital age. Amid rising concern over online and social media "influence operations" by states and their proxies, we need more research on whether and when these campaigns can actually have cognitive impacts—whether changing minds or, more likely, increasing the motivation of actors to take additional actions from what they otherwise would have done (or forgo activities, like voting, they might otherwise have normally pursued). In short, we need to know whether particular influence mechanisms are highly likely to produce the desired cognitive outcomes. And, similarly, there is value in identifying operations that qualify as "empty noise" for which states (and their resources) need not devote much, if any, attention. Assessing the cognitive implications of interference campaigns, moreover, should not focus only on the actors who launch them. Attention must also be paid to intermediaries in traditional and social media who may, unwittingly, serve as "amplifiers" or "accelerants" to an influence operation, generating a desired impact that the original authors could not achieve on their own.

Second, international lawyers are not known for their fact-finding skills. Yet, as several chapters in this volume emphasize, there are large information gaps in the foreign election interference space. For example, several chapters offer competing views on whether discovering information about influence operations targeting elections is difficult (chapter 2) or inevitable (chapter 5). Other chapters question whether the problem is election interference itself or its foreign origins. More research is needed to determine which of the competing positions is more accurate than the other or if particular assertions are actually contingent on the context in which interference occurs (i.e., will the answer vary by the author of the influence operation or the state targeted?). However such questions are resolved, there remains a need for further information on what foreign election interference looks like. We must continue to uncover and catalog the various—and constantly evolving—means by which one state (and, in some cases, its proxies) attempt to intervene into the political processes of another.[20] Nor are information gaps limited to actors with malicious intentions—as several contributors highlight, there is often a lack of transparency in how the social media platforms on which many campaigns depend respond to them (and the costs those responses incur on other values and interests). This lack of transparency extends, moreover, to states themselves, with a pronounced reluctance in the cyber

[19] *See, e.g.*, Peter Kornbluh, The Pinochet File: A Declassified Dossier on Atrocity and Accountability (2003) (historical account of U.S. interference in 1973 coup d'état in Chile); Stephen Kinzer, All the Shah's Men: An American Coup and the Roots of Middle East Terror (2d ed. 2008) (historical account of U.S. interference in 1952 coup d'état in Iran).

[20] There are already several productive examples of such efforts. *See, e.g.*, Kristine Berzina & Etienne Soula, *Conceptualizing Foreign Interference in Europe* (Alliance for Security Democracies, Mar. 18, 2020), *at* https://securingdemocracy.gmfus.org/wp-content/uploads/2020/03/Conceptualizing-Foreign-Interference-in-Europe.pdf; Laura Galante & Shaun Ee, *Defining Russian Election Interference: An Analysis of Select 2014 to 2018 Cyber Enabled Incidents*, Atlantic Council (2018), *at* https://www.atlanticcouncil.org/in-depth-research-reports/issue-brief/defining-russian-election-interference-an-analysis-of-select-2014-to-2018-cyber-enabled-incidents/; *Threat Activity Targeting Elections*, FireEye (2019), *at* https://www.fireeye.com/content/dam/fireeye-www/products/pdfs/pf/gov/eb-cyber-threat-activity.pdf.

context to identify how they understand the application of international law, let alone actually citing violators publically when they occur.[21]

Much of this contemplated cognitive and data gathering research may not actually come from the international legal discipline. True, international lawyers are well suited to search (or call) for *opinio juris*, that is, state statements on the nature and scope of their legal obligations in cyberspace. In other areas, however, international lawyers may have less facility with identifying the underlying behavior of states or their proxies that is internationally wrongful. Yet, international lawyers clearly need such information. Identifying the existence of problematic behavior is a necessary prerequisite for crafting and evaluating appropriate responses, whether through international regulation or other means. This may mean, for example, that states will need to do more to declassify evidence they possess with respect to election interference that, to date, they often keep secret. Similarly, any ability to weigh the need for, and contributions of, domestic and/or international legal responses depends on the sufficiency and effectiveness of existing responses by the social media industry. More research may help, therefore, illuminate which, if any, response mechanisms may have the most value added.

In terms of value added, several contributions in this volume have contemplated a third future direction for dealing with foreign election interference—domestic law. It is worth considering whether and how states might do more with their sovereign prerogative—to prescribe and enforce criminal laws and to oversee a system for allocating civil liabilities—in the foreign election interference context. Although jurisdictional hurdles may hamper the ability of states to hold foreign individuals accountable if they operate outside the state's territory or jurisdiction, domestic legal regimes are highly developed and experienced mechanisms for regulating human behavior. As such, even if foreign states themselves may have immunity from domestic suits, domestic law may still hold promise as a remedial device, particularly if research can unpack those tools most likely to be effective against different types of election interference.

The positive contributions domestic law might offer in the fight against foreign election interference also counsels in favor of a fourth, future direction for research relating to international law itself: further study and activity regarding its facilitative,

[21] *See, e.g.*, Dan Efrony & Yuval Shany, *A Rule Book on the Shelf? Tallinn Manual 2.0 on Cyber-Operations and Subsequent State Practice*, 112 Am. J. Int'l L. 583, 594 (2018); Duncan B. Hollis & Martha Finnemore, *Beyond Naming and Shaming: Accusations and International Law in Global Cybersecurity*, 33 Eur. J. Int'l L. (forthcoming 2020). Recently, however, a number of states have begun to make their views public in what may be a new trend toward transparency in setting the *opinio juris* for cyberspace. *See* Duncan B. Hollis, *International Law and State Cyber Operations: Improving Transparency—Fifth Report*, OEA/Ser.Q CJI/doc. 615/20 rev.1 (Aug. 7, 2020); Ministère des Armées, *Droit international appliqué aux operations dans le cyberspace* (Sept. 9, 2019), *at* https://www.defense.gouv.fr/salle-de-presse/communiques/communiques-du-ministere-des-armees/communique_la-france-s-engage-a-promouvoir-un-cyberespace-stable-fonde-sur-la-confiance-et-le-respect-du-droit-international (French views); *Letter from Minister of Foreign Affairs to President of the House of Representatives on the international legal order in cyberspace*, July 5, 2019, Appendix 1, *at* https://www.government.nl/ministries/ministry-of-foreign-affairs/documents/parliamentary-documents/2019/09/26/letter-to-the-parliament-on-the-international-legal-order-in-cyberspace (The Netherlands views); Jeremy Wright, QC, MP, *Cyber and International Law in the 21st Century* (May 23, 2018), *at* https://www.gov.uk/government/speeches/cyber-and-international-law-in-the-21st-century (U.K. views).

rather than prohibitory, functions. Certainly, international law regulates state behavior through various universal proscriptions, including the prohibition on the use of force, the principle of nonintervention, sovereignty, international human rights, and a peoples' right to self-determination. And states and other stakeholders would be well served to continue to pursue greater transparency on whether and how those rules restrict states from engaging in activities involving foreign election interference. Yet, international law can do more than prohibit the behavior of states or those for whom a state bears international legal responsibility.[22] International law may also operate to permit or facilitate behavior; to allow states to coordinate their efforts or even act collectively. States may agree, for example, in bilateral or plurilateral settings to mutual legal assistance and extradition regimes. The strength of those commitments could well improve the prospects for domestic legal responses to operate as intended. Thus, as international lawyers consider the future of the field vis-à-vis foreign election interference, it is important not to limit their work to the "big" questions about states' general proscriptive obligations, but to consider the less visible ways in which international law may permit collective action or coordinate activity to deal with the threat at multiple levels and in multiple contexts.

The value of international law in facilitating collective behavior provides a bridge to a final future direction to highlight in combating foreign election interference—continued efforts to delineate response options tailored to the diverse and distinct situations in which democratic processes exist across the globe. As noted at the outset, lawyers tend to see solutions in exclusively legal terms. And as this volume explains, there *is* value in considering the general mechanisms domestic and international law contain to respond to unlawful forms of foreign election interference (e.g., domestic criminal indictments, suits sounding in civil liability, countermeasures, and other yet-to-be enacted or agreed legal remedies). Yet, as we have been careful to emphasize, nonlegal responses hold promise as well, such as the use of political agreement to foster cybernorms. The heterogeneity of the problem set counsels in favor of building out a "menu of remedies" for foreign election interference rather than depending on a single "hammer" or other tool set.

These pointers are, however, just suggestions. It is important to recognize that this volume does not hold a monopoly on good ideas. Further research can—and must—occur to identify various regulatory response to various manifestations of foreign election interference, drawing on legal and nonlegal traditions. Such research should hopefully do more than merely identify new options, but also develop methods to measure their efficacy—whether in improving a society's resilience to foreign election interference or deterring it from occurring in the first place.

For nearly three centuries, democracies have become the preferred vehicle for avoiding the Hobbesian vision of life in a state of nature: "solitary, poor, nasty, brutish, and short."[23] The advent of the "Digital Age" has introduced tremendous new opportunities, tools, and techniques for advancing human existence and human dignity. At

[22] *See, e.g.*, Duncan B. Hollis, *Re-Thinking the Boundaries of Law in Cyberspace: A Duty to Hack?*, in CYBERWAR: LAW & ETHICS FOR VIRTUAL CONFLICTS (J. Ohlin et al. eds., 2015); Oona A. Hathaway et al., *The Law of Cyber-Attack*, 100 CAL. L.R. 817 (2012).

[23] *See generally* THOMAS HOBBES, LEVIATHAN (J.C.A. Gaskin ed., 1996) (1651).

the same time, information and communication technologies present malicious actors, including states, with new tools and techniques for causing all sorts of harm, including interfering in how peoples exercise their right to govern themselves. Ensuring that states and other stakeholders preserve the right of peoples and their democratic institutions to function as intended, free from malicious online interference, has become a national priority for all democracies. As such, government representatives, policymakers, and their lawyers must understand the nature and scope of the threat posed by foreign election interference in the digital age and the various ways to regulate and respond to it. The present volume contributes to this project by offering a necessary first step in situating foreign election interference threats into the international legal tradition alongside the lessons and experiences of other disciplines and methodologies.

PART I

ELECTION INTERFERENCE BY FOREIGN POWERS: UNDERSTANDING ITS HISTORY AND ITS HARM(S)

1

Should We Worry about Partisan Electoral Interventions? The Nature, History, and Known Effects of Foreign Interference in Elections

Dov H. Levin

I. Introduction

Although quite recent, the Russian intervention in the 2016 U.S. elections for candidate Donald Trump has already earned the dubious distinction of being one of the most well-known acts of foreign interference of the modern era. More than 36 million English language pages on the internet now refer to it in some manner.[1] Much of this discussion focused on the reasons for Russia's conduct, the possible collusion of the Trump campaign with the Russian government, and fears of future meddling of this kind in the United States and elsewhere. There has been far less discussion about the wider phenomena of which this particular intervention is just one recent example of the effects such meddling may have on its target state.

Until recently, the public conversation reflected the status of the academic literature as well. International relations, the natural home of research on this kind of cross-border phenomena in political science, has ignored it. The scant reference to such meddling in this literature usually served as a short prelude to discussions of other kinds of interventions.[2] The other social sciences have followed a similar

[1] Keywords "Russian intervention in the 2016 U.S. elections" googled September 26, 2019. In comparison, the 1953 covert coup against Iranian Prime Minister Mohammad Mossadeq gets 2.5 million references, the 1961 Bay of Pigs invasion against Cuban leader Fidel Castro gets 4.8 million references, the 2011 humanitarian intervention in Libya gets 24.3 million references, and the 2014 Russian takeover of Crimea gets 1.8 million references. Only the 2003 war (and regime change attempt) in Iraq whose bloody aftermath continued for much of the previous decade still surpasses the 2016 Russian intervention in this dubious honor with 56 million references.

[2] *See, e.g.*, Dan Drezner, The Sanctions Paradox 2–3 (1999); Kurt Gaubatz, Elections and War: The Electoral Incentive in the Democratic Politics of War 112–113 (1999); Alexander Downs & Mary Lilley, *Overt Peace, Covert War?: Covert Intervention and the Democratic Peace*, 19 Security Stud. 266, 285–286 (2010). The Comparative Politics literature on democratization and democracy promotion has, at times, briefly noted such interventions, especially those conducted in the last few decades. *See, e.g.*, Abraham Lowenthal, Exporting Democracy: The United States and Latin America (1991); David Reichhardt, *Democracy Promotion in Slovakia: An Import or Export Business?*, 18 Perspectives 5–20 (2002); Steven Levitsky & Lucan Way, Competitive Authoritarianism (2010); Valerie Bunce & Sharon Wolchik, Defeating Authoritarian Leaders in Postcommunist Countries (2011);

Dov H. Levin, *Should We Worry about Partisan Electoral Interventions? The Nature, History, and Known Effects of Foreign Interference in Elections* In: *Defending Democracies.* Edited by Duncan B. Hollis and Jens David Ohlin, Oxford University Press (2021). © Duncan B. Hollis & Jens David Ohlin. DOI: 10.1093/oso/9780197556979.003.0002

pattern. Diplomatic historians occasionally noted such meddling as part of a larger study of a certain era or a dyadic relationship and tried to assess its impact in that specific case.[3] Likewise, scholars in intelligence studies discussed a few cases of such interventions as part of a larger qualitative study of such operations by the CIA and other intelligence agencies.[4] Neither discipline has tried, however, to assess the impact of such interference in a systemic manner. Nor has there been an attempt to provide a "big picture" overview of the main methods, history, or overall trends of this specific form of meddling. Beginning a few years before the 2016 elections, and growing rapidly afterward, I and several other scholars have begun to do exactly this sort of work. Our efforts now make it possible, for the first time, to provide an overview of the known systemic effects of foreign electoral meddling as well as its overall record. That, in turn, enables us to provide a preliminary scholarly answer to the question in the title.

As will be seen in the following sections, the literature thus far on this topic indicates that such interventions are a long-standing and common phenomenon that in many situations can determine the affected election results and cause significant harm to their targets. Accordingly, concerns by democratic states about the possibility of such meddling in their elections are fully justified.

This chapter proceeds as follows. Section II reviews the main methods through which foreign powers are known to have tried to intervene in elections in other states in order to determine their results. Section III describes the history of such interference. Section IV surveys what is known so far from research on this topic about the various short- and medium-term effects of such interference on the target state. Finally, I conclude by explaining why the use of digital tools in order to conduct foreign partisan electoral interventions is unlikely, given the ways they have been used thus far, to lead to major changes in their overall negative effects and provide some guidelines for dealing with this phenomenon.

Daniela Donno, Defending Democratic Norms: International Actors and the Politics of Electoral Misconduct (2013). Nevertheless, this literature has classified and aggregated them with other neutral acts, nonelectoral external influences, or even acts by nonstate actors ignoring the unique features and effects of partisan electoral interventions.

[3] *See, e.g.*, Alexander DeConde, Entangling Alliances: Politics and Diplomacy under George Washington, chs. 13–14 (1958); James Miller, *Taking off the Gloves: The United States and the Italian Elections of 1948*, 7 Dipl. Hist. 35–56 (1983); Marc Trachtenberg, A Constructed Peace: The Making of European Settlement 129–131 (1999); Kristian Gustafson, Hostile Intent: U.S. Covert Operations in Chile, 1964–1974 (2007); James Stone, The War Scare of 1875: Bismarck and Europe in the mid-1870s, at 317–318 (2010); Michael Carley, Silent Conflict: A Hidden History of Early Soviet-Western Relations 85–86, 357–359 (2014).

[4] *See, e.g.*, Loch Johnson, America's Secret Power (1989); Christopher Andrew & Vasili Mitrokhin, The Sword and the Shield: The Mitrokhin Archive and the Secret History of the KGB (1999); Christopher Andrew & Vasili Mitrokhin, The World Was Going Our Way: The KGB and the Battle for the Third World (2005); W.J. Daughterty, Executive Secrets: Covert Action and the Presidency (2004); Jonathan Haslam, The Nixon Administration and the Death of Allende's Chile: A Case of Assisted Suicide (2005); John Prados, Safe for Democracy: The Secret Wars of the CIA (2006).

II. Definition and Methods of Partisan Electoral Intervention

One common definition of "election interference" in the literature is a situation in which one or more sovereign states intentionally undertakes specific actions to influence an upcoming election[5] in another sovereign state in an overt or covert manner that they believe will favor or hurt one of the sides contesting that election and which incurs, or may incur, significant costs to the intervening state or the intervened state.[6]

This definition does not include acts done by private citizens of a certain state on their own volition, such as campaign consultants hired for pay by a candidate or party in another state to give it campaigning advice, and so forth. Likewise, interventions by nonstate actors (transnational terrorist groups, nongovernmental organizations, international organizations, global media conglomerates, etc.) are not included unless they are directly controlled by an intervening state (via funding, etc.) or clear evidence exists that their intervention was done at the request of, or due to the pressures from, such an intervening state. The definition does include an element of intentionality to ensure that these acts result from the free will of the intervening state rather than due to outright coercion by the assisted side in the target state (say, threats to revoke an alliance treaty, or to restrict oil sales, or even to cut off foreign aid if the foreign power doesn't intervene on its behalf).

In terms of the referenced costs to the intervening state, these can be direct economic or reputational harms. They can also be derivative of the potential damage to the relationship between the intervening state and the target state that, in turn, may lead the target state to harm the intervening state in various ways (impose sanctions, withdraw from an alliance treaty, make it harder for the intervening state to use its bases in the target state, reduce its cooperation in regards to terrorism, etc.). Naturally, any immediate costs experienced by the target state as a result of the intervention may lead the targeted leader or a significant share of the target's public to want to downgrade relations with the intervening state. As a result, any costs imposed on the target state as part of such meddling, especially if the intervention fails or the "undesired" side wins a subsequent election, could be costly to the intervening state as well.

Intervening states have used a wide variety of methods both secret (covert[7]) and public (overt) to affect another state's election in the desired manner. These methods are usually carefully tailored to the circumstances of the intervened elections or the needs of the side being assisted. Nevertheless, most known methods of electoral intervention can be grouped under six main categories:

[5] Naturally, as could be understood from this definition, all such acts need to be conducted prior to election day in the target state. I have applied this definition only to activities falling within twelve months of the expected election day under the assumption that earlier acts by the intervening state usually have other goals or the state in question could have changed its mind in the interim.

[6] Dov H. Levin, *Partisan Electoral Interventions by the Great Powers: Introducing the PEIG Dataset*, 36 Conflict Mgmt. & Peace Sci. 88, 90 (2019).

[7] In a covert intervention, all of the significant acts done in order to help a particular party/candidate must have been either a secret and/or the connection between those acts and the election was not known to the average voter in the target state.

1. **Campaign Funding**: Providing campaign funding to the favored side. Such funding has been known to be given directly. This, for example, can involve the provision of cash, in-kind material aid (office equipment, newsprint for party newspaper or leaflets, vehicles for the party's campaign, etc.), or via a "padded" contract with a firm affiliated with that party. It has also sometimes been given indirectly (e.g., via "independent" organizations bringing likely voters of the preferred side to and from the polls on election day).
2. **Dirty Tricks**: Interventions using this method include acts that are designed to directly harm one or more candidates or parties competing against the preferred candidate or party. Examples of such acts have included: the dissemination of scandalous exposes or disinformation on the rival candidate or parties, physically harming or disabling rival candidates, damaging or destroying a rival's offices or campaigning materials, breaking in or spying on a rival's campaign activities and plans, disruption of a rival's fundraising efforts by threatening would-be donors, encouraging the breakup of the rival side's political coalition or party in the run-up to the election or bribing some rival candidates to leave or stay in the race. Dirty tricks also included, in a few special cases, assistance to the preferred side (usually an incumbent) in conducting voter fraud such as "creating" fake voters or manipulating voter rolls. Most of the known methods used by Russia in order to intervene in the 2016 U.S. elections, such as the hacking and leaking of "real" documents from the Democrat National Committee (DNC) and the Hillary Clinton campaign and the spreading of "fake news" about Clinton, fall under this category.
3. **Campaigning Assistance**: Increasing the capabilities or effectiveness of the assisted side's election campaign through the provision of nonmonetary or nonmaterial assistance to the election campaign. Examples include training locals (of the preferred side only) in advanced campaigning, party organization, and get-out-the-vote techniques, designing (for the preferred side only) of campaigning materials, sending campaigning experts to provide on-the-spot assistance to the preferred side's campaign in messaging, strategy, polling analysis, and so forth.[8]
4. **Threats or Promises**: Public and specific threats or promises by an official representative of an intervening state to provide or take away a thing of value to the target state or otherwise significantly harm it in the future.
5. **Giving/Taking Aid**: In terms of giving aid, intervening states might offer a sudden new provision of foreign aid or offer to significantly increase existing aid or other forms of material or economic assistance (such as loans, improved loan conditions, loan guarantees, trade treaties, preferred trading conditions, etc.). This aid can come directly or indirectly, say, via a multilateral international organization heavily funded by the intervening state.[9] In terms of taking aid, the intervening state may withdraw part or all of its aid, preferred trading conditions, loan guarantees, and so forth.

[8] This can also involve the direct provision of expert campaigning advice by officials of the intervening state's government.

[9] This also includes the provision (or increased provision) of various kinds of food aid.

6. **Other Concessions**: Interventions using this method include the provision of a costly benefit by the intervening state to the target state that is noneconomic or material in its nature or main value. One example occurred as part of the Soviet intervention in the 1956 Finnish election. In order to help Prime Minister Urho Kekkonan win the presidency, the Soviets in the run-up to the election, among other things, signed an agreement with the Finnish government promising to return the Porkkala military base in full to Finnish control and sovereignty.[10] Other known examples include support of a highly contentious claim by the target state for a particular piece of disputed territory, release of POWs or war criminals, or signing or revising an alliance treaty with the target state.

III. The Historical Record of Parisian Election Interventions

Just as the domestication of cattle led to cattle raiding, foreign powers began to conduct partisan electoral interventions almost as soon as meaningful competitive elections began to occur. Almost every major method of election interference used nowadays, including the various online variations used thus far, has antecedents going back to the eighteenth, nineteenth, or early twentieth centuries.

One of the first competitive national level executive elections ever conducted—the 1796 U.S. presidential election—was also the target of an overt French intervention designed to prevent George Washington's re-election and then (after Washington decided to retire on his own volition), the election of John Adams.[11] The French ambassador to the United States, Pierre Adet, sent a diplomatic message to the U.S. government enclosing a decree by the French government, both of which were made public in late October—a few days before the presidential elections in the swing state of Pennsylvania. The decree revoked the neutral status that American merchant ships had received from the French government during the Napoleonic wars, effectively restricting U.S. trade with much of Europe.[12] The decree, and the accompanying diplomatic message, warned that if the U.S. government continued its current foreign policies, as a Federalist administration under John Adams obviously planned to do, it would "Cross the Line of Neutrality" vis-à-vis France and instead "become its enemy."[13]

In 1797, France itself became the target of electoral interference. The British government, in an unsuccessful attempt to bring an early end to the French Revolution and eventually restore the Bourbons to power, secretly intervened in a French general election (the Election of Year V). It covertly provided approximately 10,000 pounds

[10] Max Jakobson, Finland in the New Europe 65–67 (1998).

[11] *See* DeConde, *supra* note 3.

[12] The revocation of this status permitted the French navy to board and confiscate without compensation all such U.S. ships (the main way by which this trade was conducted) and their goods were intercepted while en route to Europe—which was naturally a major (and widely known) constraint on all such trade.

[13] Jeffrey Pasley, The First Presidential Contest: 1796 and the Founding of American Democracy 367 (2013).

($1,619,000 in 2018 dollars) in campaign funding to the candidates of a conservative coalition.[14]

A different tool was used in the 1877 French election. Imperial Germany intervened to prevent the ruling monarchists, who were seen as more likely to start a war with Germany, from turning France back into a monarchy under one of its former ruling houses. As Bismarck's son, Herbert Bismarck, summarized his father's plan, "the time has come for us to influence the French elections so extensively and as forcefully as we are able in order to convince the French voter that he would be voting for war if he were to cast his ballot for the present French Cabinet." Bismarck accordingly created a full-fledged military crisis with France in the run-up to these elections complete with significant German troop increases on the German-French border and an embargo on the export of a key war material (horses)—a nineteenth-century equivalent of a Defcon 2 alert.[15]

As his invasion of Poland escalated into a worldwide conflict in 1940, Hitler became increasingly concerned about the possibility that Franklin Delano Roosevelt, if re-elected to a third term, would find a way to take the United States into the conflict. To prevent this, the Nazis began a covert intervention in the 1940 U.S. election against Roosevelt. One major aspect involved the publication in the United States of a memorandum of a conversation between Polish and American government officials in 1939, captured during the Nazi invasion of Poland, that ostensibly showed Roosevelt to be a "criminal hypocrite" and a "warmonger"—a potentially damaging revelation for the Roosevelt campaign that was then running on the promise to avoid U.S. entry into World War II if possible. To hide its role in exposing the document while assuring its wide distribution within the United States, the German chargè d'affaires in Washington, D.C., Hans Thomsen, secretly bribed the editor of an American newspaper to the tune of $5,000 ($89,680 in 2018 dollars) to publish it as an exclusive scoop, supposedly discovered by its own journalists, five days before election day on the front page of a special enlarged edition of the newspaper.[16]

During the Cold War, partisan electoral interventions became a common method of interference. Indeed, I have assembled the only comprehensive data set of such interventions currently available—PEIG.[17] It shows that the United States and the USSR/Russia intervened in this manner 117 times between 1946 and 2000—that is, in about *one of every nine* competitive national level executive elections during this period (937 elections).[18] Eighty-one (or 69 percent) of these interventions were done by the United States, while the other thirty-six cases (or 31 percent) were conducted by the USSR/Russia. This makes it one of the most common methods of interference since World War II, more heavily used by these two powers than more famous

[14] W.R. Fryer, Republic or Restoration in France? 197 (1965).

[15] Allen Mitchel, The German Influence in France After 1870, ch. 6 (1979).

[16] Landislas Farago, The Game of Foxes: The Untold Story of German Espionage in the United States and Great Britain During World War II, at 387–389 (1972).

[17] Partisan Electoral Interventions by the Great-powers. PEIG is available for download at https://www.dovhlevin.com. Another recent attempt to collect data on such meddling, by Bubeck and Marinov, is a sample of partisan interventions in only 10% of all elections between 1945 and 2012. Johannes Bubeck & Nikolay Marinov, Rules and Allies: Foreign Election Intervention (2019).

[18] Levin *supra* note 6.

methods such as major military interventions or covert violent regime change operations (such as in Iran in 1953).[19] The very well-known American electoral interventions in the 1948 Italian elections and the 1970 Chilean elections were thus merely two cases of a far wider post–World War II phenomena.

Sixty different states in every world region except for Oceania were the targets of meddling during this period. The targets were of various sizes and populations, ranging from small states such as Iceland and Guyana to major powers such as India, West Germany, and Brazil. Italy was the most common target (12 interventions) followed by West Germany (6), Japan (6), and Finland (4). The most common method used for intervening was campaign funding, followed by campaign assistance, and public threats or promises.

Nearly two-thirds of the U.S. and USSR/Russian interventions (64.1 percent) were covert—they were not known to the target state's public before election day.[20] Unlike the Russian intervention in 2016, therefore, the efforts of the intervening state to keep its covert intervention secret in practice were usually successful. Only five interventions of this kind (6.6 percent of all covert interventions) were inadvertently exposed prior to election day during this era. Another important aspect of such meddling is that 44.4 percent of all such cases were repeat interventions, in other words, cases in which the same intervening state, after meddling once in a particular state's elections chose to intervene again in (one or more) subsequent elections. Seventy-one percent of the repeat interventions occurred in consecutive elections.

The post–Cold War era did not pause such meddling or the use of varying intervention methods. In 1990, for example, the United States, in an attempt to prevent Daniel Ortega from winning the 1990 Nicaraguan elections, covertly provided German newspapers information about alleged Sandinista corruption and Swiss bank accounts. The Nicaraguan opposition then used these German news reports to great effect against Ortega.[21]

In 1994, Russia intervened in the Belarusian presidential elections to help the then leader of Belarus, Vyacheslav Kebich, stay in power. In the run-up to the election, the Russian government supplied 2 million tons of oil to Belarus at reduced prices and modified a proposed currency agreement with it to make it more favorable.[22]

A few days before the 2002 Bolivian presidential elections, U.S. Assistant Secretary of State for Western Hemisphere Affairs Otto Reich warned that American foreign

[19] During this period there were fifty-three significant military interventions (including the deployment of at least five hundred soldiers) by either the United States or the USSR/Russia. Patricia Sullivan, *War Aims and War Outcomes: Why Powerful States Lose Limited Wars*, 51 J. Conflict Res. 496–524 (2007). Likewise, during the Cold War era (1946–1989) the United States conducted fifty-nine covert foreign imposed regime changes or FIRCs (via assassinations, sponsoring *coup d'ëtats*, or arming or aiding dissident groups). Lindsey O'Rourke, Covert Regime Change: America's Secret Cold War 77 (2018). The USSR conducted another dozen or so such operations. Andrew & Mitrokhin, *supra* note 4.

[20] 23.8% of the overt interventions also included a covert component.

[21] William Robinson, A Faustian Bargain: U.S. Intervention in the Nicaraguan Elections and American Foreign Policy in the Post–Cold War Era 114–115 (1992).

[22] Kathleen Mihalisko, *Belarus: Retreat to Authoritarianism*, in Democratic Changes and Authoritarian Reactions in Russia, Ukraine, Belarus and Moldova (Karen Dawisha & Bruce Parrott eds., 1997); *see also Chernomyrdin Holds Talks with Kebich on Monetary Union*, BBC Summary of World Broadcasts (July 5, 1994).

aid to Bolivia would be in danger if Evo Morales was elected. The U.S. ambassador to Bolivia repeated this threat shortly afterward.[23]

In the 2004 Ukrainian election, in an effort to prevent the election of the candidate of the Orange parties, Viktor Yushchenko, from winning power, Russian President Vladimir Putin decided to intervene for his main opponent, Viktor Yanukovich. Among other measures, Russian campaign advisers were sent to the Ukraine and helped Yanukovich run his campaign. Likewise, one hundred and fifty tons of campaign posters were prepared in Russia and shipped for use in his campaign. Russia may have even been involved in an attempt to poison Yushchenko with dioxin, an attempt he barely survived.[24]

From the available information, it appears most meddling is done by major world powers. Yet smaller states are also known to have intervened in this manner too. Iran, for example, probably intervened in the 2010 Iraqi parliamentary elections through the provision of covert funding and campaign materials for Shiite parties that were part of the National Iraqi Alliance.[25] Libya under Muammar Kaddafi probably intervened, among other cases, in the 2007 French elections for Nicolas Sarkozy, providing perhaps as much as $62 million in covert funding to his campaign. According to one middleman, a Lebanese businessman, part of these funds, in suitcases stuffed with 200 and 500 euro bills, were secretly provided to Nicolas Sarkozy and his campaign manager during a visit to their offices.[26] Likewise, Hugo Chavez, the former leader of Venezuela, intervened in multiple elections conducted in nearby Latin American states, such as Peru and Nicaragua.[27] For example, eleven days before the 2011 Nicaraguan election, Venezuela's energy minister, during a visit to Nicaragua, warned that the continuation of Venezuela's foreign aid to Nicaragua, at the time estimated at around 8 percent of Nicaragua's GDP, was contingent upon the continuation of the "revolution" in Nicaragua, that is, a third presidential term for Ortega.

Accordingly, when Putin decided in early 2016 to intervene in the U.S. presidential elections, he was utilizing a long-standing policy tool frequently used by Russia and other states to try to affect domestic developments in other states. The United States was also a common target of such foreign meddling. The interference in 2016 was the sixth such case in American history. Accordingly, except for the inadvertent exposure of this intervention, and the digitization of some long used "analog" dirty tricks, little was special or new about it.

The fact that such meddling is a long-standing common phenomenon does not imply, of course, that it is not a potential cause for concern for democracies. Instead, it means that there is a rich vein of pre-2016, predigital history of partisan electoral

[23] Duncan Campbell, *Bolivia's Leftwing Upstart Alarms US*, THE GUARDIAN (July 14, 2002). The American election consultants working for Morales main opponent, Gonzalo Sanchez de Lozada, portrayed in a 2015 movie—*Our Brand Is Crisis*—may have been another (unacknowledged) part of this U.S. government intervention.

[24] Taras Kuzio, *Russian Policy Toward Ukraine During Elections*, 13 DEMOKRATIZATSIYA 491–517 (2005).

[25] David Ignatius, *Tehran's Vote-Buying in Iraq*, WASHINGTON POST (Feb. 25, 2010).

[26] Tracy McNicoll, *Gaddafi Relations Haunt Sarkozy in 2007 Campaign Finance Case*, FRANCE 24 (Mar. 20, 2018). This case is currently under a criminal investigation by the French government.

[27] RACHEL VANDERHALL, PROMOTING AUTHORITARIANISM ABROAD 105–106, 118–120 (2013).

interventions from which we can learn much about its effects. That is the focus of the next section.

IV. Effects

When foreign powers try to influence a key political institution in the target state—for example, the national-level elections and the process by which the executive is peacefully replaced or retained—that can naturally have many important effects. Research on this issue has so far focused on five major possible impacts: (1) their effects on political polarization in the target state; (2) their effects on the election results; (3) their effects on the target state's democracy; (4) their effects on intrastate violence in the target state; and (5) the policy reactions usually enacted and supported by the target state's public after the intervention.

A. Effects on Political Polarization

One known effect of election interference is that such meddling, when it is overt or exposed, polarizes the electorate as to its views of the intervening state. For example, Corstange and Marinov, in a survey experiment conducted in Lebanon right after the 2009 elections, found that an American intervention for the March 14th Alliance increased support for good relations with the United States by 15 percent among supporters of this camp while reducing support for good relations by 10 percent with the United States among supporters of the rival camp (March 7th Alliance).[28] A similar pattern was found by Shulman and Bloom in a survey conducted after the 2004 Ukrainian elections.[29] Although Ukrainians overall strongly disliked the perceived or actual interventions by both Russia and the West in this election (with somewhat greater dislike overall of the perceived Western meddling), there was a stark divide between the regional bases of the government and the opposition candidates. Respondents in Eastern Ukraine, the political base of the then-incumbent party of these regions, were 120 percent more likely to perceive improper Western influence than an improper Russian one, while respondents in Western Ukraine, the base of the then-opposition orange parties, were 29 percent more likely to perceive improper Russian influence than the Western one.

This pattern is not confined to relatively new or fragile democracies. Tomz and Weeks in a survey experiment conducted in the United States find that, while all respondents disapproved of foreign meddling in American elections, Republicans were 20–28 percent more likely to disapprove of such an intervention when done in favor

[28] Daniel Corstange & Nikolay Marinov, *Taking Sides in Other People's Elections: The Polarizing Effect of Foreign Intervention*, 65 Am J. Pol'y Sci. 655–670 (2012).

[29] Stephan Shulman & Stephan Bloom, *The Legitimacy of Foreign Intervention in Elections: The Ukrainian Response*, 38 Rev. Int'l Stud. 445–471 (2012).

of a Democrat than one done for a Republican. Similar patterns were found among Democratic respondents.[30]

The differential effects, real or perceived, may be derived from the identity of the rulers and the nature of the policies that they enact or maintain in the aftermath of the intervention. It may also come, in some cases, from the act of intervention itself—such as who, for example, is more likely to receive the benefits from the promised pre-election increase in foreign aid to the target state, and so forth. Like other situations where the effects of consequential laws or major domestic policies are perceived as asymmetric, interference by a foreign power leads to varying views by different parts of the population, with the beneficiaries viewing the foreign intervening state more favorably and the harmed side viewing the foreign power in a more negative manner. Likewise, supporters of the harmed side may resent such interference, even if viewed by them as inconsequential, due to the intervening state openly showing itself to be "against them" in the same manner that sports fans dislike cheering during a sports game for the rival team. Finally, even some of those who are on the benefited side with an overall dislike of such foreign meddling may perceive them as less consequential and therefore less objectionable when they are done in favor of "their side."[31]

Political polarization about the intervening state can also affect public support for important forms of interaction with it. Bush and Prather, for example, find in two survey experiments conducted in Tunisia and in the United States in the aftermath of elections in 2016 that an intervention can have significant influence on the target state's public views on economic relations with the foreign intervening state.[32] In the case of Tunisia, for example, after being told that the United States or France supported the main secularist party (Nidaa Tounes), respondents who voted for Nidaa Tounes were more likely to support an increase in trade and foreign aid with either state, while supporters for the main Islamist party (Ennahda) were more likely to oppose reception of foreign aid from either state. Likewise, in the American case, after a reference is made to the Russian intervention, Clinton voters were less interested in trade or Foreign Direct Investment (FDI) from Russia and after being told of German support for Clinton, Clinton supporters supported more FDI from Germany, while Trump supporters preferred less trade with Germany.

[30] Michael Tomz & Jessica Weeks, *Public Opinion and Foreign Electoral Interventions*, Am. Pol'y Sci. Rev. 856–873 (2020). There may be, however, a difference between developed and developing countries in the effects of education. Marinov, in a follow-up analysis of the survey experiment noted in note 28, finds that Lebanese respondents with higher levels of education and political knowledge tend to equally and strongly disapprove of foreign meddling regardless of whether it benefits or harms "their" side. Nikolay Marinov, *Voter Attitudes When Democracy Promotion Turns Partisan: A Survey Experiment in Lebanon*, 20 Democratization 1297–1321 (2013). In contrast, Tomz and Weeks, in the article cited above, find little evidence that Americans with a college degree differ in their reactions in this regard than their less educated brethren (although they also tend to disapprove a bit more of such foreign interference in general).

[31] Tomz & Weeks *supra* note 30; Sarah Bush & Lauren Prather, *Foreign Economic Partners and Mass Attitudes Towards International Economic Engagement*, American Political Science Association (Philadelphia, Aug. 2017).

[32] Bush & Prather, *supra* note 31.

B. Effects on the Targeted Election Results

Observers often claim that electoral interventions, when known or subsequently exposed, can have major effects on the targeted state election's results. For example, one day after the conclusion of the American intervention against him in the 1984 Grenadian elections, Sir Eric Gairy, a former prime minister, openly blamed his defeat on the United States, whom he claimed successfully "rigged" the elections in order to guarantee his defeat.[33] Forty years earlier, during a private conversation with American officials, a senior Japanese government official claimed that "many Japanese voted for" Prime Minister Shigeru Yoshida in the 1953 Japanese election due to the American overt intervention on his behalf.[34]

The growing literature on this question indicates that such interference can, in many situations, move the needle in favor of the side preferred by the foreign power. In the first systemic study of this question, a statistical analysis of the effects of such electoral interventions by the United States and the USSR/Russia worldwide, I found that partisan electoral interventions can have major effects on the results. Such interference on average increases the vote share of the preferred side by 3 percent.[35] Likewise, interventions done in public (or overtly) are usually more effective on this aspect than interventions done covertly, with the former on average increasing vote share by 3 percent more than covert interference.

My scholarship argues that the effects of such interference comes from the way that they are usually conducted. Most partisan electoral interventions involve close coordination and cooperation between the intervening state and the assisted side. Such interventions, therefore, tend to usually occur in marginal elections, that is, those in which the result is highly uncertain or one side lags but remains electorally viable. In such situations, election interference is most likely to have a significant effect on the results of the election. Likewise, because of these dynamics, the intervening state will usually not intervene overtly unless informed by the aided side that a domestic backlash will not occur prior to the election. When backlash is unlikely, overt interventions are expected to be more effective because the intervening state can outbid the local politicians for the target state public's support. It can also usually provide more resources to the preferred side in an overt intervention than in a covert one.

In a follow-up study, I identified one circumstance in which such meddling is ineffective, if not harmful, for the assisted side: electoral interventions in the first competitive elections after a long period of authoritarian rule or gaining independence (i.e., founding elections).[36] In those situations, the interference is counterproductive, reducing the vote share of the preferred side by 6.7 percent on average. The contrary effect in these situations is due to the inexperience of the assisted side with elections and with how to campaign effectively for office, leading it to frequently request from

[33] Oakland Ross, *Few Traces of Socialism: Euphoria Wins in Grenada*, GLOBE & MAIL (Dec. 6, 1984).

[34] 14(2) FOREIGN RELATIONS OF THE UNITED STATES, 1961–1963, at 1731; *see also Japan Holds to Conservative Line*, N.Y. TIMES (Apr. 26, 1953).

[35] Dov H. Levin, *When the Great Power Gets a Vote: The Effects of Great Power Electoral Interventions on Election Results*, 60 INT'L STUD. Q. 189–202 (2016).

[36] DOV. H. LEVIN, MEDDLING IN THE BALLOT BOX: THE CAUSES AND EFFECTS OF PARTISAN ELECTORAL INTERVENTIONS (2020).

the intervening state methods of interventions that are ineffective or counterproductive in that electoral context, thus leading to unintentional harm to itself.

My work is not the only one that finds electoral interference effective under certain circumstances. Bubeck and Marinov find, in a difference of means analysis of a sample of such American meddling, that when the United States is the only foreign intervening state in an election, and its intervention is for the incumbent, that incumbent is more likely to gain votes.[37] In contrast, when the election included a second intervening state that intervened for the other side, the effects cancel out, and neither side usually gains overall.

The closely related literature on the effects of foreign meddling on the results of referendums also finds that it has significant effects in the direction desired by the intervening state. Walter and others, for example, analyze the effects of the German and EU intervention in the July 2015 bailout referendum in Greece, finding that it increased support for the EU-proposed bailout package by 10 percent on average.[38] This effect seems to have been largely due to the overt intervention convincing many Greek voters that voting against the bailout agreement would lead to a (widely undesirable) exit from the European Union (or "Grexit")—one of the key messages which Germany and the European Union tried to convey to the Greek voters prior to the referendum. Matush discovers that the American intervention in the 2016 Brexit referendum had similar effects.[39] President Barack Obama's open threat during an official visit to Britain in April 2016 that in case of a vote in favor of leaving the European Union, the United Kingdom would be sent to the "back of the queue" in any subsequent negotiations of a separate U.S.-U.K. trade agreement, reduced support for the leave side by 11 percent on average in the areas of the United Kingdom most heavily reliant economically on their exports to the United States.[40]

Naturally, the most (in)famous recent case of such interference—the Russian intervention in the 2016 U.S. elections—has been an important site of significant research on this question. That research has been finding increasing, albeit still hotly contested, evidence that the Russian intervention indeed provided significant assistance to Trump.[41] Jamieson, for example, in a careful analysis focused mostly on

[37] Bubeck & Marinov, *supra* note 17 at 160–162. A similar result (such meddling is usually effective in bringing the assisted side to power) is found also by O'Rourke in an analysis of the short-term effects of a handful of covert American electoral interventions during the Cold War. O'Rourke, *supra* note 19, at 78.

[38] Stefanie Walter et al., *Noncooperation by Popular Vote: Expectations, Foreign Intervention, and the Vote in the 2015 Greek Bailout Referendum*, 72 Int'l Org. 969–994 (2018).

[39] Kelly Matush, *Going Public Abroad: When and Why Leaders Address Foreign Publics*, ch. 6 (2018) (unpublished PhD dissertation, University of California, San Diego).

[40] Likewise, recent research on the effects of (domestic) leaks of draft texts of trade treaties has found that such leaks frequently increase the negative media coverage of the treaty in question by more than 20%. Matthew Castle & Krzystof Pelc, *The Causes and Effects of Leaks in International Negotiations*, 63 Int'l Stud. Rev. 1147–1162 (2017).

[41] For some studies delving into various characteristics of the Russian cyber propaganda effort, see Ryan Boyd et al., *Characterizing the Internet Research Agency's Social Media Operations During the 2016 U.S. Presidential Election using Linguistic Analyses*, PsyArxiv (Oct. 1, 2018); Dan Miller, *Topics and Emotions in Russian Twitter Propaganda*, 24 First Monday (2019); Darren Linvill et al., *"THE RUSSIANS ARE HACKING MY BRAIN!" Investigating Russia's Internet Research Agency Twitter Tactics During the 2016 United States Presidential Campaign Computers*, 99 Computers in Hum. Behav. 292–300 (2019); Adam Badawy et al., *Characterizing the 2016 Russian IRA Influence Campaign*, 9 Soc. Network Anal. & Mining (2019); Philip Howard et al., *The IRA, Social Media, and Political Polarization in the United States, 2012–2018* (Project on Computational Propaganda, Working Paper 2018).

the effect of the covert Russian spread of propaganda and "fake news" through social media, estimates that this aspect of the Russian intervention had a major impact on the election results.[42] She finds that the Russian government was able to widely spread its fake news and election propaganda and target them toward the most persuadable audiences (potential or mobilizable Trump voters and "soft" or demobilizable Clinton voters). Likewise, the messages were well designed and highly congruent with the Trump campaign's own messaging and interests. As a result, she argues that the intervention probably had thrown the election to Trump.[43]

Other research on the effects of Russian cyber propaganda and fake news in 2016 has been reaching similar conclusions. A statistical analysis of the election-related propaganda covertly spread by Russia through Twitter found that increases in the amounts of retweets of such tweets sent by the Internet Research Agency[44] through its various hidden proxies in the run-up to the election accurately predicted shifts in public opinion toward Trump.[45] An increase of about 25,000 retweets of such messages (assumed to reflect just part of the wider Russian propaganda campaign) are estimated to have predicted an increase of 1 percent in polling for Trump a week afterward. The authors, however, admit that their research is unable to establish full causality in this case.[46] Likewise, Gutner and others, focusing on the effects of fake news (much of it spread by Russia) on 2012 Obama voters who switched to Trump in 2016 found significant effects of such disinformation.[47] In a survey of such voters conducted after the elections, Gutner and others discover that belief in such fake news increased the probability of defecting to Trump by 18 percent—a factor only second in its strength to whether they had positive views of Hillary Clinton or not (20 percent less likely).[48]

Another recent analysis by me[49] focused instead on the effects of the leaks of the hacked Russian documents that were spread through WikiLeaks. I found that the Russian intervention increased overall Trump's vote share by 2.03 percent—enough to give him seventy-five electoral college votes and an electoral college victory. Drilling into the effects of the leaks using pre-election survey data, the mere exposure to the leaks was sufficient, for example, to significantly reduce the probability of voting for Clinton among Independents and Republicans (by −17.6 percent and −20.2 percent, respectively), counteracting much of the negative effects of some domestic pre-election leaks against Trump (such as the "Access Hollywood" tape). Using Google keyword data, I also found significant interest in WikiLeaks throughout the United

[42] Kathleen Hall Jamieson, Cyberwar: How Russian Hackers and Trolls Helped Elect a President (2018).

[43] *Id.*

[44] A private firm located in St. Petersburg, which was covertly tasked by the Russian government to conduct this aspect of the Russian electoral intervention. Robert S. Mueller III, Dep't of Justice, Report on the Investigation into Russian Interference in the 2016 Presidential Election, vol. 1 (2019) [hereinafter Mueller Report].

[45] Damian Ruck et al., *Internet Research Agency Twitter Activity Predicted 2016 U.S. Election Polls*, 24 First Monday (2019).

[46] *Id.*

[47] Richard Gunther, Paul Beck, & Erik Nisbet, *Fake News and the Defection of 2012 Obama Voters in the 2016 Presidential Election*, 61 Electoral Stud. (2019).

[48] *Id.*

[49] Levin, *supra* note 36.

States in the run-up to the elections, including hundreds of thousands of searches each month in the three key swing states (Wisconsin, Michigan, and Pennsylvania) that gave Trump his victory.

However, most scholars of American politics[50] are still highly skeptical about these arguments.[51] For example, Sides and others following an analysis of a six wave poll of overall voting preferences before and after the elections, claimed to have observed no significant shifts in voters' views of Clinton or voting intentions as a result of the leaks of the hacked DNC documents.[52] They also argue, based on existing data on the domestic spending by both campaigns on ads of various kinds, as well as domestically produced political memes and partisan content, that the Russian-sponsored content was an "infinitesimal fraction" of the overall political content to which voters were exposed to prior to the election—and therefore quite unlikely to be of any consequence.[53] Likewise, in regard to the effects of "fake news," for example, Guess and others argue, based on a post-election survey combined with data on the respondents' actual web traffic history, that it largely reached a very small subgroup of the American population that was already highly conservative and strongly pro-Trump.[54]

C. Effects on the Target State's Democracy

Election interference, when done by the United States or by another liberal power, is frequently seen in the West as an effective tool for promoting or protecting democracy. In one recent case, in the immediate aftermath of the Arab Spring, members of the U.S. foreign policy community called on President Obama to intervene in favor of the liberal groups in the forthcoming elections of the postrevolutionary Arab states (such as Egypt and Tunisia) in order to make sure that actual or perceived antidemocratic forces in the region did not "spoil" the transition. For example, representative Howard Berman, among other members of the U.S. Congress, declared in early 2011 that "our [the United States'] job is to create an alternative" to the Muslim Brotherhood.[55] Ray Takeyh, a senior fellow at the Council of Foreign Relations, claimed in a *Washington Post* op-ed that the "U.S. must take sides to keep the Arab

[50] American politics is the subfield in political science dedicated to the study of U.S. domestic politics—including, of course, U.S. elections. Some scholars in Comparative Politics share this skepticism based on similar lines of argument as well as the supposed ineffectiveness of Russian meddling in general. Lucan Way & Adam Casey, "*How Can We Know if Russia Is a Threat to Western Democracy? Understanding the Impact of Russia's Second Wave of Election Interference,*" Stanford University, Freeman Spogli Institute for International Studies, Global Populisms and Their International Diffusion (Mar. 2019).

[51] *See, e.g.*, Andrew Guess, Jonathan Nagler, & Joshua Tucker, *Less Than You Think: Prevalence and Predictors of Fake News Dissemination on Facebook*, 5 Sci. Advances (Jan. 9, 2019); Brendan Nyhan, *Fake News and Bots May Be Worrisome, but Their Political Power Is Overblown*, N.Y. Times (Feb. 13, 2018); Levi Boxell, Matthew Gentzkow, & Jesse Shapiro, *A Note on Internet Use and the 2016 U.S. Presidential Election Outcome*, 13 PLOS ONE (2018); John Sides, Michael Tesler, & Lynn Vavereck, Identity Crisis: The 2016 Presidential Campaign and the Battle for the Meaning of America 311–312 (2018).

[52] Sides, Tesler, & Vaverck, *supra* note 51, at 311–312.

[53] *Id.*

[54] Guess, Nagler, & Tucker *supra* note 51. For a similar result by economists, *see* Hunt Allcott & Matt Gentzkow, *Social Media and Fake News in the 2016 Election*, Journal of Economic Perspectives 31.

[55] Thomas Carothers, *How Not to Promote Democracy in Egypt*, Washington Post (Feb. 24, 2011).

Spring from Islamist takeover."[56] Many others concurred.[57] Even some of the pundits who opposed the use of electoral interventions in specific cases agree with supporters that such interference, when wielded by a liberal power, can usually be an effective tool for promoting and protecting democracy.[58] In contrast, electoral interference by authoritarian powers is usually perceived as harmful for democracy.

A growing body of research on this question finds partisan election interference by either kind of intervening state to usually have quite negative effects on the target state's democracy. My own research, for example, employing a statistical analysis of the effects of such American and USSR/Russian interventions worldwide between 1946 and 2000 found that a successful intervention (i.e., one in which the assisted side won) significantly increased the chances of a democratic breakdown in the targeted state in the following five years by a factor of 2.5 to 8 times.[59] The effects of USSR/Russian interventions were a bit more harmful under some measures, but the effects of either power were both quite negative. Furthermore, interventions in relatively competitive elections in transitional or competitive authoritarian regimes[60] did not increase the chances of the target state to democratize.[61]

Tomz and Weeks, in a survey experiment conducted in the United States, find that an electoral intervention leads to serious damage to three key aspects of a healthy democracy.[62] The first is a drop in trust in the integrity of the electoral system (by between 16 percent and 53 percent). The second is a decrease in the share of the public interested in voting in a future election (by between 4 percent and 12 percent). The third is a decline in faith in American democracy overall (by between 10 percent and 33 percent). The exact identity of the foreign intervening state noted in the experiment had little effect on these results. The decrease is smaller for methods of intervention which are overt (such as pre-election threats) in comparison to methods that are usually covert, such as the release of false information about a certain candidate or party, and become public knowledge due to inadvertent exposure.

A third study, focusing on the credibility of elections (a key factor in shaping attitudes on democracy) has found a negative yet conditional effect. In a set of survey experiments conducted in Georgia and in the United States, Bush and Prather found that the effects of a public or exposed meddling depended on the perceived capabilities of

[56] Ray Takeyh, *U.S. Must Take Sides to Keep the Arab Spring from Islamist Takeover*, WASHINGTON POST (Mar. 23, 2011).

[57] *See, e.g.*, Carothers, *supra* note 55; Charles Krauthammer, *From Freedom Agenda to Freedom Doctrine*, WASHINGTON POST (Feb. 10, 2011); Robert Satloff, *U.S. Policy and Egypt's Presidential Runoff: Projecting Clarity, Not Disinterest*, 1945 POLICY WATCH (June 1, 2012). The currently available evidence indicates that President Obama rejected these recommendations and did not intervene in the elections in either Egypt or Tunisia in the immediate aftermath of the Arab Spring. David D. Kirkpatrick & Steven Lee Myers, *Overtures to Egypt's Islamists Reverse Longtime U.S. Policy*, N.Y. TIMES (Jan. 3, 2012); Josh Rogin, *State Department Training Islamic Political Parties in Egypt*, FOR. POL'Y (Nov. 3, 2011).

[58] George Will, *Egypt's Revolution to Win or Lose*, WASHINGTON POST (Feb. 9, 2011).

[59] Dov H. Levin, *A Vote for Freedom? The Effects of Partisan Electoral Interventions on Regime Type*, 63 J. CONFLICT RES. 839–868 (2019).

[60] Examples of such regimes include Iran or Yugoslavia/Serbia under Milosevic.

[61] Those are also situations, as noted in the previous section, where intervening states are least likely to succeed in securing the victory of the assisted candidate/party. LEVIN *supra* note 36.

[62] Tomz & Weeks *supra* note 30.

the meddler.[63] Respondents who perceived the intervening state as being capable of affecting elections saw the results of the election as significantly less credible and vice versa. Naturally, interventions by major powers, which are usually expected to have greater capability to affect other states' internal affairs, would accordingly be expected to cause more advertent and inadvertent harm to the credibility of the intervened target state's elections. Likewise, given that high levels of political polarization are also a well-known factor in the processes that frequently leads to democratic breakdowns,[64] the finding in section IV.A on the effects of such interference on polarization also indirectly indicates serious harm to the target state's democracy.[65]

Election interference seems to damage the target state's democracy through a few pathways. First, when the foreign intervention is public or exposed, knowledge of such interference may lead parts of the targeted public, especially on the losing side, to question how reflective of their will are the results of the elections.[66] Decreasing belief that the results of the elections accurately reflect their preferences can reduce their desire to vote or to participate in other peaceful political activities, thus sapping overall support for democracy. Furthermore, by reducing trust in the integrity of the election system and in a state's democratic institutions, electoral interventions can create a feedback loop in which such beliefs make it harder for the government to effectively govern and rally public support for its side, leading to more ineffective governance, which reduces even further the public's trust and faith in democracy.[67]

Second, when the electoral intervention is covert it can damage the target state's democracy in various ways. Due to the need for strict secrecy in order for a covert intervention to remain hidden (and the more morally dubious acts it frequently entails, such as spreading disinformation and so forth), the types of aided leaders who request such assistance are likely to have authoritarian tendencies and to try to undermine their state's democratic institutions once in power.[68] Likewise, many forms of covert intervention encourage corruption, a well-known cause of democratic breakdown.[69] This is because many types of interference that are usually done in a covert manner would usually be considered, if done by domestic actors, as serious forms of political corruption (i.e., breaking into the competing party's offices prior to an election in search of useful information, secret unreported campaign donations from local firms, etc.).[70] Furthermore, the resources provided in such meddling, due to their highly covert nature, are an extremely easy target for "skimming" by the assisted side's politicians for their personal use. As a result, the provision of such assistance can corrupt the recipient leaders, which, in turn, will spread such bad practices to their

[63] Sarah Bush & Lauren Prather, *From Monitoring to Meddling: How Foreign Actors Shape Local Trust in Elections*, American Political Science Association (Washington D.C., Aug. 2019).

[64] Bubeck & Marinov, *supra* note 37, at 226.

[65] *Id.* at 175–176 (finding a difference in means test an increase in the chances of democratization following an American intervention. However, their measure in this case also includes a large number of unrelated neutral interventions (such as election monitoring)).

[66] This is especially likely to be the case when the intervening state is believed by the target state's public to have the ability to affect the results in practice. Bush & Prather, *supra* note 63.

[67] Tomz & Weeks, *supra* note 30.

[68] Levin, *supra* note 59.

[69] Larry Diamond, Developing Democracy: Toward Consolidation 91–93 (1999).

[70] Levin, *supra* note 59.

underlings.[71] Indeed senior American officials in charge of supervising such covert interventions by the CIA were already complaining in the late 1950s that one of the effects of such meddling was "spreading a little more corruption."[72]

D. Effects on Intrastate Violence

In 1957, the U.S. government assisted with campaign funding and other methods the then-president of Lebanon, Camille Chamoun, in the Lebanese parliamentary elections (the body that, under Lebanon's constitution at the time, would be in charge of selecting Lebanon's next president a few months later). The success of Chamoun's supporters in this election, and the widespread expectation that Chamoun would use this victory to change the Lebanese constitution and subsequently have parliament select him for a second term, ignited a wave of protests throughout Lebanon, protests that escalated into a brief civil war a few months afterward.[73] Nineteen years later, the United States openly interfered in the 1976 Italian elections in favor of the Christian Democratic incumbents with, among other things, Secretary of State Henry Kissinger publicly warning in the run-up that a victory by their main opponents, the Italian Communist Party, would lead to serious damage to NATO and to other "serious consequences" for Italy. The Communist Party's defeat in this election greatly disappointed the Italian far left, a disappointment that caused some left-wing Italian radicals to give up on electoral politics and turn to terrorism. This turn led in the following four years to the creation of a new terrorist group and a significant increase in the amounts of domestic left-wing terrorism.[74]

There is growing evidence that domestic violence and instability in the aftermath of electoral interventions is no coincidence. I have found, for example, that in the aftermath of an overt foreign electoral intervention that succeeds in placing its preferred candidate or party in power increases the amounts of domestic terrorism in the target state.[75] Overall in those circumstances, the chances of a new terrorist group being created in a state rises by 10.5 percent, and the overall number of domestic terrorist incidents increase by 152 percent, an unintentional effect that is on par in their magnitude to the effects of intentional state sponsorship of terrorist groups.[76]

The success of such interference reduces the political efficacy of peaceful politics for the losing side (both in practice and in public perception), thus unintentionally increasing the utility of violent politics for some of the more radical members of that camp. Likewise, when electoral interventions are done in an overt manner they are frequently perceived by some people on the losing side as evidence that their

[71] *Id.* Covert interventions can also in a few cases harm democracy by inadvertently spreading certain "worse practices" to the target such as advanced election fraud methods *Id.*

[72] "Minutes of the special group meeting July 7, 1960," NSC Presidential Records, Intelligence Files: 1953–1961 Dwight D. Eisenhower Presidential Library.

[73] Wilbur Eveland, Ropes of Sand: America's Failure in the Middle East (1980).

[74] Richard Drake, The Revolutionary Mystique and Terrorism in Contemporary Italy 24 (1989); Ami Pedahzur & Leonard Weinberg, Political Parties and Terrorist Groups 16 (2003).

[75] Dov H. Levin, *Voting for Trouble? Partisan Electoral Interventions and Terrorism*, Terrorism & Pol. Violence (2018).

[76] *Id.*

government has effectively become a "puppet" of the intervening state and therefore illegitimate. Reduced regime legitimacy, in turn, increases the effectiveness of an existing terrorist group's propaganda and recruitment efforts while also encouraging the formation of new terrorist groups.

E. Policy Reactions to Election Interference

In the aftermath of the Russian interference in the 2016 U.S. elections, multiple senior elected officials, commentators, and former members of U.S. intelligence agencies described these Russian acts in extremely harsh terms (e.g., from "the equivalent of Pearl Harbor"[77] to "an act of war"[78] to a "9/11-Scale event"[79]). These comments implied that severe retaliation by the target state against a foreign government that interferes in its elections is a commonplace and natural reaction.

However, in practice, a careful overview of the known cases of foreign electoral meddling since World War II shows how rarely the target state attempts to "punish" the intervening state for such acts. This is the case even when the side that the foreign power intervened against nevertheless won the elections. Given the usual power differentials between the intervening state and the target state, it seems that the harmed leader usually prefers to let "bygones be bygones" when it comes to unsuccessful electoral interference rather than further inflame or ignite a rivalry with a far stronger state.[80] The American government's imposition of additional economic sanctions on Russia in the aftermath of the exposure of its intervention in 2016 is a rare exception to the usual pattern of nonreaction to meddling when it is overt or exposed.[81]

From the limited information available thus far, there also seems to usually be little public support within the target state for costly or harsh methods of retaliation to such interference. This is the case even in strong states that usually have the capability to react in this manner. For example, Tomz and Weeks in a survey experiment in the United States find little support for military retaliation even for the most egregious exposed meddling (such as the spreading of accurate or fake news or funding of one side's election campaign), with only 15 percent of the American public supporting a U.S. military strike in such a situation, and only 25 percent supporting military threats.[82] The only measures for which there is majority support are diplomatic (59 percent) or economic (72 percent) sanctions. When less egregious forms of interference (such as pre-election threats) are used by a foreign power in an American

[77] MSNBC, Feb. 17, 2018 (Representative Jerry Nadler).

[78] Daniel Chaltin, *John McCain: Russian Cyberattacks "An Act of War,"* Washington Examiner (Dec. 30, 2016); Morgan Chalfant, *Dem Senator: Russian Hacking May Have Been "Act of War,"* The Hill (Mar. 2, 2017) (Senator Jeane Shaheen).

[79] MSNBC, Feb. 14, 2017 (Thomas Friedman).

[80] Dov H. Levin, *Will You Still Love Me Tomorrow? Partisan Electoral Interventions, Foreign Policy Compliance, and Voting in the U.N.*, Int. Interactions (forthcoming 2021).

[81] And according to one recent account of the reaction of the Obama White House to the growing evidence of Russian meddling in 2016 even that retaliation only came after many months of inconclusive deliberations with many proposed reactions by various staffers being vetoed. David Shimer, Rigged: America, Russia and One Hundred Years of Covert Electoral Interference (2020).

[82] Tomz & Weeks, *supra* note 30.

election, support for military options is even lower, and there is no support among a majority of Americans for any form of retaliation. When a foreign power, especially a major power, openly interferes in an election in another state, it has a good reason to believe that, at least in the short term, it will avoid any immediate retaliation from the target state for its actions.

V. Conclusions

As this brief overview indicates, decision makers and the general public in democracies around the world have good reason to worry about election interference in their elections. Such partisan electoral interventions are quite common. They have been conducted in one out of every nine elections since World War II and utilized by many different state actors. These intervening states have used a wide repertoire of tools for this purpose, from overt threats to campaign funding and various dirty tricks. Many such interventions remained a secret for years after the interference had concluded.

The small but rapidly growing research on the effects of electoral interference already provides strong indications that it can have major effects and cause serious harm to the target state in many circumstances. Electoral interventions can frequently have significant influence on the intervened election results, enough in many plausible situations to determine the identity of the winner. They can cause serious damage to the target state's democracy regardless of the intervening state's identity and significantly increase the chances of its collapse into an authoritarian regime. Such interference also polarizes the target state's view about the intervening state. Finally, such meddling can also increase the chances of internal violence in the target state, raising, for example, the amount of domestic terrorism in the target state as well as the probability of new terrorist groups emerging there.

The number of known election interference cases using cyber tools is too small at present to analyze in any systemic manner. Nevertheless, there are two strong substantive reasons to believe that, when the data is eventually available to systematically analyze meddling conducted using cyber tools or digital methods, the effects will not be significantly different or less negative in nature then their offline or analog brethren.

First, all of the meddling methods known to have been used digitally thus far have merely been the same wine in different glass bottles. Every major component of the Russian intervention in 2016, to give one key example, could have been conducted by Russia in an alternate universe in which the internet did not exist using tried-and-true meddling methods—from using long-standing informants or compromised employees inside the DNC in order to take out some "embarrassing" documents to encouraging or bribing American journalists to publish news articles about the leaked documents or any other "fake news" about Hillary Clinton that they wanted to spread. Using the internet in the manner used thus far for electoral interventions (or other plausible future ways) is the equivalent of using Amazon.com to buy a paperback book instead of going to a local bookstore for this purpose—the product is provided to the recipient through a different method, but its nature is identical.

Second, one key factor frequently referred to in the public debate regarding the supposedly unprecedented nature of much such cyber meddling—the digital distribution methods—have some important limitations compared to the older "traditional" media at their prime. It is probably true that the use of Facebook and Twitter for the Russian intervention in 2016 sometimes led more Americans to encounter a particular piece of "fake news" in 2016 then, say, "planting" it in a few regular U.S. newspapers circa 1956 would have. However, there is a big, well-known difference: in the consumption habits of information provided through each delivery method. For example, many more people in 1956 were likely to have carefully read such a newspaper article and believed its contents than nowadays to believe one of the endless posts on their Twitter or Facebook feeds by one of the people they follow. Indeed, many people nowadays when online "like" or retweet links to articles that they have not bothered to read whatsoever. These trade-offs between these two information distribution methods probably lead overall to a more or less equal number of targeted people significantly affected by such "fake news."

Accordingly, policymakers, practitioners, and scholars in charge of formulating policy solutions for and combating online interference at home or abroad need to keep in mind a few key lessons from the research on this topic thus far. First, they need to be aware of the likely limitations the targets of such interference (or third parties) face in formulating a response to such meddling once it is known to have occurred. As noted, senior decision makers, even when they were the target of such meddling, are usually wary of trying to retaliate against the intervening state out of fear of worsening relations. Likewise, even publics in very powerful democracies, such as the United States, show little support for harsh methods of retaliation (such as military action) and may even oppose the use of sanctions of various kinds following the use of most methods of intervention against them.

Furthermore, much interference is covert and is unlikely to be detected at any level of certainty prior to the conclusion of an election and for years afterward. The case of the 2016 U.S. election where, due to Russian incompetence and what seems to be well-placed American intelligence sources,[83] both the intervention and the identity of the intervening state were quickly discovered with rather high levels of certainty, is unlikely to soon repeat itself in the future.

Second, as section IV.C shows, trying to fight fire with fire (e.g., intervening in another state's elections in order to promote democracy or to counter another state's own intervention) can have equally bad side effects. It may increase the chances of a democratic breakdown in the targeted state. A democratic intervening state can cause almost as much harm to a state's democracy as an authoritarian one in this manner. Accordingly, policy solutions meant to deal with such meddling should focus more on harm minimization and prevention rather than on retaliation, counterinterventions, or deterrence.

[83] Julian E. Barnes, Adam Goldman, & David E. Sanger, *CIA Informant Extracted from Russia Had Sent Secrets to US*, N.Y. Times (Sept. 9, 2019). The currently available evidence indicates that the Russian government invested significant resources in trying to keep this intervention covert and that the inadvertent pre-election exposure of its role was an unplanned failure on its side. *See, e.g.*, Mueller Report, *supra* note 44 (Investigation, Grand Jury Indictment July 13, 2018).

Third, policymakers must avoid the "fighting the last war" syndrome when trying to deal with partisan election meddling. Since 2016, most policymaker, practitioner, and scholarly efforts in this regard have focused on ways to detect, stop, or at least minimize the effects of the key methods used by Russia in its intervention in 2016 (such as the spreading of propaganda and fake news through social media). Naturally, efforts in this regard are quite important. However, as noted, there are a wide range of other methods or tools that foreign powers have used; "dirty tricks"—the main method used by Russia in 2016—was not even one of the most popular among meddlers. A future attempt by Russia or by other powers to meddle in the elections of democracies with "problematic" leaders or candidates may thus use a different intervention method. Accordingly, more attention must be given to dealing with those methods as well, either in their existing forms or in the possible ways by which they can be "digitized" in the future.

2
Understanding Disinformation Operations in the Twenty-First Century

Steven J. Barela and Jérôme Duberry

Although there is nothing necessarily new about propaganda, the affordances of social networking technologies—algorithms, automation, and big data—change the scale, scope, and precision of how information is transmitted in the digital age.[1]

I. Introduction

The term *dezinformatsiya* is said to have been coined by Joseph Stalin and denotes the political tactic of spreading fragments of falsehoods by design against one's adversaries.[2] One valuable source to begin understanding such actions is through the former three-star general for the secret police of Romania, Lt. Gen. Ion Mihai Pacepa, who in 1978 was one of the highest-ranking officials to defect from the Communist bloc. Our chapter will begin here as his view offers unique insights into the nature of the activity.

Beyond this basic understanding, there is a reason why the global community is witnessing a dramatic rise of state-sponsored disinformation operations carried out across international borders: the remarkable developments in information and communication technologies (ICTs) provide opportunities for spreading *dezinformatsiya* with a volume and accuracy that has never been known before. In the wake of such actions—to be labeled *disinfo-ops* in this chapter—the targeted societies have found themselves destabilized as facts and events become deeply contested among citizens. Indeed, we believe that much of the exacerbated political division we are witnessing today arises from a wide disagreement over the terms of what is actually happening in society.

Political marketing innovations have led to the emergence of a novel news ecosystem where marketeers, political parties, and criminal groups share the same tools, strategies, and expertise to access citizens' data and influence their behavior. The rapid

[1] Samantha Bradshaw & Philip N. Howard, The Global Disinformation Order: 2019 Global Inventory of Organised Social Media Manipulation, Project on Computational Propaganda 11 (2019).

[2] Lt. Gen. Ion Mihai Pacepa & Ronald J. Rychlak, Disinformation: Former Spy Chief Reveals Secret Strategies for Undermining Freedom, Attacking Religion, and Promoting Terrorism 39 (2013).

Steven J. Barela and Jérôme Duberry, *Understanding Disinformation Operations in the Twenty-First Century* In: *Defending Democracies*. Edited by Duncan B. Hollis and Jens David Ohlin, Oxford University Press (2021). © Duncan B. Hollis & Jens David Ohlin. DOI: 10.1093/oso/9780197556979.003.0003

and wide growth of social media platforms and associated marketing instruments has contributed to the emergence of a new set of vulnerabilities—exploited with the greatly enhanced *breadth*, *depth*, and targeting *precision* of digital disinformation campaigns.[3]

In the coming pages we provide a descriptive work to illustrate the essential components of this activity today, to be organized in the following manner. Section II will offer a view on Soviet-era disinformation campaigns through the eyes of Pacepa, the former Romanian intelligence chief. Sections III and IV will respectively outline the elements of information warfare and the role of today's big data and social media platforms. Then, to provide detailed insight into the practice, we will put forward an example in section V of distorted content based on foreign maneuvers being amplified in social media.

There are three important conclusions to draw from this exploration. First, because disinformation aims to twist the truth in subtle ways when key facts remain secret and unavailable, exposing an operation becomes a tedious and difficult task. Second, the new digital world of ICTs has opened the door to omnipresent operations that occur below the threshold of armed conflict and are accelerated exponentially by big data warehousing and algorithms that allow individualized targeting during an election cycle. Each of these developments requires progress in international law to regulate an activity that is different in kind from what has been previously known. Third, when disinformation operations disrupt the flow of information during a political campaign, the candidates involved and the process itself emerge with an eroded legitimacy—a sine qua non for all societies.

In addition to these insights, this study brings us to one overall important finding: breaking and distorting information flows within a foreign society goes largely untracked today. The bulk of these operations are occurring in the difficult to research space of online social media (closed for reasons of privacy and trade secrets). Consequently, section VI will close our chapter by raising a clarion call to allow access for social scientists to study what is happening in this opaque public square where ever more political understanding is being fashioned. More comprehensive empirical study promises to unlock desperately needed details still missing from the analysis of digital *disinfo-ops*.

II. *Dezinformatsiya*

Capturing the nature and essence of disinformation is by no means easy. When an operation is successful, people have been subtly influenced to accept a narrative that has been purposefully bent by external forces to accommodate a political agenda. However, very few people readily admit that they have been duped, manipulated, or even influenced by someone without their knowledge. We all cherish our intellectual

[3] In particular, we believe these three parameters should be used to give measurable and verifiable shape to the term of "coercion" as it pertains to the international law principle of nonintervention. *See* Steven J. Barela, *Cross-Border Cyber Ops to Erode Legitimacy: An Act of Coercion*, Just Security (Jan. 12, 2017); Steven J. Barela, *Zero Shades of Grey: Russian-Ops Violate International Law*, Just Security (Mar. 29, 2018).

autonomy. When such a campaign is carried out on a massive scale, proving its existence often runs against conventional knowledge of facts and events. So how do we talk about widely shared misunderstandings that have been pushed with tiny nudges from an outside force?

As a starting point it is helpful to note that this practice has been classified under various terms over the last century. One volume on intelligence history has explained that during the Soviet era, "disinformation operations against enemy special services had several [...] designations: 'actions of influence,' 'operational disinformation,' 'active measures,' 'operational games,' 'assistance measures' etc."[4] Today, "information warfare," "information confrontation," and "cyberwarfare" are terms often used to describe such subversion campaigns aiming to weaken and undermine adversary societies using ICTs.[5] Nevertheless, the existence of multiple terms already demonstrates part of the difficulty. Some scholars have pointed out that words themselves are used to obfuscate: " 'Active measures' is a historical, now somewhat imprecise term. Like many Russian terms, this one also is a façade, behind which various methods of influencing the international community are concealed."[6] Duly noting these variations, we will simplify the discussion in this chapter by largely applying "disinformation" and *dezinformatsiya* for the deep-rooted Soviet tactic, and *disinfo-ops* for today's application with new technologies.

To illuminate the discussion for our purposes we turn to Lt. Gen. Ion Mihai Pacepa and look into his 2013 book, co-authored with Ronald J. Rychlak, entitled, *Disinformation: Former Spy Chief Reveals Secret Strategies for Undermining Freedom, Attacking Religion, and Promoting Terrorism*.[7] In doing so, even briefly, it is necessary to acknowledge that many of the suggested corrections to contemporary events can produce pause. This is because successful information operations make searching for a truth that runs counter to a dominant belief onerous and time-consuming.[8] To then convince others of the need for correction becomes another daunting task entirely. As

[4] Herbert Romerstein, *Disinformation as a KGB Weapon in the Cold War*, 1 J. INTEL. HIST. 54 (2001) (citing OCHERKI ISTORYA ROSSIISKOY VNESHNY RAZVEDKI, MEZHDUNARODNIYE OTNSHENIYA, VOL. 2, at 13–14 (Y.M. Primakov ed., 1996)).

[5] *See, e.g.*, KEIR GILES, HANDBOOK OF RUSSIAN INFORMATION WARFARE 24 (NATO Defense College, 2016); THOMAS ELKJER NISSEN, #THEWEAPONIZATIONOFSOCIALMEDIA 31 (Royal Danish Defence College, 2015); Andrew Foxall, *Putin's Cyberwar: Russia's Statecraft in the Fifth Domain*, 1 Russia Studies Centre (Policy Paper No. 9, 2016); Dima Adamsky, *Cross-Domain Coercion: The Current Russian Art of Strategy*, Institut français des relations internationals 1–43 (Proliferation Papers No. 54, 2015). For discussion of what has been incorrectly termed the "Gerasimov Doctrine" from the scholar who created it, *see* Mark Galeotti, *The Mythical "Gerasimov Doctrine" and the Language of Threat*, 7 CRIT. STUD. SEC. 157–161 (2019); *see also* Mark Galeotti, *The "Gerasimov Doctrine" and Russian Non-Linear War*, IN MOSCOW'S SHADOWS (2013), *at* https://inmoscowsshadows.wordpress.com/2014/07/06/the-gerasimov-doctrine-and-russian-non-linear-war/ (Galeotti's original blog publishing the first translation by Rob Coalson of the speech by Russian Chief of the General Staff Valery Gerasimov in 2013 appearing in VOENNO-PROMYSHLENNYI KUR'ER (Military-Industrial Courier)).

[6] Jolanta Darczewska & Piotr Żochowski, *Active Measures, Russia's Key Export*, 64 POINT OF VIEW 12 (Centre for Eastern Studies, No. 64, 2017).

[7] *See* PACEPA & RYCHLAK, *supra* note 2. For similar firsthand testimony of a Czech defector from the Czech intelligence and security services, *see* LADISLAV BITTMAN, THE KGB AND SOVIET DISINFORMATION: AN INSIDER'S VIEW 50 (1985); *see also* KGB defector Yuri Bezmenov, *Warning to America*, YOUTUBE (Feb. 1, 2013), *available at* <https://www.youtube.com/watch?v=bX3EZCVj2XA>.

[8] *See* GILES, *supra* note 5, at 58 ("countering every single piece of Russian disinformation is labour-intensive out of all proportion to the result").

a result, our intention in this first section of the chapter is simply to elucidate the elusive concept of disinformation, rather than to analyze the veracity of the entire list of historical amendments presented in the Pacepa and Rychlak book.[9]

As one of the top advisers to President Nicolae Ceaușescu of communist Romania and chief of its intelligence service, Pacepa's perspective is unique. He is able to discuss the concept of disinformation from the vantage point of key meetings, access to top-secret documents, and sensitive discussions within the KGB of the Soviet era. Fundamentally, the intelligence services that Pacepa oversaw were spending a great deal of their resources curating narratives, rewriting history, and framing enemies rather than gathering information. In fact, the function of discovering what adversaries were doing was largely subordinated to the efforts of manufacturing and propagating a slightly adjusted reality to suit their government's interests: "During the Cold War, more people in the Soviet bloc worked for the disinformation machinery than for the Soviet army and defense industry put together."[10]

Even if deception has deep roots around the globe in wartime, Pacepa claims that the idea that this tactic should be elevated to the status of a permanent peacetime national policy was born in Russia.[11] As one indication of this, he recounted that the highly classified Russian training manuals on disinformation taught that it was first the fruit of Prince Grigory Potemkin's efforts to charm Catherine the Great. Many know that Prince Grigory constructed empty-façade villages to feign rural prosperity along the route she would take in Crimea in the eighteenth century—hence the term used today of a "Potemkin village."[12] These manuals that regulated and instructed Pacepa's role as an intelligence chief made special note of its Russian roots and proudly termed it a "science."[13] So sophisticated was this science that Joseph Stalin chose to even obscure its origins to the outside world by spreading the rumor that the Russian term actually only came as a translation from the French. Pacepa explains that his intelligence services were instructed to circulate this idea by their Soviet counterparts,

[9] Pacepa and Rychlak contend that the Soviet Union, followed by Russia, launched information operations that range from framing Pope Pius XII as Hitler's Pope, claiming CIA involvement in the assassination of President John F. Kennedy, fanning the flames of conflict in the Middle East, launching defamatory attacks on American soldiers in Vietnam, and advancing a socialist transformation in the United States during the Obama era. *Id.* Perhaps most troublesome for these authors is the charge of a false story put forward in the epilogue: "France and Germany accused the US of torturing the al-Qaeda prisoners held at its military prison in Guantanamo Bay, Cuba" *Id.* at 353. This has now undoubtedly been shown to be true—not *dezinformatsiya*. *See, e.g.*, Interrogation and Torture: Integrating Efficacy, with Law and Morality (S.J. Barela et al. eds., 2020). This last erroneous assertion shows an enormous difficulty caused by disinformation—it can often be dismissed as a matter of political perspective. Nevertheless, amplifying illegal, immoral, and ineffective actions by the CIA in this case can still serve the purposes of the operation to delegitimize the government of an adversary.

[10] Pacepa & Rychlak, *supra* note 2, at 38; *see also* Bezmenov, *supra* note 7 ("The main emphasis of the KGB is not in the area of intelligence at all. According to my opinion, and many opinions of defectors of my caliber, only about 15% of time, money and manpower is spent on espionage as such. The other 85% is a slow process which we call ideological subversion or active measures.").

[11] Pacepa's claim of the initial historic roots starting in Russia is less important here. More importantly, we find that other various sources suggest that for Russia today, there is little difference between wartime and peacetime. *See* Giles, *supra* note 5, at 4; Adamsky, *supra* note 5, at 29.

[12] Pacepa & Rychlak, *supra* note 2, at 36–37.

[13] *Id.* at 36.

and the operating definition is captured in the 1952 edition of the *Great Soviet Encyclopedia* that describes it as a capitalist tool:

> DEZINFORMATSIYA (from *des* and French *information*). Dissemination (in the press, on the radio, etc.) of false reports intended to mislead public opinion.[14]

While the Pacepa and Rychlak book offers general descriptions of disinformation as a means, most intricate and extensive are the dismantlings of successful Soviet operations that have taken root and grown into a narrative all their own. To carry out the task that dominates nearly half of the book—unraveling the transformation of a Christian leader who silently provided aid and saved numerous Jews during the Holocaust into "Hitler's Pope"—Lt. Gen. Pacepa worked with a co-author who is a historian and law professor. Professor Rychlak had extensively researched and written his own book on the subject of Pope Pius XII, uncovering Soviet efforts to discredit the Catholic Church and its leader.[15] The two were well suited to their task: "an in-depth, guided tour of a sophisticated, complicated, long-term, multifaceted campaign of pure lies and smears. That is the nature of disinformation."[16]

Emerging from World War II, Joseph Stalin took to framing those whom he saw as a threat as "Nazi collaborators" and removed them from the scene via arrest, trial, detention, or death. This included high-ranking figures in the Ukrainian Catholic Church. Pius XII issued an encyclical announcing that "all its bishops and many of its priests have been arrested," and assured the faithful in Ukraine that God would "calm this terrible storm and . . . bring it to an end."[17] The authors explain that this was taken as a deep affront by Stalin and an offensive disinformation campaign was launched against Pius XII along with other Catholic leaders.

One of the most dramatic operations described in the book was unleashed upon the archbishop of Hungary, Jószef Mindszenty.[18] It was lauded in the highly classified Soviet manuals of disinformation because it was meant to encapsulate a significant refrain emphasized in all caps on the first page, "IF YOU ARE GOOD AT DISINFORMATION, YOU CAN GET AWAY WITH ANYTHING."[19] That is, the KGB believed that the operation against Cardinal Mindszenty showed that it was possible to "neutralize even a saint" and was one of "our most stupendous, monumental *dezinformatsiya* operations."[20] The Roman Catholic clergyman was arrested and convicted of treason in 1949, and then later sought asylum in the U.S. embassy of Budapest, spending fifteen years in voluntary confinement there. Today the *Encyclopedia Britannica* explicates that he "personified uncompromising opposition

[14] *Id.* at 39. The *Larousse* dictionary carried no mention of the word in either its 1952 or 1978 editions.

[15] RONALD J. RYCHLAK, HITLER, THE WAR, AND THE POPE (2010).

[16] PACEPA & RYCHLAK, *supra* note 2, at 55. As seen later, the accusation of "pure lies and smears" is an exaggeration.

[17] Encyclical of Pope Pius XII to the Venerable Brethren, the Patriarchs, Primates, Archbishops, Bishops, and other Ordinaries in Peace and Communion with the Apostolic See (Dec. 23, 1945), *available at* <http://www.vatican.va/content/pius-xii/en/encyclicals/documents/hf_p-xii_enc_23121945_orientales-omnes-ecclesias.html>.

[18] Alex Last, *Fifteen Years Holed Up in an Embassy*, BBC NEWS (Sept. 6, 2012).

[19] PACEPA & RYCHLAK, *supra* note 2, at 80.

[20] *Id.*

to fascism and communism in Hungary for more than five decades of the 20th century."[21] Nonetheless, this opponent was forced into isolation.

While the Mindszenty case would appear to be more straightforward, the same cannot be said for Pope Pius XII. Indeed, successful operations are built on two pillars:[22] first, they must contain a "kernel of truth";[23] and, second, they should be planted in local sources to lend credibility to the narrative far beyond what the Soviets could achieve with their own statements.[24] When these two elements are the foundation, disentangling and proving the existence of a foreign operation are extremely difficult.

In this case, the solid grain of fact that would serve as the foundation of the campaign against Pius XII was that he never publicly denounced the persecution of Jews and anti-Semitic laws by Nazis—neither during nor after the war.[25] Of course, Pacepa and Rychlak go out of their way to document the moments when Pius XII spoke up and defended the Jews during the Holocaust.[26] However, at the same time, one moment that has been commemorated in a plaque in the historic Jewish ghetto outside the windows of the Vatican is the night of October 16, 1943, when over one thousand Jews were rounded up and deported out of Rome to Auschwitz.[27] This tragic event is a hard truth.

As for sources from the West that framed Pius XII, three are deeply analyzed by Pacepa and Rychlak to unknot an extensive campaign. One is the book *The Silence of Pius XII*, which uses "heavy-handed documentation" from a communist Croatian trial[28] that was later annulled.[29] These discredited records from Soviet secret police forces found their way into the prominent work on the subject by John Cronwell's *Hitler's Pope*;[30] Rychlak systematically dismantles his "exclusive" archival research and

[21] ENCYCLOPEDIA BRITANNICA, *József Mindszenty, Hungarian Bishop*, *available at* <https://www.britannica.com/biography/Jozsef-Mindszenty>.

[22] PACEPA & RYCHLAK, *supra* note 2, at 96 ("To ensure credibility of the lies, two things were required. First the fabrications had to appear in Western sources; and second, there had to be what Sakharosky called "a kernel of truth" behind the allegations, so that at least some part of the story could be definitely verified—and to ensure that the calumny would never be put to rest").

[23] *Id.*at 38.

[24] *Id.* at 35–36.

[25] Interview with historian and Rabbi David Dalin, *Pius XII Saved More Jews Than Schindler, Rabbi Says*, ZENIT.ORG (Aug. 28, 2001) ("His silence was an effective strategy directed to protecting the greatest possible number of Jews from deportation. An explicit and severe denunciation of the Nazis by the Pope would have been an invitation to reprisals, and would have worsened attitudes toward Jews throughout Europe.").

[26] Pinchas E. Lapide (after months of research at the Israeli consul in Italy) wrote: "The Catholic Church saved more Jewish lives during the war than all other churches, religious institutions and rescue organizations put together. Its record stands in startling contrast to the achievements of the International Red Cross and the Western Democracies ... The Holy See, the nuncios, and the entire Catholic Church saved some 400,000 Jews from certain death [the estimate was eventually increased to 860,000]." PACEPA & RYCHLAK, *supra* note 2, at 68.

[27] Lisa Palmieri-Billig, *Italy's First Holocaust Museum to Be Built in Rome*, JERUSALEM POST (Feb. 22, 2011) ("The section on Italy promises to draw extreme interest, with documentation on the country's most famous controversial wartime issues. It will explore both the positive and negative roles of the Vatican—its proverbial silence during the 1943 deportations, contrasted with the opening of its institutions to thousands of Jewish refugees; and its helping Jews by providing false documents, but also helping Nazis flee to South America after the war.").

[28] Whitall N. Perry, *Book Review: The Silence of Pius XI by Carlos Falconi*, 4 ST. IN COMP. REL. (Winter 1971).

[29] *Croatia overturns conviction of WW2 "collaborator" Cardinal Stepinac*, BBC NEWS (July 22, 2016).

[30] Jure Krišto, *Book Review Accentuation of the Known and Repetion of Untruths: About the Book John Cornwell, Hitler's Pope. The Secret History of Pius XII (1999)*, 32(1) ČASOPIS ZA SUVREMENU POVIJEST (2000)

cherry-picked citations that even suggest Pius XII was partly responsible for Hitler's rise to power and the Holocaust itself.[31] The authors additionally trace the writing and production of a play that denigrates Pius XII as a Nazi collaborator: *The Deputy. A Christian Tragedy*. They discuss its premier in Berlin and follow it to Paris, London, and New York, where it won a Tony award on Broadway (and finally made it to film).[32] And to show nefarious intent, they track the anti-Semitism and Holocaust denials, along with the promotion, reviews, and printings of the theatrical piece financed and pushed with communist and KGB connections.[33] All of this makes for tedious work to add nuance to a complicated story.

One final piece of a successful disinformation campaign should also be noted: incomplete knowledge gives life to a false storyline. As can be noted in the previous analysis, a great deal of (further) research and verification of sources is necessary to definitively prove or disprove a narrative. Disinformation thrives on conflicting stories that demand unavailable verification. Thus, effective *dezinformatsiya* aims to push a description of events, while opacity rules the day.[34]

For this reason it is important to point out that this discussion over Pope Pius XII has become polarized over the past decades—during the time when a full accounting has remained obscured.[35] The archives at the Vatican (no longer designated as "Secret" by order of Pope Francis[36]) will only now be opened to scholars in March 2020 to shed a fuller light on the matter with reports, letters, notes, and telegrams from the Vatican on decisions surrounding the highly sensitive days of Pius XII.[37] Hence, even more work is in store to present a full picture to avoid exploitation.

We now pivot to discuss weaponized information in the twenty-first century and the greatly expanded opportunities for spreading falsehoods in the cyberworld. To set the stage it is fitting to transition with two final descriptions of *dezinformatsiya*. The first comes from a volume on Russian intelligence history edited by Yevgeni Primakov, former prime minister of Russia and a prior chief of Soviet intelligence

("Cornwell's treatment of Catholic Church in the Independent State of Croatia ... is a travesty of research and objective writing. Cornwell perhaps did not know, but he could have and must have been informed, that Falconi wrote his piece on the basis of the propagandistic material given to him by the Yugoslav secret service and propagandists").

[31] Pacepa & Rychlak, *supra* note 2, at 188–195.

[32] *Id.* at 120–140.

[33] *Id.* at 141–182.

[34] We explain in the following section how the recent conflict in Ukraine, and in particular the annexation of Crimea, illustrates this point. Contradictory narratives communicated through official and nonofficial channels by Russian authorities contributed to create a veil of opacity over what was really happening in the field, and consequently bought time for Russian military troop to launch the kinetic military operation.

[35] Harriet Sherwood, *Unsealing of Vatican Archives Will Finally Reveal Truth about "Hitler's Pope*," The Observer (London) (Mar. 1, 2020) ("Mary Vincent, professor of modern European history at Sheffield University, said that much of the criticism of Pius Xll lacked nuance. 'He was a careful, austere and quite unlikable man, trying to steer a path through almost impossible circumstances. He had clear views about what he saw as the threat of Soviet communism, and his view of Italian fascism was quite a bit softer. But categorising him as good or bad is not helpful—it's about the decisions he took, and the space he had to make those decisions.' ").

[36] Nicolas Senèze, *Vatican Archives Will No Longer Be "Secret*," La Croix International (Oct. 30, 2019).

[37] Lisa Palmieri-Billig, *Opening of Pius XII Archives: To Speak or Not to Speak: That Was the Question*, La Stampa: Vatican Insider (Feb. 27, 2020); Sylvia Poggioli, *Vatican Opens Archives of World War II–Era Pope Pius XII*, National Public Radio News (Mar. 2, 2020).

services. Regardless of the many various terms that have been applied to these types of operations, it was explained: "they all were and are specific targeted actions to confuse an actual or potential adversary as regards our true intentions or capabilities, and to obtain an advantageous reaction from the 'action target' that would be practically unattainable by open means."[38] Fully capturing the design of such deception and disorder is a challenge.

Secondly, Pacepa offered useful imagery for understanding the importance of the quantitative element of these actions. He referenced a document from the head of the Soviet bloc espionage community which vividly expressed a valuable insight about *dezinformatsiya*: "a drop makes a hole in a stone not by force, but by constant dripping."[39] What we will find in the subsequent sections is that ICTs and social media platforms now afford an incessant delivery of drops that are individually crafted to leave a mark more quickly.

III. Information Warfare: A New Breadth for *Disinfo-Ops*

Information has long been considered by political decision makers as a powerful weapon to advance the interests of the state, complementary to traditional warfare approaches. This strategy is not new. Homer already described the crucial influence of poets on the mobilization of the Greeks in the war against Troy.[40] As seen previously, Russia has traditionally held this expansive view as well. More recently in 2012, President Putin and Maj. Gen. Sergei Kuralenko—then Chief of Military Art at the Academy of the General Staff—interpreted information technology as a new means for the military.[41] They argued that "the development of information technologies has caused significant changes in the ways wars are fought and led to a build-up of cyber-troops."[42]

Cyber power involves a wide range of instruments, strategies, and capacities; it is "the ability, in peace, crisis, and war to exert prompt and sustained influence in and from cyberspace."[43] It encompasses the potential impacts of strategies in cyberspace, but also in the kinetic world.[44] In other words, cyberspace is at the same time a place where states compete and defend their interests and a toolbox to achieve specific objectives.

[38] Cited in Romerstein, *supra* note 4, at 54. This description echoes the words of U.S. ambassador to Ukraine Geoffrey Pyatt in 2015: "Everyone knows the Kremlin seeks to use information to deny, deceive, and confuse," Giles, *supra* note 5, at 59 (citing Pyatt).

[39] Pacepa & Rychlak, *supra* note 2, at 350.

[40] Andrei Aliaksandrau, *Brave New War: The Information War between Russia and Ukraine*, 43 Index on Censorship 55, 56 (2014).

[41] Oscar Jonsson, The Russian Understanding of War: Blurring the Lines Between War and Peace (2019).

[42] Sergey V. Kuralenko, *Changing Trends in Armed Struggle in the Early 21st Century*, 21 Mil. Thought 29, 29–35 (2012).

[43] John B. Sheldon, *The Rise of Cyberpower*, in Strategy in the Contemporary World 306 (John Baylis, James Wirtz, & Colin Gray eds., 2018).

[44] Damien Van Puyvelde & Aaron F. Brantly, Cybersecurity: Politics, Governance and Conflict in Cyberspace (2019).

Moreover, cyber power is often considered a weapon of the weak due to the limited investment it requires to achieve substantial and tangible impact on other states.[45] Analogous to the concept of smart-power strategies developed by Joseph Nye,[46] the intended impacts can serve as a useful analytical division between information-technology and information-persuasion.[47] On the one hand, digital instruments aim to disable information technology systems and critical infrastructure, and provide new means for on-the-ground military operations. On the other hand, persuasion techniques use social media platforms and data-driven marketing tools to influence opinions abroad. This chapter focuses on the latter.

Interstate and intrastate hybrid conflicts place information at the center of defensive and offensive strategies.[48] This change is reflected by the Russian military's understanding of the emergence of a "new generation of warfare" (*voina novogo pokoleniya*), and is well illustrated by the use of information during the Russian military annexation of Crimea.[49] Persuasion techniques allow the operator to send "specially prepared information to incline [a partner or opponent] to voluntarily make the predetermined decision desired by the initiator of the action."[50] To be effective, persuasion first requires a reconnaissance phase to collect data about the targets, whether they are individuals or organizations. Thanks to this first phase of information gathering, the disinformation operators can fully exploit the vulnerabilities of the targeted populations. Data collection allows persuasion techniques not only to identify the best strategy to make their messages heard (i.e., choice of channel and format of communication, time, language, tone of the voice, name of sender) but also to craft their content according to the psychological profiling of targeted individuals or groups of individuals. Whether it is to push for a specific narrative or sow chaos, successful persuasion techniques spread content on multiple platforms and channels of communication simultaneously.

Information is used in situations of conflict today to support traditional kinetic military operations. Some examples include confrontational and contradictory statements by President Putin to give the impression of a dangerously unpredictable leadership, amplifying the narrative of war preparedness and at the same time refuting any troop movement nearby Ukraine right before the conflict.[51] For instance, contradictory information about movements of Russian troops near the eastern border of Ukraine was published before and during the conflict. This effort resulted in buying

[45] Simone Dossi, *Confronting China's Cyberwarfare Capabilities: A "Weapon of the Weak" or a Force Multiplier?*, in U.S. FOREIGN POLICY IN A CHALLENGING WORLD 357–377 (Marco Clementi, Matteo Dian, & Barbara Pisciotta, eds., 2018).

[46] Joseph S. Nye Jr., *Get Smart: Combining Hard and Soft Power*, FOREIGN AFF. 160–163 (July/Aug. 2009).

[47] Emilio J. Iasiello, *Russia's Improved Information Operations: From Georgia to Crimea*, 47 PARAMETERS 51–63 (2017).

[48] Dave Johnson, *Russia's Approach to Conflict: Implications for NATO's Deterrence and Defense*, 111 Research Division NATO 1–12 (2015).

[49] Rod Thornton, *The Changing Nature of Modern Warfare: Responding to Russian Information Warfare*, 160 RUSI J. 40–48 (2015); *see also* Nye, *supra* note 46.

[50] Timothy Thomas, *Russia's Reflexive Control Theory and the Military*, 17 J. SLAVIC MIL. STUD. 237–256 (2004); *see also* Ido Kilovaty, *Doxfare: Politically Motivated Leaks and the Future of the Norm on Non-Intervention in the Era of Weaponized Information*, 9 HARV. NAT. SEC. J. 146–179 (2018).

[51] Mason Richey, *Contemporary Russian Revisionism: Understanding the Kremlin's Hybrid Warfare and the Strategic and Tactical Deployment of Disinformation*, 16 ASIA EUR. J. 101–113 (2018).

time in the initial stages of the conflict by thickening the fog of war.[52] This led former NATO Supreme Allied Commander Europe, General Philip Breedlove, to describe Russian's information warfare in Ukraine as "the most amazing information warfare blitzkrieg we have ever seen in the history of information warfare."[53] Russia's specialized tactic further benefits from the relationship between government and broader criminal networks,[54] such as the Russian Business Network[55] and the degree of immunity they enjoy.[56]

The Russian government also supported bloggers and individuals who broadcast pro-Russian narratives on social media networks[57] and sometimes simulate anti-Russian news sources to disseminate false information about the ongoing conflict. Both refuted the presence of the Russian military behind the Ukrainian border and condemned Western media outlets for running broad informational warfare against Russia.[58] The Kremlin thus tried to inflate its military power and legitimize false facts on the ground (e.g., peace or a truce).[59]

The Russian narrative of unpredictable leadership is a key element of Russian's disinformation campaigns, as it feeds the other three objectives: (1) to trigger uncertainty about the real situation on the ground and Russia's intentions; (2) to support dissension within and among other states; and (3) to contribute to the perception of a strong Russia. It does not draw a clear line between war and peace; it conducts information warfare continuously in peacetime and wartime alike.[60] In times of peace (and, more precisely, in the West), Russia's information warfare intends to manipulate the information circulated in Western mass media, alter democratic decision-making processes, influence elites and citizens' consciousness, and foment societal tensions to strengthen its position on the international stage.[61] We saw this expressed previously by Pacepa when describing the Soviet era, and it continues to be the case. For example, one scholar explains, "the informational campaign is an uninterrupted (*bezpriryvnost*) strategic effort. It is waged during 'peacetime' and wartime."[62]

[52] James J. Wirtz, *Cyber War and Strategic Culture: The Russian Integration of Cyber Power into Grand Strategy*, in CYBER WAR IN PERSPECTIVE: RUSSIAN AGGRESSION AGAINST UKRAINE 29–38 (Kenneth Geers ed., 2015).

[53] John Vandiver, *SACEUR: Allies Must Prepare for Russia "Hybrid War,"* STARS & STRIPES (2014).

[54] Julie Anderson, *The Chekist Takeover of the Russian State*, 19 INT. J. INTELLIGENCE & COUNTERINTELLIGENCE 237–288 (2006).

[55] An internet business, based in St. Petersburg, the Network operates as a world hub for sheltering illegal activities, including child pornography, online scams, piracy, and other illicit operations. *See* Brian Krebs, *Shadowy Russian Firm Seen as Conduit for Cybercrime*, WASHINGTON POST (Oct. 13, 2007).

[56] JACK A. JARMON & PANO YANNAKOGEORGOS, THE CYBER THREAT AND GLOBALIZATION: THE IMPACT ON U.S. NATIONAL AND INTERNATIONAL SECURITY (2018).

[57] Jill Dougherty, *Everyone Lies: The Ukraine Conflict and Russia's Media Transformation*, 88 HARV. CENTER ON MEDIA 1–29 (Discussion Paper Series, 2014).

[58] Sascha Dominik, Dov Bachmann, & Hakan Gunneriusson, *Russia's Hybrid Warfare in the East: The Integral Nature of the Information Sphere*, 16 GEO. J. INT'L AFF. 198 (2015).

[59] Richey, *supra* note 51.

[60] ULRIK FRANKE, WAR BY NON-MILITARY MEANS: UNDERSTANDING RUSSIAN INFORMATION WARFARE (2015).

[61] PUYVELDE & BRANTLY, *supra* note 44.

[62] Adamsky, *supra* note 5, at 29. *See also* GILES, *supra* note 5, at 4 ("it is an ongoing activity regardless of the state of relations with the opponent").

The fact that this activity is continuous regardless of a state of conflict is particularly important from the point of view of international law. Not only does the activity occur below the threshold of armed conflict, it is omnipresent across long spans of time. In this sense, humanitarian law tools used for regulating armed conflict are ill-fitting. It is necessary to look to other legal paradigms to understand the type of damage that can be wrought, along with what sort of regulation could be effective for harnessing the activity.[63]

The concept of "reflexive control" adopted by Russia consists of influencing the opponents' perceptions to make them adopt positions advantageous to Russian objectives.[64] It is not a new concept and was applied in the past against both civilians and military targets. In fact, reflexive control is an information weapon that has "been studied in the Soviet Union and Russia for over 40 years" to persuade the targeted individual or group of individuals to make choices and carry out actions in the interest of the initiator.[65] Reflexive control encompasses a large range of instruments and strategies that are based on the knowledge of how the targeted individuals make their decisions. What differs today is the greater capacity to collect data about the opponent, which allows the initiator of the action to know their target extremely well and consequently make their persuasion more effective.

Thus, while most Western governments focused their attention on Russia's official diplomacy, the country was developing government-to-people diplomacy and its influencing capacity.[66] In Europe, Russia supported far right movements with financial backing and propaganda techniques: France's Rassemblement National, Hungary's Jobbik, Great Britain's UKIP, and the Austrian FPÖ benefited from the Russian helping hand.[67] These parties were quite instrumental for Russia to support efforts to dismantle some of the European Union's agreements and institutions, including the euro area and the Schengen Area.[68] In addition to providing Euroskeptic content, Russia produced and distributed narratives to legitimize its actions, including Crimea's secession referendum and its assistance to Syria's Bashar al-Assad regime to contain rebel groups, which led to widespread criticism for crimes against humanity.[69]

However, the Kremlin also aimed to create political discord. To do so, it generated messages with opposite views. For instance, in Germany, while Angela Merkel was under pressure to step down due to her immigration policy, the Kremlin supported

[63] *See, e.g.*, Barela, *Cross-Border Cyber Ops* and *Zero Shades of Grey*, *supra* note 3; Jens D. Ohlin, *Did Russian Cyber Interference in the 2016 Election Violate International Law?*, 95 Tex. L. Rev. 1579 (2017); Sean Watts, *Low-Intensity Cyber Operations and the Principle of Non-Intervention*, in Cyber War: Law and Ethics for Virtual Conflicts (Jens D. Ohlin, Kevin Govern, & Claire Finkelstein eds., 2015); along with the chapters in Parts II and III of this volume exploring various creative options for dealing with a threat that has morphed beyond previously known operations.

[64] Maria Snegovaya, *Putin's information warfare in Ukraine: Soviet Origins of Russia's Hybrid's Warfare*, 1 Russia Report 7 (2015).

[65] Thomas Timothy, *Russia's Reflexive Control Theory and the Military*, 17 J. Slavic Mil. Stud. 237–256 (2004).

[66] Richey, *supra* note 51.

[67] Frederik Wesslau, *Putin's Friends in Europe*, 19 Eur. Cou. Foreign Rel. (2016).

[68] *Id.*

[69] Andrew Dawson & Martin Innes, *How Russia's Internet Research Agency Built Its Disinformation Campaign*, 90 Pol. Q. 245–256 (2019).

both her and far-right movements with hashtags such as "#MerkelMustStay" and "#AfDisshit."[70] Social bots and online disinformation were also found during the 2016 Referendum in the United Kingdom,[71] the 2017 French presidential elections,[72] and the 2017 Catalan referendum.[73] The 2019 European Parliament elections also saw the presence of disinformation efforts in multiple member states, including in Italy[74] and Sweden,[75] where operators ran automated bots to distribute known junk news on Twitter.[76]

The European Union has taken disinformation campaigns seriously and set up an action plan to develop its capabilities and enforce cooperation between EU member states. In the run-up to the 2019 EU elections, it built a fact-checking portal and a database to denounce "partial, distorted, or false depiction of reality and spread of key pro-Kremlin messages."[77] Studies of media reporting and analysis by the East Stratcom Task Force[78] have found that of the 7,572 results of key pro-Kremlin messages, 1,897 involved at least one of the 27 EU member states since the creation of the database;[79] 246 directly targeted the European Union, out of which only 20 mentioned explicitly the EU elections in 2019. Other messages mainly target the United States (1,867) as well as Russia and former USSR countries: Moldova (123), Estonia (138), Latvia (122), Lithuania (173), Kazakhstan (10), Kyrgyzstan, Tajikistan (5), Turkmenistan (1), Uzbekistan (3), Armenia (71), Azerbaijan (29), Georgia (331), and Ukraine (3,063). These numbers illustrate that the current geopolitical struggles with Ukraine sit atop Russia's agenda—it is its main disinformation target. Baltic countries are also of strategic concern for Russia,[80] in particular due to the presence of the NATO Cooperative Cyber Defence Centre of Excellence in Tallinn, Estonia.[81]

Disinformation is a challenge the European Union is determined to address. EU Commission Vice President Věra Jourová, in her speech at the Opening of EU vs

[70] *Id.*

[71] Marco T. Bastos & Dan Mercea, *The Brexit Botnet and User-Generated Hyperpartisan News*, 37 Soc. Sci. Com. Rev. 38–54 (2019).

[72] Emilio Ferrara, *Disinformation and Social Bot Operations in the Run Up to the 2017 French Presidential Election*, 22 First Monday (2017).

[73] Massimo Stella, Emilio Ferrara, & Manlio De Domenico, *Bots Increase Exposure to Negative and Inflammatory Content in Online Social Systems*, 115 PNAS 12435–12440 (2018); Javier Lesaca, *Los Zombis De La Desinformación*, El País (Nov. 11, 2017); Javier Lesaca, *Why Did Russian Social Media Swarm the Digital Conversation about Catalan Independence?*, Washington Post (Nov. 22, 2017).

[74] Francesco Pierri, Alessandro Artoni, & Stefano Ceri, *Investigating Italian Disinformation Spreading on Twitter in the Context of 2019 European Elections*, 15 PLoS One 1–23 (2020).

[75] Freja Hedman et al., *News and Political Information Consumption in Sweden: Mapping the 2018 Swedish General Election on Twitter* (Oxford University, Project on Computational Propaganda, Sept. 6, 2018).

[76] Johan Fernquist, Liza Kaati, & Ralph Schroeder, *Political Bots and the Swedish General Election*, IEEE ISI 124–129 (2018).

[77] *See* EU vs Disinfo Database, *available at* <https://euvsdisinfo.eu>.

[78] *Id.*

[79] Specifically, these are Austria, Belgium, Bulgaria, Croatia, Cyprus, Czech Republic, Denmark, Croatia, Estonia, Finland, France, Germany, Greece, Hungary, Ireland, Italy, Latvia, Lithuania, Poland, Portugal, Romania, Spain, Sweden, and The Netherlands.

[80] Mark Galeotti, *The Baltic States as Targets and Levers: The Role of the Region in Russian Strategy*, 28 Sec. Ins. (2019); *see also* Greg Simons, *Perception of Russia's soft power and influence in the Baltic States*, 41 Pub. Rel. Rev. 1–13 (2014).

[81] The NATO Cooperative Cyber Defence Centre of Excellence is a multinational and interdisciplinary hub of cyber defense expertise. *See* <https://ccdcoe.org>.

Disinfo Conference, underscored disinformation's threat to democracy: "There are specific external actors—namely Russia, and increasingly China—that are actively using disinformation and related interference tactics to undermine European democracy, and will continue doing so until we demonstrate that we will not tolerate this aggression and interference."[82]

As discussed, persuasion and deception strategies are not new. What makes disinformation campaigns today more effective is the new man-made environment in which they evolve. *Disinfo-ops* are part of an information warfare that is simultaneously broader and more pervasive than before, and yet more individualized and hidden underneath a continuous flow of communications and an opaque curtain of anonymity. It is a challenge for Western liberal democracies to develop effective measures to counter such actions and to protect democratic processes.

IV. Computational Politics: A New Depth and Precision of *Disinfo-Ops* during Elections

Data is at the heart of today's political campaign strategies. The analysis of big data allows political strategists to make their argument more convincing and visible to specific groups of the population. The data sets and the techniques to collect data, track individuals, and target these persons can be employed by various domestic and foreign actors to pursue legitimate and nonlegitimate objectives—including electoral interference, as illustrated by the recent Cambridge Analytica scandal.[83] In other words, big data provides both new tools and new targets for *disinfo-ops*.

This data-centered approach to political communication stems from the marketing and advertising industries, where data has become a treasurable commodity to target potential buyers more efficiently and effectively. Thanks to data, combining credit card information, personal interests, consumption patterns, and TV-viewing patterns (among other sources), ad buyers identify and reach the people most likely to react to their messages—as narrow a target as 20 of the 1.5 billion daily users of a social network.[84]

Since users are asked to sign in with their real name and identity, social media platforms allow tech companies to permanently identify users. This identity-based targeting paradigm takes even more prominence when coupled with cross-device recognition capacity, including TV, websites, social media platforms, and mobile phones.[85] In turn, large data sets allow political communication strategists to gain unprecedented access to the mind and soul of potential voters and consequently base their contact decisions on individually microtargeted propensity scores.[86] Political

[82] Věra Jourová, *Disinfo Horizon: Responding to Future Threats* (Conference Opening Speech, Jan. 30, 2020), *available at* <https://ec.europa.eu/commission/presscorner/detail/en/SPEECH_20_160>.

[83] Carole Cadwalladr & Emma Graham-Harrison, *Revealed: 50 Million Facebook Profiles Harvested for Cambridge Analytica in Major Data Breach*, The Guardian (London) (Mar. 17, 2018).

[84] Ira S. Rubinstein, *Voter Privacy in the Age of Big Data*, 2014 Wis. L. Rev. 861 (2014).

[85] Jeff Chester & Kathryn Montgomery, *The Role of Digital Marketing in Political Campaigns*, 6 Int. Pol. Rev. 1 (2017).

[86] The term "microtargeting" is sometimes used to refer any individual-level contact performed by campaigns and sometimes refers to the data-generated propensity scores used to guide individual-level contact

parties apply computational methods to large data sets, not only to persuade and mobilize potential voters[87] but also to score, rate, and categorize citizens according to behavioral, demographic, and psychographic data.[88] In this context, psychographics means qualifying consumers according to psychological attributes such as personality, values, opinions, and attitude.[89]

Behavioral tracking is mainly based on cookies (small computational identifiers) to explore the digital trail users leave while visiting websites and social media platforms. It then associates them with data collected from other sources, including those offline.[90] That is, data onboarding describes the techniques to transfer offline data to an online environment for marketing needs.[91] They allow connection of offline customer records with online users by matching identifying information to retrieve the same customers.[92]

This unquenchable thirst for data results in a disaggregation of personal data into a myriad of publicly and privately owned databases scattered throughout the world. The data is collected from internet and mobile service providers, social media and web platforms, governmental and intelligence agencies, advertising companies, and data brokers. It is made possible by the widespread adoption of connected devices, such as smartphones and more recently the internet of things,[93] growing high-speed internet access, and the vast deployment of data centers, which allow affordable and reliable cloud-based services.[94]

This disaggregation of personal data and the large variety of sources for it makes data not only treasurable but also highly vulnerable to cyberattacks and cybercrimes—which have also become a part of hybrid war strategies.[95] Data scattered throughout the planet provides an unprecedented level of transparency into the lives, interests, and emotions of billions of citizens. The large data leaks that regularly make the news headlines illustrate how vibrant the illegal data trade has become.

decisions. In this chapter, we refer to the latter. *See* Kyle Endres & Kristin J. Kelly, *Does Microtargeting Matter? Campaign Contact Strategies and Young Voters*, 28 J. Elec. Pub. Opin. & Part. 1–18 (2018).

[87] Zeynep Tufekci, *Engineering the Public: Big Data, Surveillance and Computational Politics*, 19 First Monday (2014).

[88] Chester & Montgomery, *supra* note 85.

[89] Tufekci, *supra* note 87.

[90] Avi Goldfarb & Catherine E. Tucker, *Online Advertising, Behavioral Targeting, and Privacy*, 54 Communications of ACM 25–27 (2011).

[91] Gil Vernik et al., *Data on-Boarding in Federated Storage Clouds*, 6 Int. Conf. IEEE (2013).

[92] Santiago Gallino & Antonio Moreno, *Integration of Online and Offline Channels in Retail: The Impact of Sharing Reliable Inventory Availability Information*, 60 Mgmt. Sci. 1434–1451 (2014).

[93] The "internet of things" describes the increasing number of objects of everyday life with the capacity to communicate with one another and with their users, becoming an integral part of the internet. *See* Luigi Atzori, Antonio Iera, & Giacomo Morabito, *The Internet of Things: A Survey*, 54 Comp. Networks 2787–2805 (2010).

[94] Jiyi Wu et al., *Cloud Storage as the Infrastructure of Cloud Computing*, Int. Conf. Intel. Comp. and Cog. 380–383 (2010).

[95] Bettina Renz, *Russia and "Hybrid Warfare*," 22 Cont. Pol. 283–300 (2016); *see also* Aurel Sari, *Legal Resilience in an Era of Gray Zone Conflicts and Hybrid Threats* (Exeter Centre for International Law, Working Paper Series 2019/1); Hybrid Threats in the Grey Zone: Mapping the Terrain (Milton Regan & Aurel Sari eds., forthcoming 2021).

Thanks to the vast troves of data collected, marketers and disinformation campaign operators can follow an individual through their media and online usage and adapt the content of dynamic ads according to contextual factors such as time, location, and environment. This easily accessible personal data is the foundation of twenty-first-century persuasion techniques as it allows for more efficient and effective advertising placement and targeting. To make ads more accurate in real time, a recent marketing instrument provides an algorithm with the capacity to constantly buy and place ads with what are known as programmatic advertising platforms.[96] These are based on the analysis of big data in real time[97] and ensure that each ad precisely reflects the specific interests of a citizen anytime they are connected.[98] But their use is not neutral. This marketing innovation has had a significant impact on the media ecosystem and the incentives to produce news, content, and ads,[99] including the production of false information.[100]

Disinformation campaigns benefit from the most recent technological and marketing innovations developed by Western companies. They offer a platform for domestic, but also foreign, actors to widely and precisely micro-target citizens without much accountability. Facebook allows the creation and publication of micro-targeting ads, based on demographics and lifestyle interests, but also nonpublic "dark posts," which only show to the potential voter they are trying to influence—and then disappear.[101] This functionality makes disinformation campaigns almost impossible to track.[102]

Facebook and Google offer tailor-made products and services to political campaign leaders: they have political marketing teams aligned with each major political party to provide assistance and advice on targeting strategies.[103] By making the purchase of advertising automatic, advertisers and large web and social media platforms have enabled nefarious actors—adversarial foreign governments and criminal organizations—to distribute an unprecedented amount of false information. These marketing tools and advertising services have indeed granted visibility to the Kremlin's disinformation campaigns. Yet the same dynamic ads can be funded by a large array of actors without public scrutiny or any sort of accountability.

The distribution of such a large amount of false news is possible thanks to the generalized use of social media platforms in the world today. These platforms allow not only individual users and organizations to interact with each and publish new content, but they also enable *disinfo-ops* to spread rapidly. Thanks to the large data sets

[96] Joshua A. Braun & Jessica L. Eklund, *Fake News, Real Money: Ad Tech Platforms, Profit-Driven Hoaxes, and the Business of Journalism*, 7 Dig. Jour. 1–21 (2019).

[97] Pedro Palos-Sanchez, Jose Ramon Saura, & Felix Martin-Velicia, *A Study of the Effects of Programmatic Advertising on Users' Concerns about Privacy over Time*, 96 J. Bus. Res. 61–72 (2019).

[98] Yi-Ting Huang, *The Female Gaze: Content Composition and Slot Position in Personalized Banner Ads, and How They Influence Visual Attention in Online Shoppers*, 82 Comp. Hum. Behav. 1–15 (2018).

[99] Lucia Moses, *The Underbelly of the Internet*, Digiday (2016).

[100] Julian Thomas, *Programming, Filtering, Adblocking: Advertising and Media Automation*, 166 Media. Intl. Aus. 34–43 (2018).

[101] Jessica Baldwin-Philippi, *The Myths of Data-Driven Campaigning*, 34 Pol. Com. 627–633 (2017).

[102] Cadwalladr & Graham-Harrison, *supra* note 83.

[103] Jason J. Jones et al., *Social Influence and Political Mobilization: Further Evidence from a Randomized Experiment in the 2012 US Presidential Election*, 12 PLoS One (2017). For a systematic literature review of computational politics, *see also* Ehsan ul Haq et al., *A Survey on Computational Politics*, IEEE ACC (2019).

collected through these platforms, and the precise tracking and targeting they afford, social media platforms are instrumental to disinformation operators. Disinformation campaigns on social media platforms use three main instruments: (1) spreading false news through a large number of bots—handles or accounts that automate content distribution;[104] (2) paid, organized, and supervised trolls—individuals who falsify their true identities to promote discord;[105] and (3) the use of cyborgs—accounts managed by individuals but sometimes taken over by bots or that present bot-like or malicious behavior.[106]

Combined, these techniques aim to deceive populations and decision makers by artificially supporting what seems like a trend, a consensus, a hashtag, a public figure, a piece of news, or a view of the truth. In the area of public health, for instance, Russian trolls and bots promote simultaneously pro- and anti-vaccination content to contribute to political discord.[107]

Citizens are quite vulnerable on social media platforms when it comes to detecting and fighting against false information. They rarely have the skills or time to verify the source of dubious information. Moreover, the design of social media platforms and applications make this verification harder, flooding users with a constant feed of new information, triggering what has been called a fantasy of abundance.[108] Geolocalization targeting allows an advertiser to follow citizens not only anytime but also anywhere, whether they are driving a car, shopping at a store, or relaxing at home.[109] Yet if false content travels faster than true stories, it is not only because of bots but because of humans,[110] who are more attracted by sensational content, even when untrue.[111]

Russia's former Internet Research Agency (IRA) is now recognized for its attempts to influence the outcome of numerous recent political elections in Western countries through Facebook, Twitter, Instagram, YouTube, and stand-alone websites.[112] Their use of bots to influence discourse and sentiment online is also well documented.[113] The efforts of the IRA to set the political agenda abroad were done systematically and through the use of instruments to influence mass audiences. For instance, when examining the IRA's use of Twitter, researchers have identified five categories of

[104] Zi Chu et al., *Detecting Automation of Twitter Accounts: Are You a Human, Bot, or Cyborg?*, 9 IEEE Transc. Depen. Secure Comp. 811–824 (2012).

[105] *Troll*, Collins English Dictionary, *available at* <https://www.collinsdictionary.com/dictionary/english/troll>.

[106] Chu et al., *supra* note 104.

[107] David A. Broniatowski et al., *Weaponized Health Communication: Twitter Bots and Russian Trolls Amplify the Vaccine Debate*, 108 Am. J. Pub. Health 1378–1384 (2018).

[108] Jodi Dean, Publicity's Secret: How Technoculture Capitalizes on Democracy (2002).

[109] Son Sooel, Daehyeok Kim, & Shmatikov Vitaly, *What Mobile Ads Know About Mobile Users*, Conf. NDSS (2016).

[110] Soroush Vosoughi, Deb Roy, & Sinan Aral, *The Spread of True and False News Online*, 359 Science 1146–1151 (2018).

[111] Vincent F. Hendricks & Mads Vestergaard, Reality Lost: Markets of Attention, Misinformation and Manipulation (2018).

[112] This new context may lead to a postfactual democracy, where facts have lost their value and truth is relative: "A democracy is in a post-factual state when politically opportune but factually misleading narratives form the basis for political debate, decision, and legislation." Yavor Raychev, *Cyberwar in Russian and US Military-Political Thought: A Comparative View*, 43 ISIJ 349–361 (2019).

[113] Dawson & Innes, *supra* note 69.

trolls: Right Troll, Left Troll, News Feed, Hashtag Gamer, and Fearmonger.[114] (These five categories are not unique to the IRA and correspond to the strategies described previously to sow chaos and generate an environment of opacity.) The first category of messages did not address traditionally right-leaning topics, such as taxes and abortion, but rather distributed contentious content about moderate Republicans. The second category mainly sent out messages about cultural identities, including gender, sexual, religious, and racial identity. The third category presented itself as coming from local news agencies, while the fourth focused on playing hashtag games. The last category sent out pure fake news, fabricating crises such as nonexistent outbreaks of Ebola in Atlanta, nuclear plant accidents, and war crimes perpetrated in Ukraine.[115]

This last category of trolls specifically, in addition to the other content generated, contributes to a constant flow of information, which challenges users and fact-checkers to pinpoint a specific fact or argument, find the source of a piece of news, or simply reread a publication. The existence of this constant flow of information produces a permanent "noise" that makes it impossible to distinguish a specific voice. As some scholars have recently pointed out, "[d]isinformation campaigns thereby overwhelms the 'signal' of actual news with 'noise, eroding the trust in news necessary for democracy to work."[116] This method of bombarding voters with information has also been adopted by domestic campaigns. Journalists immersing themselves in election cyber activities have found the very same tactic present (in this case for the Trump campaign):

> What I was seeing was a strategy that has been deployed by illiberal political leaders around the world. Rather than shutting down dissenting voices, these leaders have learned to harness the democratizing power of social media for their own purposes—jamming the signals, sowing confusion. They no longer need to silence the dissident shouting in the streets; they can use a megaphone to drown him out. Scholars have a name for this: censorship through noise.[117]

The IRA was a highly professional news agency with staff dedicated to specific regions and countries and specialized for each social media platform.[118] They were in charge of producing memes, posting about fifty comments on news articles daily, running several fake accounts, maintaining six Facebook pages, and tweeting at least fifty times daily[119] and were tasked to include five specific keywords in all posts to encourage search engine pickup.[120] Staff would play opposing roles: on the one hand

[114] Darren L. Linvill & Patrick L. Warren, *Troll Factories: Manufacturing Specialized Disinformation on Twitter*, POL. COM. 1–21 (2020).

[115] *Id.*

[116] Karen Kornbluh & Ellen P. Goodman, *Safeguarding Digital Democracy. Digital Innovation and Democracy Initiative Roadmap*, DIDI ROAD 4 (2020).

[117] C. McKay, *The Billion-Dollar Disinformation Campaign to Reelect the President*, THE ATLANTIC (Mar. 2020).

[118] *One Professional Russian Troll Tells All* (Radio Free Europe broadcast, Mar. 25, 2015), *available at* <https://www.rferl.org/a/how-to-guide-russian-trolling-trolls/26919999.html>.

[119] *Russia Has a Troll Army That Is Trying to Mold Public Opinion on Internet News Sites*, HIGHER LEARNING (June 4, 2014), *at* <http://thehigherlearning.com/2014/06/04/russia-has-a-troll-army-that-is-trying-to-mold-public-opinion-on-internet-news-sites>.

[120] *Russian Troll Tells All*, *supra* note 118.

condemning the authorities, and on the other supporting them. They might post an image or a meme to defend one view, and another adding a link to contradict and fuel political discord.[121] Sometimes, to increase the visibility of a newly created Twitter handle, the IRA bought false followers, which provided more traction to the content they then published.[122] Another technique used by the IRA was to engage in follower phishing. This consists of following hundreds or thousands of new accounts, expecting them to reciprocate, and then unfollowing them in order to increase the "followers per followed" ratio and augment the account's "authority" for platform algorithms.[123] Lastly, the IRA engaged in switching narratives, meaning that a false account would change its narrative after some time, either to create confusion or to identify potential individuals for a later disinformation campaign.[124]

When we consider the size of the "disinformation machinery" during the Cold War described previously, the exponentially amplified breadth, depth, and precision of such operations take on a whole new meaning in today's online world. The use of such interference in the last U.S. presidential election was a game changer.

V. The 2016 U.S. Election and Beyond

To get a handle on how such activities unfold, it is extremely useful to provide a more recent example. We know that in 2016, hackers working for units within the Russian military intelligence (GRU) attempted to hack into email accounts, sometimes with success, belonging to the Democratic National Committee (DNC), the Democratic Congressional Campaign Committee, Hillary Clinton Campaign Chair John Podesta, other staff members, and Hillary Clinton's private email server.[125] This first part of the military operation exfiltrated massive amounts of data. But why?

This was not a traditional act of espionage aiming to learn about the enemy. As Pacepa explained, the first part of a durable disinformation campaign is to "collect as much information as possible on the target."[126] For an operation to contain the essential "kernel of truth," the most stable *disinfo-op* is built on incontestable internal documents. Hence, we subsequently saw a steady release of this cache at strategic moments during the campaign; it was timed to be most damaging to Hillary Clinton's candidacy and in turn aid Donald Trump.[127]

Intelligence reports have been publicly released to verify the foreign actions and warn the general population,[128] indictments have been filed against Russian persons

[121] *Trolling for Putin: Russia's Information War Explained*, Yahoo! (Apr. 5, 2015).

[122] *Russian Troll Tells All*, *supra* note 118.

[123] *Id.*

[124] *Id.*

[125] Robert S. Mueller III, U.S. Dep't of Justice, Report on the Investigation into Russian Interference in the 2016 Presidential Election, vol. 1, at 36–40 (2019).

[126] Pacepa & Rychlak, *supra* note 2, at 84.

[127] Mueller, *supra* note 125, at 41–48. For the first public identification of this operation, *see* Malcolm Nance, The Plot to Hack America: How Putin's Cyberspies and WikiLeaks Tried to Steal the 2016 Election (2016).

[128] Office of Dir. of Nat'l Intelligence, Assessing Russian Activities and Intentions in Recent U.S. Elections (Jan. 6, 2017).

and organizations,[129] the U.S. Senate Intelligence Committee has commissioned[130] and issued reports,[131] and Special Counsel Robert Mueller has filed an extensive report of his own detailing the activities.[132] Our intention is to build on this broader work and offer some detail and nuance by presenting one small piece of disinformation caught making its way through the information ecosystem after the election. In doing so the objective is to give further shape and form to twenty-first-century disinformation to better understand its nature.

It should not be a surprise that the information exfiltrated from the DNC continued to make its way through the U.S. courts and media landscape even after the election, and has at times been amplified, targeted, and distorted to sow discord within the population. It has been reported that the United States used its military to interrupt outside interference on the day of the 2018 midterm elections,[133] and the head of the Federal Bureau of Investigation (FBI) has warned that malign foreign influence campaigns on social media platforms have "continued virtually unabated and just intensifies during the election cycles."[134]

Of particular importance to this volume, our example is an article that strikes at the legitimacy of the election process—in this case the Democratic primaries to select the party's candidate. It must not be overlooked that free and fair elections serve the essential role of conferring legitimacy upon an authority in a democracy; targeting the process that elevates the leader of a government can inflict genuine damage, even if it is more abstract in nature.[135] These concerns were clearly outlined by the Obama administration before leaving office: "Russia's cyber activities were intended to influence the election, *erode faith* in U.S. democratic institutions, *sow doubt* about the integrity of our electoral process, and *undermine confidence* in the institutions of the U.S. government."[136] As three of these goals are of this exact character, the fact that Russian

[129] (Mueller) Indictment, United States v. Internet Research Agency et al., No. 1:18-cr-32-DLF, 2018 WL 914777 (D.D.C. Feb. 16, 2018); U.S. v. Viktor Borisovich Netyksho, et al., No. 1:18-cr-215-ABJ (D.D.C. July 13, 2018); U.S. v. Elena Alekseevna Khusyaynova, No. 1:18-MJ-464 (East. Dist. VA Sept. 28, 2018).

[130] R. DiResta et al., *The Tactics and Tropes of the Internet Research Agency* (New Knowledge, Columbia University, Tow Center for Digital Journalism, and Canfield Research LLC, 2018); P. Howard et al., *The IRA, Social Media and Political Polarization in the United States, 2012–2018* (Oxford University, Computational Propaganda Research and Graphika, 2018).

[131] 1 United States Select Committee on Intelligence, United States Senate on Russian Active Measures Campaigns and Interference in the 2016 U.S. Election, Russian Efforts Against Election Infrastructure, 116th Congress, 1st Sess., Report 116-XX; 2 United States Select Committee on Intelligence, United States Senate on Russian Active Measures Campaigns and Interference in the 2016 U.S. Election, Russia's Use of Social Media with Additional Views, 116th Congress, 1st Sess., Report 116-XX.

[132] Mueller, *supra* note 125.

[133] Ellen Nakashima, *U.S. Cyber Command Operation Disrupted Internet Access of Russian Troll Factory on Day of 2018 Midterms*, Washington Post (Feb. 26, 2019).

[134] U.S. Federal Bureau of Investigation (FBI) Director Christopher Wray Interview with Susan Hennessey, *FBI Director Wray on Combating Cyberthreats*, RSA Conference Lawfare Podcasts (Mar. 6, 2019), *at* <https://www.lawfareblog.com/lawfare-podcast-shorts-fbi-director-wray-combating-cyberthreats>.

[135] For a conceptualization of "legitimacy as a target," *see* S.J. Barela, International Law, New Diplomacy and Counterterrorism: An Interdisciplinary Study of Legitimacy (2014); for identification of the Russian operation in the U.S. 2016 presidential election as targeting legitimacy, *see* Barela, *Cross-Border Cyber Ops*, *supra* note 3.

[136] The White House, Office of the Press Secretary, Fact Sheet: *Actions in Response to Russian Malicious Cyber Activity and Harassment* (Dec. 29, 2016) (emphasis added).

bots and trolls were seen amplifying distorted stories about the validity of the election process can be understood as a continued effort to erode faith in the democratic process and the legitimacy of the leaders who emerge from it.

A. Spreading Confusion at the 2016 DNC Convention

The first discernable victim of the Russian campaign in 2016 came when the former DNC chairperson, Debbie Wasserman Schultz, was forced to announce her intention to step down after the national convention. In the days just before the event, WikiLeaks had posted material online that was pilfered from the DNC by the Russians: emails, spreadsheets, donor information, possible vulnerabilities, rebuttals, opposition research, and other documents.[137] Most pertinent at that moment was the fact that these documents revealed some bias by Wasserman Shultz and others in the DNC during the primary elections in favor of presidential candidate Hillary Clinton over Bernie Sanders.[138]

Regardless of the veracity or inaccuracy of the claim that the DNC was biased, Robert Mueller confirmed the release of the material was purposefully timed to impede the intentions behind a party convention—to consolidate support for the nominee and build momentum toward the general election.[139] Additional evidence of how this Russian operation was pushed into the mainstream media conversations is found by looking at candidate Donald Trump's Twitter handle. On the day after the release he tweeted:

> Leaked emails of DNC show plans to destroy Bernie Sanders. Mock his heritage and much more. On-line from Wikileakes [*sic*] really vicious. RIGGED![140]

Of course, the final word in all caps echoes the intention to erode the legitimacy of a leader by raising doubts about the system that brought this person to their position. Yet this cyberattack using the weaponization of exfiltrated information did not end with the election. For our purposes, the same stolen material from the DNC, and the very same wedge within the Democratic electorate, continued to be exploited in the time that followed.

[137] Thomas Rid, *How Russia Pulled Off the Biggest Election Hack in U.S. History*, ESQUIRE (Oct 20, 2016).

[138] It is not within the scope of this chapter to deeply analyze the disseminated stolen material and the validity of claiming such a predisposition by the DNC. What is relevant here is the fact that the stolen material was organized by the hackers to draw specific attention to any and all inappropriate communication within the DNC—stolen for this precise purpose. Nonetheless, it is worth noting here that some have contended that the contest was never close. One well-respected statistician on the left, Nate Silver, concluded after looking at the numbers and giving due regard to all that Bernie Sanders had achieved: "My view is that the race wasn't really all that close and that Sanders never really had that much of a chance at winning." Nate Silver, *Was The Democratic Primary a Close Call or a Landslide?*, FIVETHIRTYEIGHT (July 27, 2016).

[139] MUELLER, *supra* note 125, at 36 ("The release of the documents was designed and timed to interfere with the 2016 U.S. presidential election and undermine the Clinton Campaign").

[140] KATHLEEN HALL JAMIESON, CYBER-WAR: HOW RUSSIAN HACKERS AND TROLLS HELPED ELECT A PRESIDENT 111 (2018).

B. Disinfo Dismissed in Court

A class action lawsuit was filed in federal district court in southern Florida, and announced via YouTube,[141] just two weeks after the first disclosure of documents from Guccifer 2.0 in June 2016 (even before they became widely reported on by the press with the WikiLeaks release in July). The case was brought on behalf of all people who had donated to the DNC, those who contributed to the Sanders campaign, and all registered members of the Democratic Party, claiming that Debbie Wasserman Shultz and the party establishment were "in cahoots with the Clinton campaign and sought to tip the scales in her favor in the Democratic primaries."[142]

While there is certainly reason to believe that this was a genuine grassroots effort, it was entirely built on the cyber-poached documents from a Russian operation. As one expert explained in testimony before the U.S. Congress: "Cold War disinformation was artisanal; today it is outsourced, at least in part—outsourced to the victim itself."[143] Of course, there are many genuine and committed supporters of Bernie Sanders and it is unfair to suggest they are acting in concert with Russia here. However, it has also been pointed out that in the disinformation game, there is not only the operator and the adversary, but also the "*unwitting agent* . . . who is unaware of his true role and is exploited by the operator as a means of attacking the adversary."[144] It is also worth noting that much more pejorative language has been employed to describe those who assist in a disinformation operation without being aware of their role: "useful idiots," a terminology that plays right into the aim of sowing division.[145] Yet considering the swift dismissal of the court case, it might very well be the case here.

A summary judgment for a final order of dismissal of the case was handed down on August 25, 2017. The presiding judge decided that a trial was unnecessary because the court lacked jurisdiction and the plaintiffs did not have standing to assert each of the causes of action. Reasonable reporting, or even sharp critique, would focus on these two questions since they are the crux of the legal issues at stake.

1. A Shard of *Dezinformatsiya*

Only hours after the dismissal was handed down in Florida, an article was posted at the *Observer* entitled, "Court Admits DNC and Debbie Wasserman Schulz [*sic*] Rigged Primaries Against Sanders."[146] This particular media outlet covered the case

141 Jared H. Beck, Esq., *We Fight Back: Nationwide Class-Action filed Against Democratic Party and Debbie Wasserman Schultz*, YouTube (June 28, 2016), *available at* <https://www.youtube.com/watch?v=hU4I6C-9JZw>.

142 Wildling, et al., v. DNC Services Corp., DNC and D. Wasserman Schultz, No. 16-61511-CIV-ZLOCH (Aug. 25, 2017) 1 (U.S. D.C. of S. Dist. Fla.).

143 *Disinformation: A Primer in Russian Active Measures and Influence Campaigns*, Hearing before the Select Committee on Intelligence, U.S. Senate, 115th Congress, S. Hrg. 115–40, Pt. 1 (Mar. 30, 2017) (Statement of Thomas Rid).

144 Bittman, *supra* note 7, at 50.

145 Darczewska & Żochowski, *supra* note 6, at 15; Renée DiResta & Shelby Grossman, Potemkin Pages & Personas: Assessing GRU Online Operations, 2014–2019, at 6 (Stanford Internet Observatory, Cyber Policy Center, 2019); Alina Polyakova, *Why Europe Is Right to Fear Putin's Useful Idiots*, Foreign Pol'y (Feb. 23, 2016); Dalibor Rohac, *Cranks, Trolls, and Useful Idiots*, Foreign Pol'y (Mar. 12, 2015).

146 Michael Sainato, *Court Admits DNC and Debbie Wasserman Schulz [sic] Rigged Primaries Against Sanders*, Observer (Aug. 26, 2017).

at its filing[147] and stayed on top of the story as it progressed through the court.[148] In fact, the small media outlet released a piece only two days after the disorderly cache of material was first dumped on June 15, 2016.[149] That article claimed in its headline, "Guccifer 2.0 Leak Reveals How DNC Rigged Primaries for Clinton: Hillary Clinton didn't win the Democratic primaries through democratic means."[150] As noted previously, the large national uproar and attention only took place after the more user-friendly WikiLeaks release in July. Yet we can clearly see that each of these articles was pushing the story that the primary was "rigged" from the moment the stolen DNC information was made public.

This early, focused, and sustained attention by the *Observer* newspaper—on what would normally be a small courthouse story on a case that never panned out—makes it worth illuminating the fact that Jared Kushner had owned this outlet up until January 2017.[151] In preparation for Kushner to accept a position to work in the White House as a senior adviser to President Donald Trump, his brother-in-law took over as publisher, and interest in the paper was transferred into a family trust.[152]

Another point worth highlighting is the fact that the title of this article changed over the days that followed its first posting. But even if the headline was shifting, it was always misleading, and any of the versions could be easily shared through social media (Figure 2.1). Each of the topline descriptions of the story insisted that the court had ruled that there was a "rigging" of the primary election:

1. "Court Admits DNC and Debbie Wasserman Schulz [*sic*] *Rigged Primaries* Against Sanders";
2. "Court Concedes DNC and Debbie Wasserman Schulz [*sic*] and DNC *Rigged Primaries* Against Sanders";
3. "Court Concedes DNC Had the Right to *Rig Primaries* Against Sanders".[153]

However, at this stage of the proceedings the judge was obliged to assume as true all of the claims put forward by the plaintiff. The judge could only consider the technical matters of pleading and subject matter jurisdiction—requisite hurdles for a full trial. Consequently, the most relevant judicial findings were that "[i]t is readily apparent

[147] Michael Sainato, *Debbie Wasserman Schultz Served Class Action Lawsuit for Rigging Primaries*, Observer (June 30, 2016).

[148] *See* Michael Sainato, *Hearing Set for Class Action Lawsuit Against DNC*, Observer (Apr. 24, 2017); Michael Sainato, *DNC Lawyers Argue DNC Has Right to Pick Candidates in Back Rooms*, Observer (May 1, 2017).

[149] Guccifer 2.0, *Guccifer 2.0 DNC's servers hacked by a lone hacker* (June 15, 2016), *at* <https://guccifer2.wordpress.com/2016/06/15/dnc/>. It is worth noting that the national uproar only took place in July after the more user-friendly WikiLeaks release.

[150] Michael Sainato, *Guccifer 2.0 Leak Reveals How DNC Rigged Primaries for Clinton*, Observer (June 17, 2016).

[151] Dylan Beyers, *Jared Kushner to Transfer Observer Interest to Family Trust*, CNN.com (Jan. 9, 2017).

[152] Nathan McAlone, *Trump Son-In-Law Jared Kushner Will Step Down as Publisher of the Observer, and Have No "Ownership Stake,"* Business Insider France (Jan. 10, 2017).

[153] Emphasis added. The first two headlines were captured with a screenshot (the first is pictured in the text *supra*), and the third and final headline is still *available at* <https://observer.com/2017/08/court-admits-dnc-and-debbie-wasserman-schulz-rigged-primaries-against-sanders/>.

Figure 2.1 Original false and misleading headline moving through social media

that this Court lacks jurisdiction" and that "it is also apparent that Plaintiffs lack standing to assert each of the causes of action raised in this putative class action."[154]

Moreover, the text of the article went through changes as well. The author suggests in the second paragraph of the original version that the summary judgment "reflects a dire state of democracy in this country ... proving the DNC attorney's claims that the DNC is within their right to rig primaries." Nevertheless, this stark and grim assessment of what the judgment means disappeared in future versions of the article and no longer exists online. The article does later note that at this stage there is an assumption that "a plaintiff's allegation is inherently taken to be true."[155] Yet this point is buried in the article.

We would suggest that an extremely limited number of people would be inclined to do so, but if you follow the link in the article and read the actual judgment from the Florida court, the requirements of the proceedings are made explicitly clear by the judge:

> This Order does not concern who should have been the Democratic Party's candidate for the 2016 presidential election; it does not concern whether the DNC or Wasserman Schultz generally acted unfairly towards Senator Sanders or his

[154] Wildling, et al., v. DNC Services Corp., *supra* note 142, at 11, 12.
[155] Original version on file with authors.

> supporters; indeed, it does not even concern whether the DNC was in fact biased in favor of Hillary Clinton in the Democratic primaries. At this stage, the Court is required to construe the First Amended Complaint in the light most favorable to Plaintiffs and accept its well-pled allegations as true.
>
> [...]
>
> This Order therefore concerns only technical matters of pleading and subject-matter jurisdiction. To the extent Plaintiffs wish to air their general grievances with the DNC or its candidate selection process, their redress is through the ballot box, the DNC's internal workings, or their right of free speech—not through the judiciary.[156]

Much of the information in the article is true, so why does this qualify as *dezinformatsiya*? For one, the lawsuit itself was based entirely on the DNC material pinched by Russia.[157] Next, the changing title and content of the article leave the analyst and returning readers grasping for a moving substance that is difficult to fully understand or discuss. (Even if changed over time, the URL still reveals the original title: <https://observer.com/2017/08/court-admits-dnc-and-debbie-wasserman-schulz-rigged-primaries-against-sanders/>.) What is more, as will be discussed further later, it is currently difficult to track and know how far the original headline traveled within targeted communities who would be particularly sensitive to the "proven" accusations—that is, Bernie Sanders supporters who felt disenfranchised.

Perhaps most importantly, we can see that the term "rigged" is consistently tied to the court's judgment in the *Observer* article—along with previous articles on the case. Though this connection is demonstrably false, it is central to the narrative being propagated to erode trust in democracy itself. As for the required "kernel of truth," one expert helpfully tweeted in May 2017: "Historic note: Soviet bloc disinformation operators considered the best fact/forgery mix to be ~90% fact, ~10% fake."[158] The small percentage of falsehood here is the inflammatory allegation that a "rigging" had been proven in court—an accusation that undermines the legitimacy of the electoral system itself.

2. Russian Bots and Trolls

Finally, we can uncover further Russian involvement in this operation. To do so, a useful tool was unveiled in August 2017: the *Hamilton 68 Dashboard*.[159] This website aims to track in real time Russian-aligned propaganda on Twitter. The project was launched by the Alliance for Securing Democracy (ASD) and has involved a

[156] Wildling, et al., v. DNC Services Corp., *supra* note 142, at 8–9.

[157] *Id.* at 4–6 ("The DNC's bias, according to Plaintiffs, came to light after computer hackers penetrated the DNC's computer network. An individual identified as 'Guccifer 2.0' took credit for the hack and posted several documents purportedly taken from the DNC's servers on a publically accessible website. [...] As a result of the information 'Guccifer 2.0' released, Plaintiffs conclude that 'the DNC was anything but 'impartial,' 'evenhanded,' or 'neutral' with respect to the Democratic nominating process'").

[158] Thomas Rid (@RidT), Twitter (May 6, 2017, 4:13 AM), *at* https://twitter.com/ridt/status/860769446083911681?lang=en.

[159] <http://dashboard.securingdemocracy.org/>. The website has now been upgraded to track "the narratives and topics promoted by Russian and Chinese government officials and state-funded media on Twitter, YouTube, state-sponsored news websites, and via official diplomatic statements at the United Nations."

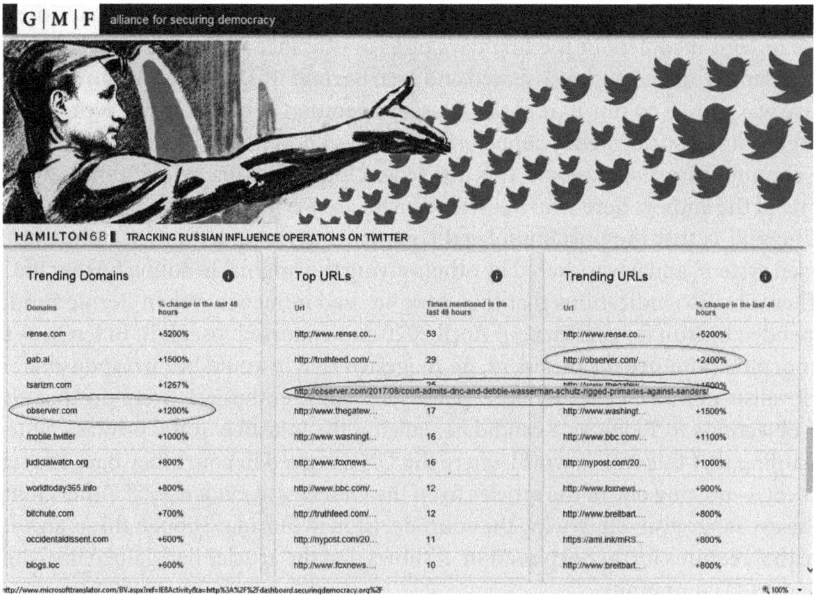

Figure 2.2 Amplification of the false and misleading material

former FBI special agent, Clint Watts, who is now Distinguished Research Fellow at the Foreign Policy Research Institute and Non-Resident Fellow at the ASD.[160] While the website has received criticism,[161] the preceding analysis indicates why this particular article is worth tracking with this tool to gather whether it was picked up by the accounts being monitored. As the dashboard moves in real time, consulting it now will only display what the bots and trolls are currently doing or have done over the previous forty-eight hours. Therefore, a screenshot taken at 20:00 GMT on August 27, 2016, establishes the amplification of this story by the *Observer* as one of its top URLs mentioned (Figure 2.2).

As can be seen, the specific URL was profiting from a boost supplied by the Russian-aligned bots and trolls the day after it had been published online. In other words, the *Hamilton 68 Dashboard* would suggest that this story was promoted because it includes "news content that supports the story Vladimir Putin wants to tell—a depiction of the West as corrupt, chaotic and collapsing."[162]

[160] *See* Clint Watts, Messing with the Enemy: Surviving in a Social Media World of Hackers, Terrorists, Russians, and Fake News (2018).

[161] Criticism has come for the backgrounds of some of its founders (e.g., Bill Kristol, a neoconservative who hyped the invasion of Iraq in 2003), and for not revealing the accounts it follows (justified at the site out of fear of spooking the account operators and changing behavior: *How to Interpret the Hamilton 68 Dashboard: Key Points and Clarifications*, *at* https://securingdemocracy.gmfus.org/toolbox/how-to-interpret-the-hamilton-68-dashboard-key-points-and-clarifications/). *See* Glenn Greenwald, *With New D.C. Policy Group, Dems Continue to Rehabilitate and Unify with Bush-Era Neocons*, The Intercept (July 17, 2017); M.C. McGrath & Glenn Greenwald, *How Shoddy Reporting and Anti-Russian Propaganda Coerced Ecuador to Silence Julian Assange*, The Intercept (Apr. 20, 2018).

[162] Watts, *supra* note 160.

This appeared to be the peak of activity (relatively high on the site at that time) by these foreign meddlers in the first days of its appearance online. Yet we don't know how far and wide the post was shared and seen beyond this. Nor do we know what increase was gained by this part of the Russian operation as this does not represent the entirety of their social media campaign. Nor do we know how targeted it was to receptive communities. For example, this article was found moving through the newsfeed of one of the authors here who has friends who are Bernie Sanders supporters. What can be said is that the post stimulated comments agreeing with the sentiment of a broken system, and it was shared by others giving the original headline further life.

There are also indications that this story has had influence. When Bernie Sanders suspended his run for president in April 2020 and endorsed Joseph R. Biden Jr. as the Democratic nominee for president, he suggested that it would be "irresponsible" for his loyalists not to support Biden.[163] Days later some enthusiasts were posting virulent objections to Biden as a candidate, voicing the injustice of the primary system, explaining that this was "a world where the DNC argued in court they have the right to cheat"—posting one of the articles from the *Observer* as evidence.[164] Others joined in the exchange also referencing the court decision in Florida. Though this is an anecdote that requires further exploration, it shows that the articles had gained life within the targeted community.

This shard of disinformation reveals several important points. First, we can see how exfiltrated information injected into the media mainstream can spur genuine activists into acting in the interests of Russia as unwitting agents. Second, the subtle manipulation of truth becomes more obvious as we see the real presence of some bias within the DNC becoming a damaging exaggeration of a "rigged" contest—pushing societal divisions and public understandings in ways that benefit Russia. Third, we see how this election interference targets the legitimacy of government and erodes faith in the institutions that are meant to establish governors of society. Finally, it is also a call for greater access to social media data and broader analysis of digital disinformation strategies.

Building off this last point, it should not be missed that we do not have tools for gauging the impact of this story moving through the information ecosystem. That is, not just how many people saw this headline in their newsfeed, but how many commented and helped it travel further by sharing it? And what did readers make of it? Did it influence them? If so, how much? We are certainly not the first to point out this problem:

> In the operations where they are used, it is sometimes difficult to define and determine their effect on the end result of these operations. There is a lack not only of research and tools to measure their effectiveness: in addition, the main limiting factor in the analytical process is the secret nature of the operations.[165]

[163] Joanna Walters & Laura Gambino, *Sanders Warns His Loyalists It Would Be "Irresponsible" Not to Support Biden*, The Guardian (Apr. 15, 2020).

[164] Screenshots of the posts on April 25, 2020, are filed with the authors.

[165] Darczewska & Żochowski, *supra* note 6, at 7. For a veritable effort to make such an assessment with the available social science tools, *see* generally Jamieson, *supra* note 140.

As a consequence, our final section will illuminate the need for fuller access to the empirical data that is now available on social platforms in order to obtain needed answers.

VI. A Clarion Call for Opening Fuller Data Access to Social Scientists

Three essential questions demand full investigation in order to wholly understand disinformation today:

- *Breadth*: How large are these operations?
- *Depth*: How deeply do they penetrate into a foreign society?
- *Precision*: How accurate (individualized) is the targeting for these operations?

Each of these queries should be answerable, in theory. However, social media companies have not allowed unfettered research on their platforms to protect their own trade secrets and the privacy of their users. This means that researchers, journalists, and regulators have not had the required access to provide sufficient answers to these vital questions.

There have been real efforts to study these quantitative research questions. In fact, the studies that have been executed thus far have created pressure on the tech companies to open up their vast troves of data. Initial literature reviews shed a great deal of light on the connection between social media, political polarization, and disinformation.[166] In other words, we are only starting to delineate what is known—and unknown—about this new phenomenon.

Some of the most trailblazing research into the Russian social media operation into the 2016 U.S. presidential election was arguably conducted by Johnathan Albright.[167] He is now the Director of the Digital Forensics Initiative at the Tow Center for Digital Journalism at Columbia University and keen attention on Albright's research into a topic of sudden political importance helped bring about his success in academia.[168] Due to the timeliness of his investigations, a great deal of it has been published online to offer immediate access.[169]

Most pertinent here, Albright's work quickly shattered the myth that Facebook attempted to promulgate when claiming that the Russian Internet Research Agency campaign had reached only 10 million people with 3,000 ads bought on the platform.

[166] Joshua Tucker et al., *Social Media, Political Polarization, and Political Disinformation: A Review of the Scientific Literature*, Hewlett Foundation (2018). This text provides a breakdown of current publications into six categories: (1) online political conversations; (2) the effects of exposure to online disinformation; (3) producers of disinformation; (4) tactics and strategies of dispersing disinformation; (5) political polarization and online content; and (6) polarization, misinformation, and democracy.

[167] Craig Timberg, *Russian Propaganda May Have Been Shared Hundreds of Millions of Times, New Research Says*, WASHINGTON POST (Oct. 5, 2017).

[168] Issie Lapowsky, *Shadow Politics: Meet the Digital Sleuth Exposing Fake News*, WIRED (July 18, 2018).

[169] *See* Albright's online portfolio at MEDIUM.COM, <https://medium.com/@d1gi>, and the research data published to back up these claims at <https://public.tableau.com/profile/d1gi#!/vizhome/FB4/TotalReachbyPage>. His Medium.com page was shortlisted for a Data Journalism Award.

Due to his previous work studying public discourse online, this figure struck him as a vast underestimate. Albright thus set out to extract data and archived content using "CrowdTangle" (Facebook's tool for social analytics) from six of the known IRA pages—Blacktivists, United Muslims of America, Being Patriotic, Heart of Texas, Secured Borders, and LGBT United. Since there were some 470 known Russian accounts, this would represent only a tiny fraction of their overall online content. Yet in analyzing 500 posts for each of these six accounts, Albright found that they had been shared a total of 340 million times and had garnered over 20 million "likes," "shares," and other reactions. When the numbers are extrapolated, this would put the potential number of views for what is currently known about the Russian operation well into the billions.

Disturbingly, the large amounts of data that Albright had scraped during this notable research were quickly removed from the platform just days after his research was published.[170] Which brings us to our final point for this chapter. Namely, there is a large hole in our full understanding of these foreign influence operations today. This gap was aptly summarized for the biggest platform as such in 2017:

> Simply put, without access to Facebook data, understanding of the spread of disinformation through social media will be incomplete. [...] a great deal more could be learned about many of the topics contained in this report if a system for sharing Facebook data with scientific researchers could be developed and implemented.[171]

With this in mind, we close our chapter with a call for extensive academic research into social media platforms so that we can wholly comprehend the scale, scope, and accuracy of foreign operations.

In fact, such a program has been launched—though it has only progressed in fits and starts. In April 2018, a partnership was initiated between Facebook and an entity named *Social Science One*. The objective is to offer researchers access to one petabyte of data (1 million gigabytes) from its platform to study "the effect of social media on democracy and elections."[172] The newly created body consists of a commission of senior academics who act as a third party to manage the envisioned industry-academic partnerships.[173] Outside scholars are able to petition data sets for study through research proposals that are evaluated by the commission (which excludes projects that violate privacy, damage a company's market position, or infringe upon other studies). The accepted researchers will receive access to privacy-preserving data and can publish their findings on agreed topics without seeking approval from the participating company.

The emergence of big data today means that while social scientists have access to more data than ever before, this only represents a substantially smaller fraction of what actually exists—resulting in incomplete outcomes that often raise more

[170] Craig Timberg & Elizabeth Dwoskin, *Facebook Takes Down Data and Thousands of Posts, Obscuring Reach of Russian Disinformation*, Washington. Post (Oct. 12, 2017).

[171] Tucker et al., *supra* note 166, at 70.

[172] Social Science One: Building Industry-Academic Partnerships, *Our Facebook Partnership, at* <https://socialscience.one/our-facebook-partnership>.

[173] The Institute of Quantitative Social Science at Harvard and the Social Science Research Council are to provide logistical help.

questions than they answer (e.g., Albright's investigation detailed previously). Hence, researchers either publish their research findings with access to only partial data, or sign away academic freedom in nondisclosure agreements by working within a company and relinquishing final control over research and publishing decisions.

In light of what has been elucidated in this chapter concerning the dearth of access and study, we believe *Social Science One* to be a potentially groundbreaking development by creating a model that can be enlarged or replicated elsewhere. Furthermore, it demonstrates the growing understanding that we need to study what is happening on personalized newsfeeds.

Unfortunately, *Social Science One* has proven much more difficult to implement than first envisioned. While the project was unsurprisingly successful in attracting viable and valuable research proposals, getting Facebook to deliver the originally specified data was challenging.[174] The Co-Chairs and European Advisory Committee of *Social Science One* eventually released a bold statement in December 2019 that keenly captures our own concerns:

> In recent years digital platforms have made independent scientific research into potentially consequential phenomena such as online disinformation, polarization, and echo chambers virtually impossible by restricting scholars' access to the platforms' application programming interfaces (APIs). The Social Science One initiative, specifically designed to provide scholars with access to privacy protected data, has made important progress over the last 18 months, but Facebook has still not provided academics with anything approaching adequate data access.
>
> [...]
>
> The current situation is untenable. Heated public and political discussions are waged over the role and responsibilities of platforms in today's societies, and yet researchers cannot make fully informed contributions to these discussions. We are mostly left in the dark, lacking appropriate data to assess potential risks and benefits. This is not an acceptable situation for scientific knowledge. It is not an acceptable situation for our societies.[175]

In addition, the authors of this statement called for specific actions: (1) Facebook should make accurate and representative data available for scientific study; (2) all

[174] The problem revolved around Facebook's legal interpretation of the General Data Protection Regulation (GDPR) from the European Union and the consent decree under which it operates with the Federal Trade Commission of the United States. The company took the position that these restrictions inhibit any analysis by researchers of individual level data, even if it is aggregated or de-identified. This legal interpretation was not shared with the co-chairs of Social Science One. *See* Social Science One, *Unprecedented Facebook URLs Dataset Now Available for Academic Research through Social Science One* (Feb. 13, 2020), *at* <https://socialscience.one/blog/unprecedented-facebook-urls-dataset-now-available-research-through-social-science-one>. Reluctance by the social media platform created such a problem that in August 2019 the funders behind the Social Science One program instituted a deadline for Facebook to share the promised data with the researchers or said they would terminate their support. *See* Social Media and Democracy Research Grants, *Statement from Social Science Research Council President Alondra Nelson on the Social Media and Democracy Research Grants Program* (Aug. 27, 2019), *at* <https://www.ssrc.org/fellowships/view/social-media-and-democracy-research-grants/update-from-ssrc-president-alondra-nelson/>.

[175] *Public statement from the Co-Chairs and European Advisory Committee of Social Science One*, Dec. 11, 2019, *at* <https://socialscience.one/blog/public-statement-european-advisory-committee-social-science-one>.

digital platforms should be required to do the same; (3) Facebook, Google, and Twitter should provide written analysis of any legal barriers that might prevent academic research; (4) European authorities should provide actionable guidance on what can and cannot be shared for research; (5) platforms and public officials should create "research safe harbors" (similar to that used for health and medical data) where scholars can access personally identifiable data with clear and robust limits; and (6) public authorities should help in creating independent verification of platform data since "[e]ven if the researchers and their analyses are considered credible, all findings rest on trust that the platforms have provided complete, accurate data."[176]

The public pressure worked. Two months later Facebook released an unprecedented URLs data set to *Social Science One*.[177] In order to comply with Facebook's interpretation of their legal obligations, an agreement was made to apply "differential privacy" to the data sets in order to prevent reidentification of individuals represented in the data through an introduction of calibrated "noise." This is not the place to delve into whether this adjustment allows full social scientific analysis without jeopardizing privacy,[178] and, in any event, it is far too early to expound upon this development as it broke while we were bringing this chapter to completion. At this point, all that can be said is that this is an enormously welcome development that holds great promise.[179]

VII. Conclusion

In this chapter, we have attempted to flesh out the central components of twenty-first-century *disinfo-ops*. One clear challenge—a holdover from the Soviet era—comes from the elusory nature of the operations themselves. As they are built on factual information with only slight distortions that are often pushed forward by unwitting agents who wholeheartedly believe in their cause, the narratives are extremely difficult to disprove—or even prove that they are part of an external campaign. Furthermore, when a belief has taken hold, demonstrating to someone that an incorrect assessment of the facts has been made largely means asking them to admit they have been improperly influenced or duped.

On top of this, we notably find vastly expanded opportunities to carry out campaigns using information and communication technologies. In the newly available political marketing/disinformation continuum, social media platforms and persuasion techniques play a key role in what has become information warfare. ICTs make persuasion techniques broader, more omnipresent, and yet more difficult to identify when hidden under millions of other messages and behind multiple identities. Moreover, the same large data set and technologies used to collect this data, track individuals, and target them with bespoke content are also used (or rented) as a service, by malevolent actors, including foreign states and criminal groups.

[176] *Id.*

[177] Social Science One, *Unprecedented Facebook URLs, supra* note 174.

[178] *See* Georgina Evans & Gary King, *Statistically Valid Inferences from Differentially Private Data Releases, at* <http://j.mp/38NrmRW>.

[179] *Cf.* Kalev Leetaru, *Facebook and Social Science One: The Academics Are Rushing to Mine Our Private Data*, FORBES (May 13, 2019).

These facts give shape to a novel type of interference that is wholly different than anything we have seen before; this calls for rethinking current international legal norms. We are seeing pervasive campaigns, operating below the threshold of armed conflict, that can cause genuine upheaval within a society as citizens vehemently disagree over the basic truths of events. And when elections and politicians running are targeted, the activity breaks down the trust that a people must have in the legitimacy of their leaders and the processes that elevate them to a position of authority.

It is hoped that this descriptive work provides useful information for prescriptive proposals of what ought to be done. It is thus fitting that this chapter appears within a volume that provides various propositions for combating foreign election interference through international law and other means. For our part, we would suggest that one place to start is by classifying such cross-border operations as a violation of the international law principle of nonintervention[180]—which certainly does not preclude the actions from transgressing other rubrics of international law at the very same time. Yet for any of these ideas to become policy, the first order of business must be governments who are ready and willing to confront today's digital *dezinformatsiya*.

We close with a potent analogy made by former Soviet leader and head of the KGB, Yuri Andropov: "[*Dezinformatsiya*] works like cocaine. If you sniff it once or twice, it may not change your life. If you use it every day though, it will make you an addict—a different man."[181] The pushers of this addictive drug have today found a way to inject a relentless flow of individually tailored content directly into the bloodstream of foreign citizens through ubiquitous handheld devices. More study must be done, yet we believe there is already enough to show that *disinfo-ops* represent a significant threat to democracy.

[180] *See* Barela, *Cross-Border Cyber Ops*, *supra* note 3; Barela, *Zero Shades of Grey*, *supra* note 3.

[181] PACEPA & RYCHLAK, *supra* note 2, at 196 (citing Andropov).

3

Weaponizing Information Systems for Political Disruption

Valeria Marcia and Kevin C. Desouza

I. Introduction

On Friday, March 20, 2020, at a coffee shop in Washington, D.C., several senior government employees worked on their government laptops after connecting to the free pul1blic Wi-Fi. Soon after, the U.S. Health and Human Services (HHS) Department suffered a cyberattack.[1] Amid the rapid spread of the pandemic COVID-19, the cyberattack on the HHS's computer system sought to undermine the agency's response to the coronavirus. It was speculated to be the work of a foreign Actor as part of a campaign of disruption and disinformation.[2]

In addition to cyberattacks on government and healthcare networks, the confusion around the coronavirus' spread is leading to the weaponization of information more broadly. From Tehran to Moscow, coronavirus is at the heart of disinformation narratives. For Iran, the coronavirus is viewed as a ploy by the United States to divide it from its neighboring Shia Brethren. For Russia, it is considered an opportunity to further its information war against the West. For China, it is an opportunity to prove that domestic autocracy is preferable to foreign democracy. For the political right, it highlights the dangers of the refugee camps within Europe's borders. And, for the left, it showcases the callousness of a right-wing government.[3]

The spread of coronavirus also represents a new technique for influencing elections through the spreading of misinformation. The February 2020 elections in Iran serve as an example of how misinformation can affect voter turnout at the polls; Iran appears to have had the lowest turnout since its 1979 Islamic revolution. CNBC reports that, according to Supreme Leader Ayatollah Ali Khamenei, the low turnout was due to the spread of false information about the coronavirus.[4] In California, the spread of coronavirus concerns prompted temporary election employees to stay home for U.S. "Super Tuesday," for fear of being in public places.[5] Subsequently, some U.S. states are

[1] Michael Krull & Jeremy Turner, *COVID-19 and Information Warfare: Through the Fog of War toward a New World*, Am. Mil. News (Mar. 23, 2020).

[2] Shira Stein & Jennifer Jacobs, *Cyber-attack Hits U.S. Health Agency amid Covid-19 Outbreak*, Bloomberg (Mar. 16, 2020).

[3] *See* David Patrikarakos, *Corona Confusion Is Being Ruthlessly Weaponized*, The Spectator (Mar. 22, 2020).

[4] Parisa Hafezi, *UPDATE 1-Iran's Enemies Tried to Use Coronavirus to Impact Vote—Khamenei*, CNBC (Feb. 23, 2020).

[5] Justin Rohrlich, *How Disinformation about Coronavirus Could Impact the 2020 U.S. Election*, Quartz (Mar. 5, 2020).

Valeria Marcia and Kevin C. Desouza, *Weaponizing Information Systems for Political Disruption* In: *Defending Democracies*. Edited by Duncan B. Hollis and Jens David Ohlin, Oxford University Press (2021). © Duncan B. Hollis & Jens David Ohlin.
DOI: 10.1093/oso/9780197556979.003.0004

evaluating the possibility of using online and mobile platforms for the elections. The use of these platforms significantly increases cybersecurity risks since foreign Actors who intend to influence election results could take advantage of this technology.[6]

Both the HHS cyberattack and coronavirus narratives demonstrate that information systems are increasingly subject to manipulation, allowing Actors to engage in information warfare's acts. These acts include direct attempts to compromise voting systems and other public infrastructure attacks via cyber operations that generate losses of confidentiality, integrity, or availability. Today, almost all facets of the public sector leverage information systems to deliver public services. Rogue Actors commonly seek to compromise this technology, thereby impacting service delivery, increasing fear and frustration in the citizenry, and creating political turmoil. Together, this serves as a common flowchart for rogue Actors that impedes the citizens' trust in their government and public institutions.[7] But the weaponization of information does not depend only on compromising information systems; a critical analysis of its role in creating political disruption reveals that information systems can be "weaponized" by foreign adversaries in order to compromise political goals and values even while the systems and networks remain protected.[8]

This chapter builds the case for why we need to understand the nuances of information systems regarding various forms of political disruption, including instances of foreign election interference. This chapter takes a critical look at: (1) how information systems can be disrupted at various levels for political purposes; (2) how nation-states respond to attacks on information systems (e.g., going beyond defense to include offensive responses); and (3) what to expect in the future given growing dependence on information systems in political processes and their economic impacts.

The chapter first offers background material on the nature of information systems disruptions to political processes and public institutions. It then elaborates on a particular taxonomy—the ALERT framework—for assessing the manipulation of information systems. The chapter demonstrates the utility of the ALERT framework using illustrative examples from the U.S. election interference context. The chapter concludes with a discussion of this novel explanatory framework, the connections between the state and non-state Actors implicated, and future research avenues.

[6] Matthew Vann, *States Worried about Mail-In Ballot Access during COVID-19 Pandemic Consider Online Voting Options*, ABC NEWS (May 7, 2020).

[7] Kevin C. Desouza et al., *Weaponizing Information Systems for Political Disruption: The Actor, Lever, Effects, and Response Taxonomy (ALERT)*, 88 COMPUTERS & SECURITY 101606 (2020).

[8] Although this chapter focuses on foreign threats to information systems, it is important to note that there are cases where information systems disruptions can be internal, such as where a government disrupts internally (e.g., blackouts to internet service) for political purposes. From India to Indonesia to Brazil, democracy and political stability are being compromised by online domestic disinformation campaigns by political parties seeking to gain an advantage. Political parties in India and Indonesia often operate through surrogates and consultancies to keep their activities at arm's length. They deploy armies of real humans managing news sites, YouTube channels, online accounts, and WhatsApp groups to produce and disseminate hyperpartisan content. Conventional political ads are tied into this nexus as well. Moreover, online campaigning is big business, with over $350,000 spent on political Facebook ads in India between March 2 and 16 alone, ahead of the six-week general election that began April 11. Arjun Bisen, *Disinformation Is Drowning Democracy*, FOREIGN POL'Y (Apr. 24, 2019).

II. Background

As a general matter, government influence on foreign elections is a practice that has repeated over time across different geographical areas. For decades, the West—including the United States and the United Kingdom—have conducted operations in this space, through both covert and overt means, including monetary support, training programs, and public relations assistance.[9] As the first chapter of this book recalls, the French organized an intervention to prevent George Washington's re-election in the 1796 U.S. presidential election. Likewise, the United States interfered in Italy's 1948 election, providing huge support to the Christian Democrats; while the Soviet Union assisted the Italian Communist Party.[10] However, the nature of such activities has undergone a radical transformation, given the advances in information systems.

Amid the broader phenomenon of election interference, there is also a history of the misuse of these information systems for political gains and denting democratic institutions. For example, countries such as Estonia, Belarus, and Moldova have contended with this issue for an extended period.[11]

Several factors account for this increasing evolution of information systems: (1) real-time generation of fine-grained data from human activities; (2) advancement of data analytics and computational skill; (3) digitization of public institutions influencing the modes of engagement with citizens and service delivery; and (4) the increased role of information systems in election campaigning and shaping public opinion. Simultaneously, the increased dependence of public institutions, public policy processes, and the governance of public goods on information systems has made them vulnerable to attacks from Actors with mala fide intentions. This situation is exacerbated by the rise of big data—that is, the collection of a multitude of fine-grained data generated from multiple sources—as an integral part of today's information systems. Algorithms created to process this data can be manipulated to produce different results. For instance, in 2012, Twitter was accused of engaging in "algorithmic censorship" of "#occupywallstreet" (the micro-blogging platform did not show the topic trending in cities where protests were being held and tweets were spiking).[12] Similarly, when Google was accused of proliferating fake news and put under considerable political pressure, the company announced that it had tweaked its search algorithm to give more weight to the authority of the source.[13]

Taken together, these advancements suggest a key point: the protection of information systems from cyberattacks is no longer a sufficient defensive posture.

[9] *See, e.g.*, Peter Beinart, *The U.S. Needs to Face Up to Its Long History of Election Meddling*, The Atlantic (July 22, 2018); Scott Shane, *Russia Isn't the Only One Meddling in Elections. We Do It, Too*, N.Y. Times (Feb. 17, 2018); Thomas Carothers, *Is the U.S. Hypocritical to Criticize Russian Election Meddling?*, Foreign Aff. (Mar. 12, 2018).

[10] James E. Miller, *Taking Off the Gloves: The United States and the Italian Elections of 1948*, 7 Diplomatic History 35–56 (1983).

[11] Oren Dorell, *Alleged Russian political meddling documented in 27 countries since 2004*, USA Today (Sept. 7, 2017).

[12] Tarleton Gillespie, *Can an Algorithm Be Wrong?*, Limn (2018).

[13] Kim Darrah, *The Troubling Influence Algorithms Have on How We Make Decisions*, The New Economy (Nov. 14, 2017).

Cyberattacks that target confidentiality, integrity, or availability are not the exclusive threat. A foreign power can still impact an electoral process by manipulating information itself, weaponizing it to compromise an adversary's goals and values to create political disruption. We use the term "information warfare" (IW) to encompass the wide range of activities involving the weaponization of information systems for political disruption.

III. A Case Study of Modern Information Warfare: Russian Troll Factories in Ghana Targeting the 2020 U.S. Presidential Elections

How has information warfare responded to the new opportunities created by the transformation of information systems? Russia, among others, has demonstrated how global information networks facilitate new forms of IW. For example, in 2019, both Facebook and Twitter discovered a disinformation campaign focused on attacking the United States, which originated in Africa. This operation was run by individuals with links to Russia's Internet Research Agency (IRA). Additionally, in November 2019, Facebook announced the removal of three networks of accounts, totaling dozens of pages related to African countries. The pages were linked to Russian businessman Yevgeny Prigozhin, touted as Putin's "chef" by the Russian media.[14]

Facebook's removal came days after President Vladimir Putin's lavish reception at a summit for fifty-four African countries in the Russian resort town of Sochi. Thus, the disinformation campaign was part of growing Russian interest in Africa—utilizing a mix of state power and private interests, including Russian companies keen to exploit Africa's energy and commodity resources and provide private military contractors to boost local security forces. Instead of using its territory, Russia chose to run its troll factories from Africa, including otherwise authentic accounts. AFRIC, one of the disabled pages, had a very real-life presence on the ground both in Russia and in Africa. Describing itself as a "community of independent researchers, experts, and activists," AFRIC was prominently featured at the Sochi forum and even announced its partnership with a foundation run by Russian propagandist Alexander Malkevich, who was exiled from the United States.

All told, Facebook detected forty-nine Facebook accounts, sixty-nine Facebook pages, and eighty-five Instagram accounts participating in the campaign. On Facebook, the relatively nascent accounts accumulated roughly 13,500 followers. On Instagram, the accounts had a following of around 265,000. On Twitter, seventy-one accounts were linked to the Russian-run operations in Ghana and Nigeria, spreading similar messages to sow discord by engaging in conversations about social issues like race and civil rights. According to Facebook, the network was in the early stages of building an audience. Local nationals, some wittingly and some unwittingly, operated it on behalf of individuals in Russia. The Russia-based campaign relied on

[14] The United States had already sanctioned Prigozhin for funding the Internet Research Agency, which U.S. prosecutors allege meddled in the 2016 presidential election. *See* Mary Ilyushina, *Russia's "Troll Factory" Is Alive and Well in Africa*, CNN (Nov. 1 2019).

Ghana-based non-governmental organizations as grassroots proxies, with some of those involved unlikely to know their work's true nature.[15]

In 2016, much of the trolling aimed at the U.S. election had operated from an office block in St. Petersburg, Russia. However, in the run-up to the U.S. 2020 presidential election the trolling was outsourced to West Africa. These new trolls focused almost exclusively on racial issues in the United States, promoting black empowerment and often displaying anger toward white Americans. The objective appeared to be directed at inflaming divisions among Americans and provoking social unrest. A CNN investigation found the accounts created in Ghana were consistently coordinated, posting on the same topic within hours of each other.[16]

The Ghana-based operation shows a new face for the weaponization of information today. A foreign Actor from one country can act in concert with other countries' gullible foreign agents using known social media networks as levers to influence the elections in a third target country. In so doing, there is an increased potential for hiding the operation's true purpose. If an information system is compromised or weaponized by Actors with mala fide intentions toward third parties abroad, it is unlikely that most individuals would be aware of the malicious Actors' concealed agendas. This circumstance is more pronounced in countries in places like Africa, where there are limited alternatives in terms of how citizens deal with their physical or social environments.

This threat, combined with increased regulatory scrutiny, has left social media companies in a bind. After being misused to run misinformation campaigns during the 2016 U.S. presidential election campaign, these platforms have started weeding out pages, posts, and accounts of people involved in jeopardizing the information in democracies. In combating one set of problems, however, these efforts raise new questions—whether these platforms' efforts come at the expense of other human rights interests like freedom of expression. To better understand the threats posed to information systems, we need to build a better framework for understanding how different sorts of IW operations are constructed and executed. One possible approach is a framework developed by one of us in previous scholarship: the ALERT framework.

IV. The ALERT Framework

Drawing on the concept of weaponization of information systems, Desouza et al. developed the ALERT tool for security policymakers and practitioners tasked with responding to political disruption.[17] It takes the first step in constructing a comprehensive analysis of how these attacks can occur and the role of Actors and information systems in perpetrating the attacks. Although there are other taxonomies in the literature (e.g., Killourhy et al., 2004,[18] Simmons et al.,[19]

[15] Taylor Hatmaker, *Russian Trolls Are Outsourcing to Africa to Stoke U.S. Racial Tensions*, TECHCRUNCH (Mar. 12, 2020).

[16] Clarissa Ward et al., *How Russian Meddling Is Back before 2020 Vote*, CNN (Mar. 12, 2020).

[17] Desouza et al., *supra* note 7.

[18] Kevin S. Killourhy, Roy A. Maxion, & Kymie M.C. Tan, *A Defense-Centric Taxonomy Based on Attack Manifestations*, INT'L CONF. DEPENDABLE SYS. & NETWORKS (2004).

[19] Charles R. Simmons, *Method and System for Configuring Network Devices, U.S. Patent No. 8,898,346* (filed Nov. 25, 2014).

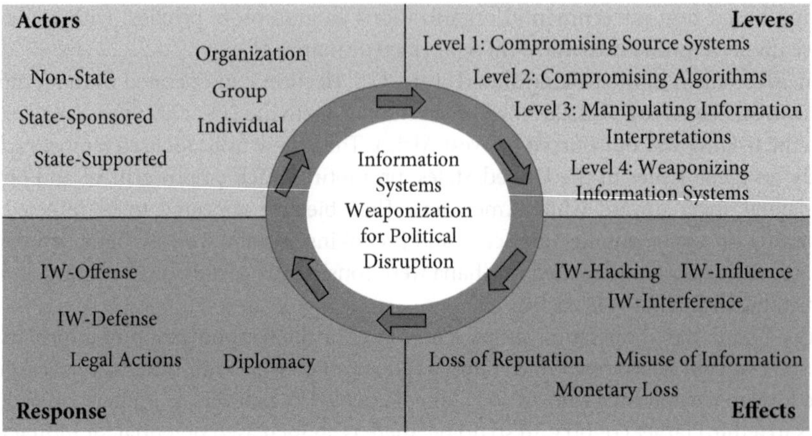

Figure 3.1 Framework for Weaponizing Information Systems for Political Disruption (adapted from Desouza et al. 2020)

Mirkovic and Reihner,[20] and Kjaerland[21]), most focus on protecting information systems and even data from cybersecurity threats. The ALERT framework goes further by looking at how information systems' goals and values can be compromised. The authors have articulated hazardous scenarios as a combination of four elements—(1) Actor; (2) Lever; (3) Effect; and (4) Response—that viewed holistically may offer a (5) Theory for assessing threats to information systems. The ALERT framework defines risk as a hazardous scenario in which the Actors adopt a vector to create an impact. "Hazardous scenario" is further defined as a combination of the agent (Actor) with the Levers. The Actor is the individual or entity that instigates, conducts, or supports an attack. The term "Lever" defines how the Actor leverages the information system to carry out the attack (the threat vector).

The ALERT framework also defines "information warfare," which includes a series of activities related to information systems' weaponization for political disruption.[22] The potential impact (Effect) can then be articulated alongside the element of Response as a mitigation measure. Figure 3.1 illustrates this theoretical framework in the context of weaponizing information systems for political disruption.[23]

[20] Jelena Mirkovic & Peter Reiher, *A Taxonomy of DDoS Attack and DDoS Defense Mechanisms*, 34 ACM SIGCOMM Comp. Com. Rev. 39–53 (2004).

[21] Maria Kjaerland, *A Taxonomy and Comparison of Computer Security Incidents from the Commercial and Government Sectors*, 25 Comp. & Sec. 522–538 (2006).

[22] Desouza et al., *supra* note 7, at 4.

[23] This is Figure 4 in Desouza et al., *supra* note 7.

A. Actors

1. Roles

An Actor is an agent or organization that either (1) instigates the attack, (2) supports any aspect of planning the attack (e.g., through the provision of funding, computing resources, and even human experts), (3) conducts the actual attack, (4) knowingly supports the concealment of the attack and/or source of the attack, or (5) unknowingly amplifies the attack due to its actions.

Russia is the primary example of an Actor that deliberately instigates IW operations for political manipulation. In their introduction to this volume, Duncan B. Hollis and Jens David Ohlin highlight how the Russian government supported bloggers and individuals to spread pro-Russia news on social media networks. The case of the Russian troll factories, described earlier in this chapter, is another example of how Russia plays a primary role in instigating attacks. Moreover, it should be noted that Russia is an Actor interfering in elections not only in the United States but also in other countries such as France[24] and Ukraine.[25]

The charges against Elena Alekseevna Khusyaynova for her alleged role in a Russian conspiracy to interfere in the U.S. political system provide an example of how Actors (whether they are states, groups, organizations, or individuals) can support the planning of attacks.[26] The definition of "Actors" also includes those who conduct a cyberattack. In September 2019, Australian intelligence identified China as the "sophisticated state Actor" responsible for a cyberattack on the Australian Parliament and three Australian political parties before the general elections.[27]

Actors can also include organizations that knowingly conceal an attack. For example, shell companies can anonymously transfer money and engage in commercial transactions such as those located not only in notorious locations like Panama and the Cayman Islands but also in Western countries like the United States.[28] News media can also be Actors as they provide the platform to the message. The media use information systems to communicate with the public. They can, therefore, unknowingly amplify an attack, being a suitable channel for divulging information. Indeed, the media may amplify and disseminate fake news. Depending on the tone and the mode of communication used, the media could even incite harmful actions. An example is what happened to Fox News regarding the spread of disinformation about the Ukrainian scandal.[29]

[24] Ninon Bulckaert, *How France Successfully Countered Russian Interference during the Presidential Election*, EURACTIV (July 17, 2018).

[25] *The Logic Behind Russian Military Cyber Operations*, BOOZ ALLEN HAMILTON (2020).

[26] *Recent FARA Cases*, THE UNITED STATES DEPARTMENT OF JUSTICE (2019).

[27] Colin Packham, *Australia Concluded China Was behind Hack on Parliament, Political Parties—Sources*, REUTERS (Sept. 15, 2019).

[28] Melanie Hicken & Blake Ellis, *These U.S. Companies Hide Drug Dealers, Mobsters and Terrorists*, CNNMONEY (Dec. 9, 2015).

[29] Luke O'Neil, *Fox News Guests Spread "Disinformation"—Says Leaked Internal Memo*, THE GUARDIAN (Feb. 7, 2020).

2. State-sponsored, State-supported, and Nonstate Actors

In addition to their different roles, ALERT divides Actors by their relations to a nation-state: for example, state-sponsored, state-supported, or nonstate Actors. An example of a state-sponsored Actor is the "APT 41" hacker group, a criminal group used by China to perform cyber espionage.[30] An example of a state-supported Actor, although no state has formally claimed responsibility, is the alleged group of Israeli and U.S. experts who worked on the Stuxnet virus in 2010.[31] On nonstate Actors, it is important to note that some may act for ideological reasons—such as ISIS—using social media as a propaganda tool.[32] Nonstate Actors can also operate for economic reasons, that is, to obtain a profit from their criminal activity.

3. Reach of the Attack

Actors can also vary in terms of their capacity to operate—that is, they can differ within the reach of their IW operations. An example of a category of Actors that weaponize information systems with massive effects is an Advanced Persistent Threat (APT). An APT is "an entity that engages in a malicious, organized and highly sophisticated long-term or reiterated network intrusion and exploitation operation to obtain information from a target organization, sabotage its operations or both."[33] For example, APT28 was associated with Russia's measures to interfere in the 2016 U.S. presidential election.[34] APTs and other Actors can operate inside the state in which they reside or outside that state. As the Ghana troll factory example shows, they can also pursue IW directly against a target state and its people or indirectly through intermediary Actors located in third states.[35]

The ALERT framework highlights the presence of a multiplicity of Actors, who can act as individuals, groups, or organizations and can have different roles. They are driven by multiple motivations, whether political, military, economic, or ideological. They are capable of carrying out attacks inside their own country or outside and can operate via cyberattacks, all aimed to disrupt the availability or integrity of information systems or via information operations aimed at influencing elections or political processes in other countries.

[30] Josh Taylor, *Chinese Cyberhackers "Blurring Line between State Power and Crime,"* The Guardian (Aug. 8, 2019).

[31] This virus represents one of the most memorable cyberattacks between Iran and the United States, which infected the Iranian uranium enrichment structures and caused their centrifuges to malfunction. Vasileios Karagiannopoulos et al., *How Real Is the Threat of Cyberwar between Iran and the US?*, IPI Global Observatory (2020).

[32] William Feuer, *Tiktok Removes Two Dozen Accounts Used for ISIS Propaganda*, CNBC (Oct. 21, 2019).

[33] Atif Ahmad et al., *Strategically-Motivated Advanced Persistent Threat: Definition, Process, Tactics and a Disinformation Model of Counterattack*, 86 Comp. & Sec. 402–418 (2019).

[34] Tom Sear, *A State Actor Has Targeted Australian Political Parties—But That Shouldn't Surprise Us*, The Conversation (Feb. 18, 2019).

[35] Where IW Actors perform attacks outside their state, it is crucial to assess what is the applicable law, and, therefore, if there are international treaties that establish jurisdiction or otherwise set a menu for responsive options.

B. Levers

Levers represent the means through which Actors can leverage information systems. According to the ALERT framework, four levels of Levers exist. Level One represents the disruption of information systems, that is, taking them offline. Level Two involves the manipulation of algorithms in information systems. Level Three is the manipulation of interpretations of meaning associated with information. In Level Four, information systems are fully weaponized.

1. Disruption of Sources of Data

The lowest Level (i.e., the least complex Level but not necessarily any less threatening) represents the disruption of data sources. An example is the broadcasters' disruption that occurred in Ukraine during the 2015 local elections. Following political turmoil and violence, the Ukraine's president decided to block separatists from participating in the 2015 elections. From Russia's point of view, the Ukrainian government's behavior was aimed at delegitimizing the separatist elections, which would have been equivalent to a violation of sovereignty by Russian allies. For this reason, Russia's intelligence agency, the GRU, conducted numerous attacks to damage servers and workstations.[36]

2. Manipulation of the Algorithms

The second level of Levers is the manipulation of the algorithms used in the processing of signals. Actors may manipulate elements that process the data, compromising it, and rendering the results useless. One example of this is the so-called "AI nudge," where humans act in unison to persuade algorithms to change their behavior.

In the electoral context, the U.S. Senate Intelligence Committee conducted a survey that revealed a systematic method by which Russian companies purchased Facebook advertisements to increase the political and racial divide in the United States. Cambridge Analytica also developed a behavioral model of over 87 million Facebook profiles intending to influence elections with a certain political result through targeted advertising.[37]

3. Manipulating Interpretations Associated with Information

At the third level, Levers can involve manipulating interpretations associated with information. Advancements in video and audio editing have introduced a suite of new opportunities to manipulate information and its interpretation. For instance, superimposing an individual's face on another individual's body is now a commonday reality, with easy-to-use tools available to the ordinary person—also known as "deepfake" technology. Deepfake technology creates videos showing politicians who say or do things they never actually said or did. A well-made deepfake video could convince voters that what the video showed actually occurred and could easily influence voter sentiment.[38] One example of this is the video of Nancy Pelosi, in which she

[36] *Logic Behind Russian Military Cyber Operations*, *supra* note 25.

[37] Anup Ghosh, *How Elections Are Hacked via Social Media Profiling*, CSO ONLINE (May 31, 2018).

[38] Grace Shao, *Fake Videos Could Be the Next Big Problem in the 2020 Elections*, CNBC (Oct. 15, 2019).

appears to be impaired. This video was widely broadcasted via social media and is one of many examples of how videos can be manipulated.[39]

4. Weaponizing Information Systems

At the fourth and final level, the information system stands fully weaponized to cause direct, political, physical, economic, and social damage. Last year, for example, the Ukrainian government accused Russia of orchestrating a distributed denial-of-service (DDoS) attack only weeks before the presidential election.[40] Another example is the DDoS attacks that Russian operators conducted three days before the elections in Montenegro. To influence the results of the elections, these attacks disrupted media websites, the country's largest communications network, the Socialist Democratic Party of Montenegro, and a nongovernmental organization that promotes democratic elections in the country.[41]

The Dark Web is also a tool in disinformation election campaigns. On the Dark Web, it is possible to find voter data and digital weapons that hackers use to subvert the election. Cryptocurrencies are the incentive that fuels cybercriminals on the Dark Web. It is estimated that Russian operators spent more than $95,000 in bitcoin to fund their operations to influence the 2016 election.[42]

The typology of attacks in Level 1 and Level 4 can be the same. DDoS attacks, for example, might qualify as such in both cases. The difference between Level 1 and Level 4 lies in the actor's motivations to carry out the attack. While in Level 1, the motivation consists of taking the systems offline, in destroying data, or requesting the ransom, in Level 4, the impulse is more sophisticated, given that the Actors intend to exploit the information systems by not only taking them offline but also using them against victims by influencing voters' behaviors.

C. Effects

Using one or more of the four Levers, Actors can produce Effects through weaponized information systems that are undesirable from the target's point of view. Whether it be a direct attack on a public service website, or disseminating disinformation or manipulated information, attacks aim to affect damage on the targeted entity.[43]

The ALERT framework categorizes such Effects into three categories. The first is IW influence Effects, where dialogue is shaped passively and through agents. The second category is IW interference Effects, where dialogue is shaped actively through bots or other entities. The third is IW hacking, where systems stand compromised or damaged with data/information stolen. IW hacking, in particular, may corrode the faith

[39] *See* CBS This Morning, *Doctored Pelosi Video Highlights the Threat of Deepfake Tech*, YouTube (May 25, 2019), https://www.youtube.com/watch?v=EfREntgxmDs.

[40] *Logic Behind Russian Military Cyber Operations*, *supra* note 25, at 12.

[41] *Id.*

[42] Dan Patterson, *The Dark Web Is Where Hackers Buy the Tools to Subvert Elections*, CBS News (Sept. 26, 2018).

[43] Such damage may vary from monetary gains to the attacker, loss of information or reputation by the target, service disruption, or undermining the confidence of citizens in their institutions.

of voters on the truthfulness of the election results. Meddling in elections can trigger suspicion in voters that the party or the person who won the election does not reflect the common democratic consensus, and that another party or person would have won if there had been no interference in the elections. Even without hacking systems, IW influence and IW interference can generate equally significant losses of voter confidence or social peace. Indeed, IW influence and IW interference could trigger riots, say, for example, via information manipulation operations in social media using fake accounts. See, for example, Indonesia's recent case, where fake news related to the 2019 presidential election caused political turmoil.[44]

D. Responses

The ALERT framework considers that the states or entities that are targets of IW have a series of options to react to the weaponization of information systems. Specifically, the taxonomy divides possible Responses of a target entity[45] into five groups: (1) IW defense, (2) IW offense, (3) diplomacy, (4) legal sanctions, and (5) economic sanctions. The IW victims may use these measures singularly or jointly. IW defense and IW offense are exercised through cyberspace, but the other three Responses encompass foreign policy, trade, economics, and legal frameworks, both within the domestic and international realms.

Defensive and offensive Responses allow countries to practice deterrence by denial. The objective of such Responses is to inflict a high cost on perpetrators to deter future attacks. Diplomacy aims to raise awareness among states of the problems that revolve around cyberspace. The use of diplomacy to deal with these problems is growing. One method that is gaining profound importance in recent years is the use of accusations that a state was allegedly involved in cyber operations having a severe impact on governments, resources, and individuals.[46] Legal sanctions tend to be more effective for offending domestic parties as they operate locally. Economic sanctions, in contrast, are more effective internationally as financial penalties applied by one or more countries to the perpetrating party. Given the wide range of Actors with varying capabilities, the Levers they can employ, and the extent of possible Effects, it is necessary to have a framework (or classification) to decide the right Response to different efforts to weaponized information systems.

1. IW Defense

IW Defense aims to make information systems immune to attack. The inputs to this type of Response generally come from experience given by previous attacks or from sharing knowledge through national and international collaboration. One relevant

[44] Kate Lamb, *Indonesia Riots: Six Dead after Protesters Clash with Troops over Election Result*, The Guardian (May 22, 2019).

[45] Both state and nonstate Actors may respond to the weaponization of information systems. See, for example, the Response of social media aimed at deleting accounts that spread messages to introduce discords in the case of Russian trolls factories in Ghana described *supra* in section III.

[46] Martha Finnemore & Duncan B. Hollis, *Beyond Naming and Shaming: Accusations and International Law in Cybersecurity*, EJIL (forthcoming 2020) (manuscript at 2).

example is the system of Defense being put in place for the 2020 U.S. elections. Based on previous attacks on the 2016 elections, technology giants are investing multiple resources in order to locate and remove fake accounts.

In response to the inappropriate use of deepfake videos, social media companies have begun taking steps to limit such manipulation. Facebook, for example, removes deepfake videos if artificial intelligence or machine learning modified the video, making it look authentic. Facebook even removes videos that have been edited in ways where an average person does not recognize the modifications, specifically if the videos would likely mislead someone into thinking that the person in the video did or said something that she did not say or do.[47]

Furthermore, Facebook recently removed a network of fake accounts, posting misleading content on Facebook. The tech giant declared that three of these networks originated in Iran, and one was based in Russia.[48] Microsoft is also offering Responses against cyberattacks. The company created a new service, called AccountGuard, as part of its Defending Democracy Program. The service aims to protect organizations that support democracy from cyberattacks. It provides notifications of cyber threats and, when it detects them, works directly with the organizations participating in the program to help them secure their systems.[49] Another example is the Hamilton 68 project, which hinders malicious Actors' actions by spreading awareness of what such Actors are doing online.[50] Taken together, such measures aim to substantially reduce IW attacks compared to those experienced during the 2016 presidential elections.[51]

Canada offers a different example of the IW defense focused on using more transparency as a defensive Response. In 2019, Prime Minister Justin Trudeau approved a set of rules on the transparency of online political advertisements and ordered intelligence services to make foreign threats public.[52] Moreover, with the Critical Election Incident Public Protocol, it became possible to inform Canadians of the presence of a threat to the integrity of their 2019 elections.[53]

2. IW Offense

IW offense consists of retaliation in response to IW attacks. In general, such Responses are in kind, using the same "information weapons" as used in the original attack.[54]

[47] Courtney Linder, *Facebook Is Banning Deepfake Videos Ahead of the 2020 Election*, Popular Mechanics (Jan. 8, 2020).

[48] Kevin Webb, *Facebook Just Removed Dozens of Fake Accounts Based in Russia and Iran That Were Spreading Misinformation and Trying to Meddle in Elections*, Business Insider Australia (Oct. 22, 2019).

[49] Tom Burt, *Protecting Democracy with Microsoft AccountGuard*, Microsoft Blog (Aug. 20, 2018).

[50] Laura Rosenberger & J.M. Berger, *Hamilton 68: A New Tool to Track Russian Disinformation on Twitter* (Alliance for Securing Democracy, Aug. 2019), *at* https://securingdemocracy.gmfus.org/hamilton-68-a-new-tool-to-track-russian-disinformation-on-twitter/.

[51] Julia Carrie Wong, *Facebook Discloses Operations by Russia and Iran to Meddle in 2020 Election*, The Guardian (Oct. 21, 2019).

[52] Alexander Panetta & Mark Scott, *Unlike U.S., Canada Plans Coordinated Attack on Foreign Election Interference*, Politico (Sept. 4, 2019).

[53] Government of Canada, *Critical Election Incident Public Protocol* (2019), *at* https://www.canada.ca/en/democratic-institutions/services/protecting-democracy/critical-election-incident-public-protocol/cabinet.html.

[54] Last June, for example, the United States launched a cyberattack that deactivated the Iranian computer systems that control the missiles and rockets' launch. The cyberattack was made in response to the shooting

During the mid-term American election in 2018, American military hackers outlined an offensive cyberattack as retaliation in the event of interference in the American elections.[55] Another example is digital incursions that the United States is carrying out on Russia's electricity grid. The United States intended these to serve as a warning to President Putin and to demonstrate how the American government is willing to retaliate with cyber tools more aggressively.[56]

3. Diplomacy

Diplomacy consists of action by different states to establish appropriate conduct to be adopted in cyberspace jointly. A vital element of a diplomatic Response is to signal that the cyberattack victim knows who the Actors authoring it are and that these activities will not be tolerated. Signaling was used, for example, during the Cold War by the United States and the Soviet Union to discourage certain behaviors. When one of the two states discovered that the other intended to violate a treaty, it was sufficient to notify the other state that the violation had been detected. The signaling was often sufficient to bring the violation to an end.[57] Signaling in cyberspace is even more essential because, in general, those who carry out a cyberattack believe that, given the well-known attribution problems online, they can do so without taking risks.

Another diplomatic Response is the expulsion of diplomats from the state that carried out the cyberattack from the territory of the victimized state. For example, Russia expelled 755 members of an American diplomatic mission in response to sanctions issued by the United States in response to Russian IW relating to the 2016 U.S. federal election.[58]

The European Union's "Cyber Diplomacy Toolbox" represents a third type of diplomatic technique. The Toolbox is a joint Response from EU member states that starts from the assumption that international law regulates cyberspace. It provides that in the event of an attack, the European Union will adopt common foreign security policy instruments. The goal of the Toolbox is to report the potential consequences of a cyberattack to potential Actors.[59] The Toolbox has been further developed with the addition of restrictive measures against cyberattacks threatening the Union or its member states.[60]

down of an American drone and attacks on oil tankers that the United States attributed to Iran. *See US "Launched Cyber-Attack on Iran Weapons Systems,"* BBC NEWS (June 23, 2019).

[55] Zachary Fryer-Biggs, *The Pentagon Has Prepared a Cyber Attack against Russia* (Center for Public Integrity, Nov. 2, 2018), *at* https://publicintegrity.org/national-security/future-of-warfare/the-pentagon-has-prepared-a-cyber-attack-against-russia/.

[56] David E. Sanger & Nicole Perlroth, *U.S. Escalates Online Attacks on Russia's Power Grid*, N.Y. TIMES (June 15, 2019).

[57] Mason Rice, Jonathan Butts, & Sujeet Shenoi, *A Signaling Framework to Deter Aggression in Cyberspace*, 4 INT'L J. CRITICAL INFRASTRUCTURE PROTECTION 57–65 (2011).

[58] Tim Stelloh, *Putin Orders U.S. to Cut 755 Diplomatic Employees in Russia*, NBCNEWS (July 30, 2017).

[59] Erica Moret & Patryk Pawlak, *The EU Cyber Diplomacy Toolbox: Towards a Cyber Sanctions Regime?* (EUISS, 2017), *at* https://www.iss.europa.eu/content/eu-cyber-diplomacy-toolbox-towards-cyber-sanctions-regime.

[60] Council Decision (CFSP) 2019/797 17 May 2019 concerning restrictive measures against cyber-attacks threatening the Union or its Member States, and Regulation (EU) 2019/1150 of the European Parliament and of the Council of 20 June 2019 on promoting fairness and transparency for business users of online intermediation services.

4. Legal Sanctions

Legal sanctions are penalties in response to law infringement. With regard to IW, criminal sanctions are of considerable importance. Information weaponization involves conduct that is often punishable based on the intent to commit (or at least negligence, in the fulfillment of) an unlawful act. The conduct is unlawful because of the presence of some domestic law provision that forbids it, describing the conduct as a crime. That said, domestic legal sanctions are limited to persons, whether natural persons or legal persons such as corporations. According to one of the main principles of the Western legal tradition, criminal liability is personal. Thus, legal sanctions may target individuals involved without penalizing the state or institution on whose behalf they did so. In February 2020, for example, the U.S. Department of Justice charged four members of China's People's Liberation Army for the 2017 data breach at Equifax, one of the largest consumer credit reporting agencies. The hack exposed the personal information of some 145 million Americans.[61] Although there is no certainty about the prosecution outcomes (those indicted remain in China and are unlikely to come within U.S. jurisdiction in the future), such charges are still significant in showing states and their representatives that victims may identify the perpetrators of a cyberattack. It is clear, however, that concerning political disruptions, legal Responses coming from criminal law are not a silver bullet solution.

The weaponization of information systems in this context implicates other legal issues beyond criminal law. International law and domestic legal regimes for data protection, constitutional law, and anti–money laundering regulations each deserve attention as well. There are also important questions (and complex debate) about the liability of Actors described in the ALERT framework besides those directing the IW (e.g., social media platforms, political campaigns).

As regards data protection regulations, in some cases, legal Responses may focus on the firm targeted in a cyberattack for failing to implement sufficient security procedures to protect users' data. Similarly, the behavior of a target entity may raise questions about possible liability in the case of IW. For example, after the Cambridge Analytica data scandal, Facebook was considered liable for breaching the U.K. Data Protection Act.[62] This type of sanction has the effect of increasing potential target entities' investments in safety and compliance with data protection laws. For instance, Facebook now makes available an "Off-Facebook Activity" tool, which lets its users manage and delete data that third-party applications and websites share with Facebook.[63]

In addition to domestic legal Responses, international legal Responses are also available in cases where technology is misused with respect to international legal rules or standards. Sometimes IW affects states' interests, especially in the matter of commerce, placing IW attacks into a broader trade war. In May 2019, the U.S. Commerce

[61] Alyza Sebenius & Chris Strohm, *U.S. Charges Four Chinese Military Members over Equifax Hack*, BLOOMBERG (Feb. 10, 2020).

[62] Alex Hern & David Pegg, *Facebook Fined for Data Breaches in Cambridge Analytica Scandal*, THE GUARDIAN (July 10, 2018).

[63] Sarah Perez, *All Users Can Now Access Facebook's Tool for Controlling Which Apps and Sites Can Share Data for Ad-Targeting*, TECHCRUNCH (Jan. 28, 2020).

Department's Bureau of Industry and Security banned U.S. companies from doing business with Huawei Technologies. The U.S. government blacklisted the company, arguing that there is a risk that Huawei could give the Chinese government access to sensitive data that goes through telecommunications networks that use its systems.[64] The U.S. government opted for blacklisting Huawei as a sort of precautionary measure aimed at avoiding possible future IW attacks. China, however, views the U.S. ban as a violation of international trade law and has folded such complaints into its larger set of international legal Responses in the ongoing trade war between the two states. Song Liuping, the chief legal officer at Huawei, contested the United States' right to ban Huawei, complaining it would set a precedent that could potentially harm many consumers, as well as cause American citizens to lose jobs.[65] James Lewis, Director of the Technology Policy Program at the Center for Strategic and International Studies in Washington, declared the U.S. ban failed in part because of the interest of European countries to maintain good relations in trade with China.[66]

International organizations may also play a key role in identifying or evolving additional international legal regimes and Responses to the information systems' weaponization. For instance, in 2019, the United Nations issued Resolution No. 74/247, which attempts to counter the use of technology for criminal purposes while reaffirming "the importance of respect for human rights and fundamental freedoms in the use of technologies." The UN General Assembly decided to establish an ad hoc committee to elaborate a convention on responses to the use of information and telecommunication technologies for criminal purposes.[67] This follows an earlier, significant example at the international level in the Budapest Convention on Cybercrime. Signed in 2001, it is the first international treaty on crimes committed via the internet and other computer networks. Today, it serves as a guideline for states to develop comprehensive national regulation against cybercrime.[68] In sum, Responses at the international level are crucial in addressing IW in an era where technology and borders have a complicated relationship.

Constitutional law becomes relevant when citizens' voting rights are compromised. In the event of Actors meddling in the elections of a democratic society, the citizens' right to vote would no longer be free and correctly informed. Accordingly, not only would the democratic system provided for by Western state constitutions be at risk but also the constitutionally guaranteed rights of the individuals that exist within that system. The case of the Russian troll factory in Ghana is an example of how not only democracy but also the individual rights of citizens can be exposed to such risks.[69]

In terms of domestic law, anti–money laundering regulation also assumes importance to verify the flows of resources to and from Actors when they have been

[64] Ian King, *Huawei Makes End-Run Around U.S. Ban by Using Its Own Chips*, BLOOMBERG (Mar. 2, 2020).
[65] *Huawei: US Blacklist Will Harm Billions of Consumers*, BBC NEWS (May 29, 2019).
[66] Todd Shields & Jordan Fabian, *Rejected on Huawei Ban, Trump Now Faces European Defiance*, BLOOMBERG (Jan. 29, 2020).
[67] G.A. Res. 74/247; U.N. Doc. A/74/247 (Dec. 27, 2019).
[68] Council of Europe Convention on Cybercrime (Nov. 23, 2001) CETS No. 185 (2001) 2296 UNTS 167.
[69] *See supra* section III.

financially supported to influence election results. An anti–money laundering regulation such as that of the European Union, for example, constitutes a legal Response in the sense that the various professionals involved (including lawyers and notaries) are responsible for the correct verification and reporting to EU authorities of suspicious transactions carried out by their clients.[70]

On the legal front, the ALERT framework[71] could be employed in the future as a reference point for developing uniform standards at the international level. These standards could fix minimum security requirements for companies to adopt in order to reduce the risk of weaponization of information systems. Further dialogue is needed before doing so, however, as this might lead to unintended consequences (i.e., imposing compliance costs on small companies, reducing their competitiveness in ways harmful to consumers) or leaving out important Actors (e.g., nonprofit organizations that process sensitive data).

Nonetheless, one legal Response that the ALERT framework would clearly favor is that in case of IW attacks, all Actors—be they nonstate, state-supported, or state-sponsored—would have a general duty to report suspicious activities or transactions to the relevant judicial authorities. There might need to be liability protections within such regulations (e.g., allowing specific institutions and professionals to report to legal authorities even with respect to their client operations). Such reporting requirements would need their own legal Responses in cases of violations (e.g., sanctions). Overall, the establishment of duty for companies that are victims of information system attacks to disclose the attack and report it to authorities could lead to the improvement of security systems, limit the risk of IW attacks, and reduce attempts by target companies to conceal such attacks. This measure could also induce consumers to prefer companies that implement these policies, thus affecting the tech business market more broadly.

5. Economic Sanctions

Economic sanctions are economic or financial penalties applied by states that are victims of the IW attack on its authors. The United States has leveled various kinds of economic sanctions in the past, specifically through: (1) the freezing of assets, (2) importing tariffs, (3) creating barriers to trade, (4) imposing travel restrictions on entities, and (5) embargoes.[72] These types of sanctions include the blocking of access to financial assets and the nonpossibility of transferring ownership of properties located in the United States.[73] Where effective, sanctions offer a Response that impacts the cost-benefit calculus of the Actors launching IW. If successful, sanctions (or the other IW Responses) may lead them to halt their IW or defer future IW campaigns.

[70] Directive (EU) 2018/843 of the European Parliament and of the Council of 30 May 2018 amending Directive (EU) 2015/849 on the prevention of the use of the financial system for the purposes of money laundering or terrorist financing, and amending Directives 2009/138/EC and 2013/36/EU.

[71] Desouza et al., *supra* note 7.

[72] An example of the application of economic sanctions in the IW context is Exec. Order No. 13,848, 3 C.F.R. § 46843 (2018).

[73] *Id.*

E. Findings of the ALERT Framework: The Dynamic Relationship between Actors and the Public Sector in the Context of Information Warfare

The ALERT framework employs its four elements to develop a dynamic theory of IW. Over time, as Actors gain maturity and experience in using Levers to disrupt political systems, the public sector will also gain experience responding to the Effects of such crises. This pushes malicious Actors to develop innovative, agile, and sophisticated methods to weaponize information systems. In turn, targeted entities—or those who defend them—develop highly sophisticated, innovative, and agile responses in return. For example, Texas has developed specific guidelines to protect elections from cyber threats and best practices related to several aspects, including the entire electoral process, staff and volunteers, computer workstations and servers, and technology infrastructure.[74] At times, the Responses of defenders will even create new opportunities for Actors to weaponize information systems. To protect political systems from disruption, defenders may introduce policies or engage in IW offensive activities that render the underlying information systems less secure and more vulnerable to weaponization. These dynamic interactions are, moreover, novel; unlike historical examples where the identity of Actors and their strategies was primarily known, the Actors of today are emergent, their networks are known to be complicated, and their attacks multifaceted. The result is a dynamic, iterative IW regime.

F. Discussion: Possible Uses of the ALERT Framework in the Electoral Context

From the analysis in this chapter, it is clear that there are a variety of ways in which information systems can be deployed to disrupt political processes and institutions. The ALERT framework is a working model to help policymakers and practitioners come to terms with the different combinations in which unrelated Actors and Levers can produce respective Effects and Responses that produce different consequences. The ALERT framework can be used to analyze previous incidents to determine successful matches between threats (Actors intending to disrupt political systems), instruments (a Lever or weaponized information system), Effects (the outcome of the incident), and Responses. That analysis can, in turn, be used to devise a risk-response strategy (what worked and what did not). It could also be used more concretely to contain the spread and reach of Effects, or in a way, even stop the escalation of Effects flowing from past IW.

One of the critical reasons for the weaponization of information systems by Actors today is the reduced level of computer network defense by public and private organizations. As regards the private sector, the presence of a reduced level of computer network defense has led to some arguments in the literature suggesting that the private sector, in particular, has not invested sufficiently to protect its infrastructure from

[74] *Election Security Best Practices Guide* (Texas Secretary of State Elections Div., 2020), *at* https://www.sos.state.tx.us/elections/forms/election-security-best-practices.pdf.

being weaponized or that governments should take a more active role in regulating the security of Information Technology platforms.[75] Governments, meanwhile, have long held that companies are rational Actors that can be expected to take the necessary actions to secure their interests. However, there are several reasons why this does not happen. The consequences of significant data breaches are long-term, whereas the focus of CEOs tends to be short-term. Most senior managers come from older generations and are not able to mitigate technology risks like they do business risk. Furthermore, the weaponization of information systems is a "negative externality" akin to environmental pollution—a category of risk that senior managers consider to be shared with others.

The reduced level of computer network defense is most noticeable when private companies provide services that have a direct or indirect impact on the public sector. The impact is direct when private companies work for the public sector through tenders; for example, the companies that program mobile apps for online voting. The impact is indirect when the lack of defense systems of private companies affects the public sector without the private company and the public body having any contractual relationship. For example, the reduced level of oversight of Facebook in the Cambridge Analytica scandal did not involve a previous contractual relationship between the social network and a public body, yet it indirectly impacted public activities. In the electoral context, these risks are exacerbated because political Actors stand up temporary information systems with a short-term focus on the coming election staffed by people with limited expertise to conduct IW defensive operations.

Returning to the pandemic, the world has yet to come to terms with its spread, its cure, let alone its prevention. Yet, the crisis has clearly revealed our collective dependence on information systems and, most importantly, their vulnerabilities to IW. Global social media platforms such as WhatsApp, Twitter, and Facebook, can be easily misused by political Actors with vested interests due to their inherent characteristics of participatory communication. In the aftermath of the coronavirus, we can expect that information systems will be used by outsiders to meddle with a nation's democratic processes, while in other instances a nation's leaders will use information systems to censor dissent.

With a lot more personal data readily available online, it is relatively easy to manipulate information systems related to individuals associated with institutions. Netizens are often co-creating information, knowingly or unknowingly—resulting in false news, fake news, and hate news that can go viral around the world within hours. The nature of misinformation, the pace at which it spreads, the Actors through which it goes have all undergone a change and will continue to do so. This ensures information systems will remain vulnerable to weaponization without incurring additional training or expenditure for those who would use IW. Today, we witness a rising exposure of vulnerabilities to mobile applications used for online voting. IW can also disrupt political processes as with a Zoom meeting of the Indiana Election Commission into which hackers introduced a pornographic video.[76] More prominently, the

[75] *See, e.g.*, Amitai Etzioni, *The Private Sector: A Reluctant Partner in Cybersecurity*, PRIVACY IN A CYBER AGE 93–100 (2015).

[76] Priscilla DeGregory, *Indiana Election Commission's Video Meeting Gets Hacked with Porno Video*, N.Y. POST (Apr. 17, 2020).

application used to tabulate the election votes in Iowa did not work correctly, showing inconsistencies and causing delays in reporting the results of the 2020 caucuses there.[77]

The ALERT framework thus opens up a potential for further research into the relationship between Levers and Effects in the IW context. We need to know more what is the causal mechanism between the two, how and why they are successfully able to create specific consequences, and what are the key technological, political, and social factors in the environment that enable an Actor to operationalize their strategy to conduct electoral interference via IW.

V. Conclusion

Information systems are vulnerable today more than ever. Rogue Actors—state and nonstate—can manipulate information systems to get political gains, disrupt democratic institutions, and perhaps most significantly, dent public trust in national institutions and political processes. In such a scenario, the first responsive step must be gaining an understanding of the threat landscape. Based on their threat perceptions, different nations can adopt different strategies to IW when it comes to electoral processes. This chapter has argued that an adequate response strategy may emerge from a distinct understanding of the Actors involved in IW; the Levers used to facilitate disruption, their Effects on information systems and the region's political situation, as well as the menu of Responses victims or their defenders may deploy. The ALERT framework thus creates a research agenda for understanding threats to information systems involved in protecting electoral processes that policymakers, governments, and practitioners in the field of information systems can, and should, pursue.

[77] Matthew Hutchinson, *For State and Local Elections, Secure Apps Are Critical*, GCN (Apr. 6, 2020).

4

Protecting Democracy by Commingling Polities: The Case for Accepting Foreign Influence and Interference in Democratic Processes

Duncan MacIntosh

I. Introduction

It is widely agreed that foreign governments are interfering in U.S. democratic elections by such problematic means as cyber hacking, deploying dark money,[1] and by campaigns of disinformation, nondisclosed identity opining, and trolling internet platforms.

It is generally thought that these efforts should be countered by various means. These include (1) educating the American populace so as to immunize it to subversive influence; (2) making social media and news platforms more responsible for the content they transmit; (3) encouraging fact-checking and cautionary addenda to sources of purported news stories and opinion; (4) censoring speech hateful and violence-inciting; (5) legally mandating transparency of political donations and transparency about authorship of news stories and opinion;[2] and (6) the legal application of coercive response to perpetrators of interference as licensed by domestic and international law.[3]

In this chapter, in section II, I review acknowledged problems with these methods and adduce a further problem. I conclude that the methods cannot work, have bad side effects, are inimical to the very idea of unfettered deliberation that is a foundation of democracy, and leave unaddressed the root issue of what motivates the subversions. In section III, I review and similarly object to a specific method that involves distinguishing influence from interference and hardening law to tackle the latter. In section IV, I identify the root issue as other nations being affected by our elections but not having a formal voice in them. I suggest that if we give them such a voice they will make arguments to us, the preferred method of issue-processing in a deliberative democracy, rather than trying to cheat the process. I then elaborate the

[1] *See generally* Ciara Torres-Spelliscy, *Dark Money as a Political Sovereignty Problem*, 28 King's L.J. 239 (2017).
[2] *See generally* chapter 11, this volume.
[3] Jules Zacher, *Using American Civil Litigation to Stop Russian Interference in the American Election* (abstract, dated November 2018, on file with author).

Duncan MacIntosh, *Protecting Democracy by Commingling Polities: The Case for Accepting Foreign Influence and Interference in Democratic Processes* In: *Defending Democracies.* Edited by Duncan B. Hollis and Jens David Ohlin, Oxford University Press (2021). DOI: 10.1093/oso/9780197556979.003.0005

case for giving them a voice and moot various methods of doing it. In section V, I deal with objections to allowing other countries this sort of power. Finally, in section VI, I recognize that some nations will still cheat; I allow that in the short term we will need coercive methods of dealing with that; but I suggest that our longer-term goal should be to deconflict our relations with these Actors to try to bring them into the fold of co-deliberative nations.

II. Problems with the Standard Methods of Defending against Foreign Influence and Interference

In this section, I review the well-known problems with the standard proposals about how to deal with foreign influence and interference in U.S. elections. I also object to them because all ignore that the facts and norms they try to force respect for are themselves the sorts of things rightly contested in elections. I conclude that the proposals are, in the aforementioned way, fascistic. I note that they have bad side effects, and they cannot work because they do not address the root problem, namely, the motivation other nations have for acting subversively.

It is widely agreed that all of the standard techniques of response to foreign interference are vulnerable to workarounds. They are therefore impermanent and expensive in perpetuity.[4] There are also further, more specific problems with each. For example, there are limits to what is possible in educating the public to be more savvy consumers of information, especially given their lack of a foundational education in critical thinking since so few are university educated. As for the proposal to make news platforms more responsible for their content, this will likely result in the platforms' algorithms filtering out legitimate information because it resembles problematic material to avoid risking running afoul of the law.[5] Meanwhile, censorship is likely to have a chilling effect on valuable free speech and is antithetical to the hoped for openness of the internet that was to continue the idea of open, democratic societies and be a force for the liberation of closed, undemocratic societies.[6] As for transparency of authorship, that may be hard to enforce and could harm those who need anonymity to maneuver against tyranny. Further, transparency about donor identity will not be enough to compensate for the larger influence available to those of extreme wealth, including the wealthy countries seeking to influence America. Besides, for all of the activities the foregoing techniques try to defend against, it is: (1) controversial in what sense some of the problematic behavior is illegal and therefore a suitable target for legal censure; (2) questionable whether its dangers rise to a level of threat permitting strong coercive responses; (3) likely that new law would have to be written to enable these sorts of response; and (4) difficult to attribute interference and so to know whom

[4] *See* Robert Chesney & Danielle Citron, *Deep Fakes: A Looming Challenge for Privacy, Democracy, and National Security*, LAWFARE (Feb. 21, 2018).

[5] Matt Burgess, *Theresa May's Fake News Unit Is Just Another Naïve Plan for the Web*, WIRED (Jan. 24, 2018).

[6] Staci Leiffring, *First Amendment and the Right to Lie: Regulating Knowingly False Campaign Speech After United States v. Alvarez*, 97 MINN. L. REV. 1047, 1047–1078 (2013).

to target.[7] It is also worrying that any coercive response would be hypocritical since the United States engages in similar interference against other countries at least three times more frequently even than Russia, and has done so more than eighty times in the last century all over the world.[8] Even in the United States, parties on both sides of various issues have used the foregoing interference and influence techniques against the other side.

Jens David Ohlin argues that just because the United States did these things to other countries does not make it okay to do them to the United States now.[9] The actions were wrong then, and they are wrong now. I reply that the fact that they were wrong then might, in some cases, make them right now, for example, if doing them to the United States now is part of redressing the wrong the United States did then. Ohlin also argues that in some of the past cases, the United States was interfering in other countries' elections benignly, helping people maneuver against forces compromising their rights of self-determination.[10] This may well be, but the fact that this is a possible motive and effect of interfering in a country's democratic processes means we must ask whether there might not be good faith, benign, or at least justified, motives or effects of some of the actions now being undertaken in interfering with U.S. democratic processes. Maybe the perpetrators are defending their own rights of self-determination, or even helping the United States in its self-determination by attacking corrupting forces within U.S. society.

At any rate, I would add a further worry about the foregoing techniques: all are premised on the assumption that the empirical facts needed for a democracy to deliberate about the issues that concern it are known; likewise the more-or-less correct normative positions on broad matters; and likewise, too, the best methods for sorting out the former issues where they are disputed. Accordingly, it is assumed, the problem of foreign interference is correctly framed as how to defend against forces that would misrepresent the facts, undermine the correct consensus about normative matters, and prevent sound deliberation where the former two things need debate. But in fact, many of these things are contestable and contested. And not just by and between nations, but also within nations—think of political tribal disagreements in the United States about what the facts are, what counts as a reasonable view, what values matter. These need to be deliberated about. Therefore, the use of the previously referenced techniques to filter and stonewall debate would be undemocratic. Moreover, for every proposal about how to implement the aforementioned ideas, there is likely to be a countervailing proposal. As I write, there are pressures on social media companies from left-wingers to filter out certain ideas, and charges from right-wingers that this is a problematic political bias. Every tribe has its obvious truths; and for each tribe there is another that thinks those things obviously false. Every generation has its eternal verities. Unfortunately, they change. And to reify them into categorical imperatives

[7] *See generally* Delbert Tran, *The Law of Attribution: Rules for Attributing the Source of a Cyber-Attack*, 20 Yale J.L. & Tech. 376 (2018).

[8] Peter Beinart, *The U.S. Needs to Face UP to Its Long History of Election Meddling*, The Atlantic (July 22, 2018); Ishaan Tharoor, *The Long History of the U.S. Interfering with Elections Elsewhere*, Washington Post (Oct. 13, 2016).

[9] *See* chapter 11, this volume, at 259.

[10] *See id.* at 259.

never to be violated in a given election cycle is fascistic. We need constant deliberation to work out what the facts are, what the correct values are, and to determine what processes and voices need to be listened to in resolving disagreements about these things. And, as we shall see later, very often the forces represented as trying to interfere in democratic processes are actually trying merely to negotiate its proper outcomes. So, for example, if, say, Russia is "interfering" in U.S. politics, arguably this is because it fears that America, left to its own devices, will be unjust to Russia. And such interests deserve to be considered. Likewise, when the United States "interferes" in other nations, it too has rights whose fulfillment may depend on the outcomes of the political deliberations of other nations.

In spite of these concerns, arguably we still need to do something about foreign influence and, more urgently, interference. This requires us to answer the question, what is the difference?

III. What Is the Difference between Influence and Interference?

In this section, I discuss attempts that have been made to distinguish between foreign influence on, and foreign interference with, elections—the hope was that identifying the later would give us a clean target for legal action with extant or new law. I suggest that (1) the distinction is difficult to draw, (2) even seeming interferences could be welcome in some circumstances, and (3) aiming to prevent interferences coercively will, again, leave the root problem unsolved and so be doomed to fail.

Ohlin and others have suggested that the difference between influence and interference is stealth.[11] If Russian President Vladimir Putin takes out an ad in the *New York Times* to argue that Americans should vote for Donald Trump, not Hillary Clinton, and if Putin signs his name, this is mere influence and is not problematic (let's say). But if he uses a fictional name, or sends his ad secretly to some Americans and not others, whether with his real name attached or not, then this is interference. The difference, supposedly, is that if you stealth your influence, you rob voters of information needed to evaluate the argumentative worth of your contribution, and so you manipulate rather than persuade them.

But this way of drawing the distinction is problematic. Transparency of authorship is neither always necessary nor always sufficient for a consumer of something authored being autonomous in evaluating it. Here is a case where it is not necessary, and where it would in fact impede autonomous evaluation. Suppose Putin has in fact got great arguments, ones which should make Americans see the mutual interest of themselves and Russia in some proposed enterprise, but he couldn't be taken seriously by Americans if they knew he was their author—they have too great a bias against him.[12] Then would not the autonomous opinion of U.S. voters be better served by his anonymity? Would not this best get them what they want and need?

[11] *See generally id.*

[12] S.I. Strong, *Alternative Facts and the Post-Truth Society: Meeting the Challenge*, 165 U. Pa. L. Rev. 137 (2017).

Indeed, I suspect something like this is in play in the current U.S. political scene. There is a long-standing enmity between Russia and the United States, one deeply embedded in their respective political classes and organizations. Both have intelligence agencies habitually maneuvering against each other, diplomats assuming the worst of each other, think tanks and branches of the military arrayed against each other, and so on. But in modern times, with the collapse of communist ideology in Russia and its replacement by crony capitalism, these animosities are out of place. Here, arguably President Trump is correct to seek better business relations with Russia, to seek the commingling of U.S. and Russian interests. But the specifics of this case apart, it would seem that whether an autonomous vote is best facilitated by an opinion's author being revealed or hidden is contingent on such things as the prior prejudices of voters, and therefore something that would vary from case to case.

Perhaps it will be replied that there is a difference between stealthed authorship being in the interest of an American and its not being an interference. Some interferences can have good effects. But if the effect is good, maybe sometimes that is more important than how the effect is achieved. And since the problem with prejudices is that they corrupt—interfere with—one's judgment, arguably anything that frees you from the influence of prejudice eo ipso frees you from interference.

I am saying, therefore, that transparency is not always necessary for autonomy. But neither is it sufficient: suppose Americans see hundreds of ads for a well-financed Republican candidate, transparently signed, but only a few dozen for a poorly financed Democratic candidate, also signed. The mere fact of transparency does not compensate for the frequency of the former messaging, which can induce people to accept a thesis merely by force of repetition rather than by cogency of argument.

I draw three lessons from this discussion. First, for any technique of affecting the outcome of an election, or of a nation's decision process more generally (acknowledging that not all nations are democracies), although that technique will in some circumstances be problematic, in others it could be salutary. Which of these it is depends on whether it conduces in the circumstances to proposals being assessed on their merits. Second, sometimes proposals about actions and policies, whether introduced by Americans or by other nations, will be better assessed on their merits by Americans if outsiders use some of the supposedly problematic techniques to hype them. Therefore, there is a case to be made that sometimes the U.S. democratic process *ought* to be "interfered with" by outside parties—in the hypothetical Putin case, the United States would be better for his stealthed efforts. Third, when we object to the use of some technique to affect the outcomes of our political process, we are not properly objecting to the technique itself. Rather, we are objecting that, as deployed in the instance in question, it is not conducing to a proposal being decided on its merits. In fact, in special circumstances, we might well feel justified in using such a technique ourselves against another country, thinking that, in *that* context, the technique will get a proposal (the one we favor, the one we think right) the uptake it deserves.

It is of course true that the default method of affecting each other's choices in political processes should be one that seeks and respects the truth about matters of fact, and that identifies and responds to the interests of all affected parties. If you fail the first measure, you are at risk of undertaking actions and policies that will be undermined by the reality with which they are meant to contend. And if you fail the second measure, you will commit to courses of action that some persons will undermine once they learn they have been disrespected and acquire the opportunity to do something about it. This is why we value deliberative democracy: it concerts us all upon the truth, and it allows all of our interests to be factored into choices.

My operating assumption is that these values are universally shared, while deliberation that seeks to find and move from facts to courses of action that respect all stakeholders is universally preferred. People only deviate from these defaults when they feel their interests are disrespected, their conception of the truth not recognized. This is what drives nations to be subversive of other nations' processes, to manipulate rather than argue.

In the remainder of this chapter, I make the case for accepting outside influence and interference, and for channeling it into the default ideals just enunciated. In the first instance, I shall make arguments about America, since it is the case of the United States that occasioned this piece. But most of what I will say would apply to any country whose political decisions are consequential for other countries.[13]

IV. The U.S. Democratic Process Ought to Be Interfered with by Outside Parties

The main reason other countries try to subvert our elections is that they have a stake in the outcomes but are not allowed a formal voice in determining those outcomes. In this section, I suggest then that the best way to prevent them from trying to subvert our elections is to give them such a voice. The hope is that this will make them co-deliberators with us about the issues that concern our several nations, encouraging them to process their issues with us by argumentation rather than trying to have their preconceived way by using argument-subverting techniques. But giving other nations a voice would also have several other positive effects (ones that will become clear as we work through objections to this proposal in section V): (1) it would bring in fresh perspectives on issues; (2) it would help average out the influence of problematic voices in America; (3) it would make U.S. policy more responsible in how it treats all affected parties; and in so doing, (4) it would result in polices that would be able to be consented to by all who are affected, rather than having to be imposed by threat or act of force. I further suggest that not just the United States but all nations whose electoral outcomes will significantly affect other nations should open their democracies to the voices of other countries for exactly the same reasons. Commingling polities

[13] I should acknowledge that some of the arguments for having foreigners mix in domestic political processes are not new, but rather only their application to the problem of nefarious influence. For previous arguments for mixing, *see* R.E. Goodin, *Enfranchising All Affected Interests, and Its Alternatives*, 35 PHIL. & PUB. AFF. 40–68 (2007); C. López-Guerra, *Should Expatriates Vote?*, 13 J. POL. PHIL. 216–234 (2005). *See also* C. LÓPEZ-GUERRA, DEMOCRACY AND DISENFRANCHISEMENT (2014); D. Owen, *Constituting the Polity, Constituting the Demos: On the Place of the All Affected Interests Principle in Democratic Theory and in Resolving the Democratic Boundary Problem*, 5 ETHICS & GLOBAL POL. 129–152 (2012); S. Song, *Democracy and Noncitizen Voting Rights?*, 13 CITIZENSHIP STUD. 602, 607 (2009); Zephyr Teachout, *Extraterritorial Electioneering and the Globalization of American Elections*, 27 BERKELEY J. INT'L L. 162, 166–173 (2009).

in this way is the way to go. Finally, I shall moot a selection of models for how this could work.

So, to begin with, it is obvious that more than just U.S. interests are at stake in U.S. elections.[14] U.S. democratically determined policy has vast consequences for the rest of the world, so arguably the rest of the world should have a say. Municipal matters at the level of pothole repair on roads in Cleveland, Ohio, are generally not of international interest. But presidential elections and the resulting positions of the United States on issues of foreign policy, including economic and military policy, are vastly consequential for the rest of the world. And any and all persons who would have to bear the consequences of decisions on a given issue should get a say on it. Policies consequential for the problem of climate change would be a paradigm.

This principle that if you have a stake you should get a say, is practically the defining rationale of democracy. And it would be odd, therefore, if one were to defend the ideals of democracy but not the idea of including as many as possible of the people who will be affected by a democratic process in the unfolding of that process.

But what form could this take?

A. Methods of Giving Other Nations a Voice in the U.S. Polity

There are several possible ways in which other countries could be given a more formal voice in the U.S. polity. First, U.S. media could be obliged to include a certain amount of foreign journalistic content—the obverse of something that happens in Canada, where there is a legal maximum on how much entertainment programming can have a U.S. source.

Second, the United States could help strengthen extant international bodies and could strengthen its commitment to following the outcomes of their deliberation.[15] It already submits its main foreign policy initiatives to examination and contestation in international forums, for example, the World Trade Organization, the United Nations, NATO, and "coalitions of the willing" in conflicts; and it already subjects the implementation of its policies to negotiation with other countries, for example, in working out what was formerly called the North American Free Trade Agreement. Now, these things are not normally seen as ways of letting other countries influence U.S. politics. But since U.S. political impulses are generated with a view to the fact that they will have to be subjected to negotiation in these bodies, that is exactly what it is; and it is important to recognize this so that we will not find the idea of allowing other countries a voice in our polity such a great departure from norms we already accept. Meanwhile, if the United States committed itself to more of this—to signing and obeying treaties other nations sign, for example[16]—other parties would not feel that they had to manipulate U.S. elections.[17]

[14] Teachout, *supra* note 13.

[15] Thanks to Jens David Ohlin for prompting this discussion.

[16] The United States is often a nonsignatory to key transnational governance regimes, for example, on treaties regarding climate change, weapons use, the use of outer space.

[17] I would bet, for example, that nations with whom the United States has less conflict in the United Nations are also less involved in subverting U.S. elections.

Third, the United States could keep the penalties for foreign interference low, so as not to overdeter those who are so desperate as to need recourse to election influencing and so who probably deserve to be heard by the U.S. polity. Or they could eliminate some of these penalties altogether, for example, by making it more legal for foreign nations to donate to the U.S. election campaigns of their choice.[18]

Fourth, U.S. politicians who accept that there is no reason why U.S. interests cannot be deliberatively reconciled with the interests of all peoples of the world could make the acceptability of proposed U.S. policy to other polities a larger issue in their campaigning and debates.

Fifth, the conveners of U.S. political debates at the presidential level could invite foreign leaders or their representatives to be participants as questioners or debaters. The United States could make much of this conditional on other countries doing likewise.

It might well happen that, were there all these official ways for other countries to affect the U.S. polity, they would have no need of the scurrilous ways. And the honest discussions so much needed could proceed.

A more radical way of having other nations influence the U.S. political process would be to let the members of other nations vote in some of America's elections. Of course, any such proposal invites many questions: How would this even be possible? How could you have a hundred nations vote in America's elections? How would people be informed enough to cast votes? And if we were to generalize this proposal, how could all nations vote in all nations' major elections?

Well, in America's case we might imagine that, just as there is a U.S. electoral college of representatives of each state in the American Union, perhaps there could be an international college. Each embassy from another country to the United States would be a member. Of course the diplomats who staff these embassies are already specialists in relations between the United States and their own country; and they already advise the United States and get guidance from their governments on which policies they would like the United States to implement; so they would be ready to cast informed votes. And they already take arguments back to their home countries as they get feedback from U.S. officials on their requests. So they would already be skilled in the presentation and representation of arguments between nations and in mediation. And each of these embassies might get a weighted vote in the international college, depending on the size of the population it represents.

The vote of the college would, in turn, have some weight among the votes of America's already established electoral college, as if the countries of the world were like states of the Union. Perhaps all the countries would be represented in one combined college vote. Perhaps there would be as many college votes as there are countries. Either way, some decision would have to be made about how much the one or the many colleges would count in determining U.S. electoral outcomes. I would suggest that, for the institution to have any meaning, it should be in principle possible for the vote(s) to be weighty enough as to marginally tip balances, in principle perhaps to break ties, and so on. But it may be that the actual weight need only be some small token. The most important thing is that the colleges would constitute pulpits from

[18] Thanks again to Jens David Ohlin for prompting this discussion.

which foreign voices could speak; and they would constitute constituencies which those running for office in the United States would want to woo. This would guarantee that foreign voices could speak and be heard.

Another, perhaps simpler, way to go would be to have these voices expressed as token members of the House, or the Senate; or to have them constitute some third body, the Assembly of Ambassadors, with some token power to affect the threshold of House and Senate votes needed to move proposals into policy. And, of course, there would have to be something similar and reciprocal so that the United States could speak to and be heard by other countries. Having politically consequential units in each other's countries would guarantee the internationalization of deliberation. Of course, there are many different governmental systems in the world, not all have anything like an electoral college, or even democracy, and so the implementation of this proposal would need to vary depending on the systems of each country. But the form matters less than that it, one way or another, incentivize listening and persuading in deliberation.

To this there are, of course, many objections. Some of these would apply to the other proposed methods of giving other nations a voice. And we will consider them in section V later. But one objection is worth mooting now, since that will elucidate a virtue with these proposals generally. The objection is that if non-American people are allowed to vote, the effect of any given American's vote will be so small as to not be worth casting, which would undermine the political process entirely.[19] (And no matter how little we weight foreign votes in any mechanism, this will to that extent dilute the influence of American votes.)

One reply is that, since the effect of any given person's vote is already so small, no one can reasonably fear its further dilution. (This is the obverse of the notorious problem of how it can be rational to vote given how small a marginal difference to outcomes one's vote makes.) It has therefore been argued that the true purpose of voting is to express your opinion, or to feel like at least you had a say, or to symbolize the sort of person you are (a tough guy, perhaps, or an empathetic person, or whatever, something you can express by the choice of policies or persons you vote for), or to be a part (however small) of a causal contribution to an outcome, rather than to have decisive influence on outcomes (a luxury had only by dictators). So long as these things have happened—you got to express, or to symbolize, or to causally contribute—it doesn't matter to what *degree* your vote shaped the outcome. It may not even matter on a given occasion, or on many such occasions, whether your side won—part of the process is you tacitly pledging to go along with the outcome provided you had a say in what it should be. If this is right, it would seem more acceptable to permit foreign votes. Especially if letting everyone vote would increase their commitment to whatever policies resulted, and so, perhaps, to everyone in the world getting behind U.S. policy.

Of course, there is the worry that letting everyone vote would change what that policy would be. But would that necessarily be bad? After all, if this does not happen,

[19] This section moots the relevance of large issues in the theory of democracy. For a start on these and their literatures, *see* Jason Brennan, *The Ethics and Rationality of Voting*, STANFORD ONLINE ENCYCLOPEDIA OF PHILOSOPHY, *at* https://plato.stanford.edu/entries/voting/#6; R.A. DAHL, AFTER THE REVOLUTION? AUTHORITY IN A GOOD SOCIETY 64 (1990).

then U.S. policy, whatever it is, will only prevail by threat or act of force, which is a strong argument that it must have been bad or unfair policy; while if the resulting policy is one widely voted for, this means people can live with it. Part of this is due to the fact that democracy is not just about voting. It is also about the deliberative processes leading up to the vote—people putting issues on the table, becoming sophisticated about them by giving each other information and arguments,[20] possible resolutions being tried out and being affirmed or rejected preliminarily in this trial balloon process. The resulting possibilities then get narrowed down so that none are so outrageous that they would be met with outright revolt should they prevail.

Many will find the foregoing suggestion about nations intervoting too radical, favoring instead at most that nations should confederate, declare some issues the responsibility of the global federal level, and then either have their populations decide such issues by global referendum, or elect officials to a global-level federal body to vote on such matters, perhaps on the model of the European Parliament.[21] In this way, it may seem that, instead of commingling their polities, nations retain their deliberative autonomy. We do not need to vote in each other's elections, because our elected representatives can do the required negotiating for us by securing binding agreements, such as those found in free trade agreements.[22] (Indeed, it might be thought that such agreements would be needed to make all of this work; for there is unlikely to be political commingling without economic integration.[23])

I reply that, functionally, there may not be much difference between intervoting and confederating (or between intervoting and, say, negotiating trade agreements). For whether directly or indirectly, each nation's citizens would be voting on policies that would affect other nations. And every nation would learn of every other nation's positions in the course of the deliberations leading to votes. Of course, if confederating and commingling by the method of intervoting are functionally equivalent, since we already have experience with forming confederations (between states, between provinces, between territories, even between countries, as in the European Union), we'd know how to commingle the polities of different nations that currently deliberate independently.

But I do not want to overfocus on the idea of voting in each other's elections, whether expressly or by functionally equivalent processes. These were just two of seven ways that I have identified of giving other nations a voice. For now, it will be enough to defend the very idea of doing that, never mind the exact method.

V. Objections

Now that we have seen what forms giving other countries a voice in our deliberations could take, I want to deal with the many standard arguments against allowing any of these things. These principally include: (1) nations do not have a right to

[20] *See* the work of Philip Pettit on the idea of deliberative democracy for more on this.

[21] Thanks to Andrew Fenton and David White for suggestions along these lines.

[22] Again, thanks to David White for this.

[23] Thanks to Robert Paul for this suggestion.

affect each other's elections because that would deprive nations of the rights of autonomy, including expression of national identity, self-determination, and the self-administration of their own property; (2) it would allow too great a voice to autocratic regimes and to America's enemies generally; (3) it would be hopeless to try to commensurate radically different societies and traditions; (4) it would overwhelm weak nations; (5) it would require more trustworthiness than is likely to be forthcoming, weakening polities who admit foreign influence without being allowed it in return; and (6) the proposals would export the problems in each other's polities into other polities.

A. Autonomy-based Objections

I begin with the autonomy based family of objections. It might be argued that the rights of sovereignty mean that only the citizens of a country should be the determiners of its fate—only Americans should participate in any way in U.S. elections.[24] But this is a highly problematic argument, since it rests on a conception of sovereignty according to which each country should be left to make its own decisions regardless of whether these are compatible with the interests of the rest of the world. Why would anyone concede to any nation the right to behave without regard for others? And how could any nation reasonably demand that right? For political scientists, legal scholars, and historians, these questions will seem odd: Are not these rights the very foundation of the Westphalian conception of nations? And yet the questions scream for answers morally. Moreover, as a matter of realpolitik, each nation that tries to subvert another's supposedly rightful deliberative process is in effect saying that the nation against which it is maneuvering has no such right, or at least not to just any conclusion to its process. Finally, all nations recognize that there are limits on the extent of harms one nation can inflict on another, limits whose violation would be a justification for war. I am, in effect, suggesting that the gray zone between one country's action not inflicting a harm on another and one country's action constituting a harm so great as to be an act of war, is the zone of issues regarding which there is currently election subverting. Such issues might be better addressed by bringing the involved nations into political co-deliberation.

A related argument against commingling—that Americans own their own country and its processes, and therefore have, by right of ownership, the right to be the exclusive operators of their polity—falls to a similar reply. Namely, why should any nation be permitted to operate on a conception of the rights conferred by being the owner of something that would allow them to make choices about what to do with that property without regard for the possible deleterious effects on other nations?

Similar rebuttals can counter arguments to the effect that being the sole determiner of the outcomes of elections is essential for the expression of individual or national identity, or to satisfy some supposed right of self-determination or autonomy.[25]

[24] *See generally* Jens David Ohlin, *Did Russian Cyber Interference in the 2016 Election Violate International Law?*, 95 TEX. L. REV. 1579 (2017).

[25] *Id.*

Why should other people or nations allow a given person or nation a right of self-expression—or autonomy or self-determination—that could be exercised at the expense of the welfare of others (or at the expense of their similar rights of identity expression or autonomy or self-determination)?[26] Indeed, it is doubtful that there is any such right as the right to self-determination. To be sure, there are real rights that are conceptually nearby, for example, the right to have one's own welfare counted in how the world is arranged, the right to live one's life as one sees fit, provided this does not collide with the similar rights of others, and so on. But these rights do not necessarily require or entitle given persons or nations to noninfluence from other persons and nations. In fact, it is in dialogue with other persons that one would work out the extent of these rights.

A more subtle objection is that arguably Americans have invested their labor and taxed contributions into systems of property and benefits that they therefore have rights to protect, specifically, to protect from other people in other nations voting or otherwise influencing themselves into an unearned share.[27] One might give specific context to the issue by asking whether non-Americans living in other countries, people who have therefore not paid U.S. taxes, should have a right to vote on how U.S.-taxed contributions should be spent. For example, should foreigners have the right to vote for laws permitting easy immigration into America? Should they have the right to vote to have money that has been taxed from Americans be used to fund, say, healthcare in their own countries? These are questions that could arise not only if one proposes that peoples of other nations have a vote in U.S. elections but also if, for example, the United States were to confederate with other nations. It would then face issues about when immigration with full citizen rights would be permitted between confederated nations; or issues about whether, when emigrating, they should have transferable funded healthcare.[28]

The question of American ownership of their own property is difficult to navigate. On the one hand, arguably Americans built up their wealth and treasure in a time before the world became massively interconnected, and in a time therefore where Americans maneuvered without moral need of regard for others, since the actions of Americans did not affect others. Americans have therefore mixed their labor exclusively with goods from nature and so should have exclusive share rights in them. On the other hand, even the great founders of the ideas of private property, for example, John Locke, recognized that, in appropriating goods for one's self from their unowned state in the state of nature, one has a duty to leave over enough goods from the natural world, and of as good quality, for all other persons to have a share.[29] And it is contestable whether the United States has done that. There is also the issue of whether the goods Americans have come to own were originally unowned parcels of

[26] *Contra* Teachout, *supra* note 13, at 185–187.

[27] Megan Reiss suggested this point to me.

[28] In fact, conceptually identical questions arise when nations negotiate trade agreements, since they are in effect negotiating what counts as fair competition, unfair government subsidies, and so on—things which affect the benefits workers will receive.

[29] For a classic discussion of Locke's theory of property and of the foregoing pretexts for doubts that one is the legitimate holder of a given piece of property, *see generally* ROBERT NOZICK, ANARCHY, STATE, AND UTOPIA (1974).

goods in nature, or whether Americans unjustly appropriated these parcels from prior owners—the Indigenous peoples of North America, for example; or from client states acquired by coercive political action. (Think of American adventurism in securing access to oil.) It is apparent that the issue of American entitlement to its wealth is complicated.[30] But even setting that aside, American wealth is now vastly connected to the lives of those in other countries. So even if Americans are entitled to their wealth, surely others have a moral right to some say in whether that wealth will be deployed in ways harmful to them.

The preceding issues connect with large issues in political philosophy about what different nations owe to each other—whether this be nothing or, at a minimum, at least noninterference, or cooperation on mutually advantageous terms, or positive help in prosecuting each other's ends. Likewise, there are connections to issues regarding what individual citizens of a given nation owe to individual citizens of other nations, and whether they owe these things directly or only by virtue of the relations of citizens to other social and political institutions. Finally, there are connections with issues in the possible foundations of any such duties, for example, Kantian universalization (act only as you could will others to act toward you), veil-of-ignorance reasoning (act only in ways you would approve if you did not know whether you would be benefited or exploited by the act), and rational bargaining for arrangements of mutual advantage.[31] I am not weighing in on specifics about any of these matters here. I *am* supposing that there are some duties of nations toward each other, and that, even if there are not, it would be understandable if nations demanded to have their interests respected by other nations. But what the present chapter is more focused on is the question of what method should be used to resolve these issues, whether subversion of other polities, diplomacy, war, or, as I am defending, direct participation in each other's political processes. I am similarly supportive of nations deliberating in and accepting the authority of international organizations and larger political units expressly tasked with working out acceptable relations between nations.

It might be objected that my proposal is absurd on grounds of leaving no purview for the individual nation or person to decide how to act. For example, if, as I say, someone should get a vote on any proposed course of action by anyone if the action could affect them, then, since consumers are affected by the decisions of labor unions, should not consumers get a vote in union affairs? But then what is the point of having a union? Likewise, a given individual may have an interest in the activities of another individual: Should the first get to dictate behavior to the second? Surely not.[32]

I reply that this exemplifies another timeless debate in political philosophy, namely, how extensive should the rights of the individual be? On almost all accounts, people should get a say in some aspects of each other's lives. Governments reserve the right to interfere with union matters when union members perform essential services that

[30] And, of course, this is a huge issue not just for the United States but also for colonial powers, much of whose wealth derives from conquest.

[31] For a nice survey of these issues and of extant positions on them, *see* Thomas Nagel, *The Problem of Global Justice*, 33 PHIL. & PUB. AFF. 113–147 (2005).

[32] Thanks to David White for this line of objection.

cannot safely be interrupted. And we all think we have a right to regulate each other's behavior in various ways (e.g., we get to dictate that no one may murder, steal, or rape).

B. Enemy-based Objections

I would move now to the objection that other nations have interests that make them the enemies of America, so that permitting influence from them would undermine America. The problem with this objection is that the idea that two countries could be such that their interests are permanently opposed is almost certainly mistaken. Perhaps there was a time when several countries intractably held ideologies requiring each to conquer the other and to impose its favored ideology. And it was understandable that each would resort to force and subversion to stop this. Holders of private property and believers in the inherent justice of such a system of property rightly feared communism, nationalizing of businesses, seizing and forcible redistribution of private property, collapse of the negative liberties that are entrained by this system of property distribution, and liquidation of the most prominent and resistant of the extant property holders. And defenders of communism rightly feared the denationalization of businesses and the collapse of guarantees of education, healthcare, employment, minimum incomes, pensions, and the weakening of the state organizations whose ostensible missions were to protect them from outside aggression and to sustain the ways of life and traditions which defined them.

But such ideological conflicts are now vastly fewer, and less consequential. As Michael Mazaar has argued, most of America's so-called enemies do not seek huge disruption in the global order nor, therefore, huge change in America. They seek only incremental changes giving them somewhat greater shares of wealth and power.[33] Most of the nations the United States sometimes regards as its enemies now endorse democratic government in some form or another, at least officially. And all endorse, in one degree or another, some form of private property and free market capitalism. To the degree that this is not true, it is because the current holders of wealth and power in various nations seek to preserve their power and increase their wealth, some by mafia-like means. But this is not an ideological conflict; and since the motives are merely wealth and power, the conflicts between these nations can be resolved by negotiated relations featuring protection of variants on the status quo, and wealth-sharing of the cooperative surpluses from future business deals. That is, there is nothing in principle non-negotiable here.

There are, to be sure, other spectra of variance between nations: for example, between more and less authoritarian; more and less fundamentally religious, Christian or Judean versus Muslim, Sunni versus Shiite; more and less individualistic; more and less favoring centralized services. But coercive evangelism about these things is now vastly less common, and the postures of nations about these things are more defensive than offensive. And even the most extreme differences, for example, between Western nations and those hostile to the West—to its Christianity and secularity, variously—are

[33] For a general defense of this position, *see* Michael Mazaar, Mastering the Gray Zone: Understanding a Changing Era of Conflict 126–137 (2015).

tractable. For almost all of the differences tend to evaporate the more educated the countries in question become. For example, many of the most intense seeming ideological and religious conflicts trace more to people seizing upon something to argue from in arguing for improved social standing or greater self-determination, for example, in the form of emancipation from colonialism, or from more recently occupying powers, or from religious or class oppression. So here again, negotiation toward a greater sharing of wealth and status will solve the problems.

Obviously, a full defense of this method of dealing with problematic interference would require a detailed analysis of the main agents of interference and their relations with America, including Russia, North Korea, perhaps China, and perhaps ISIS and its ilk. So let me just admit that if I am wrong about the commensurability of the interests of the major powers, and if these powers really are in a relation of irresolvable conflict between their interests, then we would have to go another way. And, of course, even if my analysis is correct, the method of dealing with problematic influences and interferences I have proposed would require a great deal of summitry and treaty-making. It would not be a quick fix, a fact which may recommend the more standard methods as a stopgap.

C. Objections Regarding the Impossibility of Commingling Democracies and Autocracies

Perhaps it will be objected that it is naive to expect all nations to participate in any of these process in good faith. Autocracies, for example, would have a stake in undermining democratic societies so that the autocracies could maneuver without constraint. Democracies and autocracies cannot happily coexist, and so the policies a democratic nation will favor must needs differ from those an autocratic state would favor. Therefore there could not be reconciliation of their differences by co-deliberative processes.[34]

I reply that democracies need not fall in order for alternatives to democracies to rise. Indeed, the thriving of democracies, and the thriving of their legitimate alternatives, have similar preconditions, such as stability, trading relationships, and coordination on global problems like climate change that require the participation of all nations to solve. And arguably the nurturing of these conditions would be furthered by democracies and their alternatives commingling their polities. Of course it would be interesting what form this commingling could take while yet respecting the ways in which the polities are different. Consider such plausible alternatives to democracy as societies in which, while there are no elections, affairs are run by civil servants responsive to perceived citizen need and desire as determined by surveillance-state monitoring of citizens' dialogues on social networking sites.[35] They might take democratic voting outcomes in other countries as new data for policy formation in their own countries. Meanwhile, democracies might take the surveillance-state data as

[34] Thanks to Todd Calder and Jack Whitmer for these concerns.

[35] On this, *see* Christina Larson, *Who Needs Democracy When You Have Data?*, TECH. REV. (Aug. 20, 2018).

relevant new data for policy formation in *their* respective countries. There seems to be enormous functional similarity here in the roles and goals of governments; and so there seems to be enormous room for rapprochement. For example, one can imagine Canadian and Chinese civil servants profitably interacting at conferences about how to transmute electoral votes and surveillance-determined citizen attitude data, respectively, into policy. And one can imagine a confederation of states, one of which is a conventional democracy, the other, a state run by civil servants selected and trained to be responsive to citizen will as detected by monitoring of social media, representatives of each country negotiating which federation-level policies to enact. One way or another, there could be a debates between whatever are the sovereigns of each nation. In a democracy, the sovereign is the people, in the form of the highest elected official(s). In China, it is, say, the ruling civil servants; in Russia, it is, say, the most powerful oligarchs.

In the West, we think you need democracy and a multiparty system to solve the problem of governing class corruption caused by cynical self-interest or unconscious bias in favor of the self. But there are apparently thriving nations which instead solve the problem by creating, and creating faith in, a civil servant class of technocrats. Indeed, such societies can have as an advantage over democracies that, since their ruling class is more enduring, rather than term-limited, it can take a longer view, and so can solve problems that require enduring policy commitments. Climate change is a perfect example. And it would be all to the good to have the deliberations of term-limited democracies brought into contact with the deliberations of nations with more enduring ruling bodies.

D. Objections Regarding the Inappropriateness of Commingling Democracies with Illegitimate Governments

I have been speaking about legitimate alternatives to democracies. But what of illegitimate alternatives? What of states run by malign oligarchs and autocrats, states which are little more than vertically integrated criminal organizations for the extraction of wealth from their citizens?[36] Surely the rulers of such states have no interest in having their nations converted into genuine democracies, since they would then lose power and wealth. So they will not want their citizens commingling in other nations' elections. Instead, these rulers have every interest in ruining the democracies of nations, because then they could manipulate those nations in ways that will enhance their own wealth and power.[37] So it would be wrong to allow these malign nations unfettered influence in the U.S. polity. At best, the only nations that should be allowed in are ones already established as democracies, and who therefore would be inclined to nondestructively co-affiliate with America, on the model, for example, of the European Parliament.

[36] *See generally* Sarah Chayes, Thieves of State: Why Corruption Threatens Global Security (2015).

[37] Nagel, *supra* note 31, at 136 (making a related point about the more well-off nations being reluctant to accept duties to help the less well off).

My reply is that autocrats can have the power they seek only by getting large numbers of people to do things whose products can be harvested in the form of money; and the best way to attain this effect on populations is by deliberative democracy—that is, by talking them into it. Further, oligarchs profit more from peace than war and will have a stake in attaining peace with each other. Finally, even oligarchs are better off in a world of safety and stability as secured by deliberative democracy and therefore will tend toward this system. For it is the system most likely to protect their gains, whether ill-gotten by prior predation or not, due to the inherent conservatism of the rule of law that democracies tend to exemplify.

Destroy democracies? No. Ultimately, oligarchs will want to participate in world government and will want to use their powers to have a large voice in democratic decision-making. We see this already in the titans of capitalism encouraging the formation of liberal democracies the world over. How are we to have influence on oligarchies and autocracies? In return for giving them a voice in our elections, they give us a voice with them—if they get to speak to our people in our elections, we, in the form of our leaders, pundits, and other operators of the deliberative process, get to talk to their ruling group, whether this be a politburo, a military junta, a hereditary king and his courtiers, or some mafia-like power-holding group.

E. Objections Regarding the Difficulty of Commingling Polities of Radically Different Cultures and Value Systems

Other sorts of differences between nations could make their commingling problematic. Imagine two nations with different prevailing fundamentalist religions and therefore with conflicting attitudes on central questions of morality and value. How can they profitably commingle? And if one of these nations was powerful, like America, say, what conceivable reason could a weaker state with different values and a different religion have to commingle? More generally, would not the proposal tend to result in unwelcome cultural homogenization? In fact, it might be worried that any culture that permits itself to commingle with the United States will in effect *become* America, with the result that there will simply be one large monoculture, in this case, American, with all the problems that afflict that culture (problems with which my proposal would infect the whole world).[38]

To this, there are several replies. First, even nations widely different culturally, religiously, and morally have issues it would benefit them to deal with in a shared polity (e.g., issues around trade, climate, infrastructure, health, war). So long as commingling was confined to these issues, the results could be salutary. And the resolution of these issues wouldn't necessarily require that, in other respects, the countries become alike. Second, commingling on deliberation about deep issues of morality and value could result in much-needed learning for all of the affected countries. I premise this on two possibilities. First, I assume that there may be a single truth on some of these matters (that is, some things that are, in fact morally permissible and others not)

[38] Thanks to Shirley Tillotson and Steven Burns for these worries.

and dialoguing between countries might help both to find it. But failing that, second, dialoguing might help the two countries become more tolerant of their differences; it might motivate them to form policies mutually respecting these differences and which quarantine the issues off from other issues needing resolution (issues a clear vision of which might otherwise be obstructed by the moral differences in play). On either premise, both countries would have to mindfully and more fully subject themselves to the norms of deliberative democracy and to the listening to others that this constitutively entrains. This could thus improve both cultures.

F. The Problem of Commingling Overwhelming Smaller, Weaker Nations

We have been discussing variants of the concern that the United States may have interests inherently incompatible with those of other nations and so should not open itself up to influence by them. A related family of concerns runs in the other direction: it may be bad for the United States and other large nations to have an influence in the polities of smaller, vulnerable nations, for then weaker nations and poor peoples would be overwhelmed.[39] Commingling the world's polities will merely allow powerful countries to enlarge the power they already have over weaker countries.[40] Think of Ukraine, and consider the most extreme form of polity commingling I proposed: Should Russia be allowed a vote in the affairs of a nation it seeks to annex? On the face of it, the answer is a resounding no.[41]

I reply that the weak are otherwise in danger anyway and might profit from there being deliberative norms according to which they get to represent their interests to the majority and the powerful in commingled polities. And if commingling were to be widely implemented, then states that seek to dominate smaller states would have to make their case to other powerful states that might be sympathetic to the small states. In the case of Russia and Ukraine, all the NATO nations would probably have a lot to say about what Russia should be allowed to do.

But, now tacking in the other direction, it is not necessarily true that the weaker countries should be left alone, or should have their interests be decisive against those of stronger states. Consider the smaller island nations being flooded out by human-induced global warming. Do these nations really have a right to our ceasing the industrial revolution that lifted billions of people out of poverty over the last hundred years? Do the inhabitants of these islands really have the right to insist on staying on the islands and demanding that we revise our climate posture to ensure their safety? Do they really have the right, therefore, to have their decision-making processes be safeguarded against influence from suasion by outside interests? To be sure, the welfare of those threatened by climate change ought to be taken into account. But, arguably, their opinions about policy ought to be brought into deliberative contact with the opinions of others representing larger numbers of people. At any rate, supposing we

39 Thanks to Max Dysart for this concern.

40 Thanks to Tyler Hildebrand for this objection.

41 Thanks to Fred Arsenault for this case.

think nations large and small should have certain rights, we could arrange for these to be respected by, for example, having a kind of constitution and bill of rights, laying out what is and is not to be in the autonomous purview of individual nations, what costs may and may not be imposed on them, and so forth. We could require larger majorities of voters, and larger number of countries, to be in agreement for these documents to be changed. Such rules might be drawn up where, say, confederation is chosen as the best method of commingling polities.

G. The Prisoner's Dilemma Problem for Mutual Trust in Commingling

It might be argued that all these considerations notwithstanding, movements to commingle are fraught with risk. For all nations may be in a prisoner's dilemma with each other on this matter, with all the attendant problems in finding a rationale for cooperation.[42] After all, even if both countries are better off if both let each other affect their deliberations, it is also true that if one country lets the other influence its policy deliberations, and the other country does not, the latter country has a power advantage and so will do even better. Thus, each has an incentive to try to exploit the other.[43]

I have several replies. First, countries could assess the characters and motives of other countries in deciding whether to offer them commingling, and only offer it to those expected to be trustworthy in allowing it in return. And there is a theory of rationality according to which, if it was rational on this expectation to offer cooperation to an agent, then it is rational to fulfill that offer even if there is no guaranteed enforcement mechanism. Instead of worrying about enforcing deals, we can just be careful about who we make ourselves vulnerable to in offering deals. This is often cheaper and less risky than seeking to ensure the possibility of enforcement.[44] Second, even if the foregoing proposal is too idealistic, commingling could be gradual enough that if one party is not playing along, the other could still have enough political autonomy to kill the deal. Third, countries found to be cheating will ruin their reputation for trustworthiness and so imperil their bid for inclusion in future such deals with the given country and other countries, missing out on the possibility of creating and sharing any surplus goods cooperation solving a prisoner's dilemma produces. And countries not welcomed into the club of cooperating nations will gradually wither in comparison. Fourth, many of America's so-called enemies do not seek to dominate America but only relief from oppression by it—they are aggressive to the United States only as a defense strategy. So all the United States need do to ensure trustworthy interactions with

[42] *See generally* DAVID GAUTHIER, MORALS BY AGREEMENT (1986), on the general structure of prisoner's dilemmas.

[43] Thanks to Richmond Campbell for this objection. Campbell also suggests that nations participating in each other's polities may be necessary to the moral progress that consists in bringing everyone in the world into the circle of morality—the progress that justified polities in the first place—but which now, because of the increasing interdependence of the fates of the world's political tribes, needs a tribe of tribes to enlarge the circle.

[44] For more on this theory, *see* GAUTHIER, *supra* note 42; Duncan MacIntosh, *Assuring, Threatening, a Fully Maximizing Theory of Practical Rationality, and the Practical Duties of Agents*, 123 ETHICS 625–656 (July 2013); *see generally* JENS DAVID OHLIN, THE ASSAULT ON INTERNATIONAL LAW (2015).

them is open itself to such interactions—the United States is in an assurance game where, if the United States provides an assurance of trustworthiness in the form of making its polity vulnerable to outside influence, the country thereby assured will reciprocate. Fifth, if two countries would be inclined to commingle were it not that they don't trust each other to play fair, they could give some treasure to mutually trusted third parties who would release it back only upon verified mutual cooperation, thus incentivizing cooperation. Or the countries could seek a country or a supranational organization, like the United Nations, willing to enforce deals and be a peacekeeper between them. Finally, many of the relations between countries are misrepresented as prisoner's dilemmas. Instead, the countries are in coordination problems where neither can do well unless both do their part, and so each has an incentive to do it for the surplus in shareable goods that would result from coordination. There is then no incentive to defect, since there is then no surplus for anyone.[45]

H. The Problem of Exporting the Problems with Each Other's Polities into Other Polities

One final concern is that the more we commingle, the more we will be infected with the problems endemic to each other's respective polities. Does the United States really want more exposure to Putin's mischievousness, Kim's bluster, Xi's special pleading? Does any nation want more exposure to Trump? Moreover, many nations, including America, are flawed democracies. U.S. elections are a chaotic free-for-all; Russia's and China's have only the illusion of freedom; and so on. And every nation is heavily influenced by its own oligarchs and special interests. Do other nations really want to open themselves to yet more of this? Every nation has prejudices and blind spots in its perspectives, disenfranchised peoples in its own population, and elements of its population that are undereducated, resistant to reason, or so poorly circumstanced as to be prone to manipulation.[46] Do we really want to be exposed to each other's failings and vulnerabilities in our political deliberations and to have our decisions be hostage to the flaws in other polities?

The short answer is, yes, we do—for several reasons. First, the deliberative norms of commingling polities will tend to induce greater reason in those who participate in it, because of the formality and sobriety of the process and because its whole point is to offer a forum for the exchange of arguments. Second, this sort of deliberation is inherently educative, each party bringing information and new perspectives to the other. Third, the process is inherently tolerance-enhancing, as is all exposure between

[45] For more details on the structure of coordination problems, *see* Duncan MacIntosh, *Buridan and the Circumstances of Justice (On the Implications of the Rational Unsolvability of Certain Co-ordination Problems)*, 73 Pac. Phil. Q. 150–173 (1992); *see also* Duncan MacIntosh, *Intransitive Preferences, Vagueness, and the Structure of Procrastination*, in The Thief of Time: Philosophical Essays on Procrastination 68–86 (Chrisoula Andreou & Mark D. White eds., 2010).

[46] For more on these issues in the specific case of the United States, *see* Duncan MacIntosh, *De-Weaponizing Incivility and Disinformation: Do We Need a (Virtual) Two-State Solution for America?*, prepared for the conference Navigating Law and Ethics at the Crossroads of Journalism and National Security, organized by the Center for Ethics and the Rule of Law at the University of Pennsylvania Law School, November 2017 (manuscript on file with author).

peoples who have information-deficit-based prejudices against each other. Fourth, the special interests within nations will now have to dialogue with the special interests in other nations. This will have two effects, one being dilution of their power (as they then have other forces to contend with), and the other, moderation (as each has to make compromises in order to make surpluses of shareable goods with others in cooperative ventures). They will accept these effects precisely because they carry with them the possibility of making and sharing cooperative surpluses.

VI. The Best Way of Dealing with Vestigial Problematic Influence and Interference

Perhaps some nations will not be content with having a formal voice constituted of the right to make arguments and will continue trying to interfere in U.S. political processes, violating the ideals described at the end of section III. There might be any of several reasons for or causes of this behavior: enmity and mistrust from past conflict; the worry that the outcomes of American-based deliberation are unlikely to respect their values and traditions (this making the nations incommensurable democratically); the nations being too far apart about what would be a fair distribution of some good; or the nations' leaders being pathological by virtue of being power-mad, robber barons, or psychopaths.[47]

It is not difficult to say what it is we think these nations are doing wrong: they are violating deliberative ideals, in ways we feel disrespect us. As I suggested earlier in section II, there can be no more contentful criterion than this for classing their subversive activity as wrong, since that is the kind of thing about which it is the purpose of politics to resolve contestation.

In the end, I suggest that the best defense is the improvement of the bad relations between nations that lead them to subversion. This, too, involves giving them a voice, although an argumentative voice in diplomacy, not a subversive voice in elections—against the latter we will still need coercive methods of enforcing our norms. Still, such diplomacy is itself part of safeguarding the integrity of America's democratic processes.

Thus the best way to deal with this problematic remainder of unwelcome maneuvering is to realize that it is enough that it is unwelcome—we need not trifle about whether it crosses over from influence to interference—and that the grievances in which it is based need to be allayed. The United States should seek to resolve the conflicts constructively, respecting the needs and concerns of its enemies and aiming to bring all nations into mutually beneficial arrangements which leave no incentive for subverting democratic processes. The United States should fix any long-standing conflicts with these countries by reassuring them that it will not undermine their regimes; it will help them to improve the wealth of their citizens and the stability of their societies and will encourage business relationships, education, and cultural exchange programs and other forms of commingling, so that every country has a stake in the

[47] These last explanations must be invoked sparingly. For they are simplistic, and they lead to policy that dehumanizes opponents, something usually unfair to them, and always unfair to their civilian populations.

welfare and deliberative integrity of every other country. They would then be inclined to maneuver to support each other's countries.

Such an approach would be noncoercive and based on positive incentive and agreement rather than violence and the reciprocal subversion of other countries. It would already count as legal and so could be begun without the law-revising needed for other methods discussed in sections II and III. Finally, it would result in stable associations that all parties would have motivation to preserve; there would be no need to guard against the workarounds that would perpetually be sought against coercive solutions.[48]

[48] This chapter began as a paper for a conference sponsored by the Center for Ethics and the Rule of Law at the University of Pennsylvania Law School, the Foreign Policy Research Institute, the Andrea Mitchell Center for the Study of Democracy, the Wharton School of Business at the University of Pennsylvania, the Carol and Lawrence Zicklin Center for Business Ethics Research, and the Office of Information Security. In many ways it is a response to Jens David Ohlin's contribution to this volume (chapter 11). The chapter also benefited from comments received at a colloquium at Dalhousie University, from comments from students in my class on the theory of rational decision, from written comments by Richmond Campbell, Greg Scherkoske, and the volume editors, Jens David Ohlin and Duncan Hollis. As always, L.W. and Max Dysart helped me read the moral compass. Finally, in the spirit of full disclosure, I should say that I am a Canadian trying to influence the American polity. On the other hand, I identify with the American project.

PART II

UNDERSTANDING ELECTION INTERFERENCE VIA A COMPARATIVE LENS

5

The Specter of Chinese Interference

Examining Beijing's Inroads into India's Digital Spaces and Political Activity

Arun Mohan Sukumar and Akhil Deo

I. Introduction

Banner events tend to steer scholarship and policy prescriptions. Thus, Russian efforts to manipulate the outcome of the 2016 U.S. presidential elections have dominated the discourse on election interference by foreign powers. "The Russian playbook," as it was termed by a top elected official of the American national security apparatus,[1] may well be adopted by other nation-states in the months to come. However, the impact of similar interventions—measured both in terms of their intended outcomes and the degrading of the integrity of digital infrastructure—will depend on a number of factors. The strategic and economic context in which foreign election interference occurs through digital platforms is naturally important. Traditional geopolitical rivalries, such as the one between the United States and Russia, have inspired online disinformation campaigns across regions, especially in the Middle East.[2] But the record of many of these interventions, to quote one forensic analysis, is "equivocal."[3] Governments, social media platforms, digital news outlets, fact-checking organizations, and research institutions are today more cognizant than ever of disinformation campaigns, making sustained malicious activity almost impossible to go undetected. That Russia's own attempt at influencing the 2018 U.S. midterm elections were purportedly less successful than its intervention two years previously attests to this reality.[4]

Equally important are the personnel and technical resources a foreign actor has invested in the craft of "old-world" espionage—identifying issues, communities, or constituencies most pliable to digital manipulation. Few states can bring to bear the sustained resources, attention, and expertise in orchestrating disinformation campaigns as Russia has historically done. China, however, is one such state. Its rising

[1] Julian E. Barnes, *Russians Tried, but Were Unable to Compromise Midterm Elections, U.S. Says*, N.Y. Times (Dec. 21, 2018).

[2] Nabih Bulos, *Coronavirus becomes a Weapon of Disinformation in Middle East Battle for Influence*, L.A. Times (Apr. 8, 2020); *Inside Saudi Arabia's Disinformation Campaign*, NPR (Aug. 10, 2019).

[3] Gabrielle Lim et al., *Burned After Reading: Endless Mayfly's Ephemeral Disinformation Campaign* (The Citizen Lab, May 14, 2019), *at* https://citizenlab.ca/2019/05/burned-after-reading-endless-mayflys-ephemeral-disinformation-campaign/.

[4] Barnes, *supra* note 1.

Arun Mohan Sukumar and Akhil Deo, *The Specter of Chinese Interference* In: *Defending Democracies*. Edited by Duncan B. Hollis and Jens David Ohlin, Oxford University Press (2021). © Duncan B. Hollis & Jens David Ohlin.
DOI: 10.1093/oso/9780197556979.003.0006

global economic and political clout, accompanied by the explosive growth of its technology companies, offers China both the tools and the playgrounds to effect electoral interference in foreign jurisdictions. In fact, as this chapter argues, China's success in manipulating elections may leave Russia far behind, given the many levers it has to channel propaganda and the relative lack of attention paid to disinformation in Chinese digital platforms over, say, a Facebook, WhatsApp, or Twitter.

This chapter highlights the prospects for election interference by China in the world's largest democracy, India. It charts the pathways by which China could mount a sophisticated disinformation campaign targeting India's political processes and outlines the growing incentives for Beijing to engage in such operations. Concerns around Chinese influence operations against India are not hypothetical: in 2020, the Indian government banned 224 Chinese mobile apps, including TikTok, WeChat, and Alipay, citing national security risks. This extraordinary measure, the government announced, was motivated by reports of apps "stealing and surreptitiously transmitting users' data in an unauthorized manner" outside India, and the use of such data for "mining and profiling by elements hostile to the national security and defence of India."[5] That the ban was imposed in the aftermath of a violent confrontation in the summer of 2020 between Chinese and Indian armed forces along their disputed Himalayan border is significant. While its duration is unclear, the ban reflects the Indian security establishment's heightened concern that China may weaponize its highly popular digital platforms towards cyber attacks and influence operations against an increasingly adversarial neighbor. To be sure, we do not offer a smoking gun to highlight China's complicity in, or planning of, digital interference in an ongoing or past election campaign in India. Rather, we hold up recent instances where state-based actors appear emboldened to facilitate disinformation campaigns. The objective of this chapter is to present a framework by which China's cyber operations to influence the outcome of elections—not only in India but also in other markets where Chinese companies have a growing presence—can be studied.

To the authors' best knowledge, there currently exists no systematic assessment of Chinese election interference in India: indeed, at the time of writing, there are few scholarly assessments of Chinese influence operations, even including documented ones in Hong Kong SAR and Taiwan.[6] As a 2019 study by the Oxford Internet Institute concluded, "[until recently,] China rarely used social media to manipulate public opinion in other countries."[7] As recently as 2018, Western intelligence agencies believed China would extend the same "techniques developed for domestic control [such as censorship and promotion of ideological propaganda] to foreign audiences."[8] That is evidently changing, and this chapter attempts to outline the "whys" and "hows"

[5] *Ministry of Electronics and IT—Government Blocks 118 Mobile Apps Which are Prejudicial to Sovereignty and Integrity of India, Defence of India, Security of State and Public Order*, PRESS INFORMATION BUREAU (Sep. 02, 2020).

[6] *Taiwan Election: Disinformation as a Partisan Issue* (Stanford Cyber Policy Center, Jan. 21, 2020), *at* https://cyber.fsi.stanford.edu/io/news/taiwan-disinformation-partisan-issue.

[7] Samantha Bradshaw & Philip N. Howard, *The Global Disinformation Order: 2019 Global Inventory of Organised Social Media Manipulation*, Working Paper 2019.3 2 (Oxford Internet Institute Project on Computational Propaganda, 2019).

[8] *Who Said What? The Security Challenges of Modern Disinformation*, WORLD WATCH: EXPERT NOTES SERIES 78 (Canadian Security Intelligence Services, Pub. No. 2016-12-05, 2018).

of Chinese influence operations targeted at political processes, highlighting India as a case study.

Our chapter is divided into four segments. The first section highlights the evolution of China's strategy, broadly defined, toward disinformation and influence operations in the digital age. The second fleshes out the contours of India's own maturing digital economy and the steady online migration of political activity, which we argue renders its democratic processes susceptible to election interference. The third section reviews extent practices of Chinese technology companies—which have built a vast user/ client network in India—with regards to the management and security of data, as well as their handling of malicious and false content. And finally, we hold up a number of conceivable incentives for China to intervene in India's electoral processes, both at the federal and at the state level.

Before doing so, however, a few caveats are in order. This chapter does not survey the security of India's election infrastructure such as voter rolls and electronic voting machines or attendant computer systems used in the polling process. In 2019, ahead of the country's general election, the Election Commission of India issued a series of detailed cybersecurity guidelines, which present vectors of vulnerability in India's digital networks.[9] Those vectors are susceptible to exploitation by China given the expansive role of Chinese companies in India's telecommunications infrastructure, handheld device market, and apps ecosystem. A detailed review of those vulnerabilities are in order, but this chapter does not undertake it; rather, it highlights other patent opportunities India's "digital public sphere" presents to China in order to interfere in the country's democratic processes.

II. The Evolution of China's Approach to Disinformation

Although a detailed history of China's evolving approach on influence operations is outside the scope of this chapter, it is important to recognize that China has long considered information a battleground for power. Thus, control over discourse and narratives at home has always been a core interest for the Communist Party.[10] Over the past decade, China's efforts have expanded to include discourse and narratives abroad.

Its efforts to influence global perception have taken on three distinct forms. The first is through what Chinese strategists call "borrowing the boat to sail into the ocean"—or paid inserts into foreign media publications.[11] Reports indicate, for instance, that a *China Daily* supplement is published in major newspapers across at least

[9] Election Commission of India, *Cyber Security General Guidelines for General Elections* (July 18, 2019), *at* https://eci.gov.in/files/file/10349-cyber-security-general-guidelines-for-general-election-2019/.

[10] *See generally* David Shambaugh, *China's Propaganda System: Institutions, Processes and Efficacy*, 57 China J. 25–58 (2007); Wu Xuecan, *Turning Everyone into a Censor: The Chinese Communist Party's All-Directional Control over the Media* (U.S.-China Economic and Security Review Commission, 2001); Toshi Yoshihara, *Chinese Information Warfare: A Phantom Menace or Emerging Threat?* (U.S. Army War College Strategic Studies Institute, 2001).

[11] Sam Geal & Robert Soutar, *Chinese Media and Latin America: "Borrowing a Boat" to Set Sail* (Jamestown Foundation, July 10, 2018), *at* https://jamestown.org/program/chinese-media-and-latin-america-borrowing-a-boat-to-set-sail/.

thirty countries.[12] The *Financial Times* has similarly reported China Global Television Network provides free content to nearly 1,700 media organizations around the world.[13] The second is through "Confucius Institutes," which are cultural and education organizations that are often tied to and fund universities abroad. Multiple reports have documented the opaque nature of this funding, as well as the institutes' censorship of conversations around politically sensitive issues like Taiwan and Tibet.[14] In 2018, the U.S. Congress enacted legislation prohibiting the use of Department of Defense funds for Chinese language training by Confucius Institutes.[15] The measure prompted many universities to sever ties with these institutes.[16] And the third is through diaspora management—a primary function of the United Front Work Department.[17]

These traditional levers of propaganda and influence have gradually evolved over the past two years to include a growing Chinese presence on Western social media platforms, as part of a major effort by the Xi Jinping administration to globalize Chinese media narratives. Xinhua news agency, *Global Times*, CGTN, and *People's Daily*, for example, all have a strong social media presence on Facebook and Twitter. CGTN has nearly 87 million followers,[18] with 20 million followers having been added since 2018 alone.[19] Beijing also employs a vast army of "Internet commentators"—known informally as "50C" party members[20]—to express pro-Party views on Chinese and foreign social media platforms.[21] China's diplomatic establishment and community have similarly made a concerted push onto Twitter, with reports documenting that at least thirty-two Chinese diplomats, embassies, and consulates launched their Twitter accounts in 2019 alone.[22] Unlike Russia, whose disinformation campaigns are intended to sow discord, exploit socioeconomic fault lines, and generally undermine trust in democratic institutions, China's influence efforts on foreign social media platforms have hitherto been largely directed at embellishing the reputation of the Chinese Communist Party (CCP) abroad.

[12] Louisa Lim & Julia Bergin, *Inside China's Audacious Global Propaganda Campaign*, The Guardian (Dec. 7, 2018).

[13] Emily Feng, *China and the World: How Beijing Spreads the Message*, Financial Times (July 12, 2018).

[14] Rachelle Peterson, *Outsourced to China: Confucius Institutes and Soft Power in American Higher Education* 10 (National Association of Scholars, June 2017), *at* https://www.nas.org/reports/outsourced-to-china.

[15] Racqueal Legerwood, *As US Universities Close Confucius Institutes, What's Next?*, Hum. Rts. Watch (Jan. 27, 2020).

[16] Karen Fisher, *Oldest Confucius Institute in U.S. to Close*, The Chronicle of Higher Education (Jan. 22, 2020).

[17] John Fitzgerald, *Loyalty through Links and Control: The Long History of Chinese Diaspora Diplomacy*, The Interpreter (May 11, 2016).

[18] Sarah Cook, *Beijing's Global Megaphone*, Freedom House: Special Report 6 (Jan. 2020), *at* https://freedomhouse.org/report/special-report/2020/beijings-global-megaphone.

[19] *Id.*

[20] The phrase "50C" gained popularity based on some assertions that party members were paid 50 US cents per post. Although this has since been disproved, the moniker stuck. *See* Gary King et al., *How the Chinese Government Fabricates Social Media Posts for Strategic Distraction, Not Engaged Argument*, 111 Am. Pol'y Sci. Rev. 484, 484–501 (2017).

[21] *Id.*

[22] Zhaoyin Feng, *China and Twitter: The Year China Got Louder on Social Media*, BBC (Dec. 29, 2019).

Recent events suggest, however, that this is beginning to change. Beijing has begun to adopt Russia-style tactics, as it were, in their digital operations. In two related data dumps released in August and September 2019, both Twitter and Facebook banned thousands of fake accounts and pages linked to Chinese actors for attempting to sow discord between pro- and antigovernment protestors in Hong Kong.[23] Many of the accounts linked to this campaign were created as part of an earlier disinformation campaign against Chinese dissident Guao Wengui, as far back as August 2017. Guao Wengui was a popular figure on social media, and Chinese efforts to discredit him were aimed at blunting his criticism ahead of the critical 19th Party Congress in September.[24] The campaign against Guao differs from standard Chinese efforts to influence global narratives. It marked the first time that China-based actors were traced to "inauthentic" behavior on U.S. technology platforms.[25] That Beijing actively engaged in a disinformation campaign is also notable, in contrast to its usual attempts at portraying China or the CCP in a good light.

Another illustration of China's evolving strategy of information "warfare"—and perhaps the only reported instance of China interfering in elections—is its disinformation campaign directed at Taiwan's 2020 presidential race and a related mayoral election earlier in 2018. Although Beijing has long employed different political and media-related measures to interfere in Taiwan's political processes, recent efforts to prevent the re-election of President Tsai Ing-wen by spreading disinformation about her and her policies (and overtly supporting the opposition candidate, who is perceived to be more sympathetic to Beijing), indicate a more aggressive approach.[26] Reports from 2018 suggest, in fact, that the opposition candidate Han Kuo-yu's run for local office was bolstered by inauthentic activity on Facebook and other social media platforms.[27] Although no official sources have attributed these efforts to Beijing, circumstantial evidence pointed to the involvement of the CCP, including the presence of accounts from mainland China,[28] linguistic differences in pages and accounts suspected to have been run by Chinese actors,[29] Twitter's takedown of "troll" accounts and pages related to Hong Kong, and a United Front Work Department conference on "internet influence activities"[30] weeks before the presidential elections. Once again,

[23] *Information Operations Directed at Hong Kong*, TWITTER SAFETY (Aug. 19, 2019), *at* https://blog.twitter.com/en_us/topics/company/2019/information_operations_directed_at_Hong_Kong.html; Nathaniel Gliecher, *Removing Co-Ordinate Inauthentic Behaviour from China*, FACEBOOK NEWSROOM (Aug. 19, 2020), *at* https://about.fb.com/news/2019/08/removing-cib-china/.

[24] Daniel Wood, Sean McMinn, & Emily Feng, *China Used Twitter to Disrupt Hong Kong Protests, but Efforts Began Years Earlier*, NPR (Sept. 17, 2019).

[25] Emily Stewart, *How China Used Facebook, Twitter, and YouTube to Spread Disinformation about the Hong Kong Protests*, Vox (Aug. 23, 2019).

[26] Brian Hioe, *Fighting Fake News and Disinformation in Taiwan: An Interview with Puma Shen*, NEW BLOOM MAGAZINE (Jan. 6, 2020).

[27] Kathryn Hille, *Taiwan Primaries Highlight Fears over China's Political Influence*, FINANCIAL TIMES (July 17, 2019); Paul Huang, *Chinese Cyber-Operatives Boosted Taiwan's Insurgent Candidate*, FOREIGN POL'Y (June 26, 2019).

[28] Connor Fairman, *When Election Interference Fails*, NET POLITICS (Council on Foreign Relations, Jan. 29, 2020), *at* https://www.cfr.org/blog/when-election-interference-fails.

[29] *Id.*

[30] Raymond Zhong, *Awash in Disinformation before Vote, Taiwan Points Finger at China*, N.Y. TIMES (Jan. 6, 2020).

these disinformation tactics more closely resembled the Russian campaign targeting the 2016 U.S. presidential elections than traditional Chinese activity.

The most recent incident is China's disinformation campaign, ongoing at the time of writing, around its response to the COVID-19 outbreak in the city of Wuhan and the Hubei province. Beijing has drawn ire from some states and political leaders for its early failures in tackling the outbreak of the coronavirus pandemic in Wuhan.[31] In an effort to deflect attention away from Beijing's purported failures, Zhao Lijian, spokesperson for China's Ministry of Foreign Affairs, tweeted an article titled "COVID-19: More evidence that the virus originated in the US."[32] Sourced from a website known for promoting conspiracy theories, the article suggested that the coronavirus was a bioweapon developed in the United States and subsequently smuggled into Wuhan by the U.S. military.[33] A few weeks later, China's state-run *Global Times* speculated the source of the outbreak to be in Italy.[34] Several official accounts of Chinese embassies around the world subsequently shared either Zhao's tweet or similar assertions of U.S. responsibility in smuggling the virus into China.[35] Most of these accounts were created only in late 2019. Although one analysis of China's COVID-19 social media diplomacy concluded China's state media focused largely on the swiftness of Beijing's response to the crises,[36] the Zhao Lijian incident, and the social media behavior of several other Chinese diplomats and embassies, demonstrates that China is more willing to use its state media outlets to propagate disinformation without concern of being attributed—another departure from standard practice.[37]

III. India's "Marketplace" for Influence Operations

These instances indicate a significant turn in China's efforts to influence global opinions. They also acquire salience as potential pathways for Beijing to influence political processes in states like India. There is a thriving market for disinformation in India, driven by its near-continuous federal and local election cycles, the country's young and internet-savvy demographic that has shown a voracious appetite for social media, and limited institutional oversight and accountability mechanisms over political speech. Taken together, these all make the prospects for a Chinese disinformation campaign highly lucrative. Political parties in India are currently major, if not the

[31] Ishaan Tharoor, *It's Not Just Trump Who's Angry at China*, WASHINGTON POST (Apr. 14, 2020).

[32] @zlj517, TWITTER (Mar. 13, 2020, 6.32 AM), *at* https://twitter.com/zlj517/status/1238269193427906560?s=20.

[33] Betsy Morris & Robert McMillan, *China Pushes Viral Messages to Shape Coronavirus Narrative*, WALL STREET JOURNAL (Apr. 10, 2020).

[34] Chris Chang, *China Now Implying Coronavirus May Have Originated in Italy*, TAIWAN NEWS (Mar. 24, 2020).

[35] Mark Scott, *Chinese Diplomacy Ramps Up Social Media Offensive in COVID-19 Info War*, POLITICO (Apr. 29, 2020).

[36] Vanessa Molter, *Pandemics & Propaganda: How Chinese State Media Shapes Conversations on the Coronavirus* (Stanford Cyber Policy Center, Mar. 19, 2020), *at* https://cyber.fsi.stanford.edu/news/chinese-state-media-shapes-coronavirus-convo.

[37] *See, e.g.*, *"Once Upon a Virus": China Mocks US with Video on Covid-19, Twitter Hits Back*, HINDUSTAN TIMES (May 1, 2020).

preeminent drivers of disinformation and propaganda.[38] There are plenty of incentives in the form of India's cyclical local and state elections and the bidecadal general elections. The practice of leveraging digital platforms for political campaigns went mainstream during the 2014 Indian General Elections—Prime Minister Narendra Modi's overwhelming electoral success has been partly attributed to his effective social media campaign.[39] Both the Bharatiya Janata Party (BJP) and the Indian National Congress—India's two major national political parties—were reported to have hired digital advertising companies to help bolster their digital presence.[40] It was the 2019 general elections, however, that marked a critical turning point, with candidates, political organizations, and other interest groups in India embracing and harvesting digital platforms for electoral advantage. This shift was largely enabled by rapid advances in India's digital economy in the interim. In 2014, barely 100 million Indians owned smartphones—a number that jumped threefold to 300 million by 2017.[41] The year 2015 also marked the entry of Reliance Jio into India's telecommunications sector, whose initially free and later subsidized offerings contributed to the plummeting of mobile data prices to $0.20 per gigabyte—the cheapest anywhere in the world.[42]

The deployment of digital platforms by all manner of actors to influence the outcome of the 2019 national polls was so extensive it earned the moniker "WhatsApp elections"—named primarily for the outsized role Facebook's messaging app played in spreading legitimate political content as well as patently false information.[43] A significant portion of what platforms now call "inauthentic" political propaganda in India is driven by well-structured, well-funded, and targeted organizations within political outfits—known colloquially as "information technology (IT) cells."[44] Although these organizations possess a staff of their own, their operations are often amplified by loose coalitions of volunteers—upward of a million at a time, according to some reports.[45] This well-defined administrative structure is bolstered by increasingly granular data aggregation practices, some that may rely on harvesting user and behavioral data from social media platforms, but also includes extensive analytics and profiling based on the data gathered from electoral rolls, electricity bills, and ration cards.[46] Party cadres are then placed in charge of hyperlocal content creation strategies that tailor messaging based on the profiles of individuals or communities.

[38] Snigdha Poonam & Samarth Bansal, *Misinformation Is Endangering Indian Elections*, The Atlantic (Apr. 1, 2019).

[39] Derek Willis, *Narendra Modi, the Social Media Politician*, N.Y. Times (Sept. 25, 2014).

[40] Bhavna Vij Arora, *Congress Gears Up for 2014, Awards ad Campaign to JWT with One-Point Agenda to Counter Narendra Modi*, India Today (Sept. 9, 2013); Vidhi Choudhary, Gyan Varma, & Makarand Gadgil, *The Ad Agencies behind BJP's Successful Campaign*, Livemint (Oct. 19, 2014).

[41] Pankaj Mishra, *The Real Revolution in India*, Bloomberg (Apr. 21, 2019).

[42] *India Has Cheapest Mobile Data in the World: Study*, The Hindu (Mar. 6, 2019).

[43] Priyanjana Bengali, *India Had Its first "WhatsApp election." We Have a Million Messages from It*, Colum. Journalism Rev. (Oct. 16, 2019).

[44] *See generally* Ualan Campbell-Smith & Samantha Bradshaw, *Global Cyber Troops Country Profile: India* (Oxford Internet Institute, May 2019), *at* https://comprop.oii.ox.ac.uk/wp-content/uploads/sites/93/2019/05/India-Profile.pdf.

[45] Dinesh Narayan & Venkat Ananth, *How the Mobile Phone Is Shaping to Be BJP's Most Important Weapon in Elections*, Economic Times (Aug. 23, 2018).

[46] Shivam Shankar Singh, *How Political Parties Mixed Data Analytics and Social Media for Disinformation Campaigns*, Medianama (Apr. 12, 2019).

Enabling this ecosystem is a growing network of marketing agencies, political consultancies, influencer networks, and analytics platforms. Cambridge Analytica, for instance, was hired by both national political parties in India—the Congress and the BJP.[47] News reports and interviews with current and former campaign management staff for Indian political parties suggest a longer list of such partnerships. A digital marketing firm in New Delhi, OML Logic, for instance, has similarly been hired both by the BJP and the Congress to manage social media content.[48] Such practices go well beyond national parties and include regional outfits. Reports from the southern Indian state of Andhra Pradesh suggest the Telugu Desam Party hired Pramanya Strategy Consulting Private Ltd. to manage digital campaigns.[49] There is limited information about how these firms actually operate and negligible pressure on political parties to be transparent about the type of campaigns they run. (During the 2019 general elections, the Election Commission of India included prohibitions against fake news and rumormongering in its "model code of conduct" for political parties and contesting candidates, but this has had very little discernible effect.[50]) Anecdotal evidence suggests a very similar approach to those employed by Cambridge Analytica during the 2016 American elections. One Delhi-based firm, Obiyan Infotech, boasts on its website, for instance, that it can harvest "quite a few indicators that may help predict whom a voter is inclined to vote for."[51]

That political parties were heavily leveraging both their cadre and third parties to influence India's digital spaces became apparent a month before the general elections in May 2019, when Facebook took down nearly 700 pages and accounts belonging to both the BJP and Congress for "coordinated inauthentic behavior."[52] Around 15 of the pages were managed by Silver Touch, a political consultancy linked to the BJP. Another 678 pages were linked to members of the Congress's IT cell. One of the pages that was taken down, "The Indian Eye," was a pro-BJP page that was integrated into the "Narendra Modi" application, which boasts over 10 million downloads and was promoted as a means for the prime minister to stay "in touch" with ordinary citizens.[53]

IV. Practices of China's Technology Platforms in India

Exacerbating the risk of Chinese influence operations within what is already a manipulable Indian "digital public sphere" is the rapid entry of Chinese content applications

[47] Vidhi Doshi & Annie Gowen, *Whistleblower Claims Cambridge Analytica's Partners in India Worked on Elections, Raising Privacy Fears*, Washington Post (Mar. 29, 2018).

[48] Anumeha Chaturvedi, *Ahead of General Elections, Parties Tap Social Media Influencers*, Economic Times (Mar. 1, 2019).

[49] *In Google Ad Spend, TDP Is Beating BJP Now*, Economic Times (Apr. 4, 2019).

[50] *EC's Social Media Guidelines May Not Be Enough*, Hindustan Times (Mar. 13, 2019).

[51] Obiyan Infotech, *Digital Marketing for Politicians in India: Mantra of Success*, *available at* https://www.obiyaninfotech.com/digital-marketing-for-politician/.

[52] Nathaniel Gleicher, *Removing Coordinated Inauthentic Behavior and Spam from India and Pakistan*, Facebook Newsroom (Apr. 1, 2019), *at* https://about.fb.com/news/2019/04/cib-and-spam-from-india-pakistan/.

[53] *NaMo App Promotes Fake News Factory "The India Eye" and Users Can't Block It Even If They Want To*, Scroll (Feb 7, 2019).

in India's digital economy. Consider, for instance, that in 2017, eighteen of the one hundred most downloaded apps on the Indian Google Play store were Chinese.[54] In 2018, this number rose dramatically to forty-four. Chinese applications now cut across various categories, but a significant number of them are social media–like and designed to rapidly share content. Helo and TikTok are the most popular social media apps, along with short video and live-streaming apps like LiveMe, Vigo Video, BIGO LIVE, and Kwai. TikTok's expansion has been particularly noteworthy: having launched only in early 2018, the app had reached over a third of all Indian smartphone users by the end of 2019, with Indian users now accounting for a full third of TikTok's global user base.[55]

The Indian market for content, news, and social media is increasingly becoming a two-horse race, with China-based companies aggressively competing to dislodge the dominance of American digital platforms in India. This mirrors a broader trend of Chinese technology platforms and infrastructure proliferating around the world and unseating FAANG companies (Facebook, Apple, Amazon, Netflix, and Google) from their leadership positions. An obvious concern is whether Chinese platforms in international markets, especially those with skeletal or no data protection laws, will offer perfunctory privacy policies, but no concrete safeguards for handling user data. Especially worrisome is the possibility of Beijing "weaponizing" Chinese digital platforms in India for conducting disinformation campaigns during elections. The Communist Party's influence over state-owned enterprises is well documented, but relatively sparse attention has been paid to its growing sway over its private technology sector. Many major technology companies, including Tencent, Alibaba, and Baidu have a "party committee," and many co-operate with the CCP to build surveillance infrastructure within Beijing.[56] Not only does the proliferation of Chinese technology platforms then allow the Chinese state to shape global norms and practices around speech, data protection, and surveillance, it also gives the CCP the tools to potentially interfere in the domestic politics of nations heavily reliant on its platforms.

A. Focusing on Rural Markets

Three aspects of Chinese technology companies vis-à-vis their role in India's "digital public sphere" merit attention for their potential to be wielded as disruptors of India's political and electoral processes and institutions. First, these platforms focus overwhelmingly on demographics in Tier 2 and Tier 3 cities in India, whose political and social milieu receive relatively less scrutiny by India's Delhi-centric national media.[57] Chinese applications have picked up on a trend that American technology platforms either missed or refused to give importance to: both the absolute number of rural Indian internet users and the amount of time they spend on news, social media, and

[54] Shadma Shaikh, *The Chinese Takeover of Indian App Ecosystem*, Factor Daily (Jan. 2, 2019).
[55] Rebecca Bellan, *TikTok Is the Most Downloaded App Worldwide, and India Is Leading the Charge*, Forbes (Feb. 14, 2020).
[56] Chauncey Jung, *What Communists Do in China's Tech Companies*, Inkstone (Dec. 4, 2018).
[57] Mugdha Variyar, *How Chinese Apps Are Making Inroads in Indian Small Towns*, Economic Times (Aug. 10, 2018).

online entertainment exceeds their urban counterparts.[58] Chinese platforms have catered swiftly and remarkably to local and vernacular content in India. Helo, for instance, operates in at least fifteen Indian languages.[59] So do Chinese-owned news applications like UC News, which has a staggering 100 million downloads, and News Dog, with nearly 50 million downloads.[60] The result being Chinese applications serve as the primary source of news and content for an entire generation of rural youth coming online, with their practices and consumption trends largely invisible to India's national security community (which does not possess the tools or capacity to track disinformation even on larger platforms), and also to international watchdogs, who may not have the resources to track content in local Indian languages.

Compounding the problem is the limited information available on the extent to which these platforms have gathered data on Indian users and their behavior.[61] Although platforms like TikTok and Helo have been compelled to respond to data privacy concerns—variously promising to store data locally[62]—there is no institutional effort devoted to monitoring the full extent of China's data-gathering capabilities in India. India's draft data protection law, which envisages an independent Data Protection Authority to perform such regulatory oversight, is in the preliminary stages of parliamentary deliberation. Aggravating these risks are poor cyber hygiene practices in India, which were recently highlighted by the National Cyber Security Coordinator.[63]

B. The Popularization of Chinese Platforms

The second concern is the steady migration in India of online political content to Chinese platforms given their popularity. Despite multiple political outfits calling for a ban on Chinese platforms, many now have a strong presence on them.[64] As political content and rhetoric gain momentum on Chinese applications, their operations will have to grapple with disinformation that is par for the course for any campaign. This may well allow China to leverage Russia-style tactics that rely on accentuating social and political fault lines. This risk is exacerbated by the fact that, unlike Russia, Chinese actors own the platforms on which Indian political conversations are hosted and have

[58] Hello Holdings Limited, Helo, Mobile App, Version 3.2.4.02, *available at* https://play.google.com/store/apps/details?id=app.buzz.share&hl=en.

[59] UCWeb, UC News, Mobile App, Version 3.0.5.1080, *available at* https://play.google.com/store/apps/details?id=com.uc.iflow&hl=en.

[60] News Dog Team, News Dog, Mobile App, Version 2.8.1, *available at* https://play.google.com/store/apps/details?id=com.newsdog&hl=en.

[61] For an analysis of Huawei and Vivo's privacy policies as they pertain to India, *see generally* Arun Mohan Sukumar, *Working with "Last-Mile" Data Protection in India*, Policy Paper Asie Visions No. 96 (IFRI, 2017).

[62] Megha Mandavia, *China's ByteDance to Store Indian Data Locally after MPs Raise Concerns on Privacy, National Security*, Economic Times (July 22, 2019).

[63] Sandhya Sharma, *Concerned about Global Spurt in Cybercrimes, PMO's Cyber Chief Issues Cyber-Advisory for Online Users*, Economic Times (Apr. 10, 2020).

[64] Anumeha Chaturvedi, *Political Parties Plan to Up Tiktok Presence*, Economic Times (Dec. 3, 2019).

already acquiesced to hosting manipulated content. In fact, the key to the success of almost every major content app in China has been turning a blind eye toward "racy" content—whether it is doctored videos, edgy political caricature, or downright misinformation, and even pornography.[65] The most recent reports of false news on these platforms relate to the coronavirus, with a digital analytics firm identifying disinformation targeting India's Muslim community for ostensibly conspiring to spread the virus all over India.[66] Concerns around disinformation on Chinese applications even compelled the Madras High Court to ban TikTok, a judgment that was subsequently reversed.[67] Despite repeated calls by various political parties over the years, the growing popularity of Chinese platforms has compelled these parties to host political content on them.

Adding to this concern is the gradual absorption of Chinese platforms into the market for influencers and digital advertising—one that political outfits tap into for personnel and technical resources to run their campaigns. The director of a political campaign firm, for instance, was quoted as considering "TikTok very seriously for elections" and to "try to leverage it in a way that will not seem political."[68] Chinese applications are also heavily investing in creating a market for and network of influencers and celebrities,[69] many of whom are tapped by political parties during their campaigns. One TikTok influencer was even offered a party ticket by a national political party to run for state assembly elections in 2019.[70]

C. Content Moderation

A third concern relates to content moderation on these platforms. TikTok has already come under scrutiny in the United States for suppressing or censoring content outside Chinese borders. Last year, the app was accused of having instructed moderators to suppress material created by users "deemed too ugly, poor, or disabled for the platform."[71] Concerns were heightened in the United States by reports of other Chinese platforms, like WeChat, censoring political content in jurisdictions outside of China, especially in the Southeast Asian states where it is quite popular.[72] A recent forensic analysis by the Citizen Lab alleged WeChat also censors content of accounts that are not registered to China-based phone numbers.[73] In response, platforms like

[65] Shadma Shaikh, *The Chinese Takeover of Indian App Ecosystem*, Factor Daily (Jan. 2, 2019).

[66] Ankit Kumar, *Surge in TikTok Videos Aimed at Misleading Indian Muslims over Coronavirus Precautions*, India Today (Apr. 3, 2020).

[67] Richa Taneja, *Ban on TikTok Video App Lifted by Madras High Court*, NDTV (Apr. 24, 2019).

[68] Shanthi S., *Political Parties to Cash in on India's TikTok Mania for Election Ads*, INC42 (Dec. 3, 2019).

[69] Shadma Shaikh, *Chinese Apps Scramble for India's Kardashians*, Factor Daily (Mar. 27, 2018).

[70] Soumyarendra Barik, *TikTok Celebrity Gets BJP Ticket for Upcoming Haryana Elections*, Medianama (Oct. 7, 2019).

[71] Sam Biddle, Paulo Victor Ribeiro, & Tatiana Dias, *Invisible Censorship*, The Intercept (Mar. 16, 2020).

[72] Emily Feng, *China Intercepts WeChat Texts from U.S. and Abroad, Researchers Say*, NPR (Aug. 29, 2019).

[73] Jeffrey Knockel et al., *We Chat, They Watch—How International Users Unwittingly Build Up WeChat's Chinese Censorship Apparatus* (The Citizen Lab, May 7, 2020), *at* https://citizenlab.ca/2020/05/we-chat-they-watch/.

TikTok have committed to outsource some of their content-moderation functions to jurisdictions outside of China—but the policy change seemingly applies only to the U.S. market.[74] As mentioned previously, China's ability to influence how content is ranked or censored in India has largely been ignored by state institutions and civil society. Stray media reports suggest that such actions have already taken place. When the deeply polarizing protests against the Citizenship Amendment Act first began in India in December 2019, for instance, moderators at BIGO Live were asked to "reduce visibility" of videos involving protest.[75] It is not clear yet how the India offices of Chinese platforms receive, create, or enforce these guidelines.

Although no authoritative finding or evidence of Chinese electoral influence operations in India has emerged, the preconditions to facilitate or enable such methods are certainly in place (just as they were ahead of Russia's influence operations in the 2016 American elections). China possesses a long history of information warfare and the digital tools and capacity to execute such operations, and has increasingly demonstrated a willingness to deploy these tools, although they have so far been limited to long-standing "core" interests relating to Hong Kong and Taiwan. As the next section highlights, however, there are demonstrable instances where it could turn on the "faucet" of disinformation campaigns in India, directing it against the country's political and electoral infrastructure.

V. Incentives for China to Interfere in India's Democratic Processes

The deep integration of China's social media platforms into India's digital public sphere as well as its evolving disinformation tactics animate concerns that China is now in a position to influence Indian political processes. This section will argue that China has also begun recently to exhibit its willingness to exercise these levers of influence, given the evolving nature of the bilateral relationship.

The China-India relationship has long been defined by a mix of conflict, competition, and cooperation. Even as they fought a limited boundary war in 1962, India and China have also partnered to jointly seek global governance reforms. Over the past decade, however, differences between both have been thrown into sharper relief, with the space for cooperation receding rapidly. These differences now extend across multiple domains and fronts. China has used its growing clout in multilateral institutions to work at cross-purposes with Indian interests, whether by pussyfooting UN Security Council Resolution 1267 committee sanctions on terrorist outfits based in Pakistan, or continuing to oppose India's entry into the Nuclear Suppliers Group (NSG).[76] In a similar vein, China has used economic largesse under the umbrella of the Belt and

[74] *TikTok to Stop Using China-Based Moderators to Monitor Overseas Content*, WALL STREET JOURNAL (Mar. 15, 2020).

[75] Prasid Banerjee, *Inside the Secretive World of India's Social Media Content Moderators*, LIVEMINT (Mar. 18, 2020).

[76] *China Hints It Will Continue to Block India's Bid to Join Nuclear Suppliers Group*, SCROLL (Jan. 31, 2019).

Road Initiative (BRI)[77] to try to displace India from its role as a hegemon in South Asia.[78]

Even so, India still occupies only a minor role in China's strategic calculus; it is seen largely as a regional competitor and dangerous only to the extent that it could support U.S. efforts to undermine China's rise.[79] This thinking is bound to change as India's economic rise and own evolving geopolitical calculations begin to affect China's national interests. Some trends to this effect are already visible. It is worth recalling that India was the first major country to have objected to the BRI, China's flagship twenty-first-century project to position itself as a global power, a move that catalyzed similar objections from the United States and European nations that were earlier ambivalent about the project.[80] Equally significant was India's ability to weather China's territorial aggression in Bhutan, an effort that culminated in the 2017 Doklam standoff.[81] Again, this episode marked a unique political moment in how India's foreign policy actions influenced China's global interests.[82] China has long used strong-arming tactics to expand territorial claims to the South China Sea, which have largely been successful. Doklam was perhaps the first instance where a major power intervened in the territory of a smaller state to thwart China's aggression.

It is clear a more muscular Indian foreign policy vis-à-vis China will compel Beijing to deploy new tools to mitigate India's influence and contain its rise. As its behavior in the United States, Europe, East Asia, and Australia demonstrates, China is no longer shy about wielding blunter instruments for political and electoral influence. It is necessary, then, to not only identify the tools China may use but also the political incentives that may encourage it to manipulate India's political processes.

A. Targeting Ethnic, Religious, and Social Fault Lines

We identify three major pathways. The first would be to exploit India's ethnic, religious, and social fault lines. In response to equivalencies drawn between the rise of India and China, Beijing has long argued that India's "messy" democracy would always make it an inferior power.[83] Under the Xi administration, China's rhetoric and ideological posturing against democracies have only sharpened. Indeed, China's

[77] For background on the Belt and Road Initiative, *see* Andrew Chatzky & James McBride, *China's Massive Belt and Road Initiative* (Council on Foreign Relations, Jan. 28, 2020), *available at* https://www.cfr.org/backgrounder/chinas-massive-belt-and-road-initiative.

[78] Ashlyn Anderson & Alyssa Ayres, *Economics of Influence: China and India in South Asia* (Council on Foreign Relations, Aug. 3, 2015), *at* https://www.cfr.org/expert-brief/economics-influence-china-and-india-south-asia.

[79] Yun Sun, *China's Strategic Assessment of India*, WAR ON THE ROCKS (Mar. 25, 2020); Andrew Scobell, *"Cult of Defense" and "Great Power Dreams": The Influence of Strategic Culture on China's Relationship with India*, in SOUTH ASIA IN 2020: FUTURE STRATEGIC BALANCES AND ALLIANCES 342 (Michael R. Chambers ed., 2002).

[80] Dhruva Jaishankar, *India Feeling the Heat on Belt and Road*, THE INTERPRETER (Aug 21, 2017).

[81] For background on the 2017 Doklam standoff, *see Doklam Standoff: Explaining Two Months of Tensions between India and China*, INDIAN EXPRESS (Aug. 5, 2019).

[82] Oriana Skylar & Arzan Tarapore, *Countering Chinese Coercion: The Case of Doklam*, WAR ON THE ROCKS (Aug. 29, 2017).

[83] *India's Messy Democracy Impediment in Race against China*, DECCAN HERALD (Jan. 19, 2015).

thinking on the matter has evolved over the past decade, beginning with the 2008 financial crisis and culminating with the political disruptions of Donald Trump and Brexit in 2016. Under Xi, China has expressed greater confidence about the failings of democratic systems and has offered "socialism with Chinese characteristics" as a viable political and economic alternative to emerging economies.[84]

India's economic and military rise as a major democratic power would dent the credibility of China's claims and would negatively affect its ideological and political standing in the near and far abroad.

Political entrepreneurship that harvests tensions among communities, especially along religious lines, has always been a feature of Indian democracy. However, much communal polarization and ethnic chauvinism has moved online with the advent of social media platforms. The cost of exploiting social cleavages has lowered, with digital spaces offering anonymity and deniability to political outfits. Multiple actors, local and foreign, have taken advantage of the digital medium to foment communal tensions in India.

Anecdotal evidence suggests China may well be in a position to similarly take advantage of India's social fault lines. In April 2020, for instance, reports emerged that Pakistan-based actors were posing as prominent political leaders and media personalities from the Middle East and amplifying content about the ruling BJP's mistreatment of Indian Muslims and insulting of Arab Muslim women in an effort to aggravate tensions between India's Hindu and Muslim communities.[85] At least one prominent fake account, pretending to be an Omani princess, was found to be followed by the People's Republic of China's MFA spokesperson Zhao Lijian.[86] Earlier in December 2019, reports indicated that over a thousand Twitter accounts based out of Pakistan were created to spread misinformation about India's polarized protests regarding the Citizenship (Amendment) Act, 2019.[87] One hashtag, #NaziIndiaRejected, was reportedly created by an organization called the Pakistan Tehreek-e-Insaaf Volunteer Task Force,[88] whose Twitter handle Zhao also follows.[89]

There is no evidence, at the time of writing, to indicate Chinese actors amplified, endorsed, or supported the creation of fake accounts or troll farms in Pakistan. However, Zhao's following of these accounts is not an insignificant matter. As the former deputy ambassador of the People's Republic of China to Pakistan, and now deputy director of the Chinese Ministry of Foreign Affairs Information Department, Zhao has been a vocal figure on—and savvy user of—social media. His tweets have previously been flagged by analysts, including former U.S. national security adviser Susan Rice, for attempting to exploit racial cleavages in Washington, D.C.[90] "Social media," Zhao has reportedly said, "is a weapon to counter [...] negative narratives."[91] As described earlier

[84] Jamil Anderlini, *China Is Taking Its Ideological Fight Abroad*, Financial Times (Jan. 9, 2020).

[85] Regina Mihindukulasuriya, *Many Arab Handles Slamming India Are Part of "Twitter War" from Pakistan*, The Print (Apr. 24, 2020).

[86] @Preetham_Offl, Twitter (Apr. 22, 2020, 11.27 AM), *at* https://twitter.com/preetham_offl/status/1252844364113432576?s=21.

[87] Sunny Sen, *Around 1,079 Pakistani Twitter Handles Being Used to Spread Hate Speech around Citizenship Amendment Act*, Firstpost (Jan. 8, 2020). For background on the Act and protests against the legislation, *see CAA—12 Key Points to Remember*, Press Information Bureau (Dec. 12, 2019); *Citizenship Amendment Bill: India's New "Anti-Muslim" Law Explained*, BBC (Dec. 11, 2019).

[88] *Id.*

[89] @PTI_VF, Twitter (Joined July 2016), at https://twitter.com/PTI_VF.

[90] Adam Taylor, *A Chinese Diplomat Had a Fight about Race in D.C. with Susan Rice on Twitter. Then He Deleted the Tweets*, Washington Post (July 16, 2019).

[91] Ben Smith, *Meet the Chinese Diplomat Who Got Promoted for Trolling the U.S. on Twitter*, Buzzfeed News (Dec. 2, 2019).

in this chapter, he has been one of the key promoters of the theory that the COVID-19 coronavirus not only originated in the United States but was also brought to Wuhan by the U.S. military.[92] Zhao has often cross-posted TikTok videos on Twitter, bringing to bear Chinese digital content on American platforms. His following of the malicious accounts in question can at best be described as an information-gathering exercise by a diplomat, but the fact that some of these accounts were recently created or altered for the explicit purpose of sowing discord among India's Hindus and Muslims suggests the matter necessitates further inquiry.[93]

Evidence from other parts of the world suggests autocratic states are increasingly leveraging their mutual disinformation networks and campaigns. India has already been a target of such operations. In October 2019, FireEye released a report documenting Iranian attempts at disinformation, which included nearly four thousand Hindi tweets that amplified typical Iranian foreign policy positions, including pro-Palestinian messaging and anti-Saudi Arabia or anti-U.S. content.[94] A forensic analysis of these operations by an independent cybersecurity consultant revealed at least four "Indian-sounding websites" were a part of the same Iranian networks, whose content was often shared on Indian social media with politically motivated hashtags, and were even retweeted and quoted by influential Indian political and media figures.[95] Evidence collected by researchers from the German Marshall Fund of the United States indicates Beijing is similarly "piggybacking off" this global network of propaganda networks by autocratic states—a development that could enable it to similarly exploit India's social fault lines without identification or attribution.[96]

B. Leveraging Pecuniary Interests

A second and potentially costly incentive for China would be to interfere in elections in Indian states where China has significant pecuniary interests. Beijing's strategy for political interference has evolved to take advantage of complex federal-state relations in democracies. In 2018, for instance, the Australian state of Victoria signed an MoU with China formally endorsing the latter's BRI. Canberra was caught off guard by the endorsement, was not consulted about the agreement, and had not even received a copy of its text (which was only made public after pressure from Prime Minister Scott Morrison).[97] The possibility of China attempting to influence subnational political

[92] Betsy Morris & Robert McMillan, *China Pushes Viral Messages to Shape Coronavirus Narrative*, Wall Street Journal (Apr. 10, 2020).

[93] *See* Mihindukulasuriya, *supra* note 85. The fake account of the Omani princess whom Zhao Lijian followed went earlier by the handle @Pak_Fauj and has since been deleted.

[94] Aria Thacker, *An Iranian Influence Campaign Has Been Targeting Indians on Twitter*, Quartz India (Nov. 2, 2018).

[95] Pukhraj Singh, *Planet-scale Influence Operation Strikes at the Heart of Polarised Indian Polity—Part I*, Writings of Pukhraj Singh (Nov. 26, 2018), *at* https://pukhraj.me/2018/11/26/planet-scale-influence-operation-strikes-at-the-heart-of-polarised-indian-polity/.

[96] *See* Jessica Brandt & Bret Schafer, *Five Things to Know About Beijing's Disinformation Approach* (German Marshall Fund Alliance for Securing Democracy, Mar. 30, 2020), *at* https://securingdemocracy.gmfus.org/five-things-to-know-about-beijings-disinformation-approach/.

[97] Paul Karl, *Scott Morrison Rebukes Victoria for Signing Up to China's Belt and Road Initiative*, The Guardian (Nov 6, 2018).

outcomes was apparent again in the U.S. state of Iowa, where the Chinese state-run *China Daily* ran a supplement in Iowa's largest newspaper outlining how the Trump administration's trade war would damage Iowa's large and profitable soybean trade with China.[98] These evolutions in China's political interference complement its economic statecraft, which have accelerated rapidly since the launch of the BRI.

Although India is not a signatory to the BRI, China's investments in India have nonetheless risen rapidly—with Beijing having invested a conservative $8 billion over the past three years alone.[99] Several Indian states now independently seek to attract investments from Beijing. As China's economic interests in Indian states deepen, so too will the stakes of managing India's political and business elite. Soon after China blocked India's bid for NSG membership in 2016, for instance, the Chief Minister of Madhya Pradesh—a key functionary of Modi's Bharatiya Janata Party—called for economic cooperation to continue despite political tensions.[100] He had reportedly just returned from a trip to China, where he aggressively lobbied for new investments in his state and even offered new industrial parks solely for Chinese investors.[101] Before India formally voiced its opposition to the BRI in May 2017, the then Chief Minister of Andhra Pradesh lobbied for the coastal city of Visakhapatnam to become a hub along the BRI.[102] During his 2016 visit to China, Pradesh also secured a deal with a Chinese firm to mine resources in a district where his party had failed to garner votes and had lost to the opposition in the 2014 general elections.[103] Reports indicate that the decision was based on the "spur of the moment" and that plans for such an investment had not been discussed earlier.[104] The episode is reminiscent of how Beijing bankrolled infrastructure projects in the constituency of then Sri Lankan Prime Minister Mahinda Rajapaksa in an effort to gain political currency.[105]

There are other means through which Beijing could attempt to curry favor among India's local leaders. Chinese companies, for instance, have also begun sponsoring foreign junkets for India's political and administrative elite, with Huawei reportedly having paid for telecom regulators to attend a conference on 5G in China.[106] Foreign junkets have been a useful tool for China in its efforts to buy political influence elsewhere, such as in Australia[107] and with municipal representatives in Canada.[108] Although such developments in the India-China relationship are still evolving, given that Chinese investments in India are still relatively low, evidence from around the

[98] *China Warns Iowa Soybean Farmers of "A President's Folly,"* S. China Morning Post (Sept. 24, 2018).

[99] Ananth Krishnan, *Following the Money: China Inc's Growing Stake in India-China Relations*, Brookings Institution India Center 5 (Impact Series 032020-01, 2020).

[100] Sarah Watson, *India's Centre-State Divide on China* (Observer Research Foundation, July 11, 2016), *at* https://www.orfonline.org/expert-speak/indias-centre-state-divide-on-china/.

[101] *Id.*

[102] Sandeep Kumar, *Naidu Wants China to Take the Silk Route via Visakhapatnam*, The Hindu (Nov. 23, 2015).

[103] *Naidu Gets China into AP's Kadapa District in Astute Political Move*, Asianetnews (June 27, 2016).

[104] *Id.*

[105] *China's Xi Offers Fresh $295 Million Grant to Sri Lanka*, Reuters (July 22, 2018).

[106] *Don't Let Telecom Officials Go on Huawei-Sponsored Trip to China, RSS Affiliate Urges PM Modi*, Business Today (July 31, 2019).

[107] *China Telco Biggest Sponsor of MP Junkets*, SBS News (June 26, 2019).

[108] Sam Cooper, *Canadian Mayors May Have Unwittingly Been Targets of Chinese Influence Campaign*, Global News (Mar. 9, 2020).

world suggests that Beijing's attempts to buy political influence often increase in scale and intensity. Once entrenched, they provide a lever for China to influence political and electoral outcomes in India's states, either to defend narrow pecuniary interests or to navigate anti-China sentiment at the federal level through the state administrations.

The numerous languages in which Chinese social media platforms operate in India provide a crucial vector for influence operations in local elections. Reports suggest that China has actively sought in the past to infiltrate the communications of India's strategic and diplomatic establishments. In 2015, Chinese actors targeted government, scientific, educational, and diplomatic institutions in India to steal information through phishing operations.[109] Earlier in 2009, India's then National Security Adviser M.K. Narayanan revealed his office was targeted in a cyber intrusion by Chinese actors.[110] It is worth recalling that attempts to influence the French election saw hackers release dozens of real and fake emails to smear Emmanuel Macron—not to mention the storied history of the use of *kompromat* by Russia in blackmailing foreign figures.[111] Although Beijing has not employed such tactics previously in India, its influence operations are continuously evolving: should Chinese actors possess sensitive information about India's political elite, it has, through the embedding of Chinese digital platforms in vernacular content, an effective conduit to perpetrate disinformation campaigns against their targets.

C. A Full-Court Press?

Finally, China could also attempt a full-court press, Russia-style operation to undermine Indian general elections in the future. This would certainly be an extraordinary development in global politics—but as China's actions in Taiwan show, Beijing is increasingly inclined to overlook public opinion to secure its regional and global interests, some of which have been detailed in this chapter. Should a political leader with a vocal and effective "anti-China" electoral platform emerge, Beijing may well attempt to undermine his or her bid for office. Signs of discomfort are already visible in Beijing with the Modi administration. In February 2014, Narendra Modi called on Beijing to "shed its expansionist mindset" while campaigning in the state Arunachal Pradesh, a territory over which Beijing has long claimed suzerainty.[112] Later in 2016, China took issue with the Indian government permitting the Dalai Lama to visit Tawang, a city in Arunachal Pradesh. At the time, China's MFA objected to this move by claiming that India is providing "a stage for anti-China separatist forces," further warning that it would "only damage peace and stability of the border areas and bilateral relations."[113] Similarly, in the 2019 general elections, a key state leader from the BJP claimed that

[109] Neha Alawadhi, *Chinese Hackers Targeting Indian Institutions for Data on Border Disputes, Diplomatic Matters: Report*, Economic Times (Aug. 22, 2015).

[110] *Chinese Made a Bid to Hack Our Computers, Says Narayanan*, Times of India (Jan. 19, 2010).

[111] Julia Ioffe, *How State-Sponsored Blackmail Works in Russia*, The Atlantic (Jan. 11, 2017).

[112] *China Should Shed Expansionist Mindset: Modi*, The Hindu (Feb. 22, 2014).

[113] People's Republic of China, Ministry of Foreign Affairs, *Foreign Ministry Spokesperson Lu Kang's Regular Press Conference* (Oct. 29, 2016), *at* https://www.fmprc.gov.cn/mfa_eng/xwfw_665399/s2510_665401/t1411259.shtml.

China had "retreated for the first time"[114] under the leadership of Narendra Modi, a less-than-subtle reference to the Doklam standoff to which China's state-run *Global Times* took objection.[115]

There are other sources of tension in the bilateral relationship under Modi's watch, most notably on account of India's participation in the resuscitated "Quadrilateral Initiative" and for its advocacy of a new geographical construct in Asia, the "Indo-Pacific." China sees both Indian initiatives as an effort to contain its rise, and has repeatedly warned through its state media of the consequences of India's warming ties with the United States.[116] The political constituencies that the Narendra Modi government leans on to win elections are also unfavorably disposed toward China. The Rashtriya Swayamsevak Sangh, the ideological progenitor of the BJP, has remained vehemently anti-China over the course of the BJP administration. It opposed India's entry into the Regional Comprehensive Economic Partnership because it was "China-led."[117] It has also been vocal about preventing China's telecom companies from establishing a foothold into the Indian 5G market.[118] Most recently, the Modi administration introduced new economic restrictions against Beijing, mandating government scrutiny and approvals for *all* Chinese investments.[119] In this context, it is conceivable that China's influence operations in Taiwan, which were designed to undermine the electoral bid of a candidate who was inimical to Chinese interests, may well foreshadow similar campaigns in India.

VI. Conclusion: The Widening Canvas of China's Influence Operations

As its global ambitions expand, China will likely shift from issue-based influence operations and disinformation campaigns (the BRI, the COVID-19 pandemic, protests in Hong Kong SAR and Taiwan) to more systemic ones targeting electoral and political infrastructure, especially in democracies. The calculus is apparent enough: Why expend resources on propaganda to sell American states on freer trade, when they could be mobilized to unseat the federal administration that is pursuing the "trade war" with Beijing? Emerging markets, too, have witnessed a progressive consolidation of political power by federal governments—the trend has been visible in several countries, including Brazil, India, Malaysia, Indonesia, Turkey, the Philippines, and Sri Lanka. This development presents China with the opportunity to target key political figures and outfits through digital platforms, with a view to steer entire electoral outcomes. No longer can states, advanced or developing, count on Western social media platforms alone to detect and weed out online influence operations guided by

[114] Yogi Adityanath, *China Retreated for First Time under PM's Leadership*, NDTV (Apr. 6, 2019).

[115] Zhao Gancheng, *Modi Playing China Card to Win Election*, Global Times (Apr. 29, 2020).

[116] *America's Indo-Pacific Strategy Will Cost You: China to India*, Economic Times (July 2, 2018).

[117] Neelam Pandey, *RSS Affiliate Claims Modi Govt Not Keen on RCEP Trade Deal But Civil Servants Pushing It*, The Print (Oct. 15, 2019).

[118] *RSS-Affiliated Body Writes to PM Modi against Huawei's 5G Trial in India*, NDTV (Dec. 31, 2019).

[119] *One Eye on China, Modi Govt Tweaks FDI Policy to Curb "Opportunistic Takeover" of Indian Companies*, The Wire (Apr. 18, 2020).

Beijing. China's own powerful technology companies have made significant inroads into foreign markets, gradually moving up the value chain: starting out as purveyors of physical infrastructure, they are now curators of digital content. In March 2020 alone, at the height of the COVID-19 pandemic, TikTok saw 12 million Americans join the platform—a number equal to its entire subscription base in the United States till just a few months ago.[120] The average American user spent five hours on Instagram and eight hours on TikTok in the same month.[121] An extraordinary displacement of U.S. digital platforms by Chinese companies is underway on its home turf, creating ever more vectors of (and constituencies for) influence operations led by China. Just as China has relied on disinformation networks of other autocratic states, Chinese platforms popular in Western democracies could be used as slingshots for election interference by China.

For developing economies like India, the picture is even more grim. India is reliant on the continued economic growth of China for its supply chains and investments, at least for the near future. Its digital economy has been effectively propped up by Chinese technology companies selling cheap handheld devices. Economic imperatives around 5G and foreign direct investment cannot be easily dismissed, no matter how vexatious the security dilemmas of Chinese involvement in highly sensitive sectors and industries. Even as a delicate bilateral dance ensues, India will encounter aggressive and bold influence operations from across its eastern border.

This chapter offers an analytical framework to study Chinese campaigns targeting India's election infrastructure and political processes through digital channels. A few policy prescriptions to help monitor and tackle such campaigns follow:

1. *Map the dimensions and magnitude of influence operations.* Federal and state election commissions in India have limited capacity to monitor foreign interference in democratic processes. The Election Commission of India appointed a chief information security officer (CISO) in December 2017 to assess cyber threats against polling infrastructure and offer guidelines on "social media security," broadly defined.[122] The incumbent CISO is a former official of India's National Intelligence Grid.[123] Meanwhile, state election commissioners have also appointed Cybersecurity Nodal Officers (CSNOs), who report directly to the CISO. While the CISO has done a commendable job in identifying the nature of cyber threats to India's election infrastructure and communicating them to state-level officers through "advisories,"[124] the flow of information can tend to be top-down. The CISO should curate an interagency platform comprising CSNOs, intelligence officials, and law enforcement agencies across the country, that periodically evaluates the scale and intensity of influence operations, including by

[120] Daniyal Malik, *Data Shows that U.S. Consumers Are Loving the TikTok during the COVID-19 Pandemic*, Digital Information World (May 4, 2020).

[121] *Id.*

[122] Election Commission of India, *Appointment of Chief Information Security Officer (CISO) at Election Commission of India* (Dec. 27, 2017), *at* https://eci.gov.in/files/file/1841-appointment-of-chief-information-security-officer-ciso-at-election-commission-of-india/.

[123] *Dr. Kushal Pathak*, LinkedIn (May 29, 2020), *at* https://in.linkedin.com/in/kushalpathak.

[124] *See* Election Commission of India, *supra* note 9.

Chinese actors. Maintaining an information-sharing network between federal and state agencies is an important first step in tackling foreign election interference. Particularly essential is building capacity to monitor foreign influence operations in vernacular languages through platforms like TikTok, which an interagency platform would be well poised to do.

2. *Support and champion initiatives like the Paris Call for Trust and Security in Cyberspace*. The Paris Call of November 2018 seeks to enhance the capacity of state and nonstate actors "to prevent malign interference by foreign actors aimed at undermining electoral processes through malicious cyber activities."[125] India is not formally a "supporter" of this nonbinding instrument. New Delhi's championing of such multistakeholder initiatives is essential both on account of its democratic credentials and rising prominence as one of the world's largest digital economies. Instruments like the Paris Call create soft "norms" or "rules of the road" against foreign election interference that are gradually embedded into the practice of states and private technology companies.
3. *Elevate the role of Chinese platforms to the high table of bilateral dialogue*. Despite political tensions apparent in their relationship, India and China have sustained high-level contact over the years. Prime Minister Narendra Modi and President Xi Jinping have met for two "informal summits" in Wuhan (2018) and Mamallapuram (2019)—meetings that have no slated deliverables or joint statements, giving both leaders the flexibility to discuss virtually any matter relevant to bilateral ties.[126] Cybersecurity concerns posed by Chinese technology platforms, despite their ubiquitous presence in India's digital economy, do not appear to have been addressed in these discussions.[127] Huawei's potential role in providing 5G telecommunication infrastructure in India, and its attendant security implications, has acquired considerable political visibility and could likely feature as a talking point in the next informal summit. The issue of foreign election interference routed through, or facilitated by, Chinese technology platforms should also be flagged by New Delhi at this forum. The popularity of Chinese apps and devices in India is certainly a strategic asset for Beijing were it to mount an election interference campaign. However, the reputational costs for Chinese technology companies—given their stake in the Indian digital economy—associated with being conduits for influence operations are equally significant. New Delhi should raise those costs by heightening the visibility of election interference as an issue in bilateral discussions.

This chapter has argued Chinese digital influence operations in India could exploit (1) the country's existing socioeconomic fault lines; (2) federal-state tensions; and (3) the messy and chaotic nature of its general election, traditionally held over several "phases" and weeks in the summer. As India becomes more vocal in its opposition to

[125] *The Paris Call for Trust and Security in Cyberspace* (Nov. 12, 2018), *at* https://pariscall.international/en/call.

[126] Devirupa Mitra, *Explainer: Ahead of Modi-Xi Informal Summit, Key Questions Answered*, The Wire (Oct. 10, 2019).

[127] Ministry of External Affairs, Government of India, *2nd India-China Informal Summit*, *at* https://www.mea.gov.in/press-releases.htm?dtl/31938/2nd_IndiaChina_Informal_Summit.

China's global projects, such operations are likely to intensify in frequency and scale. The theaters of influence operations too may shift, blurring the line between domestic and foreign campaigns. Twitter handles of Chinese embassies and consulates in Paris and Kolkata are today vehicles for disinformation campaigns pitting China favorably against the United States.[128] As the Indian footprint in global affairs enlarges, New Delhi should be prepared to meet challenges from China to the integrity of its democratic processes not only at home but also abroad.

[128] @AmbassadeChina, Twitter (Apr. 30, 2020, 8.24 PM), at https://twitter.com/ambassadechine/status/1255873178632687622?s=21; Mark Scott, *Chinese Diplomacy Ramps Up Social Media Offensive in COVID-19 Info War*, Politico (Apr. 29, 2020).

6

A Swedish Perspective on Foreign Election Interference

Alicia Fjällhed, James Pamment[1], and Sebastian Bay

I. Introduction

Ever since the 2016 U.S. presidential elections, *foreign election interference*[2] has emerged as a topic of public concern around the world.[3] As democracies are founded on the principle of free public participation in political debate, they tolerate a wide scope of action for domestic actors to assert individual or organized[4] communicative influence during elections. But the democratic process of public deliberation is not without vulnerabilities. There is a demonstrated risk that foreign actors with malicious intent can exploit the vulnerabilities of public deliberation processes in an attempt to achieve their own political goals.[5]

The foreign election interference issue is often presented as a whole-of-society problem by both scholars and government actors (e.g., the United Kingdom, the European Union, the United States, and Sweden).[6] As such, it is best countered through an equivalent whole-of-society response. The United Kingdom early on accentuated the need for "the executive branches in the US, Canada and European countries to develop whole-of government strategies to increase election security and combat electoral interference" along with "contingency plans for ensuring resiliency and bolstering public confidence in elections"[7] as part of initiatives to "build

[1] Participation thanks to funding from the Marianne och Marcus Wallenberg Foundation.

[2] This issue may also be discussed under broad terms such as *disinformation* or *influence operations*, or as part of a strategy for *hybrid warfare* using methods such as *bots*, *trolling*, *shilling*, and *click-baits* both online and offline where political motives are but one of several incentivizing these activities.

[3] *See* Hunt Allocott & Matthew Gentzkow, *Social Media and Fake News in the 2016 Election*, 31 J. Econ Persp. 211, 211–236 (2017); W. Lance Bennett & Steven Livingston, *The Disinformation Order: Disruptive Communication and the Decline of Democratic Institutions*, 33 Euro. J. Comm. 122, 122–139 (2018); *see also* Jens David Ohlin's contribution to this volume (chapter 11).

[4] Organized influence may occur via political parties, activist groups, or commercial lobbying.

[5] Howard Nothhaft et al., *Information Influence in Western Democracies: A Model of Systemic Vulnerabilities*, in Countering Online Propaganda and Extremism: The Dark Side of Digital Diplomacy 18–34 (C. Bjola & J. Pamment eds., 2018).

[6] *See* Daniel Fried & Alina Polyakova, *Democratic Defense Against Disinformation* (Atlantic Council Eurasia Center, Mar. 5, 2018), *at* https://www.atlanticcouncil.org/in-depth-research-reports/report/democratic-defense-against-disinformation/; Daniel Fried & Alina Polyakova, *Democratic Defense Against Disinformation 2.0* (Atlantic Council Eurasia Center, June 13, 2019), *at* https://www.atlanticcouncil.org/in-depth-research-reports/report/democratic-defense-against-disinformation-2-0/.

[7] U.K. House of Commons Digital, Culture, Media and Sport Committee, *Disinformation and "Fake News": Interim Report* 74 (July 24, 2018), *at* https://publications.parliament.uk/pa/cm201719/cmselect/cmcumeds/363/363.pdf.

Alicia Fjällhed, James Pamment, and Sebastian Bay, *A Swedish Perspective on Foreign Election Interference* In: *Defending Democracies*. Edited by Duncan B. Hollis and Jens David Ohlin, Oxford University Press (2021). DOI: 10.1093/oso/9780197556979.003.0007

resilience against misinformation and disinformation into our democratic system."[8] The European Union's "coordinated union response" is founded on (1) the Union's own capability to detect, analyze, and expose disinformation and coordinate a response; (2) the need for platform transparency (including an assessment of the threat and an action plan to deal with it); and (3) "raising awareness and improving societal resilience."[9] Widespread international consensus on the importance of societal or public resilience is also illustrated in anthological reports—such as the European Commission's European Political Strategy Centre's *Election Interference in the Digital Age: Building Resilience to Cyber-Enabled Threats*.[10] The United States has similarly pushed for public resilience in the #Protect2020 initiative ahead of its 2020 elections.[11]

This chapter focuses on the Swedish approach for safeguarding electoral processes, using the experience from its 2018 elections as a case study. The Swedish approach was based on an evaluation of previous threats assessed to have targeted the (1) integrity of the election process; (2) will and ability of the population to vote; (3) political preferences of voters; and (4) political leadership.[12] Based on this general assessment, Swedish government authorities outlined a response focusing on (1) identifying activities; (2) coordination and cooperation among authorities and agencies; (3) wide information sharing among affected stakeholders; and (4) raising awareness about the potential threat and our own vulnerabilities.[13]

As this volume demonstrates, there are wide-ranging proposals for how to address the issue of foreign election interference—from suggestions for new legal frameworks[14] and increased social media platform transparency[15] to stressing the importance of inherited national characteristics in the media, political, and economic landscape.[16] In this context, Sweden serves as a particularly interesting example due to the measures it took ahead of the 2018 election, especially its strategy of bottom-up initiatives that emphasize building societal resilience rather than a top-down government regulatory approach. Other countries have since adopted methods based on these Swedish guiding principles.[17] This chapter's central claim, therefore, is

[8] *Id.* at 3.

[9] Joint Communication to the European Parliament, the European Council, the Council, the European Economic and Social Committee and the Committee of the Regions, *Action Plan against Disinformation*, 5 JOIN 36 (May 12, 2018) (final).

[10] ELECTION INTERFERENCE IN THE DIGITAL AGE: BUILDING RESILIENCE TO CYBER-ENABLED THREATS 14 (E.P.S. Centre ed., 2018).

[11] Cybersecurity & Infrastructure Security Agency (CISA), *#Protect2020*, *at* https://www.cisa.gov/protect2020.

[12] Mikael Tofvesson, *Swedish Election—A Preliminary Assessment*, in ELECTION INTERFERENCE IN THE DIGITAL AGE, *supra* note 10, at 14.

[13] *Id.*

[14] *See* Jill Goldenziel & Manal Cheema, *The New Fighting Words?: How U.S. Law Hampers the Fight Against Information Warfare*, 22 U. PA. J. CONST. L. 81 (2019); Duncan Hollis, *Why States Need an International Law for Information Operations*, 11 LEWIS & CLARK L. REV. 1023–1062 (2007).

[15] Chapter 10, this volume, at 226.

[16] Edda Humprecht, Frank Esser, & Peter van Aelst, *Resilience to Online Disinformation: A Framework for Cross-National Comparative Research*, INT'L J. PRESS/POLITICS (Jan. 24, 2020).

[17] The Swedish handbook, which was originally written ahead of the 2018 elections, has since been translated into English and Finnish, generating further guidance and training in Estonia and Australia, among others. *See* Swedish Civil Contingencies Agency, *Countering Information Influence Activities: A handbook for communicators* (Mar. 2019), *at* https://rib.msb.se/filer/pdf/28698.pdf [hereinafter Swedish handbook]. The Swedish handbook inspired the UK RESIST toolkit, which today has been translated into Spanish and

straightforward: other actors should develop their own strategic work to counter foreign election interference cognizant of the lessons that can be drawn from Sweden's experiences of emphasizing societal resilience. By exploring the characteristics of Swedish society and the implications of Swedish efforts made prior to the 2018 general election, we present suggestions for how these insights might help other state and nonstate actors within the international community develop similar countering strategies for foreign election interference, while also addressing the dilemmas facing such an approach.

Our chapter is based on real-time continuous monitoring of the Swedish election, supported by a review of official government reports and interviews with key officials involved in the 2018 election protection efforts. Furthermore, the authors were involved in protecting that election.[18]

Section II begins by introducing the Swedish perspective on foreign election interference through the concept of *information influence*, while section III explores the concept of resilience. Section IV presents the key activities and preparatory work undertaken in Sweden before the election. Finally, section V focuses on the election itself and events that could be understood as examples of election interference. We conclude by discussing lessons learned and the challenges facing government authorities seeking to employ similar strategies in the future to counter foreign election interference in Sweden or abroad.

II. The Threat

Foreign election interference has been discussed under various headings in Sweden, including—as in many other countries—a wide debate about *fake news* or *disinformation*, in parallel with more niched discussions in relation to Swedish defense through specific concepts of *total defense*, *hybrid warfare*, *hybrid threats*, and *psychological warfare*. Zooming in on the context of *election interference*, the Swedish Civil Contingencies Agency's (MSB's)[19] terms *influence campaign* (in Swedish: *påverkanskampanj*) and *information influence* (in Swedish: *informationspåverkan*) are central to this particular debate. MSB defines "information influence" as activities that:

> involve potentially harmful forms of communication orchestrated by foreign state actors or their representatives. They constitute deliberate interference in a country's internal affairs to create a climate of distrust between a state and its citizens. Information influence activities are used to further the interests of a foreign power

Mandarin and is used in capacity-building internationally. U.K. Government Communication Service, *RESIST: Counter-disinformation toolkit* (2019), *at* https://gcs.civilservice.gov.uk/wp-content/uploads/2019/03/RESIST_Toolkit.pdf. Both handbooks also served as the basis for the EUvsDisinfo's forthcoming handbook on the same matter.

[18] James Pamment was lead author for the Swedish Civil Contingencies Agency Handbook and developed the associated training program; Alicia Fjällhed was part of this same research group; Sebastian Bay was the project manager for the MSB election protection project.

[19] MSB is the abbreviation for the agency's Swedish name *Myndigheten för Samhällsskydd och Beredskap*.

> through the exploitation of perceived vulnerabilities in society. [...] Information influence activities may be deployed separately or carried out as part of a larger influence campaign, drawing on a broad spectrum of techniques.[20]

As with many other concepts in this public debate, the term "information influence" has been described using different definitions throughout the years. Definitions often reference four key aspects: (1) the *means* as founded on communicative influence techniques; (2) the *method* focusing on the exploitation of vulnerabilities in democratic systems; (3) the *consequence* as disrupting the public debate; and (4) the *actor* as foreign (however potentially utilizing domestic proxies) with an *intent* ultimately driven by self-serving interest.[21] To support public debate in this area, in 2017 MSB commissioned a report from Lund University into current understandings of these issues with a focus on strengthening societal resilience against information influence activities.[22] In the following sections, we give a more in-depth presentation of these four key aspects and how they relate to the Swedish context; that is, the Swedish perspective on the problem of foreign election interference.

First, information influence mimics the *communicative tools* otherwise used for legitimate communicative influence in everyday settings, for example, public relations, marketing, public diplomacy, opinion journalism, and lobbying. The difference is that information influence activities involve "the systematic use of deceptive techniques to undermine democracy."[23] For example, one might create a bot for legitimate communicative purposes such as automatized sports journalism that reports on the latest scores, or private companies creating chatbots for customer services. But information influence actors use bots and other mechanisms to skew impressions of public debate with the intent to mislead the public, journalists, and those political actors influenced by the perceived public interest. The second and third criteria are closely connected, as these activities seem to be most effective in terms of producing the desired *consequences* through the *method* of exploiting vulnerabilities in the system it seeks to manipulate. Here, Western societies with a democratic system for governance share certain vulnerabilities inherent in the system that may be grouped into various common contexts, for example, *media*, *public opinion*, or *cognitive* vulnerabilities.[24] But democracies also face context-specific challenges such as "social or class tensions, inequality, corruption, security issues, or other problems central to social life," which hostile actors exploit as entry points for their information influence activities.[25] Information influence actors, per definition, seek to influence the public debate for various self-serving purposes (e.g., commercial, criminal, personal, or military purposes)[26] that ultimately create "a climate of distrust between a state and its citizens."[27]

[20] Swedish handbook, *supra* note 17, at 11.

[21] *Id.*

[22] James Pamment et al., *Swedish Civil Contingencies Agency, Countering Information Influence Activities: The State of the Art* (July 1, 2018), *at* https://www.msb.se/RibData/Filer/pdf/28697.pdf.

[23] Swedish handbook, *supra* note 17, at 12.

[24] *Id.*

[25] *Id.*

[26] Pamment et al., *supra* note 22.

[27] Swedish handbook, *supra* note 17, at 11.

Fourth, several foreign actors have been described as potential agents of information influence in Sweden. The most commonly mentioned is Russia;[28] described by several public authorities as Sweden's main military threat[29] and as having engaged in an ongoing influence campaign targeting the Swedish public starting well before the 2018 general election.[30] As the director of the Swedish Security Service (SÄPO) described the situation prior to the 2018 election: "It is very important for us to follow this and we are not shy in Sweden—we say that the biggest threat to our security in that perspective is Russia."[31] The reason behind Russian efforts are plenty, including (1) Sweden's geostrategic position; (2) the country being a symbol for the liberal values and Western society that Russia seeks to combat; (3) Sweden being an "enhanced partner" of NATO since 2014; and (4) Sweden's proactive stance toward Russia after the annexation of Crimea in 2014 that led both to Swedish defense rearmament and Sweden becoming one of the EU members most committed to Russian sanctions.[32] Among Russian interference efforts highlighted through the years, Swedish authorities and media cite Russian violations of Swedish airspace, increased Russian military activity on the Baltic Sea, suspected marine incursions, and increased foreign espionage (by Russia and other countries) in Sweden. Articles in the Swedish version of Sputnik (2015–2016) and a continued focus on Sweden in other versions of Russian

[28] While most attention during the 2018 election focused on Russian foreign influence, we recognize that since then the focus has shifted slightly to also include the threat of Chinese influence, which Swedish authorities and researchers have described as particularly aggressive in Sweden. For example, the Chinese embassy in Stockholm is accused of issuing threats against ministers, media houses, and journalists to such an extent that it prompted several political parties to demand that the Swedish government expel the Chinese ambassador. The Swedish Media Publishers Association has also called upon the Swedish government and the European Union to condemn Chinese attempts to influence the freedom of the press in Sweden. For this chapter, however, we have limited our research and analysis to the 2016–2019 period and the 2018 elections. Thus, we have largely excluded recent discussions about Chinese influence activities. For a discussion of China's shifting approach to influence operations, *see* chapter 4 of this volume.

[29] For example, the minister of defense (Peter Hultqvist) in 2016 described the issue of a "systematic diffusion of lies about Sweden's collaboration with NATO." *Peter Hultqvist: Seriously Spreading Myths about NATO Cooperation*, DAGENS NYHETER (Jan. 10, 2016). Both the minister of defense and the commander in chief (Michael Bydén) in an opinion piece from 2017 addressed the risk of influence and information operations in connection to a major military exercise. *See* PETER HULTQVIST & MICAEL BYDÉN, *DN Debatt. "Risk för Desinformation om Militärövningen Aurora,"* DAGENS NYHETER (May 15, 2017).

[30] For example, SÄPO wrote in their annual report from 2016 about unwarranted influence (in Swedish: *otillåten påverkan*) and that the agency aims to prevent crimes like illegal influence, hate crimes, and other ways in which "individuals through force, threat and harassment want to influence the foundational functions of democracy" by attempting to "influence or hinder the work of politicians, public representatives or journalists." *See* SÄKERHETSPOLISEN 2016 28 (2016), *at* https://www.sakerhetspolisen.se/download/18.1beef5fc14cb83963e73914/1489594358903/Arsbok-2016.pdf.

[31] Gordon Corera, *Swedish Security Chief Warning on Fake News*, BBC NEWS (Jan. 4, 2018).

[32] This is accentuated in academic articles, news articles, reports by various Swedish government authorities, *see, e.g.*, Greg Simons, Andrey Manoylo, & Philipp Trunov, *Sweden and the NATO Debate: Views from Sweden and Russia*, 5 GLOBAL AFF. 335–345 (2019); Geir Hågen Karlsen, *Divide and Rule: Ten Lessons about Russian Political Influence Activities in Europe*, 5 PALGRAVE COMMUNICATIONS 19 (2019); Peter Walker, *Sweden Searches for Suspected Russian Submarine Off Stockholm*, THE GUARDIAN (Oct. 19, 2014); *Wallström Wants "Stricter" Sanctions against Russia*, RADIO SWEDEN (Jan. 25, 2015), at https://sverigesradio.se/sida/artikel.aspx?programid=2054&artikel=6076681; Ingemo Lindroos, *Säpo varnar för rysk påverkan i Sverige*, YLE (2016), *at* https://svenska.yle.fi/artikel/2016/03/17/sapo-varnar-rysk-paverkan-i-sverige; *see also* the debate article by Peter Hultqvist and Mikael Bydén, *supra* note 29.

state-owned media may also be seen as part of a larger Russian campaign to influence public perceptions and attitudes inside and outside of Sweden.[33]

While foreign election interference (as well as information influence) focuses on *foreign* actors' interference in Sweden, it is important to also note a continuous debate about potential domestic Swedish proxies used by foreign actors to achieve their goals. To study the role of foreign influence campaigns during the Swedish national election in 2018, MSB commissioned a report from the Institute for Strategic Dialogue.[34] The authors mapped antagonistic narratives that identified both foreign and domestic actors. However, the report received critique for singling out the latter category as this situation challenges efforts to focus on foreign election interference and information influence by *foreign* actors. This example illustrates one of the most challenging dilemmas for countering foreign election interference. Due to domestic actors' rights to participate in political debate, foreign actors seek influence through domestic proxies—thus domestic actors could serve as a tool in a wider campaign to achieve foreign election interference. This, however, does not mean that all domestic groups promoting messages that overlap with that of a foreign power are a case of foreign interference. The problem is that of attribution—whether authorities are able to conclude that domestic actors are supported or perhaps even in the service of a foreign power with malicious intent.

Beyond these four criteria, to understand the threat of foreign election interference, one also needs to understand the political landscape influencing public debate in Sweden and how the political image of Sweden is being used in political debates abroad. Ever since the 2015 European migration crisis, a range of countries (including Sweden) have seen issues related to migration policy as one of the most important shaping the political public conversation. In this context, Sweden has been described by domestic authorities as the target of international influence activities. While these are not necessarily coordinated by a foreign state actor, there is a coherent trend where Sweden is used as a battering ram in political debates.[35] As one of the European countries that received the most asylum seekers per capita, international attention has turned to Sweden for arguments both for and against more progressive migration policy in other countries. As a result, politicians, the media, and foreign publics have spread unnuanced and sometimes false statements about Sweden as support for their pro- or anti-migration debates. An international study from the Swedish Institute described the international debate about Sweden during the migration crisis.[36] It found both widespread reporting of how Sweden managed the large intake, and political actors publishing statements on social media "describing Sweden as a country with

[33] NATO Stratcom Center of Excellence, *Disinformation in Sweden*, *at* https://www.stratcomcoe.org/hybrid-threats-disinformation-sweden.

[34] Chloe Colliver et al., *Smearing Sweden: International Influence Campaigns in the 2018 Swedish Election* (Institute for Strategic Dialogue, Oct. 2018), *at* https://www.isdglobal.org/wp-content/uploads/2018/11/Smearing-Sweden.pdf.

[35] James Pamment, Alexandra Olofsson, & Rachel Hjorth-Jensen, *The Response of Swedish and Norwegian Public Diplomacy & Nation Branding Actors to the Refugee Crisis*, 21 J. Comm. Mgmt. 326–341 (2017).

[36] Svenska Institutet, *Bilden av Sverige efter flyktingkrisen—En studie i sju europeiska länder* (2017), *at* https://si.se/app/uploads/2017/08/svenska-institutet-bilden-av-sverige-efter-flyktingkrisen.pdf (reviewing the image of Sweden in seven European countries (Denmark, Norway, Poland, the United Kingdom, Turkey, Germany, and Hungary) after the migration crisis).

substantial problems with violence and collapsing welfare due to what is described as an all too excessive asylum provision and deficient migration policies."[37] The report concludes that these narratives seem to have been spread within closed groups, while later reports from the Swedish Institute have argued that these narratives do not seem to have had a severe effect on the overall image of Sweden.[38]

This section has discussed the key aspects influencing the Swedish understanding of the *problem*. We continue our analysis by taking a closer look at the proposed Swedish *solution* of building public resilience ahead of the 2018 election.

III. Resilience

MSB covered four key aspects of information influence prior to the election by (a) commissioning independent research, guidance, and training into communicative influence techniques used in recent foreign influence campaigns adapted to the Swedish bureaucratic system; (b) efforts to better understand the methods and consequences of disrupting public debate; (c) studies of the foreign actors and domestic proxies actors likely to be involved in these activities; (d) and an understanding of recurring vulnerabilities in Swedish political debates that could be exploited as attack vectors during the election. This information was published independently and used by MSB to support a public awareness campaign that relied on the mainstream press to amplify core themes—that is, all activities described in this chapter can be understood as expressions of efforts aiming to build Swedish resilience.

While *resilience* has emerged as a cornerstone of suggested counteractions to foreign election interference, scholarly studies on the matter remain scarce. Among the few papers addressing the issue, Humprecht, Esser, and van Aelst recently described resilience in relation to the character of nations' infrastructure for public mediated communication (either through traditional or social media).[39] Resting on Hall and Lamont's understanding of resilience as "the capacity of groups of people bound together in a [. . .] community or nation to sustain and advance their well-being in the face of challenges to it,"[40] the authors present a set of factors they suggest influence societal resilience. Among these, the authors suggest that (1) *political* factors, such as the "polarisation of society" and "populist communication," (2) *media* factors, such as "low trust in news," "weak public service media," and "more fragmented, less overlapping audiences," and (3) *economic* factors, such as a "large ad market size" and "high social media use" all contribute to limited societal resilience.[41] Based on these measurements, the authors then measure and compare resilience in different countries. Sweden is ranked as neither high (like Finland, Denmark, and the Netherlands) nor low (like Italy, Greece, and the United States) in societal resilience.[42]

[37] *Id.*

[38] *Id; see also* Svenska Institutet, *Sverige i ett nytt ljus—Svenska institutet sammanfattar bilden av Sverige 2015–2017* (2018), *at* https://si.se/app/uploads/2018/06/si_sverige_i_ett_nytt_ljus_2018_1.pdf.

[39] Humprecht et al., *supra* note 16.

[40] Peter Hall & Michele Lamont, *Introduction*, in Social Resilience in the Neoliberal Era 2, 1–34 (Peter Hall & Michele Lamont eds., 2013).

[41] Humprecht et al., *supra* note 16.

[42] *Id.*

Humprecht, Esser, and van Aelst's factors are not necessarily, however, clearly established signs of resilience. From a critical standpoint, there are a few concerns to be considered. First, a certain level of "polarization" could be read as a sign of broadly accepted freedoms of opinion and expression in that particular national setting. Second, low trust in news could be a sign of a healthy level of source criticism. And finally, high social media use could be a sign of a higher national degree of *media and information literacy*, which is often described as a key for building (not limiting) resilience against disinformation.[43]

Among other studies on resilience, we welcome suggestions that societal resilience could also be built by focusing on microstructures of individual resilience and how they build the overall system, rather than the other way around.[44] Filipec, for example, presents an *organic approach* to public resilience as built on "the mental capacity and ability of citizens to recognize and work more efficiently with manipulative information."[45] Similarly, Goh and Soon argue "that a multistakeholder approach is more effective and suitable in fighting political deceit than is a top-down government-centric one" due to (1) low trust in institutions, (2) psychological biases, and (3) the need to partner with nonstate actors to address the threat.[46] In this way, we see scholars move from an analysis of how resilience could be measured in terms of societal structures (as in Hall and Lamont) to how those in charge of the nations' strategy to manage the threat should focus their efforts to engage citizens and key stakeholders in a bottom-up, co-constructive process of building structural systems of societal resilience.

For our part, we believe that resilience should be seen as something as complex as society itself—built on both the resilience of individuals and key stakeholders in society which, in turn, amounts to a whole-of-society-response for societal resilience. Achieving such societal resilience, however, is not an easy task. As we will show in the next section, it required the Swedish government to engage in various activities focused on achieving this aim. We believe that Sweden provides an example of how resilience can serve as the core of a national strategy to manage foreign election interference.

[43] Media and information literacy has been accentuated by the European Union and other government authorities such as the United Kingdom as entailing the need for the public to not only be a critical reader of information but also a skilled information researcher that understands the workings of the old and new media landscape to gain the communicative competence required for public participants in the political debate today. Moreover, as stated in Article 19 of the Universal Declaration of Human Rights, "[e]veryone has the right to freedom of opinion and expression; this right includes freedom to hold opinions without the interference and to seek, receive and impart information and ideas through any media regardless the frontiers." Universal Declaration of Human Rights (adopted Dec. 10, 1948) UNGA Res. 217 A(III), art. 19. A UNESCO publication states that media and information literacy "equips citizens with competencies needed to seek and enjoy the full benefits of this human right." Carolyn Wilson et al., *Media and Information Literacy Curriculum for Teachers* 16 (UNESCO, 2011).

[44] *See* Humprecht et al., *supra* note 16; Hall & Lamont, *supra* note 40.

[45] Ondřej Filipec, *Towards a Disinformation Resilient Society: The Experience of the Czech Republic*, 11 Cosmopolitan Civil Societies: An Interdisciplinary Journal 2 (2019).

[46] Shawn Goh & Carol Soon, *Governing the Information Ecosystem: Southeast Asia's Fight Against Political Deceit*, 21 Public Integrity 523 (2019).

IV. Preparations

Preparations to protect the 2018 Swedish elections started in the immediate aftermath of revelations of Russian interference into the 2016 U.S. presidential elections. Given the deteriorating security situation in the Baltic region, the Swedish government launched several efforts to protect society against cyberattacks and disinformation. In 2015, the Swedish government underscored the need to strengthen the ability of government agencies to identify and counter influence campaigns.[47] In 2017, the government noted that these efforts were not enough, and further efforts were invited.[48] Because of how the Swedish government system is structured, with independent agencies (and a focus on crisis coordination, rather than government led crisis management), the efforts undertaken to protect the election were largely initiated because of independent agency action, rather than government-issued orders. In many other countries, it is common for an individual minister to have the power to intervene directly in an agency's day-to-day operations. This possibility does not exist in Sweden because of a constitutional prohibition of "ministerial rule," and Swedish government ministries have no legal authority to intervene in an agency's decisions in specific agency matters. This emphasizes the importance of signaling from the government: for example, in March 2017, the Swedish prime minister detailed the threat and the plan for countering foreign election interference in an opinion piece titled *How we will protect the election from foreign state influence*.[49] Here, the prime minister described the international trend with examples from the U.S. presidential election (as well as attempts to interfere in German and French elections), noting that several actors had publicly accused Russia. Based on this development, the prime minister assessed that there was no reason to assume that Swedish elections would not be at risk, especially given recent "clear early signs of attempts to influence, for example, our security policy."[50] The prime minister argued that Sweden needed to be alert and act forcefully against attempts by foreign governments to interfere in Swedish elections, outlining a broad plan for how Sweden would address the issue proactively through a variety of activities:

1. efforts by various government agencies (the Swedish Armed Forces, the Swedish Government Offices, MSB, and the Swedish Media Council);
2. targeted efforts to raise public resilience before the elections (i.e., by commissioning MSB to create information material);
3. efforts to inform affected stakeholders about the threat (such as SÄPO informing political parties and MSB inviting representatives from the traditional and social media platforms to discuss information and cyber security issues); and
4. the prime minister inviting the party leaders to a briefing in an attempt to create a common understanding of the threat and the appropriate counterinitiatives.

[47] Prop. (2014/15:109) Försvarspolitisk inriktning—Sveriges försvar 2016–2020.
[48] Stefan Löfven, Prime Minister, *Så ska vi skydda valrörelsen från andra staters påverkan* (Mar. 20, 2017).
[49] *Id.*
[50] *Id.*

While the Swedish government took no collective government decisions specifically for the protection of the 2018 election against foreign interference, the policy speeches by the prime minister—and other ministers—focused the responsible agencies and provided them with political support and indirect guidance that likely resulted in agencies, county administrative boards, and municipalities prioritizing the issue. The political cover was exemplified in early 2018 when the prime minister reiterated that there was a clear risk for foreign interference in the elections and issued a stern warning: "To those of you who are considering influencing our elections: Stay away! We will not hesitate to expose you! [. . .] We will defend our democracy and freedom of speech with all available means at our disposal."[51] Beyond speeches, the government also took a number of decisions in the run-up to the 2018 elections that strengthened institutional resilience. In the following section, we take a closer look at initiatives taken by MSB, SÄPO,[52] the Swedish Police, the Swedish Election Authority,[53] and the Swedish Defence Research Agency (FOI).[54]

A. The Swedish Civil Contingencies Agency

When the Cold War Agency for Psychological Defence was abolished in 2008, MSB retained a number of its tasks and functions, such as research, media preparedness, crisis communication, analysis, and coordination.[55] Today, MSB is responsible for helping society prepare for major incidents, crises, and the consequences of war, supporting other agencies with coordination support, emergency resources, education, and training.[56] When the Swedish Parliament enacted the defense appropriation bill in 2015, it decided that all relevant government agencies should have a basic capacity for psychological defense within their area of responsibility.[57] MSB was tasked in the annual appropriation directive for 2016 to develop a capacity to identify and counter information influence activities, as well as to support other agencies through knowledge-building and coordination activities.[58]

After the 2016 U.S. presidential election, the U.S. Intelligence Community assessed that "[. . .] Moscow will apply lessons learned from its Putin-ordered campaign aimed at the US presidential election to future influence efforts worldwide, including against US allies and their election processes."[59] Based on this assessment as well as other internal and external information, MSB's Global Monitoring and Analysis Section decided to launch a project in February 2017 to support the protection of the 2018

[51] Stefan Löfven, Prime Minister, *Sveriges säkerhet i en ny värld* (Jan. 14, 2018).

[52] SÄPO being the abbreviation for the agency's Swedish name, *Säkerhetspolisen*.

[53] *Valmyndigheten* in Swedish.

[54] FOI is the abbreviation for the agency's Swedish name, *Totalförsvarsförsvarets forskningsinstitut*.

[55] Prop. (2014/15:109) Försvarspolitisk inriktning—Sveriges försvar 2016–2020.

[56] Förordning (2008:1002) med instruktion för Myndigheten för samhällsskydd och beredskap.

[57] Prop (2014: 15:109) Försvarspolitisk inriktning—Sveriges försvar 2016–2020.

[58] *See* Justitiedepartementet, Regleringsbrev för budgetåret 2016 avseende Myndigheten för samhällsskydd och beredskap, Ju2016 / 07888 / SSK (Nov. 3, 2018).

[59] U.S. National Intelligence Council, *Intelligence Community Assessment (ICA): Assessing Russian Activities and Intentions in Recent US Elections* (Jan. 6, 2017), *at* https://www.dni.gov/files/documents/ICA_2017_01.pdf.

election against foreign information influence activities. The project aimed to produce a situational assessment, support other relevant agencies, and develop tools and methods to identify and counter information influence activities aimed at the 2018 election. MSB shared the resulting national situational assessment with all the relevant national actors. Based on its contents, MSB also undertook several efforts to support the protection of the 2018 election, focused primarily on (1) *collecting and assessing information*; (2) *informing and educating*; and (3) *coordinating and providing operational support*.[60]

Beyond baseline *information collection and assessment*, MSB distributed guidance to all the relevant agencies with instructions for what information should be reported to MSB to enhance the interagency ability to develop a shared situational assessment for the election. In order to strengthen the ability of society to identify and analyze information influence activities, MSB commissioned FOI to assess automated behavior on social media, as well as to track and analyze online discussions about the 2018 elections.[61] MSB (as previously mentioned) also commissioned the Department of Strategic Communication at Lund University to develop counter influence guidance and training and the London School of Economics' Institute for Strategic Dialogue to investigate—and to provide an external perspective on—foreign attempts to influence the 2018 Swedish elections online.[62]

A significant proportion of the MSB work was spent *informing and educating* municipalities, regions, and public authorities to raise awareness about the increased need to protect the elections. In association with the Swedish Election Authority and the Swedish Association of Local Authorities and Regions, MSB informed most municipalities about the need for a comprehensive security analysis for the upcoming election.[63] MSB conducted high-level dialogues with Swedish media and the major social media platforms about the need to strengthen their resilience against information influence activities.[64] In cooperation with the Swedish Election Authority, MSB conducted training for journalists and media houses in order to strengthen their ability to identify information influence activities, as well as to build resilience against disinformation.[65] In cooperation with the Swedish Election Authority, the county administrative board in Västra Götaland, and 4C Strategies, MSB also undertook a joint project to develop methods, guidelines, and educational material for the election administration with a focus on antagonistic threats and information influence activities.[66]

[60] MSB, *Årsredovisning 2017* (2017); MSB, *Årsredovisning 2018* (2018), MSB, *Informationspåverkan EU-valet* (2018), *at* https://www.msb.se/sv/amnesomraden/msbs-arbete-vid-olyckor-kriser-och-krig/psykologiskt-forsvar/om-msbs-arbete-med-informationspaverkan/informationspaverkan-eu-valet/.

[61] *See* Johan Fernquist et al., Swedish Civil Contingencies Agency, *Automatiserade konton En studie av botar på Twitter i samband med det svenska riksdagsvalet* (Dec. 2018), *at* https://rib.msb.se/filer/pdf/28765.pdf; *see also* Johan Fernquist et al., Swedish Civil Contingencies Agency, *Digitala diskussioner om genomförandet av riksdagsvalet* (Dec. 2018), *at* https://rib.msb.se/filer/pdf/28764.pdf.

[62] Colliver et al., *supra* note 34.

[63] Michael Birnbaum, *Sweden Is Taking on Russian Meddling Ahead of Fall Elections. The White House Might Take Note*, WASHINGTON POST (Feb. 22, 2018).

[64] Gunno Ivansson, *MSB Ger Ut Handbok I Att Möta Påverkan*, TJUGOFYRA7 (June 18, 2018).

[65] Valmyndigheten, *Erfarenheter FråN Valen 2018* (2018), *at* https://www.val.se/download/18.3acea2511672bd8769229f0/1550219505460/Erfarenheter-valen-2018.pdf.

[66] MALIN BJÖRKLUND & 4C STRATEGIES, ETT ROBUST VAL UR ETT KOMMUNPERSPEKTIV: EN STUDIE INFÖR VALET 2018 (2018).

During the spring of 2018, MSB set up both a national *coordination* forum with all the relevant government actors, as well as a national *operational* coordination forum with SÄPO, the Swedish Police, the Swedish Election Authority, the Swedish county administrative boards, and the Swedish Tax Agency. MSB also provided funds from the national crisis preparedness fund to strengthen the technical infrastructure of the election administration. In early 2018, MSB decided to organize its election protection efforts as a special task force that enabled the agency to increase its capacity to handle any upcoming threats against the conduct of the 2018 elections. This decision was also taken ahead of the 2019 EU elections.[67]

One of the main needs identified by MSB in its national situational assessment was a desire by strategic communicators working in public sector positions to get more training and support to identify and respond to information influence activities. MSB commissioned Lund University to research and support MSB with the development of "a manual describing the principles and methods of identifying, understanding, and countering information influence activities [. . .] directed primarily toward communicators working in public administration."[68] The research, *Countering Information Influence Activities: The State of the Art*, was completed in December 2017, and the first version of the handbook, *Countering information influence activities: A handbook for communicators*, was launched in June 2018, a few months before the election. MSB and Lund University then conducted targeted training sessions based on the handbook in Sweden and abroad. In December 2018, government officials from relevant ministries in Finland and Sweden took part in a joint exercise that, based on the Swedish handbook and other material, aimed to improve the ability of government officials to identify and respond to disinformation and information influence activities.[69] Finland later adopted the same handbook prior to their 2019 elections, thereby strengthening Swedish-Finnish defense cooperation in the area of countering information influence.[70]

Also in 2018, MSB distributed a public information brochure called *If War or Crisis Comes* to 4.8 million households in Sweden. The purpose of the information was to help the Swedish population better prepare for serious incidents, extreme weather, IT attacks, or military conflicts. One part of the brochure informed the citizens that "[s]tates and organisations are already using misleading information in order to try and influence our values and how we act. The aim may be to reduce our resilience and willingness to defend ourselves."[71] The brochure then provided a few best practices for

[67] MSB, *Årsredovisning 2017* (2017); MSB, *Årsredovisning 2018* (2018), MSB, *Informationspåverkan EU-valet* (2018), *at* https://www.msb.se/sv/amnesomraden/msbs-arbete-vid-olyckor-kriser-och-krig/psykologiskt-forsvar/om-msbs-arbete-med-informationspaverkan/informationspaverkan-eu-valet/.

[68] Myndigheten för samhällsskydd och beredskap & Lunds universitet, Överenskommelse om projekt: Kunskapsöversikt (2017) (on file with MSB).

[69] Press Release, Government Offices of Sweden, *Cooperation to Increase Awareness of Information Influence Activities* (Dec. 3, 2018) (on file with Government Offices of Sweden); *see also* Press Release, Government Communications Department, *Preparedness and Encounter of Information Influence as the Theme of the Joint Exercise in Finland and Sweden* (Aug. 11, 2019) (on file with Valtioneuvosto).

[70] Opas viestijöille, Finnish Prime Minister's Office, Informaatiovaikuttamiseen vastaaminen, *at* http://julkaisut.valtioneuvosto.fi/handle/10024/161512.

[71] MSB, *If War or Crisis Comes*, *at* https://www.dinsakerhet.se/siteassets/dinsakerhet.se/broschyren-om-krisen-eller-kriget-kommer/om-krisen-eller-kriget-kommer---engelska.pdf.

protection against false information and hostile propaganda, such as not believing or spreading rumors, and is described in interviews as another product aiming to build public awareness and consequentially resilience before the election.

B. The Swedish Security Service and the Swedish Police

SÄPO is tasked to prevent and detect offenses against national security, fight terrorism and to protect the central government in order to help protect democracy and uphold national security. Therefore, the efforts to protect the 2018 election were one of its most prioritized tasks in 2018, initiating its election protection efforts in early 2017. The agency assessed that it was probable that foreign powers might conduct influence campaigns against the political process but assessed that it was unlikely that foreign powers would target the election infrastructure itself. Given historical experiences of extremist organizations attempting to influence the election process, SÄPO had to work on more than just preventing foreign powers from influencing the Swedish election. Among other things, SÄPO supported the government, relevant agencies, and all the political parties with preventive measures taken to protect their security-sensitive activities against espionage, sabotage, terrorism offenses, and other crimes that might threaten their operation. SÄPO also focused on counterespionage, countersubversion, and dignitary protection in its efforts to secure the elections.[72]

The Swedish Police structured its efforts to protect the election as a national operation with dedicated national and regional election task forces. The Swedish Police focused its efforts on countering domestic extremism, securing the safety of elected officials, protecting vulnerable areas, and countering influence operations. The task force remained active until the new government had taken office after the election.[73]

C. The Swedish Election Authority

The Swedish Election Authority started its preparations for increased protection of the election in early 2017. A range of protective security assessments and measures were undertaken to strengthen the resilience of the election. As part of the cooperation set up with other agencies (described previously), the Swedish Election Authority participated in coordination forums and provided information and training about the election system to relevant authorities and the media. Significant efforts were also

[72] SÄPO, Brett arbete för att skydda valet (Feb. 22, 2018), *at* https://www.sakerhetspolisen.se/ovrigt/pressrum/aktuellt/aktuellt/2018-02-22-brett-arbete-for-att-skydda-valet.html; SÄPO, Förebyggande arbete inför valet gav resultat (Dec. 17, 2018), *at* https://www.sakerhetspolisen.se/ovrigt/pressrum/aktuellt/aktuellt/2018-12-17-forebyggande-arbete-infor-valet-gav-resultat.html; SÄPO, Så skyddar Säkerhetspolisen valet (June 3, 2018), *at* https://www.sakerhetspolisen.se/ovrigt/pressrum/aktuellt/aktuellt/2018-07-03-sa-skyddar-sakerhetspolisen-valet.html.

[73] *See* Press Release, Polisen, Valet genomfördes under säkra former (Sept. 10, 2018) (on file with Polisen); *see also* Press Release, Justitiedepartementet, Polismyndigheten och Säkerhetspolisen ska stärka arbetet mot politiskt motiverad brottslighet inför valet 2018 (Nov. 9, 2017) (on file with Justitiedepartementet); Tünde Simó, Polisen rustar för ökad hotbild mot den demokratiska processen, SN (Feb. 11, 2018), *at* https://sn.se/nyheter/polisen-rustar-for-okad-hotbild-mot-den-demokratiska-processen-sm4548459.aspx.

launched to increase the resilience and continuity planning of the election. In 2018, the Swedish Election Authority, in cooperation with MSB, informed over three hundred journalists at eleven sessions in a targeted effort to increase the resilience of the media against disinformation targeting trust in the electoral processes.[74] For the EU election in 2019, additional European-wide coordination and cooperation mechanisms were set up in the wake of European Commission recommendations to member states to strengthen the resilience of the election by increasing efforts to strengthen cybersecurity and countering disinformation. In 2019, the Swedish Election Authority became the national contact point for the European election cooperation network and the Swedish national election forum hosted by MSB and SÄPO.[75]

D. The Swedish Defence Research Agency

Measures to counter foreign election interference in Sweden also included FOI. The agency was tasked by the Swedish government to research violent online extremist propaganda in 2016 and had therefore built significant capacity to monitor digital environments.[76] In 2017, MSB requested FOI to monitor online discussions related to the election with the intent to raise awareness about the nature of the conversation as well as to strengthen the ability of government agencies to identify and counter the any threats to the conduct of the election.[77] FOI regularly presented assessments of the online environment to relevant government agencies up until the 2018 election.

E. Strategic Communication as Deterrence

Foreign election interference can go beyond the scope of *information* campaigns (messaging strategies targeting the public conversation) to include activities

[74] Annual Report, Valmyndigheten, Valmyndighetens årsrapport för 2017 (Feb. 23, 2018), *at* https://www.val.se/download/18.574dd8aa1610997fea413f0/1519398102719/Arsrapport-Valmyndigheten-2017.pdf.

[75] *See* Report, Valmyndigheten, Valmyndighetens erfarenhetsrapport från valet 2018 (Feb. 15, 2019), *at* https://www.val.se/servicelankar/press/nyheter/nyheter/2019-02-15-valmyndighetens-erfarenhetsrapport-fran-valet-2018.html; *see also* Report, Valmyndigheten, Valmyndighetens årsrapport för 2018 (Feb. 15, 2019), *at* https://www.val.se/om-oss/vart-uppdrag/arsrapporter.html; Report, Valmyndigheten, Erfarenheter från Europaparlamentsvalet 2019 (Sept. 24, 2019), *at* https://www.val.se/download/18.177c100516cddd1ee54b35/1569238549438/Erfarenheter-val-till-Europaparlamentet-2019.pdf.

[76] *See* Assignment Statement, Justitiedepartementet, Utökat uppdrag till Totalförsvarets forskningsinstitut om våldsbejakande extremistisk propaganda (July 2018), *at* https://www.regeringen.se/regeringsuppdrag/2018/03/utokat-uppdrag-till-totalforsvarets-forskningsinstitut-om-valdsbejakande-extremistisk-propaganda/; *see also* Assignment Statement, Kulturdepartementet, Uppdrag till Totalförsvarets forskningsinstitut (FOI) att göra kartläggningar och analyser av våldsbejakande extremistisk propaganda (June 3, 2016), *at* https://www.regeringen.se/regeringsuppdrag/2016/06/uppdrag-till-totalforsvarets-forskningsinstitut-foi-att-gora-kartlaggningar-och-analyser-av-valdsbejakande-etremistisk-propaganda/ . In 2018, FOI's tasks were expanded to include assessment of threats and expressions of hatred against specific groups, such as politicians and journalists, as well as mapping and assessing violent extremist propaganda around specific events in society.

[77] *See* Fernquist et al., *supra* note 61; Johan Fernquist et al., Digitala diskussioner om genomförandet av riksdagsvalet (2018), *at* https://rib.msb.se/filer/pdf/28764.pdf.

where the adversary engages in a broader spectrum of influence techniques. These include more than campaigns using spoken or written words, covering cyberattacks and symbolic actions as well. Aware of such risks, the Swedish government, as part of the 2015 defense appropriations bill, acted to strengthen the national intelligence services and the ability of government agencies to identify and counter *influence* campaigns.[78] The government also provided funding in 2017 "to strengthen information and cyber security work and to strengthen the resilience to cyber attacks."[79]

In addition to the explicit measures mentioned in the prime minister's speech to achieve institutional preparedness,[80] we assess that the very announcement of such efforts was part of the Swedish counterstrategy—an example of deterrence. *Deterrence* is a common term in military circles, historically focused on actions preventing a foreign adversary from engaging in nuclear attacks by denying them the ability to attack (deterrence by denial) or credibly threatening punishments if they do so (deterrence by punishment). Today, deterrence is used in national security circles to proactively counter (read: discourage) hybrid threats.[81]

The prime minister's statement of Sweden's capacities to detect foreign election interference ahead of the 2018 election—and the government's intent to act forcefully against those engaging in it—was likely a clear attempt to deter actors from contemplating interference in the Swedish elections.

In addition to cyberattacks, symbolic actions may play a role in foreign election interference—based on the principle that actions speak louder than words. A cyberattack taking down a government website could communicate that the system is vulnerable and not to be trusted, and a breach of national airspace could serve as a reminder of the realness of a military threat.[82] Concrete acts thus also form a type of communicative influence. Symbolic acts, however, may run in the opposite direction as well—that is, as countering actions for foreign election interference. For example, one year ahead of the election, Sweden invited troops from both NATO and the United Nations (including several important allies, such as the United States, Finland, Latvia, Germany, and France) to hold the nation's largest military exercise in twenty-three years. As described by the minister of defense, the exercise "raises the deterrent threshold against different types of incidents and provides important data for evaluation of our military capabilities."[83]

[78] Försvarsdepartementet, Försvarspolitisk inriktning—Sveriges försvar 2016–2020 (2015).

[79] Så ska vi skydda valrörelsen från andra staters påverkan, DAGENS NYHETER (Mar. 20, 2017), *at* https://www.regeringen.se/debattartiklar/2017/03/sa-ska-vi-skydda-valrorelsen-fran-andra-staters-paverkan/.

[80] These explicit references included strengthening the nation's cyber-defense system and the Swedish defense's intelligence capacity, as well as the installment of a warning system at companies of societal value to detect ongoing attacks.

[81] Hybrid COE, *Hybrid CoE Launches a Playbook on Hybrid Deterrence* (Mar. 9, 2020), *at* https://www.hybridcoe.fi/news/hybrid-coe-launches-a-playbook-on-hybrid-deterrence/.

[82] Nothhaft et al., *supra* note 5.

[83] Swedish Ministry of Defence, *Swedish Armed Forces Exercise Aurora 17 Will Increase Military Capability* (2014), *at* https://www.government.se/articles/2017/09/swedish-armed-forces-exercise-aurora-17-will-increase-military-capability/.

V. The Election

The Swedish parliamentary election was held on Sunday, September 9, 2018, with the highest voter turnout in thirty-three years (87.18 percent). The election "induce[d] profound changes in the Swedish party system"—from the 2010 classic divide between two formalized blocs (the left-of-center and the center-right) the political landscape had changed as a result of the "radical-right challenger" (the Swedish Democrats).[84] Of the 349 seats in the Swedish Riksdag, the left-of-center bloc won 144 seats (40.67 percent), the center-right bloc 143 seats (40.26 percent), and the Swedish Democrats won 62 seats (17.53 percent).[85] After several attempts by both blocs to form a majority government, it would eventually take an unprecedented eighty days (on average new governments have formed after eighteen to nineteen days; the previous record was twenty-five days in 1979) to form a new government as Prime Minister Stefan Löfven was re-elected on January 18, 2019.[86]

A. Interference

A few days before the election, the Swedish Security Service had identified a number of attempts to undermine the credibility of the election. They specifically highlighted discussions about election fraud, hijacked and fake accounts in social media, and disinformation on social media attempting to polarize society.[87] In the run-up to the election there were also directed denial-of-service (DoS) attacks and attempted data breaches aimed at political parties and other election-related organizations.[88]

After the election, the Swedish Security Service assessed that no significant influence campaigns against the Swedish election were carried out by a foreign country. However, they did note that there were cyber incidents that could be connected to foreign governments and that foreign governments did continue to collect information about persons of interest. A possible reason for the lack of a large-scale campaign against the Swedish election could be, the Security Police assessed, a combination of the revelations of election interference in other countries (which exposed and possibly deterred further activities) as well as the increasing vigilance and awareness in Sweden as a result of the extensive preventive efforts undertaken.[89]

[84] For an introduction to the Swedish political system and political history, *see* Nicholas Aylott & Niklas Bolin, *A Party System in Flux: The Swedish Parliamentary Election of September 2018*, 42 West Euro. Pol. 1504–1515 (2019); Henrik Oscarsson & Jesper Strömbäck, *Political Communication in the 2018 Swedish Election Campaign*, 121 Statsvetenskaplig Tidskrift 319–345 (2019).

[85] Valmyndigheten, Val till riksdagen (Sept. 16, 2018), *at* https://data.val.se/val/val2018/slutresultat/R/rike/index.html.

[86] DN, *Svenska regeringsbildningen rekordlåg* (2018), *at* https://www.dn.se/nyheter/politik/svenska-regeringsbildningen-rekordlang/.

[87] Säkerhetspolisen, *Försök att påverka förtroendet för valprocessen* (2018), *at* https://www.sakerhetspolisen.se/ovrigt/pressrum/aktuellt/aktuellt/2018-08-30-forsok-att-paverka-fortroendet-for-valprocessen.html.

[88] TT & Dagens Nyheter, *Avsiktlig attack släckte valsajt*, Dagens Nyheter (Feb. 23, 2019), *at* https://www.dn.se/nyheter/sverige/avsiktlig-attack-slackte-valsajt/.

[89] Säkerhetspolisen, *Förebyggande arbete inför valet gav resultat* (2018), https://www.sakerhetspolisen.se/ovrigt/pressrum/aktuellt/aktuellt/2018-12-17-forebyggande-arbete-infor-valet-gav-resultat.html;

Several of the previously presented Swedish government authorities set up systems through which they kept track of incidents during the election. After the election, the Swedish Police concluded that several minor incidents had occurred in relation to the election. Those included a few cases of vandalism, minor public order disruptions, and some cases of illegal threats. The Swedish Police assessed that none of the incidents had an impact on the outcome of the election.[90] The Swedish Election Authority concluded in its election assessment report that the 2018 election was conducted in an accurate and effective manner in accordance with the principles of rule of law.[91] It reported that during the voting period, they experienced an increasing interest in alleged errors in the voting process from both traditional and social media as well as the public. The Election Authority further assessed that there were a number of attempts to influence the public's confidence in the Swedish electoral system, including attempts to influence online discussions. The most significant event that occurred was a DoS attack against the website of the Swedish Election Authority on election day. The DoS attack effectively took down the website and prevented public access for several hours.[92] Although the website was offline, Swedish media had access to a second system that enabled them to access and publish the election result independently of the availability of the website. As such, the DoS attack did not prevent access to the election result. Further, since the website of the Swedish Election Authority is separate from the election management systems, the DoS attack did not interfere with the conduct of the election. There were, however, limited attempts to try to discredit the election result and the Election Authority, claiming that the unavailable website had enabled electoral fraud. Swedish media quickly countered the argument, and we have found no information indicating that the disinformation attempt gained any significant support.[93] As of now, there is no publicly available information attributing the DoS attack to any specific actor.

Thus, no major incident was identified by Swedish authorities in relation to the 2018 Swedish elections nor the 2019 EU elections. The range of minor incidents were not judged to have influenced the outcome of the election by any of the actors referenced previously. All the incidents followed a pattern of similar influence attempts observed internationally, with IT attacks against party and election administration websites, a spike in online discussions about electoral fraud, the use of automated social media manipulation (such as bots), the use of anonymous social media accounts and groups, vandalism of political advertising, threats against elections officials, and

Säkerhetspolisen, *Arbetet med valet fortsätter* (2018), https://www.sakerhetspolisen.se/ovrigt/pressrum/aktuellt/aktuellt/2018-09-19-arbetet-med-valet-fortsatter.html.

[90] Polisen, *Valet genomfördes under säkra former* (2018), https://polisen.se/aktuellt/nyheter/2018/september/valet-genomfordes-under-sakra-former/; Polisen, *Polisen: 2.000 brott med kopplingar till valet*, Dagens Industri (Sept. 8, 2018), *at* https://www.di.se/nyheter/polisen-2000-brott-med-kopplingar-till-valet/.

[91] Valmyndigheten, *Erfarenheter från valen 2018*, https://www.val.se/download/18.3acea2511672bd8769229f0/1550219505460/Erfarenheter-valen-2018.pdf.

[92] *Id.*

[93] Hugo Ewald, *Faktiskt helt fel att val.se-kraschen betydde valfusk*, Dagens Nyheter (Sept. 10, 2018), *at* https://www.dn.se/nyheter/politik/faktiskt-helt-fel-att-valse-kraschen-betydde-valfusk/ (last visited May 4, 2020).

a range of borderline anonymous extremist political activity difficult to attribute. Notable examples include:

- In January 2018, a website mimicking the Moderat Party's website was launched at Moderatpolitik.nu, an address that could easily be confused with the party's official site. The website was used to spread false and manipulated campaign materials, including a genuine speech by party leader Ulf Kristersson that was edited to change the overall meaning and impact. In conjunction with the website, activists also plastered fake election posters emphasizing what they considered to be the party's weak position on immigration, and posed as Moderat party officials handing out false information and engaging in misleading conversations with voters seeking more information. A domestic far-right political activist group called Nordisk Ungdom (Nordic Youth) was identified and admitted to being behind the ruse.[94]
- In April 2018, five of the largest Swedish media houses collaborated on a fact-checking platform called Faktiskt.se (which can be translated as (F)actually.se). Two weeks prior to launch, a site using a similar design was launched on the domain Faktiskt.eu. It was later revealed that two domestic alt-right news platforms were behind the initiative, with the stated aim of being fact checkers of the fact checkers.[95]
- In June 2018, Russian state media channel RT published the documentary "Testing Tolerance," in which representatives of anti-immigration political parties and movements in Sweden were interviewed about the failures of social integration. The video received 1.6 million views on YouTube by October 2018 and was widely shared and discussed by international alt-right news platforms.[96]
- In August 2018, the Social Democrat Party's website was subjected to two targeted DDoS attacks a few hours after its election campaign officially began. According to party sources, the attack originated from five countries, Russia, North Korea, Japan, Spain, and South Africa. The first attack successfully brought down the website for several hours. A second attack the day after was successfully resisted.[97]
- Also in August 2018, it was reported that a Christian Democrat parliamentarian had his Facebook account hacked and that the hacker used the Messenger account to initiate conversations with other politicians. The hacker allegedly referred to personal information about those politicians, including the names of their children. The event was connected to a security leak that was being investigated by the politician in question.[98]

[94] Adam Westin, *Moderaterna utsatta för högerextrem plakatkupp*, AFTONBLADET (Aug. 12, 2018); Pressmeddelande Nordisk ungdom, *at* https://nordiskungdom.com/upplysningskampanj-till-moderata-valjare/; Hur Nordisk ungdom skildrar kampanjen, *at* https://nordiskungdom.com/tag/moderatpolitik/.

[95] *See, e.g.*, *A Fake Fact Checker—Again*, EUVSDISINFO (May 3, 2018), *at* https://euvsdisinfo.eu/a-fake-fact-checker-again/.

[96] *Testing Tolerance: Sweden's Ultra Liberal Migration Policy Gets a Reality Check*, RT (July 2, 2018).

[97] Attacker slog ut Socialdemokraternas hemsida, DAGENS NYHETER (Aug. 10, 2018), *at* https://www.dn.se/nyheter/politik/riktad-attack-mot-socialdemokraternas-hemsida-/.

[98] Politikers konto på Facebook kapades, SVERIGESRADIO (May 28, 2018), *at* https://sverigesradio.se/sida/artikel.aspx?programid=101&artikel=6962899; Säpo utreder riksdagsledamots kapade

- In September 2018, as the election took place, three narratives on election fraud received widespread attention. The first involved images of boxes of postal votes (some from the 1998 election) and suggested that they were being handled in an unsystematic manner. The second was a petition organized by the far-right Sweden Democrats Party claiming electoral fraud, which received two thousand signatures in twenty-four hours. The third was a rumor that spread in conjunction with the DoS attack on the Election Authority's website the night of the election (mentioned previously), claiming that the website's downtime hid efforts to change the results. Images showing results before and after the crash, purposely misrepresenting the data, circulated widely during the period in which the new government was being negotiated.[99]

As these examples show, domestic political actors were behind a number of alleged examples of interference. Many of their actions could be justified as satire or efforts to provoke debate rather than serious and widespread activities capable of affecting the integrity of the election. Where foreign actors might have had some covert involvement, their work seems to either have been cyber-oriented or in a supporting role for domestic actors. Nonetheless, the international press took an interest in the election, which enabled overt efforts to shape perceptions of both Sweden and the election itself.

B. Foreign Reporting

The Swedish election was a subject of attention in the international press. To take a few examples, the coverage in major newspapers and journals six months prior to the election was "very much event-oriented, mostly focuse[d] on the election and particularly on the performance of the Sweden Democrats." The reporting in Denmark was described as high, focusing on similar narratives such as, for example, Swedish migration politics, and references to "chaos," "crisis," "disruption," and "fragmentation" to describe Swedish politics during the election campaign.[100]

A comprehensive review was conducted by the Swedish Institute, analyzing international press coverage, as well as the social media conversation about the Swedish election.[101] The study concluded that the Swedish election received less attention than, for example, Sweden's participation in sports events such as the World Cup, cultural events such as the Eurovision Song Contest, the crisis in the Swedish Academy, and the Duke and Duchess of Cambridge's visit to Sweden.[102] Yet, even as the social

Facebook-konto, DAGENS NYHETER (Aug. 17, 2017), *at* https://www.dn.se/nyheter/politik/sapo-utreder-riksdagsledamots-kapade-facebook-konto/.

[99] Falsk information om valfusk—kommunens bilder kapade, SVT NYHETER (Sept. 13, 2018); Johan Wikén, *Tre falska påståenden om valfusk—som du inte ska sprida vidare*, METRO (Sept. 12, 2018).

[100] Swedish Institute, *Notis eller världsnyhet?: Det svenska valet 2018 i internationell nyhetsrapportering och på sociala medier* (2018), *at* https://si.se/app/uploads/2018/11/si_rapport_svenska_valet-2018_fa_web.pdf.

[101] *Id.*

[102] *Id.*

media engagement was lower for the election than many of these events, it still resulted in five times as much international engagement than the previous election in 2014. The most widely discussed topics on Twitter related to the election were information influence (18 percent), opinion polls (16 percent), electoral fraud (11 percent), election results (9 percent), migration (9 percent), crime (7 percent), and the connection to nationalism in Europe (6 percent). Discussions about information influence did not consist of actual instances or cases of information influence but rather the threat and preparations to mitigate its effects. Another recurring story was a controversy with YouTube following their decision to remove a video about the history of the Social Democratic Party uploaded by the Sweden Democrats. The controversy led to another enduring story promoted by a few prominent alternative news sites that claimed that the Swedish government had a "hotline" to social media companies to censor or even erase political content on the platforms. In reality, MSB cooperated with social media platforms to protect official government pages and accounts on social media—something that MSB sometimes referred to as a "hotline." In any case, alleged electoral fraud was most discussed on alternative news sites and generated limited engagement.

In the English-speaking international news, the Swedish Institute analysis covered over twenty thousand digital news articles from April to September 2018 concerning the Swedish elections (Table 6.1 shows the report's findings of the most shared articles about the Swedish election in English media). Here, the trending topics were the election result (31 percent), the postelection selection of prime minister (18 percent), the rise of the Swedish Democrats (18 percent), migration (11 percent), and information influence (7 percent). The discussion on information influence was primarily because of a report by FOI titled *Bots and the Swedish election.*[103] Based on a comparative study of reporting from nine different countries, the Swedish Institute also showed that news in most countries followed roughly the same trends—with some variations. Hungarian journalists, for example, more often reported about migration and crime in Sweden, while journalists in the United States placed more emphasis on issues related to society and politics.

As noted by the Swedish Institute, "[i]t is striking that, by comparison with the topics that the Swedish electorate considered the most important during the elections—healthcare, education, equality, social welfare, and law and order—none of these issues are pervasive in the English news reports."[104] This was also a topic discussed in the Swedish press. The online newspaper *The Local* (publishing articles in English about Sweden) under the heading "Sweden's Election Is Being Misreported Abroad—And This Is a Problem" described how "[b]ad foreign reporting on Sweden's election risks giving readers around the world a false impression of the state of the

[103] Swedish Defence Research Agency, *The Swedish Election and Bots on Twitter*, *at* https://www.foi.se/en/foi/news-and-pressroom/news/2018-09-12-the-swedish-election-and-bots-on-twitter.html.

[104] Report, Swedish Institute, *Notis eller världsnyhet?: Det svenska valet 2018 i internationell nyhetsrapportering och på sociala medier* (2018), *at* https://si.se/app/uploads/2018/11/si_rapport_svenska_valet-2018_fa_web.pdf (authors' translation from Swedish).

Table 6.1 Most widely shared articles about the Swedish election in English news media.

Heading	Published (2018)	Source	Shares
Journalist who infiltrated Putin's troll factory warns of Russian propaganda in the upcoming Swedish election	April 7	Business Insider (UK)	38.3 K
Swedish election: Main blocs neck and neck as nationalists gain	September 10	BBC (UK)	13.1 K
Sweden's Far-Right Party Is Poised for Major Gains in Country's Elections	August 26	The Local (SWE)	11.4 K
Sweden elections: Far-right party set for success amid migrant anger	August 26	Dailystar.co.uk (UK)	9.8 K
Sweden Election: Ruling Party Scrapes a Win as Far-Right Gains	September 9	NPR (UK)	8.2 K
Swedish election on knife edge as party with neo-Nazi roots surges	September 9	CCN (US)	7.1 K
Sweden's far-right set to hold balance of power after the election	September 8	MSN (US)	5.1 K
Swedish election: PM says voting for anti-immigration SD is "dangerous"	September 8	BBC (UK)	5.0 K
"Fury over EU's bullying of Britain over Brexit will trigger Sweden's own EU exit"	September 9	Express.co.uk (UK)	4.8 K
France's Macron Wades into the Swedish Election	September 2	Bloomberg (US)	4.7 K

[a] K = 1,000.

country."[105] The author argued, in line with the Swedish Institute report, that the increased attention from the international press in comparison to the previous election is due to the "obvious parallels" between the Sweden Democrats and Donald Trump, Marine Le Pen, and Brexit. The author also painted a picture of foreign correspondents who parachute into a country, often just a few days or weeks before the election, lacking insight into the political system, and presenting it as "simplistic, sensational journalism that is frequently just plain wrong":[106]

> Dire diagnoses of the state of Sweden permeate almost every article about the election. You expect this from hyper-partisan sites like Breitbart or state propaganda like Sputnik, but mainstream media outlets are repeating the same tropes.[107]

[105] James Savage, *Sweden's Election Is Being Misreported Abroad—And This Is a Problem*, The Local (Sept. 7, 2018).
[106] *Id.*
[107] *Id.*

VI. Concluding Discussion

The Swedish election protection efforts were unique in the sense that they were based upon a comprehensive approach to an emerging challenge that worked to a strategy of ensuring societal resilience. While it is impossible to assess if the approach was successful—if it removed vulnerabilities and deterred the aggressor—the efforts were substantial and involved a wide range of government actors. The Swedish election protection efforts were also unique because they were based on a bottom-up rather than a top-down perspective, with the government setting the tone and prioritizing the issue, but with individual agencies coordinating and developing the necessary remedy.

In total, the election protection efforts brought together 290 municipalities, 21 county administrative boards, and a range of government agencies including the Police, the Security Service, the Tax Agency, the Election Authority, the Civil Contingencies Agency, the Swedish Institute, the Defence Research Agency, the Armed Forces, the National Defence Radio Establishment, and the Media Council. Additionally, a number of universities, research institutes, think tanks, private companies, and many media houses focused on the topic by prioritizing the issue and strengthening their systems to prevent, identify, and counter election interference. The result was a comprehensive approach inspired by the government, coordinated by few, and led by no one.

The main lines in the Swedish approach can be summarized as:

1. Conduct comprehensive risk and vulnerability assessments;
2. Focus on resilience-building based on the risk and vulnerability assessments;
3. Consider deterrence factors;
4. Establish comprehensive and effective coordination and cooperation mechanisms;
5. Establish and test early warning and detection mechanisms;
6. Conduct education and training for relevant actors; and
7. Conduct strategic communication to deter antagonists.

We recognize that the Swedish method of pursuing a comprehensive approach may be difficult to copy in other political systems. However, we believe that the main lines of its approach, the priorities adopted, and the actions undertaken can be used in other countries. Indeed, the Swedish approach has already inspired a number of countries, particularly in the Nordic-Baltic region, to adopt, refine, and further develop their own approaches to election protection.[108]

Nonetheless, we do not claim that the Swedish approach is a silver bullet solution. As successful as its comprehensive approach was, Sweden did not manage to address a number of vulnerabilities identified during, and after, the 2018 election period. For starters, the online environment remained relatively sparsely researched, with a single research group following inauthentic coordinated activity online. Investigative

[108] *Cf.* Sebastian Bay & Guna Šnore, *Protecting Elections: A Strategic Communications Approach* (2019), *at* https://www.stratcomcoe.org/protecting-elections-strategic-communications-approach.

journalism revealed a major troll farm in Sweden the year before the election,[109] yet there were no systematic efforts undertaken by research groups to monitor the online space for systematic manipulation. While FOI monitored online discussions for automatic behavior, its time, resources, and data access were all limited. Thus, for future elections it will be important to provide substantial grants to research efforts and journalists to effectively monitor online and offline spaces for information influence activities. Moreover, there is also a need for greater transparency. Unless social media companies are able to provide more data to the media and researchers (or to present more public research of the issues themselves), large parts of the online discussion will remain out of sight for researchers, journalists, public officials, and the public at large. Simply put, we will not be able to verify the presence or lack of coordinated inauthentic behavior online.

Finally, IT-system vulnerabilities continue to be exploited by actors in attempts to steal, manipulate, and discredit data. Despite significant efforts to protect the website of the Swedish Election Authority, a DoS attack did manage to take it offline during several critical hours on election day in 2018, creating an opportunity for antagonists to try to influence perceptions about the credibility of the election. For future elections, antagonists will undoubtedly continue to exploit such vulnerabilities. Thus, it will become ever more important to protect the election administration against attempts to undermine its credibility. Governments need to prioritize and step up efforts to protect the election process with greater cybersecurity and a whole-of-government approach that emphasizes societal resistance for forestalling foreign election interference.

[109] Mathias Ståhle, *Så styrs den svenska trollfabriken som sprider hat på nätet mot betalning*, Eskilstuna-Kuriren (Feb. 16, 2017), *at* https://ekuriren.se/nyheter/eskilstuna/sa-styrs-den-svenska-trollfabriken-som-sprider-hat-pa-natet-mot-betalning-sm4519467.aspx.

7

When Does Election Interference via Cyberspace Violate Sovereignty?

Violations of Sovereignty, "Armed Attack," Acts of War, and Activities "Below the Threshold of Armed Conflict" via Cyberspace

James Van de Velde

I. Introduction

According to the January 6, 2017, U.S. Intelligence Community Assessment:

> Russian President Vladimir Putin ordered an influence campaign in 2016 aimed at the U.S. presidential election. Russia's goals were to undermine public faith in the U.S. democratic process, denigrate Secretary Clinton and harm her electability and potential presidency . . . Putin and the Russian Government developed a clear preference for [Donald] Trump and aspired to help Trump's election chances when possible by discrediting Secretary Clinton and publicly contrasting her unfavorably to him.[1]

Such foreign interference begs many relevant legal and political questions. Were Russian 2016 U.S. election-related malicious cyberspace activities violations of sovereignty or merely an act of "cyber vandalism," as President Barack Obama described the North Korean Sony cyberspace[2] operations in 2014?[3] Did such activity constitute an "armed attack" via cyberspace? Was such activity an act of war? And irrespective of these thresholds, was the 2016 Russian effort overall (in hindsight) a political victory or a mistake for Russia (regardless of whether it rose to the level of a violation of sovereignty, an armed attack, or act of war)—a typical, Soviet-like, heavy-handed, information warfare backfire that turned more Americans and allies against Russia and made Russia's "national brand" even more toxic worldwide?

[1] Office of the Director of National Intelligence, *Assessing Russian Activities and Intentions in Recent U.S. Elections, Intelligence Community Assessment*, ICA 2017-01D 1 (Jan. 6, 2017) [hereinafter DNI Russian Activities Assessment].

[2] Cyberspace may be defined as a global domain within the information environment consisting of the interdependent network of information technology infrastructures and resident data, including the internet, telecommunications networks, computer systems, and embedded processors and controllers. U.S. Department of Defense *Dictionary of Military and Associated Terms* 61 (Nov. 2019) [hereinafter DoD Dictionary].

[3] Eric Bradner, *Obama: North Korea's Hack Not War, But "Cybervandalism,"* CNN (Dec. 24, 2014).

James Van de Velde, *When Does Election Interference via Cyberspace Violate Sovereignty?* In: *Defending Democracies*. Edited by Duncan B. Hollis and Jens David Ohlin, Oxford University Press (2021).
DOI: 10.1093/oso/9780197556979.003.0008

Cyber vandalism is not an understood political, military, or legal term; it lacks clear antecedents and does not itself justify any particular range of consequences. Sovereignty violations, in contrast, do trigger both legal and political precedents and consequences. As significant as they may be, however, not all sovereignty violations justify a forceful response; the right to respond to malicious cyberspace activities with force depends on attaching either a legal ("armed attack") or political ("act of war") label to the activity suffered.

Section II of this chapter uses the 2016 Russian election interference to argue for an "unauthorized use" standard for violations of sovereignty violations. It also denotes how cyberspace operations that destroy systems, cause physical damage, or risk lives constitute "armed attacks" and that the president would have the legal right to mount an armed response. Section III notes how it is the commander in chief who discerns cyberspace operations that rise to the level of "acts of war" (as opposed to making "declarations of war," a congressional prerogative). Section IV examines the 2016 election interference from a likely Russian perspective, hypothesizing what ends these influence operations might have attempted to pursue. Section V assesses why the current Russian polity favors cyberspace competition (i.e., activities "below armed conflict" thresholds) and examines to what extent such Russian activity has proven fruitful or not. The chapter concludes by suggesting that Russia's own influence operations to date may have had the opposite of their intended effects and assesses how the United State may best craft and deploy its own policies to protect against foreign election interference in the future.

II. Was the 2016 Russian Activity a Violation of U.S. Sovereignty?

If the 2016 Russian influence campaign involved *only* obfuscated sponsorship of social media pages, the Russian effort should not be considered a violation of U.S. sovereignty, though even state-sponsored malicious cyberspace activity that does not violate sovereignty may be deeply concerning. Conducting only obfuscated social media campaigns would be no different than if the Russians had hired protestors to picket at a U.S. campaign rally (which they may have also done). Many acts by states that affect U.S. internal politics, such as foreign states giving money to U.S. nonprofits that advance causes in support of specific candidates, are not violations of sovereignty. Nor are false social media pages that advance certain true or false messages, though pages that post knowingly false information (disinformation) violate the Terms of Use of many private U.S. companies involved in these incidents. Thus, false Facebook or Instagram pages created by the Russian-government-sponsored Internet Research Agency in St Petersburg,[4] inserted legally via cutouts, are not violations of sovereignty.

[4] Also known as Glavset. *See* Ken Dilanian & Ben Popken, *Russia Favored Trump, Targeted African-Americans with Election Meddling, Reports Say*, NBC News (Dec. 18, 2018); William Cummings, *Senate Reports Find Millions of Social Media Posts by Russians Aimed at Helping Trump, GOP*, USA Today (Dec. 18, 2018); Page Leskin, *Russia's Disinformation Campaign Wasn't Just on Facebook and Twitter. Here Are All the Social Media Platforms Russian Trolls Weaponized during the 2016 U.S. Elections*, Business Insider (Dec. 19, 2018). Russia is the birthplace of a new, secretive, state-sponsored industry designed to spread

If the Russian government, however, had changed voter rolls surreptitiously prior to the 2016 election, which had the effect of frustrating legal voters from voting, U.S. sovereignty would have most certainly been violated. Cyberspace operations[5] conducted or sponsored by elements of the Russian government that disrupt computer programs, alter or deny voting tabulations, alter voter rolls, or technically insert false messages are indisputably violations of sovereignty.[6]

The determining factor here should be whether the activities in cyberspace were those of an authorized user. Therefore, if, in 2016, the Russian government used existing public cyber applications (such as making only Facebook and Instagram pages) but did not alter code or illegally enter U.S. networks, then its malicious cyberspace activity was not a violation of U.S. sovereignty. If so, in this case, the Russians were just conducting cyberspace-enabled influence operations, using existing public and private institutions to shape U.S. politics. This is true even if the Russians disguised themselves as the source of the messaging.[7]

In terms of actual Russian activity, the 2017 Assessment found that:

> Russia's intelligence services conducted cyber operations against targets associated with the 2016 U.S. presidential election, including targets associated with both major U.S. political parties ... In July 2015, Russian intelligence gained access to Democratic National Committee (DNC) networks and maintained that access until at least June 2016 ... The General Staff Main Intelligence Directorate (GRU) probably began cyber operations aimed at the U.S. election by March 2016. We assess that the GRU operations resulted in the compromise of the personal e-mail accounts of Democratic Party officials and political figures. By May, the GRU had exfiltrated large volumes of data from the DNC.[8]

pro-Russian propaganda, attack government critics, and sow domestic distrust about the internet. A *New York Times* article exposed this burgeoning industry, commonly referred to as a "troll factory," and described how "they work for government authorities at all levels." *See* Adrian Chen, *The Agency*, N.Y. Times (June 2, 2015); *see also* Catherine A. Fitzpatrick, *Russian Blogger Finds Pro-Kremlin "Troll Factories,"* The Daily Beast (Aug. 20, 2015); Sam Matthew, *Revealed: How Russia's "Troll Factory" Runs Thousands of Fake Twitter and Facebook Accounts to Flood Social Media with Pro-Putin Propaganda*, The Daily Mail (Mar. 28, 2015); Norman Hermant, *Inside Russia's Troll Factory: Controlling Debate and Stifling Dissent in Internet Forums and Social Media*, News (Australia) (Aug. 12, 2015).

[5] Cyberspace operations involve "[t]he employment of cyberspace capabilities where the primary purpose is to achieve objectives in or through cyberspace." DoD Dictionary, *supra* note 2, at 61. *See also* Paul Duchaine, *The Notion of Cyber Operations*, in Research Handbook on International Law and Cyberspace 214 (Nicholas Tsagourias & Russell Buchan eds., 2015) ("Suitable or not, the term cyber operations seems to become a common denominator for activities in cyberspace, undertaken with the aim of achieving objectives in or through this digital domain.").

[6] *See* Tallinn Manual on the International Law Applicable to Cyber Warfare 16 (Michael N. Schmitt ed., 2013) ("A cyber operation by a State directed against cyber infrastructure located in another State may violate the latter's sovereignty. It certainly does so if it causes damage"); *see also* Michael N. Schmitt & Liis Vihul, *Respect for Sovereignty in Cyberspace*, 95 Tex. L. Rev. 1639 (2017).

[7] *Tallinn Manual 2.0* states: "In the cyber context, therefore, it is a violation of territorial sovereignty for an organ of a State, or others whose conduct may be attributed to the State, to conduct cyber operations while physically present on another State's territory against that State or entities or persons located there. For example, if an agent of one State uses a U.S.B flash drive to introduce malware into cyber infrastructure located in another State, a violation of sovereignty has taken place." Tallinn Manual 2.0 on the International Law Applicable to Cyber Operations 19 (Michael N. Schmitt ed., 2017)

[8] DNI Russian Activities Assessment, *supra* note 1, at 2.

The Assessment later adds, "Russian intelligence accessed elements of multiple state or local electoral boards."[9]

If, indeed, the Russians entered U.S. private or public computer networks surreptitiously as unauthorized users and viewed material that was meant to be kept from them (espionage) or changed code or data, then they logically did violate U.S. sovereignty; "unauthorized access" being the logical, legal trigger. If the Russians were behind the theft of Democratic National Committee (DNC) email messages, they committed espionage and violated U.S. sovereignty.

Such violations of sovereignty, including such acts of espionage, are likely not, however, forms of cyberspace-enabled "armed attack" or a cyberspace attack of any kind. Nor are they likely to be deemed an act of war by the president. But had the Russians destroyed systems, causing physical damage or risked the lives of Americans, such as interfering with traffic lights to disrupt voting, then such violations of sovereignty would likely constitute "armed attack" and the president would have the legal right to mount an armed response.[10] The president could also deem such acts "acts of war," though, to date, no U.S. president has declared a cyberspace operation an act of war.

None of these acts short of armed attack (*influence operations*; *disruption of code that does not result in or threaten loss of life or physical damage*; *espionage*) is likely to be deemed an "act of war" by the president (though some false messages that cause rioting or civil conflict might). Such a decision ("an act of war") is a political calculation by the president, though most "acts of war" in cyberspace likely will also satisfy the international legal threshold for an "armed attack."

III. When Might Violations of Sovereignty or Influence Operations via Cyberspace Constitute an Act of War?

Although only Congress can "declare war," "acts of war" by adversaries are determined by the commander in chief—in these cases, the U.S. president. There is no legal threshold or case study analysis defining such operations. In short, President Obama could have called the North Korean cyberspace attacks on Sony Pictures acts of war. He chose to call them "cyber vandalism."[11] President Obama could have *theoretically* called massive Russian covert violations of sovereignty and theft of DNC information via cyberspace "acts of war" and could have attempted to muster enough political support to mount a response, though that response would have to be under international law proportional in scope to the offending act. (In other words, President Obama could not have attacked Moscow with destructive weapons if Russia's violations of sovereignty involved only unauthorized copying and dissemination of DNC email to foment unrest; his response would have to be commensurate to the original Russian act.) The president's right to respond with force would be significantly bolstered legally if the Russian activity also crossed the threshold of cyberspace "armed attack," though even then the response would have to be proportional to the original

[9] *Id.* at 3.
[10] *See* U.N. Charter, art. 51.
[11] David Jackson, *Obama: We're Not at Cyberwar with North Korea*, USA TODAY (Dec. 21, 2014).

act of aggression. If, however, the acts were merely violations of sovereignty (as they likely were), then the president would be strongly, politically, and legally bounded from conducting an armed attack in response.[12] Calling such espionage and influence operations an act of war would have set (and stretched) an enormous precedent, however; this is why, perhaps, no president has called such operations an act of war to date. (President Obama declined even to call the cyberspace attacks on Sony Pictures "attacks," let alone "armed attacks.")[13]

The United States has the legal right to respond to an "armed attack." As set forth in Article 51 of the Charter of the United Nations, states are permitted to use force in the face of an "armed attack" as an exercise of their inherent right of individual or collective self-defense. Therefore, unauthorized disruption of U.S. critical infrastructure, such as disruption of voter rolls (assuming these occurred), could be deemed an "armed attack" by the president. Legal disinformation operations, however, involving no unauthorized access to U.S. networks, would not be examples of armed attack.

However, just because a state commits an armed attack via cyberspace does not mean the president will necessarily consider the attack an act of war. Armed attack via cyberspace is discerned according to unauthorized and disruptive or damaging effects committed by a state or nonstate actor. However, an act of war is determined solely by the commander in chief. Acts of war are decided politically by the heads of state, on a case-by-case basis, in the context of an international environment, in a larger historical relationship among and between parties and involves primarily, if not exclusively, politics and not law.

In short, if France somehow accidentally tampered with the U.S. Federal Aviation Administration air traffic control system via cyberspace (by accidentally trolling through U.S. networks in some misguided cyberspace exercise), resulting in an air accident and death, the act would not be a (cyberspace-enabled) armed attack, and the president would most likely not call it an act of war. He would call it an accident. If China purposefully did the same to slow U.S. air support to a besieged Taiwan, in a hot crisis over the Taiwan Strait, such an act would likely be considered an "armed attack" and perhaps an "act of war" and likely called so explicitly by the president.

[12] *See* Draft Articles on the Responsibility of States for Internationally Wrongful Acts with Commentaries [2001] YBILC, vol. II (2), UN Doc. A/56/10, as corrected, art. 49.

[13] However, it is not inconceivable (though probably very unlikely) to imagine a cyberspace-based enabled information operation that did not rise to the level of "armed attack" but that could be deemed an "act of war" and result in an armed response. As a hypothetical, a state could so inflame an American majority or minority group with cyberspace-enabled disinformation that numerous members commit murders of a perceived rival ethnic group, leading to a small race riot and the deaths of hundreds. If the act could be attributed and discerned as purposeful incitement by another state, it is not inconceivable that the U.S. commander in chief could declare such an event an "act of war" and mount a proportional armed attack response, perhaps through cyberspace. *See* Robin Emmott, *Russia Deploying Coronavirus Disinformation to Sow Panic in West, EU Document Says*, REUTERS (Mar. 18, 2020). Such information operations could also wrongly involve pitting other states against Americans, precipitating violence. *See Russian Biologist and Former UN Expert Igor Nikulin: Coronavirus Is a Biological Weapon Used by Global Governments to Reduce the World's Population by 90 Percent*, RUSSIA TODAY (Feb. 27, 2020); Steve Lee Myers, *China Spins Tale that the U.S. Army Started the Coronavirus*, N.Y. TIMES (Mar. 13, 2020); Jomaa Al-Atwani, *COVID-19 Pandemic Is American Biological Warfare Against the Arab, Islamic World*, AL-NUJABA TV (Iraq) (Mar. 12, 2020); Abd Al-Wahhab, *The Jews Are Behind Coronavirus; We Should Unite in Jihad Against the Jews*, RASAEL ON YOUTUBE (Mar. 20, 2020).

Similarly, violations of sovereignty do not necessarily generate an automatic or comparable response. Indeed, there are many degrees of violations of sovereignty, both above and below the threshold of a use of force. Russian aircraft or naval ships that modestly pierce U.S. air or sea space violate U.S. sovereignty but warrant responses far short of violence. Violent invasion of U.S. territory would be on the opposite end of the spectrum. Cyberspace operations involve the entire political spectrum from minor to major violations of sovereignty (*espionage* to *cyberspace-enabled armed attack*). Given their nature, cyberspace operations also involve numerous international law regimes, such as international human rights law, the law of the sea, and space law.[14] But the Law of Armed Conflict seems entirely inappropriate to "gray zone" cyberspace operations conducted short of armed attack.[15]

Although small violations of sovereignty via cyberspace (i.e., "gray zone" conflict)[16] may appear minor, we are only now realizing their political significance. If such events, unlike air or sea violations, manifest themselves in political change—that is, if a state altered voter tabulations and caused the election of an individual who would not have been so elected without such interference—then such cyberspace acts are significant violations of sovereignty, despite no coincident physical damage or death.

The UN Group of Governmental Experts (UNGGE) has not clarified the role of international law in addressing cyberspace operations beyond when such law applies.[17] And states have so far largely avoided making clear pronouncements of what cyberspace operations would and would not violate sovereignty for precisely the obvious reason: it is better for them to leave the threshold ambiguous and allow successive heads of states to decide on a case-by-case basis.

According to March 2020 remarks by the U.S. Department of Defense (DoD) General Counsel:

> In assessing whether a particular cyber operation—conducted by or against the United States—constitutes a use of force, DoD lawyers consider whether the operation causes physical injury or damage ... Even if a particular cyber operation does not constitute a use of force, the State or States targeted by the operation may disagree.

[14] For a comprehensive compilation of how relevant international law applies, *see* generally the TALLINN MANUAL 2.0, *supra* note 7.

[15] Activity in the early phases of warfare has been described as unconventional war, guerilla war, irregular war, hybrid war, nonlinear war, next-generation war, ambiguous war, asymmetric war, limited war, shadow war, indirect war, small war, the gray zone, low-intensity conflict, and "Military Operations Other Than War" (MOOTW). The last time the United States formally declared war was June 5, 1942, against Bulgaria, Romania, and Hungary.

[16] "Gray zone" challenges or gray-zone conflicts are coercive and aggressive in nature and rise above normal, everyday peacetime geopolitical competition, "but [are] deliberately designed to remain below the threshold of conventional military conflict and open interstate war." *See* Hal Brands, *Paradoxes of the Gray Zone* (Foreign Policy Research Institute, Feb. 5, 2016); *see also* Joseph L. Votel et al., *Unconventional Warfare in the Gray Zone*, 80 JOINT FORCES Q. 101, 102 (2016); JOHN CHAMBERS, COUNTERING GRAY-ZONE HYBRID THREATS: AN ANALYSIS OF RUSSIA'S "NEW GENERATION WARFARE" AND IMPLICATIONS FOR THE U.S. ARMY 13 (2016).

[17] *See* Report of the Group of Governmental Experts on Developments in the Field of Information and Telecommunications in the Context of International Security, U.N. Doc. A/70/174, 27 (July 22, 2015). The 2017 round of the UNGGE even failed to achieve a consensus; *see* Arun Mohan Sukumar, *The UNGGE Failed. Is International Law in Cyberspace Doomed as Well?*, LAWFARE (July 4, 2017).

> For cyber operations that would not constitute a prohibited intervention or use-of-force, the Department believes there is not sufficiently widespread and consistent State practice resulting from a sense of legal obligation to conclude that customary international law generally prohibits such non-consensual cyber operations in another State's territory.[18]

Mounting a response to such operations, whether they be deemed a use of force or not, has legally and politically confounded many liberal democratic states. However, in a speech to clarify the United Kingdom's position, in 2018 Attorney General Jeremy Wright claimed that a breach of the principle of nonintervention provides victim states the ability to take action in response that would otherwise be considered unlawful, but which is permissible if it is aimed at returning relations between the hostile state and the victim state to one of lawfulness and bringing an end to the prior unlawful act.[19]

IV. Russian Influence Operations

Russian influence operations are not new; they were a staple of Soviet attempts to shape foreign policy, though social media today affords Russia new avenues for operations and greater access, as well as an enhanced ability to conceal such operations or misattribute them. Influence operations via cyberspace are elements of state "warfare" (a broad term) though they are not (legally) acts of "armed attack." "Warfare" encompasses the full gamut of hostile acts, from influence operations to armed attack.

However, it is conceivable that some influence operations are so egregious (for instance, an information operation that causes massive rioting leading to the deaths of thousands—see Rwanda[20]) that they could be deemed an "act of war" by a head of state. A Russian influence operation that caused civil disturbance in the United States, leading to the deaths of individuals, would be a similar act that does not reach the legal definition of cyberspace-enabled "armed attack," but could conceivably be deemed by the president as an "act of war."

A "cyberspace-armed attack" is triggered by an operation in which a capability—a "weapon"—is used to damage, destroy, or neuter code in another state's networks. Whereas, an "act of war" is any action (use of a weapon, disinformation leading to mass death) that the U.S. chief executive deems so egregious that he declares it an act of war.

[18] Paul C. Ney Jr., *DOD General Counsel Remarks at U.S. Cyber Command Legal Conference* (Mar. 2, 2020).

[19] Jeremy Wright (Attorney General, United Kingdom), *Cyber and International Law in the 21st Century* (May 23, 2018), *at* https://www.gov.uk/government/speeches/cyber-and-international-law-in-the-21st-century.

[20] *See* David Yanagizawa-Drott, *Propaganda and Conflict: Evidence from the Rwandan Genocide*, Q. J. Econ. (Aug. 2014); *Rwanda radio transcripts* (Montreal Institute for Genocide and Human Rights Studies), *at* https://www.concordia.ca/research/migs/resources/rwanda-radio-transcripts.html; Russell Smith, *The Impact of Hate Media in Rwanda*, BBC (Dec. 3, 2003).

2016 RUSSIAN INTERFERENCE	VIOLATION OF SOVEREIGNTY	ARMED ATTACK	"ACT OF WAR"
Influence Operations (fake social media messages only; involving no unauthorized access) (***assessed*** *by the U.S. Intelligence Community*)	No	No	Not declared
Unauthorized access/ espionage (***assessed*** *by the U.S. Intelligence Community*)[21]	Yes	No	Not declared No precedent; not likely
Unauthorized manipulation of voting technology (***not assessed*** *by the U.S. Intelligence Community*)	Would have been	Technically *yes*, though likely not publicly described as "armed attack"	Unlikely, but up to the President
Unauthorized destruction or manipulation of information leading to destruction or death (***not assessed*** *by the U.S. Intelligence Community*)	Would have been	Would have been	Could be so claimed by the president, though no cyberspace operation has, to date, been declared an act of war

The Putin government presumably had an end state in mind in conducting these Russian operations. The U.S. government has no metrics, however, to discern Russian "success" (or failure) with their operations in 2016; it has assessed only Russia's performance and judged Russia's likely intent. Moreover, the U.S. government can track Russian operations and uncover fake Facebook ads, fake email messages, cutouts, hacking, information theft, Twitter messages, and unauthorized intrusions, but it cannot (to date) discern with any precision whether or how much any of these efforts resulted in any change to U.S. voting or a lack of trust in the U.S. process. (This is the difference between "measurements of performance" versus "measurements of effect/success.") Nor can we say such Russian government efforts even added to undermining public faith in the U.S. democratic process. The country was largely divided politically before the 2016 elections and had been for a decade.

[21] DNI Russian Activities Assessment, *supra* note 1, at 2, 3 ("Russian intelligence obtained and maintained access to elements of multiple U.S. state or local electoral boards. DHS assesses that the types of systems Russian actors targeted or compromised were not involved in vote tallying.").

If Russia had *not* conducted any 2016 cyberspace-enabled information operations against the 2016 U.S. elections to advance division, would Americans be any less divided today? If not, then what "success" can we say such Russian operations had with certainty?

The U.S. government and the American people are right to be concerned, of course. As an autocracy, Russia's goals for the United States are malign. Russian attempts to affect the 2016 election were malicious at best and could have been deemed acts of war, had they led to a change in U.S. polity or civil unrest and death. They did, in any case, precipitate a significant U.S. counterreaction.

The U.S. Intelligence Community was subsequently directed by the Trump administration to collect on and defend against 2018 malign Russian efforts directed at the U.S. midterm elections and will likely remain attuned to future efforts. Further, the U.S. government, under President Trump, sanctioned Russia for its 2016 and other acts. And Democrat calls for rapprochement with the Putin government seemed to have ended as a result of the 2016 Russian effort.

We are right to be concerned over covert Russian activity to influence the 2016 elections, though we are weak on understanding any of its nuance (i.e., success). Was Russian activity designed to advance specific Russian goals, such as weaken NATO to allow for more Russian meddling in its periphery states, such as Georgia, Ukraine, Belarus, Kazakhstan, and the Baltics? Or was the goal to weaken the U.S. generally and globally? Or both? Does Putin pick favorites or just lesser enemies? Did he want Trump to win or did he just want to embarrass Hillary Clinton? Does he want Trump to make America great, or does he now hope America becomes weaker? Or do the Russian GRU (Main Directorate of the General Staff of the Armed Forces of the Russian Federation) and the Russian Internet Research Agency[22] have standing orders to make a mess of things generally in the United States and have the autonomy to do whatever they can, wherever they can, given limitations on budgets, people, and time? Or does Putin approve each operation proposed?

We may be concerned about Russian political influence via social media because we have a better understanding now about what Russia did in 2016. But perhaps the existence of these assessments pulls us wrongly toward social media influence, email theft, and voting infrastructure integrity, whereas there may have been other Russian influence operations conducted elsewhere and of more effectiveness (and never discerned), such as support to American political grassroots organizations.[23] Further, how outraged should we be toward thousands of false Russian-government-directed social media pages (which may not have changed any votes), while we continue to allow RT and Sputnik Television, which claim to be news organizations but which act as foreign agents of the Russian government, and Russian state media (not to mention China's media) to influence the U.S. electorate overtly?

Historically, Soviet disinformation campaigns often backfired spectacularly. Similarly, Russian attempts to interfere with the 2016 U.S. elections may have served to turn the Democratic Party anti-Putin. Trump appointees, already anti-Putin, were enabled by Trump's win to move forward with many anti–Russia government

[22] Also known as Glavset; it is linked to Russian oligarch Yevgeny Prigozhin and is based in St. Petersburg.

[23] *See* Jason Parham, *Targeting Black Americans, Russia's IRA Exploited Racial Wounds*, WIRED (Dec. 17, 2018); April Glaser, *Russian Trolls Were Obsessed with Black Lives Matter*, SLATE (May 11, 2018).

operations and policies. In short, despite some broad, seemingly Russia-sympathetic comments candidate Donald Trump made during the campaign, the Trump administration is severely anti-Putin and likely far more anti-Putin than a Clinton administration would have been (during the past two decades Democrat appointees have tended to be less confrontational internationally).[24]

Moreover, the Putin government likely does not have "favorite" U.S. candidates; it likely wishes to weaken the U.S. government overall. (Did the United States have "preferred" general secretary candidates of the Communist Party of the Soviet Union when Leonid Brezhnev died? If the U.S. government did have preferences, did that mean it wanted its preferred premier to make the Soviet Union strong?) Russian support for specific U.S. candidates is likely driven by an objective of thwarting any U.S. consensus and to sow division, rather than to support a specific party or candidate's platform. Putin is smart enough to know that Republican appointees under Trump were likely going to be much harder on his government than Clinton appointees, yet he may have worked to undermine Clinton nevertheless (perhaps he assumed Clinton was going to win). He may also have worked to undermine the Republican Party effort at the same time in 2016 but with less success. And if Putin did think that Trump would somehow be sympathetic to Russian policies, he judged badly.

V. The Era of Persistent Competition below the Threshold of Armed Conflict

Why is all such analysis of which cyberspace operations violate sovereignty or constitute "armed attack," "use of force," or an "act of war" particularly important? Because the political adversaries of the United States view cyberspace as the domain through which they can change political realities but not trigger a violent U.S. response. In short, we are engaged in bitter and consequential political struggle—in peacetime—through cyberspace.

Traditionally, the United States sees itself as either at peace or at war. Today, this divide is at best blurred and perhaps forever outdated. Today, we seem always to be in some sort of competition or confrontation—a condition accelerated and extended by cyberspace.

In peacetime, states used to endure status quo relations, during which they did not contest one another via the military domains. What is new today is that our adversaries specifically "fight" and stay in the "early" stage of warfare via cyberspace operations, information operations, and very limited or no kinetic conflict, careful never to escalate to state-on-state war. In short, our adversaries and competitors have embraced cyber competition precisely because they can avoid kinetic hostilities with the United States but still achieve their political objectives. Indeed, it is precisely because

[24] In contrast to his Democrat predecessor, President Trump has armed the Ukrainians with lethal aid; increased economic sanctions against Russia dramatically; ordered lethal retaliation against Russian mercenaries in Syria (killing as many as 200); increased U.S. oil and gas production in part to undermine Russia's European oil export extortion policy; publicly criticized Germany over its fuel dependence on Moscow; demanded NATO spend more on defense to check Russian political influence; left the INF missile treaty; and is rebuilding the U.S. military.

the United States enjoys dominance in many military domains that our adversaries plan and struggle against U.S. interests *short* of declared, mass, kinetic warfare, especially in the cyberspace domain.

Cyberspace has created a strategic environment through which political power can be challenged without resort to physical violence. States "fight" today in peacetime—via cyberspace—below the legal threshold of conflict. Political alliances, notions of national identity, and international regimes established since World War II are being challenged surreptitiously without violence. We are, therefore, at a pivotal moment for U.S. strategy and policy: Will the United States, its allies, and those that defend the rule of law, allow malicious cyber actors to despoil cyberspace and use it to undermine Western institutions and alliances—in effect, to violate sovereignty and change political realities without violence?

Russia, today, is conducting numerous cyberspace-enabled influence operations, including political destabilizing operations against the United States. Russia is competing worldwide for influence, undermining U.S. goals worldwide, and maligning U.S. policy wherever possible. Cyberspace operations are integrated into all aspects of Russian military operations. Information is used to confuse, paralyze, and subvert. Russia maintains its power by stealing, manipulating, and selectively injecting information via cyberspace operations.

The Russian government very likely entered the DNC's private databases and stole data.[25] The Russian government also likely leaked authentic and some forged data it had stolen to embarrass U.S. presidential candidate Hillary Clinton. States have an international legal obligation to refrain from interference in the internal affairs of other states. Russia likely violated this obligation. It is impossible, however, to discern the specific intent of the approver—in this case, likely Russian President Vladimir Putin himself—without a human source who can attest to what Putin claimed was his intent for the operation.

The selective leaking of private information is a form of influence operations—used by competing parties to effect opinion, weaken adversary morale, confuse or blind an adversary, and generally undermine the confidence of an enemy's institutions, capabilities, and national strength. Without specific intelligence, we are left to assess the Russian president's likely intent. At a minimum, Russia likely stole internal documents related to our political parties and institutions and strategically and selectively released them in order to influence our political process and confidence in our government. That may be the best we can conclude.

Currently, it is unknowable whether the winning margin in the key battleground states specifically changed their voting plans from Clinton to Trump, or suppressed turnout, based on the specific and selective leak of these documents by the Russian government. There is likely no method to discern whether the Russian influence operation alone swayed a single vote or thousands of votes or kept people at home. And even if there were anecdotal evidence (e.g., voter claims that a certain news item attributed to the Russian leak specifically changed voter preference from Clinton to

[25] *See* Eric Lipton et al., *The Perfect Weapon: How Russian Cyberpower Invaded the U.S.*, N.Y. TIMES (Dec. 13, 2016); *see also* Michael N. Schmitt, *Grey Zones in the International Law of Cyberspace*, 42 YALE J. INT'L L. ONLINE (2017).

Trump), and somehow it was possible to discern how many votes were swayed overall, what should a democracy do about it post hoc?

VI. What Interference Is Acceptable?

Who decides what state interference is acceptable or not? If the Russians gave money to the National Rifle Association or to Black Lives Matter (both of which would be legal for the Russian government), would we care? If the French government gave money to either organization, would we be similarly or less concerned or indifferent? Who decides which foreign state's involvement and what foreign influence is acceptable or not?

Such assessments, like acts of war, fall (in practice) more to the commander in chief (the chief foreign policy maker of the United States), than to the legislative or judicial branch of the U.S. government. The commander in chief could assess legal French interference as benign but Russian efforts malign. He could assess contributions from Russia as only modestly concerning, or very concerning, or an act of war in egregious cases, especially if it precipitated violence.

Of course, the best defense to this type of foreign influence is an educated U.S. public. Although cyberspace, especially social media, has afforded the Russian and Chinese governments new means to influence, the plethora of information sites also serve as a check to such new sources of influence. In other words, it may have been more effective for foreign states to influence the U.S. electorate when there were few U.S. news sources. Today, these Russian influence operations may have only served to affirm preconceptions but not change a single opinion. The electorate has an enormous pool of news sources through which voting preferences are likely formed. It is hard to imagine that any one source changes an opinion and likely impossible to devise a means to discern such influence.

In response to the 2016 Russian influence effort, the U.S. government was quite attuned to the 2018 elections influence effort and directed enormous resources, attention, intelligence collection, and cyber forensics to the concern. It is likely now that future Russian efforts to influence voter registration or voting will be contested aggressively by U.S. counterefforts. Further, subsequent Russian attempts at influence will no doubt be revealed publicly, making the Russian government look even worse than it did in 2016. Therefore, Russian 2016 election tactics, techniques, and procedures (TTPs) are likely to be checked by their sloppy (perceptible) tradecraft in 2016, which led to U.S. attention and an aggressive counterresponse (as well as public shaming). But the Russians are likely to adopt new TTPs in 2020 or may attempt the same capabilities used in 2016 but redouble efforts to remain undetected or unattributed. If so, this is the typical action-reaction phenomenon in defense procurements and intelligence, now being played out in influence operations, delivered through cyberspace—now the fifth domain of warfare.[26]

[26] The other military domains being land, sea, air, and space.

VII. Conclusion

Adversaries are attempting to take advantage of the subtleties of competition versus conflict in cyberspace. Compounding the problem is the challenge for democracies to discern appropriate and meaningful responses to such violations of sovereignty or instances of armed attack through cyberspace. Contrary to the initial assessments, cyberspace operations have not proved escalatory. In fact, the United States rarely responds with meaningful escalation or cost imposition (i.e., punishment) to malicious cyberspace operations. Thus, cyberspace remains the preferred domain for opponents of liberal democracy to change realities and avoid escalation and conflict. The United States is more often hamstrung and politically constipated in mounting a response to adversary violations of sovereignty or armed attack through cyberspace. Thus, the importance of understanding these thresholds, how our adversaries exploit cyberspace, and how we must confront such abuse of cyberspace is imperative. Until we can mount a legal, sufficient, and dissuasive response, our only hope may be that such adversary operations prove politically more counterproductive for the authoritarian states of the world than successful in effecting the political change they seek.

PART III

COMBATING FOREIGN ELECTION INTERFERENCE UNDER INTERNATIONAL LAW

8
Foreign Election Interference and International Law

Chimène I. Keitner

I. Introduction

The idea that human society can be divided into territorially distinct, self-governing nation-states has a long historical pedigree, and it continues to shape our conceptions of international political order. States continue, by and large, to retain a monopoly on the legitimate use of force in their territories, to prescribe domestic rules of conduct, and to undertake international legal obligations based on explicit or tacit consent. These undertakings can take the form of treaties, which are legally binding agreements among states that oblige states to do certain things and to refrain from doing other things. In addition to treaties, an evolving body of customary international law translates widespread and consistent state practice accompanied by a sense of legal obligation into a binding code of state behavior. Together, treaties and custom govern the relations among states in the international system. They also establish certain duties that states owe individuals. Yet, international law does not comprehensively regulate every aspect of human behavior. This chapter explores the possibilities, and limitations, of international law in regulating states' attempts to influence each other's elections.

The basic contours of the modern state system are often traced to the Peace of Westphalia in 1648. Over three and a half centuries later, in 1918, President Woodrow Wilson delivered a famous speech setting forth fourteen points that he deemed essential to making the world "fit and safe to live in."[1] Wilson appealed to "every peace-loving nation which, like our own, wishes to live its own life, determine its own institutions, [and] be assured of justice and fair dealing by the other peoples of the world as against force and selfish aggression."[2] In his view, this could only be accomplished by establishing a "general association of nations ... for the purpose of affording mutual guarantees of political independence and territorial integrity to great and small states alike."[3] The United States did not join the League of Nations created by the Treaty of Versailles, because the U.S. Senate declined to give its advice and consent to ratify the treaty. After World War II, however, the United States became a founding member of the United Nations—an international organization dedicated to furthering the core principles Wilson had identified.

[1] Woodrow Wilson, Address to Congress (Jan. 18, 1918).
[2] *Id.*
[3] *Id.*

Chimène I. Keitner, *Foreign Election Interference and International Law* In: *Defending Democracies.* Edited by Duncan B. Hollis and Jens David Ohlin, Oxford University Press (2021). © Duncan B. Hollis & Jens David Ohlin.
DOI: 10.1093/oso/9780197556979.003.0009

The basic idea that states are equal sovereigns underpins the current international system, notwithstanding the striking disparities in size and resources among the world's 195-odd states. Status as a sovereign state entitles a political and territorial entity to protection from the threat or use of force by other states under Article 2(4) of the UN Charter and under customary international law.[4] The Charter also enshrines "the principle of equal rights and self-determination of peoples" as the cornerstone of "friendly relations among nations."[5] Article 2(7) further specifies that the Charter does not authorize the United Nations "to intervene in matters which are essentially within the domestic jurisdiction of any state."[6] The principles of sovereignty, territorial integrity, political independence, self-determination, and nonintervention reflect core understandings about the attributes and entitlements of states in the international system.

This chapter begins by tracing attempts to further codify the nonintervention principle in the 1960s and 1970s, as the Cold War competition between the United States and the Soviet Union made other countries' domestic political arrangements a matter of national strategic interest. It then examines the tension produced by states' conflicting desires to preserve the greatest possible freedom of action for themselves and to develop rules that constrain the behavior of others. To date, this tension has impeded the ability to formulate explicit treaty-based solutions to the problem of foreign election interference. Identifying customary international law in this area requires inferring specific conduct-regulating rules from general principles, which can yield contested results.

Many forms of foreign influence and interference violate states' domestic laws. However, there are as yet few widely accepted international legal rules explicitly governing such activities, as long as they fall short of changing the results of ballots cast. Given the increased prevalence of misinformation and disinformation campaigns with domestic origins—let alone foreign ones—the current prospects for creating and enforcing international legal rules that more clearly prohibit attempts to influence the results of other countries' elections seem remote. In addition, there seems to be a lack of political will among certain leaders to take concrete steps to protect the integrity of their own countries' information environments that may be targeted by foreign influence operations. Incumbent politicians may perceive themselves as beneficiaries of the status quo, further complicating efforts to create international law in this area.

States are unlikely to agree to more granular, binding international rules as long as regimes currently in power benefit from constructive ambiguity. This does not mean, however, that there is a legal vacuum. Countries can prescribe legal rules prohibiting various types of foreign influence as a matter of domestic law. In the future, these rules might coalesce into a body of international law. In addition, although agreement on more concrete and enforceable international legal rules might remain elusive in the immediate term, like-minded states should emphasize the importance of supporting peoples' abilities to determine their own political destinies. This requires,

[4] U.N. Charter, art. 2(4); *Case Concerning Military and Paramilitary Activities* (Nicar. v. U.S.) 1986 I.C.J. Rep. 14 at 93–94 (Judgment of June 27, 1986).

[5] U.N. Charter, art. 1(2).

[6] U.N. Charter, art. 2(7).

at a minimum, promoting an anti-deception norm as a matter of both domestic and international law.

II. Toward a Nonintervention Principle

The principle of national or popular sovereignty has a long pedigree.[7] The idea that the "will of the people" should be formulated and expressed free from foreign influence also has deep roots. In 1787, for example, Thomas Jefferson wrote to John Adams that he shared Adams' apprehension about "foreign Interference, Intrigue, [and] Influence."[8] In Jefferson's view, the antidote was to hold fewer elections, because "as often as Elections happen, the danger of foreign Influence recurs."[9] The following year, Alexander Hamilton warned the public about "the desire in foreign powers to gain an improper ascendant in our councils."[10] President George Washington echoed this theme in his famous farewell address, when he advised: "Against the insidious wiles of foreign influence (I conjure you to believe me, fellow-citizens) the jealousy of a free people ought to be constantly awake, since history and experience prove that foreign influence is one of the most baneful foes of republican government."[11] The concern that other countries would seek to interfere in the United States' exercise of self-government loomed large in the minds of the founding generation.

To be sure, the American experiment in self-government was internally flawed from the outset. It excluded women and enslaved people from the franchise, and it unilaterally subjected peoples in island territories to an inferior legal status. Yet, the United States' founding documents remain powerful testaments to the idea of government "of the people, by the people, for the people."[12] Just as "We the People" created the United States by adopting the U.S. Constitution, so did "We the Peoples" create the United Nations by adopting the UN Charter.

The United States played a key role in creating the United Nations, which was established primarily to protect state sovereignty and to curtail the use of interstate armed force. As indicated previously, Article 2(4) of the UN Charter prohibits the threat or use of force against the territorial integrity or political independence of any state. It does not, however, explicitly proscribe other potential means of influencing foreign states. Indeed, much diplomacy aims to shape the behavior of other states, including by persuading states to change their domestic policies in matters ranging from the conduct of law enforcement activities, to the treatment of minorities, to the guarantee of free and fair elections.[13] At the time the UN Charter was drafted, countries were

[7] *See, e.g.*, Chimène I. Keitner, The Paradoxes of Nationalism: The French Revolution and Its Meaning for Contemporary Nation Building (2007) (exploring the historical and normative underpinnings of national self-determination as a basis for international political order).

[8] Letter from Thomas Jefferson to John Adams (Dec. 6, 1787), https://founders.archives.gov/documents/Jefferson/01-12-02-0405.

[9] *Id.*

[10] Federalist No. 68 (Mar. 14, 1788).

[11] George Washington, Farewell Address (Sept. 17, 1796).

[12] Abraham Lincoln, Gettysburg Address (Nov. 19, 1863).

[13] Overt unilateral efforts to shape and support other countries' domestic policies can take many forms, including diplomatic statements, conditional foreign aid, and technical assistance programs. The U.K. House of Lords catalogued these tools of "soft power" in a 2014 report. *See* House of Lords Select

focused primarily on constraining unilateral uses of military force, and avoiding interstate conflict by creating durable institutions for the peaceful settlement of international disputes.

The creation of the UN Security Council with five veto-wielding permanent members addressed concerns among powerful states that a new international organization would diminish their own sovereignty and ability to influence global affairs. In addition, Article 2(7) explicitly indicates that the Charter does not authorize the United Nations "to intervene in matters which are essentially within the domestic jurisdiction of any state." The Charter does not define what falls "essentially within [a state's] domestic jurisdiction,"[14] and it leaves open the question of whether each state can define the scope of its own "domestic jurisdiction." This ambiguity predated the Charter, and it persists to some extent today. For example, two decades before the Charter was drafted, the Permanent Court of International Justice noted that "the question whether a certain matter is or is not solely within the domestic jurisdiction of a state is an essentially relative question; it depends upon the development of international relations."[15] Two decades after the Charter's adoption, when the topic of nonintervention was foremost in the minds of newly independent countries, D.R. Gilmour observed that "[n]o one agrees on the present-day content of domestic jurisdiction," and that, relatedly, "no one has been able to produce a definition of intervention which is acceptable to all."[16] A similar observation might be made today, although certain points of consensus have emerged.[17]

The question of whether a state is entitled to define the scope of its own domestic jurisdiction or *domaine réservé* has arisen in the context of compulsory international dispute settlement. For example, the International Court of Justice (ICJ) confronted this issue in a 1957 case involving claims brought by France against Norway.[18] Norway argued that the ICJ did not have authority to adjudicate the dispute because, among

Committee on Soft Power and the UK's Influence, *Persuasion and Power in the Modern World* (2014), *at* https://publications.parliament.uk/pa/ld201314/ldselect/ldsoftpower/150/150.pdf.

[14] Georg Nolte observes that "the extent of protection against acts of the UN and against acts by individual States is not necessarily identical." Consequently, he endorses the view that "Art. 2(7) is *lex specialis* to the general principle of non-intervention" and that this general principle "can be derived from Arts 2(1) and (4) of the Charter and from customary international law." Georg Nolte, *Article 2(7)*, in The Charter of the United Nations: A Commentary 284 (Bruno Simma et al. eds., 3d ed., 2012).

[15] *Advisory Opinion, Nationality Decrees Issued in Tunis and Morocco*, PCIJ Ser. B, No. 4, at 24, *quoted in* Alfred Verdross, *The Plea of Domestic Jurisdiction Before an International Tribunal and a Political Organ of the United Nations*, 28 Z. für AöRV 33, 37 (1968). Verdross indicates that international law leaves it to domestic law to regulate "the constitution of the state, its organization, the obligations of its citizens, questions of nationality, and all other questions having an exclusively internal attachment." *Id.* at 36–37.

[16] D.R. Gilmour, *The Meaning of "Intervene" within Article 2(7) of the United Nations Charter—An Historical Perspective*, 16 ICLQ 330, 331 (1967).

[17] For example, the UN High Commissioner for Human Rights now leads efforts to protect minorities. *See* U.N.H.C.R., *Minority Rights: International Standards and Guidelines for Implementation* (2010), *at* https://www.ohchr.org/Documents/Publications/MinorityRights_en.pdf. The Organization for Security and Co-operation in Europe has spearheaded election monitoring along with other governmental and nongovernmental organizations. *See, e.g.*, OSCE, *Election Monitoring—A Decade of Monitoring Elections: The People and the Practice* (Nov. 29, 2005), *at* https://www.osce.org/odihr/elections/17165; *Declaration of Principles for International Election Observation* (Oct. 27, 2005), *at* https://www.cartercenter.org/resources/pdfs/peace/democracy/des/declaration_code_english_revised.pdf.

[18] *Certain Norwegian Loans* (Fr. v. Nor.) 1957 I.C.J. 9 (Judgment of July 6, 1957).

other reasons, France had not accepted the ICJ's compulsory jurisdiction over matters falling "essentially within the national jurisdiction" as understood by France. Norway thus claimed a reciprocal exemption from ICJ jurisdiction, which Norway contended encompassed disputes involving the terms of loans issued by Norway and Norwegian banks. In France's view, by contrast, the fact that French nationals held bonds of those loans created an international obligation for Norway to honor their terms and pay the sums due in gold value.

The ICJ agreed with Norway that, based on the requirement of reciprocity, "Norway, equally with France, is entitled to except from the compulsory jurisdiction of the Court disputes understood by Norway to be essentially within its national jurisdiction."[19] Sir Hersch Lauterpacht concurred in the conclusion that the court lacked jurisdiction, but he filed a separate opinion taking issue with the majority's view of the exception as self-judging. In his opinion, "[t]he notion that if a matter is governed by national law it is for that reason at the same time outside the sphere of international law is both novel and, if accepted, subversive of international law."[20] In other words, "[t]he question of conformity of [Norway's] national legislation with international law is a matter of international law."[21] Moreover, the ICJ Statute imposes upon the Court the duty and the right to determine its jurisdiction, which "cannot be exercised by a party to the dispute."[22] This is because "[a]n instrument in which a party is entitled to determine the existence of its obligation is not a valid and enforceable legal instrument of which a court of law can take cognizance."[23] Instead, such an instrument is merely "a declaration of a political principle and purpose."[24] This tension between creating authoritative international institutions, on the one hand, and states' unwillingness to cede their own ultimate decision-making authority, on the other, pervades attempts to articulate and enforce international legal rules.

Notwithstanding this tension, the effort to give more precise content to the principle of nonintervention in a state's domestic affairs gained momentum in the late 1960s and early 1970s. In addition to defining the scope of a state's domestic jurisdiction, states confronted the question of what activities amounted to prohibited intervention. In 1964, jurists from twenty-six states convened in Mexico City with the explicit goal of "translating the ideals of the United Nations Charter into a practical code of conduct."[25] The delegates struggled with whether "principles of international law heavily charged with political overtones would be capable of being codified."[26] As a textual matter, Article 2(4) addresses itself to states and Article 2(7) addresses itself to the United Nations. Yet both can be seen as protecting a core sphere of state activity from certain forms of external pressure. The questions inevitably arose: What falls within that core sphere, and from which forms of pressure must it be protected?

[19] *Id.* at 24.
[20] *Certain Norwegian Loans*, Separate Op., Lauterpacht J., at 37.
[21] *Id.*
[22] *Id.* at 43.
[23] *Id.* at 48.
[24] *Id.*
[25] Luke T. Lee, *The Mexico City Conference of the United Nations Special Committee on Principles of International Law Concerning Friendly Relations and Co-Operation Among States*, 14 ICLQ 1296, 1297 (1965).
[26] *Id.*

As a threshold matter, the United States expressed the view that Article 2(7) "could not be regarded as being concerned with the conduct of States," but only that of the United Nations itself.[27] The "great majority" of states, however, took the more expansive position that "the prohibition of intervention by the United Nations in the domestic affairs of member states would apply *a fortiori* to member states in their relations with each other," whether explicitly or "implicitly."[28] The delegates debated how to define the concepts of "force" and "intervention," and how to delineate permissible and impermissible forms of foreign attempts to influence another country's decision-making. Proposals on which divergent views proved irreconcilable included "a specific prohibition on war propaganda," and "a definition of 'force' to include not only armed force, but also economic, political or any other form of pressure."[29]

On the question of what constitutes "force," the United States and the United Kingdom argued that "any extension of the prohibition of 'force' beyond 'armed force' to include other forms of pressure would be unnecessary and impractical in the light of modern realities."[30] In support of this view, they noted that "political and economic pressure were techniques inevitably resorted to by states in their diplomacy every day."[31] Along with other delegates from Western countries, they took the position that:

> [I]n considering the scope of the principle of non-intervention, it should be recognized that in an interdependent world it is inevitable and desirable that states be concerned with and try to influence the actions and policies of other states; and that the objective of international law is not to prevent such activity but rather to ensure that it be compatible with other principles of international law such as the sovereign equality of states and the self-determination of their peoples.[32]

In the end, the delegates failed to reach consensus on these points, while collectively affirming that, among other things, "[e]ach State has the duty to respect the personality of other States," "[t]he territorial integrity and political independence of the States are inviolable," and "[e]ach State has the right freely to choose and develop its political, social, economic and cultural systems."[33] The emphasis on freedom of choice suggests a focus on process rather than outcome. Yet, as Jens Ohlin points out, the idea of "State" sovereignty protects nondemocratic systems, whereas an emphasis on the "people" privileges democracies that give expression to the will of the governed.[34]

[27] *Id.* at 1305.

[28] *Id.* at 1297. Earlier, the 1933 Montevideo Convention on the Rights and Duties of States had provided in Article 8 that "[n]o state has the right to intervene in the internal or external affairs of another." 165 LNTS 19 (Dec. 16, 1933).

[29] *Lee, supra note* 25, at 1301–1302; *see also* Edward McWhinney, *The New Countries and the New International Law: The United Nations' Special Conference on Friendly Relations and Co-Operation Among States*, 60 AM. J. INT'L L. 1, 8 (1966) (noting that the United Kingdom's draft resolution specifically excluded "non-military measures of the nature of economic and political pressures and ideological competition" from the definition of legally prohibited "force").

[30] McWhinney, *supra* note 29, at 10.

[31] *Id.*

[32] *Id.* at 23.

[33] *Id.* at 25–26.

[34] *See* Jens David Ohlin, *Did Russian Cyber Interference in the 2016 Election Violate International Law?*, 95 TEX. L. REV. 1579, 1598 n.73 (2017) (indicating that "this is a core difference between the sovereignty and

The core principles of sovereignty and self-determination may thus be at odds with each other.

The decolonization movement emphasized the prerogatives of newly independent states by assuming that each state embodied a self-determining people. In 1965, the UN General Assembly adopted Resolution 2131 on the "inadmissibility of intervention in the domestic affairs of states."[35] The resolution cites "the increased threat to universal peace due to armed intervention and other direct or indirect forms of interference threatening the sovereign personality and the political independence of States."[36] It urges "full observance of the principle of the non-intervention of States in the internal and external affairs of other States," and indicates that "direct intervention, subversion and all forms of indirect intervention ... constitute a violation" of the UN Charter.[37] Consistent with the emphasis on decolonization, the resolution provides that "[e]very State has an inalienable right to choose its political, economic, social and cultural systems, without interference in any form by another State," and that "the right of self-determination and independence of peoples and nations [shall] be exercised without any foreign pressure."[38]

Resolution 2131 does not further define the terms "intervention," "interference," or "pressure." These prohibitions were not understood to preclude international election monitoring, as evidenced by the practice of the UN Trusteeship Council.[39] Yet, the idea of a people's right to choose its political system pulls in potentially contradictory directions. On the one hand, it does not explicitly preclude choosing autocracy. On the other hand, it suggests an international entitlement to a government that reflects the "genuine" will of the people. Tom Franck emphasized the latter view in 1992 when he posited that democracy "is on the way to becoming a global entitlement, one that increasingly will be promoted and protected by collective international processes."[40] An introduction to the United Nations' efforts to support democracy also reflects this idea: "In 1945, many of the U.N. Member States did not endorse democracy as a system, or didn't practice it. Yet, the opening words of the Charter, 'We the Peoples,' reflect the fundamental principle of democracy—that the will of the people is the source of legitimacy of sovereign states and, therefore, of the United Nations as a whole."[41] The international community thus appears to condone and even encourage independent external efforts to ensure that governments authentically express the will of their respective peoples. But operationalizing this framework presupposes some agreement about the electoral outcome that the nondistorted will of a given people would produce.

self-determination frameworks; the concept of sovereignty leaves little room for discriminating between political arrangements").

[35] G.A. Res. 2131 (XX) of Dec. 21, 1965.

[36] *Id.*

[37] *Id.*

[38] *Id.*

[39] Thomas M. Franck, *The Emerging Right to Democratic Governance*, 86 Am. J. Int'l L. 46, 70 (1992).

[40] *Id.* at 46.

[41] *Democracy in the Founding Documents of the United Nations*, *at* https://www.un.org/en/sections/issues-depth/democracy/index.html.

Election monitoring aims to protect the integrity—and bolster the legitimacy—of the periodic expression of the will of a people at the ballot box. Tom Franck recounts that the United Nations "found bases for supervising colonial elections and referendums just prior to independence and this role gradually came to be an accepted element in legitimizing those crucial transitions."[42] Not surprisingly, however, the opponents of election monitoring worried that it would be used "to reimpose a form of neocolonialism under the banner of establishing democracy."[43] It seems difficult to reconcile the imperative of self-determination of peoples with a categorical prohibition on any form of intervention in the domestic affairs of states.[44]

The 1970 Declaration on Friendly Relations—which has become a touchstone for the nonintervention principle—also reflects this paradox without resolving it. The Declaration, which was adopted by the UN General Assembly, describes three categories of prohibited activities: (1) "the obligation not to intervene in the affairs of any other State," (2) "the duty of States to refrain in their international relations from military, political, economic or any other form of coercion aimed against the political independence or territorial integrity of any State," and (3) the obligation to refrain from "the threat or use of force against the territorial integrity or political independence of any State."[45] The operative text provides, among other things, that "[n]o State or group of States has the right to intervene, directly or indirectly, for any reason whatever, in the internal or external affairs of any other State," and that "[e]very State has an inalienable right to choose its political, economic, social and cultural systems, without interference in any form by another State."[46] It also provides that peoples have the right "freely to determine, without external interference, their political status and to pursue their economic, social and cultural development."[47] The rhetorical emphasis on freedom from external influence presupposes robust internal political processes that will give effect to the people's will.

The Helsinki Final Act concluded in 1975 by the Conference on Security and Co-operation in Europe echoes and reaffirmed the language in the Declaration on Friendly Relations. It indicates that each participating state will "respect each other's right freely to choose and develop its political, social, economic and cultural systems as well as its right to determine its laws and regulations."[48] In addition, the signatories pledge to "refrain from any intervention, direct or indirect, individual or collective, in the internal or external affairs falling within the domestic jurisdiction of another participating State," and to "in all circumstances refrain from any other act of military, or

[42] Franck, *supra* note 39, at 70.

[43] *Id.* at 82.

[44] *See, e.g.*, Keitner, *supra* note 7, at 6 (indicating that "[o]n a rhetorical level, states invoke the attributes of sovereignty and inviolability to defend themselves from internal and external political and territorial challenges. On the ethical level, these prerogatives (at least in a nation-statist framework) seem to rely on the assumption that existing states represent and embody self-determining nations. This leads to the puzzling result that states may rely for their legitimacy on a principle that can also be invoked to undermine that legitimacy, and to challenge their political and territorial integrity.").

[45] G.A. Res. 2625 (XXV) of Oct. 24, 1970.

[46] *Id.*

[47] *Id. See also* Jens Ohlin's treatment in chapter 11, this volume.

[48] Conference on Security and Co-operation in Europe (CSCE), "Final Act" (Helsinki 1975) [1975] 14 ILM 1292.

of political, economic or other coercion designed to subordinate to their own interest the exercise by another participating State of the rights inherent in its sovereignty."[49] The Helsinki Final Act also commits states to respect human rights and to "promote and encourage the effective exercise of civil, political, economic, social, cultural and other rights and freedoms" of individuals.[50]

The developments previously described support the view that a customary international law principle of nonintervention insulates certain core domestic interests from foreign control, even if certain aspects of governance (such as respect for human rights) have become matters of inclusive international concern. As the International Court of Justice indicated in its *Nicaragua* decision, "[a] State's domestic policy falls within its exclusive jurisdiction, provided of course that it does not violate any obligation of international law."[51] Yet, as explored later, the precise content of this norm remains elusive. As Lori Damrosch wrote in 1989, the existence of a norm prohibiting "nonforcible efforts to influence another state's internal politics ... is widely proclaimed, and it is commonly assumed to be a legal obligation rather than a mere practice of comity or aspirational objective."[52] However, as Damrosch also noted, "[a] conception of the [nonintervention] norm that would prohibit these forms of nonforcible involvement in domestic politics is problematic, because state practice diverges markedly from it."[53] The prohibition on the threat or use of force is clear. It remains less clear, however, what tools short of force remain lawfully at states' disposal to pursue their foreign policy goals, particularly when those goals implicate the internal decision-making processes of other states.

III. A Continuum of State Conduct

A range of possible frameworks exists for drawing the line between permissible and prohibited attempts to influence the domestic affairs of other states. Article 2(4) and its customary international law analog prohibit the threat or use of force against the "political independence" of any state. These acts lie at one end of a continuum between lawful and unlawful acts. Diplomatic statements about a state's own policy preferences (e.g. "We hope to see ..."), with no strings attached, lie at the opposite end of the continuum. A wide variety of possible acts lies in between these two extremes. The current debate centers on where and how to draw the line between prohibited and permitted acts.

Evan Wilson has observed that "[t]here is no simple policy solution to the problem of foreign interference in a democracy, because democracies by their very nature are open to influence."[54] There is also no "simple" answer to the question of where

[49] *Id.*

[50] *Id.*

[51] *Military and Paramilitary Activities* (Nicar. v. U.S.), 1986 I.C.J. 14, 131; *see also id.* at 133 (referring to "the fundamental principle of State sovereignty, on which the whole of international law rests").

[52] Lori Fisler Damrosch, *Politics Across Borders: Nonintervention and Nonforcible Influence over Domestic Affairs*, 83 AM J. INT'L L. 1, 1 (1989).

[53] *Id.* at 2.

[54] Evan Wilson, *Don't Call It a Comeback: Foreign Interference in U.S. Elections Has Been Here for Years*, WAR ON THE ROCKS (July 30, 2019).

international law draws the line. Duncan Hollis has expressed a lack of confidence that existing international law "carve[s] off and ban[s] certain [influence operations] from those that are regarded as a normal part of international discourse."[55] As Hollis notes, "[t]he problem lies not in the [nonintervention] rule's existence but in its application."[56]

Various terms have been used to characterize states' incursions into each others' presumptive spheres of autonomy. When it comes to elections, the terms "interference," "influence," and "meddling" seem to have gained the most currency. None of these terms sound in a distinctly legal register. As described previously, the available legal categories involve nonintervention, sovereignty, and self-determination. This section canvasses each of these categories in turn.

A. Nonintervention

The nonintervention principle seems the most obvious candidate for regulating foreign election interference, but its content remains underspecified. This is in part because, as Damrosch noted, states often endeavor to shape the decisions and conduct of other states.[57] For example, in the *Nicaragua* case, the ICJ acknowledged that "[t]he United States authorities have on some occasions clearly stated their grounds for intervening in the affairs of a foreign state for reasons connected with, for example, the domestic policies of that country, its ideology, the level of its armaments, or the direction of its foreign policy."[58] However, the ICJ declined to attribute legal significance to this practice, reasoning that "these were statements of international policy, and not an assertion of rules of existing international law."[59]

The United States and the United Kingdom took the position in 1964 that "any extension of the prohibition of 'force' beyond 'armed force' to include other forms of pressure would be unnecessary and impractical in the light of modern realities," and that "political and economic pressure were techniques inevitably resorted to by states in their diplomacy every day."[60] This conception continues. For example, the United States has long used economic sanctions as a foreign policy tool.[61] Whether or not certain economic sanctions should be viewed as running afoul of Article 2(4)'s prohibitions remains a matter of dispute.[62]

The United States notoriously ceased participating in the *Nicaragua* case after the ICJ decided to adjudicate Nicaragua's claims despite the United States' jurisdictional objections. Even so, the Court's opinion assessing the lawfulness of U.S. support for the right-wing Contras in their fight against the ruling socialist Sandinista regime remains a core jurisprudential reference point on the nonintervention principle. In

[55] Duncan Hollis, *The Influence of War; The War for Influence*, 32 Temple Int'l & Comp. L.J. 31, 39 (2018).
[56] *Id.* at 40.
[57] *See* Damrosch, *supra* note 52, at 2.
[58] *Military and Paramilitary Activities*, 1986 I.C.J. at 109.
[59] *Id.*
[60] McWhinney, *supra* note 29, at 10.
[61] *See* Economic Sanctions and American Diplomacy (Richard N. Haas ed., 1998).
[62] *See, e.g.*, Paul Szasz, *The Law of Economic Sanctions*, 71 Int'l L. Stud. 455 (1998).

often-cited language from that opinion, the ICJ indicated that "the element of coercion ... defines, and indeed forms the very essence of, prohibited intervention."[63] In a subsequent case, the ICJ referred back to its *Nicaragua* opinion and to the Declaration on Friendly Relations to reaffirm that "the principle of non-intervention prohibits a State 'to intervene, directly or indirectly, with or without armed force, in support of the internal opposition within a State.'"[64] Although these pronouncements were made in cases involving state support for paramilitary groups, they inform current attempts to identify the hallmarks of internationally unlawful intervention.

If the concept of "coercion" does not require military force, then identifying prohibited intervention involves distinguishing between (lawful) persuasion and (unlawful) coercion.[65] Ido Kilovaty goes one step further and argues that defining prohibited intervention to require coercion "cannot hold in an era where cyberspace is used for harmful interference that cannot, almost by definition, be coercive."[66] The terms election "interference" and election "meddling" have emerged as alternatives to "intervention" to describe such noncoercive forms of foreign influence. Yet, states have not categorically condemned such activities as violations of international law, as long as they do not actually manipulate or change the tabulation of election results.[67]

States targeted by "active measures" and "computational propaganda" may decry—but they do not necessarily foreswear—the use of these techniques. Thus, for example, Michael Schmitt suggests that "funding a hacker group that engages in destructive cyber operations could qualify as [unlawful] intervention," whereas "diplomacy and propaganda, albeit intended to cause another State to act in a certain manner, do not qualify as intervention because the target State retains the ability to choose; the decisions they are meant to affect remain voluntary, even though they may now be

[63] *Military and Paramilitary Activities*, 1986 I.C.J. at 108.

[64] *Armed Activities on the Territory of the Congo* (DRC v. Uganda), 2005 I.C.J. 165, 227, *quoting* 1986 I.C.J. at 108.

[65] *See, e.g.*, Gary Corn & Eric Jensen, *The Technicolor Zone of Cyberspace—Part I*, JUST SECURITY (May 30, 2018) (indicating that "the [nonintervention] rule is generally described as prohibiting forcible, dictatorial, or otherwise coercive measures against a relatively limited but important zone of sovereign interests falling within what is commonly referred to as the state's *domaine réservé*" and noting that this encompasses "actions involving some level of subversion or usurpation of a victim state's protected prerogatives"); *see also* Steven J. Barela, *Zero Shades of Grey: Russian-Ops Violate International Law*, JUST SECURITY (Mar. 29, 2018) (focusing on "the breadth, depth and precision of the Russian intrusion" into "the vital societal dynamic of legitimacy" in order to brand Russian activities as coercive).

[66] Ido Kilovaty, *The Elephant in the Room: Coercion*, 113 AJIL UNBOUND 87, 87 (2019); *but see* Maziar Jamnejad & Michael Wood, *The Principle of Non-intervention*, 22 LEIDEN J. INT'L L. 345, 368 (2009) (indicating in the context of funding foreign noninsurrectionary political parties that "[t]he key test remains coercion").

[67] *See, e.g.*, Attorney General Jeremy Wright, *Cyber and International Law in the 21st Century* (May 23, 2018), *at*https://www.gov.uk/government/speeches/cyber-and-international-law-in-the-21st-century(indicating that "[t]he very pervasiveness of cyber makes silence from states on the boundaries of acceptable behaviour in cyberspace unsustainable," and that the nonintervention principle would be breached by "the use by a hostile state of cyber operations to manipulate the electoral system to alter the results of an election in another state, intervention in the fundamental operation of Parliament, or in the stability of our financial system"); President Barack Obama, *Statement by the President on Actions in Response to Russian Malicious Cyber Activity and Harassment* (Dec. 29, 2016), *at* https://obamawhitehouse.archives.gov/the-press-office/2016/12/29/statement-president-actions-response-russian-malicious-cyber-activity(indicating that "Russia took actions intended to interfere with the U.S. election process," and that the United States will respond to "Russia's efforts to undermine established international norms of behavior, and interfere with domestic governance," but not stating that Russia violated international law).

suboptimal."[68] These statements suggest that, despite its intuitive appeal, the nonintervention principle cannot do all the work in differentiating between permitted and prohibited attempts to influence the outcome of another state's domestic political deliberations.

B. Sovereignty

If the nonintervention principle prohibits coercive acts that fall short of the threat or use of force, are all noncoercive acts permitted? One's answer to this question turns in part on whether one adopts the view that a state can unlawfully violate another state's sovereignty without using either force or coercion. The *Tallinn Manual 2.0* takes the position that sovereignty is an independent attribute whose violation constitutes an internationally wrongful act.[69] Some governments have endorsed this position.[70] Others have rejected the idea of "sovereignty-as-rule."[71]

U.S. State Department Legal Adviser Brian Egan noted in 2016 that "[i]dentifying how [international] law applies to specific cyber activities is more challenging, and States rarely articulate their views on this subject publicly."[72] Egan reaffirmed the principle that "a cyber operation by a State that interferes with another country's ability to hold an election or that manipulates another country's election results would be a clear violation of the rule of non-intervention."[73] Beyond that, he exhorted states to

[68] Michael N. Schmitt, *Grey Zones in the International Law of Cyberspace*, 42 Yale J. Int'l L. 1, 8 (2017); *cf.* Gary Corn, *Coronavirus Disinformation and the Need for States to Shore Up International Law*, Lawfare (Apr. 2, 2020) (noting that "[e]fforts to sow societal division and distrust do not readily lead to a finding of coercion; after all, the citizenry is free to accept or disavow the disinformation being disseminated"); Sean Watts, *Low-intensity Cyber Operations and the Principle of Non-Intervention*, 14 Baltic Y.B. Int'l L. Online 137 (Mar. 9, 2015).

[69] *See* Tallinn Manual 2.0 on the International Law Applicable to Cyber Operations (Michael Schmitt ed., NATO CCD COE, 2017), Rule 4 (indicating that "[a] State must not conduct cyber operations that violate the sovereignty of another State"); *see also* Eric Talbot Jensen, *The Tallinn Manual 2.0: Highlights and Insights*, 48 Geo. J. Int'l L. 735, 743 (2017) (indicating that, to date, "states are applying sovereignty with respect to cyberspace in a way that does not preclude cyber activities on the infrastructure and territory of another state" as long as these "do not impinge on the inherently governmental functions of another state").

[70] *See, e.g.*, Ministère des Armées (France), *Droit international appliqué aux operations dans le cyberspace* (Sept. 9, 2019), *at* https://www.defense.gouv.fr/salle-de-presse/communiques/communiques-du-ministere-des-armees/communique_la-france-s-engage-a-promouvoir-un-cyberespace-stable-fonde-sur-la-confiance-et-le-respect-du-droit-international; Bert Koenders, Foreign Minister (Neth.), *Letter to Parliament on The Application in Cyberspace of Relevant Elements of Existing International Law* (July 2019), *at* https://www.government.nl/binaries/government/documents/parliamentary-documents/2019/09/26/letter-to-the-parliament-on-the-international-legal-order-in-cyberspace/International+Law+in+the+Cyberdomain+-+Netherlands.pdf*see also* Harriet Moynihan, *The Application of International Law to Cyberspace: Sovereignty and Non-Intervention*, Just Security (Dec. 13, 2019) (defining a violation of sovereignty as "the exercise of state powers within the territory of another State without consent"); Harriet Moynihan, *The Application of International Law to State Cyberattacks: Sovereignty and Non-Intervention* (Chatham House, Dec. 2019), *at* https://www.chathamhouse.org/sites/default/files/publications/research/2019-11-29-Intl-Law-Cyberattacks.pdf(providing a detailed account of the application of international law to cyber operations).

[71] *See* Wright (U.K.), *supra* note 67; *see also* Gary Corn, *Tallinn Manual 2.0—Advancing the Conversation*, Just Security (Feb. 15, 2017).

[72] *See* Brian Egan, *Remarks on International Law and Stability in Cyberspace* (Nov. 10, 2016), *at* https://www.state.gov/s/l/releases/remarks/264303.htm.

[73] *Id.*

"do more work to clarify how the international law on non-intervention applies to States' activities in cyberspace."[74] The existing divergence in views on whether a violation of sovereignty itself amounts to an internationally wrongful act precludes using the idea of sovereignty as the touchstone for delineating lawful and unlawful attempts to influence another state's domestic decision-making.

C. Self-determination

The principle of self-determination offers an alternative normative and legal basis for proscribing foreign election interference that does not amount to "intervention" in the traditional sense. The idea of protecting the free expression of the people's will echoes the emphasis on free choice in the nonintervention principle. As Maziar Jamnegad and Sir Michael Wood indicate with respect to nonintervention: "If the target state wishes to impress the intervening state and complies freely, or the pressure is such that it could reasonably be resisted, the sovereign will of the target state has not been subordinated."[75] This formulation presumes that "the pressure" being exerted by the intervening state can be identified as coming from outside the target state. That is not always the case.

Jens Ohlin argues elsewhere in this volume that covert foreign participation in the political process violates the principle of self-determination, rather than nonintervention or sovereignty.[76] He focuses on the 2016 Russian social media campaign, in which "outside forces masquerad[ed] as inside members of the polity."[77] In his view, determining whether a particular action violates the nonintervention norm is, at best, incomplete.[78] When election interference involves impersonating members of the polity, the "key mechanism" is "deception, not coercion."[79] To remedy the harm caused by coercion, "[a]ll that needs to happen is for the interference to be unmasked as foreign in nature."[80] In Ohlin's account, *overt* efforts to influence another country's domestic political discourse "are unobjectionable because they are transparent."[81]

Examining disinformation operations through a self-determination lens seeks to protect the integrity of deliberative processes, rather than just electoral outcomes. By labeling covert nonmember participation in political discourse a harm in itself, this approach seeks to avoid the need to engage in counterfactual reasoning. Even so, any reference to distortion necessarily presumes a set of electoral preferences that would exist absent foreign deception. For example, Lori Damrosch has opined that states should not "attempt to substitute their own preferences for the natural outcome of another state's internal political dynamic."[82] This, too, presumes that there is such a thing

[74] *Id.*
[75] Jamnejad & Wood, *supra* note 66, at 348.
[76] *See* chapter 11, this volume.
[77] *Id.* at 251.
[78] *Id.* at 244–245 (indicating that this account captures the harm caused by Russian operation of a troll farm that created fake social media accounts, but not Russian hacking and dissemination of DNC emails).
[79] *Id.* at 244.
[80] *Id.* at 251–252.
[81] *Id.* at 259.
[82] Damrosch, *supra* note 52, at 50.

as a "natural outcome" of a particular electoral process. If the test of international lawfulness is whether or not a foreign state desires to *substitute* its own preferences for those of the voters, then lawfulness turns on the subjective intent of the foreign state, which could be difficult to ascertain. It might be more feasible to assess whether or not the techniques used mislead voters about the provenance of particular information or viewpoints or about the mechanics of voting (such as where and how to register or cast votes), thereby depriving them of the opportunity to self-govern.[83]

Nicholas Tsagourias seems to have the latter type of cyber operation in mind when he describes an example of activity that he views as noncoercive but still internationally unlawful:

> [W]hen a state interferes in the electoral process, for example through disinformation or "hack and leak" operations, it interferes with the structures but also with the environment that condition and facilitate the formation of authority and will by the people and substitutes the authentic process of self-determination with an artificially constructed process in order to generate particular attitudes and results aligned to the intervenor's will.[84]

This example relies on a distinction between "authentic" and "artificial" constructions of a people's political preferences, which can be difficult to disentangle. As a practical matter, states' hesitancy to rule out using influence techniques that might serve their own foreign policy interests, and their skittishness about discussing and disclosing covert actions, makes cyber influence operations a particularly difficult area for discerning or creating clear international legal rules.[85]

Notwithstanding these complications, the idea that noncoercive electoral interference violates the principle of self-determination carries intuitive appeal. So far, however, countries do not appear to have coalesced around this proposition. Ohlin anticipates this critique, which he argues "confuses the *identification* of the legal rule with the *application* of that legal rule."[86] Yet, for a legal rule to exert a meaningful compliance pull, it must be articulated and accepted with a sufficient degree of specificity.

[83] *See, e.g.*, Corn & Jensen, *supra* note 65 (noting, with respect to the prohibition on intervention, that "covertly disseminating on the eve of an election false information that a candidate for office had dropped from the race would likely deprive the victim state of a free and fair electoral process without using coercion in the most common senses of the term").

[84] Nicholas Tsagourias, *Electoral Cyber Interference, Self-Determination and the Principle of Non-Intervention in Cyberspace*, EJIL: Talk! (Aug. 26, 2019).

[85] The same might be said of other forms of covert action, such as espionage. The General Counsel of the U.S. Department of Defense has indicated on behalf of the Department that "most countries, including the United States, have *domestic* laws against espionage, but international law, in our view, does not prohibit espionage per se even when it involves some degree of physical or virtual intrusion into foreign territory." Paul C. Ney Jr., *DOD General Counsel Remarks at U.S. Cyber Command Legal Conference* (Mar. 2, 2020), *at* https://www.defense.gov/Newsroom/Speeches/Speech/Article/2099378/dod-general-counsel-remarks-at-us-cyber-command-legal-conference/. Ashley Deeks has noted several factors that have contributed to this "traditional" view, including that "public pressure to regulate intelligence activity was minimal, because spying and covert action seldom directly affected the average citizen." Ashley S. Deeks, *Confronting and Adapting: Intelligence Activities and International Law*, 102 Va. L. Rev. 599, 608 (2016); *see id.* at 679 (indicating that covert election interference poses a challenge for international law because "[t]he harms are nonphysical and diffuse, but may affect large parts of a population").

[86] *See* chapter 11, this volume, at 260.

States recognize the principle of self-determination at a high level of generality, but they continue to contest its attendant conduct-regulating rules. An international legal prohibition on deceptive practices intended to distort another polity's political discourse could certainly be codified in a treaty or emerge as customary international law. Although this has not happened to date, there is some evidence of attempts to move in this direction.[87]

As a point of reference, the U.S. Department of Defense (DoD) has taken the position that international law does not prohibit nonconsensual cyber operations in another state's territory that fall short of a prohibited intervention or use of force.[88] As a matter of domestic law, DoD does not view the First Amendment right to receive information as a categorical bar on its ability to conduct a military cyber operation "to disrupt a foreign government's ability to disseminate covertly information to U.S. audiences via the Internet by pretending that the information has been authored by Americans inside the United States."[89] DoD thus views foreign disinformation operations as a sufficient threat to election integrity to warrant disrupting them in a "content neutral" manner.[90] However, DoD does not label such operations a violation of international law unless they "coercively intervene[e] in the core functions of another State."[91] DoD's positions do not necessarily represent those of other agencies. Nevertheless, it is noteworthy that countries might not be willing to renounce the use of noncoercive, nonconsensual cyber operations as a matter of international law, even though they acknowledge that these can violate another country's domestic law.[92]

IV. Conclusion: The Limits and Potential of International Law

To date, states appear by and large to have maintained a posture of constructive ambiguity when it comes to the international lawfulness of influence operations—via cyber means or otherwise—that do not directly alter votes as they were cast.[93] Domestic legal regulation of campaign finance and the modalities of political speech remain a

[87] Examples include the Paris Call for Trust and Security in Cyberspace (Nov. 12, 2018), https://pariscall.international/en/, which includes a call "to ensure people decide freely, based on independent information, who should represent them," as well as the Charlevoix G7 Summit Communique (June 9, 2018), https://www.reuters.com/article/us-g7-summit-communique-text/the-charlevoix-g7-summit-communique-idUSKCN1J5107, which emphasizes the importance of "tak[ing] concerted action in responding to foreign actors who seek to undermine our democratic societies and institutions, our electoral processes, our sovereignty and our security." Chapter 14, this volume, at 316.

[88] Ney, *supra* note 85.

[89] *Id.*

[90] *Id.*

[91] *Id.*

[92] The same could be said of traditional forms of election meddling, although the United States has, in recent years, favored supporting democratic processes rather than promoting particular candidates in foreign elections. *See, e.g.*, Scott Shane, *Russia Isn't the Only One Meddling in Elections. We Do It, Too*, N.Y. Times (Feb. 17, 2018); *see also* Thomas Carothers, *Is the U.S. Hypocritical to Criticize Russian Election Meddling?* (Carnegie Endowment, Mar. 12, 2018), *at* https://carnegieendowment.org/2018/03/12/is-u.s.-hypocritical-to-criticize-russian-election-meddling-pub-75780 (drawing a distinction between democracy promotion and malign election interference).

[93] *See* Egan, *supra* note 72.

matter of internal law (as long as they comply with applicable international human rights guarantees, such as freedom of expression and nondiscrimination).

It seems somewhat unsatisfying to proclaim simply that the accumulation of state practice and *opinio juris* (a subjective belief that action or restraint is legally compelled) will, over time, yield more definite rules distinguishing lawful persuasion from unlawful intervention. If one had to draw a line based on reason and experience rather than international convention or custom, it seems that both domestic and international law could converge around a prohibition on deceit, in addition to the existing prohibition on actual manipulation of results. Enforcing such a prohibition would require greater transparency across all forms of media, as well as agreement on how to identify false information. Our highly decentralized media environment, combined with extreme partisanship and mutual suspicion, makes it difficult to envisage how such a prohibition—even if desirable in theory—could be implemented in practice.[94]

Another option would be to concede the limits of international law and leave the regulation of elections—including the role of foreign money and messages—exclusively to domestic law.[95] The U.S. indictment of the Internet Research Agency and Russian nationals who worked on its behalf to interfere in the 2016 election reflects a domestic law approach, even though the likelihood of apprehension and conviction remains remote.[96] Certain forms of espionage offer paradigmatic examples of conduct that violates domestic law, but that international law appears to accept as inevitable, if not desirable.[97] This does not prevent countries from calling each other out for spying and for actively seeking to disrupt each others' intelligence collection activities. However, by and large, international law develops in areas where states assess that mutual coordination and consensual self-restraint will benefit them individually and collectively. States do not yet appear to have reached widespread consensus on precisely where to draw the line regarding cyber operations, although some have condemned attempts to modify election results or to otherwise "undermin[e] … democratic processes."[98]

In the end, publicizing and stigmatizing disinformation campaigns and foreign efforts to manipulate public opinion might curb such activities and blunt their impact,

[94] Duncan Hollis has observed that international law is generally better suited to regulating at the "physical" rather than the "cognitive" level. Influence operations may be difficult for international law to regulate, especially in light of "uncertainty about evidence, causation, and motivations." Hollis, *supra* note 55, at 44.

[95] *See, e.g.*, Library of Congress Law Library, *Regulation of Foreign Involvement in Elections* (Aug. 2019) (surveying "thirteen major democratic foreign jurisdictions on laws and policies addressing foreign involvement in elections").

[96] Indictment, United States of America v. Internet Research Agency, Case No. 1:18-cr-00032-DLF (D.D.C. Feb. 16, 2018) (charging defendants with a conspiracy to defraud the United States by interfering in the 2016 presidential election); *see also* Testimony of Deputy Assistant Attorney General Adam S. Hickey at Senate Judiciary Committee Hearing, *Election Interference: Ensuring Law Enforcement Is Equipped to Target Those Seeking to Do Harm* (June 12, 2018), *at* https://www.justice.gov/opa/speech/deputy-assistant-attorney-general-adam-s-hickey-testifies-senate-judiciary-committee; Chimène I. Keitner, *Attribution by Indictment*, 113 AJIL Unbound 207 (June 24, 2019) (indicating that the practice of "[a]ttribution by indictment uses domestic criminal law, enforced transnationally, to define and enforce certain norms of state behavior in cyberspace").

[97] *See* Deeks, *supra* note 85; *cf.* Moynihan, *supra* note 70, at 46 (noting that "saying that espionage is not prohibited by international law is not the same as saying that it is lawful").

[98] Charlevoix Communique, *supra* note 87.

even absent their formal prohibition under international law.[99] Attributing cyber operations to foreign states can provide the desired transparency, as long as these operations can be detected and disclosed in real time, and as long as the act of attribution itself is not politicized.[100] As Martha Finnemore and Duncan Hollis point out, seeking to modify state behavior by naming and shaming "presupposes a norm already in place to generate shame, rarely a warranted assumption for cybersecurity."[101] Nonetheless, in their account, accusations against states can still play a constitutive role in constituting international law "in the shadows," even if they do not explicitly invoke and apply the language of law.[102] International law can most effectively be constituted in daylight. That said, the combination of domestic legal prohibitions and international accusations might bring us closer to a world in which countries renounce and condemn deceptive practices intended to shape other peoples' deliberative decision-making.

[99] *See, e.g.*, Steven Lee Myers & Chris Horton, *In Blow to Beijing, Taiwan Re-elects Tsai Ing-wen as President*, N.Y. TIMES (Jan. 11, 2019) (indicating that "[t]he vote, which was a reversal of Ms. Tsai's political fortunes, suggested that Beijing's pressure campaign had backfired").

[100] For an example of this potential dilemma, *see* Kaveh Waddell, *Why Didn't Obama Reveal Intel About Russia's Influence on the Election?*, THE ATLANTIC (Dec. 11, 2016).

[101] Martha Finnemore & Duncan B. Hollis, *Beyond Naming and Shaming: Accusations and International Law in Cybersecurity*, EJIL (Sep. 2020), https://doi.org/10.1093/ejil/chaa056.

[102] *Id.* at 5.

9

Cybersecurity Abroad

Election Interference and the Extraterritoriality of Human Rights Treaty Obligations

Ido Kilovaty

I. Introduction

Election interference carried out through election infrastructure hacking,[1] doxing,[2] online manipulation,[3] disinformation, and propaganda raises some perplexing questions about international law's role in regulating, deterring, and punishing such activities. Many of these questions were raised in the aftermath of the Russian interference in the U.S presidential election in 2016.[4] Was this prohibited intervention?[5] Did the interference violate U.S. sovereignty?[6] How can domestic computer crime statutes be leveraged to address the matter?[7]

These questions together form the conundrum of the law applicable to digital election interference. However, this contribution is concerned with a different aspect of the problem that has received insufficient attention. Suppose that international human rights law protects privacy,[8] liberty,[9] and self-determination[10] of individuals (which it does), do these human rights obligations apply extraterritorially when an infringing action is carried out via cyberspace? In other words, if State A interferes

[1] David Sanger & Catie Edmonson, *Russia Targeted Election Systems in All 50 States, Report Finds*, N.Y. Times (July 25, 2019) (describing Russian hackers' attempts to penetrate, delete, and change voter data in election infrastructure).

[2] Robert Chesney, *State-Sponsored Doxing and Manipulation of the U.S. Election: How Should the U.S. Government Respond?*, Lawfare (Oct. 21, 2016).

[3] Alex Hern, *Cambridge Analytica: How Did It Turn Clicks into Votes?*, The Guardian (May 6, 2018).

[4] *See, e.g.*, Jens Ohlin, *Did Russian Cyber Interference in the 2016 Election Violate International Law?*, 95 Tex. L. Rev. 1579 (2017).

[5] *See*, e.g., Duncan Hollis, *Russia and the DNC Hack: What Future for a Duty of Non-Intervention?*, Opinio Juris (July 25, 2016).

[6] *See, e.g.*, Sean Watts, *International Law and Proposed U.S. Responses to the D.N.C. Hack*, Just Security (Oct. 14, 2016) ("A stronger case might be made that the D.N.C. hacks amount to a violation of sovereignty").

[7] *See, e.g.*, Helen Murillo & Susan Hennessey, *Is It a Crime?: Russian Election Meddling and Accomplice Liability Under the Computer Fraud and Abuse Act*, Lawfare (July 13, 2017).

[8] International Covenant on Civil and Political Rights (opened for signature Dec. 19, 1966, entered into force Mar. 23, 1976) 999 U.N.T.S. 171, art. 17 [hereinafter ICCPR].

[9] *Id.*, art. 9(1).

[10] *Id.*, art. 1(1).

Ido Kilovaty, *Cybersecurity Abroad* In: *Defending Democracies*. Edited by Duncan B. Hollis and Jens David Ohlin, Oxford University Press (2021). © Duncan B. Hollis & Jens David Ohlin. DOI: 10.1093/oso/9780197556979.003.0010

with the election process in State B, through intrusions to election computer systems, political bots on social media, and doxing of key figures in the election process, can State B allege that State A violated its extraterritorial obligation to respect the human rights of State B's citizens?

The answer depends on two separate issues. First, do existing human rights, such as privacy, liberty, self-determination, guarantee some sort of protection from digital election interference? And if so, the second issue is whether these human rights obligations apply extraterritorially across borders, namely to state activity in cyberspace against a foreign election.

This chapter is concerned with the second issue. At present, states are able to use offensive cyberspace capabilities remotely, without exercising any physical control—whether over territory or persons.[11] Current conceptions of extraterritoriality, however, are overly focused on "effective control,"[12] presupposing physical presence of the controller and power to exercise jurisdiction, both of which are absent in a digital election interference scenario. The "effective control" standard of extraterritoriality simply does not fit in the context of remote digital election interference.

The focus of this chapter on extraterritoriality does not suggest that the first issue is unimportant or inconsequential. Pre-cyberspace human rights law suffers from a critical flaw in relation to the content of these rights and how they apply to a new global medium of communication. For example, how does the right to privacy apply in cyberspace? What is the role of private companies (social media platforms, email service providers) in ensuring that privacy, liberty, and self-determination are protected from foreign interference? What privacy-violating state activity can be justified by virtue of a superseding national or public interest? Whatever the content of existing and future human rights law may be, its efficacy in the cyberspace era largely depends on whether its specific obligations apply to transnational, border-crossing activity.

This chapter proceeds in three parts. Section II explores the current law on extraterritoriality. Section III assess the shortcomings of this existing law, in light of digital election interference. Section IV proposes an alternative extraterritoriality conception in response to the unique challenges presented by digital election interference through cyberspace. It builds out a previously proposed "virtual control" standard, supported by an effects-based approach for extraterritoriality in the cyber age.

[11] *See* Peter Margulies, *The NSA in Global Perspective: Surveillance, Human Rights, and International Counterterrorism*, 82 Ford. L. Rev. 2137, 2150 (2014) ("Notions of control that were adequate to analyze the actions in real time taken overseas by State officials or their alleged agents do not translate well into the cyber domain").

[12] *See, e.g.*, Oona Hathaway et al., *Human Rights Abroad: When Do Human Rights Treaty Obligations Apply Extraterritorially?*, 43 Ariz. St. L.J. 385, 395 (2011) (nothing that while the United States is an outlier on the issue of extraterritoriality, "[n]early every other foreign and international body examined here concludes that countries that exert 'effective control' over a territory, person, or situation must observe basic human rights obligations.").

II. The Law on Extraterritoriality of Human Rights Obligations

Human rights treaties typically contain provisions on their scope of application.[13] The terms "territory" and "jurisdiction" are largely used to limit the scope of application of the relevant treaties. State parties to human rights treaties are bound by the territorial application of the provisions contained therein, obligating such states to respect and ensure the rights recognized by the relevant treaty.[14] However, where a state party engages in an act that affects the rights of an individual outside of that state party's territory, human rights treaties might still apply extraterritorially.[15] Today, human rights law is widely understood to create extraterritorial obligations, though such application is often limited.

One example of a scope of application that facilitates extraterritorial application is contained in the International Covenant on Civil and Political Rights (ICCPR).[16] Article 2(1) of the ICCPR, which sets out its scope of application, reads: "[E]ach State Party to the present Covenant undertakes to respect and to ensure to all individuals within its territory and subject to its jurisdiction the rights recognized in the present Covenant."[17] While the plain meaning of "within its territory" *and* "subject to its jurisdiction" may appear conjunctive at first, the practice that has crystallized around this scope of application reflects a disjunctive approach.[18] In addition, the legislative history of the ICCPR suggests that a narrow territorial construction was never the intent of the state parties.[19]

While the disjunctive model is supported by an overwhelming majority of state parties, it is not without controversy. A memorandum authored by the then Legal Adviser of the Department of State, Harold Koh, argued that a prior U.S. position which read the ICCPR's scope of application as strictly territorial is indefensible.[20]

[13] *E.g.*, ICCPR, *supra* note 8, art. 2(1); European Convention on Human Rights (adopted Nov. 4, 1950, entered into force Sept. 3, 1953) ETS 5, art. 1 [hereinafter ECHR]; American Convention on Human Rights (adopted Nov. 22, 1969, entered into force July 18, 1978) 1144 U.N.T.S. 123, art. 1(1); Convention against Torture and other Cruel, Inhuman or Degrading Treatment or Punishment (adopted Dec. 10, 1984, entered into force June 26, 1987) 1465 U.N.T.S. 85, art. 2(1).

[14] *See, e.g.*, ICCPR, *supra* note 8, art. 2(1).

[15] Marko Milanovic, Extraterritorial Application of Human Rights Treaties: Law, Principles, and Policy 8 (2011).

[16] ICCPR, *supra* note 8, art. 2(1).

[17] *Id.*

[18] *See* Gabor Rona & Lauren Aarons, *State Responsibility to Respect, Protect and Fulfill Human Rights Obligations in Cyberspace*, 8 J. Nat'l. Sec. L. & Pol'y 503, 507 (2016) ("increasingly, the terms 'within its territory and subject to its jurisdiction' are being interpreted in their disjunctive, rather than conjunctive sense, at least as concerns the State's negative obligation to refrain from violating rights. Thus, the State is bound by international human rights law in relation to individuals outside of its territory but otherwise under its jurisdiction").

[19] *See* Theodor Meron, *Extraterritoriality of Human Rights Treaties*, 89 Am. J. Int'l L. 78, 79 (1995) (noting that the United States proposed "within its jurisdiction" to ensure that a state "not be relieved of its obligation under the covenant to persons who remained within its jurisdiction merely because they were not within its territory").

[20] U.S. State Department, Office of the Legal Adviser, Memorandum Opinion on the Geographic Scope of the International Covenant on Civil and Political Rights, at 4 (Oct. 19, 2010) [hereinafter Koh Memo].

For example, Koh argued that a strict territoriality interpretation of ICCPR Article 2(1) would render the meaning of "to respect" redundant, that it is grammatically problematic, and that the object and purpose of the ICCPR support the extraterritorial reach of its obligations.[21] The memorandum, however, was never adopted as the official U.S. position on extraterritoriality.

Therefore, the obligations enumerated in the ICCPR refer to individuals either within a territory of a state party or subject to its jurisdiction.

A. The Effective Control Model

This disjunctive interpretation allows for some form of extraterritoriality, in very limited circumstances.[22] This widely understood interpretation has led to an "effective control" standard, which limits the extraterritorial scope of application to cases where a state exercises a certain degree of control over an individual outside of its territory. For example, the UN Human Rights Committee (HRC) in a comment on extraterritoriality stated that "*a State party must respect and ensure the rights laid down in the Covenant to anyone within the power or effective control of that State Party, even if not situated within the territory of the State Party*."[23] In other words, to have *jurisdiction* as the ICCPR requires, a state needs to exercise a form of *effective control* abroad. This standard has been guiding certain international institutions over the years and was later applied in a UN Human Rights Council resolution on remote drone strikes.[24] Therefore, states engaged in these operations have become bound by "*international law, including the Charter of the United Nations, international human rights law and international humanitarian law*."[25]

B. U.S. Interpretation of Extraterritoriality

While this kind of extraterritoriality may seem desirable to keep state action abroad in check, this issue remains highly contested in the United States, as American officials have historically rejected an extraterritorial application of human rights treaties.[26] In his infamous legal memo, Koh rejected the interpretation that the ICCPR imposes positive obligations extraterritorially. According to Koh, protecting "*persons under the primary jurisdiction of another sovereign otherwise could produce conflicting legal*

[21] *Id.* at 9–11.

[22] *See* Ashley Deeks, *Does the ICCPR Establish an Extraterritorial Right to Privacy?*, Lawfare (Nov. 14, 2013) ("Many other states, as well as the ICCPR treaty body, assert that the ICCPR applies either when a person is within the territory of a state party or is subject to a state's jurisdiction (as when a state detains a non-national abroad)").

[23] UN Human Rights Committee, General Comment 31: The Nature of the General Legal Obligation Imposed on States Parties to the Covenant (2004), Eightieth Session, CCPR/C/21/Rev.1/Add.13 (Mar. 29, 2004).

[24] UN Human Rights Council Res. A/HRC/25/L.32.

[25] *Id.* at para. 1.

[26] *See* Charlie Savage, *U.S. Seems Unlikely to Accept That Rights Treaty Applies to Its Actions Abroad*, N.Y. Times (Mar. 6, 2014).

authorities," and therefore, the ICCPR ought to only impose extraterritorial obligations in "*exceptional circumstances*"[27] where there is "*effective control over a particular person or context without regard to territory*."[28] In comparison, positive obligations (to ensure human rights) which require affirmatively protecting individuals should only apply to individuals "*both within the territory and subject to the jurisdiction*" of the state involved.[29]

The official U.S. position on extraterritoriality was expressed in its report submitted to the HRC in 1995.[30] In that report, the United States took the view that "the Covenant [ICCPR] did not apply to government actions outside the United States. The Covenant was not regarded as having extraterritorial application. In general, where the scope of application of a treaty was not specified, it was presumed to apply only within a party's territory."[31] This was a strict territoriality reading of the ICCPR.

Koh's memo was an attempt to expand the scope of the ICCPR's application, in particular the strict territoriality reading of it, arguing that the responsibility to *respect* human rights obligations would apply to government actions abroad. However, the responsibility to *ensure* human rights would still be territorially limited to the U.S. government vis-à-vis individuals on U.S. soil. While Koh's memo was ultimately not adopted by the administration, it did influence the official U.S. position on the matter.[32] Ashley Deeks notes that it has been the view of the U.S. government that the "ICCPR does not apply extra-territorially, because the U.S. government reads the scope requirement as limiting the treaty to activity within U.S. territory."[33] These contentions over the extraterritoriality of human rights obligations, while recent, predate the majority of cyber operations affecting the integrity of elections.

C. The European Court of Human Rights Interpretation

While the extraterritorial application of human rights law has been somewhat controversial in the United States, the European Court of Human Rights (ECtHR) has largely recognized a certain degree of extraterritoriality when states operate abroad. This may partially be attributed to the language of the European Convention on Human Rights (ECHR), which reads in Article 1: "The High Contracting Parties shall secure to everyone *within their jurisdiction* the rights and freedoms defined in Section I of this Convention" (emphasis added).

One of the earliest ECtHR cases where extraterritoriality was recognized is *Loizidou v. Turkey*, where Turkey's occupation of Northern Cyprus had given the Court jurisdiction over human rights matters occurring in that territory.[34] In *Banković*

[27] Koh Memo, *supra* note 20, at 55.
[28] *Id.*
[29] *Id.*
[30] UN Hum. Rts. Comm., 53rd Sess., 1405th mtg., Mar. 31,1995 (morning), 20, U.N. Doc. CCPRIC/SR 1405 (Apr. 24, 1995) (Statement of State Department Legal Adviser, Conrad Harper)
[31] *Id.* at para. 20.
[32] Ohlin, *supra* note 4, at 1587.
[33] Deeks, *supra* note 22.
[34] Loizidou v. Turkey, 310 Eur. Ct. H.R. (Ser. A) (1995) (Judgment on Preliminary Objections).

v. Belgium,[35] the Court made clear that the "effective control" standard applied not only to occupation of foreign territory, but also to "conduct on a state's flag vessels or in its consulates and embassies, situations of arrest and detention, and analogous cases."[36]

In *Al-Skeini and Others v. the United Kingdom*, the ECtHR had to determine whether six Iraqi citizens, who had been allegedly wrongfully killed by British forces in Iraq in 2003, were under the jurisdiction of the United Kingdom under Article 1 of the ECHR.[37] The ECtHR held that the United Kingdom assumed authority and responsibility over southeast Iraq, where the killings took place, and therefore there was a jurisdictional nexus between these Iraqi citizens and the United Kingdom.[38]

The ECtHR consistency on extraterritoriality may be attributed to the language of the ECHR, which eliminates the term "territory" from its scope of application, but it is also a more pragmatic approach which does not let state parties escape accountability for actions committed on foreign territory or against people outside of their territories.

D. Human Rights' Extraterritoriality in Cyberspace

While the extraterritoriality of human rights obligations may seem a straightforward concept, state operations in cyberspace may present some difficulties to the concept. The effective control model is based by and large on a physical understanding of the world—the state may have a certain degree of physical control over foreign land or people and therefore be under an obligation to respect human rights obligations there. Cyberspace, a virtual medium created by physical infrastructure, may prove a challenge to this model of effective control.

In general, however, international law still applies in cyberspace, regardless of its virtual nature. As Harold Koh suggested in his 2012 speech before the U.S. Cyber Command, human rights law applies in cyberspace.[39] The *Tallinn Manual 2.0 on the International Law Applicable to Cyber Operations* (*Tallinn Manual*) has similarly adopted the HRC extraterritoriality standard of "within the power or effective control." Focused primarily on how international law applies to cyberspace, it clarifies that certain human rights apply "beyond a State's territory" in cases where that state "exercises 'power and effective control.' "[40] According to the *Tallinn Manual*, this control may be "over territory (spatial model) or over individuals (personal model)."[41] Yet again, effective control is understood as control over foreign *territory* and control over *persons* abroad.

35 Banković v. Belgium, 2001-XII Eur. Ct. H.R. 333, 346 (2001).

36 Hathaway et al., *supra* note 12, at 401.

37 Al-Skeini and Others v. United Kingdom (App. No. 55721/07) ECtHR (July 7, 2011).

38 *Id.* paras. 130–140.

39 Harold Koh, *International Law in Cyberspace*, 54 Harv. Int'l L.J. 1, 9–10 (2012).

40 Tallinn Manual 2.0 on the International Law Applicable to Cyber Operations 184, Rule 66 (Michael N. Schmitt ed., 2017) [hereinafter Tallinn Manual 2.0].

41 *Id.*

This approach, which analogizes the physical space to cyberspace, ignores a different kind of power that states may exert over individuals online. When operating in cyberspace, states would rarely have concurrent physical control over foreign territory or persons. This presents an important challenge: Are extraterritorial cyber operations constrained by human rights obligations?

Indeed, the *Tallinn Manual*'s International Group of Experts acknowledged this loophole in the law on extraterritoriality, which disregards new forms of control which may be manifested online.[42] It notes: "The International Group of Experts could achieve no consensus as to whether State measures that do not involve an exercise of physical control may qualify as 'power or effective control.' "[43] Mainly, such lack of consensus has to do with the lack of state practice and *opinio juris* on the question, suggesting that there may be room for legal evolution on the topic in the future, taking into account the unique characteristics of cyberspace.[44]

E. Human Rights' Extraterritoriality and Election Interference

State-sponsored interference in foreign elections raises critical human rights issues. International human rights law recognizes the rights to self-determination[45] and privacy,[46] among many other rights, which are likely to be implicated when a foreign nation interferes in an election. In addition, the ECHR recognizes the right to free elections.[47] Considering that these rights protect election integrity and free choice to a certain degree, this raises the extraterritoriality question. While the norm of nonintervention may limit what states can and cannot do with regard to foreign elections,[48] it does not answer the extraterritoriality of human rights question.

While effective control is the governing standard for human rights' extraterritoriality, it is unclear how it maps onto election interference through cyberspace. What does "effective control" mean when nations engage in remote election interference through a nonphysical medium? To answer that question, it may be helpful to consider what we mean by "election interference," and whether any of the acts constituting election interference reach the threshold of effective control.

1. Probing and Accessing Election Systems

The most direct form of election interference would be hacking the election systems themselves. By "hacking" I mean probing, accessing, and in most extreme cases—changing the votes and thus compromising the integrity of the outcome.

A Senate Intelligence Committee report found that Russia probed state election infrastructure for vulnerabilities in all fifty U.S. states.[49] Although there was no evidence

[42] *Id.* at 185.
[43] *Id.*
[44] *Id.*
[45] ICCPR, *supra* note 8, art. 1(1); International Covenant on Economic, Social and Cultural Rights (adopted Nov. 16, 1966, entered into force Jan. 3, 1976) 993 U.N.T.S. 3, art. 1(1).
[46] ICCPR, *supra* note 8, art. 17(1).
[47] ECHR, *supra* note 13, art. 3.
[48] *See, e.g.*, Ohlin, *supra* note 4, at 1587.
[49] Sanger & Edmonson, *supra* note 1.

of an integrity compromise, probing election systems for vulnerabilities represents a serious threat to future election integrity and public trust in election institutions. Consider a case where a foreign nation successfully hacks into the election infrastructure of another nation and changes the election outcome. Would such result constitute an activity falling within the scope of "effective control"?

It is unlikely that mere probing of computer systems and networks would reach the level of "effective control," since this does not represent a case of spatial or personal control as these concepts are understood by the law on extraterritoriality. Even changing the votes themselves may not reach the threshold of effective control, but rather is likely to be considered a transnational crime or a prohibited intervention. This conclusion could support the assertion that extraterritoriality, though its effective control standard, is working as intended. Or, conversely, it may be seen as a symptom of the failures of the current extraterritoriality approach.

2. Leaking Sensitive Documents

Election interference often seeks to destabilize political processes and sow public distrust in institutions and the government. Indeed, the 2016 U.S. election was rife with leaks intended to sway public opinion and potentially change the outcome of the presidential election.[50]

Emails obtained through the hacking of the Democratic National Committee (DNC) and Hillary Clinton's presidential campaign chairman, John Podesta, were made available on WikiLeaks, leading to the resignation of DNC Chairwoman Debbie Schultz and causing a public outcry.[51]

The entire process of hacking email accounts of highly ranked officials and dumping the documents obtained can be done remotely and quickly. Yet again, human rights law remains a dead letter because extraterritoriality looks at control over a territory or persons, thus missing an entire domain of potential human rights abuses.

3. Online Disinformation and Propaganda

Finally, election interference can take place through online disinformation and propaganda, particularly through social media like Facebook and Twitter, often done by political bots and fake profiles.[52] At times, such disinformation and propaganda involves fake news and conspiracy theories intended to gaslight and rile up voters.[53]

Consider a scenario where a foreign government spreads a hoax conspiracy theory about one of the candidates, alleging that they engage in scandalous and morally reprehensible behavior that warrants their disqualification from the race. While such activity can certainly tilt the scales in favor of one of the candidates, it is unlikely to be

[50] Ido Kilovaty, *Doxfare: Politically Motivated Leaks and the Future of the Norm on Non-Intervention in the Era of Weaponized Information*, 9 HARV. NAT'L. SEC. J. 146, 155–157 (2018).

[51] Anne Gearan, Philip Rucker, & Abby Phillip, *DNC Chairwoman Will Resign in Aftermath of Committee Email Controversy*, WASHINGTON POST (July 24, 2016).

[52] Jeff Roberts, *Disinformation for Hire: How Russian PR Firms Plant Stories for Companies in U.K. News Outlets, Social Media*, FORTUNE (Sept. 30, 2019).

[53] *See, e.g.*, Darin Johnson, *Russian Election Interference and Race-Baiting*, 9 COLUM. J. RACE & L. 191, 209 (2019) ("Russia's strategic use of social media platforms to disseminate disinformation and drive a wedge among the American public with race-baiting techniques has become the norm in American election cycles").

considered "control." In particular, as social media platforms are being weaponized for such activities, it is unclear against whom control is being exercised.

Part of the problem stems from the nature of the operation—using an intermediary to meddle in elections, which ultimately affects the voters of that specific political community. No extraterritorial operation in this case is directed *specifically* against individuals of that political community. While the effects of such interference on the voters are straightforward, the law of extraterritoriality is currently oblivious as to the significant adverse effects made possible by the advent of cyberspace, sophisticated election interference operations, and internet-connected election infrastructure.

These three scenarios, which are far from hypothetical, represent a crisis as to our current understanding of extraterritoriality. Where there is no territory or individuals directly controlled by a state, what extraterritoriality standard should apply?

III. A New Model for Extraterritoriality?

Election interference illustrates that state-sponsored cyberattacks may affect the rights of voters without the attacking state exerting any effective control or jurisdiction over territory or foreigners abroad. This is largely possible because emerging technologies can seriously be used to interfere with the enjoyment of rights abroad. On that point, the UN General Assembly's resolution on "the right to privacy in the digital age" expressed its concern about the "negative impact that ... extraterritorial surveillance ... may have on the exercise and enjoyment of human rights."[54] As the surveillance context suggests, these technologies may leverage the global, instantaneous, and inexpensive qualities of the internet. This form of control requires no spatial or personal control.

At its conception, international human rights law could not have envisioned that states would become capable of interfering with and violating protected human rights through a medium that defies physical political borders. Therefore, the same international human rights law does not offer a robust understanding of extraterritoriality in light of digital election interference operations and power relations online.

This sociotechnological change dictates a revaluation of the applicable extraterritoriality models. Territory, borders, new technologies, and the changing monopoly over force are all factors that contribute to this growing imperative. The following section will overview the sociotechnological change that calls for a new model of extraterritoriality.

A. Sociotechnological Change and Extraterritoriality

The reason why existing extraterritoriality models do not seem to address digital election interference is partially due to the rapid evolution of technology vis-à-vis the international legal system.[55] In other words, extraterritoriality fails to keep pace

[54] *See* U.N.G.A. Res. 68/167 "the right to privacy in the digital age" (Dec. 18, 2013).

[55] *See generally* Ryan Jenkins, *Is Stuxnet Physical? Does It Matter?*, 12 J. MIL. ETHICS 68, 69 (2013).

with technological advancements that enable cross-border election interference. At the same time, it is not only technology that has made significant advancements in recent decades, but also the nonstate actors involved in this space, who are increasingly powerful and more capable of undermining the integrity of elections abroad. Taken together, the implication is that states do not need to exercise jurisdiction or spatial control in order to unduly and substantially affect elections in a foreign states, and they do not necessarily need to target their operations directly against the foreign states' infrastructure either, due to the availability and potential use of social media platforms for interference purposes.

These shifting notions of what constitutes extraterritoriality and control are not in themselves unprecedented. The model of effective control has already been evolving to meet the challenges of modern armed conflict and global surveillance.[56] Digital election interference is yet another challenge for extraterritoriality to overcome.

To understand how extraterritoriality is currently challenged, it is necessary to explain what constitutes sociotechnological change, as the term is used in this chapter. By sociotechnological change I mean three distinct, yet interrelated, phenomena: *power diffusion and parity in the information age*, *new tools of interference*, and *democratization of power*. These three phenomena may explain why times have changed, and therefore, our current understanding of extraterritoriality is severely challenged in the wake of election interference through cyberspace. In other words, the tools of election interference and actors involved are different, which challenges existing extraterritoriality concepts.

B. Power Diffusion and Parity in the Information Age

Power diffusion and parity in the information age pertains to the increasingly substantial role of tech companies, primarily social media platforms in global politics and elections.[57] The reach, influence, and vulnerability of these platforms are unprecedented, and therefore pose a significant risk to the integrity of elections and voters' freedom of choice.

A recent example illustrating the vulnerability of tech in the context of elections was an app used by the Iowa Democratic Party that was supposed to tabulate and report results from the 2020 caucuses. The app, which was developed in a rush and not satisfactorily tested, caused a significant delay in result reporting due to software errors.[58] As elections become more tech-dependent, against experts' unequivocal recommendations, different actors find easier and more devastating ways to interfere in foreign elections through cyberspace.

According to Joseph Nye, the problem is not necessarily that nonstate entities, such as global technology corporations and platforms, become more powerful, but that "in

[56] *See, e.g.*, Deeks, *supra* note 22 ("applying concepts of jurisdiction to extra-territorial internet and telephonic privacy will be a hard task indeed").

[57] Tom Hoggins, *Election Manipulation Using Social Media Is at "Crisis" Point, Report Warns*, The Telegraph (Nov. 5, 2019).

[58] Nick Corasaniti, Sheera Frenkel, & Nicole Perlroth, *App Used to Tabulate Votes Is Said to Have Been Inadequately Tested*, N.Y. Times (Feb. 4, 2020).

today's global information age ... more things are occurring outside the control of even the most powerful States."[59] This means that interfering with these nonstate platforms, as has been done by state actors many times in recent years, could effectively interfere with elections.

This growing power of global social media platform raises another concern—that of parity. Parity asks the question of whether these online platforms are on a par with states.[60] The answer is affirmative. Tech companies are becoming powerful in their own unique way, which challenges the notions of power and control that we typically associate with states. Tech companies and online platforms do not have territories, armies, or recognition as sovereign states, but their emerging power represents a new type of sovereignty—digital rather than Westphalian. Due to how interconnected states and online platforms are, it comes as no surprise that states are also vulnerable to exploitation, manipulation, disinformation, and microtargeting online.

The diffusion of power and parity in the information age illustrates that what constitutes control is changing, and therefore the standard for extraterritoriality should adapt to this new reality. Tech companies and platforms have a lot of control over the content that their users are presented, whether these users are local or foreign. While the power of tech is increasing, states still have a significant degree of leverage against these companies and platforms. For example, states often have the authority to compel these companies and platforms to hand over information about individuals for law enforcement or national security purposes. They can also micro-target specific groups of individuals with election-related advertisements based on advertisement tools that these platforms are making available at cost. When abused, this may allow states to digitally interfere in elections abroad without exercising any form of effective control, as that standard is currently understood.

C. New Tools of Remote Election Interference

New tools of interference have to do with the growing array of means and methods of election interference, primarily enabled by emerging technologies and the global reach of the internet. It is related to *power diffusion and parity in the information age* in the sense that the impact of these tools is amplified when they are used on the internet. These new tools may be used in different contexts, including digital election interference.

In the past, election interference could be achieved through many means, including "grandfather-style methods: scatter leaflets, throw around some printed materials, manipulate the radio or television ... But, all of a sudden, new means have appeared."[61] There is a wide variety of new technological means of interference. Some examples include: (1) online manipulation enabled by microtargeting and psychographic

[59] Joseph Nye, *Power Shifts*, TIME (May 9, 2011).

[60] *See* Ido Kilovaty, *Privatized Cybersecurity Law*, 10 U.C. IRVINE L. REV. 1181, 1215 (2020); compare with Kristen Eichensehr, *Digital Switzerlands*, 167 U. PENN. L. REV. 665, 685–696 (2019).

[61] Evan Osnos, David Remnick, & Joshua Yaffa, *Trump, Putin, and the New Cold War*, THE NEW YORKER (Feb. 24, 2017).

profiling on social media platforms; (2) political bots/trolls spreading disinformation and propaganda; (3) political doxing; and (4) deepfake videos using the likeness of political figures. As technology moves forward, more tools that have never been used before in election interference will become available.

What is troubling about these new tools is that many of them may be used remotely in election interference without ever reaching the threshold of "effective control." In other words, states may infringe on the rights to privacy, liberty, and self-determination without exercising any form of physical or spatial control.

For example, hacking into a government official's email account may violate that official's right to privacy (and potentially the right to cybersecurity).[62] Distributing deepfake videos depicting candidates engaging in controversial conduct or making outrageous statements may implicate the right to seek information. And breaching election voting systems may give rise to a self-determination violation.[63]

D. Democratization of Power

Democratization of power is the result of the coupling of *diffusion of power* with *new tools of interference*. The crux of *democratization of power* is that the internet is widely available and easy to navigate, which may lead to positive outcomes via more transparency, accountability, access to information, and more.

However, this *democratization of power* is a double-edged sword. It also makes new tools of election interference widely available and (relatively) easy to master. The result is that nonstate actors are becoming more capable of interfering in foreign elections.

Some examples of these nonstate actors include: (1) hacking groups (Cozy Bear,[64] Fancy Bear,[65] and others); (2) political consulting firms, such as Cambridge Analytica;[66] and (3) data analytics companies (like Palantir).[67] All of these actors, as well as many others, now hold the means to interfere in elections. Human rights law presupposes a state actor as the one infringing on human rights of individuals. The *democratization of power* challenges this notion. In sum, *democratization of power* may involve new nonstate actors in election interference.[68]

[62] *See* Ido Kilovaty, *An Extraterritorial Human Right to Cybersecurity*, 10 Notre Dame J. Int'l Comp. L. 35 (2020).

[63] Ohlin, *supra* note 4, at 1595–1598.

[64] *Who Is COZY BEAR (APT29)?*, Crowdstrike (Sept. 19, 2016), https://www.crowdstrike.com/blog/who-is-cozy-bear/.

[65] *Who Is FANCY BEAR (APT28)?*, Crowdstrike (Feb. 12, 2019), https://www.crowdstrike.com/blog/who-is-fancy-bear/.

[66] *See* Ido Kilovaty, *Legally Cognizable Manipulation*, 34 Berkeley Tech. L.J. 457, 473–476 (2019).

[67] *See, e.g.*, Peter Waldman, Lizette Chapman, & Jordan Robertson, *Palantir Knows Everything About You*, Bloomberg (Apr. 19, 2018).

[68] Andrea Kendall-Taylor, Erica Frantz, & Joseph Wright, *The Digital Dictators: How Technology Strengthens Autocracy*, 99 Foreign Aff. 103 (2020) (where the authors observe that technological innovation and the internet is often used by autocratic regimes to consolidate their power and suppress dissent. Thus, democratization may sound on its face as a positive outcome, but the relevant technology is available equally to good and hostile actors).

E. The Ineffectiveness of Effective Control

Against the backdrop of sociotechnological change allowing digital election interference, there is a serious concern that effective control may be irrelevant. In the privacy context, Eliza Watt described the effective control standard as "unsuitable, outdated and narrow in the context of State-sponsored cyber surveillance operations."[69] The author is of a similar belief when it comes to foreign election interference: effective control is past due.

First, spatial control cannot deal with the realities of cyberspace and emerging technologies. Whether a state exercises spatial control should be irrelevant in the digital context. It is assumed that states engaging in digital election interference will almost never have a simultaneous spatial control over the state in whose election they are seeking to interfere. In any case, human rights law should attach to *persons*; territoriality should thus not play any significant role in digital election interference.[70] States can no longer claim that no state territory was impacted by their interference operations, since the effects of these operations are still felt by individuals abroad whose rights will certainly be implicated. More importantly, as Marko Milanovic aptly observes, "if virtual methods can accomplish the exact same thing as physical ones, then there seems to be no reason to treat them differently."[71] In the election interference context, the analogy would be between a foreign military restricting access to polling stations and thus influencing the outcome, and a hacking group engaged in probing election infrastructure and changing the votes.

The need to reimagine effective control is reinforced by the universality of human rights themselves.[72] The Universal Declaration of Human Rights makes an appeal to universality when it seeks to achieve "the promotion of universal respect for and observance of human rights and fundamental freedoms."[73] While universality may seem utopian and vague, it is often used by courts to justify extraterritorial application of human rights.[74]

Moving beyond territoriality may be a desirable approach for the regulation of digital election interference through human rights law, since the focus would shift from what territory or state is affected (though, not completely abandoned) to what individuals and rights are affected by an election interference operation in cyberspace. Understandably, territoriality is a burden when translated to the cyberspace domain. The internet may exist in multiple jurisdictions, with data flowing through multiple geographic points.[75] It exists "both everywhere and nowhere."[76]

[69] Eliza Watt, *The Role of International Human Rights Law in the Protection of Online Privacy in the Age of Surveillance*, 9th Int'l. Conf. on Cyber Conflict 1, 10 (2017).

[70] *See* TALLINN MANUAL 2.0, *supra* note 40, at 183.

[71] Marko Milanovic, *Foreign Surveillance and Human Rights, Part 4: Do Human Rights Treaties Apply to Extraterritorial Interferences with Privacy?*, EJIL: TALK! (Nov. 28, 2013).

[72] MILANOVIC, *supra* note 15, at 55–57.

[73] Universal Declaration of Human Rights, U.N.G.A. Res. 217 (III) A, U.N. Doc. A/RES/217(III) (Dec. 10, 1948), Preamble.

[74] MILANOVIC, *supra* note 15, at 56.

[75] Jennifer Daskal, *The Un-Territoriality of Data*, 125 YALE L.J. 326, 330 (2015).

[76] JOHN PERRY BARLOW, A DECLARATION OF INDEPENDENCE OF CYBERSPACE (1996) (where Barlow famously said, "Ours is a world that is both everywhere and nowhere, but it is not where bodies live").

According to Daskal, concepts of territoriality are challenged due to the growing prevalence and importance of data.[77] Data, Daskal says, is different from physical objects. Physical objects are constrained by the laws of physics, whereas data's location is often arbitrary, and the path it travels is "determined without the knowledge, choice, or even input of the data users."[78] Daskal's thesis—that territorial models fail in the cyber context to protect the people the law is designed to cover—is reflective of the unterritorial nature of the internet and data. Although states can still regulate and control the internet in their territory, they do not have to control foreign territory to interfere in elections elsewhere.

That cyberspace undermines physical territoriality is not a novel assertion. David Johnson and David Post famously argued that the rise of cyberspace was erasing the legitimacy of geographical-based regulation.[79] According to Johnson and Post, cyberspace "radically subverts the system of rule-making based on borders between physical spaces."[80] More recently, Jennifer Daskal referred to territoriality doctrine "in a world of highly mobile, intermingled, and divisible data" as "fiction."[81] Human rights law's territorial standard for "effective control" can therefore no longer offer an effective standard for digital election interference.

Second, the personal model for assigning international human rights also cannot hold in the era of digital election interference. The personal model generally assumes physical custody over an individual. Indeed, as Ashley Deeks points out, "Many of the 'effective control' cases involve detention—cases in which a State exercised some level of physical authority and control over the individual who claimed the rights violation."[82] As with spatial control, this physical authority and control standard is not a good fit for digital election interference simply because such interference does not require detention or other physical control over an individual or group of individuals. Digital election interference is often an operation targeting individuals as a collective. Simply put, states can use cyberspace and emerging technologies to interfere in foreign elections without exercising any physical authority or control over individuals.[83]

IV. An Adapted Virtual Control Standard for Extraterritoriality

If effective control is an ineffective standard for applying international human rights to digital election interference, then what alternative standard can take its place?

[77] Daskal, *supra* note 75, at 367.

[78] *Id.*

[79] David R. Johnson & David G. Post, *Law and Borders—The Rise of Law in Cyberspace*, 48 STAN. L. REV. 1367, 1370 (1996) ("The rise of the global computer network is destroying the link between geographical location and: (1) the *power* of local governments to assert control over online behavior; (2) the *effects* of online behavior on individuals or things; (3) the *legitimacy* of a local sovereign's effort to regulate global phenomena; and (4) the ability of physical location to give *notice* of which sets of rules apply.")

[80] *Id.* at 1370.

[81] Daskal, *supra* note 75, at 331.

[82] Deeks, *supra* note 22.

[83] *Id.* (in the right to privacy context, Deeks claims that "[i]ntercepting telephone calls and reading someone's email is a far cry from the type of State control those cases contemplate.").

The answer lies in asking what gaps in protection those models—and more recent candidates—produce. The reason why the spatial and personal models do not work is primarily because they overlook an important aspect of remote digital election interference: its effects.

In the cyber context, for example, Peter Margulies has proposed an alternative to effective control, namely, "virtual control."[84] The "virtual control" standard looks at whether a state has "the ability to intercept, store, analyse and use communications"[85] belonging to an individual. The "virtual control" standard is important in the context of surveillance, because just like "effective control," it is focused on control in a new context. While Margulies introduces the standard of "virtual control" in the context of privacy and surveillance, it could also be adapted to the broader context of election interference. A virtual control standard adapted to election interference would look at a state's *ability* to interfere in foreign elections through the hacking of election infrastructure, interception, storage, analysis, and use of communications. The focus of virtual control would be on the *ability* to achieve a certain result that would deprive individuals of their enjoyment of rights. That is certainly a step in the right direction, but it also misses the effects caused by such abilities.

The virtual control standard is a desirable development for the law of extraterritoriality, though there needs to be an additional layer of effects *actually* caused by states that use their ability to interfere. Virtual control is overly focused on states' ability to interfere with the enjoyment of human rights. It should, however, also be cognizant of the effects that such virtual control may have. Most importantly, control is still a useful benchmark for when extraterritoriality is warranted, but election interference through cyberspace may call into question what control exactly means in this nonphysical domain.

I believe it is time for a reconceptualization of extraterritoriality to meet the challenges of digital election interference. As such, I propose an adapted virtual control standard, informed by an effects-based approach. My approach would focus on the effects of digital election interference on the enjoyment of human rights, which is the result of the ability to interfere in elections. This effects-based approach takes into account the negative effects experienced by victimized groups of people. The "effective control" standard looks at whether a state controls territory or persons when an alleged violation occurs. In cyberspace, the equivalent extraterritoriality standard should look at whether the state has control not over territory but over the enjoyment of rights and the effects that individuals may experience should that state decide to carry out a digital election interference operation.

In other words, international human rights law's extraterritoriality in cyberspace must really operate post-territoriality and post-physicality. International human rights law should not ask whether a territory is under effective control of a foreign government or whether an individual is in that government's custody. Rather, it should ask whether a foreign government controls the ability of certain individuals or communities to enjoy their rights—be it the right to privacy, freedom of expression,

[84] *See* Margulies, *supra* note 11, at 2150 ("Deterrence of problematic conduct in the cyber arena requires a broader test, which I call the virtual control standard.").

[85] Watt, *supra* note 69, at 11.

freedom of opinion, due process, or self-determination. When a state is able to interfere with the enjoyment of such rights, it exercises a certain form of "jurisdiction" as the term is used in international human rights treaties.[86] An adapted virtual control approach would look at technological capacity and power, especially given the *new tools of election interference*, and not whether a state is in fact occupying a foreign piece of land or has physical control over an individual.

The following are few observations on what this effects-based approach would look like.

A. Control of What?

Extraterritoriality is concerned with control. If a state exercises *control* over territory, an individual, communications, then allegedly that state is under an obligation to respect the human rights of those individuals over whom control is asserted.

What form of *control* does a state exercise when it engages in digital election interference? Is it control over information flows? Control over advertisement space on social media platform? Control of public opinion abroad? Or, perhaps, control over the outcomes of foreign elections? There are many potential candidates for such extraterritorial *control* in the digital election interference context.

Coming up with a standard of extraterritorial control in the cyber context prompted some scholars to assert that control is not even necessarily required. Marko Milanovic, for example, argues that the negative obligation to respect human rights (refrain from violating them directly) should be "territorially unlimited" because states are "*always* able to comply with them, since they remain in full control of their own organs and agents."[87] In today's sociotechnological context, this seems to be a reasonable approach.

Moreover, control as a standard may not even be tenable given how states can leverage new tools of election interference through intermediaries such as social media platforms. What are states controlling when they engage in an online manipulation and disinformation campaign on platform like Facebook?

Nonetheless, focusing on a control-based standard seems to be desirable, given that control is an already-existing standard in human rights jurisprudence. States, the HRC, and human rights tribunals would have an easier time adapting to a virtual control approach, rather than an unexplored standard which is not currently available either in existing treaties or customary international law.

That said, while the virtual control standard would apply to most cases where states use cyberspace to interfere with human rights extraterritorially, there might be some instances where there simply isn't any control, and thus states will have to confront the question of whether human rights law is still the relevant body of law where extraterritorial state activity is devoid of control.

[86] *See* section II for further discussion of "jurisdiction."

[87] Marko Milanovic, *Foreign Surveillance and Human Rights, Part 3: Models of Extraterritorial Application*, EJIL: TALK! (Nov. 27, 2013).

B. Individual vs. Collective Rights

Digital election interference has a collective nature, as it often targets individuals at scale rather than individually. A focus on effects may help overcome control's tendency to look at whether a state exercises any form of control over an *individual*. As Jens Ohlin identified with respect to the Russian interference in the 2016 U.S. presidential election, "The interference substituted one sovereign will for the other as an outcome of the election. Doing so violated the right of the American *people* to self-determination."[88] Hence, if extraterritoriality requires a certain degree of *physical control*, it misses the fact that digital election interference, insofar as it violates self-determination, is rarely about physical control.

C. An Effects-based Approach to Support the Virtual Control Standard?

An effects-based approach of extraterritoriality focuses on whether a transborder state activity causes significant negative effects on the enjoyment of human rights abroad. This approach overcomes the limitations the existing formulation of virtual control and is far superior to the current special and personal models.

Supporting the virtual control standard with an effects-based approach would warrant the intervention of international human rights law only in cases where there is an ability *and* actual adverse and quantifiable effects. For example, when a state with significant cyber capabilities is probing and manipulating the election infrastructure, this would reach the requisite level of virtual control and effects. Conversely, where a state seeks to identify vulnerabilities in the election infrastructure in another state without actually acting on the intelligence they gather, there would likely be no significant effects on human rights, though arguably there is virtual control.

Virtual control and the effects-based approach are not limited to cyberspace, per se. There may be other cases where states have a powerful ability that has the capacity of causing adverse effects and potential human rights abuses, and this extraterritoriality threshold would be useful in such contexts as well. When technology defies territoriality, a new formulation of extraterritoriality is inevitable.

The HRC and regional human rights courts can—and should—be able to implement a new extraterritoriality standard that reflects the growing challenges stemming from cyberspace and election interference operations enabled by it.

V. Conclusion

Digital election interference fueled by sociotechnological control calls for a new standard of human rights' extraterritoriality. Primarily, this chapter argues that notions of territorial and physical control as prescribed by the existing "effective control"

[88] Ohlin, *supra* note 4, at 1596.

standard are unsuitable, irrelevant, and outdated in the context of remote, transborder election interference operations. A proposed revision to a "virtual control" test for extraterritorial surveillance equally misses the uniqueness of digital election interference and sociotechnological trends of recent years.

In this chapter, I have argued for a reconceptualization of extraterritoriality in an era of digital election interference. Namely, I propose an effects-based approach to extraterritoriality that would assess whether a state is under an obligation to respect human rights abroad if its operations have significant negative effects on the enjoyment of human rights of individuals abroad. An adapted virtual control standard informed by an effects-based approach overcomes many of the challenges associated with the physical control-based approaches and can be implemented through either widespread and consistent state practice moving forward or human rights institutions interpreting extraterritoriality in accordance with the uniqueness and novelty of cyberspace as a medium of interference.

10

The Dangers of Forceful Countermeasures as a Response to Cyber Election Interference

Jacqueline Van De Velde[1]

I. Introduction

In the wake of the 2016 U.S. presidential election, senior intelligence officials reported that Russia covertly interfered in the election with the aims of promoting one candidate and harming another.[2] The June 2017 testimony of former U.S. FBI Director James Comey confirmed the Russian election interference in no uncertain terms. "There should be no fuzz on this whatsoever," Comey pronounced. "The Russians interfered in our election during the 2016 cycle. They did it with purpose. They did it with sophistication. They did it with overwhelming technical efforts. And it was an active-measures campaign driven from the top of that government" designed "to shape the way [Americans] think, we vote, we act."[3] In response to that testimony, a U.S. Senator declared: "[A] foreign adversary attacked us right here at home, plain and simple, not by guns or missiles, but by foreign operatives seeking to hijack our most important democratic process—our presidential election."[4]

Despite the extent of Russian intrusion into U.S. elections, the United States was somewhat hamstrung in its ability to answer that intrusion. This is because international law, as it stands, offers states limited response options to cyber election interference. Article 2(4) of the UN Charter prohibits states from using or threatening to use force against other states with two limited exceptions: for self-defense and UN

[1] * Sincere thanks to Duncan Hollis, Jens David Ohlin, and Oona Hathaway for their very helpful comments and suggestions in preparing this chapter.

[2] David E. Sanger & Scott Shane, *Russian Hackers Acted to Aid Trump in Election, U.S. Says*, N.Y. Times (Dec. 9, 2016) ("American intelligence agencies have concluded with "high confidence" that Russia acted covertly in the latter stages of the presidential campaign to harm Hillary Clinton's chances and promote Donald J. Trump, according to senior administration officials.").

[3] *Full Transcript and Video: James Comey's Testimony on Capitol Hill*, N.Y. Times (June 8, 2017).

[4] *James Comey's Testimony*, *supra* note 3. Russia has argued that its actions were hardly acts of warfare or attacks. It opined that the Western media disseminates misinformation about Russia within the United States and in Europe, and that Russian distribution of propaganda is no different. *See* Lidian Kim, *Russia Having Success in Hybrid War Against Germany*, Reuters (Feb. 7, 2016). Besides, Russia intimated that the United States routinely interferes with other states' internal affairs, pointing to U.S. interference in elections in Chile, Nicaragua, and Iran, as well to alleged U.S. interference with Russian governance. *See* Ishaan Tharoor, *The Long History of the U.S. Interfering with Elections Elsewhere*, Washington Post (Oct. 13, 2016). For a discussion of U.S. and USSR/Russian partisan electoral interference between 1946 and 2000, *see* Dov H. Levin, *Partisan Electoral Interventions by the Great Powers: Introducing the PEIG Dataset*, 36 Conflict Mgmt. & Peace Sci. 88–106 (2019). And for further parsing of the effects of partisan election interference, *see* Dov H. Levin's contribution to this volume in chapter 1.

Jacqueline Van De Velde, *The Dangers of Forceful Countermeasures as a Response to Cyber Election Interference* In: *Defending Democracies*. Edited by Duncan B. Hollis and Jens David Ohlin, Oxford University Press (2021). © Duncan B. Hollis & Jens David Ohlin. DOI: 10.1093/oso/9780197556979.003.0011

Security Council–authorized activity.[5] In terms of self-defense, Article 51 of the UN Charter states that "[n]othing in the present Charter shall impair the inherent right of individual or collective self-defence if an armed attack occurs."[6] Read together with Article 2(4), a majority of states understand a "use of force" to violate the UN Charter, but only an "armed attack"[7] to trigger a state's right to use forceful self-defense.[8]

Cyber election interference fits awkwardly within this international legal framework.[9] Most cyber election interference will cause minimal, if any, kinetic impact or physical damage; it will seldom employ conventional military weapons; and it need not be directed at critical infrastructure of national importance.[10] In other words,

[5] U.N. Charter, art. 2(4) (member states "shall refrain in their international relations from the threat or use of force against the territorial integrity or political independence of any state, or in any manner inconsistent with the Purposes of the United Nations.").

[6] U.N. Charter, art. 51.

[7] The words "attack" and "armed attack" are terms of art that have two separate meanings within two separate bodies of law. In the *jus ad bellum*, the term "armed attack" is a precursor to a state's lawful use of forceful self-defense. *See* U.N. Charter, art. 51 ("Nothing in the present Charter shall impair the inherent right of individual or collective self-defence if an armed attack occurs against a Member of the United Nations, until the Security Council has taken measures necessary to maintain international peace and security.").

But in international humanitarian law, the term "attack" refers to a category of military operations. *See* Protocol Additional to the Geneva Conventions of August 12, 1949, and Relating to the Protection of Victims of International Armed Conflicts, June 8, 1977, 1125 U.N.T.S. 3, art. 49(1) (defining "attacks" as "acts or violence against the adversary, whether in offence or in defence"). For a discussion of those terms of art and their relationships to the cyber operations context, *see* Michael N. Schmitt, *"Attack: as a Term of Art in International Law: The Cyber Operations Context*, PROCEEDINGS OF THE 4TH INTERNATIONAL CONFERENCE ON CYBER CONFLICT 283–293 (Christian Czosseck, Rain Ottis, & Katharina Ziolkowski eds., 2012).

[8] The U.S. government considers any illegal use of force to trigger a state's right to forceful self-defense. *See* Harold Koh, *International Law in Cyberspace*, 54 HARV. INT'L L.J. 1, 7 (2012)(articulating the United States' position "that the inherent right of self-defense potentially applies against any illegal use of force" and that "there is no threshold for a use of deadly force to qualify as an 'armed attack' that may warrant a forcible response"); William H. Taft IV, *Self-Defense and the Oil Platforms Decision*, 29 YALE J. INT'L L. 295, 299–302 (2004). The United States' position is the minority view. *See* Military and Paramilitary Activities in and Against Nicaragua (Nicar. v. U.S.), [1986] I.C.J. Rep. 14, para. 191 (June 27) (*Nicaragua*); THE TALLINN MANUAL 2.0 ON THE INTERNATIONAL LAW APPLICABLE TO CYBER OPERATIONS 133 (Michael N. Schmitt ed., 2017) [hereinafter TALLINN MANUAL 2.0] (endorsing *Nicaragua* definition of armed attack while noting the contrary view of the United States).

[9] I use the term "cyber interference" as a catch-all for any state-sponsored interference in elections, without doing the careful work of classifying that interference under the relevant bodies of law that apply. I will use the term "cyber interference" throughout the paper as a framing mechanism. By contrast, I use the term "cyberattack" only to refer to those cyber interferences that meet the standard for use of force in Article 2(4) of the U.N. Charter.

[10] Scholarship has advanced three approaches for analyzing whether a cyberattack constitutes an armed attack or use of force: the effects-based approach, the instrument-based approach, and the target-based approach. For the effects-based school of thought, a cyberattack can constitute an armed attack if the effects of the attack are sufficiently severe. *See* Michael Schmitt, *Wired Warfare: Computer Network Attack and* Jus in Bello, 84 INT'L REV. RED CROSS 365, 368, 396–397 (2002). The instrument-based school of thought considers whether the weapon used to perpetuate the attack possesses "physical characteristics traditionally associated with military coercion." *See* Duncan B. Hollis, *Why States Need an International Law for Information Operations*, 11 LEWIS & CLARK L. REV. 1032, 1040–1041 (2007). The target-based approach treats any attack on critical national infrastructure as an armed attack. *See* David E. Graham, *Cyber Threats and the Law of War*, 4 J. INT'L L. & POL'Y 91–92 (2010). For discussion and critique of these approaches, *see* Reese Nguyen, *Navigating "Jus Ad Bellum" in the Age of Cyber Warfare*, 101 CAL. L. REV. 1079, 1117–1119 (2013); Hollis, *supra* at 1040–1042.

cyber election interference generally lacks the hallmarks of an armed attack.[11] Thus, states' right to engage in *forceful* self-defense will generally not be triggered by cyber election interference. Moreover, international law offers limited alternatives to using force under treaties and customary international law. This creates a serious dilemma: states that are victims of cyber election interference could be left suffering from uses of force to which they may not use force in return.

Within this void, the doctrine of countermeasures has received increasing attention. A countermeasure is an act by a victim state against another state that would ordinarily be unlawful, yet is permitted as a response to the offending state's unlawful activity.[12] The otherwise unlawful act is rendered lawful by the prior violation: the deeper logic being that one illegal act can justify another only if the responsive illegal act is narrowly tailored to bring the offending state back into line with its international legal obligations.[13] In the case of cyber election interference, some actors are advocating for the use of responsive countermeasures, even going so far as to suggest that those countermeasures might be forceful.

This chapter addresses international law's response to election interference through countermeasures and other legal authorities. It examines how existing treaties (e.g., the UN Charter and international human rights instruments) and customary international law (e.g., the duty of nonintervention, sovereignty) regulate both election interference and state responses to it. To the extent election interference does not trigger a right of self-defense, it surveys the primary alternative response option—countermeasures—and calls for them to be available above the use of force threshold (but below that for an armed attack).

The chapter's main contribution lies in explaining why states should resist these calls. International law should not be read to authorize otherwise unlawful, forceful acts against another state by way of addressing cyber election interference. Recognizing that the problem of election interference requires a response, I identify various alternative mechanisms states may employ, including drafting a new treaty better suited to regulating interference in the digital age.

Section II explains the features that distinguish cyber election interference from other forms of cyberattacks and categorizes different forms of cyber election interference. Section III unpacks the existing international regulation of election interference in treaties and customary international law, as well as the law's regulation of responses to its violation, chiefly countermeasures. Section IV explores some of the challenges in

[11] *See, e.g.*, Oona A. Hathaway et al., *The Law of Cyber Attack*, 100 Cal. L. Rev. 817, 821, 832–837 (2012) (concluding that most cyberattacks generally do not constitute armed attacks under the *jus ad bellum*).

[12] International Law Commission, Draft Articles on Responsibility of States for Internationally Wrongful Acts, U.N. Doc. A/56/10 (2001) [hereinafter ASR]. By resolution, the U.N. General Assembly recommended the ASR to member state governments and recognized their codification and development of international law. U.N.G.A. Res. 56/83, U.N. Doc. A/RES/56/83 (Dec. 12, 2001). In this way, the ASR "are considered by courts and commentators to be in whole or in large part an accurate codification of the customary international law of state responsibility." James Crawford, State Responsibility: The General Part 43 (2013); *see also* Tallinn Manual 2.0, *supra* note 8, at 79 (noting that the international group of experts concurred that the ASR reflect customary international law, while acknowledging that not all states view them as authoritative restatements of customary international law).

[13] *See* Lori Fisler Damrosch, *Enforcing International Law Through Non-Forcible Measures*, in Recueil des Cours: Collected Courses of the Hague Academy of International Law 54 (1992).

employing countermeasures against election interference generally and via "forceful" countermeasures in particular. The chapter concludes with brief thoughts about how nonforceful countermeasures might safely be used, as well as other alternatives states and citizens might use to address election interference within international law.

II. What Is Cyber Election Interference?

A. Distinguishing Features of Cyber Election Interference

The nature of the target and the attack distinguish cyber election interference from other attacks. As to the first, some of the most well-known cyberattacks have had kinetic impacts: that is, a state has used lines of code to damage, destroy, or cause to malfunction a piece of equipment in another state for the attacking state's benefit. One notorious example is the United States' alleged introduction of malicious code into the Iranian centrifuge system, purportedly to secure more time for negotiating a nuclear agreement favorable to U.S. interests.[14] The code instructed the centrifuges to rotate wildly, causing physical damage to the infrastructure controlled by the computer systems.[15] Another is North Korea's alleged efforts to hack and destroy Sony Pictures' computer systems to gain personal retribution for the release of a film offensive to North Korean leaders.[16] This attack also had physical effects; the hackers installed malware that erased data from Sony servers and rendered some of their computer equipment inoperable.[17]

Most forms of cyber election interference will differ from these examples in at least two ways. First, at least some cyber election interference events will target public property, like an electronic voting machine or a state's election databases. Any attack on an arm of the state raises questions about violations of sovereignty, both in the abstract, nature-of-a-state sense, and in the concrete, violations-of-borders and invasion-of-territory sense. Second, as discussed previously, the weapon of choice is sometimes code. But, more often, it is propaganda—designed not to affect computer systems but rather individuals.

As for the nature of the attack, cyberattacks are generally invisible. Given this invisibility, it is critical that states attempt to (1) identify the attack close to the moment in time that it occurs to limit its effects; and (2) correctly attribute the attack to the attacker, to exact punishments and demand recompense.

Those concerns are amplified in the election context. There, blindness to the moment of the attack and the identity of the hacker has the potential to magnify an attack's damage. Identifying security breaches and improper influences as close to the

[14] *See* Laurence J. Trautman & Peter C. Ormerod, *Industrial Cyber Vulnerabilities: Lessons from Stuxnet and the Internet of Things*, 72 U. Miami L. R. 787–797 (2018) (discussing the Stuxnet virus).

[15] *See* Jeremy Richmond, *Evolving Battlefields: Does Stuxnet Demonstrate a Need for Modifications to the Law of Armed Conflict?*, 35 Fordham Int'l L.J. 842, 844–845 (2012).

[16] Andrea Peterson, *The Sony Pictures Hack, Explained*, Washington Post (Dec. 18, 2014).

[17] *See* Clare Sullivan, *The 2014 Sony Hack and the Role of International Law*, 8 J. Nat'l Sec. L. & Pol'y 437, 445 (2016).

moment of their introduction is paramount to election integrity.[18] Postmortem identification of cyber election interference invokes a crisis of constitutional proportions. "What better way to destabilize a country without a shot being fired?" one security professional asked in response to Russian interference in the U.S. elections.[19]

Attribution of the attack to the attacker matters because if a state does not know who orchestrated or conducted a cyberattack, then that state's reprisal options are limited. To the extent that international law does speak to cyber election interference, states cannot respond or ask for reparations without knowledge of (1) who the actor is,[20] and (2) whether the actor was under state control.[21]

B. Categorizing Cyber Election Interference

Another difficulty in analyzing cyber election interference under international law is that sundry actions might be described as "hacking." States have been affected by cyber interference in their elections ranging from misinformation campaigns, to theft of information, to damage to voting machines. International law makes accessible different kinds of protections—and response options—for each one.

We can start by identifying four kinds of interference by which a state could interfere with another state's elections: (1) interference with kinetic effects; (2) the degradation or manipulation of the availability or integrity of electoral processes; (3) unauthorized or denied access to election related data; and (4) information operations. First, interventions may result in the physical destruction of voter equipment.[22] A state might cause physical damage to voting systems by infecting them with malware. A state could target objects or institutions proximate to the election machines, too, like state governments or vendors who conduct the elections.[23] The result? A state left unable to hold an election.

A second, less visible, but equally damaging method of election interference is meddling with the voting infrastructure. As just noted, a state might cause physical damage to the voting hardware: for example, by damaging voting machines. But so, too, might a state damage voting data: for example, by leveraging software vulnerabilities so as

[18] For more on the importance of transparency in cyber election interference, *see* Jens David Ohlin contribution to this volume in chapter 11, at XXX–XXX.

[19] Lily Hay Newman, *The Real Hacker Threat to Election Day? Data Deception and Denial*, WIRED (Nov. 7, 2016).

[20] For a discussion of the standards for attribution in the cyber context, *see* Monica Hakimi, *Introduction to the Symposium on Cyber Attribution*, 113 AJIL UNBOUND 189 (2019) (discussing Lorraine Finlay and Christian Payne's notion of a variable attribute scheme for *jus ad bellum*, requiring higher levels of certainty in attribution depending on the amount of force to be used in response to the attack).

[21] This inquiry is relevant to the issue of nonstate actors. States may be held responsible for nonstate actor activity when the state exercises a certain level of control over the nonstate actor. What level of control is required is contested. The ICJ has said the standard is effective control, while the International Criminal Tribunal for the former Yugoslavia (ICTY) said, for the purposes of international humanitarian law, the standard is one of "overall control." *See, e.g.*, *Nicaragua Case*, *supra* note 8, at 64–65; *compare* Prosecutor v. Dusko Tadic aka "Dule" (Judgment) ICTY, No IT-94-1-A (July 15, 1999) [131], [145]. For more detailed assessment in the cyber context, *see* TIM MAURER, CYBER MERCENARIES (2018).

[22] Brian Barrett, *America's Electronic Voting Machines Are Scarily Easy Targets*, WIRED (Aug. 2, 2016).

[23] Philip Ewing, *What You Need to Know About Foreign Interference and the 2020 Election*, NPR (Sept. 1, 2019).

to change voting registrations, rolls, or results.[24] Any reported vote-rigging has the potential to both inconvenience voters, slow down an election's results, and disrupt public perception of the democratic process.

Third, a state might also interfere in another state's elections by stealing sensitive information. Russia, for example, used state resources to acquire sensitive information from the U.S. Democratic National Committee and the Republican National Committee.[25] Or a state might use ransomware to hold election results hostage.[26] A state might simply hold on to this information as valuable intelligence or might disseminate the information on its own terms, leading to public doubt in the democratic process.[27]

Finally, there is election interference that appears both most common and least answerable under international law: information campaigns, "hostile non-kinetic activity" involving "deliberate use of information by one party on an adversary [or their populace] to confuse, mislead, and ultimately influence" their target's choices and decisions.[28] Information campaigns affecting elections merit close attention given the digital age. Twitter bots and fake social media accounts can, and do, spread misinformation among susceptible voters.[29] Intelligence specialists can stoke agitation among the electorate. (Take, for example, the occasion when Russian influence specialists scheduled rallies for groups with opposing views in the same park, on the same day, and at the same time.)[30]

Information campaigns delegitimize expert voices, undermine authoritative institutions, undercut objective data, and stifle rational discourse among citizens.[31] When targeted toward elections, those campaigns have the potential to cause voters to doubt the democratic nature of outcomes, change their voting behavior, or refrain from voting entirely.[32] At least some states have concluded that information campaigns have, in fact, been conducted with that express purpose; for example, the European Union determined that some Russian-sponsored campaigns were conducted to "suppress turnout and influence voter preferences" in European elections.[33]

[24] Miles Parks, *5 Ways Election Interference Could (And Probably Will) Worsen in 2018 and Beyond*, NPR (Jan. 27, 2018).

[25] *See* Robert S. Mueller III, Dep't of Justice, *Report on the Investigation into Russian Interference in the 2016 Presidential Election*, vol. 1 (2019) [hereinafter Mueller Report].

[26] Kartikay Mehrotra & Andrew Martin, *What Is Election Hacking, and Can It Change Who Wins?*, Washington Post (Dec. 6, 2019).

[27] In 2016, Russia engaged in this form of election interference in the U.S. presidential election by releasing the stolen emails of Clinton campaign chairman John Podesta. *See* Mueller Report, *supra* note 25, at 4–5, 36–48 (detailing Russian acquisition and dissemination of the Podesta emails).

[28] This chapter adopts the definition of information campaigns posited by Herbert Lin & Jackie Kerr, *On Cyber-Enabled Information/Influence Warfare and Manipulation*, in The Oxford Handbook of Cybersecurity 4 (forthcoming 2021).

[29] Newman, *supra* note 19.

[30] *See* Ewing, *supra* note 23 (citing Parks, *supra* note 24).

[31] Information Society Project & Floyd Abrams Institute for Freedom of Expression, Fighting Fake News: Workshop Report 2 (2017), https://law.yale.edu/sites/default/files/area/center/isp/documents/fighting_fake_news_-_workshop_report.pdf.

[32] Kathy Gilsinan & Krishandev Calamur, *Did Putin Direct Russian Hacking? And Other Big Questions*, The Atlantic (Jan. 6, 2017).

[33] European Comm'n, *Report on the implementation of the Action Plan Against Disinformation*, JOIN (2019) 12 final (June 14, 2019), https://eur-lex.europa.eu/legal-content/EN/TXT/HTML/?uri=CELEX:52019JC0012&from=EN.

These cyber election information campaigns can take at least three forms. Classifying which form they take requires looking at the nature of the information disseminated. First, there is what is known as "doxing"—what I will call the dissemination of true information. A state engages in doxing when it releases information that is verifiable—either because it was gathered as intelligence, because it was stolen in a hack, or because it was garnered some other way.[34]

The second form of cyber election information interference is via propaganda campaigns—what I define as the dissemination of normative arguments. For example, Voice of America and its affiliated broadcasters Radio Martí, Radio Free Europe/Radio Liberty, and Radio Free Asia work to "provide reliable news reports" in states without a strong and independent press with the express purpose of "promot[ing] democratic values abroad."[35] This form of propaganda campaign might be intended to change regime structures, incentivize democratic participation, or improve access to information. To that extent, propaganda is coercive in nature as well.[36]

The third form of an information campaign is a misinformation campaign (sometimes called a "disinformation campaign" or "fake news") in which untrue information is spread in order to influence elections. Misinformation campaigns are by nature coercive, because by spreading information that is either false or misleading, states indicate that their purpose is to change voters' minds, actions, or inclinations.[37] Misinformation campaigns could pertain to an electoral candidate: for example, sharing unflattering and untrue stories that make a voter less likely to throw their support behind a candidate. But misinformation campaigns might also be positive: sharing false, but flattering, stories about a candidate in the hopes of directing more voters to that candidate.[38] So, too, could an actor affect an election by sharing misinformation about the mechanics of the election itself: information that polling places are closed; telling voters the wrong polling location, hours, requirements, or

[34] There were frequent examples of this practice during the 2016 U.S. election. For example, WikiLeaks posted 20,000 emails sent or received by top officials of the Democratic National Committee. *See* Michael D. Shear & Matthew Rosenberg, *Released Emails Suggest the D.N.C. Derided the Sanders Campaign*, N.Y. Times (July 22, 2016).

[35] David Folkenflik, *An Obama-Backed Change at Voice of America Has Trump Critics Worried*, NPR (Dec. 14, 2016).

[36] This position is in opposition to that of *Tallinn 2.0*, which stipulates that propaganda is not coercive. *See* Tallinn Manual 2.0, *supra* note 8, at 318–319 (The duty of nonintervention does not cover acts of "persuasion, criticism, public diplomacy, propaganda."). Other scholars, however, agree that cyber election interference via propaganda may be coercive. *See, e.g.*, Nicholas Tsagourias, *Electoral Cyber Interference, Self-Determination and the Principle of Non-Intervention in Cyberspace*, EJIL: Talk! (Aug. 26, 2019)(pointing out that a government's will remains free insofar as its "sourcing is also free," and arguing that when a state engages in cyber election interference using propaganda, it interferes "with the environment that condition[s] and facilitate[s] the formation of authority and will by the people," thus substituting "self-determination with an artificially constructed process in order to generate particular attitudes and results aligned to the intervenors will").

[37] For example, during the 2016 U.S. presidential election, forged documents appearing to come from a senator on the Senate Homeland Security Committee circulated that included a fabricated warning of a cyberattack changing vote counts. *See* Newman, *supra* note 19.

[38] For a discussion of the potential impacts of fake news on voters, and in particular the phenomenon of "false remembering," *see* Richard Gunther, Paul A. Beck, & Erik C. Nisbet, *Fake News May Have Contributed to Trump's 2016 Victory* (Mar. 8, 2018) (unpublished manuscript) (on file with the Ohio State University), https://www.documentcloud.org/documents/4429952-Fake-News-May-Have-Contributed-to-Trump-s-2016.html.

even election day; or creating fake stories that warn about the tainting of election results.

These three categories of information campaigns can overlap; fake news could also contain propaganda via a normative argument, and doxing might be included among fake news. But it is helpful for the subsequent legal analysis to parse the flavors of information campaigns, then more thoughtfully consider what legal rights and obligations attach to each of the categories.

Both hacks on public apparatus and attacks on citizens raise substantial questions and justifiable concerns about improper intrusion into the objects (and subjects) of state power. When these kinds of questions are raised in the physical world, states do not hesitate to go to war to protect such critical targets.

III. International Law Applicable to Election Interference

A. Treaties and Election Interference

Treaties implicate foreign election interference in at least three ways. First, they can contain proscriptions that limit the legality of state cyber operations relating to foreign elections. In the cyber election context, the most prominent such limitation is the UN Charter's prohibition on the use of force. Second, treaties may contain "treaty-specific" response options applicable where a state violates its treaty commitments.[39] To date, examples of such responses are limited. Nonetheless, the possibility should be kept in mind if states adopt this chapter's recommendation of crafting a new treaty regulating cybersecurity generally or online election interference in particular. Third, treaties can accord individuals—that is, voters, citizens, and so forth—certain fundamental human rights that may provide protections against election interference and afford (quite limited) responsive measures when violations occur.

1. The UN Charter Prohibition on the Use of Force

Can an interfered-with state use lawful force against the interfering state? Intuitively, one might think the answer is yes: if another state interferes in a sovereign's democratic process—to such a degree as to change the results of its election—then the interfered-with state should have the right to defend itself. That defense might reasonably include the right to use force to defend its territorial sovereignty. But international law incorporates a deliberately high threshold to deter states from using force in any such response.

As noted in the introduction, the UN Charter outlines and limits states' abilities to use force. Article 2(4) directs that "[a]ll Members shall refrain in their international relations from the threat or use of force against the territorial integrity or political independence of any state, or in any other manner inconsistent with the Purposes of the United Nations."[40] Article 2(4) is understood to be an absolute prohibition on the use

[39] *See* Bruno Simma & Christian J. Tams, *Reacting against Treaty Breaches*, in The Oxford Guide to Treaties 576, 578 (Duncan B. Hollis ed., 2012).

[40] U.N. Charter, art. 2(4). The original intent of the authors of the text "was to state in the broadest terms an absolute all-inclusive prohibition [against the use of force]; the phrase 'or in any other manner' was

of armed force against any other state.[41] This ban on aggression is regarded as the heart of the UN Charter, and the basic rule of contemporary public international law.[42]

The Charter contemplates two exceptions to Article 2(4)'s ban. The first exception are actions authorized by the UN Security Council under Chapter VII of the UN Charter.[43] The second are actions that constitute legitimate acts of individual or collective self-defense pursuant to Article 51 of the UN Charter or customary international law. It is understood that Article 51 creates an exception to Article 2(4)'s strict prohibition on the use of force, and that its triggering "armed attack" is a narrower category than "threat or use of force." Simply put, when a state's conduct rises to the threshold of an armed attack, a victim state is entitled to go to war.[44]

Thus, international law prohibits states from engaging in election interference that constitutes a use of force. Yet as noted at the outset, this obligation is likely to prohibit only a small subset of existing election interference activities. Moreover, to the extent the International Court of Justice (ICJ) has identified an armed attack as involving "the most grave forms of the use of force,"[45] there may be even fewer instances where election interference may qualify as an armed attack triggering the right of self-defense.

2. International Human Rights Treaties

Citizens possess positive rights under international treaty law to participate in elections and states are responsible for effectuating and protecting those rights.[46] For

designed to ensure that there should be no loopholes." Edward Gordon, *Article 2(4) in Historical Context*, 10 Yale J. Int'l L. 276 (1985) (*citing* Brownlie, *The Use of Force in Self-Defense*, 37 Brit. Y.B. Int'l L. 183, 236 n.2 (1961)).

[41] *See* David K. Linnan, *Self-Defense, Necessity and U.N. Collective Security: United States and Other Views*, 1 Duke J. Comp. & Int'l L. 63 (1991). Scholars have made arguments that the term "force" in the U.N. Charter applies not only to military attacks and armed violence but also other means of affecting states. Other interpretations of the term "force" include coercion or interference. *See* Grigori Tunkin, Law and Force in the International System 82 (Progress Publishers trans., 1985) ("[i]n the literature of the socialist states on international law a broad interpretation of force is defended, while a narrow interpretation of that concept prevails in the literature of capitalist states according to which 'force' in the sense employed in the United Nations Charter refers only to armed force"). On the point of interference, *see* Quincy Wright, *Subversive Intervention*, 54 Am. J. Int'l L. 521, 528 (1960) ("Domain, like property in systems of national law, implies the right to use, enjoy and transfer without interference from others, and the obligation to each state to respect the domain of others. The precise definition of this obligation is the major contribution which international law can make toward maintaining the peaceful co-existence of states."). For an outline of the interpretations of "force," *see* Matthew C. Waxman, *Cyber-Attacks and the Use of Force: Back to the Future of Article 2(4)*, 36 Yale J. Int'l L. 425–430 (2011).

[42] The Charter of the United Nations: A Commentary, vol. 1, 116–117 (Bruno Simma ed., 2002).

[43] Chapter VII of the UN Charter gives the UN Security Council authority to label threats and uses of force as threats to international peace or security, then to determine what measures should be used to address them. According to Article 39 of the UN Charter, the Security Council must determine the existence of a threat to the peace, a breach of the peace, or an act of aggression. After such determinations are made, the Security Council may (1) make recommendations to maintain or restore international peace and security, (2) mandate nonmilitary measures such as diplomatic or economic sanctions pursuant to Article 41, or (3) mandate military enforcement measures pursuant to Article 42.

[44] *See supra* note 7; Schmitt, *"Attack" supra* note 7, at 286 ("[A]n 'armed attack' is an action that gives States the right to a response rising to the level of a 'use of force,' as that term is understood in the *jus ad bellum*.").

[45] *Nicaragua Case*, *supra* note 8, at para. 191.

[46] This chapter focuses on the protections guaranteed in the International Covenant on Civil and Political Rights (ICCPR). *See generally* discussion *supra* section III.A.2. Other human rights treaties accord distinct treaty protections of their own. *See, e.g.*, European Convention on Human Rights, Sept. 3, 1953,

example, three provisions of the International Covenant on Civil and Political Rights (ICCPR) could be implicated in election interference, each providing citizens with some remedy—albeit a limited one.

First, the ICCPR guarantees individuals a right to privacy, requiring that individuals are not "subjected to arbitrary or unlawful interference with [their] privacy."[47] To that extent, data from hacks that are made public, or even those that are kept private, but discovered, might be considered an arbitrary interference in a citizen's privacy.

Second, the ICCPR guarantees citizens of states parties the right to genuine elections. That right could be restricted if states protect voting infrastructure inadequately from unlawful interference. In addition, the ICCPR mandates that states provide such "genuine, periodic elections" without "unreasonable restrictions."[48] An election that is not genuine (because a vote count was tampered with) or hampered by unreasonable restrictions on ballot access risks falling afoul of these provisions.

Third, Article 20 of the ICCPR prohibits "propaganda for war."[49] The Commentary on this article clarifies that this principle "extends to all forms of propaganda threatening or resulting in an act of aggression or breach of the peace," and is directed "against any advocacy of national, racial or religious hatred that constitutes incitement to discrimination, hostility or violence, whether such propaganda or advocacy has aims which are internal or external to the State concerned."[50] So, a state that creates propaganda that has the result of breaching the peace, whether that peace is breached at home or abroad, may find itself in violation of ICCPR obligations.

Any analysis of human rights treaty protections, must, however, recognize states' potential territorial limitations. By the language of the ICCPR itself, the treaty obligations apply within each state party's territory.[51] It is, however, an open question whether human rights treaty obligations apply extraterritorially.[52] In other words, Russia may have no human rights obligations to respect the human rights of U.S. citizens in the United States—but Russia certainly has such obligations as to Russian citizens in Russia.

213 U.N.T.S. 222, art. 8; American Convention on Human Rights, Nov. 22, 1969, O.A.S.T.S. No. 36, 1144 U.N.T.S. 123, art. 11.

[47] International Covenant on Civil and Political Rights (Dec. 16, 1966) 999 U.N.T.S. 171, 175, art. 17m.

[48] *Id.*, art. 25. In full, this article provides that:

Every citizen shall have the right and the opportunity, without any of the distinctions mentioned in article 2 and without unreasonable restrictions:

(a) To take part in the conduct of public affairs, directly or through freely chosen representatives;
(b) To vote and to be elected at genuine periodic elections which shall be by universal and equal suffrage and shall be held by secret ballot, guaranteeing the free expression of the will of the voters;
(c) To have access, on general terms of equality, to public service in his country.

[49] *Id.*, art. 20.

[50] Human Rights Comm., *Gen. Comment 11, Prohibition of Propaganda for War and Inciting National, Racial or Religious Hatred (Art. 20)*, U.N. Doc. CCPR.29/07/1983 (July 29, 1983).

[51] ICCPR, *supra* note 47, art. 2.

[52] For a discussion of the extraterritorial scope of human rights treaties as applied to the cyber election interference context, *see* Ido Kilovaty's contribution to this volume in chapter 8; *see also* Jens D. Ohlin, *Did Russian Cyber Interference in the 2016 Election Violate International Law*, 95 Tex. L. Rev. 1579, 1587–1588 (2017).

International human rights protections speak to at least two categories of cyber election interference: (1) meddling with a vote count, and (2) theft of information. Meddling with a vote count implicates the human rights guaranteed to citizens with whose votes states have meddled. Citizens who live in states where their votes have been tampered with, where propaganda has made their election less "genuine" or where they have been denied the opportunity to compete for public service, have the potential to use the mechanisms provided within the ICCPR to seek a remedy. The ICCPR explicitly offers at least two forms of remedy. First, individuals whose rights to a fair election have been compromised may be able to bring a claim under the ICCPR. Second, states can bring a complaint under the ICCPR against another state that does not ensure the right to a fair election.

Although meddling with a vote count is clearly unlawful, it is unlikely that citizens whose elections have been implicated will be able to procure a remedy via these ICCPR options. The largest concern is jurisdictional. For citizens to be able to make individual complaints, states must have joined the ICCPR's First Optional Protocol, while ICJ suits may generate jurisdictional challenges from respondent states.[53] Many of the states that have been accused of cyber interference in elections range in their relationship to these international institutions from skeptical to hostile and have not submitted to further involvement by the Court in their internal affairs.

A theft of information affects two ICCPR provisions as well: the right to privacy and the right to a genuine election. But here again the ICCPR's remedies are limited. Given the jurisdictional challenges already noted, all that can usually be done is report violations to the ICCPR's Human Rights Committee (HRC), or appoint a Conciliation Committee.[54] If both states involved agree, they could submit a dispute to the ICJ, but that remedy is infrequently used, particularly by the states most affected through recent "election hacking."[55] Even if the ICJ or the HRC takes jurisdiction over a complaint, objections to applying the ICCPR extraterritoriality may derail the proceedings. Moreover, cyber election interference is unique in that states require some speed in receiving a remedy for interference. The HRC, however, takes all due deliberation before issuing reports or creating remedies; thus, it may not be an adequate venue for states to redress these particular harms.

In sum, individuals and states are unlikely to find a remedy within the international human rights structure established via the ICCPR. But that is not to say that the instruments are without value. Importantly, the ICCPR offers states a meaningful hook by which to call for other states' compliance with their international legal obligations. Even if the provisions providing a remedy are not complied with, a state can use the violations of the ICCPR as a means by which to name, shame, and exert diplomatic force on noncompliant states.[56]

[53] *See* Optional Protocol to the International Covenant on Civil and Political Rights (Dec. 16, 1966) 999 U.N.T.S. 171.

[54] ICCPR, *supra* note 47, arts. 40–42.

[55] Statute of the International Court of Justice (June 26, 1945) 33 U.N.T.S. 993, arts. 36, 40(1) [hereinafter ICJ Statute].

[56] However, some states will deny responsibility to provide human rights to foreign nationals abroad. The United States adopts this view. *See* Ohlin, *supra* note 52, at 1589 n.25.

B. Customary International Law Protections

International treaty protections provide few options for states faced with a cyberattack or other cyber election interference activities. States may find more protections under customary international law, and some scholars have argued that two customary international legal protections in particular might provide states protection from cyber election interference: (1) the norm of nonintervention, the notion that states may not interfere in the internal affairs of other states; and (2) the principle of sovereignty, which is recognition of a state's dominion over its own territory. Violations of customary international law are internationally wrongful acts, in response to which a state may engage in an action called a countermeasure: a proportionate action designed to bring a state into line with its international legal obligations. But as this chapter argues, international law—including countermeasures doctrine—offers no means by which states can muster a forceful response.

1. The Norm of Nonintervention

At its core, the norm of nonintervention forbids states from interfering in the internal or foreign affairs of other states.[57] The leading case defining the norm of nonintervention and violations of sovereignty is *Military and Paramilitary Activities in and against Nicaragua Case* (the *Nicaragua* judgment). There, the ICJ outlined limitations on a states' ability to interfere in the internal affairs of another state. The Court found that this principle amounted to a rule of customary international law, finding numerous expressions of state *opinio juris* on the matter, as well as documents and resolutions from international organizations that further supported this conclusion.[58]

In so doing, the Court outlined two elements of the norm of nonintervention: (1) those matters which must remain free from another state's interference (i.e., the so-called *domaine reserve*), and (2) the means by which a state is prohibited from interfering with another state. As to the first, the Court explained that the principle of nonintervention involves "the right of every sovereign [s]tate to conduct its affairs without outside interference."[59] It explained that:

> The principle [of nonintervention] forbids all [s]tates or groups of [s]tates to intervene directly or indirectly in the internal or external affairs of other [s]tates. A prohibited intervention must accordingly be one bearing on matters in which each [s]tate is permitted, by the principle of [s]tate sovereignty, to decide freely. One of these is the choice of a political, economic, social, and cultural system, and the formulation of foreign policy.[60]

The Court thus explained that the principle of nonintervention has the following elements. Intervention is forbidden in any matters that states are permitted to freely

[57] *See* Philip Kuunig, *Intervention, Prohibition of*, MAX PLANCK ENCYCLOPEDIA PUB. INT'L L. para. 9 (Apr. 2008).

[58] *Nicaragua Case*, *supra* note 8, at para. 205.

[59] *See id.*

[60] *See id.*

decide based on state sovereignty. Such matters include issues of state formation, including a state's "political, economic, social, and cultural system."[61] And the matters include elements of state interactions in the international arena, including "formulation of foreign policy."[62] And so the matters in which a state may not intervene extend to matters of state formation and to state continuation. The Court also makes clear that such matters may occur within or beyond the territory of a state. Based on all these factors, electoral processes appear bound up in the *domaine réservé* covered by the duty of nonintervention.

As to the second, the Court explained that certain manners of intervention are impermissible:

> Intervention is wrongful when it uses methods of coercion in regard to such choices [regarding matters in which each State is permitted to decide freely], which must remain free ones. The element of coercion, which defines, and indeed forms the very essence of, prohibited intervention, is particularly obvious in the case of an intervention which uses force, either in the direct form of military action, or in the indirect form of support for subversive or terrorist armed activities within another State.[63]

The Court thus explained that states may not intervene using "methods of coercion." The Court did not define coercion, although it explained that coercion would be "particularly obvious" when coupled with force—either by one state's use of force or by that state's support of other actors who use force. Nonetheless, the Court implied that it did not consider force necessary for a finding of coercion.[64]

And so the Court defined the following elements as inherent in the principle of nonintervention. First, (1) coercion must be used, (2) that coercion must be used in support of "subversive activities," with the subversion affecting a state's sovereign rights (such as political, economic, social or cultural system), and (3) that coercion must be directed to another state.[65]

Interpreting *Nicaragua*, the *Tallinn Manual 2.0 on the International Law Applicable to Cyber Operations* (*Tallinn 2.0*) suggests that coercion occurs only when a victim state is deprived entirely of its freedom of choice, forcing the state to act or to refrain from acting.[66] Under this view, almost all uses of force would be coercive. By the same token, almost no cyber espionage would be considered to violate the norm of nonintervention. However, espionage plus dissemination of information might have a coercive quality.

The debate around coercion complicates states' clarity as to the elements required for a finding of coercion—and thus a violation of customary international law. The

[61] *Id.*
[62] *Id.*
[63] *Id.*
[64] *Id.*
[65] It is an open question whether both (a) malicious cyber activity that directly coerces the targeted state and (b) malicious cyber activity that indirectly coerces the targeted state by creating conditions that lead the targeted state to act under false pretenses violate the norm of nonintervention. *Tallinn 2.0* takes the position that both indirect and direct coercion constitute such violations. TALLINN MANUAL 2.0, *supra* note 8, at 322 (citing *Nicaragua Judgment*, *supra* note 8, at para. 141).
[66] *Id.* at 103.

crux of the issue is whether coercion requires force; if it does, then states will rarely be able to cite the norm of nonintervention as a customary international law violation occurring during cyber election interference.[67] But if coercion instead refers to a degree of intervention, as suggested by the Court in *Nicaragua* and posited by other scholars,[68] then cyber election interference cases might be an appropriate realm in which to apply nonforceful countermeasures.

2. Sovereignty

A second international wrongful act to which cyber election interference might be attributed is a violation of sovereignty.

In the *Nicaragua* judgment, the Court discussed a separate but related concept under international law: sovereignty.[69] The Court indicated that its understanding of sovereignty was closely related to the notion of physical territory. For instance, the Court quoted its language in the *Corfu Channel* judgment, in which it explained that "[b]etween independent States, respect for territorial sovereignty is an essential foundation of international relations."[70] Further expounding on the notion of sovereignty, the Court explained that "the concept of sovereignty, both in treaty-law and in customary international law, extends to the internal waters and territorial sea of every State and to the airspace above its territory."[71] Thus, the Court indicated that the notion of sovereignty is closely related to the notion of dominion or control, and sovereigns exercise dominion over their territory.

Sovereignty, therefore, is conceived in the *Nicaragua* judgment as a somewhat more limited concept than the norm of nonintervention. The norm of nonintervention encompasses interference with the state's self-development or its ongoing business in the international community; sovereignty pertains to sovereign control over the territory of a state.

In cyberspace, however, whether a violation of sovereignty is an internationally wrongful act is subject to fierce and ongoing debate. Some see sovereignty as a rule of international law in cyberspace,[72] while others see sovereignty as a principle that

[67] For a discussion of the norm of nonintervention and its application to cyber election interference, *see* Ido Kilovaty, *Doxfare: Politically Motivated Leaks and the Future of the Norm on Non-Intervention in the Era of Weaponized Information*, 9 HARV. NAT'L SEC. J. 146, 160–169 (2018).

[68] *See id.* at 169 (arguing for an effects-based test for the norm of nonintervention, contending that "the norm against non-intervention is violated when the attack causes 'disruption' ").

[69] *See Nicaragua Case, supra* note 8, at para. 251 ("The effects of the principle of respect for territorial sovereignty inevitably overlap with those of the principles of the prohibition of the use of force and of non-intervention.").

[70] *See id.* at para. 202 (quoting *Corfu Channel Case*, Merits (Judgment of Apr. 9, 1949) [1949] I.C.J. Rep. 35).

[71] *See Nicaragua Case, supra* note 8, at para. 212.

[72] *See* TALLINN MANUAL 2.0, *supra* note 8, at Rule 4 ("A State must not conduct cyber operations that violate the sovereignty of another State."). The view of sovereignty-as-rule was seemingly endorsed by both France and the Netherlands. *See, e.g.*, Ministère des Armées, *Droit international appliqué aux operations dans le cyberspace* (Sept. 9, 2019) (France); *Letter from Minister of Foreign Affairs to President of the House of Representatives on the international legal order in cyberspace*, July 5, 2019, Appendix 1, at https://www.government.nl/ministries/ministry-of-foreign-affairs/documents/parliamentary-documents/2019/09/26/letter-to-the-parliament-on-the-international-legal-order-in-cyberspace (saying that the Netherlands "believes that respect for the sovereignty of other countries is an obligation in its own right, the violation of which may in turn constitute an internationally wrongful act.").

informs other rules.[73] This debate has substantial impacts on the doctrine of countermeasures as applied to cyber election interference. After all, there will be far fewer opportunities for states to deploy countermeasures if that doctrine is triggered by the duty of nonintervention alone, rather than by both that duty and a rule of sovereignty.

3. Countermeasures Doctrine

The International Law Commission's Draft Articles on State Responsibility for Internationally Wrongful Acts (ASR), outline concepts of state responsibility, including consequences for internationally wrongful acts. Articles 22 and 49–54 of the ASR set forth the concept of countermeasures.[74] Countermeasures permit states to bring an unrepentant state back in line with its international legal obligations.

Leading commentators of international law have embraced countermeasures as a promising solution to cyber election interference that falls below the threshold of an armed attack. The independent group of experts who authored *Tallinn 2.0* focused on countermeasures as an available response to unlawful cyber operations. Although a majority of these experts were of the view that countermeasures must not involve a use of force, a distinct minority "asserted that forcible counter-measures are appropriate in response to a wrongful use of force that itself does not qualify as an armed attack (whether by cyber means or not)."[75]

But are countermeasures an apt solution for cyber election interference? This chapter argues no. It argues that given the contested status of sovereignty in cyberspace, states may deploy countermeasures only for a limited number of actions—namely, those that constitute a violation of the norm of nonintervention.

Turning to that argument: a state's use of countermeasures must fall within certain limitations. These limitations govern the purpose, actors, content, and timing of countermeasures, and include:

Purpose Requirements:

- Countermeasures must be intended to bring the out-of-line state back into line with its international obligations.[76]

[73] The U.K. and U.S. governments view sovereignty only as a principle. *See, e.g.*, Paul C. Ney, *DOD General Counsel Remarks at U.S. Cyber Command Legal Conference* (Mar. 2, 2020), *at* https://www.defense.gov/Newsroom/Speeches/Speech/Article/2099378/dod-general-counsel-remarks-at-us-cyber-command-legal-conference/("[f]or cyber operations that would not constitute a prohibited intervention or use-of-force [i.e., those that might be covered by a rule of sovereignty], the Department believes there is not sufficiently widespread and consistent State practice resulting from a sense of legal obligation to conclude that customary international law generally prohibits such non-consensual cyber operations in another State's territory."); Jeremy Wright, QC, MP, *Cyber and International Law in the 21st Century* (May 23, 2018), at https://www.gov.uk/government/speeches/cyber-and-international-law-in-the-21st-century("Some have sought to argue for the existence of a cyber-specific rule of a 'violation of territorial sovereignty' ... Sovereignty is of course fundamental to the international rules-based system. But I am not persuaded that we can currently extrapolate from that general principle a specific rule or additional prohibition for cyber activity beyond that of a prohibited intervention. The UK Government's position is therefore that there is no such rule as a matter of current international law.").

[74] For a discussion of the doctrine of countermeasures, *see* Denia Alland, The Definition of Countermeasures, *in* The Law of International Responsibility 1127–1136 (James Crawford et al. eds., 2010).

[75] Tallinn Manual 2.0, *supra* note 8, at 111, 123–126.

[76] ASR, *supra* note 11, art. 49(1).

- Countermeasures may not be used to punish or exact vengeance.[77]

Actor Requirements:

- Countermeasures may be directed only at the state responsible for committing an internationally wrongful act.[78]
- Collective countermeasures are impermissible.[79] In other words, a state may not conduct a countermeasure on behalf of another state where the state deploying the countermeasure was not itself targeted or injured by the unlawful behavior.
- Third-party harms are unlawful. States may incur international legal responsibility for harms done to third parties in the course of deploying countermeasures against the targeted state.[80]

Content Requirements:

- Countermeasures must be proportionate to the violation.[81]
- Countermeasures may not affect fundamental human rights.[82]
- Countermeasures should be reversible in their effects if possible.[83]

Timing Requirements:

- Countermeasures during the pendency of a court proceeding, where the court has capacity to make decisions binding on the parties, are unlawful.[84]
- Countermeasures must be undertaken during an internationally wrongful action.[85] By extension, countermeasures taken before or after the internationally wrongful act has ceased are unlawful.

In addition, a state engaging in countermeasures must comply with certain notification requirements. Before deploying countermeasures, the state must notify the

[77] *Id.* art. 49(2).

[78] *Id.* art. 49(1).

[79] *Id.* art. 49(1). *But see* Kersti Kaljulaid, President of Estonia, *Speech at the opening of CyCon 2019* (May 29, 2019), *at* https://www.president.ee/en/official-duties/speeches/15241-president-of-the-republic-at-the-opening-of-cycon-2019/index.html(calling for permissible use of collective countermeasures in response to cyber interference); Ministère des Armées, *Droit international appliqué aux operations dans le cyberspace* (Sept. 9, 2019), *at* https://www.defense.gouv.fr/salle-de-presse/communiques/communiques-du-ministere-des-armees/communique_la-france-s-engage-a-promouvoir-un-cyberespace-stable-fonde-sur-la-confiance-et-le-respect-du-droit-international ("French Ministry of Defense Views") (rejecting Estonia's call for collective countermeasures).

[80] *See* Michael N. Schmitt & M. Christopher Pitts, *Cyber Countermeasures and Effects on Third Parties: The International Legal Regime*, 14 Baltic Y.B. Int'l L. 1, 6–8 (2015).

[81] ASR, *supra* note 12, art. 22.

[82] *Id.* art. 50(b).

[83] *Id.* art. 49(2)–(3). *See also* 4 The International Law Commission 1999–2009: Treaties, Final Draft Articles, and Other Materials 334 (Arnold A. Pronto & Michael M. Wood eds., 2011) ("States should as far as possible choose countermeasures that are reversible."); David J. Bederman, *Counterintuiting Countermeasures*, 96 Am. J. Int'l L. 817, 824–825 (2002) (discussing the reversibility requirement).

[84] ASR, *supra* note 12, art. 52(3).

[85] *Id.*

targeted state that it is being: (1) deemed responsible for an internationally wrongful act, (2) subjected to countermeasures, and (3) invited to negotiate.[86] This notification requirement may be avoided in cases of urgent countermeasures where the fact of notification could afford the targeted state an opportunity to avoid the effects of the countermeasures.[87]

In arguing that countermeasures are a permissible response to election interference, some have pointed to two potential internationally wrongful acts implicated by election interference. The first is a violation of the norm of nonintervention; the second, a violation of the principle of sovereignty.

4. Countermeasures and the Prohibition on the Use of Force

Traditionally, it has been accepted that states may not use force in deploying countermeasures. The ASR provide that countermeasures "shall not affect ... the obligations to refrain from the threat or use of force as embodied in the Charter of the United Nations."[88] In interpreting that provision, the Commentaries to the ASR take the position that forcible countermeasures are impermissible.[89]

Nonetheless, many institutions and scholars have posited that states might employ forceful countermeasures in response to unlawful cyberattacks.[90] Some have termed potentially permissible forceful countermeasures as "active defenses."[91] In the cyber election interference context, such an active defense might be a firewall that repels cyberattacks in an attempt to disable the attack's source. Proponents of a forcible response to below-the-threshold cyber operations rely on principles of necessity and proportionality to cabin the force that may be used.[92]

When it comes to countermeasures applicable to cyber election interference, states must examine whether the interference crossed *two* thresholds: (1) the threshold between things that are uses of force and those that are not, and (2) the threshold between a use of force and an armed attack. Separating the two thresholds helps identify

[86] *Id.*, art. 52.

[87] *Id.*, art. 52(2).

[88] ASR, *supra* note 12, art. 50.

[89] [2001] YBILC, vol. II, pt. II, 131–132 (stating that ASR Article 50(1)(a) "excludes forcible measures from the ambit of permissible countermeasures under chapter II"). In reaching this conclusion, the Commentaries rely on the 1970 Declaration on Principles of International Law Concerning Friendly Relations. U.N.G.A. Res. 2625 (XXV), Declaration on Principles of International Law Concerning Friendly Relations and Co-operation among States in Accordance with the Charter of the United Nations (Oct. 24, 1970) ("States have a duty to refrain from acts of reprisal involving the use of force.").

[90] Oil Platforms (Iran v. U.S.), [2003] I.C.J. Rep. 161 (Nov. 6), Separate Opinion of Judge Simma, para. 14 (raising possibility of forceful countermeasures available under customary international law).

[91] For a summary of the trend toward permitting so-called "active countermeasures," *see* Oona Hathaway, The Drawbacks and the Dangers of Active Defense, *in* 6th International Conference on Cyber Conflict 46 (2014) (Pascal Brangetto, Markus Maybaum, & Jan Stinissen eds., NATO CCD COE Publications 2014). Hathaway collects sources that have advocated for or embraced the use of active defenses in response to cyber. *See id* at 46 n.44 (citing U.S. Dep't of Def., Department of Defense Strategy for Operating in Cyberspace 2, 7 (July 2011); Comm. on Offensive Info. Warfare, Nat'l Research Council of the Nat'l Acads., Technology, Policy, Law, and Ethics Regarding U.S. Acquisition and Use of Cyberattack Capabilities 38, 142–149 (William A. Owens et al. eds., 2009); Jay P. Kesan & Carol M. Hayes, *Mitigative Counterstriking: Self-Defense and Deterrence in Cyberspace*, 25 Harv. J.L. & Tech. 415 (2012)).

[92] *See* David Wallace, *Revisiting Belligerent Reprisals in the Age of Cyber?*, 102 Marquette L. Rev. 81, 91–94 (2018).

the issue with expansive views of countermeasures. Specifically, forceful countermeasures in response to an unlawful use of force fall afoul of the generally accepted prohibition against reprisals under *jus ad bellum*.[93] Thus, permitting forceful countermeasures applicable to cyber election interference risks reading, *sub silentio*, unlawful reprisals into international law.

IV. The Problem with Applying International Legal Protections and Countermeasures in the Election Interference Context

Although international law provides clearer answers or applications as to physical destruction of voting equipment—these are internationally wrongful acts—it provides less clarity as to the repercussions for meddling with a vote count and theft of information, and almost no clarity in addressing information campaigns.

Looking for a solution, some scholars have advanced the argument that the norm of nonintervention and the concept of sovereignty (both principles under customary international law) are violated by information campaigns.[94] States may plausibly claim that an information campaign violated its sovereignty and unlawfully intervened in its domestic affairs;[95] as such, a state would conceivably be authorized to utilize nonforceful countermeasures to stop the state waging the information campaign. Perhaps this is why so much energy is coagulating around countermeasures as a solution; information campaigns are only increasing in frequency and in ferocity, but international law offers no compelling means by which to address them.

The difficulty is that international law does not necessarily care about whether information is true. Rather, it asks whether information was *coercive* for purposes of the duty of nonintervention. And this test results in strange outcomes for what information could be considered a violation of the norm of nonintervention, as well as what information campaigns are consonant with international legal obligations.

The dissemination of true information might be for the purpose of changing civilian behavior, but it might be for another purpose entirely. Take, for example, the International Religious Freedom reports released by the U.S. Department of State, which contain a summary of the status of religious freedom around the world, as understood by U.S. diplomats. The stated purpose of releasing those reports is to submit those reports to Congress and facilitate their access by nongovernmental organizations (NGOs) and the public.[96] The information is thus not released for the purpose of changing civilian behavior, but rather to inform the U.S. Congress, direct U.S. foreign

[93] *See* Shane Darcy, Retaliation and Reprisal, in Oxford Handbook on the Use of Force 1 (Max Weller ed., 2013) ("the overwhelming weight of opinion is that a use of force by way of retaliation or reprisal is generally unlawful").

[94] *See, e.g.*, Kilovaty, *supra* note 67, at 160.

[95] For a discussion of whether the information campaigns in the 2016 U.S. presidential election violated either the norm of nonintervention or the principle of sovereignty, *see* Ohlin, *supra* note 52.

[96] International Religious Freedom Act, Pub. L. No. 105-292, §§ 102–103, 112 Stat. 2787 (1998) (codified at 22 U.S.C. § 6412).

policy, assist NGOs, and educate the public. To the extent that the information in the reports changes civilian behavior, that is a spillover effect rather than a stated purpose.

Yet dissemination of propaganda or false information could be *only* spread for the purpose of changing civilian behavior, which in turn could affect the "political, economic, social and cultural system" in a manner that is coercive. This chapter is of the view that action is coercive whether it affects the state itself directly or whether it affects the state indirectly. Thus, information disseminated for the purpose of changing civilian behavior would constitute coercion, even if aimed at the state indirectly. As such, states could make a plausible argument that dissemination of false information, propaganda, or even some instances of true information constitute a violation of the norm of nonintervention—and thus engage in countermeasures in retaliation.

Engaging in countermeasures on the basis of a violation of sovereignty is likewise fraught. The ongoing debate between sovereignty as a rule versus sovereignty as principle limits states' abilities to engage in countermeasures in response to perceived violations of sovereignty due to cyber election interference.[97]

In any case, states may opt not to engage in countermeasures in response to cyber election interference out of fear of responsibility for the damages incurred. After all, a state may be liable for the harm caused if it engages in a countermeasure but is later assessed to have been mistaken in its right to use them.[98] A mistaken understanding of coercion or a wrongful assessment of the scope of sovereignty could lead to substantial damages.

A. Dangers of Countermeasures as Applied to Cyber Election Interference

Whatever the merits of nonforceful countermeasures in response to violations of sovereignty or the duty of nonintervention, application of forceful countermeasures to election interference via information campaigns is a dangerous proposition. It risks developing international law in a direction that could be feasibly used to repress much-needed NGO activity. It is dangerous, too, because it expands the lawful use of violence beyond the boundaries staked out within the UN Charter. Those risks outweigh the utility of using the doctrine.

1. Not All Coercion Is Impermissible

Many actions necessary for international relations constitute intervention. States and civil society actors influence one another—directly and indirectly, intentionally and unintentionally—through culture, economy, and scientific and technical achievement. As one scholar observed, influence is a cousin of coercion, and thus "[i]nternational law is faced with the issue: When does proper influence become illegal intervention?"[99]

[97] For an exploration of this debate, *see* Michael N. Schmitt & Liis Vihul, *Respect for Sovereignty in Cyberspace*, 95 Tex. L. Rev. 1639 (2017).

[98] ASR, *supra* note 12, Commentaries, art. 49.

[99] *See* Sean Watts, Low-Intensity Cyber Operations and the Principle of Non-Intervention, in Cyberwar: Law and Ethics for Virtual Conflicts 255 (Jens David Ohlin, Kevin Govern, & Claire Oakes

The Court in the *Nicaragua* judgment would posit that intervention is illegal when it is *coercive*. And the meaning of coercion, as used within the *Nicaragua* judgment, is contested.[100] According to Oppenheim, action is coercive if it is "forcible or dictatorial interference by a state in the affairs of another state for the purpose of maintaining or altering the actual condition of things."[101] *Tallinn 2.0* further limits coercive action to only those "affirmative act[s] designed to deprive another state of its freedom of choice, that is, to force that State to act in an involuntary manner or involuntarily refrain from acting in a particular way."[102]

Regardless of whether we measure coercion strictly or broadly, activities that we understand to be lawful—such as the work of promoting free and fair elections, promoting democracy, or supporting human rights—may well be coercive.

Should countermeasures be allowed in response to such actions? States should not have a plausible argument for engaging in otherwise unlawful acts against another state for its own or its NGOs' election monitoring, publishing of international news, or promotion of a free and fair press. The international legal order depends on these organizations being able to function, bolster domestic civil society, and participate in the creation and enforcement of international law. Because many actions that constitute normatively beneficial work in support of civil society and the international order could be construed as violations of sovereignty and the norm of nonintervention, the risk that these terms will be misapplied is too great to permit broadening the reading of countermeasures' availability.

2. An Expansion of Lawful Violence

Second, application of forceful countermeasures to information campaigns undercuts the international architecture surrounding the use of force.

As discussed previously, the international tripwire for the use of force under UN Charter Article 2(4) (and UN Charter Article 51) was deliberately set high. Embracing the doctrine of forceful countermeasures would give states additional opportunities to escalate to violence as a permissible option on the table—the opposite of what the international legal order was designed to protect. It would broaden the scope of lawful violence beyond that intended by the framers of international order, allowing states broad leeway to justify physical violence against one another.

One might argue that the use of forceful countermeasures is not an expansion of lawful violence. After all, a state may only use countermeasures in a manner that is proportionate to the harm. But the difficulty of information campaigns and election interference is that the harm caused by propaganda is both difficult to quantity, yet nonetheless significant. Consider the earlier examples of the potential costs of

Finkelstein eds., 2015) (quoting QUINCY WRIGHT, ESPIONAGE AND THE DOCTRINE OF NON-INTERVENTION IN INTERNAL AFFAIRS, ESSAYS ON ESPIONAGE 4–5 (1962)).

100 For a thorough summary of various views on coercion, *see id.* at 256–262.

101 L. OPPENHEIM, 1 INTERNATIONAL LAW: PEACE 188 (2d ed. 1912).

102 TALLINN MANUAL 2.0, *supra* note 8, at 317. This strict reading is likewise endorsed by Michael N. Schmitt, "*Virtual' Disenfranchisement": Cyber Election Meddling in the Grey Zones of International Law*, 19 CHI. J. INT'L L. 30, 49–50 (2018). By contrast, a more expansive view is embraced by Nicholas Tsagourias, *supra* note 36.

information campaigns and cyber election interference: the potential to impact citizens' faith in the democratic nature of an election, dissuade citizens from participating in an election, or even dictating citizens' votes.[103] As such, cyber interference via information campaigns could subvert Article 2(4) because nonkinetic actions could plausibly have a significant enough impact to merit violent, yet lawful, responses.

B. Solutions

Rejection of forceful countermeasures doctrine should not leave states without a remedy when facing election interference online. States must be able to address cyber election interference, and perhaps information campaigns, under international law. Cyber election interference has the potential to affect states' sovereign rights to hold free and fair elections. And international law, normatively, should concern itself with other states' actions that both (1) violate and (2) are intended to violate those rights guaranteed within the ICCPR, such as a states' ability to engage in self-determination through a government of its choosing.

States looking to respond to cyber information campaigns have some solutions at hand. First, they might consider engaging in acts of retorsion or nonforceful countermeasures only. Second, they might consider using the support of the international community to further curtail the norm of nonintervention and the concept of sovereignty. And third, they might recognize that new international treaty law might be needed to address such cyber election interference.

1. Employ Retorsions and Nonforceful Countermeasures

Rather than resort to forceful countermeasures, a state might employ retorsions or nonforceful countermeasures.[104] Retorsions are lawful but unfriendly acts a state may pursue at its unilateral discretion. Retorsions may be economic—such as withholding foreign aid or the cessation of trade—or they may involve the suspension of diplomatic relations, or the withdrawal of other benefits voluntarily given by one state to another free from any obligation.[105]

Retorsions offer several benefits to the interfered-with state. They have the benefit of employing international legal solutions to another state's interference. And they can be employed by a state unilaterally, so there is no need to wait for the collective agreement of the international community.

In addition, states might consider employing nonforceful countermeasures in response to election interference when that interference can be characterized as a violation of sovereignty or the duty of nonintervention. Nonforceful countermeasures offer an avenue for injured states to be made whole.[106] States may find nonforceful countermeasures appealing, given the otherwise limited response options available

[103] Gilsinan & Calamur, *supra* note 32.

[104] *See* Damrosch, *supra* note 13, at 54.

[105] *See* Troy Anderson, *Fitting a Virtual Peg into a Round Hole: Why Existing International Law Fails to Govern Cyber Reprisals*, 34 Ariz. J. Int'l & Comp. L. 136, 142 (2016).

[106] *See generally* Gabčíkovo-Nagymaros Project (Hung./Slovk.) (Judgment), [1997] I.C.J. Rep. 7, 55–57 (Sept. 25) (discussing the proportionality requirement in countermeasures doctrine).

under international law for election interference. They may also appreciate that employing nonforceful countermeasures gives the interfered-with state significant latitude in how to respond, within international legal limits. For example, nonforceful countermeasures might include otherwise unlawful tariffs or treaty breaches that are excused when deployed in response to a prior internationally wrongful act.

2. Take Advantage of Institutional Mechanisms—Use International Judicial Mechanisms to Redefine the Norm of Nonintervention to Exclude Civil Society Actors

But states need not go at it alone. By nature, countermeasures are private justice. States in the international community have global resources at their disposal for support, including dispute resolution and international law enforcement.

A state could, for example, bring a case to the ICJ seeking clarification of the norms of nonintervention and violations of sovereignty. A state may do this either through (1) submitting a bilateral agreement with another state party to the ICJ, requesting their jurisdiction over a dispute, or (2) submitting an application for the ICJ's jurisdiction against a respondent state.[107]

Alternatively, the UN General Assembly or other authorized UN agency may request an ICJ advisory opinion. To seek advisory jurisdiction of the ICJ, an international organization's director or secretary general must file a written request to the registrar.[108] If granted, the Court will list states and international organizations likely to be able to contribute to the Court's decision and invite them to participate in written and oral proceedings. Although advisory opinions do not have binding legal effect, they nevertheless "carry great legal weight" and are intended to develop international law.[109] International organizations have typically used advisory opinions to bring controversial issues and cases before the Court.[110] This path forward offers the ICJ a means by which to clarify, correct, and update its own working language defining the norms of nonintervention and the right of sovereignty—in particular, further elucidating the meaning of coercion. As such, it will leave less confusion for states and practitioners in determining which of several competing definitions of the norms should be supported. Moreover, this procedure is not infrequently used;[111] it is possible that an international organization—whether the UN General Assembly on behalf of the United Nations as a whole or one of its agencies—could be persuaded that this issue is significant and contentious enough to justify the ICJ's time and effort in clarifying.

[107] *How the Court Works*, Int'l Court of Justice, http://www.icj-cij.org/court/index.php?p1=1&p2=6.

[108] *Advisory Jurisdiction*, Int'l Court of Justice, http://www.icj-cij.org/jurisdiction/index.php?p1=5&p2=2.

[109] *Id.*

[110] *See, e.g.*, Concerning Legal Consequences of the Construction of a Wall in the Occupied Palestinian Territory, Advisory Opinion, [2004] I.C.J. Rep. 136; Legality of the Threat or Use of Nuclear Weapons, [1996] I.C.J. Rep. 226.

[111] *See* Teresa F. Mayr & Jelka Mayr-Singer, *Keep the Wheels Spinning: The Contributions of Advisory Opinions of the International Court of Justice to the Development of International Law*, 76 Heidelberg J. Int'l L. 425, 428 (2016) (the ICJ issued twenty-seven advisory opinions over the course of sixty-nine years).

Additionally, a state could introduce a resolution in the UN General Assembly defining sovereignty and the norm of nonintervention.[112] Such a document could reflect customary international law, even if the agreement is not concluded and ratified as a treaty.[113]

3. Refine the Scope of Nonintervention and Sovereignty by a New Treaty

Though countermeasures doctrine can be stretched to encompass cyber information campaigns, doing so responsibly requires (1) modification of the concepts of nonintervention and sovereignty, so as to protect the work of civil society in the international community, and (2) continued monitoring, such that states do not impermissibly extend and expand the scope of their violence against other states.

International law is created, inter alia, by the agreement of the parties bound to it. Understanding the content of international law, therefore, requires constant surveying of the institutions that reflect state opinion.[114] The clearest articulations and best evidence of state understanding is reflected in treaties or other agreements, as well as through the opinions issued by international tribunals.[115] Additionally, scholarly work and even the consistent and general practice of states can be used as evidence of the content of international law.[116]

It is worth noting that an alternative to modifying existing law would be creating new law; states could craft a treaty regarding state influence operations—including proscribing limits on when and how states can conduct them. This would allow states to narrowly tailor their obligations toward one another in the context of cyber election interference. By making such a treaty, states would be able to style their obligations from the outset, craft obligations to which they agree to bind themselves, and make clear how and when violence could ever be used to redress a breach of the agreement. They likewise could include treaty-specific breach provisions, giving the treaty its own mechanisms for enforcement. Most critically—and unlike countermeasures doctrine—states could contract such that the ability to resort to violence must be sanctioned by other members of the group, as it is in most other contexts (countermeasures, by contrast, would allow one state to be its own judge and jury as to the question of whether or not the state would be permitted to use force).

One reason that states might consider forming a new treaty rather than modifying old law is that a large and growing number of states have been affected by information campaigns in the context of elections. With an increasing proportion of states affected, the number of states who have found themselves interested stakeholders in the question is increasing. And because information warfare has reportedly largely been perpetrated by one state against many others, it is likely that many stakeholders will find themselves with unified interests in the content and the outcomes of such a negotiation.

[112] The Friendly Relations Declaration is an example of this phenomenon. *See* U.N.G.A. Res. 2625 (XXV), *supra* note 89.

[113] Louis Henkin, International Law: Politics and Values 29–38 (1995).

[114] ICJ Statute, *supra* note 55, art. 38(1)(b).

[115] *Id.*

[116] *Id.*

V. Conclusion

This chapter argues that hamstrung by high bars for the use of force, scholars and states have sought alternative means by which states might assert their sovereignty and defend their elections from foreign interference.

International and domestic law give states tools by which to defend themselves. In the case of physical damage to infrastructure, such as voting equipment, states can invoke the UN Charter and pursue self-defense against the hacking state. And in the case of "stealing" information, states can go to a domestic court to fight espionage. States can counter cyber election interference in defensive ways as well. They can protect voting infrastructure. They can also enlist the private sector to help counter the dissemination of information emanating from foreign adversaries.

But the rub comes, however, in the proliferation of information: true, false, and normative. Neither international law nor domestic law clearly speaks to the issue. Desperate for answers, scholars have proven willing to argue for the use of customary international law and the application of a countermeasures doctrine, including the possibility of forceful countermeasures, as a way to remedy states' harms. Forceful countermeasures are, however, particularly problematic if they expand the lawful use of violence in the international system.

Each of the solutions discussed in this chapter is, admittedly, incomplete—due in part to the framework of international law in which states operate to redress wrongdoing surrounding election interference. States' prerogative, then, should be recognition of limitations of what an international legal structure built for kinetic attacks can do. Given the limitations of the present system, states should be incentivized to contribute to the development of new law addressing cyber interference in elections whether via a judicial or conventional approach.

Cyber election interference has begun, but it's nowhere close to ending. With bodies of international law developed in an age of kinetic warfare, existing law offers no tailor-made solution for states as a means of addressing such interference. Resorting to forceful countermeasures as a lawful excuse to resort to violence is not the answer. Giving states another recourse to violence risks lowering the barriers to warfare: precisely the opposite result of what the existing international order was constructed to do.

11

Election Interference

A Unique Harm Requiring Unique Solutions

Jens David Ohlin

I. Introduction

In the immediate aftermath of the 2016 election, the Office of the Director of National Intelligence (ODNI) released a report that concluded that the Russian government interfered in the 2016 presidential election.[1] The report was notable for many reasons, though perhaps not for the same reason that gained so much public attention. At the time, journalists were focused on the fact that the conclusion of the ODNI was that Russia interfered in the election, even though President Donald Trump distanced himself from this conclusion and refused to endorse the empirical findings of his own intelligence analysts.[2] But equally surprising was the fact that the intelligence community was disclosing the interference—and detailing its scope—*after* the election, when nothing could be done to counteract the interference. During the period in time when the interference occurred, the intelligence community, and law enforcement agencies with jurisdiction over counterintelligence, said precious little about the interference.

International lawyers have had their own reaction to the election interference. Some have tried to place the Russian influence campaign in historical context, noting that the United States has engaged in its own share of electoral interference or propaganda efforts in other countries.[3] Other lawyers have argued that the First Amendment, or some broader principle of freedom of speech, protects the rights of anyone who wants to meddle in an election, even a foreign one.[4] Other international lawyers have

[1] Office of the Director of National Intelligence, *Assessing Russian Activities and Intentions in Recent US Elections* (Jan. 6, 2017) (concluding that "[w]e assess Russian President Vladimir Putin ordered an influence campaign in 2016 aimed at the US presidential election. Russia's goals were to undermine public faith in the US democratic process, denigrate Secretary Clinton, and harm her electability and potential presidency. We further assess Putin and the Russian Government developed a clear preference for President-elect Trump.").

[2] Trump first made the following ambiguous statement: "I accept our intelligence community's conclusion that Russia's meddling in the 2016 election took place. It could be other people also. There's a lot of people out there." He also said: "They said they think it's Russia; I have President Putin, he just said it's not Russia. I will say this: I don't see any reason why it would be." Trump later articulated that he believed that Russia intervened in the election. *See* Mark Landler & Maggie Haberman, *A Besieged Trump Says He Misspoke on Russian Election Meddling*, N.Y. Times (July 17, 2018).

[3] *See* Michael N. Schmitt, *"Virtual" Disenfranchisement: Cyber Election Meddling in the Grey Zones of International Law*, 19 Chi. J. Int'l L. 30, 32 (2018) ("Indeed, the U.S. has a long history of involving itself covertly and overtly in foreign elections.").

[4] *See* Joseph Thai, *The Right to Receive Foreign Speech*, 71 Okla. L. Rev. 269, 278 (2018) (dismissing the ideas that foreigners outside of the United States have a constitutional right to free speech but exploring whether Americans have a first amendment right to "receive" foreign speech). *See also* Nathaniel A.G.

Jens David Ohlin, *Election Interference* In: *Defending Democracies*. Edited by Duncan B. Hollis and Jens David Ohlin, Oxford University Press (2021). © Duncan B. Hollis & Jens David Ohlin. DOI: 10.1093/oso/9780197556979.003.0012

focused on the cyber intrusions, including the hacking of the Democratic National Committee (DNC) email server, as evidence that Russia either directly engaged in a cyberattack against the United States or was complicit in cyberattacks committed by WikiLeaks or associated individuals.[5] This has raised difficult questions about whether such cyberattacks violate the nascent norms regarding cyberlaw, which most recently was the subject of *Tallinn Manual 2.0*, an effort to articulate the customary international law rules governing cyberspace.[6]

Common to all of this discourse is an assumption that the concept of "sovereignty" is the best rubric for understanding and debating election interference, whether as a stand-alone rule or as the foundation for the duty of nonintervention. This chapter is meant as a small corrective to reorient the debate around an alternative concept, the idea of self-determination—that is, the idea that peoples have a right to select their own political destiny, a process that in democratic societies is actualized through the electoral process. I argue in this chapter that understood in this way, self-determination entails that a people have a right to enforce membership rules for elections and create a process that privileges insiders over outsiders.

Although politicians and intelligence analysts have criticized Russian interference in the 2016 and 2018 elections, international lawyers seem to be at a loss for how to understand the particular harm posed by this interference. In addition to the hacking of email accounts and disclosure of private information, the most salient aspect of the interference was the use of social media platforms, including Twitter and Facebook, to sow division and heighten nativist tendencies within the electorate. Strictly speaking, the goal of the 2016 interference was to delegitimize a potential Hillary Clinton presidency or to help elect Donald Trump as president. But far more important was the *method* used to accomplish these goals: the impersonation of American citizens during participation in the political process. This latter development points to the real harm of election interference, which has less to do with sovereignty and more to do with the collective right of self-determination. Foreign interference is a violation of the membership rules for political decision-making, that is, the idea that only members of a polity should participate in elections—not only with regard to voting but also with regard to financial contributions and other forms of electoral participation. Outsiders are free to express their opinions but covertly representing themselves as insiders constitutes a violation of these political norms, which are constitutive of the notion of self-determination, just as much as covertly funneling foreign money to one candidate. An important tool for combating this form of election interference is transparency, that is, to expose such interventions for what they are: attempts by foreigners to make political statements while pretending to be Americans. This chapter ends by cataloging the mistakes of the Obama administration in failing to expose this interference in real time, which might have nullified its insidious impact. Ex post

Zelinsky, *Foreign Cyber Attacks and the American Press: Why the Media Must Stop Reprinting Hacked Material*, 127 Yale L.J. Forum 286, 293 (2017).

[5] *See generally* Andrew Moshirnia, *No Security Through Obscurity Changing Circumvention Law to Protect Our Democracy Against Cyberattacks*, 83 Brook. L. Rev. 1279, 1279 (2018).

[6] Tallinn Manual 2.0 on the International Law Applicable to Cyber Operations (Michael N. Schmitt ed., 2d ed. 2017).

investigations, prosecutions, and countermeasures designed to deter future misbehavior are all praiseworthy policies but by themselves are insufficient to nullify the impact of electoral interference. However, recent efforts by the U.S. Justice Department and the FBI, including a new policy codified in the U.S. Attorneys' Manual, and contemporaneous indictments of Russians for interference in the 2018 election, suggest that some government actors finally understand that transparency is a key solution to election interference.

Section II of the chapter briefly describes and analyzes Russia's interference in the 2016 and 2018 elections. Section III focuses on the existing legal debate over election interference and why the existing literature has failed to capture its distinctive harm. Then, section IV outlines its distinctive harm as a violation of the membership rules for the election process, especially when outsiders masquerade as insiders in order to influence the election. Finally, section V evaluates the potential governmental responses to election interference—including retorsions, covert countermeasures, and criminal indictments—and concludes that governments must ensure transparency in the political process by exposing covert election interference in real time before the election is over. Section VI addresses objections to this account.

II. What Is Election Interference?

Prior to the 2016 presidential election, Russian intelligence services launched a major campaign to disrupt and influence the U.S. election. The interference was inspired by multiple goals: to sow discord and confusion in the U.S. political system; to encourage Americans to fight against each other along partisan divides in lieu of fighting against a common external enemy; to delegitimize Hillary Clinton if she won the presidential election; and to help elect Donald Trump as president.[7] To accomplish these goals, the Russian interference program included voter suppression efforts, election boycotts to reduce turnout, and support for third-party candidates (such as the Green Party's Jill Stein), who would draw support away from main-party candidates, especially Hillary Clinton.[8]

One possible motivation for preferring Trump over Clinton, or for delegitimizing a possible Clinton presidency, was an assumption on Russia's part that Clinton would impose an explicit or implicit policy goal of regime change in Russia, on account of corruption and human rights abuses by President Vladimir Putin. Consequently, Putin may have viewed a Clinton presidency as an existential threat and decided to launch a form of information warfare as a campaign of political self-defense. While it is unlikely that Clinton would have actually pursued regime change as official American foreign policy, there was sufficient tension between the two individuals

[7] *Assessing Russian Activities and Intentions in Recent US Elections*, *supra* note 1, at ii (concluding that "Moscow's approach evolved over the course of the campaign based on Russia's understanding of the electoral prospects of the two main candidates. When it appeared to Moscow that Secretary Clinton was likely to win the election, the Russian influence campaign began to focus more on undermining her future presidency.").

[8] *See* Jon Swaine, *Russian Propagandists Targeted African Americans to Influence 2016 US Election*, The Guardian (Dec. 17, 2018).

during Clinton's time running the U.S. State Department that Putin likely believed that Clinton was a major threat, regardless of whether that was true or not. At the start of Russia's influence operation, the goal was probably more to delegitimize Clinton and sow confusion, but as the election entered its eleventh hour, and Clinton's lead in the polls evaporated, the goal of electing Donald Trump could have played a supporting motivation for the election interference.

There were several methods used during the election interference. Chief among them was the hacking of emails belonging to John Podesta and DNC officials, and the dissemination of those emails through WikiLeaks and other outlets.[9] Trump himself famously solicited Russia to "find" Clinton's emails during a speech in Florida.[10] In addition to the hacking of email accounts, Russian intelligence services operated a troll farm that created fake Twitter and Facebook accounts. Some of these accounts involved the creation of fictitious advocacy groups, whereas other accounts simply spread inflammatory political statements. Falling within the latter camp were accounts that merely amplified other statements by either retweeting or resharing other posts, or accounts that generated their own inflammatory statements. Some of this activity was automated and the product of "bot" accounts, while others were individually created by human operators working at the troll farms.[11]

The scope of the influencing campaign was not originally well understood. In the early days after the 2016 election, when Twitter and Facebook were slow to investigate the nature of this influence campaign, Twitter initially indicated that there were roughly two hundred fake Russian Twitter accounts responsible for spreading a few thousand tweets.[12] Over time that number has grown substantially. In October 2018, Twitter announced that fake Russian accounts were responsible for more than 9 million tweets.[13]

One important factor in the Russian accounts was that the posters often pretended, either explicitly or implicitly, to be American when posting about American politics. Through the strategic use of profile photographs, profile descriptions,[14] and previously posted content, the accounts were designed to appear as if they were created and

[9] Podesta was a former White House Chief of Staff and was Campaign Chairman of the Hillary Clinton presidential campaign.

[10] *See* Ashley Parker & David E. Sanger, *Donald Trump Calls on Russia to Find Hillary Clinton's Missing Emails*, N.Y. TIMES (July 27, 2016) (quoting Trump stating in televised speech, "Russia, if you're listening, I hope you're able to find the 30,000 emails that are missing ... I think you will probably be rewarded mightily by our press.").

[11] *See* Neil MacFarquhar, *Inside the Russian Troll Factory: Zombies and a Breakneck Pace*, N.Y. TIMES (Feb. 18, 2018) (discussing the use of bots and other automated techniques in Russia social media campaigns).

[12] *See* Jessica Guynn & Erin Kelly, *Twitter Removed 200 Russian Accounts that Targeted Facebook Users During Election*, USA TODAY (Sept. 28, 2017).

[13] *See* Aja Romano, *Twitter Released 9 Million Tweets from One Russian Troll Farm. Here's What We Learned: The Massive Data Dump Reveals How Trolls Disrupt and Destabilize Local and Global Politics*, VOX (Oct. 19, 2018) ("The size of this release, however, confirms much of what experts have long suspected about the scope and function of the tweets—and further establishes that the goals of these propaganda farms, which mainly hail from Russia and Iran, involve not only the disruption of US politics but also the distortion of political debate in their own backyards."). Many of the 9 million tweets were in the Russian language and were designed to influence domestic political issues in Russia, such as the civil war in Eastern Ukraine.

[14] *See* Savvas Zannettou & Jeremy Blackburn, *How to Tell a Russian Troll from a Regular Person*, HOUSTON CHRONICLE (Sept. 5, 2018).

maintained by American citizens participating in the political process.[15] Borrowing a term from the lobbying arena, one might refer to this as "Astroturf electioneering."[16]

It is precisely these covert social media influencing campaigns that are the focus of this chapter. For the moment, I wish to keep the crime of computer hacking, and the release of DNC emails, to the side. Email hacking is a domestic crime under federal law and also raises important issues under both international law and strategy, but the use of social media influencers in the political process was the hallmark of Russia's troll farm activity during the 2016 election. The goal of this chapter is to conceptualize the harm of these efforts and outline what remedy, if any, is politically, ethically, and legally appropriate under the circumstances.

III. The Legal Framework for Evaluating Interference

According to most international lawyers, the basic rubric for evaluating legal election interference involves a resort to the basic standards for nonintervention.[17] In the context of military force, the rules regarding intervention are relatively easy to apply; military intervention is never permitted, according to Article 2 of the UN Charter, unless one of two exceptions applies (self-defense or a UN Security Council authorization). In contrast, the rules regarding nonmilitary interventions are far more difficult to articulate and even harder to apply. According to the *Tallinn Manual*, a nonmilitary intervention will violate the sovereignty of a state if the intervention involves either coercion or a usurpation of an inherently governmental conduct.[18] This articulation of the rule might sound strangely permissive in that it allows interventions in many situations that do not fall under these two exceptions (coercion and usurpation). It should be recalled, though, that state actors engage in activities every day that impact foreign states in some manner—activities that one might describe as economic, diplomatic, commercial, social, or cultural behaviors. Any one of them could, in theory, be described with the language of sovereignty, that is, one could use the language of sovereignty to say that the behavior in question is an illegal *violation* of a state's

[15] *See* Scott Shane, *The Fake Americans Russia Created to Influence the Election*, N.Y. Times (Sept. 7, 2017) (describing the social media posts of Melvin Redick of Harrisburg, Pennsylvania, "a friendly-looking American with a backward baseball cap and a young daughter" but noting that "Mr. Redick turned out to be a remarkably elusive character. No Melvin Redick appears in Pennsylvania records ... [but] this fictional concoction has earned a small spot in history: The Redick posts that morning were among the first public signs of an unprecedented foreign intervention in American democracy.").

[16] The term "Astroturf lobbying" refers to an advocacy group that pretends to be a grassroots initiative but is, in fact, created by a corporate group with an interest in influencing governmental regulation. The point of the term is that the advocacy styles itself as something—a grassroots effort—that it is not. For a discussion, *see* Anita S. Krishnakumar, *Towards a Madisonian, Interest-Group-Based, Approach to Lobbying Regulation*, 58 Ala. L. Rev. 513, 565 (2007); Jonathan C. Zellner, *Artificial Grassroots Advocacy and the Constitutionality of Legislative Identification and Control Measures*, 43 Conn. L. Rev. 357, 400 (2010). By analogy, the term "grassroots electioneering" could refer to a coordinated effort to produce fraudulent social media content that appears to be organically generated at the grassroots level.

[17] *See* Schmitt, *supra* note 3, at 50; Brian J. Egan, Legal Adviser, U.S. Dep't of State, *International Law and Stability in Cyberspace, Speech at Berkeley Law School* (Nov. 10, 2016) (arguing that an attack against election infrastructure would be an illegal infringement of American sovereignty).

[18] *See* Tallinn Manual 2.0, *supra* note 6, at 23.

sovereignty. So, the goal of legal doctrine must be to distinguish between permissible infringements of sovereignty and those which cross a line of legal significance.

It was with this task in mind that the *Tallinn Manual*, drawing on norms articulated in the International Court of Justice's (ICJ's) *Nicaragua* decision, noted that a state's sovereignty would be violated by an action that involves coercion or usurps an inherently governmental function.[19] Neither legal standard fits the facts of election interference with any degree of clarity.[20] Take coercion first. The Russian interference in the 2016 election involved a desire to achieve a particular result—the delegitimization of Hillary Clinton or the election of Donald Trump—but not through the mechanism of coercion per se.[21] The mechanism involved impersonation of U.S. citizens through social media to amplify particular social and political positions, thereby increasing partisan rancor and the type of political anger that encourages people to vote. The key mechanism here was deception, not coercion. It was not as if the Russians forced people to vote for Donald Trump otherwise certain unpleasant consequences would follow (such as economic punishments or the like).[22]

As for the second standard—usurpation—it is important to note that the *Tallinn Manual* articulated usurpation as a violation of international law as part of its larger claim that sovereignty functions as a stand-alone rule that would prohibit a state from engaging in cyber operations under certain circumstances.[23] This conceptualization of sovereignty as a "stand-alone" rule is controversial, with some international lawyers objecting that sovereignty is a background principle that informs the much more specific, and limited, rule regarding nonintervention (which requires coercion).[24] These objectors believe that sovereignty has no direct normative force outside of the context of the specific rule of nonintervention, while the *Tallinn Manual* asserts a role for sovereignty in prohibiting actions that fall outside the realm of the rule of nonintervention.

While this debate over the status of the legal norms of nonintervention and sovereignty is important for the legal regulation of cyber behavior, the dispute need not be resolved here. Simply put, even assuming that the *Tallinn Manual*'s view on

[19] *Military and Paramilitary Activities in and Against Nicaragua* (Nicaragua v. United States), Judgment, 1986 I.C.J. Rep. 14, para. 205 (June 27) (concluding that coercion "defines, and indeed forms the very essence of, prohibited intervention").

[20] Many of these standards are discussed in Oona A. Hathaway et al., *The Law of Cyber-Attack*, 100 Cal. L. Rev. 817 (2012); Patrick Franzese, *Sovereignty in Cyberspace; Can It Exist?*, 64 Air Force L. Rev. 1 (2009).

[21] This issue is also discussed in Jens David Ohlin, *Did Russian Cyber Interference in the 2016 Election Violate International Law?*, 95 Tex. L. Rev. 1579, 1592 (2017) (concluding that "there are substantial impediments to concluding that the Russian hacking in the 2016 election constituted illegal coercion").

[22] *Id.*

[23] *See* Tallinn Manual 2.0, *supra* note 6, Rule 4 ("A State must not conduct cyber operations that violate the sovereignty of another State."); Ministère des Armées, *Droit International Appliqué aux Operations dans le Cyberspace* (Sept. 9, 2019); Bert Koenders, Foreign Minister, *Netherlands, Remarks at The Hague Regarding Tallinn Manual 2.0* (Feb. 13, 2017).

[24] *See* Jeremy Wright, QC, MP, *Cyber and International Law in the 21st Century* (May 23, 2018) ("Some have sought to argue for the existence of a cyber-specific rule of a 'violation of territorial sovereignty' ... Sovereignty is of course fundamental to the international rules-based system. But I am not persuaded that we can currently extrapolate from that general principle a specific rule or additional prohibition for cyber activity beyond that of a prohibited intervention. The UK Government's position is therefore that there is no such rule as a matter of current international law."); Gary Corn, *Tallinn Manual 2.0—Advancing the Conversation*, Just Security (Feb. 15, 2017).

sovereignty is correct, the "usurpation" rule would not prohibit the type of social media election interference at issues in the 2016, 2018, and 2020 elections. Of course, election interference would violate the usurpation rule if it involved direct manipulation of vote tallies, manipulation of voter registration rolls, manipulation of the internal code of electronic vote machines, false information about when or where voting stations would be open, or any other behavior that would have compromised the bureaucratic process of holding the election or counting the votes.[25] According to the *Tallinn Manual* view (which is shared by some nations), this type of interference would be an illegal infringement against a state's sovereignty because it involves a usurpation of an inherently governmental activity.[26]

The problem is that neither of these standards (coercion or usurpation), whether under the rule of nonintervention or a stand-alone sovereignty rule, provides a good description of Russian interference in the 2016, 2018, or 2020 elections. While it remains to be seen whether more direct forms of interference might happen in the future, this chapter focuses on the information warfare that Russia and other states are using on social media platforms, which does not primarily involve coercion or usurpation.

I have argued elsewhere that this social media information warfare is illegal, not because it constitutes an illegal intervention or violates a state's sovereignty, but rather because it constitutes a violation of a people's collective right of self-determination.[27] Although self-determination is largely recognized as a central human right, codified and protected in Article 1 of the International Covenant on Civil and Political Rights (ICCPR), most international lawyers are inclined to deemphasize self-determination as a right.[28] There are many reasons for this delegitimization process; one reason might be that the right is collective, rather than individual, and therefore falls outside the basic paradigm of individual rights based on human dignity that are protected under the human rights movement.[29] Another reason is that self-determination is attributed to peoples, not states. International lawyers have a difficult time wrapping their minds around a right that is attributed neither to states nor individual human beings, but instead a collective entity whose boundaries are defined not by positive law but by human relationships. Their prevailing attitude of legal positivism, and the focuses on positive sources of law, is problematic because one cannot look to the positive sources of law to find a definition of which entities count as peoples or not. *That* determination must be made by reference to extralegal categories.[30]

[25] Schmitt, *supra* note 3, at 45–46.

[26] *See* TALLINN MANUAL 2.0, *supra* note 6, at 22 (giving the following examples: "changing or deleting data such that it interferes with the delivery of social services, the conduct of elections, the collection of taxes, the effective conduct of diplomacy, and the performance of key national defense activities").

[27] Ohlin, *supra* note 21, at 1580–1581.

[28] International Covenant on Civil and Political Rights (ICCPR), art. 1, Dec. 19, 1966, 999 U.N.T.S. 171 ("All peoples have the right of self-determination. By virtue of that right they freely determine their political status and freely pursue their economic, social and cultural development.").

[29] *See generally* ANTONIO CASSESE, SELF-DETERMINATION OF PEOPLES: A LEGAL REAPPRAISAL (1995). *See also* Gregory H. Fox, *Self-Determination in the Post-Cold War Era: A New Internal Focus?*, 16 MICH. J. INT'L L. 733 (1995) ("with the effective end of decolonization and the virtually unanimous refusal of States to recognize a right of secession, the legal norm appears to have been deprived of much of its content").

[30] For more discussion on this point, *see* Jens David Ohlin, *The Right to Exist and the Right to Resist*, in THE THEORY OF SELF-DETERMINATION 70 (F. Teson ed., 2016).

The concept of self-determination has usually been employed to entail a right of secession in situations where a people's self-determination is not actualized within their current political arrangement.[31] But the right of self-determination is so much more and runs so much deeper. It includes the right of a people to select their own political destiny, or as the ICCPR puts it, "[b]y virtue of that right they freely determine their political status and freely pursue their economic, social and cultural development."[32] In a democratic polity, the engine of that process is the work of representative government whose officials make decisions, about matters small and large, on behalf of the people that they represent. That process of representative government does not happen by divine right of kings—it happens because the people select their own governing representatives through a process of election.[33] And elections happen in a specific way, not just by engaging in a popularity contest, as in a high school election for student council, but a public debate about the normative choices required by governing. The people, in other words, vote for and select the representatives who will work to implement a political vision that the voters wish to endorse.[34] In a democratic society, this is the meaning of self-determination, and it is inextricably linked to the electoral process.

In the following section, I seek to evaluate modern electoral interference in relation to this political conception of self-determination.[35] In particular, I hope to respond to various objections that election interference involves nothing more troubling than exercising the right to free speech or the right to participate in the political process. If Americans can express political viewpoints on Twitter, why should not the Russians? More specifically, what is wrong with a troll farm in Russia employing a large group of individuals to post statements and opinions on Twitter and Facebook? Why would this behavior compromise the collective right of self-determination? Answering this question requires a more complete picture not just of self-determination but also about defining the outer boundaries of a political community, that is, who is a member of the polity. Only after we have a complete account of political membership—of who is an insider and who is an outsider, and who gets to define these terms—can we understand the role that elections play in the right of self-determination under international law.

[31] This was, for example, the conclusion of the Canadian Supreme Court advisory opinion on the question of Quebec's secession. *See* Reference re Secession of Quebec [1998] S.C.R. 217.

[32] ICCPR, *supra* note 28.

[33] *See, e.g.*, John W. Head, *Selling Hong Kong to China: What Happened to the Right of Self-Determination?*, 46 U. KAN. L. REV. 283, 291 (1998) (concluding that "the sources of law on the right of self-determination are fairly clear on this point. In referring to the means by which the right of self-determination is to be achieved, the sources consistently use such language as 'freely expressed will and desire,' 'political status freely determined by a people,' and 'free and voluntary choice ... expressed through informed and democratic processes.' ").

[34] *See Principles Which Should Guide Members in Determining Whether or Not an Obligation Exists to Transmit the Information Called for Under Article 73e of the Charter*, G.A. Res. 1541, U.N. GAOR, 15th Sess., Annex 29, U.N. Doc. A/4684 (1960).

[35] For a discussion, *see* Duncan Hollis, *The Influence of War; The War for Influence*, 32 TEMP. INT'L & COMP. L.J. 31, 43 (2018) ("applying the right to self-determination in the IO context presupposes a capacity to identify with sufficient specificity the impact of an IO like 'fake news' on a voting public").

IV. A Unique Harm

The following section will connect the harm of election interference with a core conception of self-determination. The goal is to explain, in both political and legal terms, the distinctive harm imposed by election interference and why it would count as a violation of the collective right of self-determination.

To answer this question, it is important to consider a key skeptical challenge that one often hears from international lawyers: that is, that all individuals enjoy freedom of speech, both under U.S. and international law, and that political speech of any kind is protected by the U.S. Constitution and the relevant international protocols.[36] This has led some to suggest that Russian social media trolls have just as much right to post inflammatory views on Twitter and Facebook as an individual living in California, Texas, or New York. While freedom of speech is undeniably protected by these sources of law, it is not an absolute right and it is subject to regulation. In the context of electoral politics, speech (including campaign financing) is regulated according to the background rules and principles governing participation in the political process.

We saw previously that elections fulfill the right of a people to select their own political destiny. In order to accomplish this goal, a political system will establish criteria for who can participate in the political process. For example, only citizens can vote in an election in the United States and in most democratic political systems.[37] Noncitizens are excluded from this form of political participation. Why would this discrimination be permitted, given that the government creates and enforces laws against noncitizens residents? While residents are subject to the government's coercive authority, residents have no authority to participate in the process of selecting the government.[38] The only answer is that citizens are permanent members of the polity and as such as allowed to participate in the process of selecting the polity's future direction.[39]

Campaign finance regulations rely on the same distinction between members and nonmembers of the polity.[40] Citizens are entitled to give financial contributions to any political candidate, outside contributions from foreigners are strictly prohibited.[41] Again, one might ask what justifies this categorical exclusion of foreigners from the political process. The only answer is that an election is supposed to be an expression of the polity's collective decision-making and allowing foreign contributions would turn an election into something else—an expression of the political will of the outsiders too.

[36] *See* Thai, *supra* note 4.

[37] *See, e.g.*, 52 U.S.C. § 10101; 52 U.S.C. § 10502 (abolishing durational residency requirement for voting as unconstitutional when applied against citizens).

[38] For a discussion of this issue, *see generally* Stanley Allen Renshon, Noncitizen Voting and American Democracy 4 (2009) (arguing that noncitizens should be allowed to vote but describing the association of citizenship and voting as settled doctrine).

[39] *Id.*

[40] *See* Toni M. Massaro, *Foreign Nationals, Electoral Spending, and the First Amendment*, 34 Harv. J.L. & Pub. Pol'y 663, 685 (2011).

[41] *See, e.g.*, 52 U.S.C. § 30121 (prohibiting foreign nationals from directly or indirectly contributing to a political campaign). However, those with permanent resident status (such as green-card holders) are permitted to donate to a political campaign. Presumably the theory behind the distinction is that permanent residents sufficiently belong to the polity—by virtue of the *permanency* of their residency—that they are permitted this form of political participation.

Outsiders usually belong to their own political entities and are entitled to participate there—but allowing universal participation in the political process would effectively undermine the existence of independent polities representing distinct peoples.[42]

In some situations, a polity will see fit to "suspend" membership in the polity when individuals behave particularly badly. For example, convicted felons are sometimes disenfranchised and prohibited from voting in state and federal elections. Setting aside whether such "felon disenfranchisement" statutes are advisable or not,[43] it is important to understand their basic structure.[44] In making this determination, the polity declares that membership in the decision-making class can be forfeited by felonious conduct.[45] This legal maneuver just highlights that for purposes of political decision-making, there are insiders and outsiders.[46] Elections only make sense once those distinctions are made. And chief among those distinctions is the distinction between citizens and foreigners. The underlying rationale for this distinction is that elections cease to be an expression of a polity's decision-making if outsiders are permitted to participate in them. Moreover, the *criteria* for insider membership status is determined by the polity itself. The polity determines the criteria for citizenship (e.g., *jus solis* or *jus sanguinis* or some combination of the two) and also determines the criteria for suspending that membership in the case of egregious law-breaking (felon disenfranchisement).[47]

The polity also distinguishes between insiders and outsiders by crafting rules governing immigration.[48] Immigration has been the source of intense political strife during the last administration, with Trump supporters arguing for restrictions on illegal and legal immigration, and critics arguing for immigration reform. Underlying *both* positions, however, is a recognition that a polity is entitled to manage its borders in such a way that defines who may enter and potentially join the polity, first as a lawful permanent resident and eventually as a possible citizen. Immigration control is yet another example of how a polity may legitimately define, regulate, and select its own membership.[49]

[42] *But see* RENSHON, *supra* note 38, at 4.

[43] There is a vast literature criticizing the wisdom and racial impacts of felon disenfranchisement. For a good survey of the literature, *see* Developments in the Law, *One Person, No Vote: The Laws of Felon Disenfranchisement*, 115 HARV. L. REV. 1939 (2002).

[44] *See, e.g.*, S. Brannon Latimer, *Can Felon Disenfranchisement Survive Under Modern Conceptions of Voting Rights?: Political Philosophy, State Interests, and Scholarly Scorn*, 59 SMU L. REV. 1841, 1844 (2006).

[45] *See* Roger Clegg, George T. Conway III, & Kenneth K. Lee, *The Case Against Felon Voting*, 2 U. ST. THOMAS J.L. & PUB. POL'Y 1, 17 (2008) (noting that "felon disenfranchisement laws are justified on the basis of Locke's notion of the social contract: As Judge Henry Friendly once put it, someone 'who breaks the laws' may 'fairly have been thought to have abandoned the right to participate' in making them").

[46] Indeed, the case *against* felon disenfranchisement logically depends on the idea that felons remain members of the political community, even if they have violated its rules.

[47] *See* Fox, *supra* note 29, at 760–761; Joseph W. Dellapenna, *Constitutional Citizenship Under Attack*, 61 VILL. L. REV. 477, 490 (2016).

[48] See PETER H. SCHUCK & ROGERS M. SMITH, CITIZENSHIP WITHOUT CONSENT: ILLEGAL ALIENS IN THE AMERICAN POLITY (1985).

[49] *See, e.g.*, Ayelet Shachar, *The Race for Talent: Highly Skilled Migrants and Competitive Immigration Regimes*, 81 N.Y.U. L. REV. 148, 155 (2006) ("Indeed, countries are willing to go so far as to reconfigure the boundaries of political membership in order to gain the net positive effects associated with skilled migration.").

This conception of elections as an expression of political self-determination helps explain the distinctive harm of election interference. When Russian military intelligence set up a troll farm to operate fictitious Twitter and Facebook accounts, they did so in order to make statements that would appear to come from American sources. Indeed, if the posts had transparently identified their Russian source, no one on Twitter or Facebook would have cared about the opinions that they expressed. The extreme political viewpoints posted by members of the troll farm—whether they were far-right or far-left viewpoints—gained traction because they were ostensibly expressions of real American citizens. In a highly partisan context, Americans debate each other and then go to the polls; the views of outsiders, while interesting, are not part of the electoral contest. In other words, the work of the Russian troll farms only worked because the operators impersonated Americans and their habits on social media, going so far as to adopt turns-of-phrase, iconography, and photographs that marked them out as Americans.[50] These were not Russians articulating their views as *Russians* in the electoral process, but Russians impersonating Americans and then articulating viewpoints whose political currency depended on the fiction that they were Americans.

These facts point the way to the distinctive harm of this type of election interference. By posing as Americans, the Russian troll farms sought to gain inside access to the political process and to distort the political discourse, not by injecting points of view that were not already there, but rather to amplify viewpoints that had lain dormant but were considered marginal and in many cases outside the political mainstream. By amplifying those viewpoints, the political discourse was fundamentally altered and most importantly, it was altered by individuals who were not members of the polity.

At this point one might object that there is no firm evidence that the election interference changed the *outcome* of the election.[51] This suggests an important clarification. First, it is unclear whether the outcome of the election was changed or not. The lack of any firm evidence that the outcome of the election was altered by troll farm activity simply boils down to the fact that the assertion that the election result was altered is a counterfactual statement that would be extremely hard, or impossible, to support with empirical evidence. But absence of evidence is not evidence of absence. The more credible conclusion is that it is very hard to predict how the election might have unfolded in the absence of the interference. This leaves us in a state of ignorance rather than a state of certainty that the interference was not outcome-determinative.

More importantly, however, there is another response to this objection. The argument presented in this chapter does not depend on the assertion that the election interference changed the outcome of the election. The particular harm flowed from the fact that the Russians *participated* in the electoral process while pretending to be Americans. This had a distortionary impact on the electoral process, which is

[50] *See supra* note 13.

[51] *See Assessing Russian Activities and Intentions in Recent US Elections*, *supra* note 1, at i (clarifying that "[w]e did not make an assessment of the impact that Russian activities had on the outcome of the 2016 election. The US Intelligence Community is charged with monitoring and assessing the intentions, capabilities, and actions of foreign actors; it does not analyze US political processes or US public opinion.").

problematic because an election is supposed to articulate the view of the polity, that is, a fulfillment of that polity's right of self-determination. Once outsiders insert themselves into that process, while pretending to be insiders, the election becomes a function of other-determination rather than self-determination. The election expresses the political will of outside entities rather than the entity that is holding the election.

This political account of elections as an articulation of a polity's self-determination helps explain why the *covert* nature of the election interference was crucial to its illegality as a violation of the principle of self-determination. As already explained, the individual account holders in the troll farm did not publicly disclose their status as Russians. However, in addition to this deception, Russia itself, at the state level, refused to acknowledge the existence of the troll farm or its connection to Russian military intelligence or its connection to official state policy.[52] The interference remained covert and unacknowledged at both the individual and collective levels. If, on the other hand, the Russians had admitted that they were participating in the American electoral process, that participation would have been less problematic because at least it would have been clear that the opinions expressed by the troll farm were an expression of the sovereign will of the Russian government or the Russian people. At that point, the problematic nature of the interference would have been substantially reduced. Any foreign participation in elections is potentially problematic—and rightfully prohibited by domestic statutes and domestic policies—but *covert* participation is even worse because the rest of the voting public is deceived about the participation. The result is a particularly pernicious distort of the deliberative process—a process that is protected by the international legal system under the general rubric of self-determination. Of course, if the Russians had acknowledged the interference effort, it would have lost most of its effectiveness because, as discussed previously, the logic behind the effort required that the Russians participate in the political process under the guise of membership in the American polity.

I should note that some scholars and political commentators have suggested that election interference is a violation of U.S. "popular sovereignty."[53] These invocations of "sovereignty" get at the right idea and should be viewed as quite distinct from how public international lawyers use the word "sovereignty."[54] In political theory and political science, the notion of "popular sovereignty" refers to the exercise of the political will of the nation or people, an idea that has much more in common with self-determination than it does with the technical definition of sovereignty used by

[52] President Trump made the following statement regarding his meeting with President Putin of Russia: "He said he didn't meddle. I asked him again. You can only ask so many times. Every time he sees me, he says, 'I didn't do that.' And I believe, I really believe, that when he tells me that, he means it." *See* Karen Yourish & Troy Griggs, *8 U.S. Intelligence Groups Blame Russia for Meddling, but Trump Keeps Clouding the Picture*, N.Y. TIMES (July 16, 2018).

[53] *See, e.g.*, Claire Finkelstein, *How Democracy, in the Kremlin's Crosshairs, Can Fight Back*, ZOCALO PUBLIC SQUARE (May 11, 2017) (concluding that "[i]nstitutions that are dependent on the concept of popular sovereignty are sitting ducks for foreign intervention carried out by cyberattack, cyber influence, and cyber manipulation.").

[54] *See also* Ciara Torres-Spelliscy, *Dark Money as a Political Sovereignty Problem*, 28 KING'S L.J. 239 (2017) (arguing that "[a] key factor to both sovereignty of the nation and the popular sovereignty of the American people is the soundness of the electoral process," noting that a "close corollary to sovereignty is the right of a people to self-determination," and concluding that "the concepts of sovereignty and self-determination are intertwined in a democracy, as the people in a given country decide their fate").

lawyers. Part of the problem is a translation exercise: the concepts used by lawyers, political theorists, and politicians do not always line up exactly. This should come as no surprise given that "sovereignty" is something of a cluster concept housing many different ideas within its rich but often confusing rubric. But we should be absolutely clear that in the context of election interference, invocations of popular sovereignty are on the right track and should not be lumped in with my general criticism of the legal literature's sovereignty-based discourse.

In conclusion, the real harm of election interference flows from outsiders participating in the political process of another polity but pretending to do so as insiders. An election is supposed to be an expression of that polity's collective will, as a fulfillment of their collective right of self-determination, and outside interference has a distortionary impact on the discourse and threatens to transform what would otherwise be an expression of the polity's will into an expression of some other polity's will.[55] The covert nature of the election interference is an integral part of its harm, because what is destructive about the interference is the participation of outside forces masquerading as inside members of the polity.

V. One Solution

Now comes the hard part. What solutions are available in law and policy to counteract this form of election interference? This section will defend the proposition that transparency in the democratic process is a key goal that domestic actors should strive to protect. Moreover, transparency should be protected not just in the voting process but also in the *deliberative* process, that is, the public's consideration and discussion of competing conceptions of the good and competing policy goals for the polity. Given the distinctive harm outlined in the prior section, the best way to protect deliberative democracy is for the *source* of the interference to be exposed as foreign. Most importantly, the remedy must occur in real time, because any ex post solution will probably come too late to rectify the harm done to the collective right of self-determination. Once the outsiders have participated in the electoral process and the election is held, no remedies after the fact will be sufficient to vindicate the collective right of self-determination.

If I am correct about the real harm in election interference, the "transparency" solution is easier than many might have thought. Since the harm flows from outsiders pretending to be insiders, it is not necessary for the election interference—the posting of opinions on Twitter and Facebook and other social media platforms—to be completely eliminated. All that needs to happen is for the interference to be unmasked as foreign in nature. In other words, the social media campaigns need to be identified as coming from outside the polity and recognized for what they are: outsiders

[55] Matt Vega refers to this as an "anti-distortion" rationale and uses it to justify prohibitions on campaign expenditures by foreign corporations in light of *Citizens United*. *See* Matt A. Vega, *The First Amendment Lost in Translation: Preventing Foreign Influence in U.S. Elections After Citizens United v. FEC*, 44 Loy. L.A. L. Rev. 951, 1012 (2011) ("Campaign spending by a foreign-controlled corporation is, by definition, a distortion of an exclusively American political process."). *See also* Massaro, *supra* note 40, at 688 (discussing the anti-distortion rationale for narrow restrictions on foreign spending).

masquerading as insiders. Social media platforms should promote transparency by removing content attributable to foreign government–sponsored troll farms, and where content is foreign but not attributable to a troll farm, it should be labeled as foreign in origin. The point of this social media labeling regime would be to give the public the information that it needs about the source of the political speech that it is consuming, so as to prevent the deception about foreign origin that is the foundation for troll farm success. The labeling regime would help neutralize the distortion to the political process that happens when outsiders covertly participate in the deliberative process.

Existing statutory regimes seek to promote transparency, but these regimes are patchworks and are insufficiently enforced. To take just one example, the Foreign Agents Registration Act, passed in 1938, requires that lobbyists and other foreign agents register with the federal government in order to announce their representation of a foreign sovereign.[56] The Act also covers political propaganda, thus providing a hook for regulating social media content, though there are issues of extraterritoriality to consider.[57] Also, failure to file a Foreign Agents Registration Act (FARA) registration is infrequently punished, though recent events have renewed interest in using FARA as a tool for enforcing transparency in the context of covert political influence.[58] For example, in 2018, the Justice Department indicted a Russian national for violations of FARA while working with the National Rifle Association and other Second Amendment advocacy organizations.

As a matter of computer technology and social media, transparency is not easy to accomplish. Advanced computer algorithms need to be developed to flag potentially problematic social media posts, but inevitably the process requires a massive investment of human capital to oversee and flag problematic developments. At the time of the 2016 elections, tech media giants such as Google, Facebook, and Twitter were woefully unprepared for this mission. Only since late 2018 have Facebook and Twitter begun hiring and investing resources in flagging deceptive foreign-generated content during the election cycle.[59] The 2018 mid-term elections were the first opportunity to test whether these private corporate solutions will work. While there were encouraging signs of progression, the existence of continuing election interference during the 2020 election suggests that the volume of material produced by troll farms is so massive that private firms have struggled to deal with the problem. It may be necessary for private firms to devote even more financial and human resources to their efforts.

In addition to private sector solutions, the government has a major role to play in identifying and then publicizing covert foreign election interference. Unfortunately, on this score, the Obama administration performed poorly. Although well intentioned, the strategy utilized by the FBI and intelligence agencies was outmoded and

[56] 22 U.S.C. 11.

[57] For a discussion, *see, e.g.*, Zephyr Teachout, *Extraterritorial Electioneering and the Globalization of American Elections*, 27 BERKELEY J. INT'L L. 162, 171 (2009).

[58] *See* Jahad Atieh, *Foreign Agents: Updating Fara to Protect American Democracy*, 31 U. PA. J. INT'L L. 1051, 1067 (2010) (the Department of Justice's enforcement of FARA has been abysmal).

[59] *See, e.g.*, Josh Constine, *Facebook Will Hire 1,000 and Make Ads Visible to Fight Election Interference*, TECH CRUNCH (Oct. 2, 2017).

inappropriate for this particular problem.[60] Intelligence agents, analysts, and counterintelligence agents are designed to uncover threats and then pass them on to government leaders in a confidential or even classified setting. Government leaders usually keep these intelligence assessments secret, for fear of tipping off foreign adversaries about remedial actions the United States might take, or to preserve sources and methods. In the case of most security threats, this policy makes good sense. In the case of election interference, however, this policy is not just ineffectual—it is downright harmful. It allows the election interference to continue unabated because the true source of the problematic posts remains hidden, protected yet again by the classified nature of the intelligence-gathering process and the remedies advanced by the Obama administration.[61]

The Obama administration engaged in strategic behavior designed to nullify the election interference. The administration made *private* overtures to the Russian government demanding that the meddling stop.[62] Specifically, the administration warned the Russians that meddling in the *vote tally* would be met with draconian countermeasures, but apparently said little or nothing about the social media campaign. The FBI also launched criminal investigations after the election, but an ex post remedy is no solution at all to an infringement of the collective right of self-determination. And the FBI's counterintelligence investigation was also unhelpful because it was classified and could not be disclosed to the public in any meaningful way.

The only thing that would stop the election interference from succeeding would be to expose it for what it is. Transparency is the only solution, and it requires disclosing to the American public not only the overall effort—the fact that the Russians are intervening—but also exposing the true authorship of social media activity flowing from Russian troll farms. The Obama administration did neither of these things, in part because the American government had never experienced a problem like this, on this scale, before, and therefore had little experience in counteracting it. But new threats require new solutions, and the solutions are not ones to which intelligence agencies are accustomed. Instead of more secrecy, we need more transparency. Intelligence agencies hate transparency. But there are other organs of the government

[60] James Comey gave the following explanation to NPR: "Separately, it's a really good question as to whether the Obama administration should've said more about the broader Russian effort. I offered to be the voice of inoculation to the American people in August. I drafted an op-ed to say, 'Hey, the Russians are coming for our election. Here's what we think they're doing. It's part of a broad pattern.... American people be warned.' The administration never took me up on that and didn't get around to making a decision about disclosing the broader Russian effort until October." *See* James Comey, Interview with Terry Gross on NPR's Fresh Air (Apr. 17, 2018).

[61] *See* Donie O'Sullivan, Curt Devine, & Drew Griffin, *Obama Official: We Could Have Stopped Russian Trolls*, CNN (Mar. 26, 2018).

[62] Obama described his conversation in the following way: "What I was concerned about in particular was making sure [the hack of the Democratic National Committee] wasn't compounded by potential hacking that could hamper vote counting, affect the actual election process itself... So in early September when I saw president Putin in China, I felt that the most effective way to ensure that that didn't happen was to talk to him directly and tell him to cut it out and there were going to be serious consequences if he didn't. And in fact, we did not see further tampering of the election process—but the leaks ... had already occurred." *See* Barack Obama, *Transcript of End-of-Year Press Conference*, Dec. 16, 2016. The problem with this statement should be obvious. By stating that tampering with election counting would be met with serious consequences, Obama implicitly left the impression that Russia's social media interference would have no serious repercussions for Putin. In retrospect, this was a grievous error.

that can take the intelligence assessments and publicize the threats in a way to maximize transparency. One organ is the Justice Department, though even the Justice Department has not historically focused on public communications.[63] In theory, the federal government should assign this task to a particular agency or even create a cross-agency working group with the specific task of disclosing and publicizing foreign election interference in order to neutralize it. In this context, "neutralizing" does not mean suppressing or prohibiting the speech but merely eliminating its deceptive character regarding its origin. The viewpoint expressed in the communication can still be expressed, but outsiders should not be entitled to express it with the benefit of a deceptive insider voice.[64]

One reason why the Obama administration may have decided against publicizing the Russian election interference was that it assumed, falsely as it turns out, that Hillary Clinton would win the 2016 election and any federal government statements about Russian involvement would appear to the public as favoritism to one candidate (Clinton) over another candidate (Trump). For that reason, the administration decided to stay quiet and work behind the scenes to correct the interference. Not only was the prediction in error, but the strategy was completely incoherent. Regardless of who is going to win or not win an election, the government has just as much obligation to disclose outsiders participating in the election process masquerading as insiders, as they have an obligation to prevent foreigners from funding a presidential or congressional campaign. And they should stop such efforts regardless of who might win the election. The response should not be governed by a prediction of whether one side might win the election anyway.

Luckily, there are signs that the Justice Department is starting to understand the role that public disclosure can play in nullifying the effect of election interference. In September 2018, the Justice Department announced a new policy on "Disclosure of Foreign Influence Operations," which was codified in the Department's Justice Manual:

> Our Nation's democratic processes and institutions are strong and must remain resilient in the face of this threat. It is the policy of the Department of Justice to investigate, disrupt, and prosecute the perpetrators of illegal foreign influence activities where feasible. It is also the Department's policy to alert the victims and unwitting targets of foreign influence activities, when appropriate and consistent with the Department's policies and practices, and with our national security interests.
>
> It may not be possible or prudent to disclose foreign influence operations in certain contexts because of investigative or operational considerations, or other constraints. In some circumstances, however, public exposure and attribution of foreign

[63] Comey's offer to write an op-ed article about Russia's election interference is a good example of a public communication that would have been helpful. *See supra* note 58.

[64] Some lawyers might object that such a regulation or policy would violate the First Amendment, which often protects anonymous speech. This chapter deals with these alleged First Amendment obstacles briefly in section VI *infra*. For a full argument that the policy proposals discussed here are consistent with both the First Amendment and the human right to freedom of speech, *see* JENS DAVID OHLIN, ELECTION INTERFERENCE: INTERNATIONAL LAW AND THE FUTURE OF DEMOCRACY (2020).

> influence operations can be an important means of countering the threat and rendering those operations less effective.[65]

The policy then goes on to list the circumstances when such disclosure would be appropriate. The list includes some obvious and less obvious examples. For example, the policy states that disclosure may be necessary to "support arrests and charges for federal crimes arising out of foreign influence operations, such as hacking or malicious cyber activity, identity theft, and fraud."[66] This largely codified existing policy. However, the policy also says that disclosure may be appropriate to notify technology companies that "their services are used to disseminate covert foreign government propaganda or disinformation, or to provide other covert support to political organizations or groups."[67] Disclosure would also be appropriate to "relevant Congressional committees." As for members of the public at large, the policy states that:

> To alert the public or other affected individuals, where the federal or national interests in doing so outweigh any countervailing considerations. For example, there may be an important federal or national interest in publicly disclosing a foreign influence operation that threatens to undermine confidence in the government or public institutions; risks inciting violence or other illegal actions; or may cause substantial harm, alarm, or confusion if left unaddressed. On the other hand, in some cases, public disclosure of a foreign influence operation may be counterproductive because it may amplify or otherwise exacerbate the foreign government's messaging, or may re-victimize the victim.[68]

While the statement that disclosure to the public is possible when national interests outweigh countervailing considerations, the policy includes no specific indication that disclosure of a foreign influence operation should be made to counter the harmful effects of election interference. I would argue that the policy should be updated to explicitly include a preference for, or presumption in favor of, disclosing information about foreign influence operations that involve election interference of the type discussed in this chapter. Given the failure of both the Obama administration and the Justice Department to give timely notification to the public during the 2016 election, the presumption should be stated explicitly so that future administrations do not make the same mistake.

At the same time as it introduced the policy, the Justice Department's Cyber Digital Task Force released a report that included two important statements regarding remediation efforts for election meddling. First, the report stated that:

> The FBI and IC partners may be able to identify and track foreign agents as they establish their infrastructure and mature their online presence, in which case

[65] *See* Justice Manual § 9-90.730—Disclosure of Foreign Influence Operations (2018). The Manual was previously referred to as the "U.S. Attorneys' Manual."

[66] *Id.*

[67] *Id.*

[68] *Id.*

> authorities can work with social media companies to illuminate and ultimately disrupt those agents' activities, including through voluntary removal of accounts that violate a company's terms of service.[69]

Of course, this involves taking down the posts or suspending the accounts. In some situations that might not be possible or even advisable. What about informing the population regarding the foreign intelligence meddling? On this point, the task force report states the following:

> [I]n some circumstances, public exposure and attribution of foreign influence operations, and of foreign governments' goals and methods in conducting them, can be an important means of countering the threat and rendering those operations less effective. Of course, partisan politics must play no role in the decision whether to disclose the existence of a foreign influence operation, and such disclosures must not be made for the purpose of conferring any advantage or disadvantage on any political or social group. In addition, the Department must seek to protect intelligence sources and methods and operational equities, and attribution itself may present challenges.[70]

While this paragraph nods in the direction of transparency, it certainly fails to announce an unambiguous policy in favor of announcing foreign influence operations that concern elections. Given the intensity of these influence operations and the way they can impinge the polity's collective right of self-determination, the Justice Department should have articulated that the federal government has an affirmative obligation to publicly disclose election interference in real time in order to counter the negative effects of the influence operation. This was a missed opportunity for both the cyber-digital task force specifically and the Justice Department generally.

Since the 2016 election, the Justice Department has focused on criminal prosecutions as a method of resolving foreign election interference. Some of these prosecutions arose from the investigation conducted by Special Counsel Robert Mueller. For example, in February 2018, the Justice Department announced an indictment against thirteen individuals and three corporations for running a foreign influence operation out of a troll farm connected to Russian military intelligence. Specifically, the indictment alleged that:

> Defendants, posing as U.S. persons and creating false U.S. personas, operated social media pages and groups designed to attract U.S. audiences. These groups and pages, which addressed divisive U.S. political and social issues, falsely claimed to be controlled by U.S. activists when, in fact, they were controlled by Defendants. Defendants also used the stolen identities of real U.S. persons to post on ORGANIZATION controlled social media accounts. Over time, these social media accounts became Defendants' means to reach significant numbers of Americans for purposes of interfering with the U.S. political system, including the presidential election of 2016.[71]

[69] United States Department of Justice, Office of the Deputy Attorney General, Cyber-Digital Task Force, at 12 (2018).

[70] *Id.*

[71] United States of America v. Internet Research Agency et al., indictment, at para. 4 (Feb. 16, 2018).

Central to these allegations was that the troll farm activity involved Russians posing as Americans.

Many wondered what practical effect the indictment would have. The thirteen named individual defendants are unlikely to be extradited to, or voluntarily visit, the United States, thus keeping them from the long arm of the American judicial system. In a strange twist, however, lawyers representing some of the corporate defendants appeared in federal court in the United States seeking discovery in the case.[72] This was a brilliant strategic move because the corporations have no U.S.-based assets that could be seized as part of a criminal punishment, nor are the directors of the corporations located in the United States. Consequently, the corporations could participate in the case in order to receive discovery—much to the chagrin of American intelligence agencies and the Justice Department—while effectively eliminating their risk of punishment even if they are found guilty. Strategically, the best move to block the discovery requests was to dismiss the charges against the corporate defendants, but the Justice Department was not interested in this option.

What was the value of the indictment if the thirteen named individuals could not be extradited to stand trial? One goal, of course, was "naming and shaming"—a time-honored technique, well known to human rights lawyers, that is designed to deter illegal conduct.[73] But deterrence is particularly difficult to achieve in this context, and I would submit that promoting transparency is a far more relevant goal here. The indictment told a very specific story to the American public about the allegations of Russian interference through the use of social media platforms. Although publicizing these efforts at the macro level might not help individual social media users identify which specific accounts are linked to the troll farm, nonetheless the overall effort helped publicize the nature of the foreign interference—a prosecutorial effort in service of transparency rather than criminal punishment, which is the usual goal of criminal prosecutions.

Of course, the Russian troll farm indictment was an ex post prosecution—it was announced in 2018, long after the 2016 election and the Russian meddling associated with it. Nothing in 2018 would change what happened in 2016. Moreover, vague predictions that the indictments might deter the Russian government from future interference are wildly implausible.[74] The value of the indictments stem from the publicity they bring to the overall problem, not to the deterrence value they bring to the future. Similarly, it was announced in 2018 that U.S. intelligence services had a plan which involved identifying—and notifying—Russian operatives involved in election

[72] Some of these issues are outlined in *United States v. Concord Mgmt. & Consulting LLC*, 317 F. Supp. 3d 598, 605 (D.D.C. 2018), appeal dismissed, No. 18-3061, 2018 WL 5115521 (D.C. Cir. Sept. 17, 2018).

[73] For a nuanced discussion of naming and shaming in the cyber context, *see* Martha Finnemore & Duncan B. Hollis, *Beyond Naming and Shaming: Accusations and International Law in Cybersecurity*, Eur. J. Int'l L. (2020) (introducing and examining the broader concept of "accusation" as a social, political, and legal alternative to naming and shaming).

[74] On the issue of the difficulty of developing a plan that could accomplice deterrence, *see* Anthony Cuthbertson, *Russian Trolls and Fake News Are Set to Get Even Worse, Warns Former White House Advisor*, Newsweek (Feb. 19, 2018) (quoting Virginia Senator Mark Warner as saying that "[w]e've had more than a year to get our act together and address the threat posed by Russia and implement a strategy to deter future attacks . . . But we still do not have a plan.").

interference activities during the 2018 elections.[75] Although the details are a bit unclear, it appears that the U.S. government directly contacted Russian operatives and communicated to them that their activities and identities had been discovered and they could be subject to economic sanctions or criminal indictment. However, these efforts are unlikely to induce compliance from Russian operatives who remain far afield from the coercive machinery of the American legal system.[76] Even targeted economic sanctions are likely to be ineffective in deterring state-sponsored foreign interference, unless the sanctions successfully target the individuals with the decision-making authority to suspend a foreign-influence campaign.[77]

The better option is to release an indictment *during* the election campaign to publicize the election interference when it is occurring. Although this move, by itself, fails to publicize the particular social media footprint of the indicted individual, it at least gives the public a sense of the overall effort in a way that at minimum raises the possibility of correction. For example, in July 2018, the Justice Department indicted a Russian national for running "Project Lakhta," a campaign to influence the midterm elections of November 2018. The indictment alleges that the campaign was coordinated by the Internet Research Agency, the same group named in the February 2018 election interference indictments. According to the indictment, Project Lakhta:

> Has a strategic goal, which continues to this day, to sow division and discord in the U.S. political system, including by creating social and political polarization, undermining faith in democratic institutions, and influencing U.S. elections, including the upcoming 2018 midterm election. The Conspiracy has sought to conduct what it called internally "information warfare against the United States of America" through fictitious U.S. personas on social media platforms and other Internet-based media.[78]

This is precisely the kind of real-world information that the Justice Department should be providing in order to neutralize election interference. Instead of waiting until the election is over to begin criminal investigations, the Justice Department is issuing indictments *during* the election in order to serve the goals of transparency. This is an appropriate development, though it is only the first step.

Of course, government solutions are only one piece of the puzzle. As noted previously, private technology firms have a major role to play in enhancing transparency of deliberative democracy, in particular by identifying, and possibly removing, material

[75] *See* Ellen Nakashima, *Pentagon Launches First Cyber Operation to Deter Russian Interference in Midterm Elections*, WASHINGTON POST (Oct. 23, 2018).

[76] The deterrent effect of targeted economic sanctions against the individuals is another matter. This might be effective depending on the circumstances of each case.

[77] President Trump signed an executive order creating a framework for targeted economic sanctions in response to election interference. *See* Executive Order 13848 (Sept. 12, 2018) (concluding that the "ability of persons located, in whole or in substantial part, outside the United States to interfere in or undermine public confidence in United States elections, including through the unauthorized accessing of election and campaign infrastructure or the covert distribution of propaganda and disinformation, constitutes an unusual and extraordinary threat to the national security and foreign policy of the United States"). The executive order also noted that "the proliferation of digital devices and internet-based communications has created significant vulnerabilities and magnified the scope and intensity of the threat of foreign interference." *Id.*

[78] United States of America v. Elena Alekseevna Khusyaynova, Indictment, at para. 15 (Sept. 28, 2018).

emerging from foreign social media troll farms. Some of these efforts might be mandated by statute or regulation or they might be voluntarily initiated by the private firms, perhaps through public-private partnerships in conjunction with intelligence and counterintelligence agencies. However, this section has focused on the efforts in the Justice Department, in part because the Justice Department is one of the few departments of the federal government with a specific mandate to investigate foreign election interference.

VI. Four Objections

It remains to respond to four important objections. The United States has a long history of meddling in foreign political systems.[79] In addition to supporting, planning, or funding coups and assassinations, the CIA has engaged in propaganda efforts to influence foreign politics. In some cases, the influence campaigns have been overt, through Voice of America or other government-funded media outlets. These overt efforts are unobjectionable because they are transparent. In other cases, however, the U.S. government supported covert and unacknowledged influence campaigns against foreign systems.[80] These events are often referenced during a larger argument that the Russian election interference is simply of a piece with prior American efforts and therefore neither illegal nor particularly surprising. The charge is that the U.S. government is hypocritical for complaining about foreign influence initiatives given its long history of designing and implementing such programs through the auspices of the CIA or its precursors.

There are several responses to this objection. The first is that not all of the examples of historical American meddling are problematic to the theory presented in this chapter. Many of the covert American initiatives targeted illiberal or totalitarian regimes. Those governments arguably did not have an election system that maximized their collective right of self-determination—the latter ground represents the distinctive harm of election interference. Consequently, by meddling in those political systems, the United States was not necessarily substituting its political will for the will of the domestic polity, since the latter's government was not an expression of that polity's will in the first instance.

Of course, not all cases of American interference can be classified as interference in illiberal regimes or undemocratic states.[81] At least some of those states were democratic ones, and for those, a different response is required. It is odd to say that a given prohibition is irrelevant simply because some actors have violated it before. For example, many states have violated the prohibition against using military force (in violation of Article 2 of the UN Charter), but these violations are not evidence that the norm does not exist—indeed, they are simply evidence that the norm has

[79] For a discussion, *see* Ishaan Tharoor, *The Long History of the U.S. Interfering with Elections Elsewhere*, Washington Post (Oct. 13, 2016).

[80] *See* Schmitt, *supra* note 3.

[81] *See also* Dov H. Levin, *Sure, the U.S. and Russia Often Meddle in Foreign Elections. Does It Matter?*, Washington Post (Sept. 7, 2016).

been violated. Furthermore, the fact that a state was once the perpetrator of acts of aggression does not mean that it forfeits its right to complain about acts of aggression against it. It would be odd, for example, to say to Germany that it cannot complain that it is being subjected to unlawful military force simply because Germany perpetrated crimes against peace (or in today's language, aggression) during World War II. Prior bad acts by the victim do not provide immunity for future perpetrators for future bad acts.

A second objection might be raised by international lawyers concerned about the requirements of customary international law. In evaluating whether election interference counts as a violation of the principle of self-determination, one might be tempted to look for state practice, accompanied by *opinio juris*, that supports the theory. One may ask: Have states complained about, or diplomatically protested, election interference as a violation of international law? Moreover, have any states referenced the language of self-determination in making these protests?[82] If not, the international lawyer might say, there is insufficient evidence of a customary prohibition in this area.

This objection confuses the *identification* of the legal rule with the *application* of that legal rule. Customary international law is one source of international legal rules, and in identifying a legal rule, one must apply the criteria for customary law if no other source of law (such as treaties) is applicable. However, once the legal rule is established as a valid rule of law, one can then apply it in genuinely novel situations. The application of the legal rule need not be supported by customary law as long as the application of the rule is legally sound. In other words, the source of law establishes the legal rule in question, but then lawyers must apply the rule in particular circumstances. In this case, custom and treaties establish the validity of the collective right to self-determination. The task of lawyers is to then determine what that right means in practice. This chapter has been one such exercise, showing that self-determination both protects and allows a people to determine their own political destiny and to use elections—and the membership rules that go along with them—to actualize that right.

The third objection is animated by a concern for First Amendment values. Although the First Amendment probably does not apply extraterritorially to foreign speakers located outside of the country, the First Amendment may protect the right of Americans within the country to receive or consume foreign speech. For example, although a British individual located in Britain does not have a right to free speech that is protected by the U.S. Constitution, an individual living in the United States might have a right to receive communications from the Brit. So, for example, if the government banned the importation of the *Financial Times* or another British newspaper, the American audience for that foreign speech might argue that their First Amendment rights were infringed by the regulation.

There are two important responses to this objection. The first is that this chapter is mostly about the international legal framework for responding to election interference. But even if one switches focus to domestic legal obstacles to such regulation, a second response comes to the forefront. The transparency regime articulated in this

[82] This issue is discussed in Hollis, *supra* note 35, at 42 ("Perhaps most importantly, IOs have a long—and, some would say, successful—history of interfering with foreign national elections without self-determination complaints.").

chapter would not entail banning the speech in most circumstances; it would simply seek to label that speech as foreign. Nothing in the regime would prevent Americans from consuming foreign speech; it would simply insist, either by formal regulation or more likely through voluntary adoption, that social media platforms label foreign electioneering be labeled as such.

The fourth and final objection is again animated by First Amendment values. The First Amendment not only protects speech; it also protects anonymous speech in some circumstances. A disclosure regime for foreign electioneering might impinge on the right of Americans to consume anonymous speech. There is a rich tradition in American history of creating and consuming anonymous political speech, including the *Federalist Papers*, which were published in newspapers under "Publius," the collective pen name for Alexander Hamilton, James Madison, and John Jay. Taken to its logical extreme, protection for anonymous speech might preclude regulation of foreign electioneering.

The response to this objection is that it proves too much. Congress has frequently regulated foreign behavior, including foreign speech, without running afoul of the First Amendment. FARA itself, which requires registration of those acting on behalf of a foreign power, prevents those agents from speaking and acting anonymously. The purpose of FARA is not to prevent them from acting but to require them to do so transparently; to stand up and make clear to the American audience that they are speaking on behalf of a foreign power. It seems no less reasonable to require foreign election speech to similarly be identified as having a foreign origin, especially when it is instigated by a foreign power. The need to protect the integrity of the election process is no less compelling than the need to protect national security; the need to protect the boundaries of the election process is internal to the notion of a democratic election and its goal of expressing the polity's views on the nation's future direction, or what I have referred to in this chapter as the collective right of self-determination.

The anonymous publication of the *Federalist Papers* was indeed a paradigmatic moment that helped to define American political participation in the marketplace of ideas. But imagine, just for a moment, the results for the birth of our fragile republic if an agent of the British government had anonymously authored an anti–*Federalist Papers* under the pretense of it being an authentically American document. Surely such a deceptive act, if it took place today, would not only be legitimately regulated by today's FARA but also by additional regulations designed to impose transparency with regard to foreign electioneering.

VII. Conclusion

With the discussion of recent remedial efforts of the Justice Department in mind, it is important not to obscure the central theoretical move in this chapter. The argument flowed from a particular conception of self-determination—a norm that has both political salience and legal protection. The concept of self-determination ensures that peoples have a right to select their own destiny, and I have argued here and elsewhere that this right not only entails a right to remedial secession in some circumstances but also protects peoples' right to use democratic institutions to select their political destiny. This was a novel move, because international lawyers have rarely recognized the intuitive connection between the collective right of self-determination and the protection of democratic institutions, preferring instead to consistently rely on the concept of sovereignty (alone or as the foundation for the duty of nonintervention) to frame such discussions despite the fact that sovereignty is ill-suited to this task.[83] Within our new framework, however, election interference—particularly when it involves outsiders masquerading as insiders—is now revealed to be a fundamental impingement on a people's right of self-determination. The interference interrupts the process by which the insiders express their political preferences and jointly participate in the process of selecting their political destiny. This conceptual framework is far more relevant than the concept of sovereignty, which has unfortunately dominated the discourse on election interference for far too long.

[83] *See, e.g.*, Teachout, *supra* note 57, at 187 (concluding that "[o]n the whole, concerns about sovereignty, unlike concerns about self-government, will tend to militate against extraterritorial electioneering"); Jacqueline Van De Velde, chapter 10, this volume.

PART IV

COMBATING FOREIGN ELECTION INTERFERENCE THROUGH OTHER MEANS

12

The Free Speech Blind Spot

Foreign Election Interference on Social Media

Evelyn Douek[*]

I. Introduction

What is the point of removing foreign election interference on social media? This question does not come from a place of nihilism ("Oh, what's the *point*! Let's just resign ourselves to a post-truth world!"), but is in fact of significant practical consequence. Removing "content" (known offline as "speech") from social media is not an intrinsic good; such removals should be justified as serving some legitimate aim. Deeper interrogation of what that aim is—the reason *why* foreign election interference is perceived as a threat that platforms must do more to meet—is necessary before engaging with *how* functionally they should do so.

Many foreign interference efforts against democracies are aimed not at particular political goals, but instead at undermining faith in institutions, public discourse, and democracy itself. An effective response to these campaigns, therefore, has to have at its core the goal of re-establishing trust in the online public sphere and democratic discourse. Focusing on this aim suggests that the opaque and ever-changing governance structures that currently oversee the detection and removal of foreign election interference from social media may frustrate the very goal they should be trying to achieve.

This chapter argues that the militarization of the discourse around election interference on social media, most often exhibited in rhetoric around "information operations," has created a free speech blind spot. Removal of "information operations" on social media is, in essence, the censorship of political speech. At the outset it is important to be clear: there will be circumstances where such removals are a proportionate measure to prevent harm or protect legitimate interests. But, ordinarily, essentially every manifestation of free speech law and theory requires such restrictions on speech to be supported by a clear articulation of their purpose and a showing that the way of achieving that purpose does not sweep any more broadly than necessary. Current practice does not come close to meeting this burden; instead, free speech concerns are largely absent in the conversation about dealing with information operations on social media.

[*] Thanks to Martha Minow, Ros Dixon, Duncan Hollis, Elise Thomas, and Barrie Sander, whose (in many cases, foreign and cross-border) influence was extremely helpful and most welcome. All errors remain my own.

Evelyn Douek, *The Free Speech Blind Spot* In: *Defending Democracies*. Edited by Duncan B. Hollis and Jens David Ohlin, Oxford University Press (2021). © Duncan B. Hollis & Jens David Ohlin. DOI: 10.1093/oso/9780197556979.003.0013

The difference in tone is especially notable compared with the discourse around platform "content moderation" more generally.[1] In the past few years, content moderation discourse has increasingly centered around the human rights implications of platforms unilaterally, and without any regular procedure, deciding what speech is or is not allowed on their services.[2] By contrast, the discourse around election interference on social media is "militarized,"[3] dominated by talk of "war rooms," "bad actors," "targets," "threats," and "operations." This bifurcation between types of content moderation is reflected even in the organizational structure of the front-line actors in this "war"—platforms: election interference is typically handled by threat intelligence teams distinct from the policy teams that handle a platform's speech rules more generally.[4] Reports about takedowns are done in separate documents, and affected users do not have access to the same regular appeals processes as other users to contest a platform decision. This distinctive treatment is justified by the securitization of the threat of social media information operations that paints these campaigns as if they are uniquely persuasive or akin to actions with kinetic effects.

The militarized discourse is also marked by an "invasion" framing that vilifies and denigrates the value of "foreign" speech. Rarely defined but often singled out, "foreign" interference is used to refer to transborder campaigns, whether or not they can be attributed to a state actor or indeed any particular organized group. The implicit suggestion is that certain species of foreign speech are equivalent to other interferences in self-governance, such as hacking operations, illegal campaign contributions, interference with voting procedures, or improper direct influence on political representatives. It paints foreign information operations as uniquely pernicious, justifying more exceptional responses than manipulative or misleading domestic campaigns. But this framing ignores the benefits and inevitability of "foreign" speech in a globalized information environment and the ways in which the demonization of such speech subverts the free speech values in which democratic responses to foreign influence efforts should be grounded.

What such framing does achieve, however, is the diversion of attention from far more fundamental concerns with the current structure and management of online public discourse. Focusing on the "foreign" in "foreign election interference" has prevented proper examination of what constitutes improper "election interference" on social media more generally. It has enabled the rise of opaque and ad hoc governance structures to determine what constitutes election interference and how it should be

[1] Sarah T. Roberts, Behind the Screen: Content Moderation in the Shadows of Social Media 44 (2019) ("commercial content moderation is the organized practice of screening user-generated content posted to internet sites, social media, and other online outlets.").

[2] *See, e.g.*, David Kaye, Speech Police: The Global Struggle to Govern the Internet (2019); Molly K. Land, Regulating Private Harms Online: Content Regulation under Human Rights Law, in Human Rights in the Age of Platforms 285 (Rikke Frank Jørgensen ed., 2019); Emily B. Laidlaw, Regulating Speech in Cyberspace: Gatekeepers, Human Rights and Corporate Responsibility (2015); Evelyn Douek, *Verified Accountability: Self-Regulation of Content Moderation as an Answer to the Special Problems of Speech Governance*, Hoover Aegis Series No. 1903 (2019).

[3] *See, e.g.*, Jonathan Zittrain, *"Netwar": The Unwelcome Militarization of the Internet Has Arrived*, 73 Bull. Atomic Scientists 300 (2017); P.W. Singer & Emerson T. Brooking, LikeWar: The Weaponization of Social Media (2018). *See also infra* section II.

[4] *The Lawfare Podcast: Alex Stamos on the Hard Tradeoffs of the Internet*, Lawfare (Feb. 13, 2020).

dealt with. This arrogation of unaccountable, but highly consequential, power to private companies and certain governments ignores the more fundamental distortions these very same actors themselves create in political discourse. Such a short-term solution will not serve the longer-term interests of rebuilding trust in online public discourse and democratic culture.

This chapter begins in section II by reviewing what is known (and how much is not) about the way the major tech platforms currently deal with foreign election interference. The upshot is that although pressure in recent years has led to more detail and transparency from platforms, rules about what is permissible online behavior are still vague and enforced in opaque, sometimes seemingly inconsistent ways. This creates uncertainty and gives rise to concerns that platforms might not be exercising their considerable discretion in principled or neutral ways. Such opacity and lack of constraint is at odds with ordinary free speech values, such as international human rights law's requirement that any restrictions on speech be specified clearly and based on objectively justifiable criteria. This section concludes by showing that this absence of normal free speech protections—a free speech blind spot—has been in large part facilitated by a militarized discourse that vilifies foreign speech as uniquely pernicious and dangerous, and therefore requiring exceptional measures. Section III argues that this vilification of "foreign" speech is unjustified and at odds with underlying rationales for free speech. The role of free speech in facilitating self-governance, the search for truth or individual autonomy does not justify the censorship of speech on the basis of "foreignness" alone. Nor do important goals of protecting democratic processes justify opaque singling out of categories of foreign speech as uniquely threatening. The foreign-threat framing is a distraction from more pervasive and fundamental questions about online public discourse, which are the subject of section IV. This section argues that hiding in the blind spot created by platform opacity and the militarized "invasion" framing are important questions about norms of online behavior more generally, who decides them, and how they are enforced. Without examining and answering these underlying questions, the goal that removing foreign election interference on social media is meant to achieve—re-establishing trust in the online public sphere—will remain unrealized.

II. Platform Practice: What We Know (and Don't)

Despite an explosion of scholarly and public attention in the past few years, still remarkably little is known about the way platforms formulate, monitor, and enforce their policies relating to foreign election interference.[5] Even as the standards remain unclear, enforcement action by platforms is seemingly increasing. Public pressure on platforms to take more action against foreign election interference greatly intensified in the wake of the 2016 U.S. election. Representatives of the major platforms have since been hauled before legislators around the world to explain how their services were exploited by bad actors in the past and what they are doing to improve in the

[5] This section reflects publicly available information as of April 2020.

future.[6] As a result, platforms make many more announcements of takedowns of this kind of activity.[7]

Alongside these developments has been the rise of an increasingly militaristic discourse around disinformation on social media. The relationship between the military and propaganda of course stretches back centuries,[8] and scholars have been theorizing about the category of online "information operations" for over two decades.[9] But the securitization of the threat in relation to social media platforms specifically is much more recent. In November 2016, Facebook CEO Mark Zuckerberg was still relaxed enough to be famously dismissive of the idea that false content on Facebook influenced the 2016 U.S. election, rejecting it as "pretty crazy idea."[10] But unfolding revelations about the extent of the Russian influence operation, as well as public and regulatory scrutiny, caused a rapid change in tone. In April 2017, Facebook released the first major piece of public engagement by a social media platform on the issue, a thirteen-page report titled "Information Operations and Facebook."[11] By 2018, Facebook was widely promoting its new "War Room" as evidence of its proactive efforts to counter "attacks" on elections around the world.[12] Press reports remark that the team within Facebook dedicated to countering election interference "talks about the company not as a social network, but a battlefield."[13] Representatives talk about "threat actors," the ongoing game of "cat and mouse," and the need to stay "one step ahead."[14]

This is the dominant framing in the discourse more generally. Government reports refer to "information warfare" on social media,[15] while academics talk of "cyber troops"[16] and the "weaponization" of social media.[17] It would of course be naïve to ignore the geopolitics surrounding these campaigns and pretend information operations are *simply* a free speech issue. That is not my argument. My point is that the militarized discourse has obscured the extent to which these issues do still implicate at least some free speech concerns, and especially the requirements of transparency and proportionality, and a lack of overbreadth, of response measures. Information

[6] *See, e.g.*, Evelyn Douek, *Congress' Grilling of Tech Companies in 2017 Foreshadows the Debates of 2018*, LAWFARE (Jan. 11, 2018); Evelyn Douek, *Senate Hearing on Social Media and Foreign Influence Operations: Progress, But There's a Long Way to Go*, LAWFARE (Sept. 6, 2018); Natasha Lomas, *Legislators from Ten Parliaments Put the Squeeze on Facebook*, TECHCRUNCH (Nov. 7, 2019).

[7] *See, e.g.*, *Factbox: Facebook Takedowns of "Coordinated Inauthentic Behavior" in 2019*, REUTERS (Aug. 2, 2019).

[8] Duncan Hollis, *The Influence of War; The War for Influence*, 32 TEMPLE INT'L & COMP. L.J. 31, 46 (2018).

[9] Duncan Hollis, *Why States Need an International Law for Information Operations*, 11 LEWIS & CLARK L. REV. 1023, 1028–1029 (2007).

[10] Casey Newton, *Zuckerberg: The Idea that Fake News on Facebook Influenced the Election Is "Crazy,"* THE VERGE (Nov. 10, 2016).

[11] JEN WEEDON ET AL., INFORMATION OPERATIONS AND FACEBOOK (Apr. 27, 2017).

[12] Sheera Frenkel & Mike Isaac, *Inside Facebook's Election "War Room,"* N.Y. TIMES (Sept. 19, 2018).

[13] Hannah Murphy, *Inside Facebook's Information Warfare Team*, FINANCIAL TIMES (July 5, 2019).

[14] Kevin Roose et al., *Tech Giants Prepared for 2016-Style Meddling. But the Threat Has Changed*, N.Y. TIMES (Mar. 29, 2020).

[15] SENATE S. COMM. ON INTELLIGENCE, 116TH CONG., REP. ON RUSSIAN ACTIVE MEASURES CAMPAIGNS AND INTERFERENCE IN THE 2016 U.S. ELECTION, VOLUME 2: RUSSIA'S USE OF SOCIAL MEDIA (2019).

[16] *See, e.g.*, SAMANTHA BRADSHAW & PHILIP N. HOWARD, THE GLOBAL DISINFORMATION ORDER: 2019 GLOBAL INVENTORY OF ORGANISED SOCIAL MEDIA MANIPULATION, OXFORD INTERNET INSTITUTE (2019).

[17] SINGER & BROOKING, *supra* note 3.

operations are speech, but they are often painted as if they are kinetic weapons of extraordinary power.

It is against this backdrop that platforms design their enforcement measures against such influence operations. As private actors, social media platforms generally have no legal obligation to host their users' speech or recognize individual speech rights on their services.[18] Platforms' terms of service allow essentially unfettered discretion to determine what (legal) content is or is not allowed on their sites.[19] Most major platforms have established fairly elaborate rule sets about what is and is not allowed on their services. The general transparency deficits in how platforms write and enforce rules are well known,[20] but the standards for what platforms look for and remove as unacceptable election interference are an especially opaque subset of the already notoriously obscure way platforms manage the content on their sites generally.

This section begins by reviewing the manifold transparency deficits in how platforms deal with election interference on their services. My analysis concentrates on ostensibly "organic" content (that is, content that looks like it has been posted by a user) and not paid advertising, in keeping with this chapter's focus on "pure" speech.[21] In what follows, I show that, first, the written policies platforms invoke to justify removals of election interference masquerading as organic content are ambiguous and leave room for ample discretion. Second, enforcement practices remain almost entirely opaque, and what limited transparency there is does not increase confidence that platforms are enforcing truly neutral standards. Third, platforms often (and indeed may need to) cooperate with governments to detect and remove such campaigns. But the way such cooperation currently occurs is unclear and shielded from scrutiny. Finally, I turn to how this extraordinary secrecy about censorship practices has been in part justified by using "foreign" speech as a scapegoat.

A. Policies on Paper

The explicit policies that major platforms invoke when taking down disinformation operations are broadly formulated. While these policies have expanded and become more detailed in recent years, they remain intentionally vague and leave platforms ample discretion in enforcement.

Facebook takes down election interference under its policy against "coordinated inauthentic behavior."[22] This phrase is a moniker officially introduced only in 2018 but

[18] Daphne Keller, *Who Do You Sue? State and Platform Hybrid Power over Online Speech*, HOOVER AEGIS SERIES PAPER NO. 1902, 2 (2019).

[19] NICOLAS SUZOR, LAWLESS: THE SECRET RULES THAT GOVERN OUR DIGITAL LIVES 109 (2019) ("Most terms of service documents have a clause that gives the platform a right to terminate a user's account or remove their content at any time, for any reason, or even no reason at all, at the service provider's sole discretion. They include no meaningful safeguards against arbitrary or capricious decisions, allow the platform to change the rules at any time, and provide no meaningful rights to appeal against mistakes.").

[20] For a good overview, *see* Nicolas P. Suzor et al., *What Do We Mean When We Talk About Transparency? Toward Meaningful Transparency in Commercial Content Moderation*, 13 INT'L J. COMM. 1526 (2019).

[21] Of course, election interference operations often also use paid advertising and drawing a clear line can be artificial, but this chapter focuses on unpaid influence campaigns.

[22] Nathaniel Gleicher, *Coordinated Inauthentic Behavior Explained*, FACEBOOK NEWSROOM (Dec. 6, 2018), https://about.fb.com/news/2018/12/inside-feed-coordinated-inauthentic-behavior/.

is increasingly deployed in the field as a term of art and adopted by other platforms and researchers.[23] Despite this memetic proliferation, it is not clear what the phrase means. Facebook defines "inauthentic behavior" expansively as misleading people about a range of things including the identity, popularity, purpose, or source of content or pages.[24] "Coordinated inauthentic behavior," then, is "working in concert to engage in inauthentic behavior . . . where the use of fake accounts is central to the operation."[25] A video released by Facebook "explaining" the policy, depicted in Figure 12.1, unhelpfully shows dots on a whiteboard with lines between them, as if this clarifies matters.[26]

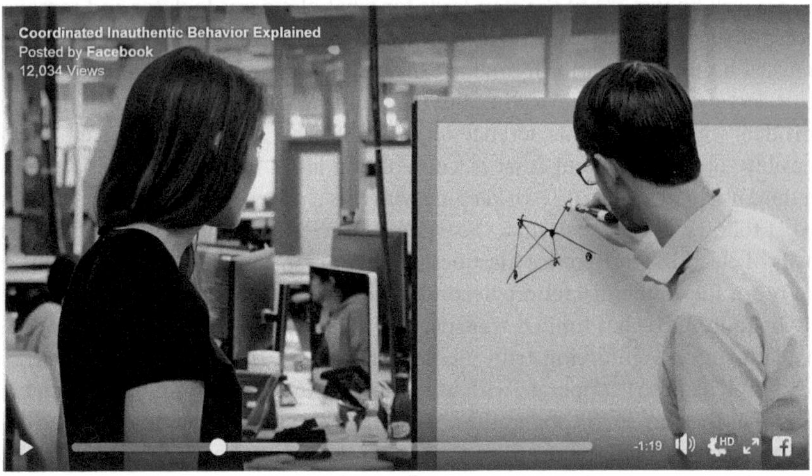

Figure 12.1 Facebook's Head of Security Policy in a video explaining their 'Coordinated Inauthentic Behavior' policy. Source: https://about.fb.com/news/2018/12/inside-feed-coordinated-inauthentic-behavior/

Facebook's policies are a useful example because they are indicative, and not because they are uniquely ambiguous. Twitter and Google's policies are just as vague, if not vaguer. Broadly, Twitter's "platform manipulation and spam policy" prohibits use of its services in a manner "intended to artificially amplify or suppress information or engage in behavior that manipulates or disrupts people's experience on Twitter," and gives a nonexhaustive list of examples.[27] Google defines "disinformation" as

[23] *See, e.g.*, Twitter Safety, *Information Operations Directed at Hong Kong*, TWITTER BLOG (Aug. 19, 2019), https://blog.twitter.com/en_us/topics/company/2019/information_operations_directed_at_Hong_Kong.html("As we have said before, it is clear that information operations and coordinated inauthentic behavior will not cease."); NATO Strategic Communications Centre of Excellence, *Falling Behind: How Social Media Companies are Failing to Combat Inauthentic Behaviour Online* (2019), https://www.stratcomcoe.org/how-social-media-companies-are-failing-combat-inauthentic-behaviour-online.

[24] *Community Standards: 22. Inauthentic Behaviour*, FACEBOOK COMMUNITY STANDARDS, https://www.facebook.com/communitystandards/inauthentic_behavior.

[25] *Id.*

[26] Gleicher, *supra* note 22.

[27] *Platform Manipulation and Spam Policy*, TWITTER HELP CENTER, https://help.twitter.com/en/rules-and-policies/platform-manipulation.

"deliberate efforts to deceive and mislead using the speed, scale, and technologies of the open web."[28] YouTube's community guidelines have "several policies ... applicable to some form of disinformation,"[29] but they are in general terms, and it is not always clear which is invoked in any particular case.[30]

There is, however, one notable element that all these policies have in common. They purport to regulate *behavior*, not *content*.[31] As Facebook's head of cybersecurity policy has explained, "most of the content shared by coordinated manipulation campaigns isn't provably false, and would in fact be acceptable political discourse if shared by authentic audiences ... *That's why, when we take down information operations, we are taking action based on the behavior we see on our platform—not based on who the actors behind it are or what they say.*"[32]

This highlights a uniquely difficult challenge in policing election interference. On its own, any individual post may not appear (or, indeed, even be) problematic. But the *campaign* as a whole is deemed to violate a norm. As a report prepared for the Senate Intelligence Committee on the Russian Internet Research Agency's activities during the 2016 U.S. election noted, "the vast majority wasn't hate speech. Much of it wasn't even particularly objectionable.... [But i]t was designed to exploit societal fractures, blur the lines between reality and fiction, erode our trust in media entities and the information environment, in government, in each other, and in democracy itself."[33] This characterization cannot be gleaned from looking at individual posts but relies on evaluating the set of posts as a whole.

Focusing on behavior also seems to offer a criterion for removal that is not based on the subject matter or viewpoint of the content. By professing content agnosticism, platforms can continue to disclaim becoming the "arbiters of truth"[34] while still showing efforts to deal with the problem of election interference.

But impermissible "behavior" is not as neutral as it superficially sounds. Defining impermissible "coordination" or "inauthenticity" online, when the internet is teeming with coordination and inauthenticity, is itself a fraught and value-laden judgment.[35]

[28] Google, *How Google Fights Disinformation*, 2 (Feb. 2019), https://www.blog.google/documents/37/How_Google_Fights_Disinformation.pdf.

[29] *Id.* at 19.

[30] Shane Huntley, *Maintaining The Integrity of Our Platforms*, GOOGLE (Aug. 22, 2019), https://blog.google/outreach-initiatives/public-policy/maintaining-integrity-our-platforms/(announcing a removal of a "coordinated influence operation," but not indicating a specific policy violation).

[31] CAMILLE FRANÇOIS, TRANSATLANTIC WORKING GROUP, ACTORS, BEHAVIORS, CONTENT: A DISINFORMATION ABC 4 (2019), https://www.ivir.nl/publicaties/download/ABC_Framework_2019_Sept_2019.pdf ("while there are significant differences in the various disinformation definitions and terms of service applicable to the issue among technology companies, the focus on deceptive behavior appears to be a clear convergence point throughout the technology industry.").

[32] Nathaniel Gleicher, *How We Respond to Inauthentic Behavior on Our Platforms: Policy Update*, FACEBOOK NEWSROOM (Oct. 21, 2019), https://about.fb.com/news/2019/10/inauthentic-behavior-policy-update/(emphasis in original).

[33] RENEE DIRESTA ET AL., THE TACTICS & TROPES OF THE INTERNET RESEARCH AGENCY (2019).

[34] *See, e.g.*, Mark Zuckerberg, *Facebook Status Update*, FACEBOOK (Nov. 19, 2016), https://www.facebook.com/zuck/posts/10103269806149061; Callum Borchers, *Twitter Executive on Fake News: "We Are Not the Arbiters of Truth,"* WASHINGTON POST (Feb. 8, 2018); Supraja Srinivasan, *We Don't Want to be Arbiters of Truth: YouTube CBO*, ECON. TIMES (Mar. 24, 2018).

[35] For analysis of the judgments inherent in Facebook's definition of "authenticity," *see* Haan, Sarah C., *Bad Actors: Authenticity, Inauthenticity, Speech and Capitalism*, Washington & Lee Legal Studies, Paper No. 2019-24, https://ssrn.com/abstract=3458795.

Coordination is "inherent to any information campaign, which by definition consists of a group of people who want to convey specific information to an audience," and distinguishing between what is or is not authentic is "not straightforward."[36] Compounding this ambiguity is the fact that account behavior is an area in which there is a "dramatic asymmetry of information between the platforms targeted by these campaigns and the rest of the world."[37] This makes verification of platform claims of neutrality especially difficult.

In short, while platform rules give notice that some forms of manipulative or misleading behaviors are prohibited, the rules as written do not confine platform discretion or present workable neutral standards in any meaningful way. They do not come close to meeting the requirement under international human rights law, for example, that restrictions on speech should be taken in accordance with "clear, pre-determined policies . . . based on objectively justifiable criteria."[38]

Such an ambiguous standard might not be as problematic if it were clarified by a transparent and illustrative record of how the policies are enforced in practice. The next section shows this is far from the case.

B. Enforcement

The extent and nature of platforms' enforcement of these policies is almost entirely opaque.[39] Disclosures are more common in recent years but are still ad hoc and "meager."[40] A major problem is that disclosures are not mandated by law but voluntary. This creates a perverse incentive: enforcement at scale is hard and mistakes are inevitable—as a result, the scrutiny that comes with transparency only facilitates justified criticism.

This dynamic is illustrated by the disclosures platforms made relating to takedowns of information campaigns targeting Hong Kong protestors in 2019. Twitter released the most comprehensive data set, including complete Tweet and user information for the 936 accounts it identified as part of the information operations.[41] The accountability that such transparency enables followed swiftly: researchers were quick to find mistakes in the takedowns, discovering evidence the account list was both over- and

[36] Franziska B. Keller et al., *Political Astroturfing on Twitter: How to Coordinate a Disinformation Campaign*, Pol. Comm. 1, 4 (2019).

[37] François, *supra* note 31, at 5.

[38] Joint Declaration on Freedom of Expression and "Fake News," Disinformation and Propaganda, The United Nations Human Rights Council (UNHRC) Special Rapporteur on Freedom of Opinion and Expression, the Organization for Security and Co-operation in Europe (OSCE) Representative on Freedom of the Media, the Organization of American States (OAS) Special Rapporteur on Freedom of Expression and the African Commission on Human and Peoples' Rights (ACHPR) Special Rapporteur on Freedom of Expression and Access to Information, FOM.GAL/3/17 (Mar. 3, 2017), https://www.osce.org/fom/302796?download=true.

[39] François, *supra* note 31, at 4 ("enforcement in this realm remains opaque throughout the major technology companies.").

[40] Sima Basel & Matt Suiche, *Facebook's Coordinated Inauthentic Behavior—An OSINT Analysis* (Jan. 11, 2020), https://si.ma/fb-cib/.

[41] Twitter Safety, *Information Operations Directed at Hong Kong*, Twitter Blog (Aug. 19, 2019), https://blog.twitter.com/en_us/topics/company/2019/information_operations_directed_at_Hong_Kong.html.

underinclusive.[42] As one researcher put it, "There's a lot of chaff in this wheat."[43] By contrast, Facebook's blog post describing its own takedowns gave high-level figures only and a few sample pieces of content.[44] Even this was generous compared with Google's blog post, which simply announced that the accounts it took down were "consistent with recent observations and actions related to China announced by Facebook and Twitter" without releasing any examples or data of what it took down.[45] As a result, there is essentially no way to know what Facebook or Google took down, what signals they used, or how they drew the line between what was impermissible and what was not in a highly charged political context that was the subject of world attention and no doubt considerable cross-border online engagement. This example is not unique; if anything, the Hong Kong information operations example is an outlier in having all three major platforms publicly acknowledge some enforcement activity.

As a result of these perverse incentive structures and the lack of transparency they create, there is little way to evaluate how platforms interpret and enforce their very open-ended election interference policies in practice. A lack of information about content moderation more generally has fueled fears that platforms are politically biased and the development of other "folk theories" about how platforms determine what content to allow or disallow.[46] In the context of election interference, there have similarly been reports that fear of political backlash has influenced at least some decisions by platforms on what to do with foreign influence, such as what to publicly announce.[47]

To the extent that there has not been more outcry or concern about potential platform bias or inconsistency in the enforcement of information operations, it is at least in part because of the securitization of the discourse. But this lack of concern is unlikely to last as scrutiny grows. Journalistic exposés have already led to disquiet. For example, one journalist highlighted a network of pages driving traffic to one of the most popular news sites on Facebook that presented the pages as independent when they were owned by a single website and all posted the same links, with the same text, at the same time.[48] Facebook did not explain why this did not fall within its prohibition on "coordinated inauthentic behavior."[49] The *New York Times* has reported that fear of political backlash drove the decision not to take action against the network

[42] Dave Lee, *Baffled Student Tells Twitter: "I'm Not a Chinese Agent,"* BBC (Aug. 21, 2019); Nick Monaco, *Welcome to the Party: A Data Analysis of Chinese Information Operations*, MEDIUM (Sept. 29, 2019), https://medium.com/digintel/welcome-to-the-party-a-data-analysis-of-chinese-information-operations-6d48ee186939.

[43] Lee, *supra* note 42 (quoting Elise Thomas from Australia's International Cyber Policy Centre).

[44] Nathaniel Gleicher, *Removing Coordinated Inauthentic Behavior From China*, FACEBOOK NEWSROOM (Aug. 19, 2019), https://newsroom.fb.com/news/2019/08/removing-cib-china/.

[45] Huntley, *supra* note 30.

[46] Nick Clegg, *An Update on Senator Kyl's Review of Potential Anti-Conservative Bias*, FACEBOOK NEWSROOM (Aug. 20, 2019), https://about.fb.com/news/2019/08/update-on-potential-anti-conservative-bias/; *What Is "Shadowbanning"?*, THE ECONOMIST (Aug. 1, 2018); Sarah Myers West, *Censored, Suspended, Shadowbanned: User Interpretations of Content Moderation on Social Media Platforms*, 20 NEW MEDIA & SOC. 4366 (2018).

[47] Craig Timberg, *How Conservatives Learned to Wield Power Inside Facebook*, WASHINGTON POST (Feb. 20, 2019).

[48] Judd Legum, *Facebook Allows Prominent Right-Wing Website to Break the Rules*, POPULAR INFORMATION (Oct. 28, 2019).

[49] Judd Legum, *Three Updates and One New Hack*, POPULAR INFORMATION (Jan. 15, 2020).

initially, a fact disputed by Facebook representatives.[50] Whatever the motivation, such incidents and the lack of transparency around them raise the specter of political considerations determining what information operations are enforced against.

Along similar lines, a *Guardian* investigation found a campaign by overseas actors to become administrators of a network of preexisting pages that they then used to post Islamophobic clickbait to drive traffic to off-platform for-profit sites.[51] The *Guardian* concluded that "Facebook's own definition of 'coordinated inauthentic activity' reads like a blueprint for the network the Guardian has uncovered."[52] But despite assurances by Facebook that it would take action, many of the pages remained months later.[53] Facebook is not alone in having apparent inconsistent enforcement practices. Swarms of inauthentic accounts conducting harassment campaigns are common on Twitter,[54] where the ability to use automated and anonymous accounts is considered a feature not a bug. Yet how Twitter identifies information operations is still ambiguous, and "[a] lot of details are yet to be unearthed."[55] Research or public disclosures from YouTube are even more rare and less detailed.[56]

These disclosure gaps and inconsistencies do not necessarily indicate platforms move the enforcement line to suit their own interests; they equally could be consistent with the line itself being illusory. Gillespie has argued that the distinction between "coordinated efforts" to game a system and the "genuine" output of users is a false one: "[m]ost contributions to the web are somewhere in the middle, where people in some way coordinate their efforts in order to help make their content visible to a search engine, out of a 'genuine' desire for it to be seen."[57] At the very least, there is good reason to believe that far more actors engage in organized social media influence campaigns than has been publicly identified by platforms.[58] As disinformation researcher Ben Nimmo put it, "[i]t's almost like wherever you look, you're finding this stuff."[59] This only highlights that when and how takedowns occur depends on where platforms prioritize looking. Often, takedowns occur as a result of tips from independent researchers, journalists, or governments—hardly a basis for enforcement that can be verified as comprehensive or neutral. All this means that beyond

[50] Roose et al., *supra* note 14.

[51] Christopher Knaus et al., *Inside the Hate Factory: How Facebook Fuels Far-Right Profit*, GUARDIAN (Dec. 5, 2019).

[52] *Id.*

[53] Christopher Knaus & Michael McGowan, *Far-Right "Hate Factory" Still Active on Facebook despite Pledge to Stop It*, THE GUARDIAN (Feb. 4, 2020).

[54] *See, e.g.*, Christopher Bouzy, *Is There a Targeted Troll Campaign Against Lisa Page? A Bot Sentinel Investigation*, LAWFARE (Jan. 22, 2020).

[55] Sima Basel & Matt Suiche, *Twitter's Information Operations—An OSINT Analysis* (Feb. 12, 2020), https://si.ma/tw-io/.

[56] Consistent with the Hong Kong disclosures described previously, for example, Google provided the least data to researchers analyzing the Russian Internet Research Agency's activities during the 2016 U.S. election: PHILIP N. HOWARD ET AL., THE IRA, SOCIAL MEDIA AND POLITICAL POLARIZATION IN THE UNITED STATES, 2012–2018, at 47 (2019).

[57] Tarleton Gillespie, *Algorithmically Recognizable: Santorum's Google Problem, and Google's Santorum Problem*, 20 INFO. COMM. & SOC. 63, 67 (2017).

[58] BRADSHAW & HOWARD *supra* note 16; Basel & Suiche, *supra* note 55.

[59] Marie C. Baca & Tony Romm, *Twitter and Facebook Take First Actions Against China for Using Fake Accounts to Sow Discord in Hong Kong*, WASHINGTON POST (Aug. 19, 2019).

the requirement of some form of coordination between accounts, it remains fundamentally unclear "if the decision to remove such activity is influenced by any other factors."[60]

In sum, the sparse details of platforms' broad rules on paper are not remedied by robust disclosures of enforcement activity establishing a course of practice. To the contrary, the haphazard and seemingly inconsistent enforcement practices of platforms raise more questions than they answer.

C. The "Long Tail" of Information Operations and Content Cartels

So far, I have focused on the policies and actions of major platforms, both because there is the most public information available about them and because they are the most systemically important. But the perpetrators of election inference operations do not take such a blinkered view. Online information operations are often sophisticated, cross-platform operations. During the 2016 U.S. election, Russia's Internet Research Agency "operated like a digital marketing agency: develop a brand . . . build presences on all channels *across the entire social ecosystem*, and grow an audience with paid ads as well as partnerships, influencers, and link-sharing. They created media mirages: *interlinked information ecosystems* designed to immerse and surround targeted audiences."[61] Another Russian intelligence operation a few years later spanned over thirty platforms and nine languages.[62] In short, influence operations view the online ecosystem as a whole, rather than platform by platform.

As a result, platforms often collaborate with each other and with certain governments in detecting and taking down these operations. This collaboration can be critical to finding and removing a campaign.[63] Alex Stamos, former Facebook Chief Security Officer, has argued that "[t]he long tail of social platforms will struggle with information operations unless there are mechanisms for the smaller companies to benefit from the research the large companies can afford."[64] But while these collaborations may be necessary, the way they currently take place has further compounded the opacity of platform decision-making and led to the creation of what I have elsewhere labeled "content cartels": arrangements between platforms, and sometimes governments, to work together to remove content or actors from their services without adequate oversight.[65] In September 2019, for example, U.S. law enforcement representatives met with Facebook, Google, Microsoft, and Twitter to discuss election

[60] Basel & Suiche, *supra* note 40.

[61] DiResta et al., *supra* note 33, at 42 (emphasis added).

[62] Nika Aleksejeva et al., Atlantic Council, Digital Forensics Lab, Operation "Secondary Infektion" 3 (2019), https://www.atlanticcouncil.org/wp-content/uploads/2019/08/Operation-Secondary-Infektion_English.pdf.

[63] *See, e.g.*, François, *supra* note 31; Jessica Brandt & Bradley Hanlon, *Online Information Operations Cross Platforms. Tech Companies' Responses Should Too*, Lawfare (Apr. 26, 2019).

[64] Alex Stamos (@alexstamos), Twitter (Dec. 7, 2019, 8:10 PM), https://twitter.com/alexstamos/status/1203240448153677826?s=20.

[65] Evelyn Douek, *The Rise of Content Cartels*, Knight First Amendment Institute at Columbia University (Feb. 11, 2020), https://knightcolumbia.org/content/the-rise-of-content-cartels.

interference ahead of the 2020 election in a secretive closed-door meeting.[66] Facebook representatives have cited such meetings as a sign of progress toward countering the threat of foreign intervention.[67] But as Camille François has observed, "defining the contours of government action in this space remains a largely unexplored policy question."[68] In few contexts would meetings about the censorship of political speech between private companies and governments behind closed doors be as uncontroversial and unexplored.

D. Whack-a-Moles and Scapegoats

This extraordinary opacity of rules, enforcement, and collaborative efforts has been facilitated and legitimized by the securitization of the discourse around election interference. The general militarized framing has been described earlier, but this securitization has two more specific themes that are worth examining separately: first, the assertion that any greater transparency would only help bad actors evade rule enforcement; and second, that the threat of foreign interference is especially pernicious and justifies exceptional measures.

As to rule evasion, a key justification for limited transparency is that any greater detail on rules and signals that platforms use to detect this kind of activity would only help bad actors learn how to game the system more effectively.[69] As in the spam or search-engine-optimization wars, platforms argue that the lack of transparency is not for their benefit, but is necessary for preventing determined actors from outfoxing rule enforcers.[70] These bad actors are painted as amorphous, but cunning. An indicative statement comes from Facebook CEO Zuckerberg, who stated that "we face sophisticated, well-funded adversaries. They won't give up, an[d] they will keep evolving."[71] Researchers similarly describe detecting interference as a "whack-a-mole" game.[72]

The fundamental obfuscation in this argument is that it completely discounts the benefits of transparency and focuses only on the costs. Transparency in this area, as in many others, is fundamentally a trade-off, but platforms do not release any information that would allow outsiders to evaluate the costs and benefits that need to be balanced. They assert that more details on signals would enable bad actors to skirt

[66] Tony Romm & Ellen Nakashima, *U.S. Officials Huddle with Facebook, Google and Other Tech Giants to Talk About the 2020 Election*, Washington Post (Sept. 4, 2019).

[67] Nathaniel Gleicher, *Elections Have Changed. So Has Facebook*, Des Moines Register (Jan. 21, 2020).

[68] François, *supra* note 31, at 4.

[69] *See, e.g.*, Google, *supra* note 28, at 3 ("we try to be clear and predictable in our efforts, letting users and content creators decide for themselves whether we are operating fairly. Of course, this is a delicate balance, as sharing too much of the granular details of how our algorithms and processes work would make it easier for bad actors to exploit them."); Sara Harrison, *Twitter's Disinformation Data Dumps Are Helpful—To a Point*, Wired (July 7, 2019) ("Twitter would not reveal any specifics about its process for this article. 'We seek to protect the integrity of our efforts and avoid giving bad actors too much information, but in general, we focus on conduct, rather than content.'").

[70] Myers West, *supra* note 46, at 4371.

[71] Mark Zuckerberg, *Preparing for Elections*, Facebook (Sept. 13, 2018), https://www.facebook.com/notes/mark-zuckerberg/preparing-for-elections/10156300047606634/.

[72] *The Lawfare Podcast: Ben Nimmo on the Whack-a-Mole Game of Disinformation*, Lawfare (Nov. 21, 2019).

the rules, but it is unclear to what extent this is true. On the other hand, transparency has consequential benefits for rebuilding trust in the public sphere and online speech governance.[73] It allows justified enforcement to not only be done but also be *seen* to be done, increasing legitimacy of and confidence in such efforts. Such benefits are not accounted for when platforms insist greater transparency would only harm efforts to combat election interference.

The second major justification for the extraordinary opacity is rhetoric vilifying "foreign speech" writ large as a scapegoat for much deeper problems with the online speech ecosystem. No platform restricts its policies banning platform manipulation to foreign interference—there are increasingly frequent head nods to the notion that domestic actors can and do perpetrate coordinated information operations.[74] But platform rhetoric and public discourse continue to distinguish between foreign and domestic efforts, with the underlying theme that foreign speech is especially pernicious.

Facebook's policy update to its inauthentic behavior policies in October 2019 is a good reflection of general sentiment: "Foreign-led efforts to manipulate public debate in another country" are singled out as one of two "particularly egregious" types of coordinated inauthentic behavior.[75] Similarly, its Community Standards have a special ban on foreign interference, even though this ban does not add anything over and above the general ban against coordinated inauthentic behavior.[76] The data set that Twitter releases of information operations it has taken down is said to be aimed at improving understanding of "foreign influence campaigns" specifically.[77] The vast majority of ad hoc blog posts that platforms release about such inauthentic behavior takedown campaigns globally are of foreign campaigns.[78] This gives rise to the impression that in the United States, for instance, platforms "have been more lenient with publishers based in the United States, out of concern that they will appear to be taking sides and stepping on the First Amendment."[79] Facebook has implied that it treats foreign speech differently in a February 2020 report which stated, without further explanation, that "the most appropriate way to respond to someone boosting the popularity of their posts in their own country may not be the best way to counter foreign interference."[80] All of this platform rhetoric may be mere signaling, but it sends a clear message that foreign speech is a distinct, and lesser, species of speech.

[73] *See infra* section IV.

[74] It is also true that in some countries and contexts, concern over domestic political manipulation dominates. I am grateful to Barrie Sander for emphasizing this point. In general, though, the emphasis on the "foreign" remains pervasive and, as discussed in section IV *infra*, is increasingly used by governments even countries where domestic interference may be a more pressing concern to justify censorship.

[75] Gleicher, *supra* note 32.

[76] *Community Standards: 22. Inauthentic Behaviour*, *supra* note 24.

[77] Twitter, *Information Operations*, TRANSPARENCY REPORT, https://transparency.twitter.com/en/information-operations.html.

[78] In Facebook's first regular monthly report in February 2020, for example, Facebook announced takedowns of five operations, four of which were exclusively foreign operations, and one which was mixed: FACEBOOK, FEBRUARY 2020 COORDINATED INAUTHENTIC BEHAVIOR REPORT (Feb. 2020), https://about.fb.com/wp-content/uploads/2020/03/February-2020-CIB-Report.pdf.

[79] Kevin Roose, *Epoch Times, Punished by Facebook, Gets a New Megaphone on YouTube*, N.Y. TIMES (Feb. 5, 2020).

[80] Facebook, *Helping to Protect the US 2020 Election* 8 (Feb. 2020), https://about.fb.com/wp-content/uploads/2020/02/Helping-to-Protect-the-US-2020-Elections.pdf.

Public discussion often similarly disproportionately focuses on foreign threats. Congressional hearings,[81] reports,[82] this very volume, all focus on *foreign* interference. A joint statement from U.S. law enforcement agencies released in advance of the Super Tuesday Democratic primaries focused exclusively on "malign foreign influence" and did not even mention the potential for manipulative domestic operations.[83] As Renée DiResta summarizes, "[f]oreign influence ... is at least clearly impermissible under emerging internet norms. But there are very few demarcations between acceptable influence and manipulative behavior for real American candidates or political activists."[84]

This perceived foreign threat is not limited to state actors: often, the only element said to make such an effort especially egregious is its "foreignness." Facebook has started breaking out influence operations into "two tiers," with the second, more serious tier, against which it will take "the broadest enforcement measures," being coordinated inauthentic behavior on behalf of a "foreign *or* government actor."[85] The decision not to confine the most robust enforcement measures to state-sponsored efforts is no doubt in part a practical decision. Attribution for acts in cyberspace generally is notoriously difficult, and information operations have proven no exception.[86] Over a year after a comprehensive update from Twitter about its investigation into Russian interference in the 2016 election, for example, it had to issue a clarification—based on a tip from an independent researcher—that over two hundred accounts it had identified as Russian were actually Venezuelan.[87] Difficulty in attribution is an important limitation on being able to create rules aimed at particular actors. At least in theory, state-backed operations could be an exception to the argument that follows in the next section that foreign speech does not deserve so much opprobrium. Whatever the merits of this argument (and I myself am sympathetic to it), current attribution capabilities do not seem to make such a carveout available in practice.

The current state of play, then, is that even as the existence of domestic election interference is increasingly acknowledged, the dominant framing remains that foreign threats are especially problematic. Contrary to the idea that this distinction serves free speech values, this singling out of foreign speech as especially pernicious gives lie to professed faith in the free speech rationales that underpin free speech jurisprudence.

[81] Douek, *Senate Hearing on Social Media and Foreign Influence Operations*, *supra* note 6.

[82] 2 S. Comm. on Intelligence, *supra* note 15.

[83] FBI National Press Office, Joint Statement from DOS, DOJ, DOD, DHS, ODNI, FBI, NSA, and CISA on Preparations for Super Tuesday, Press Release (Mar. 2, 2020), https://www.fbi.gov/news/pressrel/press-releases/joint-statement-from-dos-doj-dod-dhs-odni-fbi-nsa-and-cisa-on-preparations-for-super-tuesday.

[84] Renée DiResta, *The Conspiracies Are Coming from Inside the House*, Wired (Mar. 10, 2020).

[85] Facebook, *supra* note 78, at 2–3 (emphasis added).

[86] Cat Zakrzewski, *The Technology 202: YouTube Explains How It Will Moderate Political Falsehoods Just in Time for Iowa*, Washington Post (Feb. 3, 2020) (quoting researchers as saying "It's difficult to discern what's domestic and what's foreign-backed disinformation online in real time—and becoming harder"); Zuckerberg, *supra* note 71 (noting the frequent need to rely on signals from law enforcement for attribution).

[87] Twitter Public Policy, *Update on Twitter's Review of the 2016 US Election*, Twitter Blog, https://blog.twitter.com/en_us/topics/company/2018/2016-election-update.html; Yoel Roth (@yoyoel), Twitter (Feb. 4, 2019, 7:56 PM), https://twitter.com/yoyoel/status/1092587833020182528?s=20.

III. Free Speech Rationales and Foreign Speech

Just as it is important to ask what purpose removing election interference from social media serves in order to know how best to do so, it is important to ask the purpose of free speech in order to define its scope. Once it is accepted that free speech cannot mean literally no speech regulation, a rationale for free speech helps explain what restrictions are permissible. There are three canonical rationales for the importance of free speech: (1) free speech is necessary to facilitate democratic self-governance; (2) free speech promotes the search for "truth"; and (3) free speech is necessary to respect individual autonomy.[88] There has been remarkably little scholarship on the relationship between these rationales and foreign or transboundary speech.[89] Greater attention is overdue, however, as their relation is one of the defining challenges for modern free speech theory and practice given the unavoidable and unprecedented volume of transboundary speech that the internet facilitates every day. Properly examined, the vilification of foreign speech is at odds with each of the three rationales for the fundamental purpose of a system of free expression. It is not my goal here to advance or defend any particular rationale (and they are, in any event, nonexclusive). This section seeks to show that limiting foreign speech on the basis of its foreigners alone is inconsistent with any of the major accounts of why free speech is important.

A. Self-Governance

The idea that foreign speech can or should be limited in service of self-governance is the most intuitive: after all, if the purpose of free speech is to facilitate democratic deliberation and political sovereignty,[90] then it seems obvious that the speech that matters is that of those who need to govern themselves and not outsiders. But this does not hold up under closer scrutiny. If speech is important to self-government because it "allows people to vote intelligently and freely, aware of all the options and in possession of all the relevant information,"[91] it is not clear why the characteristic of "foreignness" should disqualify speech as irrelevant. In a world of globalization and collective action problems, foreigners' speech may well be helpfully informative about matters of public policy. Alexander Meiklejohn, the "most influential" proponent of the self-governance theory of free speech,[92] unequivocally thought that restricting speech of

[88] Adrienne Stone, The Comparative Constitutional Law of Freedom of Expression, in Comparative Constitutional Law 406, 413–414 (Tom Ginsburg & Rosalind Dixon eds., 2011); Frederick Schauer, *Free Speech, the Search for Truth, and the Problem of Collective Knowledge*, 70 SMU L. Rev. 231, 233–238 (2017) (citing Thomas Irwin Emerson, The System of Freedom of Expression 6–20 (1970)).

[89] Ronald J. Krotoszynski Jr., *Transborder Speech*, 94 Notre Dame L. Rev. 273, 477 n.16 (2018) (describing the dearth of scholarship on the topic as "startling"). For some recent exceptions, *see* Timothy Zick, The Cosmopolitan First Amendment: Protecting Transborder Expressive and Religious Liberties (2013); Joseph Thai, *The Right to Receive Foreign Speech*, 71 Okla. L. Rev. 269, 305 (2018) (concluding that First Amendment doctrine "likely preclude[s] the government from barring the entry of political speech from abroad on the ground that the speaker is foreign or that the speech is valueless or false.").

[90] *See, e.g.*, Cass R. Sunstein, Democracy and the Problem of Free Speech, at xvii (1995).

[91] Owen M. Fiss, *Free Speech and Social Structure*, 71 Iowa L. Rev. 1405, 1410 (1986).

[92] Robert Post, *Meiklejohn's Mistake: Individual Autonomy and the Reform of Public Discourse*, 64 U. Colo. L. Rev. 1109, 1111 (1993).

foreigners on matters of public policy showed a lack of faith in the importance of free expression:

> Why may we not hear what these men [*sic*] from other countries, other systems of government, have to say? ... Do We, the People of the United States, wish to be thus mentally "protected"? To say that would seem to be an admission that we are intellectually and morally unfit to play our part in what Justice Holmes has called the "experiment" of self-government.[93]

As the U.S. Supreme Court has held, "[t]he inherent worth of the speech in terms of its capacity for informing the public does not depend upon the identity of its source."[94] As such, "it is inherent in the nature of the political process that voters must be free to obtain information from diverse sources in order to determine how to cast their votes" and "[s]peech restrictions based on the identity of the speaker are all too often simply a means to control content."[95] These arguments could equally apply in any democracy. Free speech helps the project of self-governance by providing people with information, and the mere fact that such information comes from a foreign source alone does not justify removing people's ability to access it.

If anything, the argument that self-governance can or should require the restriction of foreign speech proves too much. Taken seriously, the idea that foreign speech should be restricted would lead to a dramatically less well-informed electorate. This is glaringly obvious in some cases, such as when Facebook's ban on foreign ads caused havoc in EU elections by inhibiting regional campaigning.[96] But it is generally true that the criterion of "foreignness" alone cannot render information irrelevant to self-governance. If at least one purpose of free speech protections is to "supply the public need for information and education with respect to the significant issues of the times,"[97] it cannot seriously be argued that today the "significant issues of the times" are not global in character and would not benefit from global perspectives. If that puts it too highly, then even if foreign speech is not helpfully informative, "it may still be important to know that it is being said if the people themselves are to exercise an untrammeled right to determine their own collective response to it."[98]

B. Pursuit of Truth

Closely related to the self-governance rationale for free speech is the rationale that free speech facilitates the search for truth. Here, again, it is not clear why foreign speech should be singled out or is uniquely unsuited to testing in the so-called "marketplace

[93] Alexander Meiklejohn, Free Speech and Its Relation to Self-Government, at xiii–xiv (1948).

[94] First Nat'l Bank of Boston v. Bellotti, 435 U.S. 765, 777 (1978).

[95] Citizens United v. Federal Election Comm'n, 558 U.S. 310, 341, 340 (2010).

[96] Mark Scott et al., *Facebook to Cave to EU Pressure after Row over Political Ad Rules*, Politico (Apr. 18, 2019).

[97] Thornhill v. Alabama, 310 U.S. 88, 103 (1940).

[98] William W. Van Alstyne, *The First Amendment and the Suppression of Warmongering Propaganda in the United States: Comments and Footnotes*, 31 L. Contemp. Prob. 530, 537 (1966).

of ideas."[99] Increasingly, there are concerns that the online marketplace of ideas is failing generally, whether because of unique characteristics of the internet or because of distortions created by the platforms themselves in choosing to amplify or connect certain types of content or people over others.[100] These are important and compelling arguments that deserve careful attention. Crucially for present purposes, however, these arguments do not rest on the notion that such market failures are caused by the intrusion of foreign speech into the marketplace. Nor could they: foreign speech is neither new nor is it peculiarly unhelpful in reaching truth.

John Stuart Mill's case for free speech in service of truth, perhaps the most iconic argument in this tradition, was explicitly internationalist. He decried the man[101] who was not exposed to the thinking of other countries and who was therefore untroubled by the notion that "the same causes which made him a Churchman in London, would have made him a Buddhist or a Confucian in Pekin [*sic*]."[102] He wrote passionately about how free speech facilitated the spread of ideas throughout Europe.[103]

This is the ethos that informs the prescription in the Universal Declaration of Human Rights and the International Covenant on Civil and Political Rights that everyone has the right to freedom of expression "*regardless of frontiers*."[104] Indeed, in the years following World War II, the United States and other democratic states "monotonously" refused Soviet Union demands for a treaty outlawing international war propaganda on the grounds that this would jeopardize freedom of speech.[105] The best cure for international propaganda, these states maintained, was more, not less, freedom of information.[106]

As an example of the general hold of this tradition, most legal measures against foreign interference in the United States have focused on transparency rather than censorship. The Foreign Agents Registration Act (FARA) generally imposes registration and transparency obligations on foreign actors within the United States, rather than proscribing their speech altogether.[107] The Supreme Court upheld FARA against a First Amendment challenge, stressing that it did not censor any speech and noting that the legislation "recognizes that the best remedy for misleading or inaccurate speech contained within materials subject to the Act is fair, truthful, and accurate speech."[108] This approach holds offline: at the time of writing, for example,

[99] Abrams v. United States, 250 U.S. 616, 630 (1919) (Holmes J, dissenting).

[100] *See, e.g.*, Tim Wu, Is the First Amendment Obsolete, in The Free Speech Century 272 (Lee C. Bollinger & Geoffrey R. Stone eds., 2018); Zeynep Tufekci, *It's the (Democracy-Poisoning) Golden Age of Free Speech*, WIRED (Jan. 18, 2018); Cass R. Sunstein, #Republic: Divided Democracy in the Age of Social Media (2017); Jameel Jaffer, *Facebook and Free Speech Are Different Things*, KNIGHT FIRST AMENDMENT INSTITUTE (Oct. 24, 2019).

[101] Sexism in original.

[102] JOHN STUART MILL, ON LIBERTY AND UTILITARIANISM 22 (Bantam, 1993).

[103] *Id.* at 40–41.

[104] Universal Declaration of Human Rights (Dec. 10, 1948), G.A. Res. 217 (III)A, art. 19; International Covenant on Civil and Political Rights, Dec. 16, 1966, S. Exec. Rep. 102-23, 999 U.N.T.S. 171, art. 19 [hereinafter ICCPR] (emphasis added).

[105] John B. Whitton & Arthur Larson, *Propaganda: Towards Disarmament in the War of Words* 234 (1964).

[106] *Id.* at 241.

[107] 22 U.S.C. §§ 611–621. *See* CYNTHIA BROWN, CONG. RESEARCH SERV., R45037, THE FOREIGN AGENTS REGISTRATION ACT (FARA): A LEGAL OVERVIEW (2017).

[108] Meese v. Keene, 481 U.S. 465, 481 (1987) (Stevens J).

Radio Sputnik is registered under FARA and broadcasting propaganda across Kansas City radio.[109] Even in the high-watermark case against foreign speech, in which the Supreme Court affirmed a decision upholding restrictions on foreigners making political contributions, the lower court's decision had emphasized that foreigners could still engage in issue advocacy.[110] Similarly, a U.S. Department of Justice report in 2018 emphasized that what was malicious about foreign influence campaigns was their covert nature, and that "[o]vert influence efforts by foreign governments—including by our adversaries—may not be illegal" and that what was important was that "the American people should be fully aware of any foreign government source of information so they can evaluate that source's credibility and significance for themselves."[111] Indeed, as Robinson notes, "the United States has historically greatly benefited from the free exchange of ideas across borders, whether related to the abolition or suffrage movements, or the writing of the U.S. Constitution."[112] As Jens Ohlin writes elsewhere in this volume, "[o]utsiders are free to express their opinions," and it is only "covertly representing themselves as insiders [that] constitutes a violation of ... the notion of self-determination.... The only solution to this form of election interference is transparency."[113]

The pursuit of truth is not aided by denigrating or discounting foreign speech. One does not have to believe that free speech requires there to be "no such thing as a false idea"[114] to believe that there should be no such thing as a foreign one. If "[o]nly a weak society needs government protection or intervention before it pursues its resolve to preserve the truth,"[115] to fear foreign speech speaks volumes.

C. Autonomy

The autonomy rationale for free speech also does not support broad censorship or diminishment of foreign speech. Self-evidently, the autonomy of foreigners is undermined by censoring their speech, there are also less cosmopolitan-centered inconsistencies between the autonomy rationale and the vilification of foreign speech. The autonomy tradition of free speech has long also been concerned with protecting the autonomy of the *listener* to receive information and evaluate it for themselves.[116] So understood, "[t]he freedom to speak and the freedom to hear are inseparable; they are two sides of the same coin."[117] In this vein, the right to freedom of expression in

[109] Neil MacFarquhar, *Playing on Kansas City Radio: Russian Propaganda*, N.Y. Times (Feb. 13, 2020).

[110] Bluman v. Federal Election Com'n, 800 F. Supp. 2d 281 (D.D.C. 2011); *aff'd*, 565 U.S. 1104 (2012).

[111] U.S. Department of Justice, Cyber Digital Task Force Report 6 (2018).

[112] Nick Robinson, *"Foreign Agents" in an Interconnected World: FARA and the Weaponization of Transparency*, 69 Duke L.J. 1075, 1140–1141 (2020) (citations omitted).

[113] *See* chapter 11, this volume, at 240.

[114] Gertz v. Robert Welch, Inc., 418 U.S. 323, 339 (1974) (Powell J).

[115] U.S. v. Alvarez, 567 U.S. 709, 729 (2012).

[116] Morgan Weiland, *Expanding the Periphery and Threatening the Core: The Ascendant Libertarian Speech Tradition*, 69 Stan. L. Rev. 1389, 1450–1451 (2017); Seana Valentine Shiffrin, *A Thinker-Based Approach to Freedom of Speech*, 27 Const. Comm. 283, 299–303 (2017).

[117] Kleindienst v. Mandel, 408 U.S. 753, 775 (1972) (Marshall, J., dissenting). The majority did not contest the idea that the First Amendment protected listener autonomy too, including the right to hear and receive ideas from foreign speakers, but held that the executive could refuse an entry visa in this case on national

international law explicitly includes the freedom to "*seek, receive* and impart" information.[118] To interfere with this right on the basis that foreign speech might prove to be persuasive is itself a paternalistic and manipulative denial of information that invades the would-be listener's autonomy.[119] As Balkin observed over a decade ago, "what people do on the Internet transcends the nation state; they participate in discussions, debate, and collective activity that does not respect national borders. These are valuable human activities in their own right."[120]

The securitized discourse around foreign election interference often masks the paternalistic and autonomy-infringing assumptions inherent in the framing of foreign influence campaigns as a uniquely potent force. If there is something about information operations that makes censorship a proportionate response to *preserve* individual autonomy, it is not their foreignness alone.

D. As a Means to an End?

It is important to emphasize the limited confines of my argument: the preceding sections address only foreign *speech*, and do not encompass other foreign activity that aims to interfere with democratic processes. As a matter of principle and international law,[121] and of course most domestic constitutions or regulations, every state or people has the right to noninterference and self-determination.[122] My argument is simply that foreign *speech* alone does not interfere with this right and indeed may aid its exercise by providing information or perspectives that can be engaged with, ignored, discarded, refuted, but not censored.

Narratives that suggest that the rise of big data or techniques such as "psychographic profiling" have made even speech alone an overbearing force that must be stemmed to prevent subversion of democratic processes (the "hypodermic needle" characterization of propaganda) generally inflate the role of these techniques and remain unproven.[123] In any event, if speech alone could be so potent, it is unclear why counterspeech and other domestic messaging should not be relied on to meet like with like.

security grounds: for discussion, *see* Krotoszynski Jr., *supra* note 89, at 492–495 (concluding that the case "acknowledged that the First Amendment protects the interest of a U.S. audience in receiving ideas and information from abroad.").

[118] ICCPR, *supra* note 104, art. 19 (emphasis added).

[119] David A. Strauss, *Persuasion, Autonomy, and Freedom of Expression*, 91 COLUM. L. REV. 334, 356 (1991).

[120] Jack M. Balkin, *The Future of Free Expression in a Digital Age*, 36 PEPP. L. REV. 427, 438 (2009).

[121] *See* chapter 11, this volume. *See also* Barrie Sander, *Democracy under the Influence: Paradigms of State Responsibility for Cyber Influence Operations on Elections*, 18 CHINESE J. INT'L L. 1, 44 (2019).

[122] For a discussion of the difficulties of proving a breach of this right in the context of social media influence campaigns, *see* Sander, *supra* note 121, at 43–45.

[123] Jessica Baldwin-Philippi, *Data Ops, Objectivity, and Outsiders: Journalistic Coverage of Data Campaigning*, POL. COMM. 1 (2020); David Karpf, *On Digital Disinformation and Democratic Myths*, MediaWell, SOCIAL SCIENCE RESEARCH COUNCIL (Dec. 10, 2019), https://mediawell.ssrc.org/expert-reflections/on-digital-disinformation-and-democratic-myths/.

Beyond mere speech, however, restrictions on foreign interference or participation in other democratic processes are more readily justifiable as necessary for legitimate democratic self-governance. The internet has not created a borderless world.[124] Restrictions on foreign voting, financial contributions, and other forms of immediate influence on political representatives or campaigns directly protect the mechanisms of democracy.[125] My argument for the rehabilitation of the appreciation of foreign speech does not even extend to all election meddling that occurs through cyberspace. As Sander notes, debate about cyber election meddling frequently conflates different techniques that are analytically distinct.[126] Hacking and leaking operations, for example, go beyond mere speech.[127] The categories of election interference Levin gives in this volume similarly all constitute more than mere speech.[128] But the militarization of the discourse around influence operations on social media has removed any nuance and allowed for the drawing of a false equivalence between speech and these other activities, often characterizing foreign speech as if it has kinetic effects. Of course, the line between speech and action may not always be clear-cut in practice and perhaps especially in cyberspace; but the importance of free speech is such that the distinction should not be wholesale abandoned. Today's world makes cross-border speech both inevitable and beneficial, not only for global governance but also national self-governance.

A still further objection might be that while the restriction of foreign speech may not itself serve self-governance, it is a necessary means to achieving the ends of restricting the other kinds of impermissible interference just described, such as direct influence of representatives or funneling financial contributions, or the appearance of these activities. Foreign speech threatens self-governance, this argument runs, not because of the speech itself but because such speech is a precursor to more pernicious meddling. This would be a forceful argument, and at the very least supports the kinds of transparency measures that Ohlin argues for in this volume.[129] But there are two reasons why such a consequentialist argument does not support the current way foreign speech is treated. First, this is not the argument actually made in favor of restricting this speech, which instead frames the foreign speech *itself* as harmful because of its potential persuasive effects. Given the importance of freedom of speech,

[124] Jack Goldsmith & Tim Wu, Who Controls the Internet?: Illusions of a Borderless World (2008).

[125] *See, e.g.*, Jens David Ohlin, *Did Russian Cyber Interference in the 2016 Election Violate International Law?*, 95 Tex. L. Rev. 1579, 1594 (2017) ("Everyone agrees that had the Russian government tampered with the ballot boxes, or with electronic voting, this would count as a violation of international law, because the counting of votes during an election is a paradigmatically 'governmental function,' which in that case would be 'usurped' by Russia.").

[126] Sander, *supra* note 121, at 5.

[127] *See, e.g.*, Hendrick Townley & Asaf Lubin, *The International Law of Rabble-Rousing*, 45 Yale J. Int'l L. Online 1, 4 (2020) (distinguishing online amplification of divisive issues, which they term "rabble-rousing," from both "the injection of 'fake news' into public discourse—as it need not involve false information—and from doxing and hacking—as it has no obviously illegal component under domestic law nor does it target a single individual.").

[128] *See* chapter 1, this volume.

[129] *See* chapter 11, this volume.

the burden rests on those who would restrict speech to justify it as a narrowly tailored or proportionate means of achieving the asserted aims. Neither governments nor platforms have actually asserted the consequentialist anti-avoidance aim of such restrictions, let alone shown that current measures help achieve it. Second, the present opacity around standards and enforcement—and in particular, which governments influence platform actions and to what extent—does not help achieve the goal of avoiding the appearance of improper influence. If anything, a lack of transparency undermines attempts to show that restrictions on foreign speech are neutral and not driven by geopolitical considerations or influence.

***

This section has argued that singling out foreign speech for censorship does not serve free speech values. In fact, the very inconsistency of such action with free speech rights is partly what makes platforms such an attractive choke point for governments in the fight against the perceived threat. There are practical reasons that such "[c]ollateral censorship may be especially important for states that want to encourage filtering and blocking of content from overseas, because governments cannot generally control foreign intermediaries and speakers."[130] But such collateral censorship is also a legally attractive option: it has long been recognized that platforms are the "weakest link" in protecting speech because they have limited incentive to avoid overcensorship.[131] Therefore, tech companies can be incentivized to take down content that should be protected, without having to afford the same procedural protections a government would have to provide. Overbroad and opaque censorship of foreign political speech is a clear example of exactly this kind of collateral censorship.

Beyond being inconsistent with free speech values, the denigration of foreign speech is especially incoherent as platforms rely on the very vibrancy and ease of cross-border information flows as a fundamental characteristic and advantage of their products.[132] Platforms insist that there is much to value about this new global information ecosystem, and they are right to do so. The dissonance between this and the vilification of foreign speech as especially dangerous "interference" underscores that it is not the characteristic of "foreignness" that distinguishes problematic election interference. Again, this proves too much. If the problem were foreign speech, the fix would be much simpler—a fragmented internet with resurgent national borders. But this is not a desirable or realistic future for the internet. Moreover, the focus on foreignness obscures far deeper problems about the current information ecosystem that such fragmentation would not solve. The next section turns to what is hiding in this blind spot.

[130] Jack M. Balkin, *Old-School/New-School Speech Regulation*, 127 Harv. L. Rev. 2296, 2311 (2014).

[131] Seth F. Kreimer, *Censorship by Proxy: The First Amendment, Internet Intermediaries, and the Problem of the Weakest Link*, 155 U. Penn. L. Rev. 11 (2006).

[132] *See, e.g.*, Monika Bickert, Defining the Boundaries of Free Speech on Social Media, in The Free Speech Century 254, 259 (Lee C. Bollinger & Geoffrey R. Stone eds., 2018).

IV. Hiding in the Blind Spot: Technology and Distrust

This chapter is emphatically not making the argument that nothing should be done about election interference on social media. My argument is both more limited and more far-reaching. The more limited argument is that the focus on "foreign" speech as especially pernicious is misplaced, undermines important speech interests, and has been used to justify a uniquely opaque governance regime. The more expansive argument is that by moving the focus away from "foreign" election interference, it becomes apparent that there are no clear lines about online influence in general. This more fundamental concern remains unaddressed as the "arms race" information warfare framing has allowed the conversation about election interference to be driven by actors who have a stake in how the problem is defined: platforms and governments. Ultimately, allowing the agenda for dealing with election interference to be shaped by the interests of these interested parties alone will undermine the greater project of re-establishing trust in online discourse.

This is thrown into sharpest relief by focusing on the actual harm caused by influence operations. This requires looking beyond a belief in hyperefficient digital targeting and audience manipulation. Public discourse around data campaigning in political contexts has imbued such campaigns with a power and aura of effectiveness that outpaces the limited evidence of efficacy.[133] Even years on, there remains very little evidence of direct impact by the Russian influence operation during the 2016 U.S. election.[134] This should not be surprising: political scientists have long known that political persuasion in general is extremely difficult. Translating data on "interactions" that people had with Russian-created content on social media into real-world effects is fraught. As noted earlier, most of the content was not "particularly objectionable"—we should be cautious before ascribing unusually powerful effects to otherwise unremarkable content. In many cases, foreign interference campaigns are not even crafted to push a particular ideological agenda or electoral outcome.[135] Instead, they are intended to undermine both the reality and perception of reasoned democratic discourse online. In 2016, the Russian operation primarily sought to "erode our trust in media entities and the information environment, in government, in each other, and in democracy itself."[136] This erosion of trust and belief in the possibility of productive

[133] Baldwin-Philippi, *supra* note 123.

[134] Karpf, *supra* note 123. *See also* chapter 1, this volume (stating that "most scholars of American politics, are still highly skeptical" of arguments that Russian influence operations changed the outcome of the 2016 election).

[135] *See, e.g.*, Townley & Lubin, *supra* note 127, at 4–5 (defining the category of interference of "rabble-rousing" as "simultaneous amplification of both opposing sides of a nationally divisive issue."); @DFRLab, *Top Takes: A Facebook Drama in Three Acts*, MEDIUM (Jan. 24, 2020), https://medium.com/dfrlab/top-takes-a-facebook-drama-in-three-acts-a275e037c8be (the network demonstrated no single or coherent ideological agenda; instead, the accounts seemed to be passionate about disparate political issues.... Different accounts often contradicted each other in political positioning."); Nathaniel Gleicher, *Removing Coordinated Inauthentic Behavior from Russia*, FACEBOOK NEWSROOM (Mar. 12, 2020), https://about.fb.com/news/2020/03/removing-coordinated-inauthentic-behavior-from-russia/ ("This activity did not appear to focus on elections, or promote or denigrate political candidates.").

[136] DIRESTA ET AL., *supra* note 33. *See also* U.S. DEPARTMENT OF JUSTICE, *supra* note 111, at 2.

public discourse, and not an undemonstrated number of votes changed, is a far more pervasive and demonstrable harm caused by these campaigns.[137]

Focusing on the erosion of trust as the most pressing harm to be countered in the fight against election interference highlights both how much bigger than foreign campaigns the problem is and how inadequate current solutions are. Overhyping the threat and outsourcing the response to opaque content cartels do not help rebuild trust in the online information environment. As has been discussed, platforms insist they do not detect and remove campaigns based on content, but it remains unclear what the criteria are. The lack of transparency and seemingly uneven enforcement actions that characterize the status quo have led researchers to conclude that how platforms define illegitimate manipulation is "nebulous and largely reflective of their material interests."[138]

Platforms alone should not be able to set the terms of debate for what constitutes improper election interference or manipulation. There are at least five key questions that the currently carefully circumscribed conversation avoids asking, and this itself undermines the very trust that counterinfluence efforts should be aiming to rebuild.

First, what constitutes permissible political campaigning on social media in general is unclear and requires more attention. Social media platforms remain plagued by a "fake follower" problem, where for relatively small fees thousands of followers can be purchased to make any person or idea look more popular than it really is.[139] But research into politically motivated false amplification "is still in its infancy," and its extent and effectiveness remains unknown.[140] Fake activity is only the tip of the iceberg. Teens, far less well-resourced than foreign state actors, can get nonexistent people verified as political candidates on Twitter.[141] Michael Bloomberg, candidate for president in the U.S. 2020 election, caused havoc by having the money and digitally literate campaign staff to push the lines and expose the loopholes in platforms' vague rules about political campaigning on social media.[142] Was paying influencers to post supportive messages coordinated inauthentic behavior?[143] What about seventy pro-Bloomberg

[137] *See also* PETER POMERANTSEV, THIS IS NOT PROPAGANDA: ADVENTURES IN THE WAR AGAINST REALITY (2019).

[138] Caitlin Petre et al., *"Gaming the System": Platform Paternalism and the Politics of Algorithmic Visibility*, 5 SOC. MEDIA + SOC'Y 1, 1 (2019); Bridget Barrett & Daniel Kreiss, *Platform Transience: Changes in Facebook's Policies, Procedures, and Affordances in Global Electoral Politics*, 8 INTERNET POL. REV. 1, 15 (2019) ("it is clear from our case studies that there are a number of economic incentives that underlie platform transience.").

[139] NATO Strategic Communications Centre of Excellence, *supra* note 23, at 3 ("At a cost of just 300 EUR, we bought 3530 comments, 25,750 likes, 20,000 views, and 5,100 followers. By studying the accounts that delivered the purchased manipulation, we were able to identify 18,739 accounts used to manipulate social media platforms."); Emma Grey Ellis, *Fighting Instagram's $1.3 Billion Problem—Fake Followers*, WIRED (Sept. 10, 2019); Nicholas Confessore et al., *The Follower Factory*, N.Y. TIMES (Jan. 27, 2018).

[140] Deen Freelon et al., *Black Trolls Matter: Racial and Ideological Asymmetries in Social Media Disinformation*, SOC. SCI. COMP. REV. 5 (Apr. 2020).

[141] Donie O'Sullivan, *A High School Student Created a Fake 2020 Candidate. Twitter Verified It*, CNN (Feb. 28, 2020).

[142] Sheera Frenkel & Davey Alba, *Digital Edits, a Paid Army: Bloomberg Is "Destroying Norms" on Social Media*, N.Y. TIMES (Feb. 22, 2020).

[143] Jeff Horwitz & Georgia Wells, *Bloomberg Bankrolls a Social-Media Army to Push Message*, WALL STREET JOURNAL (Feb. 19, 2020).

accounts on Twitter pushing out identical messages?[144] Was a digitally altered video of the candidate's debate performance misleading or just spin?[145] Did tweeting fictitious quotes attributed to another candidate cross a line?[146] Platforms' ad hoc and reactive ways of dealing with each of these incidents do not suggest they have any principled or enduring answers to what legitimate political campaigning looks like in the digital era. As Bridget Barrett concluded, this series of events only illustrated "the current state of play for political figures on social media: If you're big enough, bold enough, and influential enough, the rules are negotiable."[147]

Second, the lines between foreign and domestic and authentic and inauthentic influence is becoming increasingly arbitrary and difficult to draw in practice, regardless of whether it can be justified in theory. Domestic efforts are increasingly employing the methods associated with foreign influence efforts. Facebook's head of cybersecurity policy has said that most U.S.-focused election meddling is homegrown, and this should be especially concerning because "in order to run an information operation, the most important thing is that you understand the culture."[148] Benkler summarizes the problem: "the basic problem is that social networks are susceptible to coordinated efforts, whether carried out by paid agents of a government ... or by more-or-less sophisticated automated accounts."[149] As real people are drawn into interactions with "inauthentic" accounts, what is foreign or domestic, or what is fake or real, becomes harder to untangle. Individuals may not know the nature of the broader campaign that they are interacting with, but often still hold their political views genuinely and have an interest in expressing them. These tensions are only going to grow. As sophisticated digital campaigning becomes more commonplace, it is "increasingly difficult to draw some of the more traditional lines between foreign and domestic political activity, government and nongovernmental organizations, and information operations and permissible campaign activity."[150] Trying to maintain arbitrary lines that will repeatedly prove illusory will only further undermine efforts to create meaningful criteria for enforcement against election meddling efforts.

Third, platforms focus the conversation about election interference on bad actors without accounting for the profound effects they themselves have on public discourse. Their algorithms determine what kind of content gets seen, without anyone knowing exactly how they work. Platforms are built to amplify a certain type of content, and as such "[t]he platforms are not just available for misuse; they are structurally implicated

[144] Suhauna Hussain & Jeff Bercovici, *Twitter Is Suspending 70 Pro-Bloomberg Accounts, Citing "Platform Manipulation,"* L.A. Times (Feb. 22, 2020).

[145] Alex Ward, *Is This Doctored Mike Bloomberg Video Political Spin or Disinformation?*, Vox (Feb. 20, 2020).

[146] Shirin Ghaffary, *Why Twitter Says Bloomberg's Fake Sanders Tweets Don't Break Its Rules*, Vox (Feb. 25, 2020).

[147] Bridget Barrett, *What We Learned from Bloomberg's Online Campaign*, Lawfare (Mar. 6, 2020).

[148] Nancy Scola, *Experts Warn the Social Media Threat This Election Is Homegrown*, Politico (Nov. 5, 2018).

[149] Yochai Benkler, *Election Advertising Disclosure: Part 2*, Harv. L. Rev. Blog (Nov. 3, 2017), https://blog.harvardlawreview.org/election-advertising-disclosure-part-2/.

[150] Kofi Annan Commission on Elections and Democracy in the Digital Age, *Protecting Electoral Integrity in the Digital Age 83* (Jan. 2020), https://www.kofiannanfoundation.org/app/uploads/2020/01/f035dd8e-kaf_kacedda_report_2019_web.pdf.

in it."[151] Even setting aside these structural effects that result from platforms' business models, platforms make more discrete election-related decisions that fundamentally shape political campaigns. Zittrain prophetically pointed out over half a decade ago that "Facebook could decide an election without anyone ever finding out" by nudging certain demographics to vote.[152] Platforms change their rules regarding campaigning and advertising in the middle of elections around the world in a way that "increases the likelihood of hidden manipulation and, more broadly, unequal information environments.[153] There is no evidence that these decisions are politically motivated. But the fact remains that in making them, platforms radically transform political debate in a way that, as far as the biggest platforms are concerned, in every country apart from the United States constitutes a far more potent form of foreign interference than any influence operation.

Fourth, the role that various governments play in determining when and how platforms remove content remains unclear. Platforms are more responsive to some governments than others. Even in cases where platforms and government tout a good working relationship, there is no oversight and some evidence that information sharing is not systematized or consistent. In at least some cases, for example around COVID-19 disinformation, the U.S. government has publicly asserted that there are foreign-backed social media information operations occurring, without providing platforms themselves with evidence that would allow them to investigate.[154] This apparent inconsistency of when governments share their intelligence raises the specter of political bias that undermines the legitimacy of all information sharing and content removals. The total lack of independent oversight exacerbates this.[155]

Fifth, settling for incoherent or unexplained standards not only undermines domestic efforts to rebuild faith in democratic discourse and institutions but also has global ramifications. As the Kofi Annan Commission on Elections and Democracy in the Digital Age emphasized:

> A larger challenge ... is how to distinguish and protect legitimate foreign assistance for the promotion of democracy and electoral integrity from illegitimate foreign interference in elections.... The best way to counter arguments based on false equivalence is for democracies to spell out what is and what is not legitimate transnational support for democracy.[156]

The lack of such a transparently made affirmative argument of the benefits of some foreign speech has been used to justify harsh laws by repressive governments around the world ostensibly aimed at "fake news" and "foreign propaganda."[157] This repeats

[151] Tarleton Gillespie, Platforms Throw Content Moderation at Every Problem, in Fake News loc. 6682 (Melissa Zimdars & Kembrew McLeod eds., Kindle ed. 2020).

[152] Jonathan Zittrain, *Facebook Could Decide an Election Without Anyone Ever Finding Out*, New Republic (June 1, 2014).

[153] Barrett & Kreiss, *supra* note 138, at 3.

[154] Donie O'Sullivan & Kylie Atwood, *Facebook and Twitter Ask to See Government Report Linking Coronavirus Misinformation to Russia*, CNN (Feb. 28, 2020).

[155] Charlie Warzel, *Russia Wants to Meddle in Our Election. We're Helping*, N.Y. Times (Feb. 25, 2020).

[156] Kofi Annan Commission on Elections and Democracy in the Digital Age, *supra* note 150, at 87.

[157] Kaye, *supra* note 2, at 113.

previous experience with U.S. transparency laws like FARA, which other countries pointed at to justify and legitimize passing analogous legislation, which was then used to stigmatize and marginalize civil society.[158] The fear of the "foreign" exhibited by liberal democracies can be deployed to justify constricting freedom of expression in contexts where domestic manipulation likely poses a far more potent threat to self-governance.

All these factors fuel exactly the distrust in online discourse that foreign influence campaigns hope to create. As John Hart Ely identified long ago in *Democracy and Distrust*, the protection of speech rights should not be left to those who have a vested interest in the way the threat is defined.[159] This remains the reason why governmental involvement in speech regulation is regarded with suspicion. But in the digital age, there is the added problem of *technology and distrust:* platforms also have a vested interest in defining the conversation about what constitutes impermissible online coordination and influence in a way that appears carefully circumscribed and peripheral. These vested interests combined make governments and platforms especially ill-placed to decide the rules for reestablishing trust in the online public sphere. This is all the more true given the current high lack of confidence in platforms.[160] Even if their decisions are well-intentioned and unbiased, they cannot be *seen* to be without adequate oversight and transparency.

This is not to deny that there may be some trade-off between "effectiveness" of counterinfluence efforts (narrowly defined as content removals) and transparency. But given that one fundamental purpose of removing election interference from social media must be restoring trust in the online information environment and democratic discourse in general, a completely opaque system of perfect enforcement is a worse solution than a less effective but more open approach. Put another way: platforms and governments could remove all foreign election interference, but without transparency around how and why they do so, the apathy and distrust that such campaigns seek to create would still remain.

The project of rebuilding trust more generally is of course much harder. Determining the permissible types of influence and coordination online is not a story with clear "goodies" and "baddies"; it is not a "war" but a constant process of evolution and development. The answer will be highly context-dependent and will need to respond and adapt to an ever-changing online environment. But addressing this question with the necessary openness and debate cannot even begin to take place when it is obscured by a much more appealing but oversimplified narrative that centers foreign political speech as the problem. As Jennifer Daskal has observed, "we should be cautious about quick fixes that paint all foreigners as equally pernicious . . . [t]otal bans on entire categories of speakers won't solve the bulk of the problem, and they'll probably

[158] Robinson, *supra* note 112, 1081–1082.

[159] John Hart Ely, Democracy and Distrust: A Theory of Judicial Review 106 (1980). *See also* Sunstein, *supra* note 100, at 205 ("an insistence that government's burden is greatest when it is regulating political speech emerges from a sensible understanding of government's own incentives. It is here that government is most likely to be acting on the basis of illegitimate considerations").

[160] John LaLoggia, *U.S. Public Has Little Confidence in Social Media Companies to Determine Offensive Content*, Pew Research Center (July 11, 2019), https://www.pewresearch.org/fact-tank/2019/07/11/u-s-public-has-little-confidence-in-social-media-companies-to-determine-offensive-content/.

cause new ones."[161] To allow the fear of the foreign to justify overbroad or ambiguous restrictions on speech is to undermine exactly the democratic values that need to be preserved as the best defense.

V. Conclusion

A central tenet of free speech theory is that scrutiny of speech regulation should be highest when it involves political speech. Instead, when it comes to foreign election interference on social media, it is at its weakest. The outsourcing of censorship of this genus of political speech on social media to opaque content cartels defining the conversation on their own terms has been facilitated by an alarmist narrative about the threat of the "foreign." But foreign influence campaigns should not be given the power of forcing democratic states to give lie to their professed faith in the reasons free speech is important. Closer examination of these reasons shows that it is not the foreignness of speech that is most threatening but the deeper problems of an ecosystem ruled by opaque standards and subject to exploitation by a much wider variety of actors. This is a much harder problem to solve. Nevertheless, the project of restoring trust in public discourse and preserving free speech rights online requires not being distracted by the simpler but ultimately superficial militarized discourse that currently dominates discussion of election interference on social media.

[161] Jennifer C. Daskal, *Facebook's Ban on Foreign Political Ads Means the Site Is Segregating Speech*, Washington Post (Dec. 16, 2019).

13
Foreign Election Interference and Open-Source Anarchy

David P. Fidler

I. Introduction

Russian meddling in the 2016 elections in the United States sparked debates in liberal democracies about how to counter foreign election interference. These debates reveal the seriousness of the threat and the complexity of responses to it, including how to protect voting systems and what actions social media companies should take against disinformation. As other chapters in this volume explore, foreign interference in elections is not new.[1] Indeed, the United States has protected its elections against foreign influence and interfered in foreign elections.[2] However, what happened in 2016 does not simply repeat what transpired in the past. The scale and intensity of the controversies that emerged suggest that the threat of foreign election interference has changed—and that this change arises from developments in the realms of power, ideas, and technology.

Explaining why the threat of foreign election interference is different today, and the implications of this difference, can take diverse tracks. What the United States experienced in 2016 can be attributed to how hyperpartisan U.S. politics tempted foreign adversaries to interfere in the elections. Another explanation can be found in how the internet evolved into a global, accessible, and minimally regulated communication network that provided foreign actors with unprecedented incentives and opportunities to meddle in U.S. politics during an election season.

This chapter seeks to understand the contemporary problem of foreign election interference through conceptual frameworks, such as international relations theory. In the past, foreign election interference was not prominent in the study of international relations.[3] The elevation of this problem provides incentives to explore past and present foreign election interference through concepts developed to analyze international relations. The application of leading theories of international relations indicates that none adequately explains the foreign election interference challenge that

[1] *See* Part I, *Election Interference by Foreign Powers: Understanding Its History and Its Harm(s)*, this volume.

[2] 52 U.S.C. §30121 (making contributions by foreign nationals during elections illegal); Thomas Carothers, *Is the U.S. Hypocritical to Criticize Russian Election Meddling?*, FOREIGN AFF. (Mar. 12, 2018) (noting the U.S. "record of electoral meddling, particularly during the Cold War").

[3] Dov H. Levin, *Partisan Electoral Interventions by the Great Powers: Introducing the PEIG Dataset*, 36(1) CONFLICT MGMT. & PEACE SCI. 88, 88 (2019) (noting that foreign election interference has been a "blind spot in the international relations (IR) literature").

David P. Fidler, *Foreign Election Interference and Open-Source Anarchy* In: *Defending Democracies*. Edited by Duncan B. Hollis and Jens David Ohlin, Oxford University Press (2021).
DOI: 10.1093/oso/9780197556979.003.0014

democracies face. This outcome creates the need to develop other explanations of how the problem of foreign election interference reflects changes in international politics.

This chapter argues that international anarchy—a concept central to international relations theories—changes in ways that leading theories do not capture. The chapter develops the concept of "open-source anarchy" to understand how anarchy changed after the Cold War and to analyze why foreign election interference has gained prominence during the second decade of the twenty-first century.[4] In open-source anarchy, changes in the structure of material power, technologies, and ideas permit less powerful states and nonstate actors to affect more directly and significantly how anarchy functions. The concept helps explain how Russia exploited the internet and social media to interfere in elections in the United States—the world's leading democracy, foremost source of technological innovation, and most powerful country. Open-source anarchy also illuminates the struggles that the United States and other democracies have experienced in preventing, protecting against, and responding to foreign election interference.

II. Russian Interference with the 2016 Elections in the United States

The report of Special Counsel Robert S. Mueller described Russian efforts to interfere with the U.S. elections in 2016 and captured how foreign actors can influence elections in other countries.[5] Russia leaked information it obtained by hacking the computers of a presidential campaign and political party, probed the voting systems operated by state and local governments, and disseminated disinformation through social media.[6] The Russian campaign exploited nonstate actors in other countries and in the United States by leaking hacked information through WikiLeaks, using Facebook and Twitter to spread misinformation, benefiting from the mainstream media's amplification of leaked information, and mixing Russian-sourced disinformation with that U.S.-based actors circulated. These activities, however, are not the sole province of highly capable governments. Weaker states and nonstate actors can also hack, leak, and engage in information operations in order to influence political processes, including elections, in foreign countries.[7]

Each means of foreign election interference used in 2016 relied on the internet. The infrastructure, institutions, and incentives of elections have become integrated into internet-based technologies, which creates a large "attack surface." Thus, the internet has transformed the risk profile for foreign election interference. It increased

[4] The chapter builds on David P. Fidler, *A Theory of Open-Source Anarchy*, 15(1) Ind. J. Global Legal Stud. 259 (2008).

[5] Robert S. Mueller, III, Report on the Investigation into Russian Interference in the 2016 Presidential Election (Mar. 2019).

[6] *Id.* at 14–51.

[7] Samantha Bradshaw & Philip N. Howard, *The Global Disinformation Order: 2019 Global Inventory of Organised Social Media Manipulation* 2 (Oxford Computational Propaganda Research Project, 2019) (noting that countries, such as Pakistan and Venezuela, engage in foreign influence operations in addition to major powers, such as Russia and China).

the vulnerabilities of election systems, provided globally accessible and attribution-unfriendly capabilities that state and nonstate actors can exploit to intervene in foreign elections, and catalyzed the motivations of potentially more state and nonstate actors to meddle in the electoral politics of other countries.

However, the foreign election interference of 2016 is not simply a tale about technology. Russia's use of disinformation to influence the U.S. elections is merely the latest example of how states and nonstate actors have long engaged in information operations as part of competition, coercion, and conflict.[8] Governments, dissidents, insurgents, and terrorists have deployed information and disinformation in struggles for power and influence in times of war and peace. This behavior is consistent over time and always involves exploitation of the latest technologies. Similarly, before 2016, countries were hacking computers in other nations to steal information, including on foreign politics and elections, as part of espionage—just as governments had previously used every new technology to enhance spying. Explaining what happened in 2016, and what countries face in future elections, involves understanding how political and technological factors converged to produce opportunities for foreign election interference unavailable and unimaginable before.[9]

In many ways, Russia's meddling in the U.S. elections in 2016 poses a puzzle. Russia, a weaker state than the United States,[10] used the internet and nonstate actors to mount an assault on elections, something fundamental to U.S. politics, the nation's ideology, and the belief in American exceptionalism. The Russian campaign not only damaged the United States but also sent shock waves through the community of liberal democracies.[11] The incident provided other states—weak or strong—and nonstate actors with a playbook for interfering in the elections of other countries.[12] The ineffective responses of the United States enhanced the playbook's attractiveness, and Russia and other countries are preparing to interfere in the U.S. elections in 2020.[13] This episode's significance invites using international relations theory to illuminate what happened and inform debates about how to counter foreign election interference.

[8] Information operations may occur for reasons other than election interference. *See* Bradshaw & Howard, *supra* note 7; Michael J. Mazarr et al., *Hostile Social Manipulation: Present Realities and Emerging Trends* (RAND, 2019).

[9] Efforts to influence foreign elections are not always successful. *See, e.g.*, Connor Fairman, *When Election Interference Fails*, Net Pol. (Jan. 29, 2020) (analyzing measures Taiwan took to counter China's efforts to interfere with its elections in January 2020).

[10] David J. Kramer, *Russia Is No Great Power Competitor*, The Atlantic (Apr. 24, 2019); Joseph S. Nye Jr., *How to Deal with a Declining Russia*, Project Syndicate (Nov. 5, 2019).

[11] James Lamond & Tailia Dessel, *Democratic Resilience: A Comparative Review of Russian Interference in Democratic Elections and Lessons Learned for Securing Future Elections*, Center for American Progress (Sept. 3, 2019) (noting that "democracies in Europe and around the world are combating Russian election interference").

[12] Keir Giles, *Handbook of Russian Information Warfare* (NATO Defense College, Nov. 2016); Sheera Frenkel, Kate Conger, & Kevin Roose, *Russia's Playbook for Social Media Disinformation Has Gone Global*, N.Y. Times (Jan. 31, 2019).

[13] Lamond & Dessel, *supra* note 11 (arguing that "[e]very indicator suggests that Russia will . . . be actively engaged in disrupting U.S. democratic processes throughout the 2020 election cycle" and that other countries, such as China and Iran "are advancing their foreign interference capabilities").

III. Foreign Election Interference and International Relations Theory

A. Realism and Foreign Election Interference

Realist theory posits that the anarchical structure of the international system determines state behavior by forcing states to focus on material power and its distribution in the international system.[14] Realism holds that anarchy drives state behavior no matter what domestic political system a state has. Further, nonstate actors have no independent effect on state behavior. In competing for power and influence, states might co-opt nonstate actors, but states determine what such proxies do and why.

Fitting the problem of foreign election interference into realist theory proves difficult. Such interference targets a component of the domestic regimes of states that use elections to determine who exercises government authority. However, according to the theory, whether a state holds elections does not change how anarchy affects that state's behavior. Thus, under realism, foreign election interference—or any interference with the politics of another state—should not be a strategic response because the nature of a state's domestic political regime does not determine that state's behavior in an anarchical system.

States have engaged in information operations, including to influence foreign elections, in competing for power and influence in anarchy.[15] Under realism, anarchy's demands on states transforms information into a tactical instrument of power politics. Faced with serious or existential threats to their power or survival, states will weaponize information just as they modernize weapons. In such a context, whether the information disseminated is true or false does not matter. The balance of power determines strategic outcomes not the veracity of information or the quality of ideas. This perspective suggests that states will engage in information operations against rival powers that pose a serious threat or against weaker states.[16] However, one would not anticipate that a weaker state would launch large-scale information operations against a more powerful nation.

Russia's meddling in the 2016 election in the United States is, thus, hard to explain under realism. The hack-and-leak and disinformation activities constituted a significant escalation in how Russia used cyber-technologies against the United States. The U.S. government had identified Russian cyber espionage and military cyber capabilities as threats, but exploiting new technologies for intelligence and military purposes is an expected practice among states. The information operations that Russia launched during the U.S. elections were altogether different. In particular, the Russian disinformation activities utilized the capabilities of nonstate actors, such as social

[14] On realism, *see* EDWARD H. CARR, THE TWENTY YEARS' CRISIS, 1919–1939: AN INTRODUCTION TO THE STUDY OF INTERNATIONAL RELATIONS (1939); HANS J. MORGENTHAU, POLITICS AMONG NATIONS: THE STRUGGLE FOR POWER AND PEACE (5th ed. rev. 1978); and KENNETH N. WALTZ, THEORY OF INTERNATIONAL POLITICS (1979). For a recent example of realist analysis, *see* John J. Mearsheimer, *Bound to Fail: The Rise and Fall of the Liberal International Order*, 43(4) INT'L SEC. 7 (Spring 2019).

[15] Levin, *supra* note 3, at 91 (identifying disinformation as one electoral interference tactic).

[16] *Id.* at 99 (noting that great powers use electoral interventions "in order to exert political influence upon other countries").

media platforms, rather than just assets that it controlled. Although Russia has been attempting to regain great-power status,[17] it was not, in 2016, on par with the United States in terms of material power.[18]

Thus, Russia took a serious risk that the United States would use interference in its elections as a pretext to use its superior power to gain geopolitical leverage against a revanchist Russia. Under realist theory, the Russians could not expect the United States to respect international law that might limit how the Americans responded. In addition, the benefits of interfering in the U.S. elections were questionable under realism. Meddling in the U.S. election would not enhance Russia's power vis-à-vis the United States because, in realism, the nature and functioning of an adversary's political system does not determine how a state responds to anarchy.

B. Institutionalism and Foreign Election Interference

A second leading theory of international relations is institutionalism.[19] This theory accepts realism's premise that anarchy determines state behavior by forcing states to worry about the balance of power. However, institutionalism posits that states can build institutions, such as international organizations, to create cooperation that is more than expedient and ephemeral. Achieving sustainable cooperation requires, among other things, increasing the exchange of information, which produces transparency and builds more stable expectations about state behavior. In this way, institutions can have independent effect on how states behave, thus allowing states to determine aspects of their future rather than having anarchy's grim logic determine everything.

Nothing the Russians did during the U.S. elections in 2016 connects to institutionalism. Indeed, the Russian campaign exposed problems with diplomatic efforts to craft rules, norms, and processes to guide state behavior in cyberspace. In many fora,[20] Russia and other like-minded countries had long emphasized the need for activities in cyberspace to respect the international legal principles of sovereignty and

[17] *See, e.g.*, Julia Gurganus & Eugene Rumer, *Russia's Global Ambitions in Perspective* (Carnegie Endowment for International Peace, Feb. 2019).

[18] President Barack Obama expressed this perspective at the end of 2016, arguing that Russia was a smaller, weaker country. Madeline Conway, *Obama Dismisses Russia as "Weaker Country,"* POLITICO (Dec. 16, 2016).

[19] On institutionalism, *see* STEPHEN D. KRASNER, INTERNATIONAL REGIMES (1983); ROBERT O. KEOHANE, AFTER HEGEMONY: COOPERATION AND DISCORD IN THE WORLD POLITICAL ECONOMY (1984); Robert O. Keohane, *International Institutions: Two Approaches*, 32 INT'L STUD. Q. 379 (1988); Robert O. Keohane & Lisa Martin, *The Promise of Institutional Theory*, 20 INT'L SEC. 39 (1995).

[20] *See, e.g.*, Russia's participation in developing the Shanghai Cooperation Organization's International Code of Conduct for Information Security and negotiating the 2013 and 2015 reports of the UN Group of Governmental Experts on Developments in the Field of Information and Telecommunications in the Context of International Security. Letter dated September 12, 2011, from the Permanent Representatives of China, the Russian Federation, Tajikistan, and Uzbekistan to the United Nations, *International Code of Conduct for Information Security*, U.N. Doc. A/66/359, Sept. 14, 2011; Group of Governmental Experts, *Developments in the Field of Information and Telecommunications in the Context of International Security*, U.N. Doc. A68/156/Add.1, Sept. 9, 2013 (2013 GGE Report); Group of Governmental Experts, *Developments in the Field of Information and Telecommunications in the Context of International Security*, U.N. Doc. A/70/174, July 22, 2015 (2015 GGE Report).

nonintervention.[21] Russia's intervention into the U.S. elections involved the kind of domestic meddling that the Russian government had accused the United States of undertaking.[22] In 2016, Russia took matters into its own hands rather than relying on international cooperation, institutions, and norms.

Russia's accusations that the United States used its cyber power to interfere in Russian politics were not entirely without merit.[23] However, this fact underscores that the foreign election interference of 2016 belonged to a pattern of state behavior that does not reflect strong motivations to create and sustain institutions for better cooperation. Even more of a stretch would be to interpret Russia's meddling as a lawful countermeasure in response to U.S. violations of international law produced by alleged American interference in Russian affairs. Russia denies that it meddled during the 2016 elections,[24] which demonstrates that it has no interest in justifying its behavior through international law.

C. Liberal Theory and Foreign Election Interference

Liberal theory accepts that international relations occur in a condition of anarchy, but it explains what happens in anarchy by focusing on the formation of political preferences within states and how governments express those domestic preferences internationally.[25] The theory tries to understand why state interests and behavior differ when all states face the same structural environment of anarchy. According to liberal theory, explaining such variance requires focusing on the domestic political processes that generate the interests that governments advance diplomatically. This bottom-up, domestic-to-international dynamic determines what happens in the international system. The key participants are nonstate actors, including political parties, corporations, and nongovernmental organizations.

Unlike realism and institutionalism, liberal theory looks inside states at domestic politics and governance regimes in order to understand how nonstate actors produce the political preferences that states pursue internationally. The theory's approach is not confined to democracies but can be applied to understand how political interests

[21] In international law, the principle of sovereignty refers to the supreme authority that each state has over its territory. The principle of nonintervention prohibits a state from interfering with the internal or external affairs of another state in a coercive manner. For how these principles apply in cyberspace, *see* TALLINN MANUAL 2.0 ON THE INTERNATIONAL LAW APPLICABLE TO CYBER OPERATIONS 11–29, 312–327 (Michael N. Schmitt gen. ed., 2017).

[22] Concerned about the role social media played in facilitating protests following elections in 2011, Russia accused the United States of orchestrating the protests in order to achieve regime change. James Lamond, *The Origins of Russia's Broad Political Assault on the United States* (Center for American Progress, Oct. 3, 2018).

[23] Stephen F. Cohen, *The Long History of US-Russian "Meddling,"* THE NATION (Mar. 6, 2019) (describing U.S. efforts to influence Russian politics after Putin came to power in 1999).

[24] Brett Samuels, *Russian Diplomat Says Election Meddling Wasn't Discussed at White House, Contradicting Trump*, THE HILL (Dec. 10, 2019) (noting how Russian officials deny that Russia interfered in the 2016 election).

[25] On liberal theory, *see* Michael W. Doyle, *Liberalism and World Politics*, 80 AM. POL. SCI. REV. 1151 (1986); Michael W. Doyle, Liberalism and World Politics Revisited, in Controversies in International Relations Theory 83 (C.W. Kegley Jr. ed., 1995); Andrew Moravcsik, *Taking Preferences Seriously: A Liberal Theory of International Politics*, 51 INT'L ORG. 513 (1997).

develop within any state. The state remains important because domestic preferences get channeled through state organs into the international realm. However, liberal theory rejects the premise of realism and institutionalism that anarchy determines how states behave in the international system.

Under liberal theory, a state might be interested in how political preferences form in other countries and want to influence the domestic politics of rival or troublesome states, including by affecting election outcomes.[26] The theory also explains why each state opposes foreign interference in its domestic politics, a preference expressed in national laws and the nonintervention principle in international law. Under the theory, foreign interference into domestic politics, including election interference, happens when nonstate actors within the interfering state decide their government should meddle rather than respect the target country's indigenous preferences. Liberal theory appears to explain why states conduct influence operations against adversary states but are intolerant when they are the target of such operations.

Liberal theory would hold that Russia's hack-and-leak and disinformation activities in 2016 reflected the Russian government's implementation of a domestic preference to intervene in U.S. politics. This preference arose, at least in part, from anger at perceived U.S. attempts to influence Russian politics.[27] Certainly, deciphering how Russian political actors formulated a preference to intervene would be difficult, and the story would likely reveal how limited participation in such matters is under Vladimir Putin. But neither of these observations undermines the framework offered by liberal theory.

Problems with liberal theory in terms of Russia's interference in the U.S. elections arise in a different area. As noted previously, the theory explains why states have engaged in efforts to influence the domestic politics of other countries. Such efforts occurred across time regardless of the prevailing communication technologies. Russian meddling in the U.S. elections, and U.S. efforts to influence Russian politics, repeat this pattern. However, this interpretation risks marginalizing why the internet creates different political dynamics on this issue. Previous technologies that states used to influence politics in other countries, such as radio and television, confronted technical and political constraints that limited their effectiveness. These earlier technologies remained sufficiently subject to the state's sovereign control and countermeasures that their use by foreign governments did not, without other interference activities,[28] threaten to transform the functioning of the state's domestic politics. In contrast, the internet facilitates foreign election interference on a scale and at an intensity that make countermeasures difficult and that can, as a result, disrupt domestic political processes.

The historical record contains nothing to rival what happened in the U.S. elections in 2016. Foreign interference, undertaken predominantly through information operations, tainted the legitimacy of an election in the world's most powerful country,

[26] Levin, *supra* note 3, at 89 (arguing that electoral interventions are important given the "realization among IR scholars of the importance of regime type").

[27] David M. Herszenhorn & Ellen Barry, *Putin Contends Clinton Incited Unrest over Vote*, N.Y. Times (Dec. 8, 2011) (reporting on Putin's accusations that the United States incited unrest after Russian elections).

[28] Levin, *supra* note 3, at 96 (noting that states, typically the great powers, used a "variety of costly methods . . . in order to help the preferred side").

was linked to the victory of the candidate preferred by a foreign government, triggered controversies that continue to disrupt U.S. politics, and damaged the image of the United States around the world. Under liberal theory, nonstate actors participate in domestic political processes to determine national preferences that the government pursues in the international system. In 2016, a foreign government gained direct, large-scale access to the politics of another state through globally accessible technologies and exploited nonstate actors in order to achieve unprecedented interference. Simply put, a foreign state participated in the formation of political preferences within another country. This scenario poses a problem for liberal theory. It challenges the proposition that nonstate actors drive the formation of political preferences because a foreign government manipulated domestic political processes in order to produce what it preferred.[29]

D. Constructivism and Foreign Election Interference

The fourth major theory, constructivism, explains international relations by positing that socially constructed ideas determine the nature of anarchy by shaping the behavior of state and nonstate actors.[30] For constructivists, concepts in international relations—anarchy, sovereignty, and power—are socially constructed and have no fixed meaning. Constructivists acknowledge the condition of anarchy, but they argue that it cannot be explained without understanding how intersubjective processes among state and nonstate actors construct and reconstruct the idea of anarchy. In other words, human agency determines what anarchy does rather than anarchy determining what states do. Through the social construction of ideas, state and nonstate actors build structures (e.g., the system of territorial states), institutions, and processes the meanings and purposes of which remain dynamic. This approach rejects the structural determinism of realism and institutionalism, as well as liberalism's emphasis on the state as the central filtering mechanism between international and domestic politics.

In constructivism, the boundaries between the domestic and the international, and between the activities of state and nonstate actors, are permeable and fluid. Information flowing within and across borders forms part of the social construction of ideas, ideologies, and interests. Under this perspective, information operations undertaken by state and/or nonstate actors form part of the intermixing of ideas that drives human political activity. As such, information operations are both a product and producer in the social construction of ideas.

[29] Put differently, Russian interference "influenced the election to produce the sovereign will of the Russian people (or its government) rather than the sovereign will of the American people." Jens David Ohlin, *Did Russian Cyber Interference in the 2016 Election Violate International Law?*, 95(7) TEX. L. REV. 1579, 1596 (2017).

[30] On constructivism, *see* Alexander Went, *Anarchy Is What States Make of It: The Social Construction of Power Politics*, 46 INT'L ORG. 391 (1992); Jeffrey T. Checkel, *The Constructivist Turn in International Relations Theory*, 50 WORLD POL. 324 (1998); Alexander Wendt, Social Theory of International Politics (1999); John G. Ruggie, What Makes the World Hang Together? Neo-Utilitarianism and Constructivist Approaches to International Theory, in The Globalization of World Politics 234 (John Baylis & Steve Smith eds., 2d ed. 2001).

For constructivism, Russian meddling in the U.S. elections is interesting for what the episode communicates about the social construction of the ideas that led Russia to undertake this act. Clearly, the Russians decided that elections in the United States—something indivisible from American political ideology—were not untouchable because of the power and influence that the United States wields. The meddling also suggested that the Russians reconstructed their understanding of the internet, from the notion that the internet constituted a U.S.-led threat to sovereignty to the belief that Russia can control and harness the internet to advance its interests.[31] The shock of what the Russians did also started, or contributed to, debates in the United States and other countries about the internet, the responsibilities of technology companies for online political discourse, and the meaning of principles, such as freedom of expression, in the social media era.[32]

One challenge with constructivism is its lack of guidance on what ideas state and nonstate actors should socially construct and how to ensure that those ideas prevail against competition.[33] The other theories segue into policy prescriptions in ways not as apparent with constructivism. For example, the internet is, to be sure, an idea; but it is also a material capability the use of which by state and nonstate actors can have political consequences. Constructivists acknowledge that it is not "ideas all the way down" and that material power and its distribution matter in anarchy. However, the theory tends toward a relativity of ideas that struggles with answering urgent questions about how ideas mix with, and help manage, the distribution and use of material capabilities among and by state and nonstate actors.[34]

In the context of foreign election interference, the United States is grappling in the post-2016 context with the vulnerabilities its electoral processes have to internet-facilitated disruption by foreign governments or nonstate actors. Russian meddling in 2016 revealed the extent to which the internet provided Russia with the technological capability to disrupt one of the most important ideas and constitutive processes in the American republic. Here, the internet channeled ideas and power. For the United States and other democracies, the most concerning aspects of 2016 center on how Russia exploited the internet to damage the democratic process—and the ideas that inform it. The experience elevated awareness that the internet is less an idea socially constructed to favor democracies than an instrument of material power in the hands of adversaries against which democracies are vulnerable. In this context,

[31] Oleg Matsnev, *Kremlin Moves Towards Control of Internet, Raising Censorship Fears*, N.Y. Times (Apr. 11, 2019). Russia is not the only authoritarian state to assert more control over the internet. *See* Andrea Kendall-Taylor, Erica Frantz, & Joseph Wright, *The Digital Dictators: How Technology Strengthens Autocracy*, Foreign Aff. (Mar./Apr. 2020).

[32] Deanna Paul, *How Fighting Political Disinformation Could Collide with the First Amendment*, Washington Post (Mar. 30, 2019). (observing that "[e]fforts to safeguard against election interference have ignited concerns over First Amendment protections and censorship").

[33] Jack Snyder, *One World, Rival Theories*, Foreign Pol'y (Oct. 26, 2009) (arguing that constructivism is "weak on the material and institutional circumstances necessary to support the emergence of consensus about new values and ideas").

[34] Robert O. Keohane, *Ideas Part-Way Down*, 26 Rev. Int'l Stud. 125, 130 (2000) (arguing that versions of realism and institutionalism recognize "that ideas . . . play a major role in international relations" and seek to explain "how these ideas are mixed with material forces and embedded in enduring institutions, to produce variations in outcomes").

constructivism's focus on the formation and spread of ideas provides neither a persuasive explanation nor prescriptive guidance.

IV. Open-Source Anarchy

As the brief application of the aforementioned international relations theories suggest, the leading theories do not adequately explain the election interference undertaken by Russia in 2016. The Russian assault on the U.S. election has elements of power politics, but the theories that focus most on that issue—realism and institutionalism—did little to illuminate this episode. Liberal theory offered an explanation that captured elements of the Russian meddling, but this episode contained features that liberal theory could not explain. Similarly, with its focus on the social construction of ideas, constructivism did not provide a way to get to grips with how the internet provided Russia with the material capability to exploit nonstate actors in its campaign to influence elections in the United States.

As general theories, the four approaches explain international relations by having an analytical center of gravity—structural anarchy, institutions, formation of domestic political preferences, and the social construction of ideas. The messiness of history tends to show, however, that anarchy changes in terms of the relationship between power and ideas and between the roles played by state and nonstate actors. Across time, anarchy is neither as rigid as realism posits nor as fluid as constructivism holds.

To use a software analogy, anarchy can operate under different source codes, which raises the question of who writes the code. In software, source codes can be closed, proprietary programs or "open source" programs developed by many participants. In the Westphalian tradition, the most powerful states wrote, and maintained suzerainty over, the source code for anarchy.[35] The Westphalian source code is a closed, proprietary code that strong states, or coalitions of influential states, developed and controlled. Through the code, states regulated their interactions and determined how nonstate actors and new ideas would affect international relations.

Under the Westphalian source code, the international system functions like an oligopolistic market in which a small number of states determine the supply and demand for power and ideas. In oligopolistic anarchy, the great powers dominate because they have achieved economies of scale in the production, use, and projection of material capabilities, particularly military and economic power, that render them relatively invulnerable to weaker states and nonstate actors. Instead, great powers worry about each other, and, as realism and institutionalism emphasize, competition in anarchy centers on power and its distribution in the international system. The dynamic filters new ideas, norms, and technologies through the limited, distorting lens of the competition for power among states. The more intense the struggle for power among states becomes, the less space ideas emerging from state or nonstate actors have to affect how anarchy functions.[36] The great powers revise the Westphalian source code to

[35] Mearsheimer, *supra* note 14, at 9 (arguing that "[g]reat powers create and manage orders" when they write "rules to suit their own interests").

[36] *Id.* at 12 (arguing that, in bipolar or multipolar systems, "the political ideology of the great powers is largely irrelevant").

accommodate ideational and technological innovations in ways that serve their interests, including maintenance of the balance of power. Here, the relationship between material power and ideas is inelastic because ideational and technological changes have little impact on how states operate international politics.

In contrast, the concept of open-source anarchy envisions a context in which weaker states and nonstate actors participate in writing the source code for anarchy. With more "coders," the source code can reflect new ideas more than, and differently from, the Westphalian code. Conceptually, power and ideas have a more elastic relationship under open-source anarchy.[37] However, transitioning to a post-Westphalian source code cannot simply involve more ferment in the realm of ideas. Instead, the transition requires reduced competition among the great powers and increased material capabilities for weaker states and nonstate actors to influence international relations. Put differently, open-source anarchy becomes possible when changes in the structure of power, technologies, and ideas lower the barriers to entry for weaker states and nonstate actors to affect how anarchy functions.[38]

The period after the Cold War ended reflects these changes. The Soviet Union's collapse ushered in a "unipolar moment" in which the United States was the unrivaled power. A new phase of globalization began that featured the growing power and influence of nonstate actors, such as multinational enterprises, nongovernmental organizations, transnational criminal organizations, and terrorist groups.[39] Weaker states, once trapped by the bipolar rivalry between the superpowers, emerged to play larger roles by, for example, integrating into global markets, participating in tackling global threats, or attracting attention because of their vulnerabilities to malevolent nonstate actors.[40] This period also witnessed an explosion of ideational activities by weak and strong states as well as nonstate actors.[41]

The most important technological change after the Cold War was the internet and its rapid global adoption. The transformation in the balance of power removed

[37] For example, constructivism emerged when the end of the Cold War challenged the explanatory power of theories, such as realism, that had dominated the field.

[38] The concept of open-source anarchy covers what Mearsheimer calls "agnostic" and "ideological" orders. In agnostic orders, the preponderant power "accepts the heterogeneity that is inherent in political and social life and does not try to micromanage the politics of nearly every country in the world." In an ideological order, the dominant power "seeks to remake the world in its own image." Mearsheimer, *supra* note 14, at 17. In agnostic and ideological orders, ideas have more space and importance in how anarchy functions than in realist orders.

[39] *See, e.g.*, PHILIP BOBBITT, THE SHIELD OF ACHILLES: WAR, PEACE, AND THE COURSE OF HISTORY (2002).

[40] *See, e.g.*, the attention paid to newly industrialized countries and the BRICS countries (Brazil, Russia, India, China, and South Africa) as trade and investment liberalization proceeded. Alyssa Ayres, *How the BRICS Got Here* (Council on Foreign Relations Expert Brief, Aug. 31, 2017). Strategies for addressing global threats, such as pandemics and climate change, required weak and strong states, as well as nonstate actors, to participate. David P. Fidler, *The Challenges of Global Health Governance* (Council on Foreign Relations Report, May 24, 2010); HARRIET BULKELEY & PETER NEWELL, GOVERNING CLIMATE CHANGE (2d. ed., 2015). The "failed" or "fragile" state problem also gained attention after the Cold War. STEWART PATRICK, WEAK LINKS: FRAGILE STATES, GLOBAL THREATS, AND INTERNATIONAL SECURITY (2011).

[41] Other historical moments marked by significant changes in the balance of power also experienced ideational ferment reflected in how states reconstructed the international system, including the periods following the Napoleonic wars (Congress of Europe), World War I (League of Nations, principle of self-determination, restrictions on the use of force), and World War II (United Nations, Bretton Woods, European Coal and Steel Community, human rights).

geopolitical obstacles to the internet's spread and its integration into almost every human activity. In this environment, states and nonstate actors accessed and used the internet without fear that these actions would agitate the balance of power. The internet became a material capability for both state and nonstate actors, a means for new kinds of cooperation, a channel for disseminating and acting on new ideas, and an idea in and of itself.

In this tolerant geopolitical context, the internet proved transformative. State and nonstate actors used it to disrupt established patterns, challenge conventional wisdom, create innovative strategies, produce novel threats, and devise new ways of engaging in business, politics, governance, crime, and terrorism. Similarly, the internet helped make the Westphalian source code inadequate after the Cold War.[42] States increasingly had to respond to multinational corporations exploiting the internet to earn profits, nongovernmental organizations engaging in activism in cyberspace, transnational criminal groups embracing cybercrime, and terrorists spreading extremism online. Countries as diverse as China and India had to navigate between the incentives to use the internet to develop their national capabilities and the fear that Google and Facebook might be more dangerous to their sovereignty than the armed forces of the United States. Thus, the internet features prominently in the transition from Westphalian to open-source anarchy as the post–Cold War system took shape.

This prominence can be seen in the development of different perceptions about the internet. On the one hand, the internet became an ideology. The internet was global, accessible, participatory, open, democratic, and empowering. On the other hand, the internet became a threat. The internet was foreign, manipulated, interventionist, biased, imperial, and dangerous. These perspectives surfaced as state and nonstate actors grappled with writing new source code for anarchy to address the internet and its implications across almost every political, economic, and social activity. Debates, initiatives, and negotiations on internet governance, cybersecurity, the application of international law in cyberspace, and global cyber norms represented attempts to write new source code, as did efforts to have technology companies govern their platforms in light of the malevolent activities taking place, or being promoted, on them. The difficulties experienced in these areas demonstrate that open-source anarchy does not necessarily produce a better environment for diplomacy, regime creation, and global governance.

The concept of open-source anarchy encompasses more than the internet's impact on international relations. Other post–Cold War developments permitted weaker states and nonstate actors to play more prominent roles in how anarchy operated. Concerns expressed about the influence of multinational corporations stemmed from the liberalization of markets that permitted the globalization of production processes, transportation networks, capital mobility, financial services, and neoliberal economic policies. Although the internet facilitated these phenomena, the proximate cause was the collapse of the constraints on international economic activity in place during the Cold War. Worries about terrorists, insurgencies, or transnational

[42] In spreading globally, the internet bypassed the part of the Westphalian source code that states developed, starting in the nineteenth century, to manage communication technologies under an international organization, what became the International Telecommunication Union.

criminal organizations exploiting "failed" or "fragile" states arose from the realization that Cold War spheres of influence had masked vulnerabilities arising from poor state capabilities in many countries. Likewise, open-source anarchy helps explain why the United States—the world's preeminent power in the post–Cold War period—fought armed conflicts against terrorists and insurgents for much of the first two decades of the twenty-first century.

V. Foreign Election Interference in Open-Source Anarchy

Foreign election interference falls within two larger categories—meddling in the politics of another state (which can target more than elections) and conducting information operations against other states (which can target more than domestic politics). States have attempted these activities across time, including during the Cold War and post–Cold War periods. Thus, explaining foreign election interference as something only present in open-source anarchy will not work. Rather, can this concept explain contemporary foreign election interference, particularly Russia's interference with the U.S. elections in 2016, better than the leading theories of international relations?

To recap, open-source anarchy posits that weaker states and nonstate actors can affect anarchy, including by participating in determining the ideas, rules, norms, and processes that guide international relations. For this participation and impact to materialize, the balance of power in the international system needs to exhibit flexibility, and weaker states and nonstate actors must have access to material capabilities that facilitate their ability to affect the dynamics of anarchy. Put another way, a tolerant balance of power provides political space for more states and for nonstate actors to participate in writing the source code for anarchy. The level of participation and impact depends on the material capabilities that weaker states and nonstate actors can access in order to gain a seat at the table and inform the outcome.[43]

What happened in 2016 reflects what the concept of open-source anarchy posits. Although the United States no longer enjoys hegemony,[44] the rise of other powers, such as China and Russia, had not, by 2016, produced the rigid, sensitive balance of power seen in previous eras. Even though weaker, Russia sensed it had an opportunity to challenge the United States without risking punishment based on U.S. perceptions that Russia's actions threatened the balance of power. The election interference also formed part of a strategy to probe how far Russia can increase its power and influence before the United States perceived a threat to the balance of power.[45]

[43] The post–Cold War period witnessed efforts to deny terrorists material capabilities, including economic resources, traditional and nontraditional weapons, and territorial footholds. Actual or potential access to such capabilities gave terrorists the means to affect the behavior of states and nonstate actors. The institutions, rules, and processes created to address terrorism became part of the new source code for anarchy. Terrorists were "at the table," and the threat they posed shaped governance activities. For one perspective on the impact of the terrorist threat, *see* PHILIP BOBBITT, TERROR AND CONSENT: THE WARS FOR THE TWENTY-FIRST CENTURY (2008).

[44] *The End of American Hegemony*, THE ECONOMIST (Dec. 28, 2018).

[45] Dmitri Trenin, *Russia's Comeback Isn't Stopping with Syria*, N.Y. TIMES (Nov. 12, 2019).

Russia exploited the internet in interfering with the U.S. elections, drawing on its cyber competencies to infiltrate nonstate and governmental targets. In its disinformation operations, Russia used nonstate actors as willing (e.g., WikiLeaks) and unwitting (e.g., Facebook, Twitter) proxies. The Russians benefited from the impact that other nonstate actors, located within and outside the United States, achieved by using social media to spread disinformation. Thus, the Russian campaign was parasitical—it depended as much or more on the capabilities of nonstate actors, especially social media companies, to facilitate the spread of information and disinformation than on the Russia's cyber assets, such as the Internet Research Agency. This fact highlights how the internet, as a material capability, increased the importance and impact of nonstate actors, especially social media platforms, in international relations.

The U.S. reaction to the Russian election interference also supports the explanatory power of open-source anarchy. The U.S. response to a foreign government interfering in American elections by exploiting U.S. technology companies has been tepid. The Westphalian source code provided no guidance. The Obama administration did not leverage the superior power of the United States because Russia assaulted a critical component of the American political creed. The Obama administration also did not claim that Russia violated international law.[46]

Further, Russia's meddling in 2016 turned many U.S. arguments about internet governance inside out and upside down. In championing "internet freedom," the United States claimed the right to use the internet to support dissidents in nondemocratic countries and worked to protect U.S. technology companies from international and foreign-government regulation.[47] Russia's campaign gave the United States a taste of its own medicine by using the internet to interfere in U.S. politics. Russia accomplished this objective by turning largely unregulated U.S. technology companies into weapons and deploying them against the U.S. political system. In the process, Russia also exposed the cesspool that U.S. political discourse online has become, marking the 2016 election as unsavory evidence for the superiority of internet freedom.

Matters have not improved for the United States in the aftermath of that election. Controversies have raged without resolution on the cybersecurity of voting systems, the threat posed by online disinformation, whether social media companies should counter disinformation on their platforms, and even whether Russia interfered with the 2016 election. As the 2020 election approaches, warnings abound that the United States remains vulnerable to internet-facilitated election interference by Russia, other countries, and foreign nonstate actors.[48] In open-source anarchy, the United States appears unwilling and unable to address the risks it faces from weaker states and

[46] In announcing responses to Russian election interference, President Obama asserted that Russia violated "established international norms of behavior," rather than claiming that Russia violated international law. The White House, *Statement by the President on Actions in Response to Russian Malicious Cyber Activity and Harassment* (Dec. 29, 2016). *See also* chapter 8, this volume.

[47] Secretary of State Hillary Clinton, *Remarks on Internet Freedom*, Jan. 21, 2010 (stating that the State Department was working in over forty countries to "help individuals silenced by oppressive governments"); Ellen Nakashima, *U.S. Refuses to Back U.N. Treaty, Saying It Endorses Restricting the Internet*, WASHINGTON POST (Dec. 13, 2012) (reporting on U.S. opposition to changes to the International Telecommunication Regulations that could bring private-sector internet companies within the scope of the regulations).

[48] *See, e.g.*, Office of the Director of National Intelligence, *Joint Statement from DOJ, DOD, DHS, DNI, FBI, NSA, and CISA on Ensuring Security of 2020 Elections* (Nov. 5, 2019).

nonstate actors that exploit the internet to damage American politics, ideology, and prestige.

In contrast, Russia has taken steps to protect itself from dangers present in open-source anarchy. First, it has reduced its vulnerabilities to foreign interference by increasing government controls over the internet in Russia.[49] The latest phase in this strategy has been Russia's proof-of-concept tests for a national internet.[50] This strategy weakens the global internet as a material capability that foreign states and nonstate actors could use to interfere in Russia's affairs.[51]

Second, Russia has sought to revive the Westphalian source code for the internet age in order to privilege states, reduce the role of nonstate actors, and challenge the influence of the United States. Russia has promoted "internet sovereignty" to counter the internet freedom agenda, worked to give governments and intergovernmental organizations a greater role in internet governance, and supported the imposition of national controls over the internet. Although Russia has pursued such activities for most of the twenty-first century, its efforts developed more traction in the century's second decade as more countries aligned themselves with Russia as it made progress in regaining great power status.[52]

VI. Open-Source Anarchy and Addressing the Problem of Foreign Election Interference

Russian interference in the U.S. elections in 2016 produced an avalanche of analyses and proposals about how the United States and other democracies should counter foreign election interference. This outpouring reveals the extent to which foreign election interference has not been on the policy agendas of democracies for the past thirty years.[53] Areas of concern include creating deterrence against foreign election interference; integrating opposition to foreign election interference into global cyber norms; improving the cybersecurity of election systems; navigating legal constraints on government regulation of political speech; rethinking the responsibilities of social media companies in managing disinformation on their platforms; and disentangling foreign interference from domestic political activities.

These topics are sufficiently recent that analyzing their success or failure is difficult and, perhaps, premature. However, the prominence of debates about foreign election interference invites some observations. Certainly, the toxic political environment in the United States has limited progress in reducing the vulnerabilities that Russia's

[49] *Russia Internet: Law Introducing Controls Comes into Force*, BBC NEWS (Nov. 1, 2019).

[50] Lily May Newman, *Russia Takes a Big Step Toward Internet Isolation*, WIRED (Jan. 5, 2020).

[51] The Russian strategy resembles China's imposition of controls over the internet and forms part of what Freedom House calls "digital authoritarianism." Freedom House, *Freedom on the Net 2018* (Oct. 2018).

[52] As of this writing, Russia's most recent effort to advance its agenda in cyberspace involved obtaining UN support for developing a new treaty on cybercrime. Joyce Hakmeh & Allison Peters, *A New UN Cybercrime Treaty? The Way Forward for Supporters of an Open, Free, and Secure Internet*, NET POL. (Jan. 13, 2020).

[53] During this period, democracies focused on promoting the spread of democracy rather than protecting their democratic processes from foreign interference. *See, e.g.*, THOMAS CAROTHERS, AIDING DEMOCRACY ABROAD: THE LEARNING CURVE (1999).

interference in 2016 exposed. Warnings that Russia and other foreign actors will interfere with the 2020 elections demonstrate that the United States is not deterring this threat.[54] Efforts to develop global cyber norms against foreign election interference unfold as diplomacy on such norms fragments into competing processes and ideas.[55] Some consensus has formed around strengthening election cybersecurity.[56] However, in the United States, friction on this goal arises from controversies about federalism, the level of federal funding, the right mix of technologies in voting machines, the adequacy of cybersecurity within political parties and campaigns, and whether focusing on election cybersecurity is a disguised attack on the legitimacy of the 2016 election's outcome.

The situation concerning disinformation and foreign election interference is even more fraught with dissension. Under international law, information operations conducted by states do not violate the principles of sovereignty and nonintervention.[57] This interpretation reflects the interest that states have in being able to conduct information operations and the perception among states that such operations have limited impact. What happened in 2016 raised questions about continuing to apply the principle of nonintervention as if the internet has not changed the threat that information operations pose to domestic politics.[58] Initiatives to integrate opposition to foreign election interference into global cyber norms draw attention to this issue,[59] but the norms promoted are nonbinding principles rather than rules of international law.

At the domestic level, the commitment of democracies to freedom of expression creates a conundrum for addressing internet-facilitated information operations by foreign actors.[60] Support for the "marketplace of ideas" means democracies do not extensively regulate what is good or bad information in political discourse. Democracies have laws to prevent foreign involvement in domestic politics and elections, but these laws focus more on money and other things of value than on information flows.[61] The ability of foreign actors to disseminate disinformation online during an election with unprecedented scale and intensity and with disturbing consequences has forced democracies to ponder whether the marketplace of ideas requires more governance. The manner in which social media mixes disinformation from domestic and foreign sources makes crafting regulations that would pass legal muster difficult, especially

[54] Office of the Director of National Intelligence, *Joint Statement*, *supra* note 48.

[55] Alex Grigsby, *The United Nations Doubles Its Workload on Cyber Norms, and Not Everyone Is Pleased*, Net Pol. (Nov. 15, 2018) (discussing UN approval of two negotiating processes on cyber norms arising from competing U.S. and Russian proposals).

[56] *See, e.g.*, *The State and Local Election Cybersecurity Playbook* (Belfer Center for Science and International Affairs, Feb. 2018).

[57] Tallinn Manual 2.0, *supra* note 21, at 26, 318–319. *See also* Ohlin, *supra* note 29, at 1596 (arguing that Russian interference violated the international legal principle of self-determination); and Michael N. Schmitt, *"Virtual Disenfranchisement": Cyber Election Meddling in the Grey Zones of International Law*, 19(1) Chi. J. Int'l L. 30, 66 (2019) (arguing that electoral cyber meddling falls within a "grey zone of international law" that "presents a tempting environment for States that are not fully committed to the international rule of law").

[58] The internet's impact has also stimulated rethinking in other areas, including how international law deals with espionage. *See, e.g.*, Russell Buchan, Cyber Espionage and International Law (2018).

[59] *See, e.g.*, the G7 Charlevoix Commitment on Defending Democracy from Foreign Threats (June 2018); Paris Call for Trust and Security in Cyberspace (Nov. 2018). *See also* chapter 14, this volume.

[60] *See* chapter 13, this volume.

[61] *See* chapter 15, this volume.

in the United States. Hence, interest has turned to whether technology companies should regulate disinformation on their services. This question has also proved controversial, and corporate responses differ, with Twitter banning political advertisements, Google imposing some restrictions on them, and Facebook declaring that it will not police online political speech.[62]

Open-source anarchy provides ways to understand the post-2016 landscape. In open-source anarchy, the balance of power is tolerant of jostling among states for competitive advantage. For the United States to respond to Russia's meddling with deterrence by punishment would require it to perceive the meddling as a threat to the balance of power, requiring the U.S. government to escalate by, for example, undertaking offensive cyber operations that disrupt Russian governmental, political, and economic processes. Whether wise or foolish, the United States did not pursue this course of action. Instead, the focus on election cybersecurity at home attempts to strengthen deterrence by denial. This approach seeks to protect election systems from cyber interference by any malevolent actor—an "all hazards" strategy consistent with the emphasis in open-source anarchy that both states and nonstate actors pose threats.

Open-source anarchy also proves useful in understanding what has happened in the post-2016 context with efforts to create deterrence by norms against foreign election interference. As the Obama administration's response to Russian meddling in 2016 revealed, international legal principles developed for the Westphalian source code, including the principle of nonintervention, proved unhelpful. Instead, the administration claimed that Russia had violated norms on responsible state behavior in cyberspace.[63] This situation proved ironic for two reasons.

First, discussions on the application of international law in cyberspace revealed how much the United States and its allies and Russia, China, and like-minded states talked past each other about the principle of nonintervention. Russia was at the forefront in asserting that the United States violated international law by using its preponderant power in cyberspace—as enhanced by the proliferation of internet-empowered nonstate actors—to intervene in the domestic affairs of other states.[64] This threat included information operations that the United States could undertake against weaker states. The United States disagreed. References to the principle of nonintervention in reports produced by diplomatic negotiations, such as meetings of the UN Group of Governmental Experts, did not mask these differences.[65] When the United States had to confront Russian interference in its elections, the U.S. government could not

[62] Ceclia Kang & Mike Isaac, *Defiant Zuckerberg Says Facebook Won't Police Political Speech*, N.Y. Times (Oct. 17, 2019); Kate Conger, *Twitter Will Ban All Political Ads, C.E.O. Jack Dorsey Says*, N.Y. Times (Oct. 30, 2019); and Daisuke Wakabayashi & Shane Goldmacher, *Google Policy Change Upends Plans for 2020 Campaigns*, N.Y. Times (Nov. 20, 2019).

[63] White House, *Statement by the President*, *supra* note 46.

[64] This concern appears in the Shanghai Cooperation Organization's International Code of Conduct for Information Security, which warned against a state taking "advantage of its dominant position in the sphere of information technology . . . to undermine other countries' right of independent control of ICT products and services, or to threaten other countries' political, economic and social security." International Code of Conduct for Information Security, *supra* note 20.

[65] *See, e.g.*, 2015 GGE Report, *supra* note 20, at para. 28.

appeal to the principle of nonintervention without retreating from its long-standing position.

Second, the appeal to nonbinding norms of responsible state behavior in cyberspace in the wake of Russia's meddling fell flat. Efforts to advance such norms had not, before the 2016 elections, focused on foreign election interference, even in connection with the cyber norm against targeting critical infrastructure.[66] Thus, the Obama administration's claim that a norm against such interference existed raised questions that undermined the assertion. Election interference constitutes a specific type of foreign interference with the politics of another country. The Russian interpretation of how the nonintervention principle applies in cyberspace would, thus, include foreign election interference, making it unlikely that Russia would agree that the norm against such interference is only nonbinding.

In terms of open-source anarchy, these conflicting perspectives arise from how differently the United States and Russia perceived the activities and impact of nonstate actors in cyberspace. The United States wanted a multistakeholder approach where nonstate actors would participate in cyberspace governance and the writing of a post-Westphalian source code for the internet age.[67] Russia sought to reduce the influence of, or exclude, nonstate actors.[68] It believed that such actors used the internet to interfere in Russia's affairs independently or in coordination with the United States. The concept of open-source anarchy can explain why the United States and Russia spent political and diplomatic capital fighting over the role of nonstate actors in cyberspace governance.

Turning to the disinformation component of foreign election interference, open-source anarchy also helps explain what has transpired since 2016. Efforts to assess the Russian disinformation campaign and identify how to combat this type of foreign interference have encountered problems with the role of nonstate actors, especially the social media platforms that state and nonstate actors used to disseminate disinformation. In earlier eras, attempts by foreign governments or nonstate actors to spread disinformation encountered the geographical and technological fragmentation of media markets and the obstacle of editorial oversight of published or broadcast information. In such a context, a foreign government or nonstate actor would have difficulty getting disinformation cheaply, rapidly, and frequently published or broadcast at geographic scale in a timely fashion across multiple communication technologies. The internet has demolished these barriers to the rapid, cheap, frequent, widespread, centralized, and amplified spread of disinformation.

The Russian disinformation operation during the 2016 election was not the first crisis the United States faced with how the internet enables foreign-sourced

[66] For example, the 2015 report of the UN Group of Governmental Experts never addresses elections. *See id.* The United States did not declare its election systems as critical infrastructure until after Russia meddled in the 2016 elections. *See* U.S. Department of Homeland Security, *Statement by Secretary Jeh Johnson on the Designation of Election Infrastructure as a Critical Infrastructure Subsector* (Jan. 6, 2017).

[67] Megan Stifel, *Maintaining U.S. Leadership on Internet Governance* (Council on Foreign Relations Cyber Brief, Feb. 21, 2017).

[68] Julien Nocetti, *Contest and Conquest: Russia and Global Internet Governance*, 91(1) INT'L AFF. 111 (2015).

disinformation to metastasize in alarming ways. In 2014, nations confronted an online offensive by a terrorist group, the so-called Islamic State. This group's information operations unleashed policy frenzy because the Islamic State exposed how easily, cheaply, frequently, widely, effectively, and strategically foreign actors could disseminate disinformation online. States, international organizations, technology companies, and nongovernmental organizations had to cooperate on addressing the security threats that nonstate actors created by spreading disinformation through internet services operated by other nonstate actors—exactly the context open-source anarchy captures. In crafting responses, one particularly difficult problem centered on how social media companies should police their platforms to identify and remove content promoting extremism and violence. In open-source anarchy terms, states needed nonstate actors to mitigate damage being done by disinformation promulgated online by another nonstate actor that was wreaking death, destruction, and havoc across an important region of the international system. Despite all the frantic activity, the United States concluded that the Islamic State's information operations remained sufficiently dangerous that, in 2016, it launched offensive cyber operations to degrade the group's online capabilities.[69]

Like the Islamic State, Russia exploited the advantages that the internet and social media create for spreading disinformation with no meaningful barriers to entry, scale, intensity, and amplification. The Russian activities caused a policy melee as governments, international organizations, companies, political parties, campaigns, and nongovernmental organizations tussled over how to combat foreign disinformation during elections. As happened in responses to the Islamic State, debates expended much time and energy on how social media companies should govern disinformation on their platforms. With responses barely underway as the 2018 election season began, the United States launched offensive cyber operations against a Russian-government target, the Internet Research Agency, in order to disrupt its ability to interfere in the 2018 elections.[70]

The parallels between the Islamic State and Russian examples underscore how the concept of open-source anarchy provides a way to understand how internet-enabled information operations of a weaker state and a nonstate actor affected the domestic and foreign policies of one of the world's most powerful countries. The episodes also reveal the difficulties that the United States has experienced in achieving effective defenses and credible deterrence, with the U.S. government resorting in both cases to offensive cyber operations to disrupt capabilities and preempt anticipated threats.

The difficulties encountered in these incidents highlight how state and nonstate actor use of internet-facilitated interference and disinformation activities connects to balance-of-power considerations. The Islamic State threatened stability in the Middle

[69] David P. Fidler, *Send in the Malware: U.S. Cyber Command Attacks the Islamic State*, Net Pol. (Mar. 9, 2016).

[70] Julian E. Barnes, *Cyber Command Operation Took Down Russian Troll Farm for Midterm Elections*, N.Y. Times (Feb. 26, 2019).

East, creating the need to destroy its military capabilities and roll back its control of territory. The achievement of those objectives explains why the Islamic State's online behavior ceased to be an urgent priority. Similarly, with efforts to create deterrence and strengthen defenses struggling, the United States might need to frame further Russian attempts to interfere in U.S. elections as a threat to the balance of power that requires the United States to escalate its responses. As open-source anarchy posits, the nature of anarchy can change. U.S. linkage of foreign election interference with the balance of power would signal a shift back toward Westphalian anarchy.

VII. Conclusion

As of this writing, the 2020 election in the United States is only months away. Much remains unclear about whether foreign interference will mark the 2020 election as infamously as it did the 2016 elections. The United States does not appear much better prepared to deter or defend against foreign interference, which fuels predictions that Russia, other countries, and nonstate actors will attempt to disrupt the dynamics, taint perceptions, and influence the outcome of the 2020 election.[71] Continued technological developments, such as artificial intelligence and deepfakes, enhance the arsenal of states and nonstate actors interested in election interference in 2020 and beyond.[72] Nor does it help that democracies are on the defensive in ways and at a scale not seen for decades.[73]

This chapter steps back from the immediacy of this challenge in order to think conceptually about foreign election interference past, present, and future. It offers the idea of open-source anarchy to help understand why foreign election interference has become a prominent concern and explain what has happened, and what might happen, with state and nonstate actor behavior on this problem. The concept captures how changes in the structure of material power, technologies, and ideas allowed a weaker state to exploit the capabilities of nonstate actors in order to disrupt elections in the world's foremost democracy, leader in technological innovation, and most powerful nation. Open-source anarchy also illuminates why Russia's interference in the U.S. elections exposed political and technological vulnerabilities that liberal states, individually and collectively, have not yet addressed effectively.

Whatever the merits of open-source anarchy as an idea, stepping back from the urgency of the moment to think conceptually about foreign election interference heightens the moment's urgency. Foreign election interference is not only a pressing issue but also a prism on three decades of geopolitical, ideational, and technological

[71] Adam Goldman et al., *Russia Backs Trump's Re-Election and He Fears Democrats Will Exploit Its Support*, N.Y. Times (Feb. 20, 2020) (reporting that U.S. intelligence officials "warned House lawmakers . . . that Russia was interfering in the 2020 campaign to try to get President Trump re-elected").

[72] Elaine Kamarck, *Malevolent Soft Power, AI, and the Threat to Democracy* (Brookings Report, Nov. 29, 2018); William A. Galston, *Is Seeing Still Believing? The Deepfake Challenge to Truth in Politics* (Brookings Report, Jan. 8, 2020).

[73] *See, e.g.*, Freedom House, *Freedom in the World 2019* (2019) (concluding that "[d]emocracy is in retreat"); Sean Coughlan, *Dissatisfaction with Democracy "at Record High,"* BBC News (Jan. 29, 2020) (reporting on a study that recorded the highest level of dissatisfaction with democracy since the university center began monitoring such views in 1995).

change. The story of the 2016 elections in the United States brings the scale and significance of these changes into focus. Like the fall of the Berlin Wall, this episode marks an inflection point in history with implications beyond coping with foreign election interference. If so, the story of the 2020 elections in the United States will provide more clues about how the source code for a next era of international anarchy will be written and used.

14

Defending Democracies via Cybernorms

Duncan B. Hollis and Jan Neutze

I. Introduction

How can we reduce the number or effectiveness of foreign election interference incidents? To date, most answers have emphasized legal or technical tools. International law regulates nation-states directly. It restricts a state's ability to intervene in the internal affairs of another state (including its electoral processes) while obligating states to observe human rights, regulating their investigation of foreign cases, and authorizing particular consequences when internationally wrongful acts occur.[1] Domestic laws target individuals associated with election interference by criminalizing hacking, identity theft, and fraud. They can require foreign agent registration or create campaign finance regimes that make foreign election interference more difficult.[2] Social media companies can use private contract law to set terms of service and content moderation rules to block offending users or content.[3] On the technical side, voting machines may generate a voter-verified paper audit trail, while social media algorithms can flag or block disinformation and other patterns of potential concern.[4]

Although some progress has been made, for those concerned with election interference these responses are often fragmented and remain (dramatically) inadequate.[5] Rising incidents of foreign election interference encompass a wide array of tools and methods.[6] Yet international law's coverage is contested, if not absent, with respect

[1] For more on international law and foreign election interference, *see* chapters 8–11, this volume. *See also* Jens D. Ohlin, *Did Russian Cyber Interference in the 2016 Election Violate International Law*, 95 Tex. L. Rev. 1579, 1587–1588 (2017).

[2] All of these domestic law tools were on display in Robert Mueller's response to Russian election interference in the 2016 U.S. presidential election. *See* Robert S. Mueller III, Dep't of Justice, Report on the Investigation into Russian Interference in the 2016 Presidential Election, vol. 1, 3–9 (2019).

[3] *See* Kate Klonick, *The New Governors: The People, Rules, and Processes Governing Online Speech*, 131 Harv. L. Rev. 1598, 1630–1631 (2017).

[4] Ian Vandewalker & Lawrence Norden, Securing Elections from Foreign Interference 5 (Brennan Center for Justice, 2017).

[5] *See, e.g.*, International Foundation for Electoral Systems, *Annual Report 2018* 10 (June 10, 2019), *at* https://www.ifes.org/publications/ifes-annual-report-2018 ("Malign actors are increasingly deploying polarizing, technology-fueled disinformation campaigns around the globe.").

[6] We define foreign election interference online to include state and state-sponsored behavior seeking to impact electoral processes, including: (1) physical damage to electoral machinery, (2) theft, manipulation of, or denial of access to, election-related data (e.g., voter registration, votes, vote tallies), and (3) influence operations that seek to impact opinions about elections or the electoral system, including disinformation, propaganda, and doxing of otherwise confidential election-related data. For a definition focused on hacking and disinformation, *see* European Commission for Democracy through Law (Venice Commission), *Joint Report of the Venice Commission and of the Directorate of Information Society and Action Against Crime of*

Duncan B. Hollis and Jan Neutze, *Defending Democracies via Cybernorms* In: *Defending Democracies*. Edited by Duncan B. Hollis and Jens David Ohlin, Oxford University Press (2021).
DOI: 10.1093/oso/9780197556979.003.0015

to some of the most prominent categories of such interference. Domestic laws were not designed for these events, and where they address relevant subjects, jurisdictional constraints limit their effectiveness. Technical solutions face their own array of problems, including: (1) legacy voting equipment designed with security as an afterthought; (2) high barriers for new entrants due to outdated standards and regulations; and (3) a lack of transparency about whether and how social media companies are implementing their own solutions to these threats. Such inadequacies have generated a range of calls for new legal and technical solutions (including several featured in this volume).[7]

This chapter introduces an additional response mechanism for defending democracies: cybernorms. Cybernorms are socially constructed, shared expectations of appropriate behavior for members of a particular community.[8] Social science has established norms' capacity to impact state behavior in other global governance contexts.[9] We believe cybernorms may play a similar role in cyberspace. Our chapter's central claim is that affirmatively constructing international norms tailored to the challenge of online foreign election interference—and building broad multistakeholder support for such norms—are critical tools to positively affect a state's behavior.

For adherents, cybernorms can delineate both "out-of-bounds" behavior vis-à-vis foreign elections or set expectations for assistance or cooperation when such behavior occurs. Just as importantly, cybernorms may positively impact other response efforts; they can complement—rather than compete with—efforts to generate new legal or technical responses. To be clear, we do not claim cybernorms are a salve for all wounds. Indeed, like law and technology, cybernorms' features come with certain "bugs." Rogue actors can ignore their directives, while interpretation and implementation issues persist for those internalizing their contents. Nonetheless, existing gaps and challenges in the current mix of legal and technical responses counsel in favor of bringing cybernorms to the table. Simply put, states and other stakeholders should incorporate cybernorms as part of a broad, multilayered, and multidisciplinary response to the threat of foreign election interference.

Our case for cybernorms is not merely conceptual. Like-minded states and other stakeholders have already begun to embrace the cybernorms project for foreign election interference. On June 9, 2018, the G7 issued the *Charlevoix Commitment on Defending Democracy from Foreign Threats*. Among other things, that instrument contained a commitment by the member states to "[s]trengthen G7 cooperation to prevent, thwart and respond to malign interference by foreign actors aimed at

the Directorate General of Human Rights and the Rule of Law (DGI) on Digital Technologies and Elections (June 20, 2019) para. 113 [hereinafter 2019 Venice Commission Report].

[7] *See, e.g.*, chapters 6, 9, and 15, this volume; *see also* SECURING AMERICAN ELECTIONS: PRESCRIPTIONS FOR ENHANCING THE INTEGRITY AND INDEPENDENCE OF THE 2020 U.S. PRESIDENTIAL ELECTION AND BEYOND (Michael McFaul ed., Stanford University, June 2019); VANDEWALKER & NORDEN, *supra* note 4; Eileen Donahoe, *Protecting Democracy from Online Disinformation Requires Better Algorithms, Not Censorship*, NET POLITICS (Aug. 21, 2017).

[8] *See infra* section III.

[9] *See, e.g.*, Martha Finnemore & Duncan B. Hollis, *Constructing Norms for Global Cybersecurity*, 110 AJIL 425, 427–428 (2016).

undermining the democratic processes and the national interests of a G7 state."[10] Six months later, the French government launched the *Paris Call for Trust and Security in Cyberspace*. Like the Charlevoix Commitment, the Paris Call's signatories endorsed efforts in "Principle 3" to strengthen their "capacity to prevent malign interference by foreign actors aimed at undermining electoral processes through malicious cyber activities."[11] Open to both states and other stakeholders, today the Paris Call has over one thousand signatories, including states, local governments, firms, civil society organizations, and academic institutions.[12]

These are, however, only initial steps toward effective cybernorms. Cybernorms are not simply words on paper; they are dynamic social processes around which community expectations—and behavior—form. As such, they require attention, resources, and effort to develop and disperse within a given community. Without these, efforts to construct new cybernorms for protecting democracies are unlikely to succeed.

Our chapter proceeds in four sections. Section II surveys the prominent mechanisms for combatting foreign election interference today—international law, domestic law, and technical measures—and explains the gaps and challenges each faces. Section III outlines the norm concept. Section IV reviews norms' relative strengths and weaknesses as a tool of global governance for addressing foreign election interference online. Section V uses Paris Call Principle 3 as a case study, assessing its cybernorm potential, including areas in need of further effort or elaboration. We conclude with a call for more attention to the direct and indirect roles cybernorms can play in combating foreign election interference.

II. The Inadequacy of Existing Responses to Foreign Election Interference

The case for cybernorms begins with the current context. International law, domestic laws, and technical solutions each make important contributions to combatting foreign election interference. Yet, each currently faces challenges that limit their capacity to comprise a complete response either individually or collectively. These challenges establish the need for additional regulatory responses like cybernorms.

A. International Law's Incomplete (and Contested) Coverage

There is little question that international law generally applies to cyberspace.[13] As the legal regime governing behavior among states, international law can prohibit, permit,

[10] Charlevoix Commitment on Defending Democracy from Foreign Threats (2018), *at* https://www.mofa.go.jp/files/000373846.pdf [hereinafter Charlevoix Commitment].

[11] Paris Call for Trust and Security in Cyberspace (Nov. 12, 2018), *at* https://pariscall.international/en/call [hereinafter Paris Call].

[12] *The Supporters*, Paris Call for Trust and Security in Cyberspace, *at* https://pariscall.international/en/supporters.

[13] *See* UNGA Res. 73/266, U.N. Doc. A/RES/73/266 (Jan. 2, 2019) ("Confirming the conclusions of the Group of Governmental Experts, in its 2013 and 2015 reports, that international law, and in particular the Charter of the United Nations, is applicable and essential to maintaining peace and stability.");

and require various activities online. International law does not, however, have any rules tailor-made for regulating foreign election interference via cyber activities. As such, international law's application requires an extension of existing treaties and customary law provisions. Some of these rules clearly constrain state behavior: states may not use or threaten force against another state's electoral facilities nor may they intervene in another state's electoral processes.[14] Yet, in most respects, the application of current international law encounters real difficulties in the online context generally, and with respect to elections in particular. Four challenges are worth highlighting: (1) state silence; (2) existential debates; (3) interpretative disputes; and (4) attribution standards.

For starters, international law's relationship to foreign election interference is complicated by the fact that many states remain silent about how they understand international law applies to cyberspace. A few states have recently offered statements on the subject.[15] But specific invocations of international law in the context of online election-related activity remain elusive. For example, when U.S. President Barack Obama called out Russia for interference in the 2016 presidential election, he did not characterize it as a violation of international law; rather, he highlighted "efforts to undermine established international norms of behavior, and interfere with democratic

accord ASEAN–United States Leaders' Statement on Cybersecurity Cooperation (Nov. 18, 2018), *at* https://asean.org/storage/2018/11/ASEAN-US-Leaders-Statement-on-Cybersecurity-Cooperation-Final.pdf; EU Statement–United Nations 1st Committee, Thematic Discussion on Other Disarmament Measures and International Security (Oct. 26, 2018), *at* https://eeas.europa.eu/delegations/un-new-york/52894/eu-statement---united-nations-1st-committee-thematic-discussion-other-disarmament-measures-and_en.

[14] *See, e.g.*, U.N. Charter, art. 2(4). States and other stakeholders widely agree that the prohibition applies to cyber activities. *See* Group of Governmental Experts on Developments in the Field of Information and Telecommunications in the Context of International Security, U.N. Doc. A/70/174 (July 22, 2015) para. 26 [hereinafter 2015 GGE]; Group of Governmental Experts on Developments in the Field of Information and Telecommunications in the Context of International Security, U.N. Doc. A/68/98 (June 24, 2013) para. 19 [hereinafter 2013 GGE]. The precise threshold at which a use of force occurs in cyberspace is unresolved. It would seem likely to include cyber operations that generate physical damage to, say, a voting location. But it is unclear if it would include damage just to data (e.g., online voting records), and it is unlikely to cover influence operations or disinformation campaigns. As such, this rule may have more theoretical than practical value in the electoral context.

[15] *See, e.g.*, Ministère des Armées, *Droit international appliqué aux operations dans le cyberespace* (Sept. 9, 2019), *at* https://www.defense.gouv.fr/salle-de-presse/communiques/communiques-du-ministere-des-armees/communique_la-france-s-engage-a-promouvoir-un-cyberespace-stable-fonde-sur-la-confiance-et-le-respect-du-droit-international (France); Australian Mission to the United Nations, Australian Paper—Open Ended Working Group on Developments in the Field of Information and Telecommunications in the context of International Security (Sept. 2019), *at* https://s3.amazonaws.com/unoda-web/wp-content/uploads/2019/09/fin-australian-oewg-national-paper-Sept-2019.pdf (Australia); Kersti Kaljulaid, President of Estonia, Speech at the opening of CyCon 2019 (May 29, 2019), *at* https://www.president.ee/en/official-duties/speeches/15241-president-of-the-republic-at-the-opening-of-cycon-2019/index.html (Estonia); Jeremy Wright, QC, MP, *Cyber and International Law in the 21st Century* (May 23, 2018), *at* https://www.gov.uk/government/speeches/cyber-and-international-law-in-the-21st-century (United Kingdom); Brian Egan, *Remarks on International Law and Stability in Cyberspace*, Berkeley Law School (Nov. 10, 2016), *at* https://www.justsecurity.org/wp-content/uploads/2016/11/Brian-J.-Egan-International-Law-and-Stability-in-Cyberspace-Berkeley-Nov-2016.pdf (United States); Harold Koh, *International Law in Cyberspace*, 54 Harv. Int'l L.J. 1, 7 (2012) (United States). A number of states (e.g., Germany, the Netherlands) have also articulated views on how international law applies in government reports to their respective parliaments.

governance."[16] Such silence creates significant ambiguities about what acts states may *legally* pursue vis-à-vis foreign elections. In 2018, the UN International Law Commission concluded that a "[f]ailure to react over time to a practice may serve as evidence of acceptance as law (opinio juris)."[17] Here, there was a reaction, which might be enough to deny a claim that Russia's acts were lawful. On the other hand, the lack of legal rhetoric complicates that conclusion; it might suggest that the United States regarded the behavior as unfriendly, but not unlawful.[18]

Second, when states do discuss their views on how international law applies online, there are a number of "existential" disagreements—competing claims that a particular international legal rule or regime is entirely included/excluded from cyberspace.[19] In the UN context, for example, a number of states have questioned whether international humanitarian law, the right of self-defense, and the right to take countermeasures "exist" with respect to online activity.[20] At least one other state has also questioned if cyberspace has a duty of due diligence (requiring a state to respond to activities that it knows, or reasonably should know, originated in its territory or areas under its control that violate the right(s) of another state).[21]

Taking one or more of these legal regimes off the table would significantly impact international law's capacity to regulate how states interact with foreign electoral processes. If due diligence exists in cyberspace, it affords victims of foreign election interference further protections, imposing a duty on other states to ensure their networks and systems are not the source of malicious cyber activity (and to halt it if they are). Without it, victim states must depend on political will, while other states might be incentivized to use third-state networks as platforms for hacking foreign election targets (e.g., campaigns, voter rolls) or influence operations. The availability of

[16] White House Press Release, *Presidential Statement on Actions in Response to Russian Malicious Cyber Activity and Harassment* (Dec. 29, 2016), *at* https://obamawhitehouse.archives.gov/the-press-office/2016/12/29/statement-president-actions-response-russian-malicious-cyber-activity.

[17] *See* ILC, *Draft Conclusions on Identification of Customary International Law*, U.N. Doc. A/CN.4/L.908 (2018) (Conclusion 10(3): "Failure to react over time to a practice may serve as evidence of acceptance as law (*opinio juris*), provided that States were in a position to react and the circumstances called for some reaction"). Note, some states objected to this ILC conclusion so its status as an accurate reflection of the law remains indeterminate.

[18] *See, e.g.*, Barrie Sander, *Democracy Under the Influence: Paradigms of State Responsibility for Cyber Influence Operations on Elections*, 18 Chinese J. Int'l L. 1, 53 (2019). For more on how accusations construct international law, *see* Martha Finnemore & Duncan B. Hollis, *Beyond Naming and Shaming: Accusations and International Law in Global Cybersecurity*, 33 EJIL (forthcoming 2020).

[19] On existential arguments in international law, *see* Duncan B. Hollis, The Existential Function of Interpretation in International Law, in Interpretation in International Law 78–79 (A. Bianchi et al. eds., 2015).

[20] Arun Mohan Sukumar, *The UN GGE Failed. Is International Law in Cyberspace Doomed as Well?*, Lawfare (July 4, 2017); Michael Schmitt & Liis Vihul, *International Cyber Law Politicized: The UN GGE's Failure to Advance Cyber Norms*, Just Security (June 30, 2017).

[21] Thus, the idea of due diligence was framed in aspirational terms in the 2015 GGE Report. 2015 GGE Report, *supra* note 14, para. 13. In contrast, states like France and the Netherlands have labeled due diligence an international legal rule that requires a state to act against cyber activities violating the international legal rights of third states. *See, e.g.*, Ministère des Armées, *supra* note 15; Letter from Minister of Foreign Affairs to President of the House of Representatives on the international legal order in cyberspace, app. 1 (July 5, 2019), *at* https://www.government.nl/documents/parliamentary-documents/2019/09/26/letter-to-the-parliament-on-the-international-legal-order-in-cyberspace [hereinafter July 2019 Dutch Letter]. On the duty of due diligence generally, *see Corfu Channel Case; Assessment of Compensation* (United Kingdom v. Albania) [1949] I.C.J. Rep. para. 22 (Apr. 9).

countermeasures (otherwise unlawful acts permitted when done in response to some prior, unlawful act) has similar significance for international law's capacity to deter unlawful election interference activities by foreign states.[22]

Third, even where states accept that a particular international legal regime applies in cyberspace, substantial interpretative questions restrain its ability to effectively regulate foreign election interference online.[23] For example, there is widespread agreement on a duty of nonintervention in international law[24] that is applicable to cyberspace.[25] As Rule 66 of the *Tallinn Manual 2.0* states it: "A State may not intervene, including by cyber means, in the internal or external affairs of another State."[26] A state's "electoral processes" should easily qualify as part of a state's internal affairs (also called the *domaine réservé*). But it is not clear just how many activities targeting an election qualify as a prohibited "intervention." International law defines intervention as "coercion," requiring activity that would deprive the victim state of its freedom of choice, forcing it to act (or not act) in specific ways.[27] The duty of nonintervention does not cover acts of "persuasion, criticism, public diplomacy, propaganda."[28] Thus, it will only prohibit foreign election interference activities deemed coercive (e.g., manipulating vote totals) but is unlikely to cover influence operations on social media or elsewhere that do not force individuals (let alone a state) to a particular course of (in)action.

Even broader interpretative questions loom over the concept of sovereignty, a core architectural feature of the international legal order.[29] Sovereignty serves as a foundational principle for some of the international legal rules already mentioned (e.g.,

[22] If countermeasures are available in response to internationally wrongful acts in cyberspace, international law conditions their use on a variety of preconditions and restrictions. They must be proportionate to the original internationally wrongful act; they should be reversible if possible; they may not affect fundamental human rights; they must not harm third parties; and the state engaging them should notify the targeted state that they are doing so except in "urgent" cases. *See* Draft Articles on the Responsibility of States for Internationally Wrongful Acts with Commentaries [2001] YBILC, vol. II (2), U.N. Doc. A/56/10, as corrected, arts. 49–54.

[23] Human rights are a paradigmatic example. States appear comfortable with the mantra that "the same rights that people have offline must also be protected online, including the right to privacy." U.N.G.A. Res. 68/167, U.N. Doc. A/Res/68/167 para. 3 (Jan. 21, 2014). Yet, precisely how states must guarantee freedom of speech or privacy online remain open questions, especially when it comes to a state's obligation to respect the human rights of foreign nationals outside its territory. *See, e.g.*, Al-Skeini & Others v. United Kingdom, App. No. 55721/07 (ECtHR, July 7, 2011) para. 142; Bankovic & Others v. Belgium and Others, App. No. 52207/99 (ECtHR, Dec. 12, 2001) para. 80; Coard et al. v. United States, IACommHR, Case 10.951, Rep. No. 109/99 (Sept. 29, 1999); Ryan Goodman, *UN Human Rights Committee Says ICCPR Applies to Extraterritorial Surveillance: But Is That So Novel?*, Just Security (Mar. 27, 2014).

[24] *See, e.g.*, *Case Concerning Armed Activities in the Territory of the Congo* (Democratic Republic of the Congo v. Uganda) (Jurisdiction and Admissibility) [2006] I.C.J. Rep. 6, [46]–[48]; *Military and Paramilitary Activities in and against Nicaragua* (Nicaragua v. United States) [1986] I.C.J. Rep. 14, [205]; Declaration on Principles of International Law concerning Friendly Relations & Co-operation among States, U.N.G.A. Res. 2625 (XXV), U.N. Doc. A/RES/25/2625 (Oct. 23, 1970).

[25] 2015 GGE Report, *supra* note 14, para. 26; 2013 GGE Report, *supra* note 14, para. 20.

[26] *See* Tallinn Manual 2.0 on the International Law Applicable to Cyber Operations 312 (Michael Schmitt ed., NATO CCD COE, 2017) [hereinafter Tallinn 2.0].

[27] *Nicaragua*, *supra* note 24, para. 205 (coercion "defines, and indeed forms the very essence of the prohibited intervention.").

[28] Tallinn 2.0, *supra* note 26, at 318–319.

[29] *Island of Palmas* (Netherlands v. United States of America), 2 R.I.A.A. 829, 838 (1928) ("Sovereignty in the relations between States signifies independence. Independence in regard to the portion of the globe is the right to exercise therein, to the exclusion of any other State, the functions of a State.").

the prohibition on the use of force, the duty of nonintervention). In lieu of a background principle, in certain contexts, sovereignty operates as a separate rule (e.g., a foreign aircraft entering another state's airspace without permission violates its sovereignty).[30] It is not clear, however, whether sovereignty operates as a rule in cyberspace. In 2018, the U.K. Attorney General took the view that sovereignty was a principle that informed other rules, not a rule of international law itself, a position subsequently echoed (at least in part) by the General Counsel of the U.S. Department of Defense.[31] In contrast, the French and Dutch governments have both labeled sovereignty as a stand-alone rule.[32]

Whether sovereignty is a rule or not has significant implications for foreign election interference since so much of the activity witnessed (e.g., doxing campaigns, influence operations) would not violate either the prohibition on the use of force or the duty of nonintervention. Sovereignty's meaning will also impact other potential international legal rules. Any due diligence obligation would significantly expand if states had to police against sovereignty violations via their networks (as opposed to just prohibited interventions). Similarly, countermeasures would become more widely available if they could be employed in response to sovereignty violations.[33]

Of course, even for those who regard sovereignty as a rule, significant questions remain as to which operations violate it. Sovereignty appears to protect all infrastructure within a state, both public and private.[34] But what impacts trigger the rule remains open for debate. The *Tallinn Manual 2.0* suggests an operation might violate another state's sovereignty if (1) the foreign actor's behavior has physical consequences within the victim state (e.g., causing a loss of functionality to infrastructure where some physical components must be repaired/replaced); or (2) where the

[30] *See, e.g.*, Michael N. Schmitt & Liis Vihul, *Respect for Sovereignty in Cyberspace*, 95 TEX. L. REV. 1639, 1640 (2017).

[31] *See, e.g.*, Wright, *supra* note 15 ("Some have sought to argue for the existence of a cyber-specific rule of a 'violation of territorial sovereignty' . . . Sovereignty is of course fundamental to the international rules-based system. But I am not persuaded that we can currently extrapolate from that general principle a specific rule or additional prohibition for cyber activity beyond that of a prohibited intervention. The UK Government's position is therefore that there is no such rule as a matter of current international law."); Paul C. Ney, *DOD General Counsel Remarks at U.S. Cyber Command Legal Conference* (Mar. 2, 2020), *at* https://www.defense.gov/Newsroom/Speeches/Speech/Article/2099378/dod-general-counsel-remarks-at-us-cyber-command-legal-conference/("[f]or cyber operations that would not constitute a prohibited intervention or use-of-force [i.e., those that might be covered by a rule of sovereignty], the Department believes there is not sufficiently widespread and consistent State practice resulting from a sense of legal obligation to conclude that customary international law generally prohibits such non-consensual cyber operations in another State's territory."); *see also* Gary Corn, *Tallinn Manual 2.0—Advancing the Conversation*, JUST SECURITY (Feb. 15, 2017) (lawyer for U.S. Cyber Command, writing in a personal capacity, contests sovereignty as a rule).

[32] *See* Ministère des Armées, *supra* note 15; July 2019 Dutch Letter, *supra* note 21, app. (Netherlands "believes that respect for the sovereignty of other countries is an obligation in its own right, the violation of which may in turn constitute an internationally wrongful act."). These views accord with the *Tallinn Manual*. *See* TALLINN MANUAL 2.0, *supra* note 26, Rule 4 ("A State must not conduct cyber operations that violate the sovereignty of another State.").

[33] In addition to countermeasures, all states may respond to election interference with retorsions—unfriendly but lawful acts (i.e., withdrawing financial assistance a state was never legally obligated to provide; restricting visas; declaring diplomats *persona non grata*, etc.).

[34] TALLINN MANUAL 2.0, *supra* note 26, at 18 ("the principle of sovereignty encompasses cyber infrastructure located in a State's territory irrespective of whether it is governmental or private cyberinfrastructure").

foreign activity "usurps … inherently governmental functions."[35] As with the duty of nonintervention's *domaine réservé*, electoral processes are likely to qualify as inherent governmental functions. The question is what foreign activity qualifies as usurpation. Usurpation might cover attempts to supplant actual election results with results designed by a foreign actor, but it is less clear if sovereignty is implicated by campaign-related doxing efforts, disinformation, or undisclosed state-sponsored advertisements in social media.

Fourth and finally, the question of attribution looms large. Attribution requires knowing who did what in cyberspace. Technically, this remains difficult, especially on short time horizons. Legally, international law generally only regulates behavior attributable to states.[36] An act of a government or any of its agencies may be attributed to a state even if the state agent acted without domestic legal authority. Acts by nongovernmental actors, however, are usually not attributable to a state unless the state exercised control over that actor. The amount of control required may vary depending on the context, with the International Court of Justice (ICJ) suggesting a standard of "effective control" (i.e., acting under the instructions, direction, or control of a state).[37] Not all state support for nonstate actor behavior qualifies as control; simply funding the nonstate actor, for example, is not usually enough. This raises significant challenges for international law's operation vis-à-vis electoral interference. For example, sophisticated states aware of international law's thresholds may facilitate nonstate actor behavior without "controlling" it to achieve some election interference without triggering international legal restrictions (or consequences).

To be clear, international law applies in cyberspace and does so with respect to a state's electoral processes. Thus at least some foreign election interference activity online is currently (and obviously) unlawful. Yet the patchwork of existential and interpretative disputes, combined with the challenges of state silence and attribution, means that even if international law applies, it fails to do so effectively. As such, it is not surprising to see calls to adjust the law. Projects at the United Nations and the Organization of American States (OAS) seek greater transparency on how states understand international law's application.[38] States have proposed new contours for

[35] *Id.*, at 17–18, 21–22. Debates persist, however, whether sovereignty violations can occur for activities impacting functionality temporarily (i.e., without requiring equipment replacement) or where the effects are cognitive rather than kinetic. *Id.* The *Tallinn Manual*'s Independent Group of Experts agreed that "in addition to physical damage, the remote causation of loss of functionality in cyber infrastructure located in another State sometimes constitutes a violation of sovereignty, although no consensus could be achieved as to the precise threshold at which this is so." *Id.* at 20–21. Moreover, "no consensus could be achieved as to whether, and if so, when, a cyber operation that results in neither physical damage nor the loss of functionality amounts to a violation of sovereignty" including operations "causing cyber infrastructure or programs to operate differently." *Id.* at 21. Thus, it's not clear if changing data in a voting system or corrupting data in an electronic pollbook would satisfy the *Tallinn Manual*'s first, damage-based standard for violating sovereignty, even as those activities would likely interfere with governmental functions (thus satisfying its second basis for a sovereignty violation).

[36] It also regulates other subjects of international law, including international organizations, and, in certain egregious cases (e.g., international criminal law), individuals.

[37] *See, e.g.*, *Nicaragua*, *supra* note 24, at 64–65; *compare* Prosecutor v. Dusko Tadic aka "Dule" (Judgment) ICTY, No IT-94-1-A (July 15, 1999) [131], [145] (test is "overall control").

[38] *See, e.g.*, U.N.G.A. Res. 73/266, U.N. Doc. A/RES/73/266 (Dec. 22, 2018) (authorizing a new Group of Governmental Experts on information security to examine how international law applies to the use of information and communications technologies, including an annex containing "national contributions of participating governmental experts on the subject of how international law applies"); Duncan B. Hollis,

existing doctrines (e.g., Estonia's call for permitting "collective" countermeasures).[39] Scholars have sought to adjust the existing law (i.e., redefining the meaning and need for coercion in interventions) or repurpose old principles (e.g., Jens Ohlin's suggestion that self-determination might protect democracies).[40]

International law, however, remains a creature of state consent. Treaties only bind states parties. Custom requires a general and consistent practice of states done out of a sense of legal obligation.[41] This means that these new proposals may be difficult to enact, while any successes will take time. Today, international law offers no more than a partial response to the threat of foreign election interference online. Pending a successful resolution of its current ambiguities and disagreements, the effective defense of democracies must also look to other response mechanisms.

B. The Reach—and Limits—of Domestic Law in Defending Democracies

Whereas international law comprises the law among nation-states, domestic laws involve a state's internal exercise of sovereign authority. Each state has its own domestic law, which regulates people, things, and events within or otherwise connected to that state. States can exercise this authority in manifold ways relevant to foreign election interference. Criminal and administrative laws allow states to target individuals accountable for such interference even if they are foreign nationals operating outside the state's territory.[42] In the United States, for example, it is clearly illegal for any "foreign national" to directly or indirectly make any contribution "in connection with a Federal, State, or local election."[43] Most states also have "cybercrime" laws that outlaw unauthorized access to a computer system, including efforts to hack computer systems

Rapporteur, *Fifth Report: Improving Transparency—International Law and State Cyber Operation*, 96th Reg. Sess., Organization of American States, CJI/doc. 615/20 rev. 1 (July 17, 2020) (reporting on questionnaire submitted to member states on how international law applies to state cyber operations).

[39] *See* Kaljulaid, *supra* note 15. Other states (notably, France) have suggested collective countermeasures are not consistent with existing international law. *See* Ministère des Armées, *supra* note 15.

[40] *See, e.g.*, Michael N. Schmitt, *"Virtual Disenfranchisement": Cyber Election Meddling in the Grey Zones of International Law*, 19 Chi. J. Int'l L. 30 (2018); Nicholas Tsagourias, *Electoral Cyber Interference, Self-Determination and the Principle of Non-Intervention in Cyberspace*, EJIL: Talk! (Aug. 26, 2019). On self-determination, *see* Ohlin, *supra* note 1, at 1580.

[41] *ILC Draft conclusions on customary international law*, *supra* note 17, Conclusion 2.

[42] International law provides that a state can (but is not required to) prescribe criminal jurisdiction based on behavior in its territory, by its nationals, or threatening the state's own security or integrity. The last basis is known as the "protective principle" and should permit states to criminalize behavior that seeks to negatively impact its electoral processes even if performed by foreign nationals outside the state's own territory. *See* Iain Cameron, International Criminal Jurisdiction, Protective Principle, in Max Planck Encyclopedia of Public International Law (R. Wolfrum ed., July 2007). A separate basis of jurisdiction known as the "effects doctrine" may also justify extraterritorial criminal laws where acts occur outside the state's territory but have effects within it. *See generally* Restatement (Fourth) of the Foreign Relations Law of the United States § 409 (American Law Institute, 2018).

[43] *See* 52 U.S.C. § 30121.

relating to a campaign or an election, whether to manipulate the data on those systems or later dox it in some way.[44]

Other domestic laws may reach various aspects of election interference operations. The U.S. Justice Department, for example, indicted individuals and entities involved in Russia's social media campaign in the 2016 presidential election using laws prohibiting identity theft and participation in a conspiracy to defraud the United States by undermining the work of federal agencies charged with regulating foreign influence in U.S. elections.[45] The Foreign Agent Registration Act makes it illegal to act as an agent of a foreign principal (including a foreign state) in certain political activities in the United States without prior registration with the U.S. Attorney General.[46]

In lieu of targeting bad actors, states can also seek to regulate intermediaries, restricting social media companies, for example, from hosting disinformation. In 2018, France enacted two anti-fake news laws to rein in false information during election campaigns following allegations of Russian meddling in the French 2017 presidential vote.[47] Alternatively, a state may use its domestic laws to regulate the targets of election interference. States can, for example, designate elections infrastructure as national critical infrastructure[48] and develop (voluntary or mandatory) minimum standards for the technical infrastructure used in elections.[49] They can also regulate how campaigns operate, including campaign finance laws and regulations.[50]

In addition to their criminal laws, domestic laws may regulate private relationships in ways that can defend democracies. Victims can invoke domestic tort laws such as the invasion of privacy to respond to the doxing of campaign communications.[51]

[44] *See, e.g.*, Computer Fraud and Abuse Act (CFAA), 18 U.S.C.A. § 1030 (2012) (United States); Computer Misuse Act 1990, ch. 18, §§ 5(2)(b), (3)(b) (United Kingdom); Penal Code § 202a(1) (Germany); Information Technology Act 2008 § 43(a) (India); Cybercrime Act 2001, Act No. 161 of 2001 (Australia).

[45] Department of Justice Press Release, *Grand Jury Indicts 12 Russian Intelligence Officers for Hacking Offenses Related to the 2016 Election* (July 13, 2018), *at* https://www.justice.gov/opa/pr/grand-jury-indicts-12-russian-intelligence-officers-hacking-offenses-related-2016-election; United States v. Internet Research Agency et al., No. 18-cr-32 (D.D.C.); *see also* 18 U.S.C. § 371 (1994); 18 U.S.C. § 1028A(c) (2004); 18 U.S.C. § 1030 (2008); 18 U.S.C. § 3559(g)(1) (2006).

[46] 22 U.S.C. §§ 611–621; *see also* 18 U.S.C. § 951 (making it illegal to act in the United States as an agent of a foreign government without providing notice to the attorney general). With the exception of Paul Manafort, however, none of the Russian election interference in the United States in 2016 violated these statutes. MUELLER, *supra* note 2, at 183.

[47] James McAuley, *France Weighs a Law to Rein in "Fake News," Raising Fears for Freedom of Speech*, WASHINGTON POST (Jan. 10, 2018).

[48] *See* Press Release, Dep't Homeland Sec., *Statement by Secretary Jeh Johnson on the Designation of Election Infrastructure as a Critical Infrastructure Subsector* (Jan. 6, 2017), *at* https://www.dhs.gov/news/2017/01/06/statement-secretary-johnson-designation-election-infrastructure-critical; *see also* Allaire M. Monticollo, *Protecting America's Elections from Foreign Tampering: Realizing the Benefits of Classifying Election Infrastructure as Critical Infrastructure under the United States Code*, 51 U. RICH. L. REV. 1239, 1240–1241 (2017).

[49] *See* U.S. Elections Assistance Commission (EAC), *Voluntary Voting System Guidelines, at* https://www.eac.gov/voting-equipment/voluntary-voting-system-guidelines.

[50] *See, e.g.*, 52 U.S.C. § 30101 *et seq.* (U.S. campaign finance laws); Political Funds Control Act, Act No. 194 of 1948, amended by Act No. 69 of 2014 (Japan); Representation of the People Act 1983, c. 2, § 75 (Eng.); Canada Elections Act, S.C. 2000, c. 9 (Can.).

[51] Charlie Savage, *Trump Campaign Is Sued Over Leaked Emails Linked to Russians*, N.Y. TIMES (July 12, 2017) (invasion of privacy lawsuit filed against Trump campaign for alleged involvement in WikiLeaks doxing of DNC campaign data).

Separately, contract law provides social media companies an important lever for ensuring that users honor their terms of service.[52]

Taken together, domestic laws provide a first-order response mechanism to online foreign election interference. They benefit, moreover, from several features absent in international law. Domestic laws are (usually) created via well-defined processes that do not require the specific consent or practice of the law's subjects the way international law does. Nor is the existence and interpretation of domestic law subject to the levels of ambiguity or contestation evident in international law. Constitutional structures delineate what laws exist (whether by statute, regulation, or judicial decision), and there are well-tried legislative and judicial processes for ironing out interpretative ambiguities.

For all these features, domestic law has its own suite of challenges that preclude it from operating as a "silver bullet" solution to online foreign election interference. Critically, domestic laws regulate individuals and entities, not states or governments. International law accords "sovereign immunity" to every state, protecting it from both the criminal and civil jurisdiction of other states' courts.[53] Sovereign immunity provides a significant barrier to using domestic laws to regulate foreign election interference by states. The U.S. Justice Department, for example, has limited its indictments concerning Russian electoral interference to individuals and entities, not the Russian government nor its head, Vladimir Putin.[54] And Russia actually invoked sovereign immunity in the Democratic National Committee's (DNC's) civil suit alleging interference in its 2016 campaign communications.[55]

Holding foreign individuals and entities accountable for election interference online is further complicated by limits on states' enforcement jurisdiction. As the ICJ noted in its famous *Lotus* decision, "the first and foremost restriction imposed by international law upon a State is that—failing the existence of a permissive rule to the contrary—it may not exercise its power in any form in the territory of another State."[56] In short, states cannot enforce their domestic laws abroad absent the permission or cooperation of the state where the enforcement action is sought. Thus, even as states like the United States indict foreign individuals for online election interference

[52] *See, e.g.*, Klonick, *supra* note 3, at 1632–1633. For an example of election-related terms of service, *see* Twitter, *Civic Integrity Policy—Overview* (May 2020), *at* https://help.twitter.com/en/rules-and-policies/election-integrity-policy.

[53] Many states have restricted sovereign immunity for certain types of state conduct (e.g., commercial activities, terrorist acts), but none of these exceptions appear well-suited to election interference. For example, the United States denies sovereign immunity when a state is engaged in a noncommercial tort, but U.S. courts have required that all the tortious conduct occur within U.S. territory, a criterion easily avoided in the context of foreign election-interference. *See* Foreign Sovereign Immunities Act, 28 U.S.C. §§ 1603–1605 (1976); Democratic Nat'l Comm. v. Russian Fed'n, 392 F. Supp. 3d 410, 427 (S.D.N.Y. 2019) (citing Doe v. Fed. Democratic Republic of Ethiopia, 851 F.3d 7, 10 (D.C. Cir. 2017)). In addition to sovereign immunity, status-based immunities for heads of state and foreign officials may also limit the ability of domestic law to regulate foreign state activity directly (although these immunities are harder to apply to non-state actor behavior).

[54] Mueller, *supra* note 2, at 5.

[55] Ingrid Wuerth, *Russia Asserts Immunity in the DNC Case*, Lawfare (Nov. 16, 2018). Nor was this an exceptional situation. *See* Rebecca Crootof, *International Cybertorts: Expanding State Accountability in Cyberspace*, 103 Cornell L. Rev. 565, 592 n.118 (2018) (domestic tort law usually grants immunity to sovereign states).

[56] *The Case of the S.S. "Lotus"* (France v. Turkey), 1927 P.C.I.J. (Ser. A) No. 10, at 18–19.

activities, they have not been able to detain and prosecute those individuals.[57] This inability to enforce domestic laws marks its most visible weakness as a tool for defending democracies.

States have devised transnational cooperation mechanisms to deal with these enforcement problems, including mutual legal assistance treaties (MLATs) and extradition treaties. Relying on such treaties, however, creates a patchwork of enforcement options. Not all states have made the requisite bilateral commitments.[58] And where they do exist, they often have limited value. The required MLAT formalities mean that requested assistance can take months, if not years, to arrive; a timeline at odds with the highly dynamic nature of online malicious cyber behavior.[59] Moreover, MLATs and extradition treaties contain various exceptions by which the requested state can decline to cooperate; such exceptions have played a large role, for example, in limiting U.S.-Russian cooperation under their MLAT.[60]

It would be a mistake, however, to denounce these and other restrictions on domestic law enforcement cooperation absolutely. Domestic laws may constitute an important response to the threat of online foreign election interference, but they can also facilitate authoritarian control. Under the guise of protecting state security, some states have domestic laws that regulate speech or invade privacy inconsistent with what other states (and international law) view as fundamental human rights.[61] Simply put, domestic laws on election-related speech can mask repressive behavior. As a response tool, therefore, domestic laws require careful balancing of a state's security interests with the privacy and free expression rights of its citizens.[62]

Yet, even where domestic laws are carefully calibrated (and manage to avoid or overcome issues of immunity, enforcement jurisdiction, and transnational cooperation), they may still come up short. As U.S. Special Counsel Robert Mueller's comprehensive accounting of Russian election interference shows, much of the Russian campaign targeting the 2016 U.S. presidential election did not violate any U.S. domestic

[57] *See* Department of Justice Press Release, *supra* note 45.

[58] Iran and the United States, for example, have no MLAT or extradition treaty to further U.S. investigations of alleged Iranian hacking into U.S. campaigns. *See* Nicole Perlroth & David E. Sanger, *Iranian Hackers Target Trump Campaign as Threats to 2020 Mount*, N.Y. Times (Oct. 4, 2019).

[59] *See* Jennifer Daskal, *The Un-Territoriality of Data*, 125 Yale L.J. 326, 393–394 (2015) (referring to the MLAT system as "historically slow" and "clumsy").

[60] Christopher Painter, *Putin's "Incredible Offer" Lacked Any Credibility*, RealClear Defense (July 23, 2018).

[61] *See, e.g.*, International Covenant on Civil & Political Rights (1966) 999 U.N.T.S. 171 (ICCPR), art. 17 ("No one shall be subjected to arbitrary or unlawful interference with his privacy, family, home or correspondence, nor to unlawful attacks on his honour and reputation"), and art. 19 (providing for both freedom of opinion and freedom of expression, including "freedom to seek, receive and impart information and ideas of all kinds, regardless of frontiers, either orally, in writing or in print, in the form of art, or through any other media of his choice.").

[62] *See* 2019 Venice Commission Report, *supra* note 6, at 10 ("Democratic elections are not possible without respect for human rights, in particular freedom of expression and of the press, freedom of circulation inside the country, freedom of assembly and freedom of association for political purposes, including the creation of political parties."); *see also* European External Action Service Election Observation Missions (EUEOMs), *Compendium of International Standards for Elections* 23 (July 14, 2016), *at* https://eeas.europa.eu/topics/election-observation-missions-eueoms/6698/compendium-international-standards-elections_en.

laws.[63] There were no publicly known campaign finance violations associated with the foreign interference, nor did the social media advertisement purchases run afoul of U.S. laws.[64]

As with international law, therefore, it is not surprising to see that the challenges and gaps in domestic law have led to various legislative and regulatory proposals. There are now calls for mandating certain capabilities for voting systems in the United States as well as federal funding support for U.S. states to improve the resiliency of their electoral processes.[65] Others have suggested a need for fair and reasonable guidelines for online advertising in political campaigns, including the regulation of foreign actors in this domain. Some in the United States would extend existing restrictions on foreign governments and nationals in traditional advertising (e.g., newspaper, radio, television) to the online domain.[66] Other states have witnessed similar calls, generating anxiety over their potential human rights implications.[67] The diversity and range of these proposals reinforces the challenges of relying on domestic law in warding off foreign election interference whether alone or alongside international legal mechanisms. Other solutions must be brought to bear, including efforts by the information and technology industry itself.

C. Technical Measures—A Partial but Incomplete Solution

When it comes to democratic processes, technology can be used both for good and ill. In many ways, technology now presents an indispensable component of organizing democratic processes. Even in voting scenarios that consist of predominantly hand-marked paper ballots, technology is often used to register voters, generate ballots, and report election results. Modern political campaigns in democratic countries are quickly becoming heavily dependent on maximizing the highly effective amplification and targeting technology that social media platforms offer. In short, conducting elections in democratic countries without the use of technology has—like many other aspects of daily life—become unthinkable.

[63] Mueller, *supra* note 2, at 22–24 (citing Office of the Director of National Intelligence, *Russia's Influence Campaign Targeting the 2016 US Presidential Election* 1 (Jan. 6, 2017)).

[64] For more on the loopholes in existing domestic law, *see* Ian Vandewalker and Lawrence Norden, chapter 15, this volume. As they recount, the FBI did open an investigation into whether a Russian banker with ties to President Vladimir Putin used the National Rifle Association's dark money arm to secretly spend on the 2016 election.

[65] McFaul, *supra* note 7, at v (Recommendation 2.1: calling for new federal legislation to require all vote casting systems have the capability to provide a voter-verified paper audit trail); State Cyber Resiliency Act (SCRA), S. 1065, 116th Congress (as referred to the Committee on Homeland Security and Governmental Affairs, Apr. 8, 2019); Vandewalker & Norden, *supra* note 4, at 6 (supporting the need for the SCRA).

[66] S.1989—Honest Ads Act, *at* https://www.congress.gov/bill/115th-congress/senate-bill/1989; McFaul, *supra* note 7, at 31–32 (Recommendations 3.1, 3.2).

[67] *See, e.g.*, *Malaysia Parliament Scraps Law Criminalising Fake News*, Al Jazeera (Oct. 9, 2019); On Amendments to Legislative Acts of the Russian Federation regarding the Regulation of the Activities of Non-profit Organisations Performing the Functions of a Foreign Agent [UK RF] [Criminal Code] (Russ.); Anton Troianovski, *In Russia, an Updated Law with New Restrictions on Freedom of Speech*, N.Y. Times (Dec. 2, 2019); Foreign Influence Transparency Scheme Bill 2018 (Austl.); Elections Modernization Act, S.C. 2018, c. 31 (Can.).

The challenge for most democracies, however, is that as the adoption of technology starts to underpin democratic processes and institutions, it also increases the attack surface that can be exploited by bad actors. Similarly, pluralistic information ecosystems, while central to the functioning of a robust democracy, present a major threat vector for foreign interference in elections.

Important innovations are currently underway to help secure the technical infrastructure of elections and political campaigns against cybersecurity threats as well as to counter foreign influence operations in the information space. At the same time, the dynamic innovation of technology suggests that these efforts will at best be an interim or partial step forward in mitigating the threat of foreign election interference.

1. Securing Technical Elections Infrastructure

When releasing the U.S. National Academy of Sciences (NAS) 2018 report, *Securing the Vote*, its co-chair called the 2016 U.S. presidential election "a watershed moment in the history of elections—one that exposed new challenges and vulnerabilities that require the immediate attention of state and local governments, the federal government, researchers, and the American public."[68] Compiled over two years by leading election security experts, the NAS report outlines long-standing concerns about outdated voting equipment and the threat of cyberattacks against these systems while outlining a series of recommendations for how to address these challenges.

Outdated electronic voting equipment is often listed among the principal challenges by numerous election security experts such as those at the Brennan Center for Justice.[69] The Brennan Center estimated that in the 2018 U.S. midterm elections, 34 percent of all local election jurisdictions were using voting machines that were at least ten years old as their primary polling place equipment.[70] These systems are often running software that is no longer supported by the manufacturer; this can limit the availability of security patches, leaving these machines potentially exposed to digital exploitation.

Other challenges include electronic voting systems that do not produce a paper record, which means election officials and the public cannot confirm electronic vote totals.[71] While the deployment of these types of systems has been significantly reduced in recent years, approximately 16 million voters in the United States will still vote in the U.S. 2020 election on systems that will not produce a paper record.[72] Moreover, it is critical to conceive of election security more broadly than electronic voting systems. Vulnerabilities can also exist in voter registration and election-night reporting systems, even in jurisdictions where the voting itself is done by hand-marked paper ballots. And such challenges go well beyond the United States. In a 2019 report, the

[68] National Academy of Sciences, *Securing the Vote* 12 (Sept. 2018), *at* https://www.nap.edu/catalog/25120/securing-the-vote-protecting-american-democracy.

[69] Andrea Cordova McCadney, Elizabeth Howard, & Lawrence Norden, *Voting Machine Security: Where We Stand Six Months Before the New Hampshire Primary* (Brennan Center for Justice, 2020), *at* https://www.brennancenter.org/our-work/analysis-opinion/voting-machine-security-where-we-stand-six-months-new-hampshire-primary.

[70] *Id.*

[71] *Id.*

[72] *Id.*

Canadian government noted that "half of all OECD countries holding national elections in 2018 had their democratic process targeted by cyber threat activity."[73]

How could technology respond to these vulnerabilities? One solution involves pairing it with a "hands-on" alternative. Thus, one of the NAS report's central recommendations is the use of paper ballots that "may be marked by hand or by machine" and that "may be counted by hand or by machine."[74] The report also recommends the use of "risk-limiting audits"—that is, examining a statistically appropriate random sample of paper ballots—prior to the certification of an election result. Risk-limiting audits, the report argues, can "determine with a high level of confidence whether a reported election outcome reflects a correct tabulation of the votes cast."[75] If implemented effectively, the use of paper ballots could help increase some aspects of election security. It is not, however, a silver bullet solution, especially given potential drawbacks from a voting accessibility perspective (depending on the type of voting method employed).[76]

Beyond paper ballots and risk-limiting audits, the NAS report also recommends technology capable of "end-to-end-verifiable election systems in various election Scenarios."[77] According to the report, an election is end-to-end-verifiable (E2E-V) "if it achieves three goals: 1) voters can obtain assurance that their selections have been properly recorded; 2) any individual can verify that their ballots have been included in vote tallies; and 3) members of the public can verify that the final tally is the correct result for the set of ballots collected."[78] Importantly, E2E verifiability enables not only detection of external threats but also detection of internal threats, including errors or tampering by election officials, corrupted equipment, or compromises originating with equipment vendors.[79]

Although there were prior attempts at implementing this concept,[80] the first major effort at doing so in a highly secure, yet easy to use manner, is Microsoft's *ElectionGuard* technology.[81] *ElectionGuard* was developed by Microsoft's Defending Democracy Program in 2019. The technology was based on long-standing research by Josh Benaloh, a senior cryptographer in Microsoft Research, whose doctoral dissertation in 1987, "Verifiable Secret-Ballot Elections,"[82] introduced the use of homomorphic encryption to enable E2E-V election technologies.

[73] Canada Communications Security Establishment (CSE), *2019 Update: Cyber Threats to Canada's Democratic Processes* (2020), *at* https://cyber.gc.ca/en/guidance/2019-update-cyber-threats-canadas-democratic-process.

[74] *Securing the Vote*, *supra* note 68, at 6.

[75] *Id.*

[76] Matt Vasilogambros, *How Voters with Disabilities Are Blocked from the Ballot Box* (Pew Trusts, Feb. 1, 2018), *at* https://www.pewtrusts.org/en/research-and-analysis/blogs/stateline/2018/02/01/how-voters-with-disabilities-are-blocked-from-the-ballot-box.

[77] *Id.*

[78] *Id.* at 97.

[79] *Id.*

[80] Susan Bell et al., *STAR-Vote: A Secure, Transparent, Auditable, and Reliable Voting System*, 1 USENIX J. Election Tech. & Systems (Aug. 2013).

[81] Tom Burt, *Protecting Democratic Elections through Secure, Verifiable Voting*, Microsoft Blog (May 6, 2019), *at* https://blogs.microsoft.com/on-the-issues/2019/05/06/protecting-democratic-elections-through-secure-verifiable-voting/.

[82] Josh Benaloh, *Verifiable Secret-Ballot Elections* (PhD Thesis, Sept. 1987), *available at* https://www.microsoft.com/en-us/research/publication/verifiable-secret-ballot-elections/.

Working with partners, Microsoft was able to pilot its *ElectionGuard* system in February 2020 when voters in Fulton, Wisconsin, were the first to use it in an actual election: 398 votes were cast in a statewide judicial election as well as in a local school board election. When the final votes were tallied, *ElectionGuard*'s electronic tally matched and counted the tally of paper ballots by the local election officials, demonstrating that the E2E-V system worked. As part of their voting experience, voters received a printed "tracking ID," each containing a unique code that can be used to follow an encrypted version of each vote through the entire election process via a web portal provided by election authorities. This "tracking ID," which contained no information about the voter or whom they voted for, enabled each voter for the first time to personally verify that their votes had indeed been counted.[83] *ElectionGuard*, which is free of charge, was developed as an open-source software development kit on GitHub for manufacturers of election systems to incorporate into their voting equipment.[84]

2. Protecting Political Campaigns from Cyber Threats

Political campaigns, their advisers, and affiliated political parties have regularly been the target of nation-states using cyber means to "hack and leak" sensitive information about a candidate or their campaign effort. Following the experience of the 2016 U.S. presidential campaign, as well as cyberattacks against French political parties in 2017, many technology companies have been working to provide additional security to political campaigns and parties. We highlight three of the most prominent here.

First, in May 2018, Google-affiliate Jigsaw was among the first to pioneer cybersecurity services for political campaigns, parties, journalists, and non-governmental organizations (NGOs) in the form of additional protection against distributed denial-of-service attacks via *Project Shield*.[85] Second, in August 2018, Microsoft's Defending Democracy Program rolled out its *AccountGuard* service in the United States, which provides enhanced detection and notification services for suspected nation-state cyberattacks for Microsoft Office 365 customers.[86] Since then, the service, which covers political campaigns, elected officials, parties, and NGOs, has been expanded to thirty countries. Third, in October 2019, Facebook launched a program called *Facebook Protect*.[87] It offers candidates, elected officials, federal and state departments and agencies, and party committees, as well as their staff, additional protections to further secure their Facebook and Instagram accounts.

As useful as these technical tools may be, however, they are not without challenges. For starters, although these efforts offer significant security enhancements at no cost, a key challenge for most companies has been to get eligible users to adopt these services across the board. Even as they face an outsized cybersecurity threat, campaigns and

[83] Tom Burt, *Another Step in Testing ElectionGuard*, Microsoft Blog (Feb. 17, 2020), *at* https://blogs.microsoft.com/on-the-issues/2020/02/17/wisconsin-electionguard-polls/.

[84] Microsoft, *What Is ElectionGuard*, *at* https://news.microsoft.com/on-the-issues/2020/03/27/what-is-electionguard/.

[85] Jigsaw/Google, *Project Shield*, *at* https://projectshield.withgoogle.com/landing.

[86] Tom Burt, *Protecting Democracy with Microsoft AccountGuard*, Microsoft Blog (Aug. 20, 2018), *at* https://blogs.microsoft.com/on-the-issues/2018/08/20/protecting-democracy-with-microsoft-accountguard/.

[87] Facebook, *Facebook Protect*, *available at* https://www.facebook.com/gpa/facebook-protect.

political parties often lack the cybersecurity savvy to embrace these services to their fullest extent. While this situation is slowly improving (for example, some U.S. presidential campaigns in the 2020 cycle hired dedicated cybersecurity personnel), the reality is that there is likely always going to be a mismatch of those trying to defend IT-assets against well-organized and sometimes military-grade attackers.

3. Countering Foreign Influence Operations and Emerging Disinformation Challenges

In addition to cybersecurity threats, modern democracies increasingly face a slew of disinformation campaigns. While the social media disinformation efforts of Russia's Internet Research Agency (IRA) are well documented,[88] it is important to understand that many other nation-states (and nonstate actors) are copying the IRA's playbook, or simply writing their own. In one of the most comprehensive research efforts to date, Diego Martin and Jacob Shapiro identified fifty-three unique influence campaigns targeting twenty-four different countries from 2013 through 2018.[89] According to Shapiro's study, 72 percent of these foreign influence campaigns were conducted by Russia, with China, Iran, and Saudi Arabia accounting for most of the remainder.[90]

Technology companies have tried to address these challenges by significantly expanding their capacity to identify what Facebook calls "coordinated inauthentic behavior,"[91] using both human review and automated detection tools. However, disinformation efforts on social media platforms continue to pose a significant challenge. They provide a low-cost and nearly consequence-free way of sowing discord in politics and exploiting often preexisting social divisions in society. And while social media companies have enacted a range of updated content policies and use automation and new tools to better police their platforms, significant questions about transparency and accountability remain, impacting democratic processes not just in the United States but around the world.[92]

Governments across democratic countries have started to look closely at what kind of (self-)regulatory tools can be employed by technology companies in response. In September 2018, the European Union adopted a "Code of Practice" to address the spread of online disinformation.[93] The Code, which was signed by key social media and technology companies, asks them to report out on a regular basis the actions they have taken to "improve the scrutiny of ad placements, ensure transparency of political and issue-based advertising and to tackle fake accounts and malicious use of bots."[94]

[88] For further discussion, *see* chapters 2 and 13, this volume.

[89] Diego A. Martin & Jacob N. Shapiro, *Trends in Online Foreign Influence Efforts* (Empirical Studies of Conflict Project, July 2019), *at* https://scholar.princeton.edu/sites/default/files/jns/files/trends_in_foreign_influence_efforts_2019jul08_0.pdf.

[90] *Id.* at 3.

[91] Nathaniel Gleicher, Head of Cybersecurity Policy, *Coordinated Inauthentic Behavior Explained*, Facebook (Dec. 6, 2018), *at* https://about.fb.com/news/2018/12/inside-feed-coordinated-inauthentic-behavior/.

[92] For further information, *see* The Kofi Annan Foundation's Commission on Elections and Democracy in the Digital Age, *Protecting Electoral Integrity in the Digital Age* (Jan. 2020), *at* https://www.kofiannanfoundation.org/app/uploads/2020/01/f035dd8e-kaf_kacedda_report_2019_web.pdf.

[93] EU Code of Practice on Disinformation (2018), *at* https://ec.europa.eu/digital-single-market/en/news/code-practice-disinformation.

[94] *Id.*

In May 2019, the Canadian government launched its "Declaration on Electoral Integrity Online."[95] Numerous other governments have since been developing similar approaches.

National regulatory approaches can certainly have merit in this domain. But even if these approaches nudge technology companies to more advanced tools and techniques for combating foreign election interference, we anticipate parallel advancements in terms of the tools and techniques of those seeking to undermine democratic processes through sophisticated disinformation efforts.[96] Simply put, technology must always be part of the solution to foreign election interference, but it will always be a part of the problem as well.

One of the most prominent new technological challenges relates to the malicious use of synthetic media or "deepfakes" (which combines the terms "deep learning" and "fake"). Malicious use of deepfakes seems to manifest itself to date primarily in two areas: nonconsensual pornography and elections. While election campaigns in liberal democracies have not yet seen the onslaught that some predicted of manipulated video, audio, or photographs of candidates and/or their associates, the technology to do just that certainly does exist.[97]

Deepfakes use different underlying artificial intelligence (AI) technology, such as generative adversarial networks (GANs) and autoencoders. The challenge with the adversarial nature of GANs is that any effort at improving their detection can be used by those building deepfakes to improve detection avoidance. This "arms race" means that deepfake detection tools are an intermediate solution—the longer-term approach will likely need to focus on creating a new ecosystem for authenticated content where provenance of a media file can be tracked every step of the way.

Technology companies as well as leading media and publishing companies have started to explore deepfake mitigation efforts to help ensure content on their platforms is trustworthy in terms of its origin and provenance. Adobe, the maker of one of the leading image-manipulation technologies, recently launched its Content Authenticity Initiative in partnership with the *New York Times* and Twitter. Facebook, Microsoft, and the Partnership on AI ran a Deepfake Detection Challenge intended to bring together researchers globally to help develop deepfake detection tools.[98] Such efforts offer some promise of using technology to defeat the threat to democracies deepfakes pose.

That said, we should be clear: technology solutions alone are not a panacea for election interference. As the move for more transparency on disinformation responses shows, these solutions must be complemented by legal and policy measures. To curb the impact of malicious deepfakes, for example, numerous draft bills have been proposed in the United States both at the state and federal level, and some have been

[95] *Canada Declaration on Electoral Integrity Online* (May 27, 2019), *at* https://www.canada.ca/en/democratic-institutions/services/protecting-democracy/declaration-electoral-integrity.html.

[96] As noted, further clarifications or applications of international law may prove useful, although we believe they are likely to be inadequate, hence our additional call for broader cybernorm efforts.

[97] *What Is a Deep Fake*, The Economist (Aug. 7, 2019).

[98] Adobe Communications Team, *Introducing the Content Authenticity Initiative*, Adobe Blog (Nov. 4, 2019), *at* https://theblog.adobe.com/content-authenticity-initiative/; Deepfake Detection Challenge, *at* https://deepfakedetectionchallenge.ai/.

adopted.[99] At the policy advocacy level, the Transatlantic Commission for Election Integrity in February 2019 launched a "Pledge for Election Integrity," by which political candidates could endorse five principles aimed at "not aid[ing] and abet[ing] those who seek to undermine democracy."[100]

Taken together, international law, domestic law, and technology each provide a set of existing functions and features that can be deployed to combat foreign election interference online. At the same time, when considered in isolation, each regime faces significant gaps in terms of its coverage, enforcement, or effectiveness. Such shortfalls may be mitigated by looking to have these efforts work in concert. The sum of technological innovation, international and domestic law, and self-regulation may well be greater than the parts. At the same time, however, we do not believe that these options exhaust the menu of responsive measures to foreign election interference. States and other stakeholders need to consider the value of getting powerful actors to accept a global minimum standard of acceptable online behavior—a norm—when it comes to foreign election interference. Doing so can further enhance the collective response to this threat matrix. And, without it, all other measures are likely to remain constrained or of limited utility.

III. Unpacking the Norm Concept

Norms represent an additional tool of global governance beyond technology and law. They order expectations based on social relationships. Different social groups have different norms. We expect students to follow certain norms (attend class, read assigned material, take—and pass—final exams) while other groups (e.g., doctors, lawyers, corporate board members) have norms that set different behavioral expectations for group members. Other social relations lead to norms for organizational entities, ranging from firms to nation-states.

Social scientists define norms as "collective expectations for the proper behavior of actors with a given identity."[101] From this definition, four essential ingredients of a norm become apparent: (1) identity; (2) behavior; (3) collective expectations; and (4) propriety.[102]

For starters, norms guide behavior based on the actor's *identity*; their association with a particular group or community. Actors who want to establish or maintain their relationship with the group conform to its norms, not necessarily because of the norms' contents, but because they value their relationship with the group.[103] As such,

[99] For an overview of deepfakes-related legislation in the United States, *see* Matthew Ferraro "*Deepfake Legislation: A Nationwide Survey* (Wilmer Hale, Sept. 25, 2019), *at* https://www.wilmerhale.com/-/media/files/shared_content/editorial/publications/wh_publications/client_alert_pdfs/20190925-deepfake-legislation-a-nationwide-survey.pdf.

[100] Alliance of Democracies, *The Pledge for Election Integrity*, *at* https://electionpledge.org/.

[101] Peter J. Katzenstein, Introduction: Alternative Perspectives on National Security, in The Culture of National Security: Norms and Identity in World Politics 1, 5 (P.J. Katzenstein ed., 1996).

[102] *See* Finnemore & Hollis, *supra* note 9, at 438–444.

[103] Alastair Iain Johnston, *Treating International Institutions as Social Environments*, 45 INT'L STUD. Q. 487, 500 (2001). Socialization often has a strong status element, with lower-status actors seeking to meet expectations (and adopt the norms) of high-status actors. *Id.*

whatever the group (e.g., democratic states), relevant actors must self-identify with it for its norm to affect their behavior. The extent of such effects can vary depending on how closely the actor identifies with the group. Goodman and Jinks suggest, for example, that the strength, immediacy, and size of a group determine how much a group member will conform to its norms.[104] They cite research suggesting that the most effective norms relate to groups of three to eight members, with the efficacy of compliance for larger groups dropping off rapidly.[105] That said, there are cases where a small group coalesces around a norm that then expands and cascades to a broader group to which the small group members belong.[106]

Second, norms always address some *behavior*, whether action or inaction. Like international law, norms can be *proscriptive*, telling group members what *not* to do. Others may be *prescriptive*, demanding positive behavior from group members. Norms may also be *permissive*, setting expectations that behavior is proper even if undertaking it remains within the discretion of group members.[107]

Third, norms always involve *collective expectations*. Norms are not unilateral edicts; they do not arise by fiat. They are intersubjective—socially constructed, shared understandings about appropriate behavior held by members of the designated group. They exist because people believe they exist. The extent of this intersubjectivity can vary. Some norms are fully internalized, so ingrained that few, if any, question whether and why they occur.[108] Fully internalized norms generate conformance independently, without monitoring or threat of sanctions. Witness, for example, how certain cultural norms mean that a person may decline to cross an untrafficked and empty street late at night until the electronic "walk" sign is displayed.

Other norms are less internalized. Some are, what Cass Sunstein calls "incompletely theorized"—where group members share behavioral expectations but diverge on *why* they conform to these.[109] In other cases, group members exhibit "insincere conformity"—that is, giving lip service to the norm but not conforming their actual behavior to it.[110] Such insincerity may initially appear problematic, but, over time, lead actors' behavior toward greater conformity, whether to reduce cognitive dissonance or in response to organizational platforms established to promote the norm.

[104] Ryan Goodman & Derek Jinks, Socializing States: Promoting Human Rights Through International Law 28 (2013). "Strength" refers to the importance of the group to the accused; "immediacy" to the accused's awareness of and interactions with that group; and "size" to the number of members in the group. *See id.*

[105] *Id.*

[106] In other words, the "cascade" effect by which norms form suggests that small groups can evolve into much broader coalitions. *See generally* Martha Finnemore & Kathryn Sikkink, *International Norm Dynamics and Political Change*, 52 Int'l Org. 887 (1998).

[107] Finnemore & Hollis, *supra* note 9, at 438–439. In the internet context, use of TCP/IP serves as a good example of a permissive norm. No one is required to use TCP/IP; its use is voluntary for those seeking to join the Internet. *Id.*

[108] *See, e.g.*, Lawrence Lessig, Code and Other Laws of Cyberspace 190 (1999).

[109] Cass R. Sunstein, *Incompletely Theorized Agreements in Constitutional Law*, 74 Soc. Res. 1 (2007). Sunstein's idea shares some similarities with Rawls's ideas of overlapping consensus. John Rawls, *The Idea of an Overlapping Consensus*, 7 Oxford J. Legal Stud. 1 (1987). Sunstein uses religious liberty as an example: everyone may believe in it, but for vastly different reasons. Some favor religious freedom to preserve their own beliefs, some view it as a moral command, some accept its existence on utilitarian grounds, while others may see it as a matter of national security—a way to preserve social peace. Sunstein, *supra*, at 1–2.

[110] Finnemore & Hollis, *supra* note 9, at 434.

The Soviet Union's response to the Helsinki Accords' norms serves as a prominent example of this latter possibility.[111]

Yet, even if greater conformity does not follow, it would be a mistake to dismiss a norm's public affirmation entirely. Consider speed limits. In many communities, the existence of a speed limit may receive lip service as most drivers still speed. Yet even for such speeders, the speed limit remains an important reference point; speeders do not drive as fast as their cars can go, but rather speed in relation to the set speed limit.[112] In other words, even if they are repeatedly violated, norms can continue to cabin violations by limiting the extent of deviations that occur.

Finally, *propriety* refers to the basis on which norms label behavior as proper or improper. Norm propriety can derive from different bases, including politics, religion, culture, professional standards, and, importantly, law. In the cyber context, the norms discourse has often focused on promoting "voluntary, non-binding" norms as an *alternative* to international or domestic law.[113] But law and norms are not mutually exclusive. Laws can be normative (indeed, it is the goal of those who enact law that its legitimacy—with or without a threat of sanctions for violators—will create a collective expectation of proper behavior among the law's subjects). And those who promote norms often pursue their instantiation into law as an important goal. In other words, laws can be a basis for generating norms just as norms can generate laws. At the same time, laws may fail as norms where actual behavior diverges from the law's contents (e.g., jaywalking). The power of norms thus does not derive from the law so much as the actual social expectations that accompany it. Norms are inherently *social* constructs that emerge and spread by processes of interactions among particular groups of actors in specific contexts.[114] As a result, they are a discrete mechanism for dealing with social problems that concretely impact what behavior(s) do (or do not) occur.

How do norms arise? Some emerge spontaneously out of habit and repetition.[115] When group members do the same thing for long enough, a norm may emerge even without conscious thought or decision. Sophisticated states and others are aware of this possibility. Thus, they may strategically object to behavior if only to block any developing sense that it is permissible.

[111] *See generally* DANIEL C. THOMAS, THE HELSINKI EFFECT: INTERNATIONAL NORMS, HUMAN RIGHTS AND THE DEMISE OF COMMUNISM (2001). Risse, Ropp, and Sikkink's "spiral model" of human rights change provides a more detailed theorization of this process. THOMAS RISSE ET AL., THE POWER OF HUMAN RIGHTS: INTERNATIONAL NORMS AND DOMESTIC CHANGE 17–35 (1999).

[112] *See* F. Mannering, Effects of interstate speed limits on driving speeds: Some new evidence, in Compendium of Papers CD-ROM, Transportation Research Board 86th Annual Meeting 3 (Jan. 2007) (Indiana drivers "reported average normal driving speed was nearly 66 mph on interstates posted with 55 mph speed limits, about 74 mph on interstates posted at 65 mph and almost 78 mph on interstates that are posted at 70 mph," while in Texas, "a 5 mph increase in the speed limit was associated with a 3.2 mph increase in average speeds."). We do not mean to suggest that driving speeds depend entirely on speed limits; other factors clearly matter (e.g., driver safety concerns, speed of other drivers). Yet, the speed limit appears to remain a relevant factor implicating actual driving speeds even in cases where drivers have decided to violate it.

[113] *See, e.g.*, 2015 GGE Report, *supra* note 14, paras. 9–10.

[114] *See* Finnemore & Sikkink, *supra* note 106, at 909–915.

[115] *See* Robert Sugden, *Spontaneous Order*, J. ECON. PERSP. 85–97 (1989).

Beyond habits, processes catalyzed by so-called "norm entrepreneurs" may also generate norms.[116] Anyone from civil society advocates to nation-states may have a norm to promote. Norm entrepreneurs may, moreover, promote a norm for a group in which they are members or offer norms for some other community to adopt. As targeted group members begin to conform their behavior to the norm, it may eventually reach a tipping point where it "cascades" throughout the whole group. Anti-smoking and anti-littering norms in the United States testify to the power of norms to spread and become ingrained in complex and large societies.[117] Alternatively, norms may emerge out of "cycles" where dissatisfaction with an existing norm leads to interactions within the group or between group members and others from which a revamped or entirely new norm emerges.[118] In international relations, for example, over time, the norm allowing states to use military force to collect debts abroad cycled into a new norm prohibiting that very behavior.[119]

Norm entrepreneurs have a range of tools to promote and spread their norms. They can use material incentives (whether positive or negative) to coerce members to abide by their preferred norm. Alternatively, they can use persuasion, that is, arguments that frame and link the norm to issues that lead group members to accept it and conform their behavior accordingly.[120] Or, norm entrepreneurs can employ socialization tools (e.g., professional training, naming and shaming) to socialize group members about internalizing norm conformance.[121] Norm entrepreneurs often celebrate group members who champion a norm or label nonconformers as "rogues" who are not to be trusted, thereby threatening their status and reputations within the group.

In addition to incentives, persuasion, and socialization, norm entrepreneurs often create *organizational platforms* to sustain their efforts.[122] Some build a new

[116] *See, e.g.*, Finnemore & Sikkink, *supra* note 106, at 887–917; Stacie E. Goddard, *Brokering Change: Networks and Entrepreneurs in International Politics*, 1 INT'L THEORY 249 (2009); Amitav Acharya, *How Ideas Spread: Whose Norms Matter? Norm Localization and Institutional Change in Asian Regionalism*, 58 INT'L ORG. 239 (2004); Harold Hongju Koh, *Why Do Nations Obey International Law*, 106 YALE L.J. 2599, 2630–2634 (1997); Cass Sunstein, *Social Norms and Social Rules*, 96 COLUM. L. REV 903, 929 (1996).

[117] *See, e.g.*, Hope M. Babcock, *Civic Republicanism Provides Theoretical Support for Making Individuals More Environmentally Responsible*, 23 NOTRE DAME J.L. ETHICS & PUB. POL'Y 515, 525 n.64 (2009); Alex C. Geisinger, *A Group Identity Theory of Social Norms and Its Implications*, 78 TUL. L. REV. 605, 641 (2004); Luís Sílvia & José Palma-Oliveira, *Public Policy and Social Norms: The Case of a Nationwide Smoking Ban Among College Students*, 22 PSYCHOL. PUB. POL'Y & L. 22, 26 (2016); Richard H. McAdams, *The Origin, Development, and Regulation of Norms*, 96 MICH. L. REV. 338, 383 (1997).

[118] CASS R. SUNSTEIN, FREE MARKETS AND SOCIAL JUSTICE 38 (1999) (describing norm cascades after a tipping point); WAYNE SANDHOLTZ & KENDALL STILES, INTERNATIONAL NORMS AND CYCLES OF CHANGE (2008); WAYNE SANDHOLTZ, PROHIBITING PLUNDER: HOW NORMS CHANGE (2007) (examining norm development in cycles).

[119] *See* Jorge L. Esquirol, Latin America, in The Oxford Handbook of the History of International Law 553, 568 (2012); MICHAEL TOMZ, REPUTATION AND INTERNATIONAL COOPERATION: SOVEREIGN DEBT ACROSS THREE CENTURIES, 151 n.89 (2007).

[120] In the electoral context, for example, the OSCE has argued for states and other stakeholders to standardize the norms for election observers. *See* OSCE Office for Democratic Institutions and Human Rights (ODIHR), *Declaration of Principles for International Election Observation* (Oct. 27, 2005), *at* https://www.osce.org/odihr/16935?download=true.

[121] These processes are intertwined, and scholars use varying typologies. Goodman and Jinks focus on material inducement, persuasion, and acculturation. GOODMAN & JINKS, *supra* note 104, at 4. Johnston cites persuasion and social influence. Johnston, *supra* note 103. Checkel emphasizes strategic calculations, role playing, and normative suasion. Jeffrey T. Checkel, *International Institutions and Socialization in Europe: Introduction and Framework*, 59 INT'L ORG. 801 (2005).

[122] Finnemore & Sikkink, *supra* note 106, at 887–917.

organization for this purpose, as Henry Dunant and his colleagues did in launching the International Committee for the Red Cross.[123] Others "graft" their efforts onto existing organizations to ease the norm's institutionalization and dissemination.[124] Looking at the cyber context, several states have grafted efforts to promote cybernorms of responsible state behavior to the existing "Group of Governmental Experts" framework in the UN General Assembly's First Committee.[125]

Norm cultivation culminates when behavioral expectations become "normal"—taken for granted by actors as just "how things are done." That said, norms are not static products; they remain quite dynamic. The various processes—incentives, persuasion, and socialization—lead to repeated interactions among actors that ensure various adjustments or alterations to a norm's meaning. Even fully internalized norms may evolve as the context, the group members' shared identity, and bases of propriety shift and evolve.

Finally, no norm exists in isolation; it is always situated alongside other norms. Multiple norms usually apply to actors with a given identity. These norms may be aligned, but may alternatively cut against each other.[126] Moreover, most actors, including states, have multiple identities—they identify with different groups simultaneously. The United States, for example, identifies itself as a part of (1) the group of most powerful states (e.g., economically, the G7, or politically, as one of the five permanent members of the UN Security Council); (2) liberal-democratic states; and, more broadly, (3) the community of all nation-states. These different groups each have different norms that may be partially or completely incompatible.

Success in norm creation and distribution can mean concrete impacts on global governance problems. Witness the success of the campaign to ban land mines, which generated not only the Ottawa Convention but also a broader expectation that states would endeavor to give up this weapon of war. Indeed, even the United States, which never joined the Ottawa Convention, has reduced its usage of land mines to the Korean Peninsula.[127]

But norm promotion efforts will not always succeed; failure is possible and, for many, may be the default position. To succeed, norm entrepreneurs need to adopt a strategic calculus. They must decide what combination of ingredients—which group

[123] *See* Francois Bugnion, *The International Committee of the Red Cross and the Development of International Humanitarian Law*, 5 Chi. J. Int'l L. 191, 191–192 (2004).

[124] *See* Acharya, *supra* note 116, at 243–245; Richard Price, *Reversing the Gun Sights: Transnational Civil Society Targets Land Mines*, 52 Int'l Org. 613, 617 (1998).

[125] The 2015 GGE Report called on states to support various peacetime cybernorms, including not conducting or knowingly supporting ICT activity that intentionally damages critical infrastructure, not knowingly targeting another state's CSIRT, nor using their own CSIRTs for malicious activity. 2015 GGE Report, *supra* note 14, para. 13(f)–(h).

[126] The "regime complex" literature addresses issues of multiple, often competing, configurations of norms. *See generally* Karen J. Alter & Sophie Meunier, *The Politics of International Regime Complexity*, 7 Persp. Pol. 13 (2009); Kal Raustiala & David G. Victor, *The Regime Complex for Plant Genetic Resources*, 58 Int'l Org. 277 (2004); Laurence R. Helfer, *Regime Shifting: The TRIPs Agreement and New Dynamics of International Intellectual Property Lawmaking*, 29 Yale J. Int'l L. 1 (2004).

[127] *See* The Convention on the Prohibition of the Use, Stockpiling, Production and Transfer of Anti-Personnel Mines and on their Destruction (1997) 2056 U.N.T.S. 241; White House Press Release, *Fact Sheet: Changes to U.S. Anti-Personnel Landmine Policy* (Sept. 23, 2014), *at* https://obamawhitehouse.archives.gov/the-press-office/2014/09/23/fact-sheet-changes-us-anti-personnel-landmine-policy.

identity, what behaviors, at what level of collective expectations, and on what basis of propriety—they will base their efforts. Similarly, they need to decide in what organizational forum they will pursue the norm and which mix of incentives, persuasion, and socialization tools to bring to bear. And they must do all this while paying attention to the broader context, attending to the other norms (and norm candidates), as well as the current state of international law, domestic law, and the state of technology itself.

IV. Promoting Cybernorms to Defend Democracies

A. Setting Normative Expectations for Foreign Election Interference Online

The success of norms in other contexts suggests that norms could play an important role in defending democracies. Norms are a sophisticated social instrument that may be carefully calibrated to the problems at hand. For starters, the diverse group identities to which norms attach provide a wider range of targets than other tools like law and technology. International law only governs states; domestic laws only reach individuals and entities within the legislating state's jurisdiction; technology is only open to those who engineer it. In contrast, norms can be promoted for a wider range of stakeholders. Norms can, of course, be pitched to the community of nation-states. But they can also target other groups that have a stake in particular aspects of foreign election interference. Social media platforms may aggregate around norms to address problems of foreign political advertisements or disinformation.[128] Election infrastructure vendors may devise norms to improve the security of the casting or counting of votes. Campaign officials can adopt norms on the security of their data or the use of doxed data of opponents.[129]

Norms thus provide a nuanced mechanism for introducing social controls to the group best situated to redress particular aspects of the problem set. Online threats to democracy take such a diversity of forms that there is no single group that can effectively redress them all alone (not even states). Different group behaviors will have greater (or lesser) impacts on different aspects of the problem set. Whether and how social media platforms control election-related content matters to those concerned with propaganda or disinformation, but those platforms' behavior will have little impact on the security of voting machines.

Nor do norms always have to come from a preexisting group. The Christchurch Call's constitution of a new group—coordinating behavioral expectations among a group of states, civil society representatives, and information and communication technology companies with respect to the threat of online violent extremism—demonstrates how new groups may form and associate membership with particular

128 2019 Venice Commission Report, *supra* note 6, at 39 ("[Internet] intermediaries should provide access to data on paid political advertising, so as to avoid facilitating illegal (foreign) involvement in elections, and to identify the categories of target audiences.").

129 *See, e.g.*, the *Pledge for Election Integrity*, *supra* note 100, as one such normative effort.

norms.[130] In other words, a normative approach can coordinate behavior across otherwise discrete stakeholder groups, unlike the multilateral setting of international law, which addresses states exclusively. Moreover, these groups can exist in a transnational context without regard to the jurisdictional constraints that bound the reach, and enforcement, of domestic law.

When it comes to behavior, norms exhibit a similar diversity. As noted, norms may adopt a proscriptive, prescriptive, or permissive cast. All three forms can contribute to defending democracies. By proscribing certain behavior—namely, online election interference by foreign actors—as improper for group members, norms may convince those members who value their relationship in the relevant group to forgo such activity.[131] Alternatively, norms can prescribe positive behavior, such as coordinating defensive strategies or requiring assistance to those threatened by malicious cyber activities targeting electoral processes.[132] In some cases, norms may even clarify the propriety of behavior that might otherwise be questionable for group members. The latter may have particular importance if it could signal how much content moderation is acceptable for defending democracies without undercutting human rights.

Even as norms coalesce within groups combating foreign election interference online, those groups may also work to forestall the creation of norms permitting such activity. Indeed, U.S. claims of Russian election interference (and similar charges from France, Germany, and the United Kingdom) may disrupt momentum for any claim that online foreign election interference is appropriate.[133] Indeed, U.S. coyness about its own participation in past foreign election interference incidents may exhibit a similar logic, that is, seeking to avoid precedents that might "normalize" such behavior to which the United States is now demonstrably vulnerable.[134] As with group identity, therefore, the complexity of foreign election interference, compounded by the manifold online mechanisms for perpetuating it, counsels in favor of multiple norms regulating behavior in diverse ways.

The flexibility of norms extends to the bases on which norms might emerge for protecting democracies. Norms are social facts—they arise from social interactions without necessitating any particular process or pedigree. Norms can thus emerge based on shared cultural or political ties. These may be particularly useful where

[130] *See* New Zealand Ministry of Foreign Affairs and Trade, *The Christchurch Call*, *at* https://www.christchurchcall.com/.

[131] For an early example of UN efforts to restrict foreign election interference, *see* U.N.G.A. Res. 56/154, U.N. Doc. A/RES/56/154 (Feb. 13, 2002) (Respect for the Principles of National Sovereignty and Non-Interference in the Internal Affairs of States in Electoral Processes: "*Calls upon* all States to refrain from financing political parties or other organizations in any other State in a way that is contrary to the principles of the Charter and that undermines the legitimacy of its electoral processes.").

[132] The OAS, for example, has pushed a set of norms for defending democracies, albeit with a focus on internal threats to democratic processes rather than foreign interference. *See* Organization of American States, *Inter-American Democratic Charter* (Sept. 11, 2001), *at* https://www.oas.org/charter/docs/resolution1_en_p4.htm.

[133] *See* Michael Carpenter, *Countering Russia's Malign Influence Operations*, Just Security (May 29, 2019); CSIS, *Russian Malign Influence in Montenegro: The Weaponization and Exploitation of History, Religion, and Economics*, CSIS Briefs (May 14, 2019), *at* https://www.csis.org/analysis/russian-malign-influence-montenegro.

[134] On the history of U.S. (and Soviet) election interference, *see* chapter 1, this volume; Dov H. Levin, *Partisan Electoral Interventions by the Great Powers: Introducing the PEIG Dataset*, Conflict Mgmt. & Peace Sci. (Sept. 19. 2016).

international law's consensual foundations complicate efforts to devise new rules and the extant law suffers from silence, existential disagreements, and attribution difficulties. Nor must norms hew to domestic law processes for enacting legislation (or authorizing consent to a treaty).

How can cybernorms defending democracy emerge? Of course, they may come out of practice—common behaviors, repeated over time. Studies show that common practices do exist that may reflect norms for the conduct of democratic elections.[135] Alternatively, norm entrepreneurs may push for election-related cybernorms. As in other areas of global governance, entrepreneurship may come from within the group to which the norm would be associated. This would be the approach the G7 adopted in the Charlevoix Commitment.[136] Among industry groups, similar norm entrepreneurial efforts for cybersecurity include the Charter of Trust and the Cybersecurity Tech Accord.[137] As noted, however, norm promotion can also begin without any buy-in from the targeted group. "Outsider" norm entrepreneurs (e.g., in international organizations or civil society) can push states, campaigns, or other stakeholders to adopt and internalize norms relevant to electoral processes.[138]

These entrepreneurs, moreover, can bring to bear whatever resources they have on hand to advance their normative agenda. This does not mean, however, that only powerful actors with lots of incentives can succeed. As the success of the International Campaign to Ban Landmines coalition showed, "weaker" actors can employ powers of persuasion and socialization quite effectively. Similar efforts might advance election-related norms even in the face of resistance from powerful states or industry players.[139]

Taken together, norms provide a flexible and dynamic tool suited to respond to the complexity and diversity of risks associated with online election interference activities by foreign states and state-sponsored actors. Norms can develop within groups of states and stakeholders that consolidate expectations about what behavior is proper and improper. If these expectations become "social facts," they will impact behaviors without having to overcome the hurdles of consent or legislative approval that cabin international and domestic legal approaches. They can also adjust human behavior (and through them, organizations and states) to revise or forgo the architecture and operation of relevant technology. Just because algorithms might control all online speech does not mean that social media companies (or states) should do so.[140] Norms

[135] *See, e.g.*, EUEOMs, *supra* note 62, at 22 ("[It] is possible to identify a number of distinct features, namely: the right to vote and the right to stand as a candidate, genuine as well as periodic elections, universal as well as equal suffrage, the secrecy of the ballot and the free expression of the will of the electors.").

[136] *See supra* note 10, and accompanying text.

[137] Cybersecurity Tech Accord, *Tech Accord, at* https://cybertechaccord.org/; SGS, *The Charter of Trust Takes a Major Step Forward with Cybersecurity* (Feb. 15, 2019), *at* https://www.sgs.com/en/news/2019/02/the-charter-of-trust-takes-a-major-step-forward-with-cybersecurity.

[138] *See, e.g.*, 2019 Venice Commission Report, *supra* note 6; Council of Europe, European Commission for Democracy through Law (Venice Commission), *Code of Good Practice in Electoral Matters: Guidelines and Explanatory Report* (Oct. 18–19, 2002); International Foundation for Electoral Systems (IFES), *Social Media, Disinformation and Electoral Integrity* (Aug. 14, 2019).

[139] Andreas Schedler, Electoral Authoritarianism, in The SAGE Handbook of Comparative Politics 382–384 (Todd Landman et al. eds., 2009).

[140] For example, technology has existed for decades to have civilian aircraft operate without pilots, yet members of the aviation industry have a norm that avoids such behavior.

provide a mediating path for balancing the need to protect democracies with the need to ensure the underlying human rights these governments seek to serve.

B. Challenges for Cybernorms Defending Democracies

In advocating for cybernorms combating foreign election interference activities online, we do not mean to suggest doing so will provide a complete or unproblematic path forward. Like other responses to date, cybernorms are imperfect instruments. Even as they avoid some of the challenges facing existing legal and technical approaches, they encounter challenges of their own in terms of (1) identity failures, (2) application, and (3) permanence.

Identity failure refers to the possibility that a group might adopt and internalize a norm, but its membership may not be capable of effectively addressing the underlying problem. This may be because the group is not the one from whom conformance is most needed. For example, the Charlevoix Commitment may signal a G7 norm prohibiting states from engaging in malign interference aimed at undermining democratic processes, but the G7 does not include the actors (e.g., Russia, Iran) most often cited as engaging in such behavior.[141] Even if a similar norm existed for *all* states, however, the problem of rogue actors remains—that is, states that do not value their identity as a member of the community of nations in good standing sufficiently to follow norms associated with that standing. Whatever their strengths, cybernorms are unlikely to constrain marginalized actors like North Korea or Russia, which do not value their ties or reputation within the global community sufficiently to accommodate its norms.

Beyond identity issues, cybernorms may encounter issues in application. As with international law, even where a cybernorm exists, setting expectations in a general sense, the particulars may prove contentious; interpretative challenges may lead to competing interpretations as to what constitutes appropriate normative behavior or the norm may be framed in such general terms as to not require or prohibit behaviors that adequately remove or mitigate digital threats to democracies.[142] In other cases, cybernorms may exist for certain purposes—for example, norms favoring anonymity exist to protect freedom of expression and online privacy—but may apply in practice in ways that facilitate election interference. Alternatively, actors may internalize a norm but remain unsure about how to implement it in practice. It is one thing, for example, for a social media company to endorse a norm of removing disinformation online while preserving freedom of expression and quite another to actually do it.

[141] *See* Martin & Shapiro, *supra* note 89; MUELLER, *supra* note 2, at 3–9; Ohlin, *supra* note 1, at 1587–1588. *See also* Rebecca Falconer, *Security Agencies Warn Russia, China, Iran Aim to Interfere in 2020 Election*, AXIOS (Nov. 6, 2019); Jason Abbruzzese, *Mark Zuckerberg: Facebook Caught Russia and Iran Trying to Interfere in 2020*, NBC NEWS (Oct. 21, 2019).

[142] *Cf., e.g.*, how Twitter and Google have responded to the problem by prohibiting political ads with Facebook's decision not to do so. *See* Danielle Abril, *Google and Twitter Changed Their Rules on Political Ads. Why Won't Facebook?*, FORTUNE (Nov. 22, 2019); Garrett Sloane, *Facebook Breaks from Twitter and Google with Permissive Political Ads Policy*, ADAGE (Jan. 9, 2020).

Finally, the dynamic quality of norms can be a bug rather than a feature. International law favors stability and thus changes rarely come quickly; treaties require formal amendment processes, and customary international law requires a general practice of states done out of a sense of legal obligation. Domestic laws can be ever stickier, requiring a new law to supersede or supplant existing ones. Like technology, norms may move without formalities and where tipping points arise, do so quite quickly. In 2015, for example, it looked like a norm was emerging prohibiting espionage for commercial advantage; U.S. President Obama reached a "common understanding" to that effect with Chinese President Xi Jinping that later received endorsement from the G20.[143] Yet, by 2019, such espionage had resurged, undermining claims to the earlier understanding's normative status.[144] In other words, cybernorms may exhibit temporal fragility. Unfortunately, the converse problem is also possible—norms may evolve so slowly that when internalization occurs, the underlying problem set may have already shifted to make the norm ineffective or insufficient.

None of these problems, however, should preclude the pursuit of cybernorms for defending democracies. Rogue actors, for example, are a problem in legal settings as much they can be in social ones. Like laws, norms can still have value as a social control over a majority of actors who value their identity in the group enough to undertake the norms associated with it. And even among those actors inclined to lip service, norms can operate, like speed limits, to cabin the extent to which actors deviate from their contents.

Moreover, those who are not rogue actors may find value in devising norms that coordinate and defend against the risks such actors pose. It is noteworthy, for example, that the Charlevoix Commitment's norm proposal was not simply to prohibit malign election interference by foreign actors but rather to "[s]trengthen G7 cooperation to prevent, thwart and respond" to such threats.[145] Interpretative and application issues are, moreover, pervasive in all forms of regulation. Resolutions on both fronts are possible, even if they require careful attention and resolve. Moreover, where the dynamic quality of norms poses more risks than rewards, norm entrepreneurs can seek to shift the basis of propriety from informal, social mechanisms to more formal (i.e., legal) ones. In short, cybernorm challenges are significant, but not insurmountable.

[143] *See* Office of Press Sec'y, *Fact Sheet: President Xi Jinping's State Visit to the United States* (Sept. 25, 2015), *at* https://obamawhitehouse.archives.gov/the-press-office/2015/09/25/fact-sheet-president-xi-jinpings-state-visit-united-states.

[144] The reasons why the norm emerged remain unclear. For some, it was a response to U.S. incentives. *See id.* For others, it was endorsed to centralize control and reduce corruption within the Chinese government. *See* FireEye, *Red Line Drawn: China Recalculates Its Use of Cyber Espionage* (June 21, 2016), *at* https://www.fireeye.com/blog/threat-research/2016/06/red-line-drawn-china-espionage.html (citing President Xi's desire to reign in freelancing Chinese ministries as motivation for forgoing commercial cyber espionage). Similarly, the reasons why the norm did not last remain murky; was it a norm limited by personalities, such that China did not feel the norm held once President Trump replaced President Obama? Or, did other factors in the relationship undercut its internalization on the Chinese side? *See* Lorand Laskai, *A New Old Threat: Countering the Return of Chinese Industrial Cyber Espionage* (Council on Foreign Relations, Dec. 6, 2018), *at* https://www.cfr.org/report/threat-chinese-espionage.

[145] Charlevoix Commitment, *supra* note 10.

C. The Complimentary Potential of Cybernorms

A key, if underappreciated, feature of cybernorms is their capacity to complement other regulatory responses. To be clear, norms need not align with law or technology—there are plenty of examples where law contemplates certain behavior (not violating copyright protections) and the actual norm another (i.e., ignoring copyright protections). Yet, the converse is possible; in addition to regulating behavior directly, norms may indirectly facilitate the development of law or technological responses.

For example, neither the Charlevoix Commitment nor Paris Call Principle 3 have any legal foundation—they are "political" commitments, proposing norms that rest on shared political expectations.[146] States are thus not legally bound to behave in accordance with their contents.[147] This is not to say, however, that norm-conforming activity will lack any legal significance. To the extent states conform their behavior to a norm, it constitutes an example of a general practice—one of two requirements for a rule of customary international law.[148] Over time, repetition of such behavior may lead states to understand the behavior as legally required. In other words, norm promotion and internalization may constitute the first stages in the creation of new customary international law. Alternatively, sufficient internalization of a norm among some group of states may lead them to promote a treaty to codify its existence.[149] Moreover, where states belong to a multilateral or multistakeholder group that endorses a norm, individual states may ensure its internalization through domestic law. Thus, some states have made the normative "Kimberly Process"—a certification system designed to restrict trade in "blood diamonds" used to finance civil wars and other conflicts—into a domestic legal regime.[150]

Norms may even complement technological responses to election interference. The social quality of norms often requires interaction among group members. Where norms emerge for information and communication technology companies, it often means regular interactions and interpretations. These behaviors may provide opportunities for information sharing and coordination that create more opportunities for technical fixes than companies would identify operating in isolation. It may even facilitate innovations that would not have been possible without collaboration. Nor must these technical improvements depend only on norms from industry itself; the regular use of organizational platforms by norm entrepreneurs, including states, suggests that there may be opportunities for experts to interact in such settings in similar ways.

[146] For more on the distinction between legally binding and nonbinding agreements, *see* Duncan B. Hollis, Rapporteur, *Binding and Non-binding Agreements: Seventh Report*, Inter-American Juridical Committee, OEA/Ser.Q/CJI/Doc.614/20 rev. 1 (Aug. 4, 2020).

[147] As a legal matter, states might be precluded from behaving under these norms in ways that violate domestic or international law. Yet, from a normative perspective, such limitations could prove unavailing if group identity ties trump members' respect for the rule of law.

[148] *ILC Draft conclusions on customary international law*, *supra* note 17, at 124 ("Conclusion 2: To determine the existence and content of a rule of customary international law, it is necessary to ascertain whether there is a general practice that is accepted as law (opinio juris)").

[149] For example, the prior informed consent procedure laid out in the Rotterdam Convention originally began as a voluntary system devised by states and the chemical industry to address the import and export of hazardous chemicals. *See* Convention on the Prior Informed Consent Procedure for Certain Hazardous Chemicals and Pesticides in International Trade (Sept. 10, 1998) 38 I.L.M. 1.

[150] *See, e.g.*, Clean Diamond Trade Act, Public Law 108–119 (Apr. 25, 2003).

Witness, for example, efforts following the Christchurch Call to revamp the Global Internet Forum to Counter Terrorism into a stand-alone organization that may include a research and development arm; this could, over time, generate new technological approaches to the problem set.[151] States and other stakeholders should consider the potential of similar efforts in the fight to defend democracies.

V. A New Cybernorm for Defending Democracies? Paris Call Principle 3

On November 12, 2018, French President Emmanuel Macron issued the *Paris Call for Trust and Security in Cyberspace*. The Paris Call is a political commitment establishing nine voluntary cybersecurity principles to advance cooperation on meaningful rules of the road in cyberspace. Today, it is the largest multistakeholder document on cybersecurity, with over 1,000 signatories, including 76 states, 26 local governments, 631 companies, and 343 civil society and academic institutions.[152]

Among its nine principles, Principle 3 provides that signatories will:

> [A]ssist one another and implement cooperative measures . . . [to] . . . Strengthen our capacity to prevent malign interference by foreign actors aimed at undermining electoral processes through malicious cyber activities.[153]

Paris Call Principle 3 clearly represents an effort at norm entrepreneurship—seeking to identify a set of behaviors that are proper and others that are improper for a specific group of actors. It is interesting to see the strategic choices that lay behind this effort as well as the challenges that lie ahead.

Rather than target a specific preexisting group for norm development, the Paris Call represents a new community, and the largest multistakeholder one formed to date. Yet, the Paris Call community is notable for who lies outside its orbit—it does not include key players like the Russian Federation, or even the United States itself.[154] As such, it seems unlikely to impose any concrete conformity expectations on those actors (or their proxies). On the other hand, Principle 3 is, like the Charlevoix Commitment, framed to focus on strengthening signatories' capacity via both assistance and cooperative measures to prevent malicious cyber activity leading to malign electoral interference by foreign actors. Thus, its value may lie more in coordinating defensive and responsive measures than in proscribing behavior.

[151] Microsoft, *Global Internet Forum to Counter Terrorism: An Update on Our Progress Two Years On*, Microsoft on the Issues (July 24, 2019), *at* https://blogs.microsoft.com/on-the-issues/2019/07/24/global-internet-forum-to-counter-terrorism-an-update-on-our-progress-two-years-on/.

[152] The seventy-six states include every member of the European Union, as well as Japan, Qatar, and Canada. Local governments, including the U.S. states of Colorado, Virginia, and Washington, have also signed on. Industry participants include Microsoft, Facebook, and Huawei, while civil society representatives include Access Now and the Internet Society. *See Supporters*, *supra* note 12.

[153] Paris Call, *supra* note 11.

[154] China's role may be a bit more ambiguous; in the summer of 2019, Huawei signed onto the Paris Call. Huawei, *Huawei Joins Paris Call for Trust, Security in Cyberspace* (July 2019), *at* https://www.huawei.com/en/press-events/news/2019/7/huawei-joins-paris-call.

Even for those who have signed, it is still young enough that the strength and immediacy of signatories' ties to the group may be shallow. Combined with the large size of the group, therefore, Goodman and Jinks's research might suggest that we should not expect too much internalization from this sort of effort.[155] On the other hand, the nature of the foreign election threat may require coordination across groups rather than leaving states, industry, civil society, and the academy to work on these problems in their respective silos. Simply put, it may be neither practical nor effective to isolate cybernorm projects to small groups given the heterogeneity of the threat matrix presented.

That said, it is worth emphasizing that particular norm entrepreneur "champions" have emerged for Principle 3. On the Paris Call's one-year anniversary, Microsoft and the Alliance for Securing Democracy announced the creation of the "Paris Call Community on Countering Election Interference."[156] In May 2020, they were joined in this effort by the government of Canada.[157] The "community" is a multistakeholder project focused on implementing Paris Call Principle 3 by working to clarify the principle's contents, identifying best practices in applying it, and building capacity to strengthen defenses against foreign electoral interference.[158] It is too soon to know whether this new "community" will prove effective, but by culling together a group of like-minded stakeholders, there is the possibility that if they can achieve shared expectations of where to draw the lines of propriety, those lines may cascade throughout the broader Paris Call community.[159] Indeed, the creation of an organizational platform for these efforts is a practice that has had success in other settings.[160]

Ultimately, the future of Paris Call Principle 3 as a cybernorm will depend on its actual behavioral expectations. Looking at the text more closely, it appears to contain at least three, separate norm candidates.

- First, it delineates a zone of unwanted behavior—"*malign interference by foreign actors aimed at undermining electoral processes*";
- Second, it proscribes specific means for engaging in such behavior: "*through malicious cyber activities*"; and
- Third, it commits signatories to positive acts to "*prevent*" this proscribed behavior, namely: (1) *assistance* and (2) implementation of "*cooperative measures*" that (3) "*[s]trengthen*" their capacity for such prevention.

Paris Call signatories may internalize all three directives, although, as noted, the third has the highest potential to prove effective in combatting foreign election interference

[155] GOODMAN & JINKS, *supra* note 104, at 28.

[156] John Frank, *Paris Call: Growing Consensus on Cyberspace*, MICROSOFT BLOG (Nov. 12, 2019), *at* https://blogs.microsoft.com/on-the-issues/2019/11/12/paris-call-consensus-cyberspace/.

[157] Government of Canada, *FAQ—The Paris Call for Trust and Security in Cyberspace* (May 2020), *at* https://www.canada.ca/en/democratic-institutions/news/2020/05/frequently-asked-questions---paris-call-trust-and-security-in-cyberspace.html.

[158] *Id.*

[159] *See* Finnemore & Hollis, *supra* note 18, at 26–27.

[160] *See supra* note 111, and accompanying text.

(presumably, most of the signatories already forgo the activities in the first two directives).

Still, there is ample room for interpretative issues to arise even among like-minded participants. At present, signatories lack common definitions for key concepts like "electoral processes." Does that term only cover elections themselves (e.g., voter registration, candidate selection, and actual voting)? Does it also include all campaign activity or even anything that might constitute political speech? Similar challenges lie behind wording such as "undermining electoral processes"—while some activity would seem clearly covered (e.g., preventing an election or manipulating its results), its coverage of other activities (e.g., an influence campaign to persuade voters to favor or drop a particular candidate) is open to debate. The definition of "malign" may raise similar issues—for example, would foreign support of political groups with the intention of facilitating their participation in a domestic political process qualify as malign? In short, the Paris Call "community" has real work to do to assist the development of a multistakeholder community's shared expectations of what it means to proscribe electoral interference by malicious cyber activities and strengthen capacities to prevent or defend against these.

Of course, even if these meanings can be clarified, application issues also loom in the coming months and years. For example, does Principle 3's call for strengthening capacity sanction precursor efforts at *detection*, identifying the existence of foreign malign cyber activities? And how can we measure whether any assistance or cooperation that is covered will (or will not) "strengthen the capacity" to prevent the unwanted interference?

Interactions among adherents may work through these issues, even as no state (nor any stakeholder) will be legally bound to apply Paris Call Principle 3. At the same time—like other cybernorms, Principle 3 may indirectly support other moves to improve legal and technical responses to the threat of foreign election interference online. As noted, to the extent state signatories undertake concrete acts (and refrain from other acts) to conform with the Paris Call, it will constitute "state practice" that may contribute to the formation of new customary international law.[161] Such activity may also lead those same states (perhaps in concert with industry, civil society, and academic signatories) to revisit domestic legal regimes.[162] The Paris Call also provides a platform from which information and communication technology (ICT) companies can share their technical solutions. By spreading awareness (and perhaps even use) of tools like the Alliance for Securing Democracy's *Hamilton Dashboard*,[163] Microsoft tools such as *AccountGuard* and *ElectionGuard*, Jigsaw/Google's *Project Shield*, and *Facebook Protect*, the Paris Call may provide a forum for solidifying the use of technologies to protect campaigns and voting from malign interference.[164]

Ultimately, the Paris Call is a normative "work in progress"—it represents a concrete effort to employ the power of norms to defend democracies. While it is not without

[161] *See supra* note 148, and accompanying text.

[162] *See supra* notes 150, and accompanying text.

[163] Alliance for Securing Democracy, *Hamilton 2.0 Dashboard*, *at* https://securingdemocracy.gmfus.org/hamilton-dashboard/.

[164] *See supra* notes 81–87, and accompanying text.

limitations, it provides a rallying point for cooperation and assistance in defending against foreign election interference through online means. As the Community of Interest evolves, it may provide a menu of tools to group members, be they states, ICTs, or civil society. If successful, it could further instantiate and effectively internalize a norm to protect democracies from foreign actors bent on interfering with elections and/or undermining the very concept of democracy itself.

VI. Conclusion

Foreign election interference, including various manifestations of it online, pose a significant challenge to the functioning of democratic states. It is a multilayered, heterogeneous problem set, ranging from threats to online resources, voting machines, electoral processes themselves, and the various information and communication ecosystems through which political discourse occurs. Existing regimes may help respond to this threat matrix, including key portions of international law (e.g., the duty of nonintervention), domestic law (e.g., criminal law, contractual terms of service), and technological platforms (e.g., E2E verifiability).

Yet it is also clear that each of these regulatory responses are insufficient in and of themselves as responsive tools. International law lacks tailor-made rules for election interference, while the application of other existing rules and regimes suffers under current conditions of state silence, existential debates, interpretative disputes, and attribution. Domestic law avoids many of these difficulties, but faces its own set of problems, from sovereign immunity to limited prescriptive and enforcement jurisdiction. And while there is heightened attention to security in new technological tools, achieving widespread adoption while keeping up with evolving innovations by those bent on attacking voting processes or producing disinformation suggests technology alone cannot constitute a panacea.

In this chapter, we have made the case for adding an additional regulatory vehicle—cybernorms—to the menu of responsive measures for online foreign election interference. As socially constructed collective expectations for proper behavior by specific communities, cybernorms provide a flexible and dynamic tool. If successful, they can change the behavior of relevant actors, whether by convincing members of a community to forgo unwanted election interference or by having states and other stakeholders internalize the need to cooperate and respond to stave off such interference by others. Cybernorms can, moreover, do so without detracting from other regulatory responses, whether in international law, domestic law, or the technical sphere.

At the same time, we are not claiming that cybernorms are guaranteed to work—failure remains an option, particularly given problems of rogue actors, application, and impermanence. Nor do we claim that advancing cybernorms will produce better outcomes than other new international or domestic legal candidates, let alone technical innovations. Such a claim would require further research and analysis. And while that would be an interesting project, it is not the present one.

Our claim is more modest. We believe that cybernorm projects can provide an *additional* avenue for the fight to defend democracies. Importantly, this includes much-needed normative capacity building measures that can help with broader socialization, understanding, and ultimately adherence to cybernorms. Efforts like Paris Call Principle 3 (and the work of its champions) provide a template for identifying clear rules of behavior as well as a toolkit of best practices that various actors, including states, industry, and civil society, may adopt to more effectively defend against online election interference and disinformation. Whether states and other stakeholders will clarify Paris Call Principle 3's contours in ways that can have real-world consequences remains to be seen. Careful cultivation and strategic choices will be required to move from normative ideas to fully internalized sets of behavioral expectations for relevant actors. And it may be the case, that other cybernorm projects and those focused on their implementation and adherence will be needed in the future to address shifting tools and techniques. For now, we simply want to establish the value of such efforts. Cybernorms offer an additional "social" approach for combating foreign election interference that states and other stakeholders should deploy alongside existing regulatory efforts in law and technology.

15

Using Campaign Finance Reform to Protect U.S. Elections from "Dark Money" and Foreign Influence

Ian Vandewalker and Lawrence Norden

I. Introduction

In the months leading up to U.S. Election Day in 2016, a hostile foreign power attacked the United States with a multifaceted campaign designed to influence the election.[1] Among other things, this election interference included covert spending directed by Russian President Vladimir Putin on online political ads designed to sway public opinion. In 2018, the U.S. Department of Justice charged a Russian with alleged ties to the Kremlin of conspiring to interfere in the 2018 midterm elections.[2] Investigations revealed Russian trolls disguised as Americans attacking candidates, telling audiences how to vote, and even soliciting donations to a political committee. And in 2020, researchers and journalists found a network of trolls targeting U.S. politics that was acting on behalf of Russia, even though it was operating in—and employing people from—Ghana and Nigeria.[3]

The menace is only likely to intensify in upcoming elections.[4] U.S. Department of Homeland Security (DHS) Undersecretary Christopher Krebs predicted that hostile action by foreign adversaries in 2018 was just the "warm-up" for the "big game" in 2020.[5] In late 2019, the leaders of seven federal defense, intelligence, and law enforcement agencies issued a joint statement warning:

[1] *See* U.S. Department of Justice, Office of Special Counsel Robert S. Mueller III, Report on the Investigation into Russian Interference in the 2016 Presidential Election, vol. I, 14–36 (2019); U.S. Senate Select Comm. on Intelligence, *Russian Active Measures Campaigns and Interference in the 2016 U.S. Election*, vol. 2; Russia's Use of Social Media, S. Rep. 116-XX (2019); Office of the Director of National Intelligence, *Assessing Russian Activities and Intentions in Recent U.S. Elections*, ICA 2017-01D (2017).

[2] Pete Williams & Tom Winter, *Russian Woman Charged with Attempted Meddling in Upcoming U.S. Midterms*, NBC News (Oct. 19, 2018). Defense Secretary Jim Mattis confirmed that the Kremlin interfered in the midterms in 2018. Lara Seligman, *Mattis Confirms Russia Interfered in U.S. Midterm Elections*, Foreign Pol'y (Dec. 1, 2018).

[3] Clarissa Ward et al., *Russian Election Meddling Is Back—Via Ghana and Nigeria—And in Your Feeds*, CNN (Apr. 11, 2020).

[4] The 2018 Worldwide Threat Assessment of the U.S. Intelligence Community, presented to Congress in February, predicted that Russia will "continue using propaganda, social media, false-flag personas, sympathetic spokespeople, and other means of influence to try to exacerbate social and political fissures in the United States." Daniel R. Coats, Director of National Intelligence, *Worldwide Threat Assessment of the US Intelligence Community* 11 (2018).

[5] Daniel Chaitin, *Top DHS official: Hackers Using Midterms as "Warm-Up" for "Big Game" in 2020*, Washington Examiner (Oct. 18, 2018).

Ian Vandewalker and Lawrence Norden, *Using Campaign Finance Reform to Protect U.S. Elections from "Dark Money" and Foreign Influence* In: *Defending Democracies.* Edited by Duncan B. Hollis and Jens David Ohlin, Oxford University Press (2021).
 DOI: 10.1093/oso/9780197556979.003.0016

> Our adversaries want to undermine our democratic institutions, influence public sentiment and affect government policies. Russia, China, Iran, and other foreign malicious actors all will seek to interfere in the voting process or influence voter perceptions. Adversaries may try to accomplish their goals through a variety of means, including social media campaigns, directing disinformation operations or conducting disruptive or destructive cyber-attacks on state and local infrastructure.[6]

Any such action, regardless of whether it can be pinpointed as the proximate cause of an election result, represents a threat to national security and popular sovereignty—the exercise of the American people's power to decide the course their government takes.

U.S. law has banned election spending by foreign individuals and entities for more than fifty years. The ban was originally motivated by concerns that "foreign governments had attempted to influence U.S. policy through techniques outside normal diplomatic channels."[7] Its current incarnation in the federal campaign finance regime prohibits foreign individuals, companies, and governments from contributing to candidates or parties or spending money "in connection with" an American election.[8] In 2012, the U.S. Supreme Court upheld the ban in the face of a constitutional challenge, affirming the decision of a lower court that held: "It is fundamental to the definition of our national political community that foreign citizens do not have a constitutional right to participate in, and thus may be excluded from, activities of democratic self-government."[9]

Yet despite the ban on foreign spending in U.S. elections, twenty-first-century upheavals—namely, the rapid development of the internet and the drastic deregulation of campaign finance (and in particular the rise of dark money groups and direct corporate political spending, which until recently were generally prohibited)—have created huge weaknesses in the legal protections against foreign meddling. These loopholes must be closed to make the ban work as intended.

A. The Internet

The first vulnerability stems from the quick rise of the internet as a mass medium and the failure of regulation to keep up. As the amount of time Americans spend online has jumped, so has the importance of the internet as a medium for political

[6] Joint Statement from DOJ, DOD, DHS, DNI, FBI, NSA, and CISA, *Ensuring Security of 2020 Elections* (Nov. 5, 2019).

[7] Lori Fisher Damrosch, *Politics Across Borders: Nonintervention and Nonforcible Influence over Domestic Affairs*, 83 Am J. Int'l L. 22 (1989). Numerous statements from members of Congress on the Senate and House floor show a concern about foreign entities and principals using political spending as "nondiplomatic means" to influence American policies. Bruce D. Brown, *Alien Donors: The Participation of Non-Citizens in the U.S. Campaign Finance System*, 15 Yale L. & Pol'y Rev. 509–510 (1996).

[8] 52 U.S.C. § 30121(a)(1). There are various exceptions. *See* FEC, *Foreign Nationals*, https://www.fec.gov/updates/foreign-nationals/.

[9] Bluman v. FEC, 800 F. Supp. 2d 281, 288 (Dist. D.C. 2011) (three-judge court), *aff'd*, 565 U.S. 1104 (2012) (noting the interest in excluding foreigners from activities "intimately related to the process of democratic self-government" (quoting Bernal v. Fainter, 467 U.S. 216, 220 (1984)).

advocacy.[10] Campaign spending online has increased dramatically; the $1.4 billion spent online in the 2016 election was almost eight times higher than in 2012.[11] There is every reason to believe that it will increase even more. It's not surprising that foreign powers would look to the internet to meddle.

Russia's interference in the 2016 election provides a stark illustration. A company in St. Petersburg called the Internet Research Agency (IRA) employed "trolls" to spread divisive messages about U.S. politics.[12] The company was funded by an oligarch with close ties to Russian President Vladimir Putin.[13] The operatives bought online ads through fake accounts whose owners pretended to be Americans, and messages from the fake accounts were seen by hundreds of millions of people in the United States. The ads appeared on all the major internet platforms, including Facebook, Gmail, Google's search engine, Twitter, and YouTube.[14]

B. Dark Money

The second key weakness comes from the ability of some political spending groups to hide their donors' identities. These dark money organizations have flourished since a series of Supreme Court rulings invalidated many campaign finance regulations, and the Federal Election Commission (FEC) has become dysfunctional due to partisan stalemate and failure to reach a quorum.[15] While there is currently no public evidence that Russia violated the ban on foreign national spending by illegally directing funds to dark money groups, the FBI opened an investigation into whether a Russian banker with ties to President Putin used the National Rifle Association's dark money arm to secretly spend on the 2016 election.[16]

[10] Americans today are more inclined to get their news online, with 43% often looking to the internet for news. Jeffrey Gottfried & Elisa Shearer, *Americans' Online News Use Is Closing in on TV News Use* (Pew Research Center, Sept. 7, 2017). The most popular websites attract hundreds of millions of visitors; 53% of the adult U.S. population visits Facebook every day, and 54% of American adults use Google several times a day. Morning Consult, *National Tracking Poll #170923*, 192 (Sept. 29–Oct. 1, 2017). Pew has found that 21% of American adults use Twitter. Shannon Greenwood, Andrew Perrin, & Maeve Duggan, *Social Media Update 2016* (Pew Research Center, Nov. 11, 2016). The hundreds of millions of Americans reached by online platforms dwarf the audience of the most watched TV broadcast of all time. Robinson Meyer, *Facebook Is America's Favorite Media Product*, The Atlantic (Nov. 11, 2016).

[11] Sean J. Miller, *Digital Ad Spending Tops Estimates*, Campaigns & Elections (Jan. 4, 2017).

[12] Mueller, *supra* note 1, at 14–36.

[13] *Id.* at 4.

[14] Elizabeth Dwoskin, Adam Entous, & Craig Timberg, *Google Uncovers Russian-Bought Ads on YouTube, Gmail and Other Platforms*, Washington Post (Oct. 9, 2017).

[15] Decreased transparency has resulted from the Court's deregulatory decisions even though the Court has consistently upheld laws requiring disclosure of political spending. Daniel I. Weiner, *Citizens United Five Years Later* 7 (Brennan Center for Justice, 2015).

[16] Peter Stone & Greg Gordon, *FBI Investigating Whether Russian Money Went to NRA to Help Trump*, McClatchy (Jan. 18, 2018). The Russian banker, Alexander Torshin, was tied to Maria Butina, who was convicted of acting as an unregistered agent for Russia by seeking to influence U.S. politics through National Rifle Association activities. Kenneth P. Doyle, *Russia-Meddling Uproar Worsens as Probe of NRA's Role Is Dropped*, Bloomberg (Aug. 20, 2019).

C. Corporate Spending

Third, corporations and other business entities are currently allowed to spend on American elections even when their owners would be prevented from doing so by the foreign spending ban. There are various examples of foreign nationals using domestic companies to engage in secret election spending.[17]

D. Solutions

This chapter offers practical reforms to make it far more difficult for any foreign power to engage in political spending in American elections in each of these three areas.[18] All these reforms are permissible under current Supreme Court doctrine. Most importantly, we recommend both federal and state lawmakers take the following steps:[19]

- **Update political spending laws for the internet** with the framework used for television and radio ads: requiring disclosure of funding sources and explicitly banning foreign spending for ads that mention candidates before an election.
- **Eliminate dark money** by requiring any organization that spends a significant amount on elections to disclose its donors.
- **Extend the ban on foreign spending** to domestic corporations and other business entities that are owned or controlled by foreign interests.

II. Update Political Spending Laws for the Internet

Although candidates, political consultants, and even trolls connected to foreign states have shown they understand the power of the internet for political advocacy, the law has not kept up with the rapid technological and cultural developments of the internet age. Unlike television spots, internet ads are cheap to produce, they can either be disseminated widely or be precisely targeted at little or no cost, and it is easy to hide their

[17] For example, a Mexican businessman hid the foreign origin of his funds by passing money through a shell company incorporated in the United States before spending on the 2012 San Diego mayoral race. Greg Moran, *Feds Say Azano Wanted to "Buy A Mayor,"* San Diego Union-Tribune (July 27, 2016).

[18] For a fuller discussion, refer to our white paper: Ian Vandewalker & Lawrence Norden, *Getting Foreign Funds Out of America's Elections* (Brennan Center for Justice, 2018).

[19] Members of Congress have introduced bills that incorporate some of these policies. The bipartisan Honest Ads Act, sponsored by Senators Amy Klobuchar (D-Minn.), Lindsey Graham (R-S.C.), and Mark Warner (D-Va.), and in the House by Representative Derek Kilmer (D-Wash.), would bring online ads under existing rules for political spending and strengthen disclaimer rules. Honest Ads Act, S.1356, 116th Congress (2019); Honest Ads Act, H.R.2592, 116th Congress (2019). The DISCLOSE Act of 2019, introduced by Senator Sheldon Whitehouse (D-R.I.), would eliminate dark money and apply the ban on political spending to corporations that are foreign owned or controlled. Democracy Is Strengthened by Casting Light On Spending in Elections (DISCLOSE) Act of 2019, S.1147, 116th Congress (2019). Versions of both pieces of legislation were included in omnibus legislation passed by the House of Representatives in 2019. For the People Act of 2019, H.R.1, 116th Congress (2019).

true source. Yet the law fails to reflect current reality. Congress last updated campaign finance law in 2002, and the FEC's last substantial rulemaking was in 2006.[20]

Russia's sprawling effort to influence the 2016 election through online ads illustrates the dangers of failing to update our campaign finance regime to fully include the internet. The expenditures of the IRA were not publicly reported anywhere at the time. Neither the accounts nor the ads contained any outward clue as to the Russian source of the spending; on the contrary, they were made to disguise the speakers as Americans. The same actors have interfered in the 2018 and 2020 elections.[21] Social media platforms and researchers have uncovered similar activity originating in Iran and Venezuela.[22]

The reach of online trolls can be vast. Paid posts from IRA accounts reached tens of millions of Americans across multiple social networks in 2016. Plus, unpaid, or "organic," posts from the same accounts reached several times more Americans, appearing in their Facebook and Twitter feeds, among other places. Trolls employ paid ads and organic posts in concert with ads driving audiences to organic content—for example, if a Facebook user "likes" an ad, they are automatically signed up to follow that account and will see its posts in their feed.[23] Trolls also use ad buys, which come with analytics about audience responses, to refine messages for organic content. Because trolls use paid ads and unpaid posts in these interdependent ways, the regulation of ads can address foreign influence operations that heavily use organic content.

To help prevent foreign states from using online tools to interfere in U.S. elections, we recommend five discrete reforms to bring election spending laws into the information age: (1) rules requiring disclosure of ads mentioning candidates in mass media should be expanded to apply to online ads; (2) rules requiring disclaimers in ads stating who paid for them should apply online, even to small ads on social media; (3) political ads online should be entered into a public database; (4) companies that sell political ads should be required to work to block foreign purchases; and (5) purchases of political ads with credit cards should use the address verification system to confirm a U.S. address.

[20] In the rulemaking, the FEC required disclaimers on paid online ads, but not on content shared for free. 11 C.F.R. § 100.26; *see also* Cynthia L. Bauerly, *The Revolution Will Be Tweeted and Tmbl'd and Txtd: New Technology and the Challenge for Campaign-Finance Regulation*, 44 U. Tol. L. Rev. 530–535 (2013). In the 2004 election, political spending online was only about 2% of what it was in 2016. Patrick Quinn & Leo Kivijarv, *US Political Media Buying 2004*, 24 Int'l J. Advertising 131–134 (2015).

[21] *See, e.g.*, Young Mie Kim, *New Evidence Shows How Russia's Election Interference Has Gotten More Brazen* (Brennan Center for Justice, Mar. 5, 2020). The criminal complaint filed by federal prosecutors against an employee of the IRA contained evidence of IRA trolls targeting the 2018 elections. United States of America v. Elena Alekseevna Khusyaynova, 1:18-MJ-464 (Virginia 2018). *See also Truth on the Ballot: Fraudulent News, the Midterm Elections, and Prospects for 2020*, PEN America 39 (2019).

[22] *See, e.g.*, Tony Romm, *Facebook Disables Russian and Iranian Efforts to Manipulate Users, Raising New 2020 Election Fears*, Washington Post (Feb. 12, 2020); Donie O'Sulllivan, *Facebook and Twitter Remove Thousands of Fake Accounts Tied to Russia, Venezuela and Iran*, CNN (Jan. 31, 2019).

[23] Mike Isaac, *At Facebook, Hand-Wringing over a Fix for Fake Content*, N.Y. Times (Oct. 27, 2017) (noting that liking an account's promoted post will subscribe a user to that account on Facebook); Jonathan Albright, *Instagram, Meme Seeding, and the Truth about Facebook Manipulation, Pt. 1*, Medium (Nov. 8, 2017) (discussing Russian accounts use of user engagements to increase reach on Instagram).

A. Solution: Expand Rules to Include Candidate Mentions Online

As federal law stands now, online expenditures on "express advocacy" that explicitly supports or opposes a candidate's election must be disclosed. Of course, the law clearly prohibits foreign nationals from engaging in such advocacy. But advertisers are clever about crafting messages that skirt express advocacy. These "sham issue ads" typically attack or praise a candidate on some divisive subject without explicitly calling for a vote for or against the candidate. Spending on this type of ad close to an election must be disclosed if the ad is run on television or radio, but not if it appears on the internet.[24]

Congress should extend the disclosure rule to include internet ads that mention candidates in the final weeks before an election. Facebook and Google have called for this reform,[25] and the Honest Ads Act, pending in Congress, would accomplish it.[26]

B. Solution: Broaden Disclaimer Requirements

Disclaimer requirements (sometimes called "stand by your ad" rules) put information about who paid for an ad in the content of the ad itself. Disclaimers are vital to transparency because they inform audiences about who is speaking at the moment the communication takes place. Under current law, only ads that are already illegal for foreign nationals to buy must contain disclaimers.[27] But even if foreign powers illegally buy political ads and lie in the disclaimer, the information can provide clues for law enforcement and others to follow.[28]

The FEC has not updated its disclaimer regulations for the current era of internet communication. Paid posts on social media are not adequately covered, and the rules do not deal with the need for disclaimers to follow organic "shares" or "retweets" of paid ads. Disclaimer rules must fully cover the internet's use by political advertisers and close the social media loophole by ensuring that source information remains with the content of any promoted post however it is shared by users.

[24] The 2002 McCain-Feingold law created the category of "electioneering communications," which requires disclosure of any expenditure of more than $10,000 on ads that mention candidates within a specified window, such as sixty days before a general election. 52 U.S.C. § 30104(f). The definition excludes news stories. 52 U.S.C. § 30104(f)(3)(B)(i).

[25] Letter from Colin S. Stretch, General Counsel, Facebook, to Neven F. Stipanovic, Acting Assistant General Counsel, FEC, Nov. 13, 2017, at 4–5 ("Facebook supports policymakers' efforts to extend the disclaimer requirement to include digital or online communications."); Comments of Google LLC re: Internet Communication Disclaimers, Nov. 9, 2017, at 7 ("Congress should extend the definition of electioneering communication for purposes of the Foreign National Ban so that it applies to communications placed for a fee on another person's web site.").

[26] Honest Ads Act, S.1356, 116th Congress (2019). The substance of the Honest Ads Act was included in legislation passed by the House. For the People Act of 2019, H.R.1, 116th Congress (2019).

[27] Campaign finance law requires source disclaimers on anything paid for by a campaign committee, messages that include express advocacy, and electioneering communications.

[28] Special Counsel Robert Mueller, for example, took advantage of aliases and other information that could be revealed by disclaimers in charging the Russian trolls with various federal crimes. Indictment, United States v. Internet Research Agency LLC, et al., No. 1:18-cr-00032-DLF, 2018 WL 914777 (Dist. D.C. Feb. 16, 2016).

C. Solution: Create a Public Database of Online Political Ads

Even an expanded issue ad disclosure rule would leave online ads unregulated if they—like the great majority of the ads from the IRA in Russia[29]—do not mention candidates, meaning there is a need for further transparency. Television and radio broadcasters are currently required to maintain a public "political file" of ad purchases that discuss national political *issues*.[30] This file supplies journalists with the chance to fact-check claims and gives the public the power to hold speakers accountable for inflammatory or false rhetoric.[31] Congress should craft a similar requirement for paid internet political content.

The Honest Ads Act would extend the "political file" requirement to online ad sellers like Facebook and other popular websites. The bill would require major platforms to disclose information about ads that discuss either a candidate or "national legislative issues of public importance."[32] A machine-readable database would allow the public to see crucial information, including the ad itself, the audience targeted, the timing, and payment information.[33]

We recommend the creation of a single, standardized database maintained by the government. Having data from across all platforms in a consistent format would make the data most useful to researchers, journalists, and civil society groups to analyze and synthesize information for the public.

A handful of states have created online political file requirements since the 2016 foreign meddling was revealed. California and New York have enacted new statutes requiring online platforms that sell ads to make public disclosures about ad transactions and ad buyers' identities.[34] Regulators in Washington State drafted new rules in 2018 to accomplish the same.[35]

[29] Alex Stamos, *An Update on Information Operations on Facebook* (Facebook, Sept. 6, 2017). The ads were "dark posts," which are only seen by the targeted audience, so journalists, law enforcement, and the broader public don't know what's being said, never mind how much is spent or by whom. *See* Garett Sloane, *No More "Dark Posts": Facebook to Reveal All Ads*, AdAge (Oct. 27, 2017).

[30] The file includes information about the content of the ad, when and where it was aired, the cost, and the buyer's identity. 47 C.F.R. § 73.1212.

[31] *See* Christopher S. Elmendorf, Ann Ravel, & Abby Wood, *Open Up the Black Box of Political Advertising*, San Francisco Chron. (Sept. 22, 2017); Daniel Kreiss & Shannon McGregor, *Forget Russian Trolls. Facebook's Own Staff Helped Win the Election*, BuzzFeed (Oct. 3, 2017); Siva Vaidhyanathan, *Facebook Wins, Democracy Loses*, N.Y. Times (Sept. 8, 2017).

[32] Honest Ads Act, S.1356, 116th Congress (2019), § 8.

[33] *Id.* The FEC could set forth a standard format in regulations, since consistency will make the data most useful for industry-wide analyses. Regulations could also provide standards for when different versions of the same ad are similar enough that only one needs to be included in the database. Online advertisers frequently make small changes to things like font or background color; not all variations need be captured in the database.

[34] Maryland also enacted a law increasing disclosure requirements for political ads online. The law was prevented from being applied to a group of newspapers that challenged it in court. Although the court recognized the importance and legitimacy of transparency requirements for online political ads, it rejected the specific way Maryland structured its law, which would have required newspaper websites, even with very small circulation, to publish data about ad transactions. Washington Post v. McManus, 944 F.3d 506 (4th. Cir., 2019).

[35] Wash. Admin. Code § 390-18-050. *See also* Eli Sanders, *Washington Regulators Stand Up to Big Tech in Final Rule on State Political Ads*, The Stranger (Nov. 29, 2018).

D. Solution: Require Ad Sellers to Work to Block Foreign Purchases

Congress should enlist the help of the entities in the best position to stop illegal foreign ad buys: the ad sellers themselves, whether social media platforms, search engines, other websites, or traditional media like television. The Honest Ads Act would do this by requiring companies that sell ads to make reasonable efforts to prevent foreign nationals from purchasing political ads.

Facebook, Google, and Twitter have already announced that they will demand better verification of ad buyers' identities, showing that improvements on this score are feasible.[36] The platforms should be transparent about their procedures for identifying ineligible buyers and have a robust and transparent appeals process for buyers who are incorrectly blocked.[37]

E. Solution: Verify Credit Card Addresses

Finally, Congress should consider the potential benefits of the credit card industry's address verification system (AVS), which allows merchants to fight fraud by comparing address information entered by the customer with the cardholder's address on file. Although it is designed to catch fraudsters who have stolen someone's credit card number, the AVS system could be used by companies that sell political ads to verify whether the cardholder has a U.S. address. An analogue can be found in pending legislation that would require political committees to check for a U.S. billing address before accepting a contribution.[38] This relatively simple tool would, of course, only serve as a partial solution, since sophisticated foreign individuals or entities may be able to obtain a credit card with a U.S. billing address. But closing this door to those who try to disguise their foreign source is an easy step in the right direction.

III. Eliminate Dark Money

There is another major loophole in political spending that applies to political expenditures of all types, not just the internet. Dark money, or spending by groups that do not have to reveal their donors, offers foreign powers ways to hide their activity from American voters and law enforcement. Dark money was virtually nonexistent until after 2007, when the Court decided *Wisconsin Right to Life v. Federal*

[36] *Extremist Content and Russian Disinformation Online: Working with Tech to Find Solutions, Before the Subcomm. on Crime and Terrorism*, 115th Congress (2017) (statements of Colin Stretch, General Counsel of Facebook; Richard Salgado, Senior Counsel, Google; and Sean J. Edgett, Acting General Counsel of Twitter, Inc.).

[37] A joint report from Harvard's Berkman Center for Internet & Society and the Center for Democracy & Technology provides a set of recommendations for adequate appeals processes. Erica Newland et al., *Account Deactivation and Content Removal: Guiding Principles and Practices for Companies and Users* (Berkman Center for Internet & Society and the Center for Democracy & Technology, 2011).

[38] Stop Foreign Donations Affecting Our Elections Act, S.1660, 115th Congress (2017).

Election Commission, which freed corporations and unions to engage in sham issue ads mentioning candidates in the weeks before elections.[39] Then, in 2010, the Court decided *Citizens United*, which further expanded the abilities of entities to spend unlimited sums in elections.[40] As a result, secret spending has skyrocketed in the last decade. Since the 2008 election cycle, more than $1 billion in dark money spending has been reported in federal elections.[41]

Improving transparency would help address the threat posed by covert foreign election spending. First, there will be fewer places for illegal foreign spending to hide.[42] Second, even where foreign spenders lie to hide their identities, greater transparency will provide more information to allow the government, media, and public to investigate suspicious spending.[43]

It is impossible to know whether agents of Russia or other foreign powers have used dark money groups as vehicles for secretly spending in American elections. There is, however, evidence of Russian government agents spending on other countries' politics. For example, a Russian bank with links to the Kremlin provided the French far-right party Front National with a $10 million loan in 2014.[44]

Ever since dark money began to proliferate, critics have worried that foreign money could be secretly seeping into the political system.[45] And over the years, a handful of investigations have revealed examples of dark money groups accepting money linked to foreign governments. For example, the American Petroleum Institute, an oil industry trade association, is financed in part by member dues from a Saudi Arabian state-run oil company. The institute gave almost half a million dollars to politically active nonprofits in 2011.[46] The U.S. Chamber of Commerce, a nonprofit trade organization, was put on the defensive when a 2010 report revealed it took dues payments from many foreign firms, including state-owned or state-run companies in Bahrain,

[39] 551 U.S. 449 (2007).

[40] Citizens United v. FEC, 558 U.S. 310 (2010).

[41] *Dark Money Basics*, Center for Responsive Politics, https://www.opensecrets.org/dark-money (last visited Feb. 21, 2018) (chart showing outside spending with no disclosure of donors since 2008 election). Decreased transparency has resulted from the Court's deregulatory decisions even though the Court has consistently upheld laws requiring disclosure of political spending. Daniel I. Weiner, *Citizens United Five Years Later* 7 (Brennan Center for Justice, 2015).

[42] *Cf.* SpeechNow v. FEC, 599 F.3d 686, 698 (D.C. Cir. 2010) ("[R]equiring disclosure of [contribution] information deters and helps expose violations of other campaign finance restrictions, such as those barring contributions from foreign corporations or individuals.").

[43] *See* Independence Inst. v. FEC, 216 F. Supp. 3d 176, 191 (D.D.C. 2016) ("[L]arge-donor disclosures help the Commission to enforce existing regulations and to ensure that foreign nationals or foreign governments do not seek to influence United States' elections.").

[44] Henry Samuel, *Marine Le Pen's Links to Russia under US Scrutiny*, THE TELEGRAPH (London) (Dec. 21, 2016). Various ties, financial and otherwise, have been noted between Russia and far-right parties in Europe. Adrienne Klasa et al., *Russia's Long Arm Reaches to the Right in Europe*, FINANCIAL TIMES (May 23, 2019). The Kremlin also reportedly funded the Alternative for Germany party through below-market gold sales. Andrew Rettman, *Illicit Russian Money Poses Threat to EU Democracy*, EUOBSERVER (Apr. 21, 2017).

[45] As a *Mother Jones* article put it in 2012: "These outfits . . . can take money from foreign citizens, foreign labor unions, and foreign corporations, and they don't have to tell voters about it." Andy Kroll, *How Secret Foreign Money Could Infiltrate US Elections*, MOTHER JONES (Aug. 8, 2012).

[46] Lee Fang, *Saudi-Led Oil Lobby Group Financed 2012 Dark Money Attack Ads*, THE NATION (Nov. 29, 2012). In addition, the American Chemistry Council, a major money spender in federal elections, announced in 2018 that a state-owned Chinese firm, Wanhua Chemical, will become a dues-paying member. Lee Fang, *Chinese State-Owned Chemical Firm Joins Dark Money Group Pouring Cash into U.S. Elections*, THE INTERCEPT (Feb. 15, 2018).

India, and Abu Dhabi.[47] The Chamber, which has spent around $30 million in support of GOP candidates in every federal election cycle since 2010, responded that foreign money is segregated and not used for political spending but refused to discuss how the money is kept separate.[48]

The lack of transparency makes it impossible for the public to know whether the funds were spent on elections.

A. Solution: Strengthen Disclosure for All Political Spending

Transparency about the financing of election campaigns is important for several reasons, as recognized in the Supreme Court's jurisprudence.[49] Information about the sources of spending helps inform voters.[50] At the time they see a political message, they deserve to know who is trying to influence them—which can give clues to how much trust to place in the message.[51] In addition, information about which interests are supporting which candidates gives voters information about the candidates' relationships, beliefs, and likely actions once in office. Requiring political spenders to disclose their activity serves these goals, as well as fighting corruption by deterring it and making it easier to find after the fact.[52]

The DISCLOSE Act, versions of which have been introduced in Congress since 2010, would eliminate dark money.[53] At its core, the legislation would require any group that spent above a threshold amount on elections to disclose its major donors of $10,000 or more. This would fix the problem that the law currently allows groups to choose to organize themselves as nonprofits rather than political committees in order to hide their donors. Under the DISCLOSE Act, the way a group organizes itself under the tax code is irrelevant; rather, it is the act of engaging in political spending that triggers disclosure requirements.[54] Versions of these rules are already in effect in some states, such as California and Washington.[55]

[47] Lee Fang, *Exclusive: Foreign-Funded "U.S." Chamber Of Commerce Running Partisan Attack Ads*, Think Progress (Oct. 5, 2010).

[48] Viveca Novak, *The Chamber and Foreign Contributions*, FactCheck.org (Oct. 8, 2010).

[49] *See* Citizens United v. FEC, 558 U.S. at 366-67 (upholding disclosure against constitutional challenge); *see also* Doe v. Reed, 561 U.S. 186, 199 (2010) ("Public disclosure also promotes transparency and accountability in the electoral process to an extent other measures cannot."); Abby K. Wood, *Campaign Finance Disclosure*, 14 An. Rev. L. & Soc. Sci. 11 (2018) (surveying empirical literature on disclosure).

[50] Citizens United v. FEC, 558 U.S. at 369.

[51] Chisun Lee et al., *Secret Spending in the States* 10 (Brennan Center for Justice, 2016).

[52] The Supreme Court has recognized government interest in "providing the electorate with information, deterring actual corruption and avoiding any appearance thereof." McConnell v. Federal Election Comm'n, 540 U.S. 93, 196 (2003).

[53] *See, e.g.*, Democracy Is Strengthened by Casting Light On Spending in Elections (DISCLOSE) Act of 2019, S.1147, 116th Congress (2019).

[54] In addition, the bill would crack down on the use of intermediary organizations to hide funding sources. Current law invites donors to hide their identity by funneling money through a secretive organization before it ends up in the account of the group that actually spends on politics. The DISCLOSE Act addresses this problem by providing that certain transfers of funds to political spending groups trigger donor disclosure. If one group gives funds to another with reason to know they will be spent on elections, the donor group is required to reveal the major sources of its funding.

[55] California requires all groups, including nonprofits, to report political expenditures, as well as the identities of recent donors. When one group makes significant political expenditures, other groups that have

IV. Ensure Spending by Businesses Is Funded Domestically

The Court's decision in *Citizens United* to allow corporations to spend in elections opened another door for foreign money. A domestic corporation can be financed by, or be a subsidiary of, a foreign corporation.[56] It does not appear the Court intended to grant foreign corporations the right to spend in American elections, since it upheld the ban on foreign individuals' political spending just two years later.[57] But the new possibilities for corporate political spending created by *Citizens United* have the unintended effect of increasing the risk of foreign funds influencing domestic elections.

Although corporations cannot give directly to candidates or parties, they can give to political committees, including super PACs, and make their own expenditures supporting or attacking candidates.[58] Under the federal foreign money ban, corporations organized or based in foreign countries are banned from spending money in American elections. Yet current law allows foreign-owned companies incorporated in the United States to make political expenditures as long as the money derives from domestic operations and the spending decision is not made by a foreign national.[59]

This leaves open the possibility that foreign interests will secretly direct political spending through corporations they own or control.[60] American firms have no shortage of foreign investment. Corporations with majority ownership by foreigners controlled more than $12 trillion in assets in the United States in 2012.[61] Expert

donated to it may also be required to disclose donors. Cal. Gov't Code § 84222; Linda Sugin, *Disclosure, and State Law Solutions for 501(c)(4) Organizations*, 91 Chi.-Kent L. Rev. 895, 904–907 (2016). The state uses a last-in-first-out system of identifying donors to be disclosed; organizations must disclose donations in reverse chronological order until the disclosed contributions are sufficient to account for the political expenditure. Cal. Gov't Code § 84222(e)(1)(C). Donors of less than $1,000 or who indicate that their contributions may not be used for politics are exempt from disclosure. Washington State enacted its own bill to address dark money in March of 2018. *New Bills Are Intended to Spur Voting in Washington*, KXRO News (Mar. 20, 2018).

56 Jon Schwarz & Lee Fang, *Cracks in the Dam: Three Paths Citizens United Created for Foreign Money to Pour into U.S. Elections*, The Intercept (Aug. 3, 2016).

57 Bluman v. FEC, 565 U.S. 1104 (2012). When President Barack Obama in his 2010 State of the Union address lamented that the *Citizens United* decision would allow foreign corporations to spend in U.S. elections, Supreme Court Justice Samuel Alito was caught on camera mouthing "not true" in response. Martin Kady, *Justice Alito Mouths "Not True,"* Politico (Jan. 27, 2010).

58 PACs or "political action committees" are groups that have the primary purpose of spending on elections. They must register with the FEC and are subject to, among other restrictions, limits on the amount of money they can accept from each individual. Super PACs are a type of political committee that was made legal by a lower court decision interpreting *Citizens United* in 2010; they are allowed to take contributions of any amount, including from corporations and unions, in contrast to the contribution limits imposed on other political committees, including candidate committees. SpeechNow.org v. FEC, 599 F.3d 686 (D.C. Cir. 2010). They are supposed to operate independently of candidates and parties.

59 FEC, *Foreign Nationals*, *supra* note 8; Federal Election Commission, Advisory Opinion 2006-15 (May 19, 2006).

60 This is especially so given the fiduciary duty of a subsidiary's managers to pursue the best interests of the owners. Memorandum from Ellen L. Weintraub, Commissioner, Federal Election Commission, Sept. 28, 2016.

61 John C. Coates IV et al., *Quantifying Foreign Institutional Block Ownership at Publicly Traded U.S. Corporations*, Discussion Paper No. 888 11 (John M. Olin Center for Law, Economics, and Business, Harvard University, 2016).

estimates put the portion of U.S. corporate stock owned or controlled by foreigners from 25 percent to 35 percent.[62]

A. Solution: Ban Political Spending by Foreign-owned Firms

Congress should clarify and expand the breadth of the definition of "foreign national" in the statutory ban to restrict the ways that corporations with foreign ownership or control can spend on American elections.[63] The proposed DISCLOSE Act of 2017 provided that a firm is banned from election spending if a foreign national owns or controls 20 percent or more of the corporation's voting shares, or if a foreign government owns or controls 5 percent or more of the voting shares.[64]

The DISCLOSE Act approach is a good one, but it can be strengthened. The risk of foreign money entering elections through business entities is not limited to corporations. Therefore, the rule should apply to other types of organizations, such as limited liability companies (LLCs) and partnerships. Any bill that would regulate corporations according to the percentage of shares with foreign ownership should make explicit that it also applies to LLCs that have publicly traded shares.[65] More generally, LLCs and partnerships—which are governed by state laws determining the ownership interest of each member or partner[66]—can be subjected to a rule providing

[62] Steven M. Rosenthal, *Slashing Corporate Taxes: Foreign Investors Are Surprise Winners*, Tax Notes (Oct. 23, 2017) ("I estimate that foreigners now own about 35 percent of U.S. stock ...."); John Coates, *Statement to the FEC Forum on Corporate Political Spending and Foreign Influence* (June 23, 2016) ("Back to 1982 about 5% of all U.S. corporate stock was held or controlled by foreigners. Now, it's now up to 25.").

[63] *See, e.g.*, Get Foreign Money Out of U.S. Elections Act, H.R. 1615, 115th Congress (2017). The FEC could also address the problem by changing its interpretation of the statutory language, as Commissioner Ellen Weintraub has proposed. Memorandum from Ellen L. Weintraub, Commissioner, Federal Election Commission, Sept. 9, 2016, at 4; *see also* Memorandum from Ellen L. Weintraub, Commissioner, Federal Election Commission, Sept. 28, 2016 (elaborating further on issues concerning potential FEC regulation of foreign-owned corporations). The FEC deadlocked on the proposal, so it has not yet been developed further. Other FEC commissioners have also tried to change the agency's permissive stance toward domestic subsidiaries. Memo from Ann M. Ravel, Commissioner, to the FEC, Aug. 9, 2016 (moving to rescind the advisory opinion allowing domestic subsidiaries of foreign corporations to spend on politics); Memo from Steven T. Walther, Vice Chairman, to the FEC, Sept. 15, 2016 ("The potential influx of foreign money into the American political system has the potential to shake the foundations of the electoral process.").

[64] Democracy Is Strengthened by Casting Light On Spending in Elections (DISCLOSE) Act of 2017, S.1585, 115th Congress (2017). There are other factors that would make a corporation subject to the ban, such as a foreign national having the power to direct the decision making process of the firm. By limiting the triggering percentage to 5% or more, the bill minimized the compliance burden, since purchases of 5% or more, along with the buyer's citizenship, must already be reported to the Securities and Exchange Commission within ten days of the purchase. 17 C.F.R. § 240.13d-101. SEC, *Schedule 13D*, https://www.sec.gov/fast-answers/answerssched13htm.html ("When a person or group of persons acquires beneficial ownership of more than 5% of a voting class of a company's equity securities registered under Section 12 of the Securities Exchange Act of 1934, they are required to file a Schedule 13D with the SEC.").

[65] The FEC's regulations treat LLCs as corporations if they have publicly traded shares or chose to file with the IRS as corporations. Other LLCs with multiple members are treated as partnerships. 11 C.F.R. § 110.1(g).

[66] An LLC's operating agreement determines the ownership interest of each of its members. A partnership agreement typically sets the ownership of each partner, with default rules set by statute in cases where there is no agreement. Ciara Torres-Spelliscy, personal communication, Feb. 5, 2018.

that 20 percent or more ownership by foreign nationals disqualifies the firm from spending on elections.[67]

V. Conclusion

For decades, foreign nationals have been technically banned from spending money in connection with any election. But the ban is out of date and not sufficient to counter today's threat. Russian trolls proved that in 2016. Yet more than four years later, Congress and the FEC have done nothing to close the holes in America's defenses, and only a handful of states have taken action. And the trolls continue to try to influence U.S. elections.

The comprehensive package of election spending reforms described here will not only bring some desperately needed reinforcement to the now-flimsy foreign-spending ban, it will bring added transparency to some spending that remains hidden. There is no silver bullet, but taken together, efforts from all of these corners can greatly reduce the ability of a foreign government to manipulate the sovereign right of the United States to conduct its democracy without interference.

[67] Louisiana's ban on contributions from casino interests hinges in part on a test of ownership "of an interest which exceeds ten percent of any legal entity." LA. STAT. ANN. § 18:1505.2(L)(3)(b)(i). New York's charitable trust governance prevents entities with any individual trustee, affiliate, or relative of the trustee who holds more than 35% ownership interest from participating in certain activities. N.Y. EST. POWERS & TRUSTS LAW § 8-1.9. The Small Business Administration runs a business development program for firms owned by socially and economically disadvantaged individuals. 13 C.F.R. § 124.105. Firms are eligible if disadvantaged individuals own at least 51% of the business. U.S. Small Business Association, *Ownership Eligibility*, https://www.sba.gov/partners/lenders/7a-loan-program/terms-conditions-eligibility.

16
Conclusion: An Outsider Looks In

Herbert Lin

I. Introduction

When Duncan Hollis and Jens Ohlin asked me to pen a conclusion, I reminded them that even if I do cyber analysis and scholarship, I was hardly an international lawyer. They said that was a feature rather than a bug. So, with that disclaimer in mind, I want to employ this conclusion to accomplish two things. First, I start by identifying some law-related issues raised for me by the chapters in this remarkable volume on defending democracies and combating foreign election interference in a digital age. I have grouped my comments into four buckets: (1) thoughts on certain chapters' scoping efforts; (2) the idea of more transparency as a solution to foreign election interference; (3) the possibility of government regulation of platform content moderation; and (4) what I call a "potpourri" of additional reactions. Second, I use these comments as a point of departure (along with reactions to several of the remaining chapters) to introduce a set of research questions for future work by international lawyers (and others) in this nascent field. I end with a nod to the value that international law, and international lawyers, hold for complex problems like foreign election interference.

II. Scoping the Issue

The Hollis and Ohlin introduction contrasts an emphasis in international legal scholarship on matters such as the use of force in cyberspace (and other traditional topics like international humanitarian law) to a scarcity of work on election interference. Hollis and Ohlin note that election interference could in theory constitute an illegal use of force in violation of the UN Charter or an attack under international humanitarian law. Yet, as editors, they made the deliberate choice to focus this volume on nonforceful aspects of election interference. In my view, that was the right choice. Indeed, most of the interesting action and intellectual challenges in this area today are well below lines that might be drawn with respect to any plausible international legal definition of armed conflict, use of force, or armed attack.

Dov Levin's chapter raised for me several issues of concern—not about the scope or content of his analysis, but rather about how he reports scholars of American politics approach the topic of election interference. Contrary to his own views, he notes that "most scholars of American politics are still highly skeptical" that Russian

Herbert Lin, *Conclusion: An Outsider Looks In* In: *Defending Democracies.* Edited by Duncan B. Hollis and Jens David Ohlin, Oxford University Press (2021). © Duncan B. Hollis & Jens David Ohlin. DOI: 10.1093/oso/9780197556979.003.0017

intervention in the 2016 election had any meaningful impact—apparently equating "tipping the election" to "meaningful impact."[1]

But changing voting behavior is not necessarily the only meaningful measure of impact. For myself, I am not sure whether Russian interference "tipped" the election. Yet, I am quite certain that Russian interference further undermined trust and confidence in the election process and increased national polarization.

Levin also cites arguments for American political scholars' "minimal impact on the 2016 election" conclusion based on the fact that Russian-sponsored content was an "infinitesimal fraction" of the overall political content to which voters were exposed prior to the election—and therefore quite unlikely to be of any consequence. But this conclusion is reasonable only if all information were equally important in shaping voter perceptions and beliefs. To illustrate, imagine a hypothetical case in which 99 percent of the information from a campaign were broadcast in Latin, and 1 percent in English. In this case, it would not be surprising that a primarily English-speaking audience receiving all of the campaign's information would be influenced primarily by the 1 percent of the content broadcast in English.

The reader may believe that this example is attacking a straw man. Yet, a substantial body of research in social cognition—and recognized by three Nobel Prizes—has shown that most people do not process all kinds of information "equally." Rather, the default information processing of human beings relies on heuristics that substitute superficial cues for deep analysis of information.[2] For most information processing tasks of everyday life, such processing is adequate. But it is not adequate for making decisions requiring deliberation and analytical reason, even as such decisions are only a small fraction of the decisions one encounters in life. Further, today's information environment—with search engines, social media, and always-on mobile computing devices—is largely optimized to cater to heuristic rather than analytical processing. In short, we should not underestimate the impact of Russian-sponsored content merely because of its relative volume.

In chapter 2, Steven J. Barela and Jérôme Duberry invoke Soviet-era disinformation campaigns as a way to understand how today's election interference differs from its historical antecedents. Comparing Soviet-era disinformation and modern disinformation over Twitter and Facebook, they find a difference in degree, but not in kind. They claim that the digital tools of today enhance the effectiveness of disinformation operations, even if these operations are based on the "old" concepts and strategies of Soviet days.

But as Stalin (or Lenin, or Mao) was once alleged to have said, quantity is a quality all its own. If you are 20 percent richer than I am, we are likely to be able to afford

[1] *See* chapter 1, this volume, at 32.

[2] For a primer on heuristic versus deliberate thinking (also known as System 1 and System 2 thinking), *see* Daniel Kahneman, THINKING, FAST AND SLOW (2011). More scholarly references include HEURISTICS AND BIASES: THE PSYCHOLOGY OF INTUITIVE JUDGMENT (Thomas Gilovich, Dale W. Griffin, & Daniel Kahneman eds., 2002); Shelley Chaiken, *Heuristic versus Systematic Information Processing and the Use of Source versus Message Cues in Persuasion*, 39 J. PERSONALITY & SOC. PSYCHOL. 752 (1980); Richard Petty & John Cacioppo, *The Elaboration Likelihood Model of Persuasion*, 19 ADVANCES IN EXPERIMENTAL SOC. PSYCHOL. 123, 125 (1986). For a contrary view on dual-system cognitive theory, *see* Arie W. Kruglanski & Erik P. Thompson, *Persuasion by a Single Route: A View from the Unimodel*, PSYCHOL. INQUIRY 83–84, 88 (Nov. 9, 2009).

comparable lifestyles, even if your lifestyle may be somewhat more luxurious than mine. But if you are 20,000 percent richer than I am, you will be able to afford a lifestyle that is completely different from mine in almost every way. And the difference between the information technology available for information production, targeting, and distribution available in the Soviet era to what is available today is much more comparable to the latter scenario than the former. Figure 16.1 demonstrates an airbrushed photograph produced with Soviet-era tools. Such pictures can also be produced today. What is significant about them now, however, is that they can be produced by rank amateurs using off-the-shelf software.

In chapter 3, Valeria Marcia and Kevin C. Desouza make the key point that "the protection of information systems from cyberattacks is no longer a sufficient defensive posture [for elections]."[3] Cybersecurity professionals typically identify confidentiality, integrity, and availability as the key attributes of information that their efforts need to protect. Thus, cybersecurity measures generally seek to prevent the hacking of computer and communications systems that manage and handle information. But an actor can also manipulate information itself, "weaponizing it to compromise an adversaries' goals and values to create political disruption."[4] Doing so is not an effort to hack a computer, but rather an effort to hack the all-too-human minds of voters, often by taking advantage of vulnerabilities in human cognition (heuristic thinking) that are difficult or impossible to fix. While cyber hackers take advantage of *flaws* in information technology (aka vulnerabilities), information weaponizers take advantage of the design *features* of information technology and use them in unexpected ways.

Together, chapters 1 through 3 underscore a point made by Hollis and Ohlin in their introduction. By targeting and amplifying societal fault lines (race, class, ethnicity, and so on), the most important impact of foreign interference in an election may be the resulting social division and distrust in the targeted government and/or in its electoral processes, rather than any particular electoral outcome.

Duncan MacIntosh's proposal in chapter 4 to solve the problem of foreign election interference by simply allowing it is puzzling, even if one accepts the basic premise (which I do not) that other nations should have a say in how one nation's political system is constituted. He argues that a United States working to alleviate the conditions that lead other nations to want to intervene in U.S. elections would reduce the need for them to do so. But he articulates no limiting principle to determine how far the United States should go in accommodating the concerns of other nations, and absent such a principle, it is hard to see how any amount of accommodation would fully satisfy another nation. Short of full capitulation to their concerns, other nations would still have incentives to intervene, clandestinely or otherwise.

In chapter 5, Arun Mohan Sukumar and Akhil Deo extend this volume's scope beyond Russian activities to include a rising player, China, examining the way its state-owned social media enterprises may enable it to interfere in Indian elections. In particular, the high integration of Chinese digital platforms into the day-to-day technology usage patterns of many Indian citizens gives Chinese information campaigns significantly greater access to these citizens than to others who do not rely on Chinese

[3] Chapter 3, this volume, at 75.

[4] *Id.*

Figure 16.1 Soviet Cosmonauts circa 1970.

Source: http://www.jamesoberg.com/vanishing_cosmonauts_with_photos.pdf. Images not copyrighted, but supplied courtesy of James Oberg.

(Note the missing person in the top row of the bottom image as compared to the top.)

digital platforms. This is a welcome reminder that the specific content of disinformation campaigns is only one aspect of malign influence efforts.

But what is "malign influence"? A somewhat cynical but nevertheless true-to-life definition would be that malign influence is any activity undertaken by a hostile adversary to gain an advantage, whereas exactly the same activities conducted by the good guys against an adversary would be promoting freedom, democracy, and the rights of the people to govern themselves as they see fit. Still, an activity classified as malign influence may not necessarily be characterized only by hostile intent. For example, it may in fact be driven by a profit motive instead. What the presumption of hostile intent does do is provide a high-level rubric to explain a broad set of activities. In the Chinese case, malign influence is used to include activities as diverse as the Chinese Belt and Road Initiative, Chinese promotion of Huawei products for telecommunications infrastructure, sponsorship of the Confucius Institutes around the world, and Chinese targeting of economic sanctions on U.S. states that are critical to President Trump's political base.[5]

In Chapter 7, James Van de Velde concludes that Russia's 2016 interference was not only *not* an act of war, but that it also was likely a failure—it did not manifestly change the outcome of the election but it did "precipitate a significant U.S. counter reaction."[6] Indeed, he pins his hopes on the possibility that "adversary operations [to interfere in U.S. elections] prove politically more counterproductive for the authoritarian states of the world than successful in effecting the political change they seek."

An analogy could be the assertion that the attack on Pearl Harbor was a strategic failure for Japan. Indeed, that attack in 1941 instantly unified an American people divided on the merits of war abroad and ultimately led to the unconditional surrender of Japan four years later. But this "strategic failure" for Japan wound up costing over one hundred thousand American lives,[7] and Pearl Harbor is hardly regarded by Americans as a Japanese failure but rather as a tremendous success for Japan. Similarly, in the wake of senior Russian officials celebrating the Trump victory and congratulating themselves on the outcome immediately after the 2016 election,[8] the installation of Donald Trump as president has contributed to the decline of American influence around the world and markedly increased tensions toward America's most stalwart allies. Both outcomes have served important geopolitical objectives for Russia. Whether the Russian intervention will ultimately be a failure for Russia is unclear at this time. Yet, at a minimum, it will take a long time to restore lost American influence and trust among allies and neutrals alike regardless of who the next U.S. president is, even if such restoration is among that president's goals.

III. On Transparency

With this volume's central thrust focused on examining international law's coverage of foreign election interference, it is interesting to see international lawyers themselves finding that law comes up short. Both Chimène I. Keitner (chapter 8) and Jens

[5] Edward Helmore, *Chinese Retaliatory Tariffs Aim to Hit Trump in His Electoral Base*, The Guardian (June 24, 2018).

[6] Chapter 7, this volume, at 171.

[7] *The Japanese Surrender*, Encyclopædia Britannica (Dec. 2, 2019), *at* https://www.britannica.com/topic/Pacific-War/The-Japanese-surrender#ref337330.

[8] Adam Entous & Greg Miller, *U.S. Intercepts Capture Senior Russian Officials Celebrating Trump Win*, Washington Post (Jan. 5, 2017).

David Ohlin (chapter 11) conclude that international law is inadequate for addressing election interference and arrive at roughly similar solutions. Ohlin advocates a transparency regime in which parties attempting to interfere with elections are publicly identified *in real time*, thus preventing foreign actors—such as Russian troll farms—from engaging in political speech while masquerading as Americans.[9] Keitner argues that "publicizing and stigmatizing disinformation campaigns and other efforts to manipulate public opinion might have as much effect as attempts to prohibit them."[10]

Keitner's claim may well be true, though surely not in the sense that she intended. Attempts to prohibit election interference through international legal means may well be ineffective for a variety of reasons, and drawing public attention to foreign attempts at manipulating public opinion is similarly likely to be ineffective because of the various limitations on human cognition described previously.

Ohlin's proposal takes for granted that real-time identification of interfering actors is possible and that such information will be disseminated widely and in a timely fashion to the affected electorate. But with proxy accounts, domestically based "useful idiots," and accounts established long before the election, recognizing foreign interference, to say nothing of attribution to a particular state, may well be difficult and time-consuming. Indeed, it is all too easy to imagine that identification and/or attribution would occur after an election took place, especially if the foreign interfering party was supporting an incumbent administration with a vested interest in taking advantage of such support.

Further, how will news of such information be distributed? And will it be believed in particular by those who are being supported by the interfering party? There is no particular reason to expect that mainstream media news of intelligence community findings, for example, will have anywhere near the reach of the mis- or disinformation carried out by the perpetrator. Indeed, one might also expect further disinformation efforts after the release of transparency-related information to drown it out or to shift the public's attentional focus.

IV. On Government Intervention in Content Moderation

Several chapters interrogate responses to foreign election interference focused on the role that other actors—platforms, the voting public—may play in responding to such interference. In chapter 12, Evelyn Douek concludes that suppression of material intended to interfere with an election violates free speech norms that are prominent in democracies. The norm of free speech has often been associated with Justice Louis Brandeis' concurring opinion in the 1927 U.S. Supreme Court case *Whitney v. California*, which stated that:

> no danger flowing from speech can be deemed clear and present unless the incidence of the evil apprehended is so imminent that it may befall before there is opportunity for full discussion. If there be time to expose through discussion the falsehood and

[9] Chapter 11, this volume, at 251.
[10] Chapter 8, this volume, at 194.

fallacies, to avert the evil by the processes of education, the remedy to be applied is more speech, not enforced silence. Only an emergency can justify repression.[11]

Justice Brandeis' conclusion relies on citizens having the "opportunity for full discussion" and time to "avert the evil by the processes of education." Such opportunity and time are, however, in short supply today given the vastly increased volume and velocity of information and cyber-enabled influence operations exploiting these characteristics of the information environment. Moreover, the opinion was written in 1927 without the benefit of an important body of scientific research in social cognition that has emerged only in the last few decades. As noted, that research demonstrates the inability of people to consistently apply deliberate and analytical thought to the information they receive. In short, given these constraints, it is simply no longer obvious that the cure for bad speech is more speech.

Douek is quite right that governments may not be the best actors to sanitize today's information environment. As I have argued elsewhere, the likelihood of U.S. government action against the cyber-enabled proliferation of false, misleading, or inauthentic statements designed to manipulate and distort the political process is exceedingly low under current interpretations of the First Amendment.[12] Nor is it desirable—imagine a Ministry or Department of Internet Information subject to the direction of the present administration (in 2020).

On the other hand, if one concludes—as I do—that today's information environment is incompatible with the Brandeis free speech norm, that leaves only the platform companies to take action. Douek expresses particular concern about such action because their criteria for doing so are neither well understood nor subject to public scrutiny in the same way that similar government action would be. And perhaps more importantly, the present business model for most platform companies is based on selling advertisements—an approach whose effectiveness increases as user engagement increases. In this context, negative and divisive content (and emotionally satisfying content) are more effective drivers of user engagement than true or useful content. Platform companies thus have few financial incentives to take action to enhance the integrity and civility of the information environment. I return to this point later in section VI. F.

In chapter 6, Alicia Fjällhed, James Pamment, and Sebastian Bay focus on Swedish use of an independent agency operating at arm's length from political oversight to take responsibility for responding to election interference, relying on a strategy designed to warn the public about the danger of misinformation on social media platforms. They conclude that the 2018 Swedish election—the first to be conducted with this agency in place—proceeded appropriately.

Whether or not the counterstrategy was responsible for Swedish success, it is hard to imagine the same approach working in the United States. Complaints about a "deep state" that is unresponsive to the will of the people and to elected government officials are already pervasive in American political discourse. Rather than those complaining

[11] Whitney v. California, 274 U.S. 357 (1927).

[12] Herbert Lin, *On the Organization of the U.S. Government for Responding to Adversarial Information Warfare and Influence Operations*, 15 I/S: J.L. & Pol'y for Info. Soc'y 1 (2019).

of a deep state accepting the resiliency-building role of such an agency, it is more likely that any American analogue would be the first entity that they would target in an election. For example, in the wake of the U.S. Food and Drug Administration's withdrawal of its emergency use authorization for chloroquine and hydroxychloroquine as treatments for COVID-19 (an application actively promoted by the White House), an adviser to the Trump administration said that "[t]his is a Deep State blindside by bureaucrats who hate the administration they work for more than they're concerned about saving American lives."[13]

V. A Potpourri of Other Responses

The remaining chapters propose a variety of other responses that do not group easily into a single category. Indeed, they span a wide range, including extraterritoriality, appeals to the international community to address foreign election interference, and the use of campaign finance laws to prevent foreign sponsorship of campaign ads.

In chapter 9, Ido Kilovaty suggests that cyber operations by Nation X can extend the domain of X's effective control beyond X's physical borders—that is, X's activities affecting cyberspace denizens within the physical borders of Nation Y are under the control of Nation X. Thus, he argues that human rights law protecting the right to self-determination has some degree of extraterritorial application—and thus that Nation X may be accountable under human rights law for electoral intervention in Nation Y. I am both intellectually and politically sympathetic to this argument. But from an operational point of view, it seems no more (and probably less) practical than the extraterritorial application of U.S. domestic law as demonstrated in the indictments handed down in concert with the Mueller report.[14]

In chapter 10, Jacqueline Van De Velde rules out the idea "forceful" countermeasures in response to election interference on both international legal and policy grounds. In her view, forceful countermeasures are both contrary to international law and unwise because of the consequences of allowing them. She suggests three alternatives: (1) acts of retorsion or nonforceful countermeasures; (2) garnering the support of the international community for modifying notions of nonintervention and sovereignty to address explicitly how and to what extent, if any, these notions regulate cyber-enabled election interference of various kinds; and (3) developing a new international treaty regime on such interference.

Of these options, she herself points out that only the first can be undertaken unilaterally—an advantage in a time when working through diplomatic channels is torturous, slow, and unlikely to result in relief of any sort, let alone prompt relief. Sometimes unilateral actions are the only option available to seek redress, and it is for this reason that I am not so quick to dismiss active defense or some other damaging or disruptive cyber operation against perpetrators as possible appropriate responses.

[13] Sheryl Gay Stolberg, *A Mad Scramble to Stock Millions of Malaria Pills, Likely for Nothing*, N.Y. Times (June 16, 2020).

[14] *See* Robert S. Mueller III, Dep't of Justice, Report on the Investigation into Russian Interference in the 2016 Presidential Election, vol. 1 (2019).

To the extent that international law is not clear on such measures, perhaps diplomatic action could focus on what limits short of outright prohibitions should be placed on such responses. In any event, I see no reason to expect that in the long run, all states will refrain from taking forceful countermeasures. If so, it makes some sense to get ahead of such events now and make international law's position more clear.

In chapter 15, Ian Vandewalker and Lawrence Norden assert that the most appropriate way to combat foreign election interference is to use campaign finance laws to target foreign sponsorship of political ads and to expand the definition of what counts as a regulated ad. None of the things that Vandewalker and Norden propose are inherently wrong, and we would be in a better place with them than without them. Nevertheless, I fear that definitional issues of what must be regulated will stymie their intent. In a 1976 decision, *Buckley v. Valeo*, the U.S. Supreme Court created two broad categories of political advertising: express advocacy and issue advocacy.[15] Express advocacy is "Vote for George in the upcoming election" (i.e., it explicitly advocates the election or defeat of a candidate). As the court recognized, such advocacy is easy to recognize and thus easier to regulate under campaign laws. Issue advocacy is harder to recognize; it is ostensibly intended to educate the public on issues broader than just the election of a candidate and thus constitutes protected speech under the First Amendment. For example, it would be issue advocacy to pay for an advertisement claiming that individuals with dark skin are genetically predisposed to violence. For purposes of regulation, it is irrelevant that the content of the ad just happens to align with George's well-known disparagement of those with dark skin, as long as the ad never mentions the upcoming election or George's name.[16]

Many of the Vandewalker and Norden proposals could circumvent the definitional problems simply by abandoning the requirement that ads must be political. For example, it should not contradict any tenet of First Amendment jurisprudence to require the creation of an internet-accessible database of *all* advertisements, rather than just political ones. With appropriate search tools and the like, interested parties could identify even narrowly targeted issue advocacy advertisements and publicize them accordingly.

The vast majority of ads contained in such a database would not be remotely connected to politics or elections, but that simply raises the question of whether such a database could be useful to any other party. At first glance, such a database could be enormously useful for the Federal Trade Commission (FTC), one of whose primary charges is to enforce laws against unfair or deceptive advertising in any medium. Indeed, one could even imagine that financial penalties collected by the FTC could be used to help fund the creation and maintenance of the database.

[15] For an overview of campaign finance issues as understood today, *see* Tammera R. Diehm, Katherine A. Johnson, & Jordan E. Mogensen, *Campaign Finance Issues in Election Communications: An Explanation of the Current Legal Standard and Modern Trends*, 104 MINN. L. REV. 1 (2020).

[16] This example is a long way from the (fuzzy) border separating express and issue advocacy. Some examples coming much closer to the border fall into the category of "electioneering communications," regulated by the Federal Election Communications Act (FECA), 2 U.S.C. § 431 et seq. This term is defined as a broadcast, cable, or satellite communication (but notably not print) that refers to a clearly identified candidate for Federal office; is made within sixty days of an election for that office (or thirty days before a primary or convention); and is targeted to the electorate for that office. The FECA imposes certain restrictions on such communications, but these are not as stringent as those for express advocacy.

VI. Looking Forward—Some Questions for Research

In their introduction, Hollis and Ohlin describe this volume as "an opening salvo in the engagement of international law with the problem of foreign election interference... [that will] spawn further areas for research and dialogue."[17] Taking that salvo seriously, I identify in the following a dozen research questions grouped into six categories that I believe warrant further exploration.

A. The Impact of Social Cognition on the Development of More Effective Remedies

Hollis and Ohlin argue that more research is needed on whether cyber-enabled influence campaigns can actually change minds or votes, or otherwise increase the likelihood that voters or others will do (or not do) things that they otherwise would not have (or would have) done. But understanding the cognitive psychology (often known as social cognition) of such campaigns also has implications for the effectiveness of the remedies proposed in this volume.

- **Research question**: What does research in social cognition say about the likely effectiveness of the various remedies proposed in this volume? How might these predictions be tested empirically?

As an example, Ohlin and Keitner both presume that people care about foreign interference. Certainly some do, and it would be wonderful if those people were sufficiently numerous to turn an election. But would knowledge of foreign interference actually make a difference to committed partisans? If I feel strongly about X, why should I care if another source, foreign or not, appears to support X? The utility of transparency regimes rests on the assumption that a voter will for all practical purposes ignore content that is publicly associated with a foreign actor—and a substantial body of social cognition research indicates the opposite, namely that people are much more likely to remember content of a message without remembering its source. More research on this topic in the election interference context would thus be highly valuable.

B. Disjunction and Commonality between Foreign Election Interference and Domestic Political Processes

A second question Hollis and Ohlin raise explicitly is hidden in plain sight in this volume's title, namely, how can the *foreign* aspect of foreign election interference be separated from domestic politics? In the age of an internet designed to be borderless, alignment of certain domestic and foreign interests, and useful idiots that can be

[17] Introduction, this volume, at 12.

recruited or unknowingly co-opted into carrying an interfering nation's water, can the *foreign* ever again be separated from the *domestic*?

- **Research question**: How and to what extent, if any, do the interests of various factions in the United States (as one example) align with the interests of would-be foreign actors that might be motivated to interfere in U.S. elections? What is the scope and nature of connections between them, if any? How easy or difficult is it for domestic actors to pursue activities that are directly or indirectly shaped by would-be election influencers?

Lastly, Hollis and Ohlin point out that "identifying the existence of problematic behavior is a necessary prerequisite for crafting and evaluating appropriate responses, whether through international regulation or other means."[18] True enough. Thus, the following question:

- **Research question**: In the absence of an intelligence apparatus that can provide insight, what evidence would suggest that foreign election intervention is taking place?

C. Possibilities for the Further Evolution of International Law

David P. Fidler's point (in chapter 13) that traditionally "weaker" states can use modern information technologies to generate outcomes of strategic consequence for stronger ones raises some of the most interesting challenges for international law (and indeed not just for international law). Fidler cites Russian interference in the 2016 election as a demonstration of the possibility that strategic effects can result from a series of substrategic events or incidents, even if no one specific event in a long campaign can be said to be determinative of a bad outcome.

International law—and law more generally—is much better suited to making judgments about individual events. For the most part, law does not deal well with a series of legal events that cumulatively add up to an illegal outcome. It is for this reason, among others, that U.S. cyber strategy today emphasizes cyber operations under the legal threshold of an armed conflict, that is, that adversary cyber operations below this threshold are important to counter, and that U.S. cyber operations—including offensive cyber operations—can be conducted with greater legal ease below this threshold.[19]

[18] *Id.* at 14.

[19] *Command Vision for US Cyber Command: Achieve and Maintain Cyberspace Superiority*, U.S. Cyber Command (2018), *at* https://www.cybercom.mil/Portals/56/Documents/USCYBERCOM%20Vision%20April%202018.pdf?ver=2018-06-14-152556-010. It is notable, moreover, that much of the recent attention of states and scholars has sought to identify additional legal prohibitions below the use of force threshold (e.g., under the principle of nonintervention, a rule of sovereignty). To the extent such efforts are successful, they establish constraints on cyber operations even outside the use of force context.

- **Research question**: How can and should international legal jurisprudence be adjusted, if at all, to address multiple unfriendly but legal acts that may result in cumulative strategic harm to the nation that is the target of such acts?

A related point is that law does not deal well with activities that are tolerable in small numbers but intolerable in large numbers, a problem that is exacerbated by the rise in information technologies. One primary reason for adversaries to use information technology is to take advantage of its ability to accomplish information handling and transmission tasks at low cost and high speed, that is, to amplify the volume and velocity of the underlying information content being distributed through cyberspace. The result is a technology-enabled conundrum—the amplification of messages that are likely quite harmless in onesies and twosies but potentially quite harmful when distributed on scales larger by several orders of magnitude.

- **Research question**: How can and should international legal jurisprudence be adjusted, if at all, to accommodate the qualitative changes in the information environment wrought by ever more sophisticated information technology?

D. The Relationship between Norms and Customary International Law

Duncan B. Hollis and Jan Neutze in chapter 14 offer cybernorms (that is, expectations of proper behavior in cyberspace that are shared by nations) as an additional tool to defend against election interference. However, as "social" expectations of behavior, cybernorms are different from international law about cyberspace. Absent treaties, customary international law (CIL) would define the rules for cyberspace based on the widespread and consistent state practice conducted because of a sense of legal obligation by states that they must comport themselves in such a manner.

Customary international law imposes more stringent requirements on state behavior and is less forgiving of violations than a regime based on norms (e.g., violations of customary international law can be met with countermeasures, which are unavailable in response to merely unfriendly acts). Yet, it seems to this untrained observer that CIL must emerge out of norms that have governed state practice for so long and in such ways that they come to *seem* like legal obligations to those states in the absence of formal, written agreement.

Hollis and Neutze note that some norms arise spontaneously out of habit and repetition, pointing out that "when group members do the same thing for long enough, a norm may emerge even without conscious thought or decision."[20] They also observe norms can emerge from processes catalyzed by so-called "norm entrepreneurs," who may range from civil society advocates to nations. Among nations, Hollis and Neutze

[20] Chapter 14, this volume, at 335.

point to the example of a norm allowing states to use military force to collect debts abroad evolving into a new norm prohibiting that very behavior.

Alas, they are silent on how a norm turns into CIL, a process that begs for further inquiry.[21]

- **Research question**: What are the mechanisms through which norms can evolve into CIL? How can those mechanisms be exploited to promote CIL regarding election interference?

E. Developing Domestic Norms against Foreign Election Interference

One particular norm of interest regarding cyber-enabled interference in elections is how the various sides in an interfered-with election respond to it. An environment in which one side openly embraces the idea of foreign activities in pursuit of victory—or even more, seeks it—is very different from one in which both sides overtly and sincerely condemn such activities and strongly reject any benefits that might accrue to them. If the latter could become the norm of behavior in elections, foreign election interference would at least be driven into the shadows to a greater extent. Foreign actors would have fewer expectations that a candidate they supported might reward them out of gratitude for helping with his or her victory.

- **Research question**: How might nations promote within their own domestic constituencies a universal norm of behavior that condemns foreign interference in elections regardless of the side that such interference might assist?

Almost all of this volume takes as a given the idea that democracies—especially the United States—have been the victim of foreign election interference. That perspective is undeniably valid, but it is notably incomplete. As Dov H. Levin explains in chapter 1, democracies—including the United States—do not have entirely clean hands in this regard. They have undertaken a variety of activities in the past century to influence elections in other nations. Indeed, even the United Kingdom made a concerted effort to intervene in the 1940 U.S. presidential election, one that has eerie similarities to the Russian intervention in 2016.[22]

Of course, since the advent of the internet, social media, mobile smartphones, and the World Wide Web, the United States is not known to have attempted to apply

[21] The UN International Law Commission (ILC) stated that state practice contributes to the formation or expression of rules of customary international law (Conclusion 4). It also elucidated a number of forms of state practice; this list did not mention norms of behavior as an example of state practice, though admittedly the list was explicitly not exhaustive. *See* ILC, *Identification of Customary International Law: Text of the draft conclusions as adopted by the Drafting Committee on second reading*, U.N. Doc. A/CN.4/L.908 (May 17, 2018).

[22] *See, e.g.*, British Security Coordination: The Secret History of British Intelligence in the Americas 1940–1945 (William S. Stephenson ed., 1998).

cyber tools to influence elections in other nations, at least not covertly.[23] But since the United States has neither acknowledged that its past interventions were improper nor pledged to never conduct such interventions in the future, how might any of the counterinterference measures proposed in this volume affect possible U.S. activities in this regard?

- **Research question**: What might be the impact of the various remedies to foreign election interference on the United States or other Western democracies, should they try to intervene in elections elsewhere in the world?
- **Research question**: What international impact on other nations' willingness to intervene in U.S. elections would follow from a U.S. acknowledgment of error in conducting previous electoral interventions and a pledge to refrain from doing so in the future?

F. Business Models to Combat Foreign Election Interference

This volume is essentially silent on the applicability of international law to the governance of multinational corporations, specifically the platform companies whose services lie at the heart of the most critical aspect of cyber-enabled election interference. This is not surprising—international law governs *nations*, not corporations. Yet, certain corporations have influence and power in certain domains that far outstrips those of many nations.

- **Research question**: How and to what extent, if any, can the tools of international law be used to guide and/or regulate activities of multinational platform companies that might impinge on the conduct of elections?

I have argued above that only platform companies are today in a position to impose any kind of moderating influence on the information environment in which elections and political discourse are embedded. But, as I also noted, their revenue models are based on the assumption that they will not exert such influence. This is not to say

[23] The World Wide Web came of age in the early 1990s, but its global penetration in its early days was only a small fraction of what it is today. A few U.S. election intervention efforts since then are known publicly. The United States supported the election of Boris Yeltsin in Russia in 1996. *See Interview with Thomas Graham*, FRONTLINE, *at* https://www.pbs.org/wgbh/pages/frontline/shows/yeltsin/interviews/graham.html. President Bill Clinton acknowledged trying to help Shimon Peres win Israel's general election in 1996 against Benjamin Netanyahu. *See* Times of Israel Staff, *Bill Clinton Admits He Tried to Help Peres Beat Netanyahu in 1996 Elections*, TIMES OF ISRAEL (Apr. 4, 2018). The United States also worked quietly (and unsuccessfully) to keep Hamid Karzai from winning the 2009 election in Afghanistan. *See generally* ROBERT GATES, DUTY: MEMOIRS OF A SECRETARY AT WAR (2014). But none of these actions are known to have used cyber tools as we understand the term today. Additionally, the United States has openly conducted activities to promote democracy abroad. The line between democracy promotion and election interference can be fuzzy at times. For example, in 2000, the *Washington Post* reported that the United States was conducting a \$77 million effort to strengthen the democratic opposition to Yugoslav President Slobodan Milosevic in anticipation of an election in the fall of 2000. These activities were conducted under a rubric of building a broad base of democratic institutions, and yet they clearly handicapped the incumbent Milosevic. *See* John Lancaster, *U.S. Funds Help Milosevic's Foes in Election Fight*, WASHINGTON POST (Sept. 19, 2000).

that platform companies would be *legally* forbidden from adopting revenue-reducing business models that could in the long-term result in a more stable business environment. For example, management could take such action on the basis of an argument that a business model prioritizing and promoting integrity and civility of the information environment would help its talent-recruiting efforts or build public trust. But those companies would have to be willing to endure the (presumably short-term) revenue loss that such action might entail.

Such action might also push up against the limits of free speech norms, even though as nongovernmental actors, private platform companies are free to moderate traffic on their platforms in any way that is consistent with their terms of service for users. Indeed, as this chapter is being written, large platform companies are taking quite active roles in suppressing misinformation related to the COVID-19 pandemic. For example, *BuzzFeedNews* quoted Monica Bickert, Facebook's head of global policy management, as saying: "We decided we would remove content that directly contradicted [the World Health Organization] and could contribute to risk of imminent physical harm."[24] As of May 23, 2020, Facebook had removed hundreds of thousands of posts already violating this policy, according to Bickert, and reduced distribution on tens of millions of others.

In principle, advertisers could bring pressure on platform companies to take action to clean up today's information environment by threatening to withhold advertising dollars if they did not do so. It is an empirical question as to which and how many companies would constitute a sufficient critical mass to pressure platform companies to take action. Yet, at first glance, it may not be an insurmountable task. The Internet Advertising Board reported that in FY 2019, ten companies accounted for 76.6 percent of internet advertising ($95.5 billion out of a total of $124.6 billion).[25]

In 2019, a number of companies banded together with platform companies (including Facebook, YouTube, and Twitter) under the rubric of the Global Alliance for Responsible Media to take action to address "harmful and misleading media environments and to develop and deliver against a concrete set of actions, processes and protocols for protecting brands."[26] Initially, these actions were focused on disassociating company advertisements with harmful content. In addition, and as this chapter is being written, a number of large companies have suspended advertising on certain social media platforms, citing concerns about hate speech and misinformation.[27] As new initiatives, the success of these efforts remains to be seen, and the fact that the top 100 advertisers on Facebook represent less than 20% of advertising revenue may call into question the likelihood of their success.[28] But it may turn out that collective action

[24] Alex Kantrowitz, *Facebook Is Taking Down Posts That Cause Imminent Harm—But Not Posts That Cause Inevitable Harm*, BuzzFeedNews (May 23, 2020).

[25] PwC, *Internet Advertising Revenue Report*, Interactive Advertising Bureau (IAB) (2020), *at* https://www.iab.com/wp-content/uploads/2020/05/FY19-IAB-Internet-Ad-Revenue-Report_Final.pdf.

[26] World Federation of Advertisers, *Global Alliance for Responsible Media*, *at* https://wfanet.org/garm (last visited June 24, 2020); Hadas Gold, *These Brands Spend Nearly $100 Billion on Ads. They Want Facebook and Google to Raise Their Game*, CNN Business (Jan. 23, 2020).

[27] *See, e.g.*, Tiffany Hsu, *The Brands Pulling Ads from Facebook over Hate Speech*, N.Y. Times (June 26, 2020).

[28] Facebook, Inc., First Quarter 2019 Results Conference Call, April 24th, 2019, https://s21.q4cdn.com/399680738/files/doc_financials/2019/Q1/Q1-'19-earnings-call-transcript-(1).pdf.

on the part of a sufficiently large number of advertisers will influence the actions of the platform companies. Indeed, although Facebook maintains that it will not make policy changes tied to revenue pressure (and that it sets policies based on principles rather than on business interests[29]), Facebook also said that going forward, it would continue to carry posts from politicians if they are newsworthy, but if their content otherwise violated Facebook policies for content, it would include a label noting that fact.[30] It is not publicly known whether the timing of this change in policy is related to the fact that two large advertisers, Verizon and Unilever, announced temporary suspensions of their advertising on Facebook around the time of this announcement.[31]

- **Research question**: Is it possible to develop a profitable business model that would prioritize reasoned political discourse and societal unity? If so, what would be its nature and logic? How might such a model become commercially dominant given the prominence of today's business models that do the opposite?

Going beyond the specifics in this volume, an authoritative statement from U.S. Department of Defense General Counsel Paul C. Ney, Jr., on March 2, 2020, at the U.S. Cyber Command Legal Conference highlights an additional, very interesting question relating to the public silence of many states regarding cyber intrusions into their networks. Ney writes: "[T]here is not sufficiently widespread and consistent State practice resulting from a sense of legal obligation to conclude that customary international law generally prohibits such non-consensual cyber operations in another State's territory," citing as evidence that "many States' public silence in the face of countless publicly known cyber intrusions into foreign networks precludes a conclusion that States have coalesced around a common view that there is an international prohibition against all such operations (regardless of whatever penalties may be imposed under domestic law)."[32] That which is not prohibited under international law (whether customary or treaty) is presumed to be allowable in the sense that, by definition, it is not a violation of international law. This suggests that the United States is willing to conduct cyber operations in legal "gray areas" until there is such a consensus. Indeed, this is the legal basis on which the Department of Defense cyber strategy of "defending forward" to counter foreign cyber activity targeting the United States rests.

- **Research question**: What authoritative public statements have been made by *any* nation about the legality under international law of offensive cyber operations conducted against it?[33] To the extent that few such statements have been

[29] Suzanne Vranica, *Facebook Tries to Contain Damage as Verizon Joins Ad Boycott*, Wall Street Journal (June 26, 2020).

[30] Rachel Sandler, *In Reversal, Zuckerberg Says Facebook Will Label Newsworthy Posts That Violate Its Rules*, Forbes (June 26, 2020).

[31] Hsu, *supra* note 27; Vranica, *supra* note 29.

[32] Paul Ney, *DOD General Counsel Remarks at U.S. Cyber Command Legal Conference*, U.S. Dep't of Defense (Mar. 2, 2020), *at* https://www.defense.gov/Newsroom/Speeches/Speech/Article/2099378/dod-general-counsel-remarks-at-us-cyber-command-legal-conference/.

[33] I know of two such statements. In 2012, the Minister of Foreign Affairs of the Islamic Republic of Iran stated at the High Level Meeting on Countering Nuclear Terrorism that "sabotage in nuclear facilities or to compel a nation to do or refrain from doing an act" constitutes nuclear terrorism, and that an act of nuclear terrorism "committed by a State, is a . . . a grave violation of the principles of UN Charter and international

made, what does that say about the legality of offensive cyber operations of the intensity and impact of those that have occurred to date? Put differently, how and to what extent, if any, would the lack of complaint in international forums regarding cyberattacks imply a norm that such behavior is not forbidden under international law?

VII. Closing Thoughts

In their introduction, even as they focus on it, Hollis and Ohlin point to international law as just one of a number of areas of intellectual specialization that can contribute to solving the problem of foreign election interference. But there's one important sense in which I believe this perspective sells itself short. It is hard for me to believe that any one nation—even the United States—can solve this problem unilaterally through technology, domestic law, regulation, military force, education, or any combination of these means. That means it will have to act cooperatively with at least some other nations to fight foreign election interference. International law is one means of facilitating cooperative action among nations, even if it is not the only means (as Hollis and Neutze suggest in chapter 14).

Nativist nationalistic populism is on the rise today, even in established democracies, a sign that does not bode well for international engagement and cooperation. Thus, I wish that Hollis and Ohlin had commissioned at least one more chapter on how to strengthen international law and make it more binding on state behavior in an era where support for international engagement seems to be falling. It is a question relevant not just to foreign election interference today. For global problems such as the threat of nuclear war, climate change, and biological pandemics such as COVID-19, such engagement will be necessary if we as a species are to have any chance for long-term survival.[34]

law." *Statement by H.E. Dr. Ali Akbar Salehi, Minister of Foreign Affairs of the Islamic Republic of Iran on behalf of the Non Aligned Movement* (Sept. 28, 2012), *at* https://dagobertobellucci.wordpress.com/2012/09/29/statement-by-h-e-dr-ali-akbar-salehi-minister-of-foreign-affairs-of-the-islamic-republic-of-iran-on-behalf-of-the-non-aligned-movement-n-y-28-september-2012/. Also, in 2018, the National Cyber Security Centre of the United Kingdom stated that "Cyber attacks orchestrated by the GRU have attempted to undermine international sporting institution WADA, disrupt transport systems in Ukraine, destabilise democracies and target businesses" and that "[the] campaign by the GRU shows that it is working in secret to undermine international law and international institutions." *See* National Cyber Security Center (NCSC), *Reckless Campaign of Cyber Attacks by Russian Military Intelligence Service Exposed* (Oct. 4, 2018), *at* https://www.ncsc.gov.uk/news/reckless-campaign-cyber-attacks-russian-military-intelligence-service-exposed. I am grateful to Duncan Hollis for pointing out the 2018 accusation.

[34] For a more extended argument in favor of international engagement as an essential element of dealing with existential problems, see the Doomsday Clock statements from the Bulletin of the Atomic Scientists for 2019 and 2020. Full disclosure—I was involved in writing both of them. *See* Science and Security Board, *2019 Doomsday Clock Statement—A New Abnormal: It Is Still 2 Minutes to Midnight*, Bulletin of the Atomic Scientists (Jan. 24, 2019); Science and Security Board, *2020 Doomsday Clock Statement—It Is 100 Seconds to Midnight*, Bulletin of the Atomic Scientists (Jan. 23, 2020).

In short, international law is an important vehicle for promoting cooperation and combating the worst forms of human (and other) behavior. And, if so, we are going to need international lawyers going forward to help us scope out problems, identify a range of solutions, and compare and contrast their costs and benefits. So—hooray for international law and lawyers! From outside your discipline, I salute you.

Index

For the benefit of digital users, indexed terms that span two pages (e.g., 52–53) may, on occasion, appear on only one of those pages.

Printed in the USA/Agawam, MA
May 25, 2022
793482.014